Course   Criminal Investigation
Course Number   **CJE 2600**
Special Edition Miami Dade College
School of Justice

http://create.mheducation.com

ISBN-10: 1308143559   ISBN-13: 9781308143552

Contents

Credits

◄ Sir Robert Peel (1788–1850), whose efforts led to the establishment of the London Metropolitan Police in 1829. English police officers are still referred to as "Bobbies," a play on Peel's first name.

(© The Granger Collection, New York)

1

THE EVOLUTION OF CRIMINAL INVESTIGATION AND FORENSIC SCIENCE

CHAPTER OBJECTIVES

1. Define "investigator."
2. Define the most fundamental purpose of investigation.
3. State four additional objectives of the investigative process.
4. Explain the importance of the Bow Street Runners.
5. Discuss the contribution of Sir Robert Peel's reform to early policing in the United States.
6. Explain the history and contributions of the Pinkerton National Detective Agency.
7. Identify the first major federal investigative agencies and their responsibilities.
8. Explain the Supreme Court's "due process revolution" and its impact on policing.
9. Discuss Bertillon's method of anthropometry.
10. Summarize the historical development of fingerprint identification.
11. Explain the concept and practice of DNA typing.
12. Outline the milestones in the development of firearms identification.

An investigator is someone who gathers, documents, and evaluates evidence and information. This is accomplished through the process of investigation. The most fundamental purpose of criminal investigation and forensic science is to discover the truth. By making this purpose the cornerstone of their behavior, investigators can remain faithful to their oath of office and the accompanying ethical standards. Four additional objectives of the investigative process are to (1) establish that a crime was actually committed; (2) identify and apprehend the suspect(s); (3) recover stolen property; and (4) assist in the prosecution of the person(s) charged with the crime.

JURISDICTION

The authority of law-enforcement officers is limited by such factors as the Constitution, court decisions, federal and state laws, departmental policies, and jurisdiction, which can be thought of as both a *geographical area* and the laws for which an agency has *enforcement responsibility*.

The general rule is that the *geographic jurisdiction* of police officers is limited to the area governed by their employer. Law-enforcement officers employed by state agencies and county, as well as metropolitan and city police departments, follow this general pattern. Depending on the state, Sheriffs' deputies and county police departments usually patrol the unincorporated portions of a county, although by contract they may provide law-enforcement services to municipalities. Sheriff's deputies may or may not have jurisdiction outside their home counties. Investigations beyond the governing authority's geographical boundaries usually are conducted with the assistance of the appropriate law-enforcement agency. Some states have statutorily extended the jurisdiction of peace officers—for example, allowing investigation beyond their normal jurisdiction for offenses committed within the investigating officers' regular jurisdiction, when viewing serious misdemeanors or felonies, or assisting another law-enforcement officer.

The FBI provides a good illustration of *enforcement responsibility*. It has primary enforcement responsibility for all federal criminal laws, except cases for which responsibility is by statute or otherwise assigned specifically to another agency. As a practical matter the enforcement responsibility of the FBI is limited to roughly 200 laws.

CRIMINAL INVESTIGATION AND FORENSIC SCIENCE

For present purposes, the roots of criminal investigation can be traced back to England in the eighteenth century, a period marked by significant social, political, and economic changes. These changes were important to the development of the first modern detective force, the **Bow Street Runners.** In addition, London was the home of the first police reformer, Robert Peel. Both of these factors contributed to the subsequent development of police organizations and criminal investigation in the United States.

Forensic science draws from diverse disciplines, such as geology, physics, chemistry, biology, and mathematics, to study physical evidence related to crime. If it is suspected that a person has died from poisoning, for example, a toxicologist, who specializes in identifying poisons and their physiological effects on humans and animals, can assist in the investigation. Experts in other areas, such as botany, forensic pathology, entomology, and archaeology, may also provide helpful information to criminal investigators.

Over hundreds of years many people have made contributions to the fields of criminal investigation and forensic science. To recognize all of them is beyond the scope of this chapter and requires setting some limits. This chapter presents a brief history of criminal investigation and forensic science. Many volumes have been written about these entwined topics, but the space that can be devoted to them here is limited. Sufficient broad perspectives and supporting details, however, are included in this chapter to enable readers intrigued by these subjects to independently pursue their interest armed with a working knowledge of the basics.

THE EVOLUTION OF CRIMINAL INVESTIGATION

THE IMPACT OF THE AGRICULTURAL AND INDUSTRIAL REVOLUTIONS

During the eighteenth century, two events—an agricultural revolution and an industrial revolution—began a process of change that profoundly affected how police services were delivered and investigations conducted. Improved agricultural methods, such as the introduction in 1730 of Charles Townshend's crop rotation system and Jethro Tull's four-bladed plow, gave England increased agricultural productivity in the first half of the eighteenth century.[1] Improvements in agriculture were essential preconditions to the Industrial Revolution in the second half of the eighteenth century, because they freed people from farm work for city jobs. As the population of England's cities grew, slums also expanded, crime increased, and disorders became more frequent. Consequently, public demands for government to control crime grew louder.

THE FIELDINGS: CRIME INFORMATION AND THE BOW STREET RUNNERS

In 1748, **Henry Fielding** became chief magistrate of Bow Street and set out to improve the administration of justice. In 1750, he established a small group of volunteer, non-uniformed home owners to "take thieves." Known as the **"Bow Street Runners,"** these Londoners hurried to the scenes of reported crimes and began investigations, thus becoming the first modern detective force. By 1752, Fielding began publishing *The Covent Garden Journal* as a means of circulating the descriptions of wanted persons. On his death in 1754, Henry Fielding was succeeded by his blind half-brother, **John Fielding,** who carried on Henry's ideas for another 25 years.[2] Under John Fielding, Bow Street became a clearinghouse for information on crime,

and by 1785 at least four of the Bow Street Runners were no longer volunteers but paid government detectives.[3]

THE METROPOLITAN POLICE ACT OF 1829

In 1816, 1818, and again in 1822, England's Parliament rejected proposals for a centralized professional police force for London as different political philosophies clashed. One group argued that such a force was a direct threat to personal liberty. The other group—composed of reformers such as Jeremy Bentham and Patrick Colquhoun—argued that the absence, rather than the presence, of social control was the greater danger to personal liberty. Finally, in 1829, owing in large measure to the efforts of **Sir Robert Peel,** Parliament passed the **Metropolitan Police Act,** which created a metropolitan police force for London. Police headquarters became known as "Scotland Yard," because the building formerly had housed Scottish royalty. Police constables were referred to as **"Bobbies,"** a play on Peel's first name.[4]

Because French citizens had experienced oppression under centralized police, the British public was suspicious of, and at times even hostile to, the new force. In response to the high standards set for the police force, there were 5,000 dismissals and 6,000 forced resignations from the force during the first three years of operations.[5] This record was a clear indication to the public that police administrators were requiring officers to maintain high standards of conduct. Within a few years, the London Metropolitan Police had won a reputation for fairness, and it became the international model of professional policing. Despite the growing popularity of the uniformed Bobbies, however, there was fear that the use of **"police spies"**—detectives in plain clothes—would reduce civil liberties.

In the years immediately following 1829, some Metropolitan Police constables were temporarily relieved from patrolling in uniform to investigate crimes on their beats.[6] As the distinction between the use of uniformed constables to prevent crime and the use of plainclothes detectives for investigation and surveillance became clear, the public became uneasy. Illustratively, in 1833, a **Sergeant Popay** was dismissed following a parliamentary investigation that revealed that he had infiltrated a radical group, acquired a leadership position, and argued for the use of violence. In 1842, a regular detective branch was opened at **Scotland Yard** (Figure 1-1), superseding the Bow Street force.[7] Initially, the detective force was limited to no more than 16 investigators, and its operations were restricted because of a distrust of "clandestine methods."[8]

AMERICAN INITIATIVES

The success of Peel's reform in England did not go unnoticed in the United States. **Stephen Girard** bequeathed $33,190 to Philadelphia to develop a competent police force. In 1833 Philadelphia passed an ordinance creating

▲ **FIGURE 1-1 New Scotland Yard**
In 1890 the Metropolitan Police left their original quarters and were housed in New Scotland Yard, pictured above. Subsequently, in 1967 the Metropolitan Police moved again, to their present facilities, which are also referred to as New Scotland Yard.

America's first paid, daylight police force. Although the ordinance was repealed just three years later, the concept of a paid police force would reappear as American cities staggered under the burdens of tremendous population growth, poverty, and massive crime. In 1836 New York City rejected the notion of a police force organized along the lines advocated by Peel. The committee studying the idea concluded it was better in emergencies to rely on citizens than "despotic governments."[9]

Thus, before mid-century, few American cities had police service, and those that existed were inadequate. Many cities had paid police departments only at night or treated day and night police services as entirely separate organizations. Finally, in 1844 the New York state legislature created the first unified police force in the country, although New York City did not actually implement the measure until a year later. Other cities rapidly followed

New York's lead: Chicago in 1851, New Orleans and Cincinnati in 1852, and Baltimore and Newark in 1857. By 1880 virtually every major American city had a police force based on England's Peelian reforms of 1829 and pioneered in this country by New York City.

If one of the problems of the London Metropolitan Police had been getting the public to accept some constables' working out of uniform as detectives, in the United States the problem was getting the police to wear uniforms in the first place. American officers believed that a uniform made them easy targets for public harassment and made them look like servants. Only after the Civil War did the wearing of a uniform—invariably Union blue—become widely accepted by American police officers.

PINKERTON'S NATIONAL DETECTIVE AGENCY

America needed reliable detectives for several reasons: (1) graft and corruption were common among America's big-city police officers; (2) the jurisdiction of sheriffs' offices and municipal officers was limited; and (3) there was little information sharing by law-enforcement agencies. Thus, offenders often fled from one jurisdiction to another with impunity. Information sharing has vastly improved in the last 150 years but is an area that still requires further development.

In 1846 seeing the need for reliable investigators, two former St. Louis police officers formed the first recorded private detective agency.[10] However, the major private detective agency of the nineteenth century was formed by **Allan Pinkerton** (1819–1884, Figure 1-2.). In 1850, after working as a Chicago detective and a U.S. mail agent,[11] Pinkerton formed a private detective agency with attorney Edward Rucker.[12] Pinkerton's trademark was an open eye above the slogan "We never sleep."[13] The trademark gave rise to the use of the term "private eye" in reference to any private investigator.[14] The Pinkertons enjoyed such enormous success in the United States and throughout the world that some people thought "Pinkerton" was a nickname for any American government detective.[15]

The list of achievements by Pinkerton is impressive. Pinkerton reportedly discovered and foiled an assassination attempt on President-elect Lincoln in Baltimore.[16] At the outbreak of the Civil War in 1861, Pinkerton organized a Secret Service Division within the army (not to be confused with the U.S. Secret Service) and worked closely with General McClellan.[17] He infiltrated Confederate lines in disguise on several occasions and usually functioned as a military analyst.[18]

Following the Civil War, the Pinkertons were primarily engaged in two broad areas: (1) controlling a discontented working class, which was pushing for better wages and working conditions, and (2) pursuing bank and railroad robbers.[19] Unrestricted by jurisdictional limits, Pinkerton agents roamed far and wide pursuing lawbreakers. In a

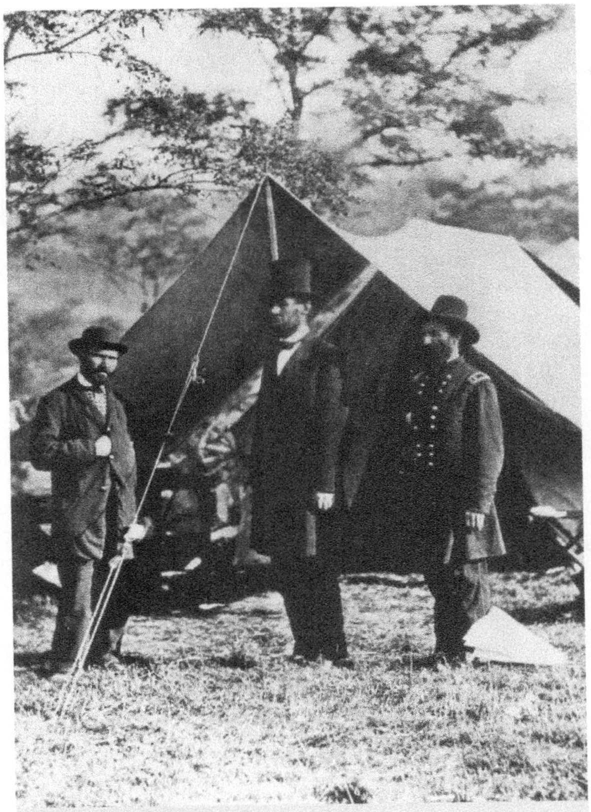

▲ **FIGURE 1-2 Pinkerton at work**
Allan Pinkerton, President Lincoln, and General McClellan at Antietam, Maryland, about October 3, 1862. Born in Scotland, Allan Pinkerton was the son of a police sergeant. He found employment as a barrel maker and advanced to supervisor. At the same time, this red-headed, strong-willed man advocated more voice in government for ordinary people, a position that resulted in him becoming a wanted man. Narrowly avoiding arrest on his wedding day, Pinkerton and his wife fled to America, surviving a shipwreck while en route. He started a successful barrel-making company. While owner of that business, his initiative led to the arrest of counterfeiters. This gave him an appetite for police work, his father's profession, and changed his life and American policing forever. **(Courtesy Pinkerton's Archives)**

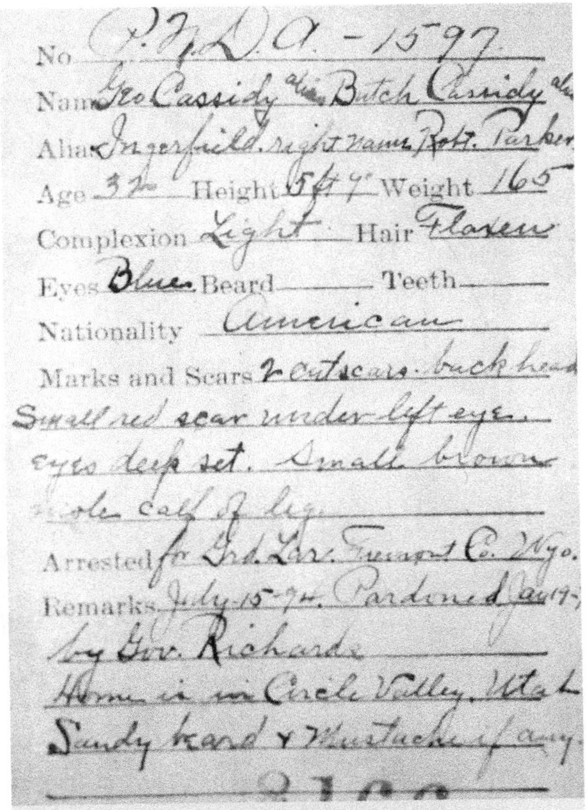

No. P.N.D.A. - 1597
Name Geo Cassidy alias Butch Cassidy
Alias Ingerfield, right name Robt. Parker
Age 32 Height 5 ft 9" Weight 165
Complexion Light Hair Flaxen
Eyes Blue Beard ——— Teeth ———
Nationality American
Marks and Scars 2 cut scars back head
Small red scar under left eye.
eyes deep set. Small brown
mole calf of leg.
Arrested for Grd. Lar. Fremont Co. Wyo.
Remarks July 15-94. Pardoned Jan 19-
by Gov. Richards
Home is in Circle Valley, Utah
Sandy beard & Mustache if any.

▲ **FIGURE 1-3 Butch Cassidy's Pinkerton record**
Note the "P.N.D.A." initials on the first line, which stand for Pinkerton National Detective Agency. Pinkerton agents were highly successful in combating the bank and train robbers of the Old West, such as the Hole in the Wall gang, so named because of the small opening through rocky walls that led to the valley in Johnson County, Wyoming, used as their hideout. As many as 40 bandits may have lived there in six cabins. Butch Cassidy and the Sun Dance Kid were both members of the Hole in the Wall gang at various times. **(Courtesy Wyoming State Archives and Historical Department)**

violent time, they sometimes used harsh and unwise methods. For instance, suspecting that they had found the hideout of Jesse James's gang, Pinkerton agents lobbed in a 32-pound bomb, killing a boy and injuring a woman.[20]

Pinkerton understood the importance of information, records, and publicity and made good use of all of them. For example, in 1868, Pinkerton agent Dick Winscott took on the Reno gang. Winscott located Fred and John Reno and, after a drinking bout, persuaded them to let him photograph them.[21] He sent the photographs to Pinkerton files, and within a year the Reno gang was smashed.[22] Pinkerton also collected photographs of jewel thieves and other types of criminals and photographed horses to prevent illegal substitutions before races.[23] The Pinkertons also pushed Butch Cassidy (Robert Parker) and the Sun Dance Kid (Harry Longabaugh) into leaving the United States for South America, where they were reportedly killed by Bolivian soldiers at San Vincente in 1909 (Figure 1-3.) Because of their better-known antilabor activities, the Pinkertons' other work often is overlooked. But they were the only consistently competent detectives available in this country for over 50 years[24] and provided a good model for government detectives.

◄ FIGURE 1-4
NYPD rogues' gallery
Uniformed officers of the New York City Police Department maintaining a rogues' gallery in the detective bureau, circa 1896. Police departments have used rogues' galleries since the late 1850s.
(Library of Congress)

THE EMERGENCE OF MUNICIPAL DETECTIVES

As early as 1845 New York City had 800 plainclothes officers,[25] although not until 1857 were the police authorized to designate 20 patrol officers as detectives.[26] In November 1857 the New York City Police Department set up a **rogues' gallery** (Figure 1-4)—photographs of known offenders arranged by criminal specialty and height—and by June 1858, it had over 700 photographs for detectives to study so that they might recognize criminals on the street.[27]

Photographs from rogues' galleries of that era reveal that some offenders grimaced, puffed their cheeks, rolled their eyes, and otherwise tried to distort their appearance to lessen the chance of later recognition.

To assist detectives, in 1884 Chicago established this country's first municipal Criminal Identification Bureau.[28] The Atlanta Police Department's Detective Bureau was organized in 1885 with a staff of one captain, one sergeant, and eight detectives.[29] In 1886 Thomas Byrnes, the dynamic chief detective of New York City, published *Professional Criminals in America,* which included pictures, descriptions, and the methods of all criminals known to him.[30] Byrnes thereby contributed to information sharing among police departments. To supplement the rogues' gallery, Byrnes instituted the **Mulberry Street Morning Parade.** At 9 o'clock every morning, all criminals arrested in the past 24 hours were marched before his detectives, who were expected to make notes and to recognize the criminals later.[31]

FEDERAL AND STATE DEVELOPMENTS

From its earliest days, the federal government employed investigators to detect revenue violations, but their responsibilities were narrow and their numbers few.[32] In 1865 Congress created the U.S. Secret Service to combat counterfeiting. In 1903—two years after President McKinley was assassinated by Leon Czolgosz in Buffalo—the previously informal arrangement of guarding the president was made a permanent Secret Service responsibility.[33]

In 1905 the California Bureau of Criminal Identification was set up to share information about criminal activity, and Pennsylvania governor Samuel Pennypacker signed legislation creating a state police force. Widely regarded then by labor as "strikebusters on management's side," the Pennsylvania State Police nevertheless was the prototype for modern state police organizations (Figure 1-5). New York and Michigan in 1917 and Delaware in 1919 adopted the state police concept. Since then, state police forces have assumed the function of providing local police with help in investigations.

Although Virginia, Kentucky, and Arkansas have a State Police, there are none in the deep South. To a large degree, their use in that area has been foiled by politically potent sheriffs seeking to maintain autonomy.

Where State Police agencies do not exist, a common arrangement is to have a department that focuses primarily on traffic enforcement and another for criminal investigation—for example, in North Carolina there is a

▲FIGURE 1-5   The Pennsylvania State Police
Troop D, Pennsylvania State Police, Punxsutawney, Pennsylvania, 1906. Note that both plainclothes and uniformed personnel are represented. (Courtesy Pennsylvania State Police)

State Highway Patrol and the State Bureau of Investigation (SBI). In such arrangements the crime laboratory may be a separate department or part of the state investigative agency. Similarly, casino gaming enforcement may be a function of a state police agency or a state gaming commission.

After Prohibition was adopted nationally in 1920, the Bureau of Internal Revenue was responsible for its enforcement. Eventually the ranks of the bureau's agents swelled to a massive 4,000.[34] Because the Bureau of Internal Revenue was lodged in the Department of the Treasury, these federal agents were referred to as T-men.

In 1908 U.S. Attorney General Charles Bonaparte created the embryo of what was later to become the Federal Bureau of Investigation (FBI) when he ordered that investigations were to be handled by a special group. In 1924 J. Edgar Hoover (1895–1972) assumed leadership of the Bureau of Investigation; 11 years later Congress passed a measure giving the FBI its present designation.

When Prohibition was repealed by the Eighteenth Amendment to the U.S. Constitution in 1933, many former bootleggers and other criminals turned to bank rob-

bery and kidnapping.[35] During the Depression, some people saw John Dillinger, "Pretty Boy" Floyd, and Bonnie and Clyde (Figures 1-6 and 1-7) "as plain folks" and did not grieve over a bank robbery or the kidnapping of a

►FIGURE 1-6   Bonnie Parker
Texas-born Bonnie Parker (1910–1934) was part of the murderous Barrow gang, which robbed and murdered its way across Oklahoma, Missouri, Texas, and New Mexico. In 1930, she smuggled a gun into the Waco (Texas) County Jail, helping Clyde Barrow and a companion to escape. From 1932 until 1934, Bonnie and Clyde left a deadly trail before they were stopped. (Courtesy FBI)

▲ **FIGURE 1-7   Clyde Barrow**

Clyde Barrow (1909–1934) was captured after his escape from the Waco County Jail and served two years in prison. Upon his release, he and Bonnie began their rampage. Outside of Black Lake, Louisiana, they were killed by law-enforcement officers who had persistently been pursuing them.
(Courtesy FBI)

millionaire.[36] Given the restricted roles of other federal investigative agencies, it became the FBI's role to deal with these criminals.

Under Hoover, who understood the importance and uses of information, records, and publicity as well as Allan Pinkerton had, the FBI became known for investigative efficiency. In 1932, the FBI established a crime laboratory and made its services available free to state and local police (Figure 1-8). In 1935 it started the **National Academy,** a training course for state and local police. In 1967 the **National Crime Information Center (NCIC)** was made

operational by the FBI, providing data on wanted persons and property stolen from all 50 states. Altogether, these developments gave the FBI considerable influence over law enforcement throughout the country. Although some people argue that such federal influence is undesirable, others point out that Hoover and the FBI strengthened police practices in this country, from keeping crime statistics to improving investigation.

The Harrison Act (1914) made the distribution of non-medical drugs a federal crime. Enforcement responsibility was initially given to the Internal Revenue Service, although by 1930 a separate Federal Bureau of Narcotics (FBN) was established in the Treasury Department. In 1949 a federal commission noted that federal narcotics enforcement was fragmented among several agencies, including the Border Patrol and Customs, resulting in duplication of effort and other ills. In 1968 some consolidation of effort was achieved with the creation of the Bureau of Narcotics and Dangerous Drugs (BNDD) in the Department of Justice, and in 1973, with the creation of its successor, the **Drug Enforcement Administration (DEA).**

Today the DEA devotes many of its resources to fighting international drug traffic. Like the FBI, the DEA trains state and local police in investigative work. The training focuses on recognition of illegal drugs, control of drug purchases, surveillance methods, and handling of informants.

In 2002 several federal agencies were consolidated to form Immigration and Customs Enforcement (ICE) in the Department of Homeland Security (DHS).

THE POLICE AND THE U.S. SUPREME COURT

As the highest court in this country, the Supreme Court is obligated to review cases and to make decisions that often have considerable impact. From 1961 to 1966, a period known as the "due process revolution," the

◀**FIGURE 1-8**
FBI crime laboratory
In 2003 the FBI occupied its 463,000 square foot state-of-the-art crime laboratory, which cost $130 million.
(© AP Photo/Charles Dharapak)

Supreme Court became unusually active in hearing cases involving the rights of criminal suspects and defendants. Its decisions focused on two vital areas: (1) search and seizure and (2) the right to legal representation. Among those cases was *Miranda* v. *Arizona* (1966), which established the well-known "Miranda rights." *Miranda* and other decisions infuriated the police, who felt that the Supreme Court had "tied their hands."

So what did the due process revolution and subsequent Supreme Court decisions really change? Questionable and improper police procedures and tactics were greatly reduced. In turn, this created the need to develop new procedures and tactics and to make sure that officers were well trained in their uses. To no small extent, this cycle has hastened the continuing professionalization of the police while also asserting the principle that the action of police officers anywhere may be subject to close scrutiny by the Supreme Court.

HISTORICAL MILESTONES OF FORENSIC SCIENCE

The origins of criminalistics or forensic science are largely European. Forensic science draws from diverse disciplines, such as geology, physics, chemistry, biology, and mathematics, to study physical evidence related to crime. The first major book describing the application of scientific disciplines to criminal investigation was written in 1893 by **Hans Gross,** a public prosecutor and later a judge from Graz, Austria.[37] Translated into English in 1906 under the title *Criminal Investigation*, it remains highly respected today as the seminal work in the field.

The Frenchman **Edmond Locard** established the first forensic laboratory in Lyon in 1910. All crime scenes are searched on the basis of Locard's exchange principle, which asserts that when perpetrators come into contact with the scene, they will leave something of themselves and take away something from the scene, for example, hairs and fibers. Expressed somewhat differently, Locard's exchange principle states that there is something to be found. He is also recognized as the father of poreoscopy, the study of pores and for advocating that if there were 12 points of agreement between two compared fingerprints the identity was certain.

Forensic science enjoys periods of stability, but on the whole it is dynamic and in constant progress. To illustrate this principle of dynamic change, the histories of two commonly used services—biometric-based personal identification and firearms identification—are traced in this section.

BIOMETRIC BASED PERSONAL IDENTIFICATION

Biometrics is from the Greek meaning life measurement. The most important goal of biometric measurements is to uniquely identify, or verify the identity of, an individual through characteristics of the human body. Biometrics is superior to eye witness identification because it has a scientific foundation.

Historically, there have been three major scientific systems of biometric-based personal identification of criminals in wide use: anthropometry, dactylography, and deoxyribonucleic acid (DNA) typing. The first was relatively short lived. The second, dactylography, or fingerprint identification, remains in use today throughout the world. The third, DNA, is a relatively contemporary development.

Anthropometry

Anthropometry was developed by **Alphonse Bertillon** (1853–1914), who is rightly regarded as the father of criminal identification (Figure 1-9). The first method of criminal identification that was thought to be reliable, **anthropometry** "was based on the fact that every human being differs from every other one in the exact measurements of their body, and that the sum of these measurements yields a characteristic formula for each individual."[38] Figure 1-10 depicts a New York City police detective taking one type of measurement used in the "Bertillon system."

▲ **FIGURE 1-9   Bertillon**
Alphonse Bertillon (1853–1914), the father of personal identification. In 1882, he began using his system on those incarcerated in Paris's Palais de Justice. **(Courtesy Jacques Genthial)**

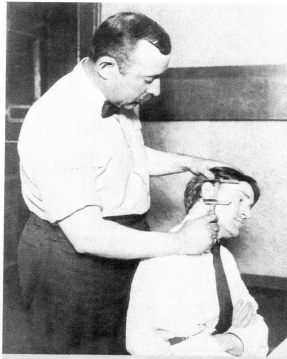

▲ **FIGURE 1-10   Taking a Bertillon measurement**
A New York City Police detective taking a Bertillon measurement of the right ear, one of the 11 measurements that made up anthropometry. This photograph was taken around 1896. Note in this photo and the one that immediately follows that the right ear is consistently part of the measurements made. **(Library of Congress)**

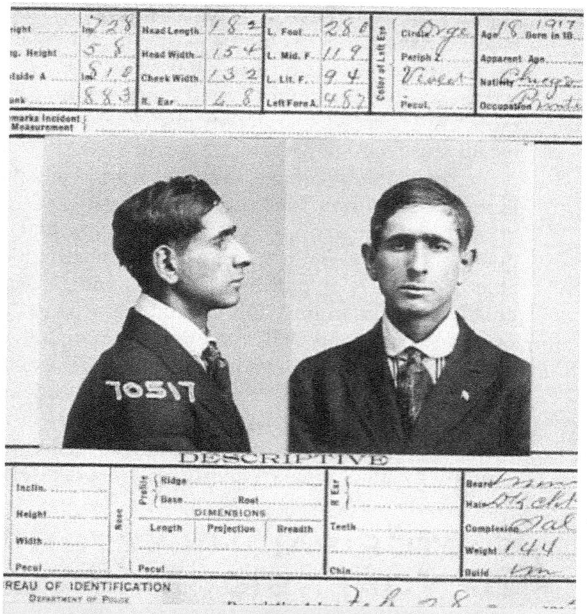

▲ **FIGURE 1-11   Early identification card**
A Bertillon-style identification card, combining both personal measurements and photographs, prepared on February 28, 1917, by the Chicago Police Department. **(Courtesy Chicago Police Department)**

There was little in Alphonse Bertillon's early life to suggest that he would later make significant contributions. He was the grandson of a well-known naturalist and mathematician and the son of a distinguished French physician and statistician, who was also the vice president of the Anthropological Society of Paris.[39] Despite the advantages Bertillon had, he failed in a number of jobs. He was, therefore, able to obtain only a minor position in 1879, filing cards on criminals for the Paris police, because of his father's good connections.[40] The cards described criminals so vaguely that they might have fit almost anyone: "stature: average . . . face: ordinary."[41]

Bertillon wondered why so many resources were wasted on a useless system of identifying criminals.[42] He began comparing photographs of criminals and taking measurements of those who had been arrested.[43] Bertillon concluded that if 11 physical measurements of a person were taken, the chances of finding another person with the same 11 measurements were 4,191,304 to 1.[44] His report outlining his criminal identification system was not warmly received. After reading it, the chief said "your report sounds like a joke."[45]

Yet in 1883 the "joke" received worldwide attention, because within 90 days of its implementation on an experimental basis, Bertillon correctly made his first criminal identification. Soon, almost all European countries adopted Bertillon's system of anthropometry. In 1888 Bertillon's fertile mind produced yet another innovation, the *portrait parlé* or "speaking picture," which combines full-face and profile photographs of each criminal with his or her exact body measurements and other descriptive data onto a single card (Figure 1-11).

After the turn of the century, many countries abandoned anthropometry and adopted the simpler and more reliable system of fingerprints instead. Bertillon himself was not insensitive to the potential of fingerprints. In 1902, he solved the murder of Joseph Riebel when he discovered the prints of Henri Scheffer on the pane of a glass cupboard.[46] Yet Bertillon's rigid personality would not allow him to acknowledge the clear superiority of dactylography to anthropometry. Even so, Bertillon's place in history is secure as the father of criminal identification.

Dactylography

Dactylography is the study of fingerprints. Fingerprints were used on contracts during China's T'ang Dynasty in the eighth century as well as on official papers in fourteenth-century Persia and seventeenth-century England.[47] In the first century, the Roman lawyer Quintilianus introduced a bloody fingerprint in a murder trial, successfully defending a child against the charge of murdering his father.[48]

In a scientific context, in 1684 in England, Dr. Nehemiah Grew first called attention to the system of pores and ridges in the hands and feet.[49] Just two years later, Marcello Malpighi made similar observations.[50] In 1823, John Perkinje, a professor at the University of Breslau, named nine standard types of fingerprint patterns and outlined a broad method of classification.[51] Despite these early stirrings, it was not until 1900 that a country, England, used dactylography as a system of criminal identification.

The Herschel-Faulds Controversy. Beginning in 1858 William Herschel, a British official in India, requested the palm prints and fingerprints of those with whom he did business, thinking that it might awe people into keeping agreements.[52] Over the next 20 years, Herschel noted from his records that the patterns of the lines on the fingerprints never changed for an individual. Excited by the prospects of applying this knowledge to the identification of criminals, Herschel wrote in 1877 to the inspector general of the prisons of Bengal. The reply made it clear that the inspector general was not interested. Discouraged, Herschel made no further efforts to pursue his discovery. Henry Faulds, a Scottish physician at the Tsukiji Hospital in Tokyo, had been interested in fingerprints for several years before 1880. When a thief left a sooty print on a whitewashed wall, Faulds was able to tell that the person in police custody was not the thief[53] and to match another suspect's fingerprints with those on the wall.[54] Faulds reported his findings in the journal *Nature* in 1880. Herschel read the account and published a reply, claiming credit for the discovery over 20 years before. A controversy broke out that was never resolved to anyone's satisfaction. Because there was also no official interest in using fingerprints, both Herschel and Faulds were even further frustrated.

Galton's and Vucetich's Systems. In 1888 **Sir Francis Galton** (1822–1911) turned his attention to criminal identification.[55] When Galton contacted the editor of *Nature* for both Herschel's and Faulds's addresses, he was by chance sent only Herschel's. Contacted by Galton, Herschel unselfishly turned over all his files in the hopes that this revived interest would lead to practical uses of fingerprints.[56] In 1892 Galton published the first definitive book on dactylography, *Finger Prints.* It presented statistical proof of the uniqueness of fingerprints and outlined many principles of identification by fingerprints.[57] In Argentina, in 1894, **Juan Vucetich** (1858–1925) published *Dactiloscopia Comparada*, outlining his method of fingerprint classification. In 1892 a disciple of Vucetich's,

Inspector Alvarez, obtained South America's first criminal conviction based on fingerprints by using Vucetich's system to convict a woman of beating her two children to death.[58]

The Henry System. The final breakthrough for the fingerprint method of personal identification was made by **Edward Henry.** At the age of 23 he went to India and by 1891 had become the inspector general of police of Nepal, the same province in which Herschel had worked some 15 years earlier.[59] Subject to many of the same influences as Herschel, but apparently working independently, Henry developed an interest in fingerprints[60] and instituted Bertillon's system with the addition of fingerprints to the cards. In 1893, Henry obtained a copy of Galton's book and began working on a simple, reliable method of classification. The governor general of India received a report from Henry in 1897 recommending that anthropometry be dropped in favor of Henry's fingerprint classification system. It was adopted throughout British India just six months later.[61] In 1900 Henry's system was adopted in England. The next year, Henry enjoyed two personal triumphs, the publication of his *Classification and Use of Finger Prints* and his appointment as assistant police commissioner of London,[62] rising to the post of commissioner two years later.

Faurot and "James Jones." In 1904 New York City Detective Sergeant Joseph Faurot was sent to England to study fingerprints, becoming the first foreigner trained in the use of the Henry classification system. Upon Faurot's return, the new police commissioner told him to forget about such "scientific notions" and transferred him to walking a beat.[63] In 1906 Faurot arrested a man dressed in formal evening wear but not wearing shoes, as the man crept out of a suite in the Waldorf-Astoria Hotel.[64] Claiming to be a respectable citizen named "James Jones," the man demanded to see the British consul and threatened Faurot with nasty consequences.[65] Faurot sent the man's fingerprints to Scotland Yard[66] and got back a reply that "James Jones" was actually Daniel Nolan, who had 12 prior convictions of hotel thefts and who was wanted for burglarizing a home in England. Confronted with this evidence, Nolan confessed to several thefts in the Waldorf-Astoria and received a sentence of seven years.[67] Newspaper stories about the case advanced the use of fingerprints in this country.

The West Case. Despite the fame achieved by Faurot, the most important incident to advance the use of fingerprints in this country was the **West case** (Figure 1-12). In 1903, Will West arrived at the U.S. penitentiary at Leavenworth, Kansas. While West was being processed in through identification, a staff member said that there was already a photograph and Bertillon measurements for him on file. But a comparison of fingerprints showed that despite identical appearances and nearly identical Bertillon

	William West	Will West
Bertillon: Measurements (in centimeters)		
Height	177.5	178.5
Outstretched arms	188.0	187.0
Trunk	91.3	91.2
Head length	19.8	19.7
Head width	15.9	15.8
Cheek width	14.8	14.8
Right ear	6.5	6.6
Left foot	27.5	28.2
Left middle finger	12.2	12.3
Left little finger	9.6	9.7
Left forearm	50.3	50.2

▲ **FIGURE 1-12** **The Two Wests**
William West had been in Leavenworth Prison since 1901; Will West arrived two years later. Given their similar appearances and nearly identical anthropometry measurements, one can understand the confusion created upon Will West's arrival. **(Courtesy FBI)**

measurements, the identification card on file belonged to a William West, who had been in Leavenworth since 1901. The incident accelerated the recognition that fingerprints were superior to anthropometry as a system of identification.

Rivalry of Vucetich's and Henry's Systems

Vucetich's book on fingerprint classification was published in 1894, seven years before Henry's, but Henry's system has become much more widely used. However, some experts think that Vucetich's system was superior.[68] The rivalry between partisans of the two classification systems deserves attention.

In 1911 the provincial government of Buenos Aires passed a law requiring fingerprint registration for all adults subject to military service and eligible to vote.[69] By 1913 Vucetich had completed the task and decided to travel. In his travels, he was showered with decorations for his classification system. But when he visited Bertillon to pay his respects to the father of criminal identification,[70] Bertillon kept Vucetich waiting and finally opened the door just long enough to yell, "Sir, you have done me great harm," before slamming it shut again.[71] They were never to meet again. On his return to Argentina, Vucetich was to face further humiliation. When Buenos Aires planned an expansion of fingerprint registration, there were strong protests. In 1917 the Argentine government canceled registrations, seized Vucetich's records, and forbade him to continue his work.[72] In 1925 much as Bertillon

had in 1914, Vucetich died a disappointed man. Although Vucetich's system is in use in South America today, Vucetich did not live long enough to see the vindication of his life's work.

In contrast, Henry became the head of what was then the world's most prestigious police organization and enjoyed the support of his government. These advantages, coupled with Vucetich's loss of support in his own country, meant that the Henry classification would become adopted virtually throughout the world.

DNA

DNA as "Blueprint"

Although **deoxyribonucleic acid (DNA)** was discovered in 1868, scientists were slow to understand its role in heredity.[73] During the early 1950s, James Watson and Francis Crick deduced the structure of DNA, ushering in a new era in the study of genetics.[74] Such developments were seemingly of peripheral interest to forensic scientists until 1985, when research into the structure of the human gene by Alec Jeffreys and his colleagues at Leicester University, England, led to the discovery that portions of the DNA structure of certain genes can be as unique to individuals as are fingerprints.[75] According to Jeffreys, the chance of two persons having identical DNA patterns is between 30 billion and 100 billion to 1.[76]

In all life forms—with the exception of a few viruses— the basis for variation lies in genetic material called

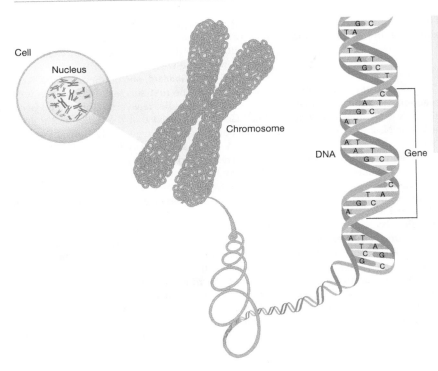

◄ **FIGURE 1-13**
DNA Structure
The long, stringy DNA that makes up genes is "spooled" or coiled within chromosomes. If unspooled and connected, the DNA is a person's body would stretch approximately 67 billion miles. (Courtesy National Institute of General Medical Sciences, 2010)

DNA.[77] This DNA is a chemical "blueprint" that determines everything from hair color to susceptibility to diseases[78] (Figure 1-13). In every cell of the same human that contains DNA, this blueprint is identical, whether the material is blood, tissue, spermatozoa, bone marrow, tooth pulp, saliva, or a hair root cell.[79] Thus, with the exception of identical twins, every person has distinctive DNA.

The Enderby Cases

The first use of DNA in a criminal case was in 1987 in England.[80] In 1983 Lynda Mann, age 15, was raped and murdered near the village of **Enderby.** This case was unsolved. Three years later, another 15-year-old, Dawn Ashworth, was a victim in a similar offense. Comparing the DNA "fingerprints" derived from semen recovered from both victims' bodies, investigators realized that the same man had raped and killed both women. A 17-year-old man was initially arrested and a sample of his blood was subjected to DNA analysis. This man's innocence, however, was clearly established by the lack of a DNA match, and he was released. Subsequently, all males in the Enderby area between 13 and 30 years of age were asked by the police to voluntarily provide blood samples for DNA typing. Of 5,500 men living in the area, all but two complied with the request. A man then came forward and told the police that he had used false identification to supply a blood sample in the name of a friend. This friend, Colin Pitchfork, was subsequently arrested and convicted of Ashworth's murder,

with DNA evidence playing a crucial role in the prosecution's case.

The Orlando Cases

During 1986 a series of rapes and assaults occurred in Orlando, Florida, that resulted in the first use of DNA in criminal investigation cases in this country.[81] The crimes shared a common pattern: the attacks occurred after midnight, in the victims' homes, by a knife-wielding perpetrator. The perpetrator was quick to cover the eyes of the victims with a sheet or blanket, so none of them could give detailed descriptions of their assailant. During early 1987, investigators staking out a neighborhood in which it was believed the rapist might strike saw a blue 1979 Ford speeding out of the area. They followed the car for a short distance before it crashed into a utility pole while making a turn.

The suspect, Tommie Lee Andrews, lived just 3 miles from the home of the first victim, who identified him at a photographic lineup the next morning. The prosecutor's case was certainly not ironclad. The identification rested on the victim's having seen the defendant for 6 seconds in a well-lit bathroom nearly a year before the photo lineup. Standard forensic tests comparing characteristics of the suspect's blood with characteristics derived from the semen found on the victim suggested that only Andrews could have committed the offense; but 30% of the male population of the United States shared these same characteristics. In short, there was enough evidence to prosecute, but a conviction was by no means a certainty.

However, on learning about the Enderby cases, the prosecutor secured DNA processing of the evidence and Andrews was convicted.

DNA Analysis

In 1988 the FBI became the first public-sector crime laboratory in the United States to accept cases for DNA analysis.[82] Private firms also offer DNA testing, including Orchid Cellmark, with forensic labs in Nashville, Tennessee and Dayton, Ohio

Although DNA analysis of blood and other evidence from humans in criminal investigation cases is widely understood and used, there was no application of "genetic fingerprinting" to plant evidence in criminal cases until the 1992 **palo verde seedpod case** in Phoenix, Arizona.[83] Joggers found the body of a female who had been strangled. At the scene, investigators found a beeper, which led them to a suspect. The suspect admitted that (1) he had been with the victim the evening she disappeared, (2) the victim had been in his vehicle, (3) he and the victim had had sex, and (4) he and the victim had struggled. However, the suspect also maintained that the victim had run off with his beeper when he refused to help her to get drugs and that he had not been anywhere near the place the body was found in 15 years. Investigators had found two seedpods from a palo verde tree in the bed of the suspect's truck. A University of Arizona plant geneticist was asked to determine if the seedpods came from a palo verde tree at the scene. The Maricopa County Sheriff's Office collected a total of 41 samples of palo verde seedpods from the crime scene and the surrounding region. The geneticist was able to exactly match the seedpods from the bed of the suspect's truck with those seized from the crime scene as part of the sample of 41 seedpods. Additionally, none of the 41 seedpods exactly matched another. This evidence was admitted at the trial. The defense attacked the evidence, properly arguing that the findings from a study based on 41 trees had substantial limitations and did not establish conclusively that the suspect could have gotten the seedpods only at the crime scene. However, along with other evidence, the testimony given by the geneticist had sufficient weight for the jury to convict the suspect.

FIREARMS IDENTIFICATION

Biometric based personal identification grew as several rival systems. Anthropomorphy lost credibility; Henry's system of fingerprint identification substantially eclipsed Vucetich's, and DNA remains widely used. In contrast, firearms identification moved forward in a series of successive steps.

In the United States, the frequency of shootings has made firearms identification extremely important.[84] As a specialty within forensic science, firearms identification extends far beyond the comparison of two fired bullets. It includes identification of types of ammunition, knowl-

edge of the design and functioning of firearms, restoration of obliterated serial numbers on weapons, and estimation of the distance between a gun's muzzle and a victim[85] when the weapon was fired.

In 1835 **Henry Goddard,** one of the last of the Bow Street Runners, made the first successful attempt to identify a murderer from a bullet recovered from the body of a victim.[86] Goddard noticed that the bullet had a distinctive blemish on it, a slight gouge. At the home of one suspect, Goddard seized a bullet mold with a defect whose location corresponded exactly to the gouge on the bullet. When confronted with this evidence, the owner of the mold confessed to the crime.[87]

Professor Lacassagne removed a bullet in 1889 from a corpse in France. On examining it closely, he found seven grooves made as the bullet passed through the barrel of a gun.[88] Shown the guns of a number of suspects, Lacassagne identified the one that could have left seven grooves. On the basis of this evidence, a man was convicted of the murder.[89] However, any number of guns manufactured at that time could have produced seven grooves. There is no way of knowing whether the right person was found guilty.[90]

In 1898 a German chemist named Paul Jeserich was given a bullet taken from the body of a man murdered near Berlin. After firing a test bullet from the defendant's revolver, Jeserich took microphotographs of the fatal and test bullets and, on the basis of the agreement between both their respective normalities and abnormalities, testified that the defendant's revolver fired the fatal bullet, contributing materially to the conviction obtained.[91] Unknowingly at the doorstep of scientific greatness, Jeserich did not pursue this discovery any further, choosing instead to return to his other interests.

Gradually, attention began to shift from just bullets to other aspects of firearms. In 1913 Professor Balthazard published perhaps the single most important article on firearms identification. In it, he noted that the firing pin, breechblock, extractor, and ejector all leave marks on cartridges and that these vary among different types of weapons. With World War I looming, Balthazard's article was not widely read for some years.

Calvin Goddard (1858–1946, Figure 1-14), a U.S. physician who had served in the army during World War I, is the person considered most responsible for raising firearms identification to a science and for perfecting the bullet-comparison microscope. To no small degree, Goddard's accomplishments were contributed to heavily by three other Americans—Charles Waite, John Fisher, and Phillip Gravelle—working as a team on firearms identification. In 1925, Goddard joined Waite's team and upon Waite's death a year later, Goddard became its undisputed driving force and leader.[92] Like those of many pioneers, Waite's contributions are often overlooked. He had been interested in firearms since 1917, and from 1920 on he visited firearms manufacturers to get data on those manufactured since 1850. Because of Waite, the first significant

▲ FIGURE 1-14 Calvin Goddard, an American pioneer in the study of ballistics

▲ FIGURE 1-15 Atomic Force Microscope (AFM) image of fingerprint on cartridge case. (Courtesy of University of Leicester, Forensic Research Centre, England)

cataloged firearms collection in this country was assembled. Nonetheless, ultimately it was Goddard who raised firearms identification to the status of a science.

OTHER CONTRIBUTORS

There are many other contributors to the evolution of investigation and forensic science. For example, in 1910 **Albert Osborn** (1858–1946) wrote *Questioned Documents*, which is still regarded as a definitive work. **Leone Lattes** (1887–1954) developed a procedure in 1915 that permits blood typing from a dried bloodstain, a key event in forensic serology. Although more an administrator and innovator than a criminalist, **August Vollmer** (1876–1955), through his support, helped **John Larson** produce the first workable polygraph in 1921. Vollmer established America's first full forensic laboratory in Los Angeles in 1923.

In 1935 **Harry Soderman** and **John O'Connell** coauthored *Modern Criminal Investigation*, the standard work for the field for decades until the publication of *Crime Investigation* by **Paul Kirk** in 1953. A biochemist, educator, and criminalist, Kirk helped develop the careers of many criminalists.

RECENT DEVELOPMENTS

The knowledge base, facilities, and capabilities for both criminal investigation and forensic science are constantly advancing. A few illustrations are provided here and other developments are discussed in the appropriate chapters.

If fingerprints are left on cartridge cases which are then fired, attempts to recover fingerprints are successful only 1% of the time using conventional methods. However, in 2009, a new capability, using Atomic Force Microscope (AFM) imaging, was announced by researchers at the University of Leicester, England. When fingerprints come into contact with a polished metal surface, such as a cartridge case, a residue is left behind. This initiates a reaction that continues even if the print is wiped away, and the heat from discharge of a bullet actually enhances the interaction.[93] AFM examinations of fingerprints on polished surfaces produce extremely high-resolution 3-D images of them (Figure 1-15). AFMs also have applicability to the examination of documents.

Research using functional magnetic resonance imaging (fMRI), electroencephalography (EEG), and near infrared light (NIL) on the brain's electromagnetic signals has produced some tantalizing results.[94] Analysis of brain activity suggests that there are different patterns when people are lying, and it appears that brain activity can also reveal whether people are familiar with unpublicized details of crimes.[95] In *United States* v. *Semrau* (2010), a federal district court excluded fMRI evidence at trial because it lacked sufficient scientific support.

There continues to be strong interest in biometrics. Among the biometric-based methods of identifying individuals that are in use or on the horizon are hand geometry, iris scans, ear matching, facial and voice recognition, vein patterns, human body odor, and brain activity. The use of iris scanning presents some challenges, because the iris is affected by alcohol, drug use, pregnancy, and aging. Veins in subcutaneous tissue, the loose flesh immediately under the skin, are unique to each person. Several systems for imaging them are available, such as Vein Viewer and Palm Secure. Vascular pattern recognition (VPR) is focused on palm and finger subcutaneous veins. Electronic noses (E-Noses) have many applications, including food quality control and air pollution measurement. There is some evidence that E-Noses are effective in detecting and classifying human body odor. In 2006, in Nanjing, China, the Chinese government began gathering an odor database, reporting success in using it to solve cases.

"Biometric signatures" also receive research attention. Although handwriting analysis has long been used, examples of applications in development include identifying computer users by the pattern, speed, and rhythm of their keystrokes and gait or walking analysis, which presents analytical problems, because gait can be disguised or difficult to discern if long, loose-fitting clothing is worn.

KEY TERMS

anthropometry	Goddard, Calvin	O'Connell, John
Bertillon, Alphonse	Goddard, Henry	Osborn, Albert
biometrics	Gross, Hans	palo verde seedpod case
Bobbies	Henry, Edward	Peel, Robert
Bow Street Runners	investigator	Pinkerton, Allan
dactylography	Kirk, Paul	"police spies"
deoxyribonucleic acid (DNA)	Larson, John	Popay, Sergeant
Drug Enforcement Administration (DEA)	Lattes, Leone	rogues' gallery
Enderby cases	Locard, Edmond	Scotland Yard
Fielding, Henry	Metropolitan Police Act (1829)	Soderman, Harry
Fielding, John	Mulberry Street Morning Parade	Vollmer, August
forensic science	National Academy	Vucetich, Juan
Galton, Francis	National Crime Information Center (NCIC)	West case
Girard, Stephen		

REVIEW QUESTIONS

1. What is the most fundamental purpose of investigation?
2. What are four other objectives of investigation?
3. Who were the Bow Street Runners, and of what historical importance are they?
4. Why did the British public object to the use of detectives after enactment of the Metropolitan Police Act of 1829?
5. Why did the profession of detective in this country basically evolve in the private sector?
6. Of what significance is the work of Pinkerton and his National Detective Agency?
7. What is a rogues' gallery?
8. Allan Pinkerton and J. Edgar Hoover have what similarities?
9. What is anthropometry, and why was it abandoned in favor of dactylography?
10. What are the milestones in the development of dactylography?
11. Why does the Henry classification system enjoy greater use than Vucetich's system?
12. What are the different human sources of DNA material identified in this chapter?
13. Of what significance is the palo verde case?
14. What are the milestones in the development of firearms identification?

INTERNET ACTIVITIES

1. Research your local, county, and state police agencies. Do these agencies have a criminal investigation unit? Do "general investigators" investigate all types of crimes? Or, in contrast, is there investigative specialization—for example, a homicide unit? How many investigators are assigned to such units? Do officers have to meet a certain criteria to be assigned to these units? How are officers selected? Is there any history on the creation of these units?
2. Find out more about the FBI's Biometric Center of Excellence (BCOE) by visiting *www.biometriccoe.gov*.

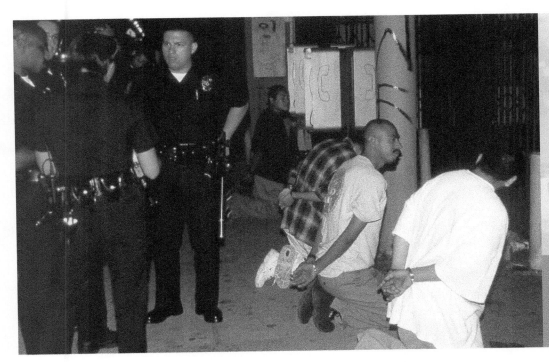

◀ Officers discuss the causes of a major gang fight while arrested gang members await transport to jail or youth centers. The suspects' handcuffed, kneeling, and facing-away position enhances officer safety.

(© Michael Newman/PhotoEdit)

2

LEGAL ASPECTS OF INVESTIGATION

CHAPTER OBJECTIVES

1. Explain the historical evolution of the laws of arrest and search and seizure from the Bill of Rights through the Fourteenth Amendment.

2. Describe and diagram the flow of constitutional rights to a defendant in a federal criminal trial and a defendant in a state criminal trial.

3. Outline the requirements of a valid arrest warrant.

4. Describe whether a "John Doe" arrest warrant is ever valid, and if so, under what circumstances.

5. Define probable cause.

6. Describe the evolution of the Exclusionary Rule.

7. Explain the "Silver Platter" doctrine.

8. Describe the reasons for a search incident to a lawful arrest.

9. Explain the limitations on the search of a motor vehicle incident to an arrest.

10. Describe at least five circumstances that justify a search under exigent circumstances.

11. Define the law-enforcement policy issue that determines whether an inventory search is lawful.

12. Identify the primary requirement that makes a plain view seizure lawful.

13. Describe the limitations of a stop and frisk encounter.

14. Explain the circumstances that would cause application of the Fruits of the Poisonous Tree doctrine.

INTRODUCTION

All law-enforcement officers, uniformed and plainclothes, conduct investigations. That is a statement of fact. There are, of course, differing concentrations of the investigative process and varying responsibilities among different units and different people.

Every law-enforcement officer must have a working knowledge of the criminal laws that he or she is charged with enforcing. The greater the knowledge, the better overall job one can do as an investigator. This will become apparent throughout the remainder of this text. It will be reinforced over and over because the criminal law is the foundation on which every investigation is built.

Criminal law is divided into two major components that are interrelated yet serve different functions. The **substantive criminal law** deals with those elements that describe and define a crime. When an investigator has the needed proof to satisfy the particular elements of an offense, it can then be said that the crime did occur.

The other component of criminal law is **procedural criminal law.** It is not enough to know whether a crime has been committed. The investigator must understand what and how things need to be done with the people involved in an investigation, be it a victim, a witness, an informant, or a suspect. Thus, the procedural part of criminal law defines what can and cannot be done with, or to, people. The procedural law changes much more rapidly than does the substantive criminal law. Procedural law deals with processes of arrest, search and seizure, interrogations, confessions, admissibility of evidence, and testifying in court. Some of these topics will be discussed in other portions of this book because they are relevant to specific subject matter covered. Legal matters dealing with interrogations and confessions are dealt with in the chapter on interviews and interrogation. Rules regarding admissibility of evidence and testifying in court round out the book, because they come into play when an investigation is completed and the case is submitted for prosecution. This chapter concerns the concepts of arrest and search and seizure. But knowing the current case law on these topics is not enough. The student must also understand the historical constitutional principles that got us to where we were, where we are, and, perhaps, where we are going tomorrow.

THE BILL OF RIGHTS AND THE STATES

An examination of constitutional history reveals that the powers yielded by the states were specifically granted for the purpose of establishing a national government. However, final ratification of the new constitution was delayed because some states wanted guarantees that individual liberties would be safeguarded from potential oppression by the newly formed government. This desire was based on the experiences of the colonists who supported the Declaration of Independence and fought the revolutionary war that won independence and created the United States of America, all of which occurred because the King of England was oppressing the colonies. The guarantees came in the form of the first ten amendments to the Constitution known as the Bill of Rights (Figure 2-1).

The Bill of Rights, however, restricts actions only by the federal government. It does not apply to, nor guarantee, the same protections from state governments. In addition, the Bill of Rights does not protect people from abuses by others who are not government officials or working on behalf of government officials. Thus, a private citizen could conduct an unreasonable search and seizure, then turn the results over to a government agency for use in court. Despite the fact that the seizing person may be criminally or civilly liable, the evidence seized could be used in court.[1]

The liberties protected by the specific clauses of the Bill of Rights are not exhaustive. One clause of the Fifth Amendment has been interpreted to leave the door open for additional protections. The **due process clause** provides: ". . . nor [shall any person] be deprived of life, liberty or property without due process of law." **Due process** is one of those concepts that has long been the subject of judicial controversy and has no universally accepted definition. The American concept of "fairness" is probably the closest one could get to an acceptable definition, in layman terms, without burdening the effort with reams of judicial history and philosophy. Thus the Supreme Court has the latitude to interpret the Constitution in any manner it

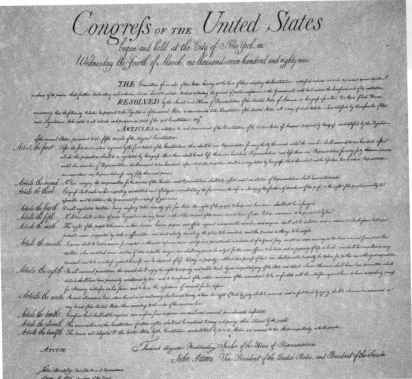

◄ FIGURE 2-1   The Bill of Rights
The Bill of Rights restricts actions only by the federal government.
(© The Granger Collection, New York)

deems to be fair and just under the American judicial system.[2]

During this time period and until the last part of the nineteenth century, the federal courts could insure fairness only in federal criminal proceedings.

EVOLUTION OF THE FOURTEENTH AMENDMENT

The Civil War was over. Slavery had been abolished. The Thirteenth, Fourteenth, and Fifteenth Amendments were all designed to guarantee the freedoms and equal protection of the laws for all citizens, especially the former slaves.

Interpretations given portions of the Fourteenth Amendment provide the foundation for much of modern criminal procedure in the United States today. The relevant portions of the Fourteenth Amendment read:

> No state shall make or enforce any law which shall abridge the privileges and immunities of citizens of the United States; nor shall any state deprive any person of life, liberty, or property, without due process of law; nor deny any person within its jurisdiction the equal protection of the laws.

The first three words of this quote provide the cornerstone to the foundation. Until this amendment was ratified in 1868, the people of the United States had never before granted the federal government the power to tell the states what they could or could not do. This section contains the Fourteenth Amendment's due process clause. This shift in power and authority was enhanced by another part of the Fourteenth Amendment. The first clause of Section 1 of the amendment reads:

> All persons born or naturalized in the United States, and subject to the jurisdiction thereof, are citizens of the United States and the state wherein they reside.

This wording creates what is commonly referred to as "dual citizenship" and gives the federal government the power to tell the states they cannot abuse the freedoms of those people—us; all of us.[3]

A few years after ratification of the Fourteenth Amendment, the United States Supreme Court was asked to determine the meaning of that amendment's due process clause. In the 1884 case of *Hurtado* v. *California*,[4] the defendant urged the Supreme Court to declare that the due process clause of the Fourteenth Amendment incorporated all the guarantees of the first eight amendments to the Bill of Rights. Hurtado was charged with a capital offense in the state court upon an Information filed by the District Attorney. He was convicted and sentenced to hang. The Fifth Amendment expressly requires that capital cases must be based on an indictment or presentment by a grand jury, but because Hurtado was being tried in a state court on a state charge, the Fifth Amendment was not applicable, as it would have been if he were being tried for a federal offense in federal court. He urged the high court to provide him the same guarantees in state court. This attempt to require carte blanche application of the first eight amendments to the states through the due process clause of the Fourteenth Amendment was rejected by a majority of the Court in this case and in many cases that followed. This attempted process became known as the "shorthand doctrine." The Supreme Court in rejecting the "shorthand doctrine" said that if the people and the states had intended for the Fourteenth Amendment to encompass the rights protected in the Bill of Rights and make them mandatorily applicable to the states, this would have been specified in the wording of the Fourteenth Amendment.[5]

Instead of adopting the "shorthand doctrine," the Supreme Court has reviewed cases on a case-by-case basis, determining whether the particular issue of the case calling into question a clause of the Bill of Rights should be made mandatorily applicable to the states through the due process clause of the Fourteenth Amendment. Although the Supreme Court rejected the quick way, the truth is, today, it doesn't matter anymore, because virtually everything in the first eight amendments has been ruled to apply to the states through the due process clause of the Fourteenth Amendment. It is still important to understand the relationship between the federal government and the states with respect to the Fifth and Fourteenth Amendments to the Constitution of the United States of America.[6] This relationship is diagrammed in Figure 2-2.

Let's now look at some of these processes as they have evolved.

THE FOURTH AMENDMENT

In part, the Fourth Amendment reads:

> The Right of the people to be secure in their persons, houses, papers, and effects, against unreasonable searches and seizures, shall not be violated, and no warrants shall issue, but upon probable cause, supported by oath or affirmation, and particularly describing the place to be searched, and the persons or things to be seized.

It is a common misconception that search and seizure is the sole topic covered by the Fourth Amendment. However, the authority for the laws of arrest is also derived from this amendment, as is seen in the last clause that provides: *"and the persons . . . to be seized."*[7]

By strict construction of the Fourth Amendment, the only time an arrest can be made or a search and seizure be conducted is under the authority of a warrant. However, the courts have not been that stringent in their interpretation of this amendment.

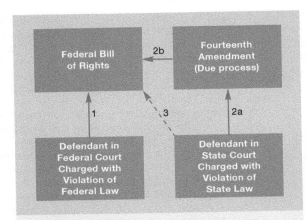

▲ **FIGURE 2-2**
Federal and State constitutional relationships in criminal cases
This chart represents the legal procedure a defendant would follow to claim a violation of constitutional rights in a criminal case. Line 1 represents a defendant claiming his rights in federal court directly from the Bill of Rights. Lines 2a and 2b are the correct procedure followed by an accused in a state court. Line 3 would be an incorrect attempt by a defendant to claim violation of constitutional rights directly from the protections guaranteed in the Bill of Rights.
(Source: Neil C. Chamelin, Vernon B. Fox, and Paul M. Whisenand, *Introduction to Criminal Justice*, 2nd Edition, Copyright 1979, reprinted with permission of Pearson Education, Inc., Upper Saddle River, NJ)

ARREST

There are a number of definitions of the term **arrest.** They range from "any interference with a person which, if not privileged, would constitute false imprisonment," to "interfering with the freedom of a person who is suspected of criminal conduct to the extent of taking him to the police station for some purpose," to "the taking of custody upon sufficient and proper evidence for the purpose of prosecution."[8] Each of these definitions is valid and depends on context. For example, what may appear to be a simple street stop or field interrogation may, in fact, constitute an arrest according to the first definition. Taking a person to the police station or sheriff's department for interrogation may fit the second definition. When an investigator intends to incarcerate and charge a person with a crime, the third definition applies.

INGREDIENTS OF ARREST

There are three essential ingredients of an arrest:

1. Intention
2. Authority
3. Custody

The officer must have the intention of taking the suspect into custody. This factor distinguishes an arrest from a lesser form of detention, but actual or expressed intention is not always the controlling factor. The intention may be inferred by a court if its estimate of all the conduct and circumstances indicates that an arrest occurred, despite any contrary intent on the part of the law-enforcement officer.

The officer must have real or assumed legal authority for taking the person into custody. The officer must have the actual authority to make a legal arrest or at least believe this to be the case. For example, an investigator may make an arrest under a defective warrant but not know about the defect. The third ingredient is that the person arrested must come within the custody and control of the law. This element can be satisfied either by physical restraint or by the arrestee's voluntary submission to the custody and control of the arresting officer.

ARREST DISTINGUISHED FROM DETENTION

Detention is a temporary and limited interference with the freedom of a person for investigative purposes. Sometimes called investigative detention, it is also commonly referred to by law enforcement as a "street stop" or "field interrogation." In this instance, police are justified in employing **"stop and frisk"** measures—patting down the outer clothing—if they suspect that the person being questioned may be armed and their safety is in jeopardy.[9] This issue of "stop and frisk" is covered later near the end of the search and seizure section of this chapter.

There is a fine line between detention and arrest. Because an officer does interfere with the freedom of the individual stopped, even for only a few minutes, some theorists view any such action as constituting arrest. Most people and most courts recognize the validity of street stops and uphold them as not being arrests if conducted properly.

A valid detention must be brief and made for good reason. The officer must limit questioning and investigation and must then either release the subject or decide to arrest. Detention for an undue length of time could be construed as an arrest if later challenged in court.

ARREST DISTINGUISHED FROM CHARGING

As noted earlier, one definition of arrest is to interfere with the freedom of a person suspected of involvement in a crime to the extent that the person is taken to the police station. But investigators do not always intend to prosecute or have the ability to prosecute at that time. Formally **charging** a suspect with a crime does not automatically flow from an arrest. Charging follows a decision to prosecute. This decision may be made by the police, by the prosecutor, or by both. But they may also decide not to bring charges. For example, the evidence that justified the arrest may not be sufficient to warrant formal charges, because the prosecutor believes he or she cannot prove the case beyond, and to the exclusion of, every reasonable doubt. Perhaps additional information may come to light after the arrest that points to the accused's innocence. Maybe an arrest was unlawful or evidence was obtained in violation of constitutional standards.

ARREST PROCEDURES

The laws of most jurisdictions permit an arrest in at least three and sometimes four types of situations:

1. When a warrant has been issued.
2. When a crime is committed in the presence of an arresting officer.
3. When an officer has probable cause to believe that the suspect being arrested has committed a felony.
4. In statutorily created instances.

THE ARREST WARRANT

The preferred method of effecting an arrest is under the authority of a warrant. In fact, if one were to read the constitutional requirements in their strictest sense, arrests can be justified only if made with a warrant. Of course, the courts have chosen to be more liberal in their interpretation so that warrantless arrests can be made in certain situations. But there are sound reasons for both the warrant requirements and the exceptions created by judicial case law, and, in some instances, by legislation. In the U.S. constitutional system, the functions of government—executive, legislative, and judicial—are each the responsibility of a separate branch. The police function is an executive one, whereas the judicial responsibility obviously belongs to the courts. Although the mechanism of arrest is an executive function, it is subject to judicial scrutiny and review. This position is supported by the very wording of the Fourth Amendment to the U.S. Constitution:

> . . . and no warrant shall issue, but upon probable cause, supported by oath or affirmation, and particularly describing the . . . person . . . to be seized.

The two major benefits derived from securing prior judicial approval for arrests through the warrant process are that the approval relieves law enforcement of the burden of proving the legality of the arrest—so that officers need not fear charges of false arrest, malicious prosecution, or other civil suits—and getting a warrant provides for an independent evaluation of the evidence.

Even the most objective, well-trained, and well-intentioned investigators sometimes become so involved in a case that their involvement may affect their ability to evaluate the case's merits objectively. Presenting the case before a qualified judge has the benefits of allowing an independent third party, with no emotional involvement in the investigation and with the knowledge of legal standards that must be met, to assist the investigator in determining whether those standards have been achieved. It is also logical to assume that the validity of an arrest made after this review and the issuance of a warrant is more likely to be upheld if later challenged in court than an arrest based solely on an officer's own determination of the sufficiency of the evidence. The wise law-enforcement officer recognizes the value of obtaining a warrant whenever practical. The word "practical" has significance with regard to the propriety of securing an arrest warrant. The law recognizes that the innumerable situations encountered by law-enforcement officers in daily activities and the variety of conditions inherent in the nature of the law-enforcement function make it impossible and unrealistic to expect an officer to obtain a warrant in every situation before effecting an arrest—hence, the exceptions to the warrant requirement.

The procedure required for obtaining a warrant is often time-consuming and inconvenient. Frequently, the process in major felony cases requires that the investigator seek out the prosecutor; present the facts, which will be reduced to paper in affidavit form for a probable cause determination; find a judge who is authorized to issue warrants; present the case again for a determination of the sufficiency of the grounds for arrest; and then wait for the warrant to be typed up and signed. In many cases, the procedure can take several hours, even during the normal workday. On weekends and late at night, it may take even longer, as the prosecutor, judge, or both are located or roused from bed. As a consequence, officers sometimes tend to take the easy way out by making a warrantless arrest, hoping they are right and believing they have sufficient grounds to act. By conducting themselves in this manner, they neglect the basic rule of thumb—get a warrant—and its underlying rationale. But the warrantless arrest is not always a shortcut. As clear as the law may appear to be on the need for warrants, each case must rest on its own facts. There are relatively few cases in which it is obvious that an arrest can be made without a warrant. Similarly, the clear-cut instances for which a warrant is absolutely needed are relatively few. The majority of cases fall within that vast plane requiring evaluation of the merits of each case. An arrest without a warrant, however, does not save time. In reality, the time an officer spends on justifying this decision in motion hearings demanded by the defense attorney will equal or exceed the time it would have taken to get a warrant in the first place. The potential consequence is that the case may be dismissed for want of a valid arrest or that important evidence, seized as a result of the arrest, may be suppressed.

The investigator is not relieved of all responsibility for the legality of the arrest simply because a warrant was obtained. The investigator must be aware of what constitutes a valid warrant to ensure that the one he or she possesses permits a legal arrest.

An **arrest warrant** is a judicial order commanding the person to whom it is issued or some other person to

▲ FIGURE 2-3   Review of affidavit for arrest warrant
Investigator and judge review the paperwork prepared by
the investigator in support of seeking the arrest warrant.
(© Mike Karlsson/Arresting Images)

▲ FIGURE 2-4
Swearing or affirming to contents of affidavit for arrest
warrant
When the judge is satisfied that the arrest warrant affidavit is
in order, and probable cause to arrest exists, he places the
investigator under oath and the affidavit becomes a sworn
document. (© Mike Karlsson/Arresting Images)

arrest a particular individual and to bring that person
promptly before a court to answer a criminal charge. The
arrest warrant generally must be written. By legislation,
some jurisdictions allow for verbal authorization supported by written authorization in warrant form that is
issued later (Figures 2-3 and 2-4).

In most cases, particularly major felonies, the warrant
must be issued by a judge who personally reviews the
facts to determine the existence of reasonable grounds as
required by the Constitution. The warrant must be supported by an **affidavit**—a written statement of the information known to the officer that serves as the basis for
the issuance of the warrant. In major cases, the requirements vary on whether the warrant must be issued in the
county in which the offense occurred, but once issued,
major case warrants can be served anywhere in the state.

The form and contents of an arrest warrant usually
include:

1. The authority under which the warrant is issued
   (the name of the state).
2. The person who is to execute the warrant (generally addressed to any peace officer of the state).
3. The identity of the person to be arrested.
4. The designation of the offense.
5. The date, time, and place of the occurrence.
6. The name of the victim.
7. A description of the offense and how it occurred.

Blank warrants are not constitutionally valid. Before a
warrant can be issued, the identity of the perpetrator
must be known. The mere fact that a crime has been committed by someone unknown will not support a warrant's issuance. The Constitution requires that the warrant
contain a particular description of the suspect. This
description must be specific enough to permit an officer
not acquainted with the case to identify the person to be
arrested with reasonable certainty. Aliases may be used.
If the suspect's name is not known, "John Doe" may be
used provided there are other methods of describing the
person to be arrested, such as place of residence, occupation, and a physical description.

A reprint of an Associated Press story appeared on the
web on August 8, 2004, reporting that in Boston, prosecutors found a way to prevent the 15-year statute of limitations from destroying the possibility of bringing rapists

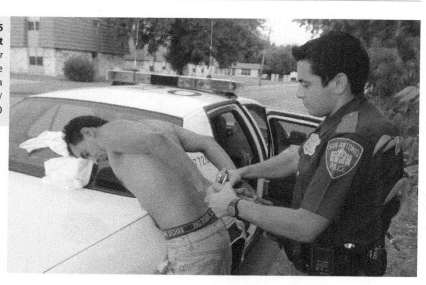

▶ **FIGURE 2-5**
Placing felon under arrest
A San Antonio, Texas, police officer arrests a person he has probable cause to believe just committed a felony battery. (© Bob Daemmrich/ PhotoEdit)

to trial. In cases that have DNA evidence, prosecutors are obtaining indictments against "John Does" based on their DNA profiles. Massachusetts followed the lead of Wisconsin that started doing this in 1999. New York has also begun using the process. In a Wisconsin appellate case challenging the constitutionality of the statute claiming that the indictment does not specifically name the defendant, the court said that DNA evidence was the best method of identification available.

Herring v. *United States*[10] involved a warrant issued on erroneous information that the police did not know was in error. Officers in one Alabama county arrested Herring based on a warrant that was listed in a neighboring county's database. Search incident to arrest yielded drugs and a gun. It was then learned that the warrant had been recalled months earlier but someone forgot to remove the warrant from the neighboring county's database. Herring was tried on federal gun and drug possession charges. The federal district court refused to suppress the evidence and Herring was convicted. The U.S. Supreme Court held: When police mistakes leading to an unlawful search are the result of isolated negligence leading up to the search, rather than systematic error or disregard of constitutional requirements, the exclusionary rule does not apply.

Crime Committed in Presence

Any offense committed in the presence of an officer, whether felony or misdemeanor, can be the basis of an arrest without a warrant. The in-presence requirement is usually thought of in the narrow context of sight. However, to satisfy the legal requirements, perception of some or all of the elements of an offense as they occur, through the use of any or all of the five senses—sight, hearing, taste, touch, or smell—can justify a warrantless arrest.

PROBABLE CAUSE

The third major category in which a lawful arrest is generally permitted involves offenses not committed in the officer's presence and for which a warrant has not been issued. The law allows an officer to make warrantless arrests in felony cases provided reasonable grounds or probable cause exists to make the arrest (Figure 2-5). (As previously noted, probable cause also must be shown in an affidavit to support the issuance of a warrant.)

Probable cause is a difficult term to define, because in no two instances are circumstances identical. One acceptable definition of **probable cause** is that it is more than suspicion but less than actual knowledge. It is suspicion plus facts and circumstances that would lead a reasonable person exercising ordinary caution to believe that a crime has been, is being, or is about to be committed (see Figure 2-6).

Probable cause may be based on a number of sources of information, not all of which have to be the kind of evidence admissible at trial. However, if prosecution is an aim of the arrest, there must also be sufficient evidence to take the case to court. In addition, the probable cause must exist at the time the arrest is made and may not be developed by subsequently acquired evidence.

Mere suspicion is not enough to justify an arrest; there must be supporting facts and circumstances. Certain factors may help to decide the existence of probable cause. The most common is the personal knowledge of the officer/ investigator. Information obtained from informants also may be of value, although that information may not be admissible at a subsequent hearing or trial. The investigator must be able to establish the reliability of the information and the informant by indicating the length of time the investigator has known or dealt with the informant, the general character and reputation of the informant, the

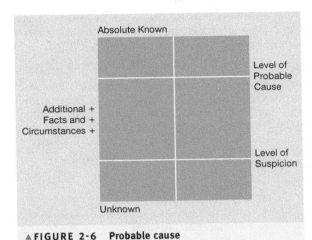

▲ **FIGURE 2-6   Probable cause**

(Source: Neil C. Chamelin, Vernon B. Fox, and Paul M. Whisenand, *Introduction to Criminal Justice*, 2nd ed. Copyright 1979, reprinted with permission of Pearson Education, Inc. Upper Saddle River, NJ)

number of tips received from the informant in the past, the accuracy of previous information, whether the informant is paid for the information, and the informant's motives for volunteering the information. One of the current common instances is the use of confidential informants to make drug buys.

Other sources of probable cause include information from a police department or from other law-enforcement agencies, such as notice of outstanding warrants, the past criminal record of the suspect, physical evidence found at the scene of the crime, other evidence detected in the follow-up investigation, crime laboratory analyses, and reports of victims and eyewitnesses.

There is a third exception to the warrant requirement for a valid arrest. By legislation, states allow officers to make arrests in nonfelony cases even though the offense is not committed in the officer's presence. Examples include domestic violence situations, violations of injunctions against domestic violence, and cases of battery.[11]

SEARCH AND SEIZURE

The evolution of the law of **search and seizure** illustrates the relationship described earlier between federal and state court systems and between the Bill of Rights and its application to the states through the due process clause of the Fourteenth Amendment.[12]

Under early English common law, an illegal search and seizure that produced incriminating evidence was allowed, and the evidence obtained was admissible in court. Surprisingly, federal law-enforcement officers in the United States were permitted to follow the same rule until 1914. Up to that time, the search and seizure practices

of federal officials had not been scrutinized in light of the wording of the Fourth Amendment. In 1914 the case of *Weeks* v. *United States*[13] was decided by the United States Supreme Court. Weeks was charged by federal agents with using the mails for transporting materials that represented chances in a lottery. After his arrest for this federal offense, Weeks's room was searched twice without the authority of a valid search warrant. But Weeks had been arrested at his place of employment, not his home. During the **search,** the agents found and seized various incriminating papers and articles. This evidence was admitted at his trial for the federal violation, and Weeks was convicted. On appeal to the United States Supreme Court, the Court established what became known as the "Federal Exclusionary Rule." The Court ruled that any evidence unreasonably obtained by federal law-enforcement officers could no longer be admissible in federal prosecutions. The Court made it quite clear that, because this was a federal case, the decision was applicable only to federal law-enforcement officers and federal courts and was in no way applicable to the states. But this decision, as do many Supreme Court decisions, left a number of unanswered questions. Out of one question arose the "Silver Platter Doctrine." The *Weeks* decision prohibited federal officers from illegally seizing evidence but it did not prevent law-enforcement officers of the states from illegally seizing the evidence and handing it over to federal agents on a "silver platter" for use in federal courts. This method of circumventing the Federal Exclusionary Rule remained unchallenged until 1960. In that year, the Supreme Court prohibited the introduction in federal courts of all illegally seized evidence obtained by state officers in violation of the Fourth Amendment.[14]

After the *Weeks* decision, very few states adopted their own exclusionary rule applicable within their own state. It was not until 1949 that a serious attempt was made to seek mandatory application of the exclusionary rule to the states through the due process clause of the Fourteenth Amendment. In *Wolf* v. *Colorado*,[15] the defendant was charged with abortion. Based on suspicion of similar prior offenses, officers searched Wolf's office, arrested him, and seized certain documents that were later admitted into trial. Wolf appealed his conviction contending that the unreasonable search and seizure was a denial of due process under the Fourteenth Amendment, as it would be under the Fourth Amendment had he been in federal court. The Supreme Court held that unreasonable searches and seizures by state officials in state cases did not constitute a denial of Fourteenth Amendment due process but added that the Court did have the authority to rule otherwise if the Justices so desired. The interesting point in this case seemed to be that the Court was giving the states fair warning that they disapproved of unreasonable searches and seizures by state authorities and that sooner or later they would rule in favor of incorporating the Fourth Amendment protection in the due process clause of the Fourteenth Amendment. Many states took the hint.

By 1961 only 18 states had not adopted an exclusionary rule. In that year, the warning that the Supreme Court had given 12 years earlier in the *Wolf* case came to pass. In May 1957 three Cleveland police officers arrived at Dolree Mapp's residence in that city with information that a person who was wanted for questioning in a recent bombing was hiding out in her home and that there was a large amount of gambling paraphernalia being hidden in the home. The officers knocked on the door and demanded entrance, but Ms. Mapp, after telephoning her attorney, refused to admit them without a search warrant. The officers advised their headquarters of the situation and undertook a surveillance of the house. Some three hours later, the officers, with reinforcements, again sought entrance. When Ms. Mapp did not come to the door immediately, one of the doors was forcibly opened and the officers gained entry. Ms. Mapp demanded to see the search warrant. One of the officers held up a paper that he claimed was the search warrant. She grabbed the paper and stuffed it down the front of her dress. A struggle ensued in which the officers recovered the piece of paper and handcuffed Ms. Mapp for her "belligerency" in resisting the attempt to recover the "warrant." A subsequent widespread search of the entire premises disclosed obscene materials. Ms. Mapps was convicted for possession of these materials. No search warrant was ever produced at the trial.

Following Ms. Mapp's conviction and the denial of her appeals in the state courts, her case was appealed to the United States Supreme Court. *Mapp v. Ohio,*[16] decided in 1961, established the rule that any evidence unreasonably searched and seized would no longer be admissible in any court—state or federal. The Exclusionary Rule was now applicable in all courts at all levels.

Among the many unanswered questions created by the *Mapp* decision, the crucial question revolved around the definition of the word **unreasonable.** It did not take the state courts long to find the loophole. In order to avoid applying the decision in the *Mapp* case to instances arising in state courts, state officials merely called previously unreasonable searches and seizures reasonable searches. Because no standards had been set for determining what constitutes a reasonable or unreasonable search, many of the state courts felt free to make their own determination on this issue. In effect, *Mapp* had little impact on these states. However, within two years of the *Mapp* decision, the Supreme Court had the opportunity to rule on this matter. The Court held in *Ker v. California*[17] that the state court judges were still free to determine the reasonableness of searches but that in making those determinations they would now be guided by the same standards as had been followed in the federal courts, which were established in the line of cases decided since the *Weeks* case in 1914. In essence, the Court said that states would be held to federal standards in search and seizure matters.

The long line of cases evolving since *Mapp* and *Ker* have essentially revolved around the single issue of what constitutes a reasonable search in instances where law-enforcement officers act with or without a warrant.

LEGAL SEARCHES AND SEIZURES

As is true for arrests, the Fourth Amendment also recognizes searches and seizures only by government agents under the authority of a warrant. The United States Supreme Court recognizes judicially created exceptions. Thus, legal searches and seizures can be made:

1. when a warrant has been issued;
2. with consent;
3. incident to an arrest;
4. of a motor vehicle;
5. when an emergency (exigent circumstances) exists;
6. to conduct an inventory.

There are two additional areas that are closely related but can't truly be called searches and seizures—plain view seizures and stop and frisk encounters. These will also be covered.

SEARCH WITH A WARRANT

A **search warrant** is a written order, in the name of the state, signed by a judicial officer, exercising proper authority, and directing a law-enforcement officer to search for certain specific property and bring it before the court. To be valid, the warrant must be signed by one who is authorized to sign. Normally, this is a judicial officer. In rare instances, state law may allow a prosecutor or law-enforcement officer to sign the warrant to expedite the process but only after the facts and circumstances have been reviewed over the telephone by a judicial officer, being later subject to that judicial officer's signature. In no case is a prosecutor or law-enforcement officer permitted to sign a warrant without that judicial review. The independent impartial review is what provides the warrant with validity.

A warrant to search must be based upon probable cause. In this instance, probable cause can best be defined as facts and circumstances that would lead a reasonable person to believe that the place to be searched and the things to be seized are to be found. The probable cause is established by a written affidavit prepared by the law-enforcement officer/investigator, stating all those known facts and circumstances. As is true for an arrest warrant, probable cause may be established by any number of sources, including information supplied by informants. In drug cases, probable cause is often established by confidential informants who make repeated drug buys from a specific house or store. The affidavit is then presented to the judicial officer, who independently evaluates it and, if she or he finds it sufficient, issues the warrant. As is pretty evident from the process described so far, probable cause must be established before the warrant is issued. Anything found as a result of the service of the warrant cannot be used to establish the probable cause.

The search warrant must particularly describe the place to be searched. Although the Constitution does not define "particularly," the description must be sufficient to distinguish the place from all others. Normally, one might think of a building on a piece of property as a place to be searched. Using the legal description is not necessary; however, a street address may not be sufficient. There are many appellate cases involving invalid warrants because the address failed to distinguish between two identical numbers on houses on "Main Street" because one was on "North Main" and the other on "South Main." In addition, numbers may be missing from the house or mailbox causing problems. What happens when a warrant is issued for "999 Main Street" but the numbers have come loose and flipped over at "666 Main Street" and now read "999"? Have investigators ever served a warrant at the wrong location? The appellate cases are full of examples. The warrant should contain information such as the color of the house, the type of floor plan (for example, ranch style home); apartment on the third floor, east side of a brownstone tenement; cream colored, vinyl siding, one story house with green trim, green shutters, an American flag on a pole in the front yard, and so forth.

The phrase "particularly describe" also applies to the things to be seized. This governs the extent of the search. For example, if the affidavit and warrant are for the search and seizure of drugs in a house, the search can be pretty extensive. Thus, it would be permitted to search closets, under beds, in dresser drawers, in medicine cabinets, and in kitchen cupboards—and anything found, even evidence of other crimes, may be properly seized and considered admissible. For example, the search turns up a firearm; but the occupant of the house, being a previously convicted felon, is not allowed to possess firearms. The discovery of the weapon could be the legal basis for adding a charge of illegal possession of a firearm. But if the warrant is based on the belief that the house contains stolen tires, the places that can legally be searched in that same house are significantly reduced. A search of dresser drawers, kitchen cupboards, and medicine cabinets would be improper, and, if the firearm in the previous example is found under the pillow on the bed occupied by the suspect, its seizure would be improper unless the investigator could convince the court, during a hearing on a motion to suppress the seizure of the firearm, that the investigator reasonably believed there might have been a stolen tire under the pillow.

In another example, a law-enforcement officer went outside the scope of his authority to search when, with consent, while searching for a stolen boat motor and a shotgun, picked up and opened a tackle box that contained drugs and drug paraphernalia. This served as the basis for charging. The court stated there was no reasonable belief the boat motor or shotgun was in the tackle box.[18]

Normally, investigators should include in their affidavits in support of a search warrant the justification for

▲ **FIGURE 2-7   Preparing to serve a search warrant**
An investigator and a uniformed officer, each positioned to react if trouble should occur, are the advance party for the service of a search warrant. Other investigators wait to see if anyone inside opens the door. (© Tony Savino/The Image Works)

searching persons found at the place where the warrant is to be executed and the search conducted. In the absence of such authority in the warrant, persons found on the scene may not be searched unless they are first lawfully arrested.

Once issued, a warrant must be executed within whatever time limits the law of the state requires; time of day/ night limits are applicable. In some instances, the warrant may specify that it may be served at nighttime if the probable cause supporting the warrant can justify that the specific criminal activity only occurs at night. Until recently, state laws required officers/investigators executing warrants to knock, announce their purpose and the fact that they were in possession of a warrant, and giving the occupants a reasonable time to answer and open the door (Figure 2-7). In 2006 the Supreme Court ruled in *Hudson* v. *Michigan*[19] that violation of the knock and announce requirement for the service of a search warrant will no longer result in the suppression of evidence found during execution of the search warrant. The Court said the social cost of applying the exclusionary rule to knock and announce violations was considerable.

▶ **FIGURE 2-8**
Investigators conducting a search
Investigators conduct a home search. Note that while one of the investigators searches, another records the location where each piece of evidence was found, and a third officer packages and marks each piece of evidence. All these steps are important in maintaining and protecting the chain of custody.
(© Mike Karlsson/Arresting Images)

During the search, particularly if several investigators are involved, one investigator should be designated the property custodian. A detailed record must be kept of each piece of evidence, with a specific description, where it was found, and by whom. This list then becomes part of the return on the warrant that must be brought back and presented to the judge for review. It, of course, also becomes part of the case file (Figure 2-8).

In 2005, in *Muehler* v. *Mena*,[20] the Supreme Court held that officers executing a search warrant of a house seeking weapons and evidence of gang membership in the wake of a drive-by shooting acted reasonably by detaining the occupants of the house in handcuffs during the search, especially since there were only two officers to watch over four people.

SEARCH WITH CONSENT

One of the most common situations arising today is when a uniformed officer, in encountering a citizen during a traffic stop or other routine activity, asks the person if he/she has any weapons or drugs on his/her person or in the vehicle. Sometimes the person says yes, and that might lead to an immediate arrest. Often the person says no, and the officer may then ask if he/she can search the person and/or the vehicle. If the person gives affirmative consent, the search may be conducted. If the person denies consent, which he/she has the right to do, no search may be made unless there is probable cause to conduct a search under one of the other exceptions to the warrant requirement. A refusal to allow a search, standing alone, does not constitute probable cause to justify any further action.

The crux of a consent search is that the consent must be voluntarily given. It can't be based on intimidation or threats of any kind.

A person may give consent to the search of his/her home, but in the case where there are roommates living in the same house or apartment and each has his/her own bedroom, an occupant may give consent to the search only of his/her private room and any area shared in common by the roommates, such as the kitchen or living room.

Once consent is given for search of a home, car, office, or any other place, it may be withdrawn at any time by the person who had the authority and gave the consent. When consent is withdrawn, the search must stop. Any incriminating evidence found after consent is withdrawn is illegally seized and is not admissible.

It is always wise to get documentation of the consent to search. Figure 2-9 is a generic form that may be used.

SEARCH INCIDENT TO ARREST

The courts have regularly recognized the right of law-enforcement officers to search people who have been arrested without a warrant. Such searches are justified for officer safety and to preserve evidence.[21] In 1969 the United States Supreme Court limited the scope of a search when it ruled in *Chimel* v. *California*[22] that a warrantless search of the defendant's entire house, following his lawful arrest in the house on a burglary charge, was unreasonable. This case set the benchmark for searches incident to a valid arrest by holding that such searches may be made of the person arrested and the area under his/her immediate control from which he or she might obtain a weapon or destroy evidence. Initially, searches were reasonable only if conducted in conformity with *Chimel*. Over the years, case law has expanded the allowable area of search following a legal arrest, particularly as applied to automobile searches, but as to searches of an arrestee's home, *Chimel* is still followed closely. In

PERMISSION TO SEARCH AND SEIZE

I, _____, agree to permit members/officers
of the _____ to search my
(agency name)
vehicle(s)/apartment/house/other structure(s) or other areas as described below, which
are in my control.

Area to be Searched: Located At:

_____

And I further agree to permit members/officers of the _____
(agency name)
_____ to remove from the above listed areas any item(s) of
property they deem relevant to their investigation. It is further understood that I will
receive a receipt for any and all items removed by the _____
(agency name)
_____.

I am giving this written permission to the _____
(agency name)
freely and voluntarily, without any threats or promises having been made to me, and
after having been informed that I have a right to refuse to permit this search and
seizure. I further understand that any item(s) seized, may be used in a court of law
during a criminal procedure/prosecution.

Signed: _____

Address: _____

Date: _____ Time: _____

Witness: _____

Witness: _____

FIGURE 2-9
Consent to search form—generic

Maryland v. *Buie*,[23] a 1990 case, the Supreme Court reported that:

Two men committed an armed robbery. The police obtained warrants for their arrest. Buie was one of the people to be arrested. The officers went to Buie's home to arrest him. When they entered, they found Buie coming from the basement. That is where he was arrested. One of the officers went into the basement, allegedly on a protective sweep, to make sure no one else was down there. While in the basement he saw "in plain view" a red running suit that matched the description of clothing that witnesses said one of the robbers was wearing. The officer seized the suit and it was used in evidence to help convict Buie.

The Supreme Court said that:

. . . as an incident to the arrest of the accused, the officers could, as a precautionary measure and without a search warrant, probable cause, or reasonable suspicion, look in closets and other spaces immediately

adjoining the place of arrest from which an attack could be immediately launched . . .[24]

As to conducting protective sweeps, the Supreme Court went on to say:

. . . beyond that, the Fourth Amendment permits a warrantless protective sweep in conjunction with an in-home arrest—extending only to a cursory inspection of those spaces where a person may be found, lasting no longer than is necessary to dispel the reasonable suspicion of danger, and in any event no longer than it takes to complete the arrest and depart the premises—when the searching officer possesses a reasonable belief based on specific and articulable facts which, taken with the rational inferences from those facts, would warrant a reasonably prudent officer in believing that the area to be swept harbors an individual posing a danger to those on the arrest scene.[25]

The Court made it clear that the officers had the right, pursuant to the arrest warrant, to search anywhere in the house, even the basement, until they found Buie.[26]

SEARCH OF A MOTOR VEHICLE

The search of a motor vehicle, sometimes referred to as the automobile exception to the requirement that a search be conducted with a warrant, really involves two distinct legal issues under modern law. The first can be traced back to a 1925 Supreme Court case. In *Carroll* v. *United States*,[27] the Court created the "moveable vehicle" rule. The Court held that if there was sufficient probable cause to get a warrant, but, because the vehicle was moveable, it might be gone if time were taken to get a warrant, a warrantless search was justified. In this case, the vehicle was moving and contained bootleg whiskey during Prohibition. The search of the entire vehicle, including the trunk was justified in this case.

In *Chambers* v. *Maroney*[28] a service station was robbed by two armed men. About the time of the robbery, two teenagers saw a blue station wagon circling the block around the service station and later sped off with four men. The service station attendant described one of the robbers as wearing a green sweater and the other wearing a trench coat. Sometime after, a vehicle fitting the description, carrying four men, one of whom was wearing a green sweater, was stopped. A trench coat was seen in the car. The occupants were arrested, and the car was searched without a warrant. The money, guns, and other evidence of the robbery were found. The Supreme Court approved of the search under the motor vehicle exception. The motor vehicle exception is still very viable.

In *Maryland* v. *Dyson*,[29] the Supreme Court continued to follow the ruling in *Carroll*. But it is not necessary that the vehicle actually be moving to justify such a warrantless search. Early on, the Supreme Court held that where a car was legally parked, agents did not have to speculate as to when the owner would return and whether there was time to obtain a search warrant.[30]

The second issue involves the search of a vehicle incident to a lawful arrest. Keeping in mind the foundation principle of the *Chimel* case, that a search may be made of the area under the arrestee's immediate control, the Supreme Court ruled in the 1981 case of *New York* v. *Belton*[31] that when a police officer makes a lawful custodial arrest of the occupant of an automobile, the officer may search the vehicle's passenger compartment as a contemporaneous incident of arrest. The right to search includes any open or closed containers found in the passenger compartment. It does not include the trunk.

On May 24, 2004, the Supreme Court decided *Thornton* v. *United States*.[32] In 2001 Officer Nichols was driving behind Thornton's Lincoln town car. He ran the town car's license plate. The response from the Department of Motor vehicles (DMV) reported that the tag belonged on a 1982 Chevrolet. Before Nichols had a chance to pull the car over, Thornton drove into a parking lot, parked, and got out of his car. Officer Nichols saw Thornton leave his vehicle as he pulled in behind him. The officer parked, got out of his car, and accosted Thornton. He asked Thornton for his driver's license and told Thornton that the license plate did not match the vehicle to which it was properly attached. Nichols then asked Thornton if he could pat him down. Thornton agreed. Nichols felt a bulge in Thornton's left front pocket and again asked him if he had any illegal narcotics on him. This time Thornton said that he did and pulled out two bags, one containing marijuana and the other crack cocaine. The officer handcuffed Thornton, informed him that he was under arrest, and put him in the back seat of the patrol car. Officer Nichols then searched the vehicle and found a 9-mm handgun under the driver's seat. Thornton was charged with federal firearms and drug offenses. He was convicted. His case was affirmed on appeal by the district court of appeals and then was appealed to the Supreme Court.

In brief, the Supreme Court said that the right to search the passenger compartment of a car still exists even if the officer does not make contact until the person arrested has left the vehicle (Figure 2-10). The issue in this case asked the question on the reasonableness of the search whether the defendant was inside or outside the vehicle when first contacted and subsequently arrested. The opinion points out that the length of time the person had been out of the car and how far away from the vehicle the person was may all come into play in determining reasonableness of a search. Interestingly, in this case, the defendant had already been secured and was in the back seat of the patrol car when this search took place. This, of course, was pointed out by the dissenting Justices, who said there was no longer any chance to obtain a weapon or destroy evidence and the officer should have obtained a warrant before searching.

Five years after *Thornton* and 28 years after *Belton*, the Court seemed to revert to the *Chimel* foundation. In *Arizona* v. *Gant*,[33] the Supreme Court said that *Belton* had been expanded beyond what the Court intended. Although the majority opinion doesn't specifically overrule *Belton* and *Thornton*, the holding severely limits the situations in which law enforcement may search incident to a lawful arrest. Gant was arrested for driving with a suspended license. He was handcuffed and locked in the back seat of a patrol car. Two other individuals were with Gant. They were also secured in patrol vehicles. Then the passenger compartment of his vehicle was searched and officers found cocaine in the pocked of a jacket in the back seat. Gant was charged and convicted of possession of cocaine and a related charge. The Supreme Court held that once the scene was secured, that is, the driver was handcuffed and locked in the back of a patrol car, he

◄**FIGURE 2-10**
**Officer and investigator searching
the passenger compartment of a
motor vehicle**
Uniformed officers search a vehicle
in a warehouse district after making
a major bust of cocaine traffickers.
(© James Shaffer/PhotoEdit)

could no longer reach a weapon to harm an officer or reach to destroy any potential evidence. Consequently, a search and seizure, without a warrant, under these circumstances would be reasonable. However, the Court waivered slightly by concluding "that circumstances unique to the automobile context justify a search incident to arrest when it is reasonable to believe that evidence of the offense of arrest might be found in the vehicle." Thus, when a person is arrested on a traffic charge and secured, there would be no evidence in the vehicle related to the charge. But if the vehicle driver is arrested on a drug charge, there may be evidence in the vehicle related to that charge and a search may be reasonable even though the driver is secured in the back of a patrol car. In *Belton*, there were four people in the vehicle. They were separated and were away from the vehicle at the time of the search but were not secured and not under arrest. That was the narrow context in which the Court intended *Belton* to be applicable. The Court pointed out that at least eight states followed the narrow interpretation based on state constitutional provisions. The states were Vermont, New Jersey, New Mexico, Nevada, Pennsylvania, New York, Oregon and Wyoming. In *Thornton*, the driver was away from the vehicle when arrested on a drug charge after a consent pat down. Thornton was secured and placed in a patrol car but, because this was a drug case, search of the vehicle incident to arrest was reasonable and evidence found was admissible.

A vehicle search is not reasonable if conducted pursuant to stopping a vehicle for a traffic violation and writing a citation. A citation is not an arrest and no right to search arises. Does the same rule hold true if an officer issues a summons (sometime called a Notice to Appear)? Generally, the answer is yes; but consider the case of *Virginia* v. *Moore*,[34] decided by the Supreme Court in 2008. Moore was arrested for driving on a suspended license. He was searched and cocaine was found on his person. He

was charged with the possession of cocaine and convicted. The kink in this story is that Virginia law specified that when officers stopped the vehicle Moore was driving, he should have been given a summons. Had that been done, there would not have been a search. But when they arrested him instead, they searched incident to the arrest. The Supreme Court held that police did not violate the Fourth Amendment by arresting Moore instead of following state law requiring the issuance of a summons, thereby making the search and seizure reasonable.

EMERGENCY (EXIGENT CIRCUMSTANCES)

The **exigent circumstances** exception recognizes that a warrantless entry by law-enforcement officials may be legal when there is a compelling need for official action and no time to get a warrant. The exception covers several common situations including: danger of flight or escape, loss or destruction of evidence, risk of harm to the public or police, mobility of a vehicle (discussed earlier), and hot pursuit.[35] In *Warden* v. *Hayden*,[36] two taxi drivers reported seeing an armed robber run into a residence. Police arrived within minutes, entered the house without a warrant, found the defendant in an upstairs bedroom where he was arrested, and then conducted a search. They found and seized a shotgun and a pistol in the adjoining bathroom flush tank. They also seized a jacket and pants that were of the type witnesses said the robber was wearing. Hayden was convicted, and when the case reached the Supreme Court, it held the search and seizure was legal. The Court said that speed was essential to find out if other people were in the house who might be in danger and to protect the officers themselves by insuring they had possession of all weapons that could be used against them or to effect an escape. In all cases of exigent circumstances, there must be an emergency that justifies the warrantless search.

Officers responded to a residence after receiving two 911 calls saying that there was loud arguing and numerous shots had been fired. On arrival, a husband and wife were on the porch of their mobile home. Officers, while behind their vehicle doors and with weapons drawn, ordered the people off the porch and told them to lie down with their palms facing up. After finally getting compliance and securing the pair along with a neighbor who appeared from the side of the house, officers entered the house to see if anyone was inside and hurt. In the process, when stepping on the porch, they found a shotgun leaning against the side of the mobile home about 3 feet from where the defendant had been standing and a number of expended shells on the porch and ground nearby. These were seized. The defendant was convicted of possession of a firearm by a convicted felon. He challenged the officers' actions of stepping on the porch as an illegal search.

When the case finally reached the Supreme Court, the search and seizure was upheld under exigent circumstances. The Court reasoned that there certainly was a reasonable belief by the officers that there might be injured people inside the home based on the multiple calls that shots had been fired. This emergency justified the warrantless entry and the seizure of the weapon that formed the basis of the charge.[37]

In *Brigham City* v. *Stuart*,[38] the Supreme Court held that law-enforcement officers may enter a home without a warrant when there is an objectively reasonable basis to believe that an occupant is seriously injured or imminently threatened with serious injury.

In *Michigan* v. *Fisher*[39] officers arrived at Fisher's home in response to a call for service by a couple who reported that Fisher was "going crazy." The officers found the homestead trashed and a pickup truck in the driveway was smashed. There was blood on the hood and on clothes inside the truck. Fence posts along the side of the property were damaged, and three windows to the house were smashed. Through the window, officers could see Fisher smashing things in the house. The back door was locked and Fisher had pushed a couch against the front door. The officers knocked but Fisher would not answer the door. The officers saw a cut on Fisher's hand and asked him if he needed medical attention. Fisher told officers to get a search warrant. One officer forced his way in but he retreated when Fisher pointed a rifle at him. Officers entered the house and finally subdued Fisher. He was charged with assault with a deadly weapon and possession of a firearm in the commission of a felony. Fisher argued that the entry of the police was an unreasonable search and seizure and anything he said to a police officer should not be admitted. The trial court agreed, and the State appealed. After several remands and reversals, the case ended in the U.S. Supreme Court. The Court cited the *Brigham City* case for the proposition that an "emergency aid" exception exists justifying an entry into a residence without warrant. The State courts in this case

found that an "emergency" did not exist. The Supreme Court, however, said that officers did not need iron-clad proof that a serious injury had occurred. There was ongoing violence and an objective basis for believing that medical attention was needed. Therefore, the officers were justified in entering without a warrant. The case was remanded, and the trial court was required to deny the defendant's motion to suppress the statements made by the defendant to officers who entered his home.

Conducting an Inventory

Law-enforcement agencies have not only the right but also the obligation to inventory property taken from a person arrested. This includes property taken from the person and from their presence, such as a motor vehicle. The inventory is done for the purpose of protecting the property of the person arrested and documenting what was found with a receipt given to the person arrested. In this manner, law enforcement can prevent accusations of stealing an offender's money or property. Similarly, law enforcement should inventory a vehicle that was impounded pursuant to an arrest. This includes the contents of the trunk (Figure 2-11). If contraband or evidence of a crime are found by virtue of a valid inventory search, the results are admissible. To justify admissibility of the fruits of an inventory search, the agency must have a standing policy that specifies the inventory in all cases. If such a policy does not exist, but this particular vehicle was inventoried, it will be ruled a pretext for a warrantless search and will be deemed unreasonable.

PLAIN VIEW SEIZURES

If an investigator/officer is lawfully in a place and sees contraband or evidence in plain view, the investigator may seize the evidence, and it will be admissible. For example, investigators were called to a hotel room door, because the occupant wanted to turn himself in on an outstanding warrant. When the defendant opened the door, officers could see crack cocaine lying on the counter inside the room. Their entry and seizure was lawful. Investigators are not required to turn their backs on a crime being committed in their presence. It is critical that the officer has a lawful right to be where she/he can see the evidence in plain view. An investigator on the street outside a house who looks in a window and sees contraband can legally seize it, but if that same investigator is standing on a box, peering inside a window overlooking the backyard, he/she cannot expect any subsequent seizure to be upheld.

Consider this example: The men's restroom in a local club, frequented by young adults, is known for drug use. Users go in the stalls, lock the doors, and ingest cocaine. Off-duty, uniformed officers check out the whole club, including the men's room. Underneath the stall door they see an individual's feet turned sideways to the toilet. It's pretty obvious that the person is not using the toilet for

◄FIGURE 2-11

Officer and K-9 partner inventorying trunk of impounded vehicle

A police officer and his K-9 partner conduct an inventory search of an impounded vehicle's trunk. The driver of the vehicle had been arrested for selling large quantities of MDMA, better known as Ecstasy. Pursuant to departmental policy, all vehicles impounded are inventoried to protect the possessions of the arrested person. In drug-related arrests, dogs are used. (© Bob Daemmrich/PhotoEdit)

its intended purpose. The officer looks through a crack between the stall door and the frame and sees the individual snorting cocaine. The officer tells the man to open the door, then arrests him for possession of cocaine. Whether this is a plain view seizure depends on two things. First, is a person in a public bathroom stall entitled to an expectation of privacy? Second, was the officer in a place where he had a lawful right to be when he viewed the offense? The answer to the first question is yes. A person does have a right to expect privacy in a bathroom stall. That's why there are stalls with doors on them. It doesn't matter that it was a restroom used by the public. The answer to the second question is a little trickier. If the opening between the door and the frame was small and, in order for the officer to see what was going

on, he had to get right up to the door and peek in through the small space, this will likely be found to be an unwarranted invasion of privacy and in violation of the Fourth Amendment. However, if the space was large enough that anyone walking by might see what the accused was doing from a couple of feet away from the stall, there is no reasonable expectation of privacy, and a subsequent seizure would be reasonable.

STOP AND FRISK

Earlier in this chapter, the stop and frisk topic was mentioned to distinguish arrest from detention. There is, of course, a search and seizure aspect to this concept. In *Terry* v. *Ohio*[40] (Figure 2-12), Cleveland Police Officer

◄FIGURE 2-12

Officer frisking a suspicious person

An officer conducts a "stop and frisk" of the outer clothing of a man to determine if he is armed, as authorized by *Terry* v. *Ohio*. This individual was driving on a back road near the Mexican border, acting very nervous, continually looking out the side window toward a distant point, and frequently checking his rearview mirror. (© Bob Daemmrich/The Image Works)

►FIGURE 2-13
Investigator checking identification
An investigator checks the identification of a young person in an abandoned house. Originally thought to be burglary suspects, these youths, it was discovered, were looking for a place to smoke marijuana. (© Kwame Zikomo/SuperStock)

McFadden observed three men walking back and forth in front of a jewelry store. Believing the men were casing the store for commission of a crime, he approached them. The defendant, one of the three, was acting strangely and the officer, concerned for his own safety, patted down the defendant's outer clothing for weapons. The officer removed a pistol from the defendant's overcoat pocket. Over the defendant's objection, the weapon was introduced in evidence. The appellate process took the case to the Supreme Court. The defendant's challenge was that the officer conducted an unreasonable search because he did not first arrest Terry and there was no probable cause or exigent circumstances justifying a search. The Court ruled that under circumstances where a person is acting suspiciously and the officer is concerned about his own safety when approaching such an individual, the officer may pat down the outer clothing to determine if the person has a weapon even though there was no arrest. If a weapon is found, it may be seized, and, if its possession is a violation of the law, it is admissible in a subsequent proceeding. The Court said that officer safety in a detention situation justifies the frisk. The Court held that an officer cannot frisk for illegal drugs but only for weapons. If, however, the officer feels something that she/he believes might be a weapon but turns out to be contraband, it is admissible. However, if it is readily apparent that the item is not a weapon, its seizure is unreasonable. To illustrate, in the case of *Minnesota* v. *Dickerson*,[41] officers stopped the defendant whose actions were evasive when approached by police just after he left a building known for cocaine traffic. One officer conducted a pat down and found no weapon, but he did feel a lump in the defendant's jacket pocket. After feeling it and examining it with his fingers, the officer believed it to be crack cocaine. He reached into the pocket and withdrew a bag containing cocaine. The Supreme Court held that even though the detention and frisk were lawful under the *Terry* doctrine, it was obvious to the officer that the lump in the pocket was not a weapon. Therefore, the seizure of the cocaine was based on an unlawful search and should not have been admitted into evidence.

In an interesting collateral issue to a *Terry* stop, the Supreme Court, in 2004, upheld a conviction under a Nevada statute that requires a person to identify himself, when so requested, during a *Terry* stop. When the defendant refused to identify himself after 11 requests by the officer, he was arrested and charged with violating the statute.[42] In addition to Nevada, the following states have **stop and identify** statutes: Alabama, Arkansas, Colorado, Delaware, Florida, Georgia, Illinois, Kansas, Louisiana, Missouri, Nebraska, New Hampshire, New Mexico, New York, North Dakota, Rhode Island, Utah, Vermont, and Wisconsin[43] (Figure 2-13).

FRUITS OF THE POISONOUS TREE

A final point is necessary to fully comprehend the consequences of an unreasonable search and seizure. The **fruits of the poisonous tree doctrine** provides that evidence obtained from an unreasonable search and seizure cannot be used as the basis for learning about or collecting new admissible evidence not known about before. Not only is the evidence obtained from the unreasonable search and seizure inadmissible; any evidence resulting from the unreasonably seized evidence is also tainted and is not admissible as fruits of the poisonous tree. This doctrine resulted from a 1963 decision of the high court in which a confession was obtained from the defendant after evidence was produced that had been obtained unreasonably.[44]

KEY TERMS

affidavit
arrest
arrest warrant
charging
detention
due process

due process clause
exigent circumstances
fruits of the poisonous tree doctrine
procedural criminal law
probable cause
search

search and seizure
search warrant
stop and frisk
stop and identify
substantive criminal law
unreasonable

REVIEW QUESTIONS

1. Define *arrest*.
2. Distinguish arrest from detention.
3. Distinguish arrest from charging.
4. What are the benefits to a police officer and the case if an arrest is made under the authority of a warrant?
5. Is a "John Doe" arrest warrant valid under any circumstances? Explain.
6. Define and describe *probable cause*.
7. During an ongoing criminal investigation, what factors must the criminal investigator consider in deciding whether to make an arrest and when to make it?
8. Explain how the laws of arrest and search and seizure flow from the Bill of Rights.
9. Distinguish the effects of the Fifth and Fourteenth Amendments on defendants in criminal cases.
10. List the requirements of a valid arrest warrant.
11. What is the Exclusionary Rule, and how did it evolve?
12. Describe the "Silver Platter" Doctrine. Is it still followed? Why or why not?
13. Under what circumstances may a search be conducted without a search warrant?
14. For what reasons do the courts allow searches incident to a lawful arrest?
15. What limitations have judicial cases placed on the search of a motor vehicle incident to a lawful arrest?
16. Give five examples justifying a search under exigent circumstances.
17. How does a law-enforcement agency's policy affect the lawfulness of an inventory search of a motor vehicle?
18. What is meant by a plain view seizure, and what are the requirements for conducting such a seizure by a law-enforcement officer?
19. What are the limitations on a law-enforcement officer conducting a stop and frisk?
20. Explain the "fruits of the poisonous tree" doctrine.

INTERNET ACTIVITIES

1. Locate the requirements in two states for the legal issuance of a search warrant. These requirements can be found as a list or on a blank search warrant form. How alike or unalike are the two? What explanation do you have for your conclusion?
2. In this country and abroad, newspaper stories about defendants alleging unlawful arrest by police are not uncommon. Take three such stories from this country and three from foreign countries and compare the fact situations for the arrest. Are there common denominators? For example, in some countries people are arrested because their speaking or writings are critical of a totalitarian government or "strong man" regime or they advocate for greater civil rights for citizens.

► Crime scene personnel documenting the scene of a murder. The number of yellow "tents" indicates numerous evidence items were found. The use of "Police Line" tape creates a buffer zone to keep bystanders from interfering with the investigation.

(© Gary Listort/New York Daily News)

3

INVESTIGATORS, THE INVESTIGATIVE PROCESS, AND THE CRIME SCENE

CHAPTER OBJECTIVES

1. Understand the skills and qualities needed by investigators.
2. Identify the objectives of crime scene investigation.
3. Distinguish between the preliminary and follow-up investigations.
4. Explain the importance of crime scene coordination.
5. Explain the factors that may affect crime scene processing plans.

6. Discuss three broad categories of evidence.
7. Explain the "rules" for crime scene investigators.
8. Identify crime scene health issues.
9. Summarize the four major considerations that dominate the crime scene search.
10. Identify different methods of visually documenting the crime scene.

INTRODUCTION

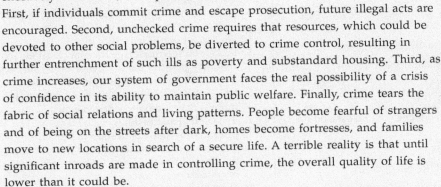

Although crime is a national problem, its control is primarily the responsibility of local government. When officials cannot prevent or deal effectively with crime, other problems are created. First, if individuals commit crime and escape prosecution, future illegal acts are encouraged. Second, unchecked crime requires that resources, which could be devoted to other social problems, be diverted to crime control, resulting in further entrenchment of such ills as poverty and substandard housing. Third, as crime increases, our system of government faces the real possibility of a crisis of confidence in its ability to maintain public welfare. Finally, crime tears the fabric of social relations and living patterns. People become fearful of strangers and of being on the streets after dark, homes become fortresses, and families move to new locations in search of a secure life. A terrible reality is that until significant inroads are made in controlling crime, the overall quality of life is lower than it could be.

Certain qualities are common to successful investigators, such as good communication skills, strong ethics, initiative, and resourcefulness. All crimes assigned to investigators must be investigated effectively and thoroughly. This responsibility includes not only complete preliminary and follow-up investigations but also understanding the importance of physical evidence in a criminal investigation. The contributions of physical evidence to an investigation are diminished primarily by the inability, unwillingness, or failure to locate, properly collect, mark, and preserve the evidence, and by the drawing of improper conclusions from its analysis.

TYPES OF OFFENSES

A **crime** is the commission (doing) of any act that is prohibited or the omission (failing to do) of any act that is required by the penal code of an organized political state. There can be no crime unless there is advance notice that the conduct is prohibited or required.

Legislatures enact criminal laws that distinguish between felonies and misdemeanors. In most states, a **felony** is an act punishable by imprisonment for a term of one or more years, or by death. Generally, violations of the criminal code that are not felonies are designated as **misdemeanors,** lesser offenses that may be punishable by a fine, ordinarily not to exceed $500, and/or imprisonment for no more than a year. Some states have a third crime category called **violation** (for example, criminal littering), which is punishable only by a fine, usually no more than $250.

THE INVESTIGATOR AND THE IMPORTANCE OF INVESTIGATION

In the search for truth, the most important skill of an investigator is the ability to converse equally well with a wide range of people, from corporate executives to the homeless. This is essential because much of what we learn during an investigation comes from people. The

CHAPTER OUTLINE

Introduction

Types of Offenses

The Investigator and the Importance of Investigation

Types of Crime Scenes

Organization of the Crime Scene Investigation

Types of Evidence

Typical Crime Scene Problems

Rules for the Crime Scene Investigator

Infectious Disease Risks and Precautions for Investigators

The Crime Scene Search

Suspended Searches, Debriefing, and Release of the Scene

Collection and Care of Evidence

Visual Documentation of the Crime Scene

Submission of Evidence to the Laboratory

Investigative Success

competent investigator is aware of the difference between knowing things and doing things. Such an investigator will therefore consistently translate his or her special knowledge into actual investigative behaviors.

The investigation of any crime places significant responsibilities on the investigator. These responsibilities are particularly heavy during an arrest for a violent felony, since the investigator may have to use deadly force: investigators cannot legally use such force prematurely, but from a tactical standpoint they cannot be even a split second too late in responding to deadly force directed at them. When a person is arrested, whether for a felony or a misdemeanor, the arrest is often publicized, and the person, even if not convicted, incurs economic and/or social costs. The more heinous the charge, the greater these costs will be. If a criminal charge is sustained, the person may suffer any of the penalties authorized for conviction of a felony, misdemeanor, or violation, which run from a fine to execution. This means that investigators must evaluate information accurately and use sound judgment in making investigative decisions.

ESSENTIAL QUALITIES OF THE INVESTIGATOR

Some investigators have a reputation of being lucky, and good fortune sometimes does play a role in solving a case. Most often, however, the "lucky" investigator is someone with strong professional training and solid experience who, by carefully completing every appropriate step in an investigation, leaves nothing to chance. By doing so, he or she forfeits no opportunity to develop evidence. In addition, successful investigators:

1. Invariably have a strong degree of self-discipline. It is not the presence or absence of a supervisor that causes them to get things done.
2. Use legally approved methods and are highly ethical.
3. Have the ability to win the confidence of people with whom they interact.
4. Do not act out of malice or bias.
5. Include in their case documentation all evidence that may point to the innocence of the suspect, no matter how unsavory his or her character.
6. Know that investigation is a systematic method of inquiry that is more science than art.
7. Realize that successful investigations are not always produced by rote application of the appropriate steps and therefore supplement the investigative procedures with their own initiative and resourcefulness.
8. Have wide-ranging contacts across many occupations.
9. Are not reluctant to contact experts from many different fields to help move the investigation forward.
10. Use both **inductive** and **deductive reasoning.** Inductive reasoning moves from the specific details to a general view. It uses the factual situation of a case to form a unifying and logically consistent explanation of the crime. In contrast, deductive reasoning creates a hypothesis about the crime. The explanation is tested against the factual situation. If the fit is not good, the hypothesis is reformulated and tested again. The process is repeated until everything "fits together."
11. Know that inductive and deductive reasoning can be distorted—by untenable inferences, logical fallacies, the failure to consider all alternatives, and bias—and self-monitor themselves to ensure effective use of these reasoning processes.
12. Learn something from every person with whom they come into contact, knowing that the wider their understanding of different lifestyles, occupations, vocabularies, views, and other factors, the more effective they will be.
13. Have the empathy, sensitivity, and compassion to do their job without causing unnecessary anguish (for example, when interviewing a rape victim).
14. Avoid becoming calloused and cynical from their constant contact with criminals, keeping in mind that the criminal element does not represent everyone. The failure to keep this distinction in mind can be the precursor of unethical behavior.

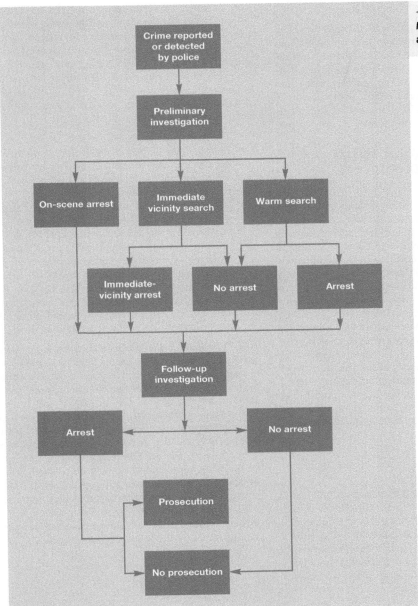

ORGANIZATION OF THE INVESTIGATIVE PROCESS

The major events in the investigation of crime are depicted in Figure 3-1. These elements provide an overview of the investigative process and introduce concepts covered in greater detail in subsequent chapters.

Once a criminal offense has been committed, three immediate outcomes are possible; it may: (1) go undetected, as in the case of a carefully planned and conducted murder by organized-crime figures, in which the body is disposed of in such a way that it will remain undiscovered; (2) be detected, but not reported, for example, because the loss is minor or the victim wants to avoid contact with the police, or (3) come to the attention of the police through their observation, a complaint by the victim or witnesses, or a tip.

Regardless of the outcome, a crime has occurred in each of the three preceding instances. However, only in the last case, when it is both detected and reported, is the offense of concern to the investigator, because only at that time does it become subject to formal processing.

THE PRELIMINARY INVESTIGATION

The actions taken by the first officer to arrive at the scene of a crime after its detection and reporting are collectively termed the **preliminary investigation.** The **follow-up investigation** is the police effort expended after the initial incident report is completed until the case is ready for prosecution. Normally the preliminary investigation is conducted by a uniformed officer from the Patrol Division and consists of the following steps:

1. RECEIPT OF INFORMATION, INITIAL RESPONSE, AND OFFICER SAFETY PROCEDURES

a. *Note all dispatch information:* time, date, type of call, location, names of parties involved, their descriptions, past history of incidents at the location, and, if known, whether any weapons are involved in this call.[1] Rough **field notes** must be made intermittently throughout the preliminary investigation. In those notes, the condition and placement of people and things at the scene are recorded, for example, where was the victim, assailant, and witnesses, what were they doing, what types of weapons were where, and what was said as you arrived. Often the type of call to which you are dispatched is actually what happened at the scene. However, people who call 911 may be excited, confused, misinformed, or have only partial information. In turn, dispatchers may have a hard time hearing or understanding callers or fail to get sufficient information. Finally, what is going on at the scene at the time of the call may have violently escalated by the time officers arrive:

A solo unit was dispatched to a domestic disturbance in progress. The caller reported that it involved a man and a woman arguing on the small porch of a home. A backup was also dispatched. When the first unit arrived, the officer saw the man stab the woman. When the second unit arrived, less than 20 seconds later, the man had already stabbed the first officer and was attempting to stab him again.

b. *Be alert for people and cars leaving the crime scene or its immediate proximity and note their numbers and descriptions.* Information about the factors needed for full descriptions are identified later on in Section 4, in the context of issuing an APB (All Points Bulletin) or BOLO (Be-On-The-Lookout) for persons and vehicles identified by victim or witness interviews as being involved in a crime to which a patrol officer is the first responder. Do not deviate from going to the call to which you are assigned, except for the most compelling reasons, for example, being fired on or discovering a violent crime in progress.

c. *Approach the scene cautiously,* scan the entire area thoroughly, assess the scene, and be aware of people and vehicles in the vicinity that may be related to the call. Consider suspect may have hidden near the scene or be within the building in which the crime occurred. Prioritize what needs to be done. Wait for or request backup as needed.

d. *In assessing the scene, use all your senses:* look, listen, smell (Figure 3-2). Be alert for:

- *The possibility that violence is still ongoing.*
- *Dangers from "ordinary" people,* for example, a backup gunman for bank robbery was dressed as a nun and shot a policeman in the back as he ran past the "nun" toward the scene.
- *Dangers from special hazards,* for instance, natural gas leaks, and the possibility of one or more other bombs yet to explode). The first arriving officer must inform other responders about dangers and request specialized help and equipment, for example, hazmat and canine teams, the bomb squad, fire department, and EMTs, as the situation dictates. Maintain a safe distance from special hazards. Do not just rush in; you cannot warn other responders if you are incapacitated or dead.

e. *Determine whether a tactical situation exists,* such as a barricaded subject with a gun or a robber who took a hostage because police arrived before he/she could flee the scene. Get help from other officers or specialized units as needed.

f. *Remain alert and attentive.* Assume that the crime is in progress until you can safely conclude—not assume—that it is over and the suspects are no longer on the scene.

g. *Make sure that you follow departmental contact protocols* for notifying supervisors or others immediately in special situations, for example, requesting approval for crime scene processing or the notification of the medical examiner.

h. *Treat the location as a crime scene until you conclude otherwise.* Sometimes this is not an easy determination, as demonstrated by the following case histories:

A badly wounded man called the police and reported an assailant had tried to rob him and his pregnant wife and that she had been shot in the head. With two victims, no gun at the scene, and no witnesses, the husband's version of events initially held up. However, there were lingering questions about what the two victims were doing in that area late at night. The wife died in the hospital as the investigation continued. Ultimately, the investigation established that the husband had been the shooter. His brother reportedly took the gun from the scene. When the husband's story unraveled, he committed suicide.

◄**FIGURE 3-2 Crime scene odor**
A quiet neighborhood was plagued with strong stench. Ray's Sausage Shop, next to this house, was first thought to be the source of the odor. The drainpipe was flushed and a sewer line replaced. Still, the smell persisted. Investigators searching the house, where a convicted sex offender lived, discovered the bodies of 11 murdered women. Note the investigator at the left covering his nose and mouth. (© AP Photo/The Plain Dealer, John Kuntz)

◄**FIGURE 3-3
Conducting a search of a suspect**
The investigator in the right foreground is handing a weapon discovered on the subject he is searching to the investigator at his immediate left. Note that he carefully keeps his finger outside the trigger guard. However, the proper action to take is to have the partially visible covering investigator at the left side of the picture approach the investigator who found the weapon, who would hand it directly back to him. The action depicted distracts both investigators and keeps an unsecured weapon near the suspects, making the situation more dangerous. (© Mike Karlsson/Arresting Images)

For over a year, a woman was tormented by a person dubbed the "Poet" because he sent threatening mail in verse form to her, as well as committing other acts. Among the acts reported to the police were having her telephone line cut, chunks of concrete thrown at her home, and being abducted and stabbed. When the woman was discovered mailing a "Poet" letter to herself at the post office, along with her normal bills, the truth came out. A psychologist speculated that the "Poet" incidents were motivated by the prior victimization of the woman, at that time age 16, when she was drugged, assaulted, and branded on both thighs by an assailant.[2]

i. *If suspect is still at the scene, arrest him/her,* conduct a search of his/her person, seize weapons, drugs, fruits of the crime, and other evidence (Figure 3-3). Legal rules apply as to just how far you may search a person beyond his or her actual person (for example, the immediate area, other rooms, and any vehicle involved). Make sure you know and follow such rules. If you intend to interrogate suspects, make sure they are given their Miranda warnings and document this action. In some situations (for example, a growing hostile crowd), you may need to have suspects removed immediately from the scene.

►FIGURE 3-4
Crime scene interview
Detectives question a shooting victim as EMTs prepare to transport him. Note the yellow crime-scene barrier tape in the left rear of the photo.
(© Seth Gottfried)

j. *An officer's field notes should also include information about a variety of scene conditions* initially observed that may prove to be significant later. Illustrations include what doors or windows were open or unlocked, what light switches were on, the condition of appliances (on-off, warm-cold, open-shut), and the general condition of the scene (for example, clothes and items thrown about and temperature). If the victim has a motor vehicle, is the engine cold, warm, or hot?

2. EMERGENCY CARE

a. If there are no satisfactory options to causing or allowing the contamination or destruction of evidence, remember that *saving the victim's life has a higher value than preserving physical evidence.*

b. *Assess level of injuries to the victim and request any needed medical assistance,* which is usually provided by emergency medical technicians (EMTs). You may need to provide first aid, taking appropriate precautions, to the victim until EMTs arrive.

c. *Point out potential evidence to medical personnel,* and ask them to have no contact with it or to have minimum contact with it. Instruct emergency personnel to preserve all clothing and personal effects; do not allow them to cut clothing through or along bullet holes or knife openings. Document all movement of people and items (for example, furniture and blankets, weapons) by medical personnel. Also make note of things EMTs may have added to or left at the scene, such as hypodermic needles and bandage wrappings, as well as personal items, such as jackets. Restrict the movement of the EMTs to areas at the scene where they are actually needed.

d. *Obtain as much information as possible from the victim before he/she is moved to the hospital by EMTs* (Figure 3-4).

e. *Do not allow EMTs to clean the scene,* because they may eradicate trace or larger types of evidence.

f. *Get the names of attending medical personnel, as well as their locator information,* including their employer, telephone numbers, and email addresses. Find out to which hospital the victim will be taken and send an officer, whenever possible, in the ambulance with the victim to get additional information. If that is not possible have an officer check with the transporting EMTs regarding any statements made by the victim or suspect. If this is not done on a timely basis, it may be 24 hours or more before the EMTs are available to be interviewed and valuable information could be lost.

g. *If there is a chance that the victim may die, attempt to get a dying declaration.* Also document other statements, comments, and spontaneous exclamations by victims, suspects, EMTs, and witnesses.

3. SECURE SCENE AND CONTROL PERSONS AND EVIDENCE

a. *As rapidly as possible, identify the boundaries of the crime scene and secure it* (Figure 3-5). Establishing the boundaries could entail checking an open field for additional bodies and physical evidence or all the rooms in a structure to determine if there are multiple scenes. A classic example of multiple scenes occurred in 1966 in a Chicago townhouse, where Richard Speck killed eight student nurses in different rooms. Checking for multiple scenes may also identify other victims who are still alive and require medical attention. On rare occasions, such victims or witnesses

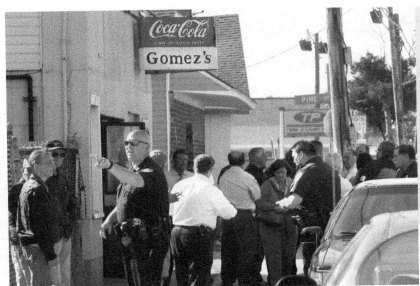

may have hidden themselves in closets or elsewhere, fearing the return of their assailant, as did a ninth nurse who eluded Speck. Crime scene control is also covered in different contexts, for example, dealing with the news media, in subsequent portions of this chapter.

b. *In defining the scene, officers must make sure that they also identify possible or actual lines of approach to, and flight from, the scene and protect them also.* These lines may contain shoe or tire impressions or residues, weapons, discarded fruits of the crime on which fingerprints may have been left, or other things which may provide investigative leads.

c. *Maintaining* **crime scene control** *is a crucial element in the preliminary investigation.* To the extent possible while meeting emergency care and other responsibilities, prevent individuals at the scene from committing any acts of theft, altering/destroying evidence, or attacking others. Identify all individuals at the scene, such as suspects, victims, bystanders, family, and friends.

Do not delay medical treatment for victims to identify them or accomplish other investigative tasks. Occasionally, situations will dictate seizing evidence before it is photographed for safety reasons:

An officer arrived at a bar where a shooting had just occurred. The victim was lying on the cement floor and had been shot several times in his upper thighs and lower groin area by a small caliber pistol, which was lying on the bar. Two seats down the bar, his girlfriend was having a drink. When she saw the officer she spontaneously said, "Yea, that's right, I shot the son-of-a-bitch, caught him with another woman and me

working and paying all the bills." Friends of the victim and the shooter were shouting back and forth and emotions in the crowd were running high. The officer immediately seized the weapon.

d. *Separate any potential combatants* to avoid violence; *separate persons arrested* so they cannot "get their story together"; and *separate witnesses* so they don't contaminate each other's recollection.

e. *Set up a physical barrier to protect the scene, prevent the contamination or theft of evidence and for your own safety.* Use yellow crime scene tape or employ natural barriers such as doors, walls, gated areas, request additional personnel as needed. Cover fragile evidence with a box or other container that will not disturb or contaminate the evidence.

f. *Maintain a crime scene entry log of persons coming to and leaving the scene* (Figure 3-6). Brief those entering on the situation and any special conditions or hazards.

4. ISSUE A BE-ON-THE-LOOKOUT

a. If the suspect is not arrested at the scene, conduct interviews and issue an **APB/BOLO (All Points Bulletin/Be-on-the-Lookout),** which is broadcast to other officers. The APB/BOLO is crucially important, because without its information other officers could be caught in the situation of approaching someone whom they think is a minor traffic violator when they have actually stumbled on a violent criminal fleeing the scene.

b. *Whenever possible, an APB/ BOLO should include* the following points: number of suspects, age, race, sex, height, weight, build, coloration, birthmarks, hair color

▶ **FIGURE 3-6**
Crime scene entry log sheet

CRIME SCENE ENTRY LOG SHEET

ALL PERSONS ENTERING THE CRIME SCENE MUST SIGN THIS SHEET

AGENCY: _____   INCIDENT #: _____

SCENE LOCATION: _____

NOTE: Officers assigned to maintain scene security must also log in and out on this sheet and should state their reason as "Log Officers."

NAME & TITLE	INITIALS	AGENCY	IN DATE / TIME	OUT DATE / TIME	REASON FOR ENTERING
			/	/	
			/	/	
			/	/	
			/	/	
			/	/	
			/	/	
			/	/	
			/	/	
			/	/	
			/	/	
			/	/	
			/	/	
			/	/	
			/	/	
			/	/	

Copyright 2000, Imprimus Forensic Services, LLC - This form may be reproduced for law enforcement purposes only.   Page_____of_____

and length, mustaches and beards, names and/or nicknames, clothing, hats, scars, marks, tattoos, jewelry worn, deformities (for example, missing finger), any prosthesis, and accent, as well as whether the suspects were unarmed or armed, numbers and descriptions of weapons, the method and direction of flight, and a full description of their vehicle, including year, make, model, color, stickers, damage, things hanging from the mirror, and loud mufflers. The importance of details in APB/BOLOs is demonstrated by the following case:

A convenience store was hit by an armed robber. The first responding officer determined that a toy gun may have been used and that the suspect's vehicle had a white "hard hat" on the rear shelf. This information was included, along with a description of the suspect and his vehicle on the BOLO. Another officer found a vehicle matching the suspect's behind a tavern. A toy gun box was found on the rear floorboard, and a white hard hat was on the rear shelf. The bartender said a man matching the suspect's description had entered the tavern, called a taxi, had a quick drink, and left in the taxi when it arrived. The cab company reported that the fare was taken to the airport. There it was learned that he had boarded a flight to another city, where he was arrested when he got off of the plane.

5. CONDUCT NEIGHBORHOOD AND VEHICLE CANVASS

A **neighborhood canvass** is an attempt to locate witnesses who may have heard, seen, or smelled something of investigative importance. The "neighborhood" may be other tenants in an apartment building, business owners and their employees in a commercial district, or some similar grouping. The neighborhood canvass may be conducted by uniformed officers, investigators, or some combination thereof. It may occur while the crime scene is still being processed. If not conducted at the time of the preliminary investigation, the investigator assigned to do the follow-up will determine whether the fact situation warrants one. All results of the canvass, both positive and negative, should be carefully recorded because information that seems unimportant to the canvasser may have significance to someone else (Figure 3-7):

BUILDING / NEIGHBORHOOD CANVASS

AGENCY: _____   **INCIDENT#:** _____

INSTRUCTIONS: Document whether or not all occupants of the residence were interviewed. Document locations where no persons were contacted. If available, list pager and / or cellphone numbers in the remarks column. Use the back side of this sheet for notes.

MULTIPLE UNIT OCCUPANCY: Address _____   **Number of Units** _____

(List only unit numbers below)

ADDRESS (indicate residence, business, etc.)	PERSON CONTACTED	DOB	HOME TX#	WORK TX#	REMARKS (pager / cell phone)
# OF OCC.					☐ FOLLOW-UP RQ'D ☐ NOTES ON BACK
# OF OCC.					☐ FOLLOW-UP RQ'D ☐ NOTES ON BACK
# OF OCC.					☐ FOLLOW-UP RQ'D ☐ NOTES ON BACK
# OF OCC.					☐ FOLLOW-UP RQ'D ☐ NOTES ON BACK
# OF OCC.					☐ FOLLOW-UP RQ'D ☐ NOTES ON BACK
# OF OCC.					☐ FOLLOW-UP RQ'D ☐ NOTES ON BACK
# OF OCC.					☐ FOLLOW-UP RQ'D ☐ NOTES ON BACK
# OF OCC.					☐ FOLLOW-UP RQ'D ☐ NOTES ON BACK
# OF OCC.					☐ FOLLOW-UP RQ'D ☐ NOTES ON BACK
# OF OCC.					☐ FOLLOW-UP RQ'D ☐ NOTES ON BACK
# OF OCC.					☐ FOLLOW-UP RQ'D ☐ NOTES ON BACK
# OF OCC.					☐ FOLLOW-UP RQ'D ☐ NOTES ON BACK
# OF OCC.					☐ FOLLOW-UP RQ'D ☐ NOTES ON BACK
# OF OCC.					☐ FOLLOW-UP RQ'D ☐ NOTES ON BACK
# OF OCC.					☐ FOLLOW-UP RQ'D ☐ NOTES ON BACK
# OF OCC.					☐ FOLLOW-UP RQ'D ☐ NOTES ON BACK
# OF OCC.					☐ FOLLOW-UP RQ'D ☐ NOTES ON BACK

CANVASSING OFFICER (Print): _____   **INITIALS:** _____   **DATE:** _____   **START TIME** _____   **TIME END:** _____

▲ **FIGURE 3-7 Building/neighborhood canvass**
(Courtesy of Imprimus Forensic Services, LLC)

On a Sunday morning, a residential burglary resulted in the theft of $3,800 in rare coins. The uniformed officer making the original investigation received permission to conduct the neighborhood canvass. Usually the follow-up investigator did the canvass, but the uniformed officer was allowed to do it. The victim's home was situated on a cul-de-sac along with four other homes with some view of the victimized premises. There were no homes to the rear of the victim's residence. After interviewing residents of the four neighboring homes, including a teenage boy, the uniformed officer recorded the identities and statements of those with whom he had talked in his report. All indicated they had seen nothing. Because of the value of the property taken, the case was referred for follow-up investigation.

The investigator assigned to the case recently had been transferred from the Youth Services Bureau to the Burglary Section and recognized the name of the youth identified in the interview section of the uniformed officer's report as an individual with an extensive juvenile record for breaking and entering. Investigation revealed that the youth had committed the offense, and all coins taken were recovered.

Interviews should be conducted first at businesses or dwellings with a clear view of the crime scene and at the suspect's avenues of approach and flight. When there are substantial numbers of locations involved, several teams of officers canvassing simultaneously are helpful.

If the crime was committed near a public transit system, visit the system at the same time and on the same day of the week as the time and day of the crime. If victims and witnesses have been intimidated or otherwise dissuaded from testifying investigators should notify their supervisors and protective services considered.

It is estimated that a systematic neighborhood canvass soon after the commission of an offense results in information of investigative value in approximately 20% of all cases. The extent of the canvass depends on variables such as the type of offense, time of day, and characteristics of the crime scene. The timing of a neighborhood canvass is an important consideration. People not only move randomly through areas but also ebb and flow on a variety of schedules. To mistime a neighborhood canvass by 30 minutes, for example, may mean eliminating the possibility of locating persons who regularly catch a bus at a particular time and who, on the day of an offense, might have seen something of considerable investigative value.

Offenders may have driven near to the scene to commit their crimes, but not have sufficient time to get back to their car afterwards. Alternatively, the co-conspirator who was to drive the suspect from the scene may have panicked as he/she saw or heard police cars approaching and walked away from the "get-away" car. The **vehicle canvass** makes a record of all vehicles in the area to provide another investigative avenue (Figure 3-8). The address or location of each vehicle must be recorded, as well as its description and plate/tag number. Anything unusual about a vehicle should be noted, such as bullet holes; blood; odd appearance of the interior; recent damage; noteworthy stickers; unusual articles; items hanging from the rearview mirror, and whether the car is hot, warm, cold, muddy, or clean.

6. ADMINISTRATIVE PROCEDURES FOR PROCESSING CRIME SCENES

Procedures for handling specific types of evidence are discussed in Chapter 4, "Physical Evidence." This section discusses the administrative procedures for crime scene processing.

a. In smaller departments that do not have specialists, roughly those with 20 or fewer sworn personnel, the responding officer must recognize and identify physical evidence, document its location through sketching and photographs, collect it and mark it, package it (Figure 3-9), and take it to the station for storage in the evidence room, where a written receipt for it will be given to the officer. This receipt is then attached to the incident/offense report, which the officer subsequently writes. When serious crimes are committed in smaller jurisdictions, assistance with the crime scene may be available through mutual aid agreements with larger agencies or from the state investigative agency.

b. At all stages of handling the evidence, the chain of custody or control of it must be established. The **chain of custody** is the witnessed, unbroken, written chronological history of who had the evidence when. It also accounts for any changes in the evidence, noting, for example, if any portion was used for laboratory analysis.

c. In larger agencies that have sworn and/or civilian crime scene technicians, these specialists will process the crime scene. More detailed information about this subject is presented later in this chapter.

d. One or more plainclothes investigators may also come to the scene, depending on the severity of the crime. If they do, the first responding officer has the following crime scene turnover responsibilities: (1) briefing the personnel taking charge, (2) assisting in controlling the scene, (3) turning over responsibility for starting another crime scene entry log, and (4) remaining at the scene until relieved.

7. THE INCIDENT/OFFENSE REPORT

The officer assigned to the call must prepare an **incident/offense report** on his or her part in the investigation. (Additional information on this subject is presented in Chapter 6, "Field Notes and Reporting.") A supervisor reviews and approves the incident report; the case may be

VEHICLE INFORMATION CANVASS

AGENCY: _____ **INCIDENT#:** _____

INSTRUCTIONS: Document all vehicles in the area you have been assigned. Include vehicles parked in the streets, driveways, alleyways and yards. Under "Remarks" list anything unusual noted about the vehicle (manner of parking, warm engine, fresh damage, etc.)

For vehicles without license plates, enter the VIN in the "Remarks" column.

ADDRESS (indicate alley, driveway, street, etc.)	MAKE	MODEL	COLOR	PLATE	REMARKS (VIN)

CANVASSING OFFICER (Print): _____ **INITIALS:** _____ **DATE:** _____ **START TIME** _____ **TIME END:** _____

FIGURE 3-8 Vehicle information canvass
(Courtesy of Imprimus Forensic Services, LLC)

▶ **FIGURE 3-9**
Crime scene investigators
handling physical evidence
A crime scene investigator examines
blood-stained clothes before placing
them in an evidence bag. Note that
the investigators are going to place
the clothes in a paper evidence bag,
which is the appropriate action when
seizing blood soaked clothing; each
article should be placed in a separate
bag to avoid cross-contamination.
(Chapter 4, "Physical Evidence" has
additional information on identifying
and collecting such evidence.)
(© Seth Gottfried)

retained in the patrol division for further investigation,
referral to the investigative division for follow-up, or inactivated and receive no further investigative effort unless
new information is received.

TYPES OF CRIME SCENES

From Chapter 1, we recall that the fundamental assumption on which crime scene searches are carried out is
Locard's principle: there is something to be found. We usually think of a crime scene as one particular place.
Although this is often true, consider the 1988 terrorist
bombing of Pan Am Flight 103 over Lockerbie, Scotland.
Among the dead were 259 people on the plane and
11 people on the ground. Evidence from the explosion
rained down over 800 square miles. In one of the greatest
investigations ever, evidence was collected that led to the
identification, arrest, and conviction of the bomber, who
was a former Libyan intelligence officer.

Crime scenes vary in regard to the amount of physical
evidence that is ordinarily expected to be recovered, for
instance, a murder scene will yield more than a yard from
which a lawn mower was stolen. At the most basic level,
a **crime scene** is the location where the offense was committed. As discussed earlier, the search of the crime scene
for physical evidence must include a wider area, such as
the perpetrator's lines of approach to, and flight from, the
scene.

The basic definition of a crime scene works well for
many crimes, such as a burglary or a robbery at a liquor
store. But where was the crime scene for Pan Am Flight
103? On a much smaller geographic scale, consider the
example of a victim who is abducted from a mall parking
lot and raped by one accomplice while the other one
drives the van from one county to another. Later, the vic-

tim is taken to a secluded area, removed from the van,
further abused, and executed, and her body is dumped
into a ravine in yet another jurisdiction. Clearly, we need
additional ways to think about what a crime scene is.

1. Criminal incidents may have more than one crime
scene. The **primary scene** is the location where the initial
offense was committed; the locations of all subsequent
connected events are **secondary scenes.**[3] Illustrating this
statement is a Utah case in which a husband shot his wife
while she was sleeping. He disposed of the body in a
trash bin that ended up in a landfill. After 33 days of
picking through 4,600 tons of compacted garbage up to
20 feet deep, investigators located the body (Figure 3-10).

2. On the basis of size, there are macroscopic and
microscopic scenes.[4] A **macroscopic scene** is the "large
view." It includes such things as the relevant location(s),
the victim's and the suspect's bodies, cars, and buildings.
The **microscopic scene** consists of the specific objects and
pieces of evidence that are associated with the commission of the crime, including knives, bite marks, hairs and
fibers, shoe and tire impressions, cigar butts, blood, and
so on.[5]

3. Other useful ways of thinking about crime scenes
are based on the type of crime (larceny versus aggravated
assault), the location (indoors or outdoors), the condition
of the scene (organized or disorganized), and the type of
criminal action (active or passive). Some further breakdown of these types may also be useful, such as if outside, whether the body is on the surface, buried, or
underwater.[6]

The usefulness of having several frames of reference
for crime scenes is that they can help organize your thinking about how to approach and process a crime scene. If
there are multiple crime scene locations, the primary and
secondary scenes may be located in different legal jurisdictions, a situation requiring a high level of cooperation

◄**FIGURE 3-10**
Crime scene investigation
Officers from the Salt Lake City Police Department search for the body of murder victim Lori Hacking, which was finally found three months after her death. Her husband subsequently pleaded guilty in the case. (© George Frey/Getty Images)

and informational exchange between agencies. In cases where a serial offender is active and working across several jurisdictions, the case may be assigned to a standing interagency investigative task force, or a special one may be created. In such situations, it is important that departmental jealousies, the issue of who is going to get credit for solving the case, and other factors do not impede the success of the operation.

ORGANIZATION OF THE CRIME SCENE INVESTIGATION

Crime scene investigation is purposeful behavior and is intended to accomplish specific objectives:

1. Establish what happened; for example, was the purpose of the murder to kill the home owner or did she surprise a burglar when she came home unexpectedly? Or, more difficult, to often impossible, to determine, was it a murder-suicide versus an accidental discharge followed by a remorseful suicide?
2. Determine the sequence of events.
3. Find out what the suspect did or didn't do at the scene.
4. Establish the modus operandi, the method of operation, used by the suspect.
5. Determine what property was stolen and what articles were left by the suspect.
6. Note inconsistencies. For example, if the crime appears to be a home invasion that resulted in a murder, why wasn't the victim's cash and jewelry taken? Did the perpetrator panic and flee the scene before taking them, or is something else at work, such as a love triangle?

7. Locate and interview witnesses.
8. Document and recover physical evidence.[7]
9. Provide investigative leads.

Some of these objectives may not be attainable during the crime scene investigation phase and will require the services of specialists. At a complex scene with multiple victims and considerable evidence, determining the sequence of events, for example, in what order were the victims killed, may only be possible when autopsy and lab reports are available. Even then, the subsequent services of a crime scene reconstructionist may be needed. Lurking behind Point 6 in the preceding list is the determination of the motive for the crime, ordinarily the work of a specialist in criminal profiling. (Crime scene reconstruction and criminal profiling are discussed in Chapter 7, "The Follow-up Investigation and Investigative Resources.")

To achieve the objectives of crime scene investigation, the work at the scene is divided into three major functions: (1) overall coordination of the scene, (2) forensic services, and (3) investigative services.

OVERALL COORDINATION

The senior criminal investigator assigned to a case usually has overall responsibility for what happens at a crime scene. In order to fulfill this responsibility he/she must conduct a visual inspection, the "walk through," of the scene and develop a preliminary plan for its investigation. Members of the investigate team typically know their jobs and little direct "standing over their shoulder" supervision is required or desired, although the senior investigator may direct that additional processing be done or otherwise provide investigative direction.

A crucially important task for the senior investigator is coordination (Figure 3-11). It is usually accomplished by the senior investigator as he/she moves from one point to another. Some scenes may be so large or victims

► FIGURE 3-11
The need for scene coordination
Maine State Police searching multiple sites for human remains in a forest. Without coordination, the investigative effort can lose focus and fail to capitalize on opportunities for locating physical evidence. (© Bangor Daily News/Bill Trotter)

so numerous that layers of coordination may be needed, which may require using a mobile incident command van or a temporary "headquarters" such as a tent or a building (Figure 3-12).

The senior investigator at the scene is also responsible for requesting whatever types of additional resources are needed—for example: (1) obtain a search warrant; (2) if there is a dead body, the medical examiner or the coroner must be called to the scene. Generally, this official has jurisdiction over a dead body, which should not be searched or removed from the scene without his/her prior consent;[8] (3) fire truck ladders may be needed to search rooftops for evidence; (4) transportation of vehicles to impound lots; (5) aerial photography of scene; and (6) personnel with specialized knowledge and experience, such as being able to interpret gang graffiti/tattoos/markings.

The senior investigator must ensure that all the members of the crime scene team are briefed simultaneously so that everyone hears and knows the same thing. The senior investigator is also responsible for ensuring that there is a continuous flow of information between members of the team as evidence is recovered. Other duties include making his/her own evaluation of potential

► FIGURE 3-12 **NYPD Temp Headquarters**
When there is an unusual event, such as a barricaded criminal or a hostage situation, an incident commander comes to the scene to take control. In fast-moving situations, the incident commander may have to operate out of his/her assigned vehicle until a mobile command van arrives. In other situations, the police use an existing building, with the permission of the owner, as a point from which to operate. Following the attack of September 11, 2001, members of the New York City Police Department established a temporary headquarters near ground zero. (© Andrea Booher/FEMA News Photo)

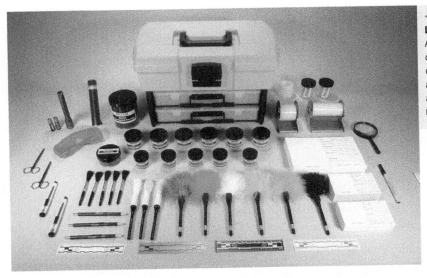

◄**FIGURE 3-13**
Latent fingerprint kit
A latent fingerprint kit, which includes
different color powders, several types
of brushes, scales, clear lifting tape,
and cards to which the lifted prints
are affixed. (Courtesy of Mike Grimm Jr./
Evident, Inc.)

◄**FIGURE 3-14**
**Police department mobile crime
scene unit**
The inside of a crime scene van; note
the portable Kawasaki generator on the
left and the light on the right. The
balance of the van is filled with various
types of equipment needed at crime
scenes, such as gunshot residue,
blood, fingerprint, and other collection
kits. Many departments buy prepared
evidence kits; others assemble kits to
better meet their specific needs and
capabilities. (Courtesy Chief Jack Lumpkin,
Athens Clarke County (Georgia) Police
Department)

safety issues, reviewing the actions of the person who conducted the preliminary investigation, allocating resources among the primary and any secondary scenes, establishing a secure area for the temporary storage of evidence, and establishing a command post and media function if the situation warrants them. The senior investigator also does a walk through of the scene with those responsible for forensic services to make sure there is a common understanding of how the scene will be approached and processed.[9]

FORENSIC SERVICES

Forensic services is the responsibility of the senior representative of the department's central crime laboratory or a crime scene processing unit. He/she may arrive to pro-

cess the scene carrying one or more crime scene investigation kits (Figure 3-13) or have the more substantial resources carried in a crime scene van (Figure 3-14). Some jurisdictions also have a mobile crime laboratory in which technicians can carry out limited scientific tests.

Figure 3-15 is a list of supplies and equipment that are available for crime scene processing. Although law-enforcement agencies are varied, the core tasks that need to be completed at scenes dictate that they will use many of the supplies and equipment listed, but there will also be some variation in what is actually used. Because at least 92% of all law-enforcement agencies in this country use **digital cameras** their use is specified in Figure 3-15.[10]

Advanced methods of crime scene documentation, laser scanning, and panoramic cameras are discussed later in this chapter.

▶ FIGURE 3-15
Crime scene supplies and equipment

Crime Scene Security

- Barrier tape—for example, "Police Line Do Not Cross," in locally spoken languages, such as Spanish, "La Linea de la Policia No Cruza"
- Scene flags—such as "Sheriff's Line Do Not Cross" and "BioHazard Line Do Not Cross"
- Waterproof tarps and tents
- Sawhorses
- Chalks—standard/reflective/fluorescent spray/assorted colors
- Spray paint/standard/fluorescent/assorted colors
- Marked police vehicles
- Cord, rope
- Flares, chem-lites
- Preprinted signs—such as "Command Center" and "Media Relations" and poles
- Traffic cones

Safety/Personal Protection Equipment (PPE)

- Reflective vests and gloves
- Neoprene, Latex, nitrile (synthetic latex), polyvinyl, and cut/puncture resistant gloves, such as TurtleSkin®
- Disposable air-filtering masks/respirators
- Safety glasses/chin length face shield/coveralls/shoe covers
- First responder spray—such as MyClyns™ for potential pathogenic exposures
- EPA registered wipes/spray (for example, Sporicidin) and bleach (for instance, Ultra Clorox Germicidal Bleach)
- Chemical/Biological/Radiological/Nuclear (CBRN) threat environments require specialized PPE
- First aid kit/insect repellant

Washington County (Maine) Sheriff's Deputy searching underwater for stolen guns using a metal detector. (© Bangor Daily News/Diana Grattinger)

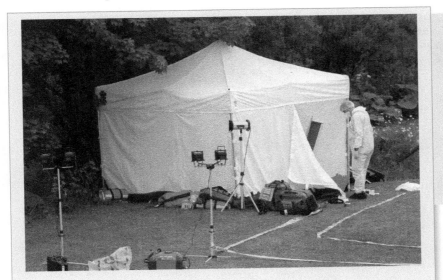

An investigator in Rothbury, England examines the scene where a fugitive shot himself, dying later in a hospital. The tent shields public observation of the process. Note the high-intensity lights, the carefully lined path, and the coveralls, hair net, gloves, and air-filtering mask being worn. Gun ownership rates are low in England, and suicide by them there is therefore rare. (© Dan Kitwood/Getty Images)

Telecommunications

- Cell/smart phones
- Fax machine
- Tablet/netbook/laptop/computers
- Copier/printer
- Teleconferencing capability
- Departmental handheld radios
- Key telephone numbers/telephone directories

Miscellaneous Equipment

- Audio recorder
- Consent search forms
- Large magnet
- Handheld Global Positioning System (GPS)
- Magnetic compass
- Portable generator
- High-intensity lights—for example, two 750-watt halogens/telescoping arm/adjustable legs
- Evidence refrigeration capability
- Flashlights/spare batteries
- Numbered evidence location marking cones/tents/flags
- Metal detectors
- Thermometers
- Logbooks
- Tents/tarps to protect evidence/personnel/equipment from inclement weather
- Extension cords/adapters
- Ladders
- Privacy/body screen
- Area map
- Pruning shears/wood saws/axes to clear vegetation from core search area
- Rakes/shovels/trowels/paintbrushes
- Soil probe
- Business cards

Equipment for Basic Crime Scene Photography

- Digital single-lens reflex (DSLR) camera for still photography
- Memory cards/extras
- Gray card/other color checker
- External flashes and cords
- Remote shutter release

▶ **FIGURE 3-15**
Crime scene supplies and equipment (*continued*)

- Various lens, macro/normal/wide-angle/telephoto
- Lens filters
- Supplemental light meter
- Digital video recorder
- Lens cleaning material
- Tripods
- External rechargeable battery packs/extra batteries
- Auxiliary lighting
- Scales/adhesive scales/rulers
- Owner's manuals for cameras
- Stepladder
- Numbered evidence location marking cones/tents/flags

Equipment for Basic Crime Scene Sketching/Diagramming

- Sketching/drafting board
- "T" square, assorted transparent triangles: 45/90 and 30/60 degrees
- Drafting compass/dividers/protractor/straight-edge rulers
- Paper/tape/pencils/pens
- Several retractable tape measures, 6- to 100-feet lengths, steel, and fiberglass
- Distance measuring wheel with visible reader for longer distances up to 1,000 feet
- Laser/ultrasonic measuring device
- Magnetic compass
- Laptop computer/crime scene diagramming software, for example, The Crime Zone
- Sketching templates

▶ **Sketching templates**
Two types of templates used in sketching crime scenes: the Human Figure Template (*left*) and the Crime Scene Template (*right*).
(Courtesy Lynn Peavey Company)

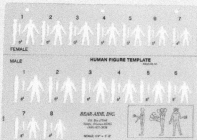 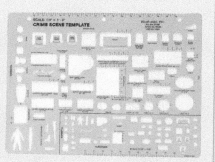

General Evidence Collection Equipment

- Stainless steel/disposable tweezers/forceps/hemostats/metal probes/scalpel
- Hard-metal scribes
- Tongue depressors
- Nets for flying insects
- Framed sifting screens and tubes
- Utility knife/scissors
- Assorted tools, wire and bolt cutters/hacksaw, extra blades/hammers/screwdrivers/wood and metal chisels/pliers/wrenches/pry bar/vise grips/drills, bits
- Mirror with telescoping arm
- Magnifying glasses

Specialized Evidence Collection Kits and Material

- Sexual assault
- Gunshot residue (GSR)
- DNA/biological evidence
- Laser trajectory
- Entomology/insect
- Latent fingerprint
- Trace evidence vacuum
- Latent fingerprint
- Blood spatter
- Presumptive field tests, for example, blood and drugs
- Body excavation
- Electrostatic lifting for dust and residue prints

- Forensic light source(s)/goggles
- Adjustable casting frames for foot/shoe/tire impressions
- Casting preparation materials/dust, sand, and dirt hardeners/wax hardener for snow impressions/snow print powder (red) to contrast impression to be photographed with surrounding snow
- Casting materials, for instance, Durocast, silicone, dental stone, low-density impression foam such as BioFoam, and Mikrosil. AccuTrans, a silicone product, which won an innovation award in 2006, is finding favor as a casting medium. The silicone is dispensed from a chalk-gun-like gun, dries in four minutes, is highly flexible after drying, and captures fine details. Self-contained kits for casting tire and shoe impressions, such as Shake-N-Cast, are also gaining in popularity. The Shake-N-Cast kits contain dental stone and a water vial in the same pouch; the vial is broken while inside of the pouch and the kit massaged, producing the same correct consistency to pour into an impression each time.

Evidence Packaging Materials

- Evidence tags/general identification labels
- Evidence control/chain of custody labels
- Sharpie permanent markers, assorted colors
- Assorted sizes of Kraft paper evidence envelopes/bags
- Rolls of Kraft/butcher paper
- Assorted adhesive/"sticky" labels—for example, "Biohazard" and "Latent Print Evidence"
- Weapons and other sized boxes
- Clear plastic tubes for syringes and knives
- Clear plastic jars, assorted sizes
- Antistatic bags for computer and other digital evidence
- Nylon bags and metal cans for arson evidence
- Evidence sealing tape, sensitive to tampering efforts, ½" to 3" wide
- Document sleeves
- Polyethylene evidence tubing
- Assorted sizes of Ziploc bags
- Heat sealer for polyethylene/nylon bags
- Sterile swabs/swab boxes
- Blood tubes, with, and without, preservative coating
- "Peel and Seal" evidence bags, which cannot be opened without destroying the bag

Source: Content drawn from Henry C. Lee, Timothy M. Palmbach, and Marilyn T. Miller, *Crime Scene Handbook* (San Diego: Academic Press, 2001), pp. 321–324; Technical Working Group on Crime Scene Investigation, *Crime Scene Investigation* (Washington, D.C.: U.S. Department of Justice, 2001), pp. 33–36; National Institute of Justice, *Crime Scene Investigation: A Reference for Law Enforcement* (Washington, D.C.: NIJ, June 2004), pp. 55–57 and additional content from the authors.

FIGURE 3-15
Crime scene supplies and equipment (concluded)

Evidence located in areas that are "open-view" to the public are ordinarily processed first and then the out-of-view areas. Similarly, fragile evidence should be documented and collected before more durable physical evidence. The open-view "rule" is especially important when bodies are in plain sight because common talk and potential news media photography will cause family members and friends great pain (Figure 3-16).

The forensic services function includes (1) establishing a central point to collect trash generated by processing the scene, including biohazard bags for the collection of disposable evidence equipment and personal protection equipment (PPE); (2) establishing a decontamination point as needed; and (3) carrying out the identification, documentation, collection, marking, packaging, and transmission of physical evidence to the evidence room or the crime laboratory.

A variety of factors shape the initial plan for processing crime scenes, which may need revisions in light of new information/developments. Among these factors are these:[11]

1. Remote or difficult terrain—for example, steep ravines, swamp areas, and forested areas with thick underbrush. In 2002 a man walking his dog found the remains of murder victim Chandra Levy in a remote part of Washington D.C.'s 2,000-acre Rock Creek Park. The Federal Bureau of Prisons intern had disappeared a year earlier. Based on information in the victim's computer, police thought she may have disappeared in the park. Although the police had twice searched much of it, they did not search the park's most remote area, judging it unlikely to yield results.

►FIGURE 3-16
Use of privacy screen to shield body
St. Tammany Parish, Louisiana, Sheriff's Office investigators use a privacy screen to shield the body of a homicide victim from morning rush hour traffic. A second victim was found on the same highway, two miles away. Gunshots killed both victims and investigators proceeded on the theory of a double homicide. (© David Grunfeld/Times-Picayune)

►FIGURE 3-17
Maine State Police, Department of Inland Fish and Wildlife wardens, and officers from several municipalities reach a small island on which a light plane had just crashed, unsure if their mission is rescue or body recovery. Aluminum canoes were the safest choice to cross the water because of increasing ice in it. In extreme cold, hypothermia is a risk factor for investigators. (© Bangor Daily News/ Kevin Bennett)

2. Physical hazards that imperil crime scene technicians—for instance, downed power lines, unsafe structures, and booby traps.
3. A hostile crowd.
4. Human remains that are widely scattered because of animal predation.
5. Weather, including rain/sleet/snow, extreme heat/ cold temperatures (Figure 3-17), blowing sand/ dust, and nearby lightning strikes.
6. Potential presence of chemical/biological/ radiological/nuclear (CBRN) weapons agents—for example, following the attacks on September 11, 2001, a biological agent, anthrax, was mailed to several dozen recipients, including two members of Congress.
7. Presence of dangerous chemicals and vapors—for example, at meth labs or from fields recently sprayed with agrichemicals.

8. Limited personnel or the availability of additional personnel—such as cadets from a police academy.
9. Infectious disease risks, which have led some law-enforcement agencies to require crime scene investigators to undergo health screening twice each year as a precaution. (Infectious disease risks and the precautions investigators should take regarding them are discussed in detail later in this chapter.)

INVESTIGATIVE SERVICES

Investigative services include: (1) interviewing witnesses; (2) conducting and documenting the neighborhood canvass; (3) a field interrogation of the suspect if he or she is in custody; and (4) carrying out and recording the results of a vehicle canvass.

TYPES OF EVIDENCE

There are three broad categories of evidence in which investigators have a particular interest: (1) corpus delicti, (2) associative, and (3) tracing. The task of developing such evidence is spread across the three main crime scene functions, but the data from the different types of evidence are combined to create a larger and more unified picture of the crime. This picture helps determine, to a large extent, how the follow-up investigation will be conducted.

CORPUS DELICTI EVIDENCE

Each criminal offense contains a distinct set of elements whose commission or omission must be demonstrated to have occurred in order to prove a case; **corpus delicti evidence** substantiates these elements. Thus, at each crime scene the investigator must keep in mind the unique requirements of proof for the case and attempt to locate related evidence.

ASSOCIATIVE EVIDENCE

Associative evidence is bidirectional in that it connects the perpetrator to the scene or victim, or connects the scene or victim to the suspect. A case history illustrates this:

A silent burglar alarm was triggered at a bar in a high-crime area. Officers responding to the scene found a point of forced entry at a rear window of the building. An individual was detected hiding in a small shed attached to the building. His statement was that when walking up the alley, he suddenly saw police cars, panicked, and hid in the shed. The search of this person following his arrest revealed the presence of valuables and materials taken from the burglarized premises, connecting the suspect with the scene.

TRACING EVIDENCE

The identification and location of the suspect are the goals of **tracing evidence;** corpus delicti and associative evidence may also serve these purposes:

A 20-year-old female was at a laundromat washing her clothes. A male loitered nearby, observing her. When the woman was alone, he walked rapidly to the laundromat and entered the men's room. A few minutes later, with his pants and underwear around his ankles, he approached the woman, shook his genitals at her, pulled up his clothing, and ran off. The officer who responded to the call found a man's wallet on the floor of the men's rest room. A records check on the identification contained in it revealed that the owner of the wallet had a history of sex offenses and lived in the neighborhood of the laundromat. When the victim identified the suspect from a series of photographs, a warrant for the suspect's arrest was obtained.

TYPICAL CRIME SCENE PROBLEMS

Although the procedures to be followed at a crime scene investigation may be neatly delineated in theory, any number of conditions may render their accomplishment a good bit less orderly than the ideal. In a perfect world, every crime scene would be fastidiously processed. In reality, the scenes of misdemeanor offenses receive a cursory examination and even the thoroughness with which felony crime scenes are processed is frequently affected by the severity of the offense. A crime scene processing unit cannot be called out to process every crime scene. To victims, the crime committed against them is important regardless of the severity. To investigators, that crime may be important or "just another report to fill out." Regardless of the situation, officers must convey a genuine interest in the complainant's situation.

At the scenes of violent crimes, especially those that are interracial, emotions may run high. Even a small crowd may add considerable confusion to the process of ascertaining what has happened and along what lines the investigation should proceed. In such situations, it is not unusual for witnesses to be lost, for their versions and perceptions of what occurred to be altered by contamination through contact with the crowd, or even for so-called witnesses to be added. In this last circumstance, a bystander may hear actual witnesses talking and suddenly believe they personally know something they should tell the police.

Police officers and supervisors occasionally make investigations more difficult when they drop by to see if they "can be of help," when in reality they are simply curious. Too many people at the scene can lead to confusion of assignments or the accidental alteration or destruction of evidence.

RULES FOR THE CRIME SCENE INVESTIGATOR

Regardless of the type of crime involved, five fundamental rules must be observed.

MAINTAIN CONTROL

Although mentioned previously in this chapter, the issue of control is so important that it warrants further elaboration. Without control, a life might be lost, evidence destroyed, assignments overlooked, or the investigation conducted in a generally haphazard manner. At the scene of sensational crimes, such as bank robberies, criminal homicides, or those involving well-known victims, members of the news media typically arrive shortly after the investigation begins and immediately attempt to quickly obtain information and/or videotape investigators, witnesses, or bystanders in order to meet their deadlines. Unless properly handled, this situation has the potential to create both confusion and complicate the investigative process.

The person in charge of the crime scene should cooperate with the press, but the scope of cooperation is limited by the need to avoid interference with the investigation, to protect the legal rights of a suspect, avoid placing a witness in danger, and other factors. All investigators should have a thorough knowledge of their agency's media relations policy.

Although some states have enacted "shield laws" so that news media personnel are not required to divulge their sources, as a general matter reporters have no legal rights beyond those granted each citizen. Although news officials may be permitted to enter a crime scene, they do so at their own risk; if their presence in any way jeopardizes police operations, it should not be allowed. The arrest of a news media worker at a crime scene should be made only on the most serious provocation and with full awareness of the adverse publicity that is certain to follow.

News media personnel may photograph or report anything that they observe while legally at a crime scene or covering any other incident involving the police. If in this process they obtain information that could endanger people or adversely affect the investigative process, both they and their supervisors should be notified of the possible consequences.

When suspects have been interviewed but not arrested, their identities should not be disclosed. It is appropriate for the crime scene coordinator to *generally* describe to reporters the physical evidence found at the scene, proceeds of the crime, weapons involved, and the issuance of warrants. However, detailed descriptions of evidence, proceeds, or weapons should not be disclosed, nor should information pertaining to how physical evidence, proceeds of the crime, or weapons were located.

It is also appropriate to withhold certain details about the crime scene, such as how a victim was mutilated, messages left at the scene by the perpetrator, particular types of evidence seized, or the exact words spoken to a rape victim. Such information could be vital in solving the case, evaluating informants' tips, or determining the authenticity of statements or confessions made by subse-

▲**FIGURE 3-18 Investigations and the media**
Washington, D.C. Police Chief Cathy Lanier speaks at a press conference following the 2009 shooting attack at the Holocaust Museum, which resulted in the death of a security guard. A persistent question is whether news media coverage helps or hinders investigations. The answer is that it all depends on the fact situation, but that excessive details revealed in the news media can hamper investigations.
(© Alex Wong/Getty Images)

quently identified suspects. If a suspect has been identified and an identity established or a likeness generated by an artist's sketch or by facial composite software (see Chapter 12, "Robbery"), it may be advantageous to widely publicize this information if it is not likely to hinder apprehension of the suspect.

Relevant information can be supplied in **media statements** if it cannot be characterized as being prejudicial to a fair trial for the defendant (Figure 3-18). Among the actions and statements that are permissible and impermissible under the policies of many departments are these:

1. If a suspect is not in custody, investigators may:
   a. Release the type of call received and the time of dispatch.
   b. Disclose known facts and circumstances related to the commission of the crime to the extent it will not hinder or prejudice investigation and prosecution.
   c. Give a general description of the suspect(s).
   d. State the age, race, sex, and occupation of the suspect(s).
   e. Provide the name(s) of the suspect(s).

f. Release the number, sex, and age of the victim(s) unless a juvenile is involved.

g. Give general information about injuries.

h. Release the identities of deceased victims if the families have been previously notified.

i. Provide the identities of the investigators assigned if this does not place them at risk or hinder the investigation.

j. If a victim has been transported to a hospital, refuse to release the name of that facility to the news media.[12]

k. At this or any other stage, refuse to release information or reports that reveal information about confidential informants, or other information, such as medical conditions, which is privileged.

2. If a suspect is in custody, investigators should not do the following for the media:

a. Require the suspect to pose for photographers.

b. Give detailed descriptions of suspects or evidence that may jeopardize the successful conclusion of an investigation or prosecution.

c. Reenact the crime.

d. Provide the suspect's prior criminal record of arrests or other criminal charges that did not result in a final conviction.

e. Disclose that the suspect told where weapons, proceeds of the crime, or other materials were located.

f. Use derogatory terms to refer to the suspect, such as "depraved character," "real no-good," "sexual monster," and other terms.

g. Reveal that the suspect declined to take certain types of tests or that the suspect did take certain tests (for example, a blood alcohol test to determine the degree, if any, to which the suspect was under the influence of drugs or alcohol).

h. Tell the results of any tests to which the suspect submitted.

i. Make statements as to the guilt or innocence of a suspect.

j. Release the identities of prospective witnesses or comment on the nature of their anticipated testimony or credibility.

k. Release information about the existence or content of any confession, admission, or statement given by suspects in custody.

l. Make statements of a purely speculative nature about any aspect of the case.

3. If a suspect is arrested, it is permissible in most states to release the following types of information about him/her:

a. The defendant's name, age, sex, residence, employment, marital status, and similar background information, unless the defendant is a juvenile.

b. The nature of the crime for which the arrest was made and the identity of the complainant (as long as disclosing this information does not create a danger for the complainant and is not seriously embarrassing to him or her—as can be the case for victims of sexual offenses—or does not run counter to other reasons of good judgment or applicable laws).

c. The identities of any other agencies participating in the investigation, and/or making the arrest, as well as those of the individual officers involved.

d. The circumstances surrounding the arrest, such as the time and place, the extent of any pursuit, amount of resistance, possession and use of weapons, injuries to an officer (notification of the family should precede disclosing an individual officer's identity), and a general description of items seized at the time of arrest.

CONCEPTUALIZE EVENTS

Outside the Bar Code nightclub, a 24-year-old man was shot five times and killed. Other shots were also fired. By conceptualizing how the crime was committed, Washington State Police officers believed that the face of the club might contain places where bullet evidence could be recovered, but which they could not see. They called in for a bucket truck and were successful in locating important evidence (Figure 3-19).

Even experienced investigators may not take the time to conceptualize how a crime was committed. Or they develop a premature concept of how the crime was committed. This often results in available evidence not being recovered, as happened in the Chandra Levy murder. During the course of an investigation facts known to investigators and inferences they have made must be periodically reviewed. This facilitates the reconstruction of the offense and identification of the perpetrator's method of operation, suggests the possible existence of certain types of physical evidence, and assists in establishing appropriate lines of inquiry:

Multiple female murder victims were found strangled and stabbed in an apartment. The lead investigator studied the crime scene very carefully. One of the victims was lying near the doorway to one of the bedrooms with a pillow under her head. The investigator concluded that the perpetrator may have touched the very lowest portion of the door to steady himself as he stood up after killing that victim. The crime scene technician processed that portion of the door and located the only fingerprint of the suspect found at the crime scene. The suspect was identified by this print and subsequently convicted of the murders.

►FIGURE 3-19
Investigators searching for bullet holes
Investigators from the Washington State Police Crime Laboratory search for bullet holes in the front of the Bar Code, a local club. Note WSP officers in the "bucket," which can be moved to search higher spots. (Courtesy The Olympian.com. Photo by Ron Soliman)

Without the investigator's thoughtful examination of the crime and reconstruction of how the perpetrator may have acted, that lower portion of the door would not have been dusted for fingerprints because it would have been illogical to expect to find a fingerprint there. Consequently, the most important piece of evidence would never have been located.

Assumptions that are made must be checked for accuracy as quickly as possible. The failure to do so may result in an offender's escaping prosecution and in embarrassment for the investigator and the department. It may also produce confusion in, or misdirect, the investigation:

A woman was murdered in her apartment. The investigators assumed that the woman's husband had thoroughly searched the apartment for their missing infant child when he first arrived and found his wife's body. Thus, they further assumed that the baby had been kidnapped. Some four days later the baby's body was found by the grandmother in the apartment under a sofa cushion.[13]

Human behavior is rich in its variety; in reconstructing the crime, investigators must be alert to the danger of imparting their own probable motives or actions to the perpetrator unless there are solid grounds for so doing. Alternatively stated, this proposition dictates that simply because, under the same or a similar set of circumstances, we would not have acted in a particular fashion does not preclude the possibility that the perpetrator may have acted in that way. Two cases illustrate the importance of this point:

In Woodbridge, New Jersey, a series of burglaries was solved when it was established that two inmates had been breaking out of a correctional facility to commit the offenses, and then returning nightly to the facility.[14]

In Palm Beach, Florida, a guard at a bank was surprised one night by an intruder who took $50,000 in gold coins. Unable to find a point of entry, investigators were puzzled until they received an anonymous tip that the intruder had shipped himself into the bank in a crate and broken out of it after the regular employees had gone home.[15]

Large physical evidence, such as a handgun used in a criminal homicide, is often easily found at the crime scene and requires little in the way of conceptualization. However, there is the possibility that much smaller types of evidence are also present; these will be located only if the investigator is able to conceptualize events:

A university student claimed that several hours previously her date had raped her at his apartment. This had been their second date. In addition to being able to identify her assailant, the victim showed the investigator a digital photograph taken on her phone earlier in the evening of her and her assailant. In examining the photograph, the investigator noticed that the victim was wearing a sorority pin in the photograph, but the victim's pin was now missing. Believing that the pin could have been lost at the crime scene, the investigator went to the suspect's apartment. The suspect's version of events was that he told the victim he no longer wanted to date her and she swore to get even for "being dumped." The suspect also said that the woman had never been in his apartment and consented to a search. The investigator found the missing sorority pin in the perpetrator's bedroom, and the suspect subsequently gave her a confession.

It does not take a great deal of conceptualization to recognize larger items of evidence at a crime scene. Where this ability pays substantial dividends is in locating **trace evidence,** which is present in extremely small or limited amounts. Such evidence may be, but is not exclusively, microscopic in size.

Often this trace evidence is located using **alternative light systems (ALSs)** (Figure 3-20). Illustrations include the Polilight, BlueMaxx, and Luma-Lite. As illumination from ALSs sweep over a crime scene, the various lights cause many types of evidence to fluoresce. Trace evidence that reacts to such illumination includes fingerprints, bodily fluids, hairs, fibers, drugs, glass and metal fragments, bite marks, bruises, human bone fragments, and gunshot residues. The following case illustrates the value of ALSs:

A small leaf was found on the windowsill where a burglar entered the building. The burglar had worked barefoot, and investigators located a portion of his footprint on the leaf using a Luma-Lite. Confronted with this and other evidence, the suspect pled guilty.[16]

Portable **trace-evidence vacuums** are also quite useful in locating very small items of evidence. To prevent the accidental contamination of the evidence, the nozzle and the evidence filter unit (which sits on top of the vacuum's nozzle) is packaged and sealed at the factory's "clean room." At the crime scene, as each different area is vacuumed, the nozzle and the filter are detached and sealed as evidence. These systems are particularly effective in gathering hairs, fibers, and certain types of drug evidence, such as cocaine. Thus, trace-evidence vacuum systems can often be effectively used in assault, rape, and some drug cases. If clothing is seized as evidence and fiber, hair, or other evidence from the suspect or victim may be on it, crime laboratories generally prefer that the clothing not be vacuumed at the scene but instead be sent to the laboratory for processing to prevent the possibility that other valuable evidence may be lost during the vacuuming.

PROCEED WITH CAUTION

Many crime scenes provide an immediate focus; in criminal homicide, for example, there is a tendency to move directly to the body. Such action, when the person is obviously deceased, has a number of disadvantages. In approaching the point of focus, small but extremely important evidence may be altered or destroyed, the area to be searched may be too rapidly defined, and other areas that might be fruitfully explored are overlooked or given only a cursory examination.

APPLY INCLUSIVENESS

The rule of inclusiveness dictates that every available piece of evidence be obtained and, where there is a question as to whether a particular item constitutes evidence, be defined as such. The rationale is that mistakes made

◄**FIGURE 3-20   Forensic light**
Forensic light illuminating latent finger fingerprints. Chapter 4, "Physical Evidence," contains a major section on fingerprint evidence. Such illumination helps to find fingerprints that might otherwise be overlooked. **(Courtesy Chief Jack Lumpkin, Athens Clarke County (Georgia) Police Department)**

in excluding potential evidence often cannot be rectified. One cannot always return to the crime scene and recover evidence. Sound judgment is required in applying the rule of inclusiveness. If you pick up everything that remotely could have some evidentiary value, scarce laboratory resources are going to be wasted.

The rule of inclusiveness also requires that standard samples and elimination prints always be obtained when appropriate. If, for example, a burglary has been committed and a safe inside the building successfully attacked, exposing the insulation of the safe, then standard samples of the insulation should be obtained. This will ensure that if at some future time a suspect is identified, comparisons can be made between the standard sample of safe insulation and any traces of safe insulation that might be recovered from the soles of the suspect's shoes or his or her car floor mat.

Elimination prints are useful in determining whether a latent fingerprint found at a crime scene belongs to the suspect. In the case of a residential burglary, for example, if a latent print was discovered inside the house on the window ledge where the perpetrator entered, the residents of the household should be fingerprinted and a comparison made between the latent fingerprint and those of the residents. If the latent fingerprint does not belong to any of the residents, it may belong to the perpetrator. In some instances, the fingerprint might belong to someone having authorized access to the dwelling. In cases where this is found to be true, however, the possibility cannot be overlooked that the person with authorized access may be the perpetrator. An example of this is the case of a licensed real estate dealer operating in the Washington, D.C., area who may have entered more than 100 homes that were being offered for sale, stealing furs,

tape recorders, silverware, and other valuables worth between $200,000 and $300,000.[17]

MAINTAIN DOCUMENTATION

Documentation of the crime scene is a constant activity, starting with the rough, shorthand record created by field notes. Other types of documentation that need to be maintained include:

1. The **crime scene entry log,** which was shown in Figure 3-6.
2. The **administrative log,** which is the responsibility of the crime scene coordinator and details such things as who is assigned to what function at the crime scene and the sequence of events at the scene, including its release.
3. **Assignment sheets,** which are completed by each individual who is given specific work to do and which document the results—both positive and negative.
4. The incidence/offense report, which is the responsibility of the first officer on the scene.
5. **Photographic logs,** detailing who took which shots, from where, when, and under what circumstances, for example, type of lighting (Figures 3-21a and 21b). Separate logs are kept for each camera used.
6. The rough sketch of the crime scene; the data used to prepare the finished or final diagram, which may be drawn by hand or by computer.
7. The **evidence recovery log,** which lists each item of evidence; the names of the collector and witness; the location, date, and time of the collection; and documentation such as photos or diagrams (Figure 3-22).

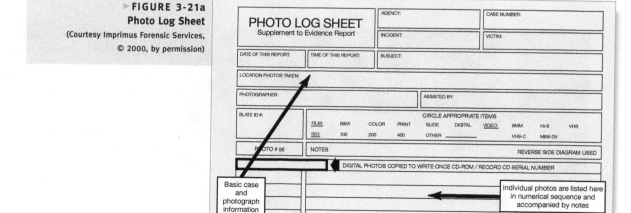

▶ **FIGURE 3-21a**
Photo Log Sheet
(Courtesy Imprimus Forensic Services, © 2000, by permission)

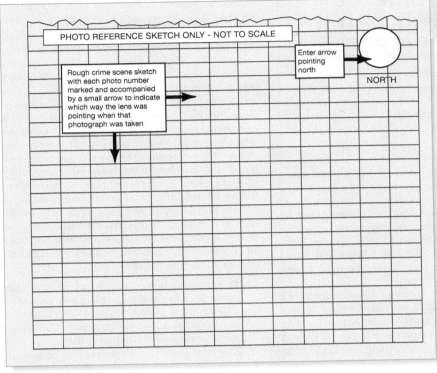

◄ **FIGURE 3-21b**
Photo Log Sheet (*continued*)

PHOTO REFERENCE SKETCH ONLY - NOT TO SCALE

Rough crime scene sketch with each photo number marked and accompanied by a small arrow to indicate which way the lens was pointing when that photograph was taken

Enter arrow pointing north

NORTH

◄ **FIGURE 3-22**
Evidence recovery log
(Courtesy Imprimus Forensic Services, © 2000, by permission)

Incident #		Offense:		Victim:		Location:					
Item No.	Description	Collector	Witness	Location	Time/Date Collected	Photos		Diagramed			
						Y	N	Y	N		
1											
2											
3											
4											
5											
6											
15											

Recorded by:
Name: _____
ID No.: _____
Unit: _____

Date:
Start Time:
End Time:

Recorded by:
Name: _____
ID No.: _____
Unit: _____

Page___of___Pages

8. Emergency medical personnel documents.
9. The **lifted-prints log,** which contains the same type of basic information as the evidence recovery log.
10. If applicable, the consent search form or search warrant.

In lesser offenses, a single officer may be the only representative of the police department at the scene. Thus, everything that is learned will be a result of his/her investigation. In such cases, the only documentation that may exist is the officer's field notes and the incident/offense report.

INFECTIOUS DISEASE RISKS AND PRECAUTIONS FOR INVESTIGATORS

On a daily basis, investigators are at risk of exposure to infectious pathogens (disease-causing agents), such as HIV, hepatitis B, hepatitis C, and tuberculosis. These diseases and the precautions that can be taken are discussed in the sections that follow.

HIV/AIDS

The **human immunodeficiency virus (HIV)** is a blood-borne pathogen that is also present in some body fluids—that is, blood, semen, vaginal secretions, and breast milk. In the United States it is most commonly transmitted by vaginal and anal intercourse. Less commonly, some HIV mothers may pass the pathogen to their baby at birth. The exposure risk from blood transfusions and organ transplants is extremely remote given the rigid testing associated with those procedures.[18]

If HIV progresses into acquired immunodeficiency syndrome (AIDS), the body's natural defenses against many types of diseases are substantially reduced, leaving victims vulnerable to "opportunistic infections," such as pneumonia, from which they ultimately die. There is no HIV/AIDS vaccine.

HIV is not spread from casual contact. You cannot get it from toilet seats, telephones, swimming pools, door knobs, a drinking fountain, or air.[19] There is no present evidence that HIV is spread through sweat, tears, saliva, or urine.[20] However, the co-presence of blood is not always obvious in such materials, nor may blood be immediately apparent on clothing, guns, knives, cars, drugs, and hypodermic needles; therefore, consistent caution is always warranted. It should be noted that HIV (and hepatitis B and C) can also be spread through shared razors, toothbrushes, and other personal care items. Biting insects, such as mosquitoes, do not transmit HIV.[21]

HIV/AIDS and Investigator Precautions. In general, the risk of HIV infection after an accidental needle stick is extremely low.[22] However, given the frequency with which investigators deal with special populations, such as intravenous drug users (IDUs), homosexuals, and prostitutes, the risk for them may be somewhat greater because of repeated exposure. The greatest danger to officers arises when they are making arrests, seizing drug-related evidence, and processing crime scenes and accidents where blood and other bodily fluids are exposed.

At all crime, accident, and other scenes with a potential or known HIV risks, investigators should use the appropriate personal protective equipment provided by their departments. If they have a suspected exposure it should be immediately reported to their supervisor and all treatment and decontamination protocols followed (Figure 3-23). Additionally:

1. Be cautious when conducting all types of searches; never put your hands anyplace you cannot see. Instead, use a mirror, or probe with a flashlight, pen, wooden dowel, or metal rod. Disinfect these items immediately after using them.
2. The most important protective barrier against HIV infection is intact skin. Even the slightest opening in the skin can be a portal through which HIV enters the body. Protect skin wounds, abrasions, and openings with 360-degree fluid-proof bandages.
3. About 20% of AIDS patients develop raised, purplish-colored lesions (Kaposi's sarcoma), which may be present anywhere on the body (Figure 3-24). Most commonly these are seen on the head, neck, and oral cavity. Some of these are "weeping lesions" that let out an HIV-carrying fluid. You should be particularly careful around such lesions.

▶ **FIGURE 3-23**
HIV post-exposure–prevention (PEP)

The risks of HIV exposures are well understood by law-enforcement agencies. The responsibilities of the officer at risk and the obligations of the employing department are detailed in policy manuals. Such policies usually require that exposures be reported immediately and medical treatment obtained where there has been a significant blood or other body fluid exposure to a known high-risk individual.

However, such policies typically stop short of identifying potential medical interventions. An HIV post-exposure-prophylaxis (PEP) treatment, a combination of several antiretroviral drugs, may be appropriate in some fact situations. PEP has been available since 1996 and changed as newer drugs became available. Although study results vary, its efficacy is about 75%. The treatment lasts four weeks and its side effects include headaches, vomiting, diarrhea, and fatigue. Some people cannot tolerate the full course of treatment.

The Chandler (Arizona) Police Department has a model policy that emphasizes rapid screening for PEP treatment. Its "Hazardous Body Fluid Exposure Control Plan" requires officers to report high risk exposures *within 15 minutes* to the agency's designated health provider. Although the Centers for Disease Control (CDC) advise that treatment started as late as 72 hours after an exposure may have benefit, needed treatment started within hours is more promising.

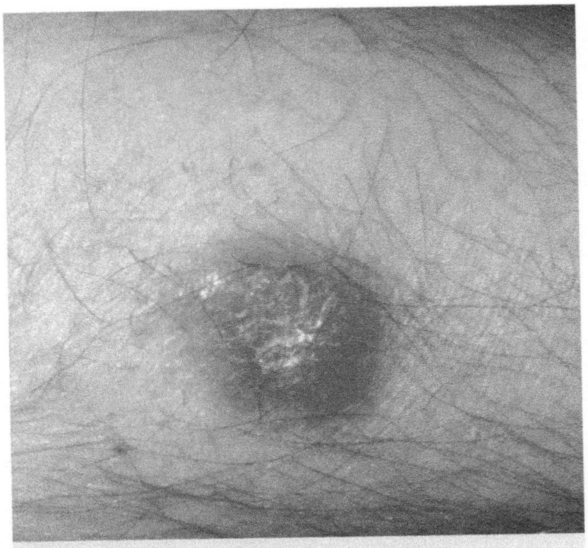

▲ **FIGURE 3-24 AIDS purple-colored lesion**
(© SPL/Photo Researchers, Inc.)

Another condition, pseudo–Kaposi's sarcoma, or acroangiodermatitus, has a similar appearance but is not HIV related.

4. If you are bitten by a suspect, have a medical assessment made. Do not place your mouth to the bite area. There are only a few, rare reports of transmission of the HIV virus by biting, although other types of infections may result.[23]

5. Bites, needle sticks, cuts, or similar incidents involving broken or punctured skin, however slight, should be washed immediately with soap in warm water for at least 30 seconds and treated medically.[24]

Use soap from a dispenser, not a shared bar. Some agencies recommend the use of germicidal wipes approved by the Environmental Protection Agency (EPA). There is no evidence that squeezing or "milking" wounds reduces the risk of HIV.

6. If splashed in the eyes or on mucous membranes (for example, inside the nose), flush the area for 15 minutes using water, sterile water, or a saline solution.

7. Do not attempt to recap hypodermic needles seized as evidence, and use care when seizing any other sharp items (for instance, knives, razor blades, broken glass, scissors, and metal pieces) at crime scenes. When handling sharp objects, use disposable tongs or forceps and place the objects in appropriate rigid, puncture-resistant containers.

8. The use of latex or nitrile gloves significantly reduces exposure from body fluids and may reduce the amount of blood transferred by an accidental needle stick by 50%.[25] To prevent the possibility of piercing your gloves, remove any rings before placing them on your hands. When wearing gloves, check them frequently for wear and tear; replace them often. When you remove gloves, wash your hands and use an approved germicidal wipe on them. High risk/cut-resistant gloves further reduce chance of accidental needle sticks and other wounds.

9. In addition to gloves, other **personal protection equipment (PPE)** may be necessary at high-risk scenes with exposed body fluids. Examples of such equipment are listed in Figure 3-25.

10. All disposable worn PPE should be placed in a biohazard waste bag when you have completed your work at a crime scene. When removing PPE, do so in a manner that does not contaminate your clothing. Clean your hands in the appropriate manner immediately afterward.

- Gloves—cotton, latex (natural rubber), nitrile, polyvinyl chloride (PVC), and neoprene. Each of these has different characteristics and limitations; more detailed information on this can be obtained by referring to the FBI's Forensic Science Handbook, which is available on the Internet.
- Cut-resistant glove liners.
- Protective or impermeable "booties" or shoe covers, disposable gowns, coveralls or jumpsuits, aprons, hoods, chin-length face shields, eyewear with side shields.
- Masks—infiltration masks for protection from highly contagious people and situations; nuisance odor masks for reduction of unpleasant odors; and half-mask particulate respirators for protection from fumes, particulate/dust, and airborne pathogens. Self-contained breathing apparatus (SCBA).
- EPA-registered bleach, germicidal disinfectants, and wipes.
- First-aid kit.
- Biohazard bags.
- Insect repellant.

Source: Content drawn from Henry C. Lee, Timothy M. Palmbach, and Marilyn T. Miller, *Crime Scene Handbook* (San Diego: Academic Press, 2001), pp. 321–324, and Technical Working Group on Crime Scene Investigation, *Crime Scene Investigation* (Washington, DC: U.S. Department of Justice, 2000), pp. 33–36; additional content supplied by the authors.

◄ **FIGURE 3-25**
Crime scene personal protection equipment (PPE)

11. Maintain a high sense of personal awareness at potential HIV scenes. When you are wearing gloves, do not handle personal items (such as your pen or clipboard), and do not put your hands in your pockets, touch your face, or scratch your head.

    If you do touch personal items or body areas, they should be immediately disinfected.

12. Always carry a flashlight, even during daylight hours, so that you can search dark areas more safely.

13. Do not eat, drink, smoke, handle contacts, or apply lip balm or cosmetics at HIV-risk crime scenes.

14. Contaminated evidence should be collected, marked, and packaged as appropriate for the particular type of evidence. If the evidence might be contaminated, mark it prominently as such or apply a "Biological Hazard" sticker.

15. Carefully follow department policy regarding decontamination of your uniform, equipment, and vehicle.

16. Make sure you understand federal and state confidentiality laws that pertain to disclosing information about HIV to others, including the news media.

Hepatitis B and C. **Hepatitis B (HBV)** is the most common serious disease in the world and is the leading cause of liver cancer; about 500,000 people die annually from liver cancer and another 5,000 from chronic HBV and associated complications.[26] It also results in cirrhosis (scarring) of the liver and liver failure. Symptoms include appetite loss, fatigue, nausea, vomiting, pain over the location of the liver, stools that are pale gray or clay colored, and dark urine with a tea or cola color. Since 1982 there has been a safe and effective HBV vaccine.

HBV is a major health concern. It is spread by contact with the blood or body fluids of an infected person, for example, blood to blood contact; unprotected sex; sharing earrings; nail-clippers; toothbrushes; razors, and unsterile needles. Well regulated acupuncture, tattooing, and body piercing services are not viewed as a serious risk. In the absence of precautions, officers are 100 times more likely to contract HBV than HIV.[27]

Hepatitis C (HCV) may be transmitted from an infected woman to her newborn during delivery. Also at risk are persons with an HIV infection, accidental needle sticks, recipients of blood transfusions and organ transplants before 1992, and chronic hemodialysis patients. There is no vaccine for HCV.

Unless effective new therapies are developed, deaths due to HCV will double or even triple over the next 15 to 20 years simply because 80% of those infected have no signs or symptoms and therefore may have been infected for a long time without knowing it.[28] The symptoms are similar to those of HBV: jaundice—the yellowish coloring of the skin and whites of the eyes, dark urine, fatigue, abdominal pain, nausea, and loss of appetite.[29] There is no vaccine for HCV. Neither HBV nor HCV is spread by casual contact.

Tuberculosis. **Tuberculosis (TB)** is a chronic bacterial infection that is spread by air. Accountable for more deaths worldwide than any other infectious disease, it usually infects the lungs, although other organs may be involved.[30] One third of the world's population is infected with TB, although most will never develop active TB. The mortality rate for treated cases is about 10%.[31] The existence of some drug-resistant strains of TB is of concern to public health officials.[32]

When a person with active TB coughs into the air, infectious droplets are released; repeated exposure to them can cause the disease. People who eat healthy diets and lead healthy lifestyles are less at risk than others when such exposure occurs. Conversely, the homeless, alcoholics, drug addicts, and people in poor health are at greater risk.

A vaccine (BCG) is given to infants in some parts of the world where the disease is common; the effectiveness of BCG in adults varies widely, and in the United States its general use is not recommended.[33] Several drug therapies are available for people who have a high risk of developing active TB, that is, those who are in close contact with persons who are infected with TB or have active TB.[34]

The Americans with Disabilities Act. Investigators who contract the infectious diseases discussed previously may be covered by the federal **Americans with Disabilities Act (ADA)**. Under this act, it is illegal to discriminate against an otherwise qualified employee in regard to employment actions—such as assignments and promotions—solely because the employee is thought to have, or actually has, a covered disability. Employers may be required to make "reasonable accommodations" for such employees. Reasonable accommodations include redesigning jobs, offering part-time hours, and modifying equipment and facilities. The legal provisions of ADA are broad and cover more than just infectious diseases; additional information is readily obtainable in personnel offices, from police unions, and on the Internet.

As a final note, some police agencies have taken the view that if an officer cannot fully perform all the functions required of a certified peace officer, she or he may be separated from the service or placed on involuntary medical retirement, depending on the situation. Other police departments have chosen to inventory their positions each year in order to determine how many of them could, with reasonable accommodations, be staffed by persons covered by ADA.

THE CRIME SCENE SEARCH

The purpose of the crime scene search is to obtain physical evidence useful in establishing the fact that an offense has been committed, identify the method of operation employed by the perpetrator, reduce the number of suspects, and identify the perpetrator. Four major considerations dominate the crime scene search.

1. BOUNDARY DETERMINATION

In terms of the boundary of the crime scene, it is useful to think of an inner perimeter and an outer perimeter. The inner perimeter delineates the area where the specific items of evidence are known to be, along with the lines of entry into, and exit from, the scene. The outer perimeter is set farther back than the inner perimeter and helps establish control of, and entry into, the scene.

The crime scene coordinator is responsible for deciding the positions of the inner and outer perimeters, which are determined by the locations of the primary and any secondary crime scenes—such as the perpetrator's lines of approach to and from the scene. Along these lines, the perpetrator may have accidentally left or dropped valuable evidence, such as items taken from the scene, the perpetrator's wallet or distinctive jewelry, matches from an establishment he or she works at or frequents, a water bottle the perpetrator drank from while waiting for the victim, and the butt from a cigarette he or she smoked. Saliva traces from the bottle and the butt could yield DNA evidence.

For an indoor crime scene, the physical limitations of the building can help determine where the inner and outer boundaries should be. More problematic is determining the boundaries for an outdoor crime scene. As a general rule, in such situations, it is better to establish the perimeters more broadly. Although doing so may result in some "wasted" search effort, items of evidence are occasionally found.

2. CHOICE OF SEARCH PATTERN

There are five basic **crime scene search patterns** from which the crime scene coordinator may choose:

1. The spiral, depicted in Figure 3-26(a) is usually employed in outdoor scenes and is normally executed by a single person. The searcher walks in slightly decreasing, less-than-concentric circles from the outermost boundary determination toward a central point. This pattern should not be operated in the reverse—beginning at some central point and working toward the perimeter of the crime scene in increasing, less-than-concentric circles—as there is a real danger that some evidence may be inadvertently destroyed while walking to the central point to initiate the search.

2. The strip/line search, diagrammed in Figure 3-26(b), involves the demarcation of a series of lanes down which one or more persons proceed. On reaching the starting point, the searchers proceed down their respective lanes, reverse their direction, and

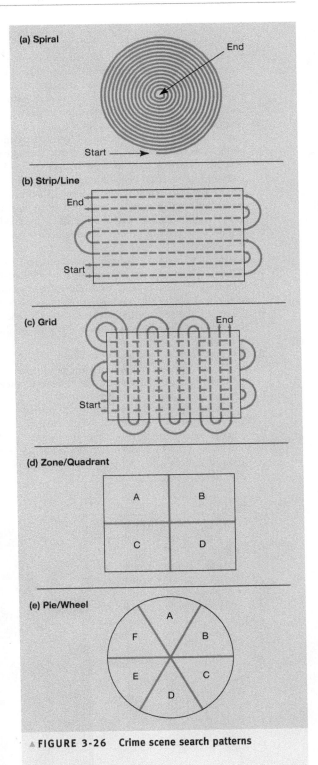

▲ **FIGURE 3-26**   **Crime scene search patterns**

continue in this fashion until the area has been thoroughly examined. If multiple searchers are being used, then whenever physical evidence is encountered, all searchers should stop until it is properly handled and they have received information with respect to its nature. The search is then resumed in the fashion described previously.

3. The grid search is a variation of the strip/line pattern and is depicted in Figure 3-26(c). After completing the strip pattern, the searchers double back perpendicularly across the area being examined. Although more time-consuming than the strip search, the grid offers the advantage of being more methodical and thorough; examined from two different viewpoints, an area is more likely to yield evidence that might otherwise have been overlooked.

4. Figure 3-26(d) shows the zone/quadrant search pattern, which requires that an area be divided into four large quadrants, each of which is then examined using any of the methods already described. If the area to be searched is particularly large, each of the quadrants can be subdivided into four smaller quadrants.

5. The pie/wheel search, shown in Figure 3-26(e), entails dividing the area into a number of pie-shaped sections, usually six. These are then searched, usually through a variation of the strip method.

   In practice, both the spiral and the pie search patterns are rarely employed. When the area to be searched is not excessively large, the strip or grid pattern is normally used. When the crime scene is of significant size, the zone search pattern is normally employed.

3. INSTRUCTION OF PERSONNEL

Although instruction of personnel was mentioned earlier in the chapter, its importance requires some further elaboration. Even when the same type of criminal offense has been committed, the variation among crime scenes may be enormous, for example, the murder weapon may be recovered at the scene or in a distant body of water (Figure 3-27.) These variations are due to such factors as the physical settings, the manner and means that the perpetrators used to execute the offenses, and the lengths to which they may have gone to eliminate or destroy evidence. Thus, it is of paramount importance that the crime scene coordinator call together all the individuals who will be, in various capacities, processing the scene and share with them all the available information concerning the case. Doing so serves to minimize the possibility of excluding any available evidence. On receipt of this information, the members of the crime scene processing team may then begin their work.

4. COORDINATION

As discussed earlier, one of the most important responsibilities of the person in charge of the crime scene is integrating the efforts of those assigned to the technical and investigative service functions, along with ensuring the timely flow of pertinent information. For example, if a suspect is in custody and the interrogation yields information concerning the weapon or tool that may have been used, or where it may be located, then the crime scene coordinator should rapidly relay this information to those involved in crime scene processing so that they will be alert to specific possibilities for the recovery of

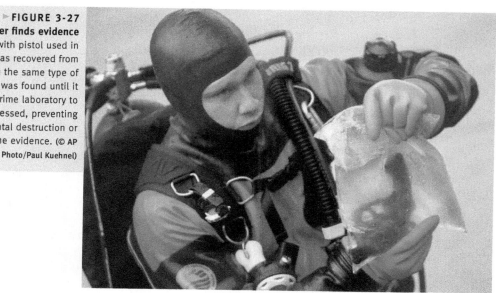

▶ FIGURE 3-27
Police diver finds evidence
Police scuba diver with pistol used in murder case that was recovered from a lake. It is kept in the same type of water in which it was found until it arrives at the crime laboratory to be properly processed, preventing the accidental destruction or contamination of the evidence. (© AP Photo/Paul Kuehnel)

physical evidence. Conversely, as significant physical evidence is recovered, the information should be conveyed to the crime scene coordinator, who can then transmit it to other investigators so they can move toward apprehending a suspect or use the information during the interrogation of a possible perpetrator already in custody.

SUSPENDED SEARCHES, DEBRIEFING, AND RELEASE OF THE SCENE

Occasionally, it may be necessary to suspend an operation temporarily. In one of the most common situations, a priority crime with evidence subject to decay requires the temporary diversion of personnel from another scene where delayed processing will not result in any loss of physical evidence. If it becomes necessary to stop the examination of a scene for a time, that scene should be secured in such a fashion that there is no possibility of contamination, alteration, or accidental destruction of any evidence that may exist.

Immediately before the **crime scene release,** the coordinator calls all team members together. In addition to ensuring that assignments were properly executed, the coordinator checks to make sure that all equipment brought to the scene has been retrieved and that all trash generated in processing the scene has been removed. Because each participant shares information during the debriefing, additional opportunities to develop evidence may be identified allowing all parties to leave the scene with a common understanding of the crime and of what the next steps are going to be. When the scene is finally released, the name of the party to whom it is released and his/her locator information should be noted in the administrative log.

Once a scene is released, the person to whom it is released will usually clean it up. Additionally, if the person is living there, the countless small things he/she does each day will alter and contaminate the scene, so that returning to it for further processing is not a viable option. Therefore, the decision to release a scene must be well thought out. An absolute must is to photograph the scene again just before it is turned over to the responsible party. These photos will counter claims that the police "tore my sister's house apart when they were there."

COLLECTION AND CARE OF EVIDENCE

The location of physical evidence during the crime scene search merely marks the first step in its long journey toward presentation in court. To satisfy legal require-

ments related to its introduction in a judicial proceeding, investigators must be able to:

1. identify each item of evidence they collected or handled;
2. describe the location and condition of the evidence at the time it was collected;
3. state who had contact with or handled the evidence;
4. state when, or during what time periods, the evidence was handled;
5. declare under what circumstances, and why, the evidence was handled;
6. explain what changes, if any, were made to the evidence.[35]

The essence of packaging any evidence is to do it in a way that will make any tampering with it clearly evident. For example, if evidence is placed in a plain Kraft envelope, the envelope should be sealed with tamper-evident evidence tape. As a further measure, when the officer signs her or his initials or signature, the writing can start on the envelope, cross the tape, and go back onto the envelope. Using a preprinted label or otherwise just writing on the envelope, the following information should be provided: type of offense and agency case number; the item number, the date recovered/received; and the investigator's name and badge number/departmental identifier. The entries made on evidence, and strong evidence room procedures, such as the use of bar codes to track evidence handling, can eliminate many barriers to introducing evidence in a courtroom.

VISUAL DOCUMENTATION OF THE CRIME SCENE

Occasionally, the value of an otherwise excellent investigation is reduced by improper or inadequate visual documentation of the scene. People process information differently, so the more ways a crime scene is properly documented, the greater the likelihood that other people will accurately understand the scene and what happened there.

This section examines three basic methods of documenting crime scenes: (1) digital video recording, (2) digital still photography, and (3) sketching. In general, the methods should be used in that order with documentation progressing from the general to the more specific. More advanced crime scene digital imaging techniques are discussed later in the chapter.

DIGITAL VIDEO RECORDING

Using **digital video recording** to document the crime scene offers several advantages. Such cameras are relatively inexpensive, they incorporate audio, their use can be quickly learned, the motion of videotapes holds the attention of viewers, and the images collected can be

▶**FIGURE 3-28**
Police officer photographing the body of a 29-year-old mother of six who was found murdered in a parking lot. The words on the yellow crime scene tape are hard to read because they are printed on the opposite side, but they can be plainly seen by people approaching the crime scene. (Courtesy Lexington Hearld-Leader. Photo by Pablo Alcala)

played back immediately. On the downside, neither the resolutions nor the color accuracy can compete with those of digital still photography. Video recorded images are not an acceptable alternative to high-resolution digital photographs. Several protocols should be followed when video recording a crime scene:

1. Keep the camera's lens clean to produce sharper images.
2. To avoid dragging electrical cords through the scene, battery packs should be used for the camera and portable lights. Use the camera's title generator and make sure that the time/date indicators are correct before recording begins.
3. The recording should begin with an identification of the location, case number, type of offense, and other pertinent information. It should progress to what viewers will be seeing. Some agencies display a simple overhead view of the scene during the narration to help orient viewers.
4. After the narration ends a dummy microphone plug should be inserted in the camera to avoid recording unwanted and potentially embarrassing extraneous comments being recorded.
5. Once recording begins, the camera should be kept running; gaps may be hard to satisfactorily explain to jurors.
6. Most crime scenes can be documented within 30 minutes. Pan each area in 360 degrees.
7. The use of a rolling tripod or shoulder brace with the camera will produce smoother, less jerky images.
8. The most common mistake in video recording is going too fast; the speed you think is right may be as much as 50% too fast. Take your time and use the camera's capabilities for wide-area pans, close-ups, and very tight shots of the evidence.

DIGITAL STILL PHOTOGRAPHY

Digital (DSLR) still photography is the primary means of documenting major crime scenes. Although digital video recordings capture images, they are supplemental to the four classes of photographs that must be taken with digital still cameras; they are often taken in this progression:

1. *Orientation*—long/longer range shots, general views of the entire scene.
2. *Relationship*—medium range, photos of evidence and their positional relationship to each other (see Figure 3-28).
3. *Identification*—close-ups that show specific features, such as the serial number on a firearm.
4. *Comparison*—close-ups that document characteristics for future laboratory examination, for example, 1:1 shots of developed fingerprints.[36]

These general guidelines are appropriate for still photography of almost any scene; some previously mentioned points in this chapter are reiterated to consolidated them:[37]

- Photograph the crime scene as soon as possible.
- Prepare the photographic log.
- Photograph from eye level to represent the normal view.
- Photograph the most fragile areas of the crime scene first.
- Photograph all stages of the crime scene investigation, including discoveries.
- Photograph the condition of evidence before recovery.
- Take all photographs intended for examination purposes without a scale, and then with one.
- Photograph the interior crime scene in an overlapping series using a normal lens, if possible. Overall photographs may be taken using a wide-angle lens.

- Photograph the exterior crime scene, establishing the location of the scene by a series of overall photographs including a landmark. Photographs should have 360 degrees of coverage. Consider using aerial photography, when appropriate.
- Photograph entrances and exits from the inside and the outside.
- Photograph important evidence twice: (1) a medium-distance shot that shows the evidence and its position to other evidence and (2) a close-up shot that includes a scale and fills the frame.

Some law-enforcement agencies have concluded that although many crimes committed do not warrant full crime scene processing, there is a need to supplement some reports with photographs—for instance, a misdemeanor assault that produces visible injuries. In those departments low-end "point and shoot" digital cameras are issued to officers or to their Sergeants.

DIGITAL IMAGE MANAGEMENT SYSTEMS

Whether digital video recordings or still digital photographs, digital images from different crime scenes should not be comingled on the same storage media. These images are evidence and should be handled as such. Many agencies use **Digital Image Management System (DIMS)** software to help accomplish this. DIMS have a digital authentication capability that verifies that the images from the storage media and those uploaded are exactly the same. The initial storage media can then be wiped clean and reused at another scene, although many agencies also treat the original storage media as evidence. Other DIMS capabilities include setting levels of user access and image searching across the entire database.

One DIMS uploaded copy is kept as the "electronic negative" and others can be processed for analytical/investigative purposes, for example, alterations of the color contrast to make visible what otherwise could not be seen; image enhancement/sharpening, and resizing. Each processing or transformation of an image must be logged; some software, such as Adobe Photoshop, automatically compiles this data. Although the original image is never altered, the ability to "manipulate" digital images has resulted in some legal changes to them. Departments must have standard operating procedures (SOPs) regarding their digital image capturing and processing practices, as well as specifying how the images are managed and their integrity maintained.

The existence of a DIMS SOP does not guarantee compliance with its provisions. One department lost over 600 digital crime scene photographs because they were not backed up. The responsibility for ensuring compliance must be fixed; that person is usually the head of the crime laboratory, or in smaller agencies, whoever supervises the person capturing the images.

CRIME SCENE SKETCHING AND FORENSIC MAPPING

A **crime scene sketch** is a basic diagram of the scene showing important points, such as the locations where various pieces of physical evidence were located. Often, the sketch is not drawn to scale. Sketches made by hand in the field are called **"rough sketches"** as opposed to the more polished **"smooth or finished" sketches** typically drawn in the office. Finished sketches may also be drawn by hand, although it is often done using specialized computer software. Although there is a learning curve with any software, once the package is mastered computer generated sketches produce substantial reductions in the time required to make them—perhaps 75%–versus traditional sketching methods.

Forensic mapping is the process of taking and recording the precise measurements of items of evidence to be drawn or "fixed" on the sketch.[38] In theory, a crime scene sketch and associated mapping data should allow someone to return to the crime scene and place an item of evidence in exactly the same place as it was recovered. As a practical matter, the sketch allows the positioning of the evidence back into its original location with a reasonable degree of accuracy because there is some variation in the precision of sketching methods. The process of mapping the scene inherently intrudes into the scene, because the investigator must move through and around the scene taking and recording measurements.[39] This process requires a degree of caution in order to prevent the accidental moving, alteration, or destruction of physical evidence, all of which have the potential to confuse or misdirect the investigation.

It is critical that the entries on the sketch be as accurate as possible. Errors noted call into question not only the accuracy of the sketch but also the investigation as a whole. For example, distances should not be paced off and then recorded as so many feet and inches. Distances may be measured using rulers or tape measures, as well as by using more sophisticated methods, such as laser devices. Sketching and mapping methods are covered in the sections that follow.

Sketching Views

Regardless of the method, sketches typically employ one of three different views: (1) **overhead** or **bird's-eye view** (Figure 3-29), which is the most common; (2) the **elevation view** (Figure 3-30), which shows heights; and (3) the **cross-projection view** (Figure 3-31), which "lays" the walls to a room down so objects of interest in the wall can be mapped.[40]

Forensic Mapping Methods

The choice of mapping methods can be influenced by a variety of factors, including the nature and the amount of evidence, the overall size of the crime scene, the number of personnel available, the number, size and types of

▶ **FIGURE 3-29**
Overhead or bird's-eye view of a crime scene
No measurements are included in this sketch because it is intended merely to portray the overhead or bird's-eye view. Occasionally it is also called a floor-plan sketch. As a convention, North is usually oriented toward the top of the sketch.

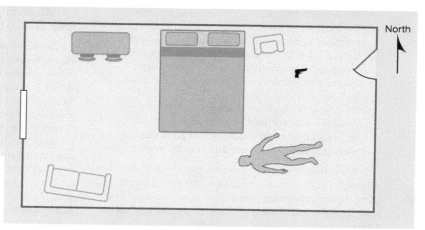

▶ **FIGURE 3-30**
North wall elevation view of the crime scene
In common language, *elevation* refers to the height of something above a reference point. In this view, the reference point is the floor. An elevation view represents the front, sides, or rear of a building. It is an excellent tool to record evidence on vertical surfaces. This view shows the North interior wall using the following legend: A: Apparent bullet hole in glass window. B: Apparent bullet hole in glass window.

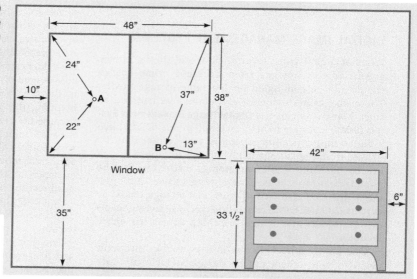

line-of-sight-obstructions, and weather conditions.[41] It is not necessary to map everything that you can see; it is important to show the location of the items of physical evidence and any decedent(s). Typically, each crime scene sketch employs only one of these mapping methods; the choice begins with the seriousness of the crime. More severe crimes dictate the use of more precise mapping methods.[42]

This section summarizes major mapping methods, including: (1) rectangular coordinates, (2) triangulation, (3) baseline coordinates, (4) polar coordinates, and (5) the grid system.

1. *Rectangular Coordinates*. This method is the best to use with scenes having clear and specific boundaries, such as interior walls, because **rectangular coordinates** can

be measured fast and accurately, especially if one is using a laser measuring device.[43] The crime scene investigator (CSI) usually takes two measurements at right angles from the center mass of the evidence to the two nearest walls. It has one deficiency: Although evidence can be fixed at a particular location, the orientation of the evidence can be changed simply by rotating it on the axis where the two measurements intersect. In the case of Figure 3-32, this means the knife's tip could point in 360 different degrees.[44] This deficiency can be overcome by taking and recording additional measurements or, as is the more usual case, by using a different sketching technique, such as triangulation.

2. *Triangulation*. The **triangulation** method is useful both for interior scenes in buildings, as well as for outdoor

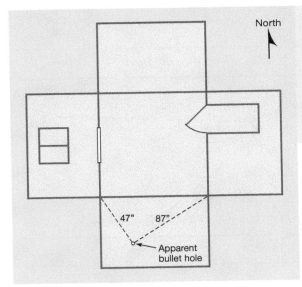

North

47" 87"

Apparent
bullet hole

The cross-projection, or "exploded," view "lays" the walls down flat, as though the room had been unfolded like a box. The purpose of doing this is to be able to show points of interest in the wall, which can also be done with an elevation sketch. The advantage of using the cross-projection method is that when there are multiple points of interest in several different walls, they can be displayed simultaneously in one sketch, as opposed to having to make and refer to multiple elevation sketches.

(1) top of the foremost portion of the gun barrel and (2) nearest portion of the grip, fixing the location of the handgun with precision.[46]

In the aftermath of the 1992 Ruby Ridge shootout, the FBI was criticized for not using triangulation to memorialize the location of physical evidence, a remark that failed to take into account the limitations of using it when the terrain is very uneven.

3. Baseline Coordinates. "The baseline method of fixing evidence is very similar to the rectangular coordinates process."[47] **Baseline coordinates** can be used both inside and outside. Figure 3-34 depicts its use in an interior location. Establishing a straight baseline in a room is straightforward; once it exists, the distance on a right angle (90 degrees) between the center mass of the evidence and where it intersects with the baseline is recorded. The distance from this intersection along the baseline to a fixed

scenes, where measurements must spring from distinct, "permanent" features or landmarks, such as the corner of a home, telephone, mailbox and lighting poles, fences, stop sign posts, the intersections of paved driveways and roads, and other similar features (Figure 3-33). Each pair of measurements is anchored by a reference point (RP), forming two sides of the triangle.[45] In Figure 3-33, two measurements from separate points were made to the

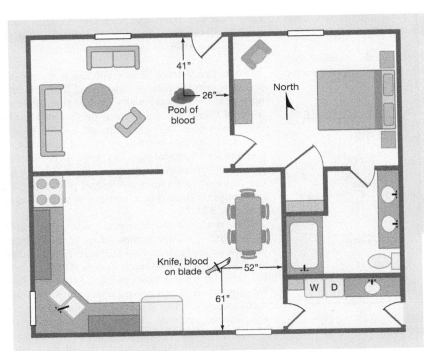

41"

26"

Pool of blood

North

Knife, blood on blade 52"

61"

W D

◄ **FIGURE 3-32**
Rectangular coordinates
In this example the legend block is blank, because the two items of evidence were drawn in the sketch. If numbers or letters had been used to indicate the locations of the evidence, then the legend would read: 1, pool of blood, and 2, knife with blood on blade. Some investigators prefer to use letters rather than numbers to indicate the location of evidence, because letters are more easily differentiated from the measurements that appear in the sketch.

▶ **FIGURE 3-33** **Triangulation**

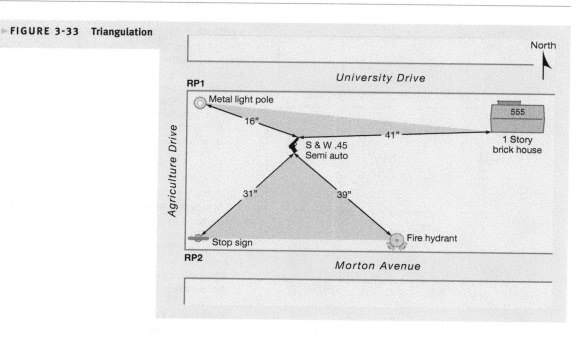

point is also recorded. If greater precision in fixing the location of the Glock 40 in Figure 3-34 was desired, several 90-degree measurements from distinct parts of the Glock back to the baseline and then, respectively, along the baseline to the West wall could be made. Without those additional measurements, the orientation of the Glock could be rotated in the same manner described earlier regarding the use of the rectangular coordinates method.

When this method is used outside, the baseline may be established by running a string or non-stretching tape

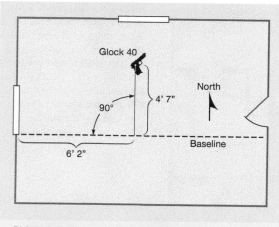

▲ **FIGURE 3-34** **Baseline coordinates**

measure between distinct features or landmarks. Some agencies do not use baseline coordinates when the distance from the physical evidence back to the baseline is more than 30 feet, because as the distance to be measured increases, so does the potential for error.[48] However, this error potential may be greater with handheld tape measures than with lasers and other very accurate measuring devices. Therefore, it should be considered a rule of thumb rather than an iron-clad requirement.

4. Polar Coordinates. When you are mapping outdoor scenes at which evidence is scattered over a fairly large open area, the **polar coordinate** method is an effective tool; it is not useful at scenes where the line of sight is limited.[49] For example, when human remains in an open field are dispersed because of animal predation, polar-coordinates are useful in fixing them. At its simplest, the polar-coordinates method requires measuring the straight line distance from a known reference point along a direction (angle) to the physical evidence to be fixed, as shown in Figure 3-35.[50]

The starting or **datum point** for polar coordinates may be established using a number of methods, including the baseline or triangulation, or in the absence of other possibilities, a global positioning system (GPS) can establish the datum point at which a metal rod may be driven into the ground as it can subsequently be located using a metal detector.[51] The distance from the datum point to the physical evidence may be measured using steel or fiberglass tapes, which are not subject to stretching or shrinkage, while the angle may be set by a handheld

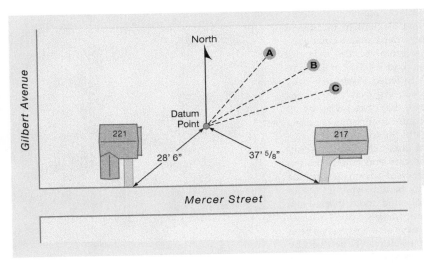

◄**FIGURE 3-35**
Polar coordinates
The datum, or starting point, is established by triangulation using the points at which two paved driveways intersect with Mercer Street to form the base of the triangle. In this example, no elevation measurements were taken. Elevation is measured as the difference between the elevation of the datum point and each item of evidence.

compass or protractor. Because of its greater accuracy, a surveyor's transit or similar device, which can also establish the elevation of evidence if this is important, is preferred to a handheld compass. In Figure 3-33, triangulation is used to establish the datum point from which the angles and distances to the evidence is determined.

5. Grid Systems. A **grid system** (See Figure 3-36) is an excellent tool to use when there is a large outdoor scene with no significant features or landmarks.[52] For many years archaeologists have used grid systems to record where artifacts are found at a site; during the mid-1980s, there was a noticeable transfer of this technology as archaeologists instructed investigators on using the grid system and other techniques to process buried body scenes.[53] Both archaeologists and crime scene investigators typically lay out grids with sides of 3 meters or 10 feet, although they may be of any dimensions so long as they are of uniform size; grids as large as 30 feet to a side have been used. When dealing with buried bodies or human remains scattered in a relatively compact area, a grid system of smaller dimensions may be useful.[54]

The boundary of each grid is fixed by a metal or wooden stakes; smaller sized grids may be connected using twine, although this may be impractical with large grids. If several search teams are working, each should be responsible for certain grids and as they find physical evidence, information about it should be immediately communicated to all other search teams. Laying out the grids and marking the boundaries of each is time consuming, but essential;[55] evidence may be fixed within the grids by employing whatever method is most useful; this is an exception to the earlier guideline that typically each crime scene sketch uses only one mapping method; another exception is the use of triangulation to establish the datum point for the polar coordinates method.

Automated Digital Imaging of Crime Scene

Although digital video recording, digital still photography, and sketching are the predominant methods of crime scene documentation, there appears to be some potential for a slow and quiet convergence of them, fueled by advances in two methods of digital imaging: (1) laser

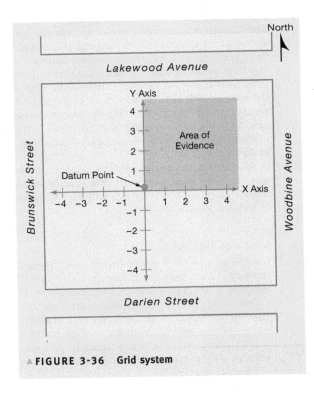

▲**FIGURE 3-36   Grid system**

scanning and (2) panoramic (360-degree-view) cameras. Originally conceived of as a supplement to traditional sketching and photography, some departments are experimenting with them as an alternative. The systems, depending on their capabilities, cost $40,000 to $250,000 and are often purchased with forfeited assets seized by law-enforcement agencies and federal government grants. They are automated in the sense that once set up by an operator, the systems do not require continuous handling as with video recordings and still photography.

Although the capabilities of laser scanning and panoramic camera imaging systems vary and require the use of specialized software, their *combined* advantages include these: (1) The systems can easily be deployed; (2) scenes can be documented very rapidly and more thoroughly; (3) the 3-D models and panoramic images created are easily stored and can be referred to days after a scene has been released up to years later; (4) the results can be accessed by investigators working similar cases at a distant precinct or across the country; (5) questions that were not fully explored or contemplated at the scene can be carefully studied later; (6) investigators can view the crime scenes, panning left and right and zooming in and out; in 3-D models they can "walk" through the virtual crime scenes to any location for any viewpoint; (7) bullet and blood spatter trajectories can be inserted; (8) victims can be captured and displayed in the precise location they were found; (9) animation of the actions of the assailant and victim can be created; (10) with a DSLR, hundreds of still photographs could be taken and still not produce the complete coverage of these newer techniques; (11) if one points at and clicks on any two different points, their precise distance apart is calculated and shown as if the scene still existed; and (12) in addition to being powerful tools for courtroom presentations and training, they are being used by some agencies as part of the interrogation process. Whichever technology is used, place the imaging unit in several locations at the scene to completely capture the scene. Specific equipment for laser scanning and panoramic imaging of crime scenes is discussed in the sections that follow as examples of what is available in the market place.

Although a number of *combined* advantages for these two methods were discussed, the specific advantages actually acquired by an agency will depend on the type of imaging system selected.

Laser Scanning

The DeltaSphere-3000 is a 25-pound easily portable **laser scanning** system that can be set up in 10 minutes and complete a 360-degree scan in 3 to 15 minutes. Through a data-fusion process, the DeltaSphere "marries" data from its two major components: (1) high-resolution panoramic photos and (2) millions of data points ("point clouds") measured by a laser scanner to produce photorealistic 3-D computer graphics models accurate to 0.25 inch (Figure 3-37).

▲ **FIGURE 3-37**

A DeltaSphere 3-D laser scan model of a mock crime scene with mannequins as two victims. The white lines above the woman's head show the major axes of the blood spatters on the wall. The blue line is perpendicular through their point of intersection. The red lines are the blood spatter trajectory. Where the red and blue lines intersect appears to be the woman's position when she was shot. In a working model, a click on the "Officer A" annotation at the left of the image would produce the same field of view the first arriving responder had. (Courtesy of Dough Schiff, 3rdTech, Durham, North Carolina)

Training for use of the DeltaSphere is conducted over a three-day period. The first half-day is devoted to setting up and using the equipment, that is, capturing the data, and the remaining time is spent using the associated SceneVision 3-D software building the 3-D computer graphics model, annotating the model and images with measurements and notes, making diagrams, linking close-up photographs, and preparing viewpoints, and the "walk through." The final step is creating the finished presentation.

Panoramic Cameras

A **panoramic camera** provides an unbroken, continuous view of the area that encircles it. The PanoScan rotates a full 360 degrees as it takes high-resolution photographs of the crime scene, a process of about 11 minutes. Individual photographs can be studied or they can be viewed as a seamless image of the entire the scene. Investigators can scene, pan left and right, and zoom in on features (Figure 3-38). Return to Scene (R2S) software bundles the

◄FIGURE 3-38   PanoScan
These images were captured by the PanoScan panoramic camera and include a general view as well as a demonstration of the ability to zoom in on an evidence item. (Image courtesy of Panoscan)

ultra-high resolution images with full measurement capabilities. Users can insert "hotspots" into the images to indicate the position of relevant features, for example, fingerprints and other forensic evidence, and links to associated files, such as laboratory reports.

SUBMISSION OF EVIDENCE TO THE CRIME LABORATORY

As a preamble to discussing the submission of evidence to the crime laboratory, we note that there is some potential for our country's laboratory system to be significantly restructured within the near-term future. In 2009 the National Research Council issued a report highly critical of this country's forensic laboratory system. The report called for forensic laboratories to be separated from law enforcement and placed under a new federal body—the National Institute of Forensic Science (NIFS)—that would oversee their operation. At least one Congressional hearing has been held to review the report's recommendations. They are further discussed in Chapter 8, "The Crime Laboratory".

Faced with exploding demands for service, the FBI made a policy decision several decades ago to accept only those state and local law-enforcement requests for evidence examinations that involved violent crimes and to virtually cease accepting their property crimes evidence. For example, the FBI no longer accepts evidence from state and local law-enforcement agencies for burglaries, thefts and frauds involving losses of less than $100,000, arson and explosive incidents involving unoccupied premises, auto thefts not involving a ring, and hit-and-run automobile accidents not involving personal injury.[56] However, if a property crime involves personal injuries or the intent to cause them, the FBI may examine the associated evidence.

When a heart artery becomes clogged and narrowed, new blood vessels, collateral arteries, develop to help circulate the blood. Much like collateral arteries, when the FBI reduced the scope of its services state and local units of government developed new capacities for the analysis of forensic evidence, creating stronger central laboratories at the state level and smaller regional ones, reducing their dependence on the FBI. In the longer view, the FBI's policy shift was a positive development.

The result is that procedures for submitting evidence for examination are similar, but varied, across the country. Evidence submitted to a crime laboratory is most often transmitted by courier, air express, or registered mail. In the ideal situation, the investigator most knowledgeable about the case takes it to the laboratory so he/she can discuss the case with appropriate examiners. Given the caseloads all crime laboratories have, this situation is the exception. In general, the method of transmitting evidence is determined by the nature of the evidence and the urgency of getting an analyst's conclusions.

Rules established by federal and state agencies regulate how some special classes of evidence must be sent. Examples of these classes are chemicals, blasting caps, flammable materials, and biological and chemical agents. Check with laboratories before submitting these types of evidence.

Unsurprisingly, many state and local laboratories leverage resources through the use of Laboratory Information Management Systems (LIMS) software for various tasks, including the automated tracking of physical evidence and reporting examination results. Laboratory internet sites provide information useful to investigators, such as an *Evidence Handbook* on acceptable procedures for collecting, marking, and packaging evidence and guidance on submitting it.

Laboratories may have one "universal form" or separate forms for different types of evidence on their Internet site and/or require a letter on agency letterhead stationary formatted in a specific way. Either way, an investigator submitting evidence will need to provide the following information:

- The investigator's name, agency, address, telephone number, and email address.
- Copies of any previous correspondence about the case, including any pertaining to other evidence that was examined earlier.
- The type of criminal act and the basic case facts related to each item of evidence.
- The name(s) and descriptive data about the individual(s) involved (subject, suspect, victim, or a combination of those categories) and the agency-assigned case number.
- A list of the evidence being submitted.
- What type(s) of examination is requested.
- Where the evidence should be returned and where the laboratory report should be sent.
- A statement if the evidence was examined by another expert in the same field, if there is local controversy, or if other law-enforcement agencies have an interest in the case.
- Any reason(s) justifying an expeditious examination request.
- The name and locator information for the assigned prosecutor, if designated already.

Some law-enforcement agencies maintain a list of crimes that the Patrol Division may retain for follow-up investigation. This list adds variety to patrol duties, creates skills that will be useful if the officers become detectives, and preserves the resources of the Investigative Division. If cases are retained for further investigation by the Patrol Division, the submission of evidence to the lab usually requires the approval of a supervisor. For cases referred for follow-up investigation, the assigned investigator often makes that decision. If submission to a private lab for analysis is contemplated a supervisor's approval is typically required because of the cost involved.

INVESTIGATIVE SUCCESS

The public thinks an investigation is a success when the perpetrator is arrested, property recovered, and the perpetrator convicted. However, law enforcement considers a case successful if it can be administratively classified in one of two different ways:

1. **"Cleared by exceptional means,"** meaning that the police can demonstrate who committed the crime

but for any of several reasons cannot pursue the case further. Examples of this are when the suspect is dead, witnesses refuse to testify, and another jurisdiction refuses to extradite. Two common reasons for one state declining to extradite a suspect to a second state are he/she will be tried on more serious charges in state one or is already incarcerated there on serious charges.

2. **"Cleared by arrest,"** meaning that the perpetrator has been arrested and there is sufficient evidence to file criminal charges against him/her. Note that this definition of success does not require a conviction.

Table 3-1 shows that many types of crimes committed do not result in arrest and conviction. This is frustrating to investigators who want to take violent, predatory, and other offenders off the street. In these situations, police have to accept the fact that some crimes are simply not going to be solved because of insufficient evidence or legal restrictions. In such situations, investigators have to draw comfort from knowing they did their best, pursued all lines of inquiry, and then go on to the next case. Ultimately, time is on the side of law enforcement and eventually many suspected offenders will commit acts for which they can be arrested. The tragedy, of course, is the harm they do between when they first come to the attention of investigators and when they are ultimately arrested.

If investigators allow case disappointments to get the best of them, they run the risk of slipping into cynicism, an unattractive trait, and over a period of years will become vulnerable to engaging in unethical behavior, such as planting evidence or committing perjury.

TABLE 3-1	Crimes Cleared by Arrest or Exceptional Means	
OFFENSE		PERCENTAGE CLEARED
Murder/Non-negligent Manslaughter		66.6%
Aggravated assault		56.8
Forcible rape		41.2
Robbery		28.2
Larceny-theft		21.5
Motor vehicle theft		12.4
Burglary		12.5
Arson		18.5

Source: Federal Bureau of Investigation, Crime in the United States—2009 (September 2010), Table 25, no page number, *www.FBI.gov/about-us/cjis/ucr/crime-in-the-u.s./2009*.

KEY TERMS

administrative log
All Points Bulletin (APB)
alternative light systems (ALSs)
Americans with Disabilities
    Act (ADA)
assignment sheet
associative evidence
baseline coordinates
be-on-the-lookout (BOLO)
chain of custody
cleared by arrest
cleared by exceptional means
corpus delicti evidence
crime
crime scene
crime scene control
crime scene entry log
crime scene release
crime scene search patterns
crime scene sketch
cross-projection view
datum point
deductive reasoning

digital camera
Digital Information Management
    System (DIMS)
digital video recording
elevation view
elimination prints
evidence recovery log
felony
field notes
follow-up investigation
forensic mapping
grid system
hepatitis B (HBV)
hepatitis C (HCV)
human immunodeficiency
    virus (HIV)
incident/offense report
inductive reasoning
laser scanning
lifted-prints log
Locard's principle
macroscopic scene
media statements

microscopic scene
misdemeanor
neighborhood canvass
overhead or bird's eye view
panoramic cameras
personal protection
    equipment (PPE)
photographic log
polar coordinates
preliminary investigation
primary scene
rectangular coordinates
rough sketch
secondary scenes
smooth or finished sketch
trace evidence
trace-evidence vacuums
tracing evidence
triangulation
tuberculosis (TB)
vehicle canvass
violation

REVIEW QUESTIONS

1. What skills and qualities are needed by investigators?
2. What are the objectives of crime scene investigation?
3. How would you describe the "lucky" investigator?
4. What are preliminary and follow-up investigations?
5. How are inductive and deductive reasoning used in investigation?
6. Why is crime scene coordination so important?
7. What factors can shape or impact a plan to process a crime scene?
8. What are the three broad categories of evidence?
9. How is a crime scene entry log properly used?

10. What is a neighborhood canvass?
11. What are the "rules" for crime scene investigators?
12. What four considerations dominate the crime scene search?
13. Define *primary scene* and *secondary scene(s)*.
14. What are macroscopic and microscopic scenes?
15. What infectious disease risks are faced by crime scene investigators?
16. What methods are available to visually document the crime scene?
17. Draw a rough crime scene sketch of your bedroom, assuming that there are two shell casings on the floor and one bullet hole in the west wall.

INTERNET ACTIVITIES

1. Visit the Crime Scene Investigator Network website at *www.crime-scene-investigator.net.* Read the section on "Crime Scene Response."

2. Learn more about laser and panoramic camera imaging of crime scenes at *www.3rdTech.com* and *www.panoscan.com.*

► Weapons are often found at the scene of a crime. Here, a large "bolo" type knife is found at the exit of the front door leading to the living room where a young woman was murdered in a domestic quarrel. This is the eighth piece of physical evidence found at the scene. A rigid ruler is included to give an indication of size and proportionality.

(Courtesy Dallas Texas Police Department)

PHYSICAL EVIDENCE

INTRODUCTION

If physical evidence is to be useful in exonerating the innocent and pursuing suspects it must be treated in accordance with its importance. The evidence must be located, its position documented, be collected, be identified by marks/writing on it and/or on the package in which it is placed, and be transmitted to the evidence room or the crime laboratory while the collector maintains the chain of custody.[1] This chapter describes the proper protocols of dealing with various types of physical evidence. Adherence to approved procedures maintains the potential that the evidence can be a powerful part of the investigative process and avoids the embarrassment that careless handling is sure to bring. Even more serious is the possibility that but for the careless handling of evidence the prosecutor would have filed charges against a suspect.

CHAPTER OUTLINE

CLASS VERSUS INDIVIDUAL CHARACTERISTICS

To fully appreciate the potential value of physical evidence, the investigator must understand the difference between class and individual characteristics. Characteristics of physical evidence that are common to a group of objects or persons are termed **class characteristics.** Regardless of how thoroughly examined, such evidence can be placed only into a broad category; an individual identification cannot be made because there is a possibility of more than one source for the evidence.[2] Examples of this type of evidence include all unworn Nike athletic shoes of a particular model, the new, unmarked face of a manufacturer's specific type of hammer, and soil. In contrast, evidence with **individual characteristics** can be identified, with a high degree of probability, as originating with a particular person or source (Figure 4-1).[3] The ability to establish individuality distinguishes this type of physical evidence from that possessing only class characteristics. Some examples of evidence with individual characteristics are fingerprints, palm prints, and footprints.

Conceptually, the distinction between class and individual characteristics is clear. But as a practical matter, the crime scene technician or investigator often may not be able to make this differentiation and must rely on the results

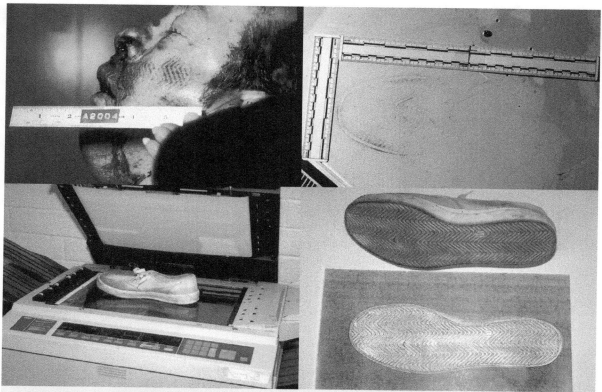

▲FIGURE 4-1   Individual class evidence
(*Top left*) Shoeprint left on face of murder victim; (*top right*) shoeprint left on hood of car at scene; (*bottom left*) duplicating the bottom of a shoe seized from suspect; (*bottom right*) wear patterns and slight nicks in the shoe's tread made it individual characteristic evidence. Additionally, DNA from blood caught in the shoe tread and the victim tied the shoe to contact with the victim. **(Courtesy Detroit Michigan State Police)**

yielded by crime laboratory examination (Figure 4-1). Thus, although the investigator must recognize that physical evidence that allows for individualization is of more value, he or she should not dismiss evidence that appears to offer only class characteristics, because it may show individual characteristics through laboratory examination. Furthermore, a preponderance of class-characteristic evidence tying a suspect (or other items in the suspect's possession) to the scene strengthens the case for prosecution. Note also that occasionally class-characteristic evidence may be of such an unusual nature that it has much greater value than that ordinarily associated with evidence of this type. In an Alaska case, a suspect was apprehended in the general area where a burglary had been committed; the pry bar found in his possession contained white stucco, which was of considerable importance, since the building burglarized was the only white stucco building in that town.[4] Finally, class-characteristic evidence can be useful in excluding suspects in a crime, resulting in a more effective use of investigative effort.

COMPARISON SAMPLES

Much of the work of forensic science involves comparing various types of samples. Special terms are used to refer to these samples, and you must know what they mean to communicate with the laboratory and understand its reports. At the most general level, comparison samples may be from **unknown or questioned sources** or from **known sources;** each of these two main categories has three subcategories.

Unknown or Questioned Samples

1. *Recovered crime scene sample whose source is in question:* This evidence may have been left, for example, by either victims or suspects. A typical question is "Whose fingerprints are on the window used as the point of entry?"
2. *Questioned evidence that may have been transferred to an offender during the commission of a crime and been*

taken away by him or her: When compared with the evidence from a known source, this evidence can be used to link the suspect to a person, vehicle, tool, or weapon. For example, the question might be "Do any of the hairs combed from the suspect's hair match those of the victim?"

3. *Evidence from an unknown or questioned source that can be used to link multiple offenses:* This material might link crimes that were committed by the same person, tool, or weapon. Assuming that a suspect is arrested at a murder scene with a pistol in his overcoat, the question raised could be "Did this gun fire the bullets recovered from the victims of a double homicide a week ago?"[5]

Known Samples

1. *Standard or reference sample:* This is material from a known or verifiable source. It is compared to similar material from an unknown source to determine whether an association or linkage exists between a crime scene, a victim, and the offender. For example, a sample of blood is taken under medical conditions from the suspect so that it can be compared with blood on the victim's shirt.

2. *Control or blank sample:* This is material from a known source that was uncontaminated by the crime (for example, carpet fibers taken from the far corner of a room in which a body was found). It is used to make sure that the material on which evidence was deposited—for instance, carpet fibers, under the body, on which there is blood, does not interfere with laboratory testing.

3. *Elimination sample:* This type of sample is taken from a source known to have had lawful access to the crime scene, such as a police officer, medical technician, or the occupant. It is compared with unknown samples of the same type from the scene so that matches can be eliminated, thereby highlighting non-matches. An example is elimination prints. If latent fingerprints recovered at a crime scene do not match the fingerprints of those who have lawful access to the area, they immediately become of investigative interest in terms of determining whose prints they are.[6]

SOIL AND POLLEN

Soil can be the natural accumulation of earth materials, such as weathering rocks, minerals, and decomposing plants, pollen, bacteria and fungus.[7] It may also contain human-made materials, including pieces of brick, glass, and paint. By comparing color, texture, and composition in soil examinations, one can determine whether soils share a common origin.[8] Although soil is class-characteristic evidence, its analysis can help focus investigations and discredit alibis:

A man was arrested and charged with the beating of a young girl. The scene of the crime was a construction site adjacent to a newly poured concrete wall. The soil was sand, which had been transported to the scene for construction purposes. As such, it had received additional mixing during the moving and construction process and was quite distinctive. The glove of the suspect contained sand that was similar to that found at the scene and significantly different in composition and particle size from that in the area of the suspect's home. This was important because the suspect claimed that the soil on the gloves came from his garden.[9]

An elderly woman was robbed and murdered in a Washington, D.C., park, and her body was found under a park bench. Within a short time, a suspect was apprehended as a result of a description given by a witness who had seen the person leaving the park on the night of the murder. It was obvious that the suspect had been involved in a struggle and had soil adhering to his clothing and inside his trouser cuffs. He claimed to have been in a fight in another part of the city and gave the location of the fight. Study of the soil near the park bench and of that collected from the scene of the alleged fight revealed that the soil from the suspect's clothing was similar to soil near the park bench but did not compare favorably with samples from the area of the described fight. These comparisons strongly suggested that the suspect had been in contact with the ground in that area and cast strong doubt on his statement that he had not been in the park for years. Furthermore, the lack of similarity between the clothing soil samples and those from the area in which he claimed to have been fighting questioned the validity of his alibi.[10]

The pollen in soil or on plants and grass can also be very significant in determining whether or not a suspect was at the scene:

In a case of alleged sexual assault, the pollen content of samples from a grassy crime scene were compared to pollen recovered from the suspect's clothes and shoes. A very strong correlation with the variety of pollens present on the suspect's clothing and the sample collected at the scene strongly supported the conclusion that the suspect was at the scene.[11]

Although soil and pollen are class-characteristic evidence, their specificity can approach the level of individual characterization:

In a rape case, the knees of the suspect's trousers contained encrusted soil samples; the sample from the right knee was different from that collected from the left. In examining the crime scene, investigators found two impressions in the soil corresponding to a right and a left knee; samples taken from these two impressions were different. The soil sample from the left-knee impression compared with that removed from the left trouser knee of the suspect, as did the right-knee impression and the right trouser knee soils. The significant difference in soil type between the two knee impressions and their consistency with samples obtained from the suspect's trousers strongly indicated his presence at the scene.[12]

LOCATING AND HANDLING SOIL EVIDENCE

Soil residues and smears on such surfaces as clothing, people, and vehicles may not be of sufficient quantity for analysis. Unless the suspects were apprehended at the scene or in very close proximity to it, the soil on their feet/shoe soles and the tires of their cars may have been contaminated, and therefore may not be of evidentiary value.[13]

Soil evidence may be important when the suspect drives or walks on unpaved areas, since it is picked up by tire treads or the bottom of shoes and the cuffs of pants. It may also be recovered in a number of other places, such as on the floorboard of the subject's car or on articles in the trunk of the vehicle, including shovels and blankets. In hit-and-run accidents, soil samples may be encountered, for example, in one unusual case, a solid soil sample in the rough shape of a triangle with 3-inch sides was found and later substantially matched to a space on the underside of the suspect's vehicle. The guidelines shown next should be followed in handling soil evidence:

1. Soil conditions at the scene can change, so gather the soil as quickly as sound action permits.
2. Collect soil not only from the crime scene but also from the logical points of access to, and escape from, the scene. Place the samples in clean plastic vials and labeled with the date, time, name of the crime scene technician, and the case number, if known.
3. Collect soil samples where there are noticeable changes in color, texture, and composition.
4. Collect soil samples from a depth that is consistent with the depth at which the questioned soil may

have originated. In most cases, samples will be a tablespoon of material taken no more than ½ inch from the surface.
5. When possible, collect soil samples from alibi areas, such as the worksite, yard, or garden of the suspect.
6. Make a detailed drawing or map documenting where and at what depth you collected each soil sample.
7. Do not remove soil adhering to shoes, clothing, and tools. Do not process tools for latent prints at this time. Air dry the soiled garments and package them separately in paper bags. Avoid jostling and transport to the crime lab for analysis and further processing.
8. Submit unknown or questioned soil and known samples in separate leak-proof containers such as film canisters or plastic pill bottles. Avoid the use of paper envelopes or glass containers. If there are lumps in the soil, pack it in a way that keeps the lumps intact.[14]
9. In packaging soil or other types of evidence, take care to avoid **cross contamination** of the samples.
10. Soil impressions made by footwear should be photographed to scale and cast before any soil samples are taken.
11. At indoor crime scenes, special vacuums may be used to collect soil samples from carpets and floors that may have been introduced by the suspect(s). Collect and document each procedure before transporting the contents to the crime lab.[15]

The guidelines for collecting pollen evidence are consistent with those for soil evidence. It may be necessary to take grass or other clippings from different heights.

FOOTWEAR, FOOT, AND TIRES: PRINTS AND IMPRESSIONS

Prints may be made from (1) footwear, including shoes, boots, and sandals; (2) the soles of feet; and (3) tires, and all are common types of evidence.[16] These prints are formed when the soles of footwear, soles of feet, and tires are contaminated with foreign matter such as blood or dust and leave a print on a firm base, such as a floor, the seat of a chair, paper, or cloth (Figure 4-2).[17] Such prints are called **residue prints.** In contrast, **impressions** result from footwear, feet, and tires treading in some moldable material, such as earth, clay, and snow.[18] For residue prints and impressions the sequence is always photograph and then collect the evidence.

Residue and impression evidence can provide investigative leads, such as the number of suspects at the scene, where they walked in the scene, some indication of the

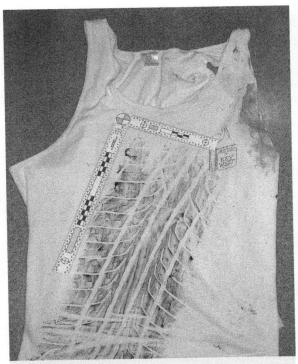

▲ FIGURE 4-2
Tire print left on pedestrian victim's shirt by hit-and-run vehicle
Police located a potentially involved vehicle. Tire print and other physical evidence established it struck the pedestrian. However, the car's owner still needed to be put behind the wheel. Confronted with the evidence, he confessed. (Courtesy Seattle Washington State Police)

▲ FIGURE 4-3   Footwear impression photography
A crime scene technician documenting a footwear impression. The impression runs left to right, roughly between the front legs of the tripod. The white slip of paper "North" of the impression has the case number and other information on it. (Courtesy Nassau County, New York Police Department)

sequence of events, the direction taken by the suspects as they left the scene, the type and brand of shoe or tire, and the type of vehicle involved.[19] Although European agencies report collecting footwear evidence in over 70% of their cases, its use in this country is much less, possibly due to a lack of awareness and proper training by crime scene technicians.[20]

A number of software programs, such as SICAR, can compare footwear and tire evidence. **SoleMate** contains the records of 24,000 sports, work, and casual footwear. Its purpose is to identify footwear prints recovered at a crime scene. It is updated continuously and distributed on CD to users quarterly. **CrimeShoe** has a collection of 23,000 shoe and sole images representing 950 brands. Using the Internet, investigators can upload their prints. If CrimeShoe cannot make an identification or provide other relevant information there is no charge. **TreadMate** is a reference collection of 8,500 tires, available for a fee on CD issued annually.

PRESERVING RESIDUE PRINTS

Residue prints are two dimensional; they have a length and a width and no appreciable height. They may be from a dry origin, such as dust, or a wet one, for example, stepped in oil.[21] Residue prints may or may not be readily visible. If they are not immediately apparent, turn off the lights and search for prints using a flashlight held close to, but obliquely from, the surface you are examining or use a forensic light source. When you find prints:

1. Take general crime scene photos showing the location of the prints.
2. Take photos from directly overhead using lighting and a tripod. A photo with a label near the print should be taken to correlate photos with the photo log (Figure 4-3). Subsequent shots should include a scale near the print. Ideally, "L"-shaped footwear/tire photographic scale should be used to capture

width and length dimensions. Alternatively, two regular scales can be crossed and used for the same purpose. These directions also apply to photographing impressions.

There are several methods by which residue prints can be recovered. The best approach is to send the original evidence to the lab. It should be taped in a rigid container so that there is no opportunity for accidental erasure of the footwear print; do not wrap it in plastic, because this can cause a partial erasure of the image.

Residue prints may be collected by using a large transparent adhesive lifter and then mounting the lifter on an appropriately colored card. Similarly, an appropriately colored and sized rubber-gelatin lifter can be employed. Coated with a thin film of very sensitive gelatin, the lifter is carefully placed over the print and then removed. Transparent, black, and white lifters are available. Transparent and white lifters can be used for dark prints; a black lifter should be used for light prints.[22] Residue prints can also be lifted through the use of an electrostatic dust print lifter (EDPL) (Figure 4-4). The resulting image must be photographed as soon as possible, since it is in dust and therefore not permanent.

PRESERVING IMPRESSIONS

Impressions are three-dimensional; they have a length, width, and height (see Figure 4-5). Impressions are physically preserved by casting. Plaster of Paris is no longer recommended for use in casting impressions. **Dental stone** or die stone—for example, Traxtone—is the most used casting medium because of greater strength, quicker setting time, and ease of use; also, cleaning casts made doesn't result in any loss of detail, and provides more detailed impressions. Because of the strength of dental stone and die stone, the cast does not need to be reinforced.

The first step in casting is the preparation of the impression. The rule is that the impression should not be disturbed. Thus, if twigs, leaves, or other materials are stuck *in* the impression, they should remain there. Only loose material lying *on* the impression, such as leaves, should be moved. If the impression to be cast is in sandy soil, hair spray may be used to "fix" the details, taking care not to disturb them as it is applied. The use of a casting frame may not be necessary if the ground is fairly level.

In Chapter 3, "Investigators, the Investigative Process, and the Crime Scene," impression casting materials were identified—for instance, Shake-N-Cast, which has all the mixing materials preassembled in one bag. This section covers preparing and using dental stone "from scratch" to cast a shoe impression. About 2 pounds of dental stone and 12 ounces of water are needed.

Place the dental stone in a 1-gallon Ziplock bag and add the water.[23] Massage the Ziplock bag; you want to reach a consistency of thick paint or pancake batter. The

▲ FIGURE 4-4
Use of electrostatic dust print lifter (EDPL)
(*top*) A lifting mat is laid over a shoe dust print and electrically charged using the high voltage power supply unit on the right side of the mat. An insulated roller systematically is moved across the silver side of lifting mat. (*bottom*) The dust print is transferred to the dark-colored underside of the lift mat. (Courtesy SIRCHIE Fingerprint Laboratories, Inc.)

dental stone is then poured alongside the impression and allowed to flow into it as opposed to pouring it directly on the impression. Make sure you pour it so that the contents of a single Ziplock bag cover the entire impression.

◄FIGURE 4-5
Footwear impression
A footwear impression is found in the dirt, a cast is made, and its examination holds the potential to provide important investigative information or evidence, such as matching the footwear of someone in custody. (Courtesy SIRCHIE Fingerprint Laboratories, Inc.)

Otherwise, there will be a lap mark in the cast that is likely to cause a loss of detail.

Dental stone sets fairly rapidly. Die stone sets up quicker, in 12 to 15 minutes. Soil evidence should be collected from the bottom of the impression after the cast is removed.

If there is standing water in the impression, the following steps should be taken: (1) place a casting frame around the impression so that a cast 2 inches deep can be made; (2) gently sift dental stone that has not been mixed with water directly into the impression to a depth of about 1 inch; (3) add enough mixed dental stone to form a second 1-inch layer; and (4) allow the cast to set in place for at least 1 hour.[24]

The crime scene technician or other person casting the footwear impression should enter her or his initials, the date, and other relevant details on the bottom of the cast before it dries.[25] For submission to the laboratory, wrap the cast in tissue, clean paper, packing peanuts, or multiple paper bags. The laboratory examiner will clean the cast and examine it after it has dried for 24–48 hours.

PRESERVING SHOE IMPRESSIONS IN SNOW

Dental stone is also the preferred material for casting impressions in snow, replacing the more difficult and time-consuming process of using sulfur, which had to be heated. Impressions in snow should first be photographed in the manner previously described; however, impressions in snow are difficult to photograph because of a lack of contrast.[26] To overcome this, lightly spray several layers of red-colored Snow Print Wax (SPW) or spray paint over the impression at a 45-degree angle from the surface (Figure 4-6). Pause briefly between layers to let the SPW dry; in addition to coloring the impression, SPW leaves a waxy surface on it that prevents the small amount of heat generated by the drying dental stone from erasing the fine details of the impression. To combat heat formation when casting in snow, use snow or cold-water mix in the dental stone.

The spray nozzle should be held 24 inches to 36 inches from the impression so the force of the aerosol doesn't alter it. An impression highlighted in this manner will absorb heat from the sun and should be shielded until ready to photograph and cast. Because some heat is generated when dental stone is mixed, a box should be placed over the cast for at least 1 hour as it dries.

PAINT

Paint evidence may be encountered in many types of investigation, but perhaps most commonly it is transferred from one source to another in burglaries and hit-and-run accidents. Paint is transferred as fresh smears, dried chips, or "chalking" from old, dry paint. Many burglaries involve a tool that was used to pry a door or window open, transferring paint from the building to the suspect's tools or clothing. In hit-and-run accidents, paint from the fleeing vehicle may be found on a pedestrian or another car.

In hit-and-run cases, the make and model of the involved vehicle might be identified by comparing paint evidence to the records in the FBI's National Automotive Paint File on original-manufacturer finishes. **Paint Data Query (PDQ),** another database, is a global information system on the paint used by the original manufacturer. Each of the roughly 22 countries participating in this system maintains a central point of information; in

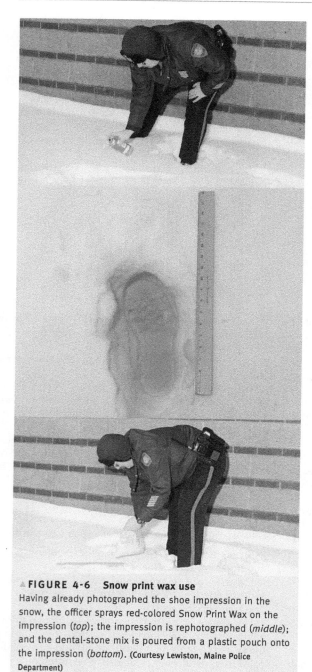

> A 53-year man was hit by an unidentified vehicle and dragged more than 200 feet, dying from his injuries. No witnesses were present, and the police did not have any other leads regarding the suspect vehicle. A gold metallic painted plastic fragment recovered from the scene was sent to the lab, along with the victim's clothing containing gold metallic paint particles.
>
> The PDQ system found one color, Aztec Gold, which closely matched the paint particles recovered from the victim's clothing. It was used on 11,000 Ford Mustangs made in 1997. Only two of these vehicles were registered in the jurisdiction of the offense. An officer located a 1997 Aztec Gold Ford Mustang with scratches on its hood and a piece of painted plastic missing from the flair molding on the left side. The flair molding and paint samples were collected from the vehicle and submitted for comparison to the materials recovered from the scene and victim's clothing. The painted plastic piece was physically fitted together with the flair molding and the recovered gold metallic paint particles were consistent with paint samples taken from the suspect vehicle.
>
> Although these results provided some closure to the victim's family, the suspect had been deported for other reasons several days before the vehicle was located.[27]

FIGURE 4-6 Snow print wax use
Having already photographed the shoe impression in the snow, the officer sprays red-colored Snow Print Wax on the impression (*top*); the impression is rephotographed (*middle*); and the dental-stone mix is poured from a plastic pouch onto the impression (*bottom*). (Courtesy Lewiston, Maine Police Department)

Usually, paint is class-characteristic evidence, although in some cases it reaches the level of individual evidence. If the chips are large enough, it may be possible to make a fracture match between a questioned and a known source (Figure 4-7). A **fracture match** occurs when it is established that two physical items were once co-joined. For example, a paint chip recovered from a tool in a burglary suspect's possession exactly fits an area on a paint sample recovered from the point of forced entry in a burglary. If a building or car has been painted multiple times, the layer structure of a questioned sample can be compared to a known source as to the number of layers, the sequence of colors, the thickness of each layer, and the chemical composition of each layer (Figure 4-8).[28] Thus, when one is recovering paint chips, one must go all the way to the base surface.

If paint evidence is collected from a burglary's point of entry, the samples should be collected from an area immediately adjacent to the area damaged by the suspect while forcing entry.[29] This principle also applies to taking paint samples from automobiles that have been involved in a hit-and-run. Each chip sample taken should be packaged separately. One rule of thumb is to collect four

the United States and Canada it is the FBI and the Royal Canadian Mounted Police (RCMP).

The value of paint evidence is seen in the case study that follows.

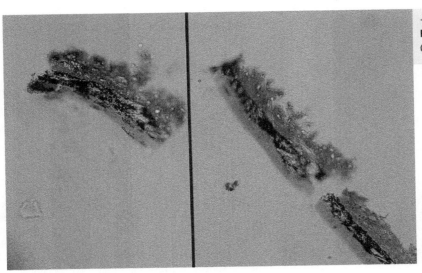

▲ **FIGURE 4-8   Side view of a multilayered paint chip**
(Courtesy Wisconsin Dept of Justice - State Crime Laboratory)

samples around each separate area that is involved with the incident.

A new razor blade or evidence scalpel should be used for each paint chip recovered to avoid contamination. Burglary tools that may contain paint evidence should be carefully wrapped and submitted to the lab without disturbing the evidence. Similarly, the clothes of a burglary suspect arrested at the scene or in its vicinity and the clothes of a pedestrian hit-and-run victim should be submitted to the lab without attempting to collect paint evidence. Paint smears may also be useful, and it is desirable to submit the item on which the smear is found—for example, a car's bumper, to the laboratory.

Do not collect paint chips or particles with transparent tape or use it to fix the evidence to a card. Paint chips and particles should not be placed in plastic bags, because they will develop a static electrical charge that makes them hard to handle. Placing paint chips in cotton is not good practice, because separating them is difficult and

they are often fragile. A clear solid plastic container is ideal for packaging a paint chip, because it can be seen. Paper envelopes are acceptable if they are properly sealed and protected from being bent or compressed.

The sheets placed under and over hit-and-run victims in the ambulance while they are being transported may also be a good source of paint evidence; the clothing and sheets may have fresh blood on them. These items should be allowed to air dry naturally in properly ventilated lockers. Before hanging these items in the lockers or other secure place, place fresh paper under the items so any evidence that falls as the drying occurs can be recovered. When dried, place the items separately in their own paper bag and submit them to the laboratory.

GLASS

Generally, glass is class-characteristic evidence, although in some fact situations it may be individual class. Glass is important as physical evidence because it is so common. Suspects may take it from the scene in their clothing or hair. Laboratory examination of glass evidence may be able to determine:

1. the type of glass, such as tempered or container;
2. the direction of force used to break the glass (Figure 4-9);
3. the direction and sequence of shots fired through a closed glass window;
4. similarity between evidence glass and standards;
5. a fracture physical match, establishing that the pieces were formerly joined (Figure 4-10).[30]

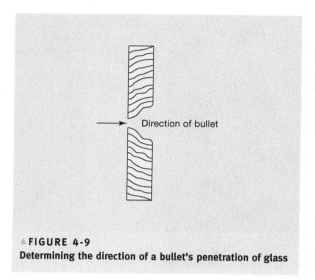

▲FIGURE 4-9
Determining the direction of a bullet's penetration of glass

Police were called to a home where the occupant alleged that while standing in the living room someone standing outside of the house fired a shot at him. The complainant dropped to the floor, crawled to a nearby desk, and retrieved his revolver. After a short time he stood up and the person outside fired a sec-

ond and third time. At that point the complainant fired a single shot at the outsider, whom he recognized as a man who lived nearby. The alleged shooter had a different version of events. He was walking past the complainant's house and was shot at three times before he shot once in self-defense at the man in the house. All shots passed through the glass of a single window. Both man said there was "bad blood" between them.

Figure 4-11 illustrates the four bullet holes found in the window by the police. When a glass window is broken by a shot, both **radial fracture** and **concentric fracture** lines may develop. Radial fractures move away from the point of impact; concentric fracture lines more or less circle the same point. From Figure 4-9 we know that shot B came before shot A, because the radial and concentric fracture lines of shot B stop those of shot A. From 4-11, we know nothing of the relationship of holes C and D. However, as shown in Figure 4-9, we can determine the direction from which a bullet penetrated glass: on the side opposite the surface of initial impact, there will be a characteristic cone-shaped area. In the case being illustrated, shots A, B, and D all contained a cone-shaped characteristic on the inside of the window, indicating that these three shots had been fired from the outside. Shot C had the cone-shaped area on the outside, revealing that it had been fired from inside the house. Thus the physical evidence substantiated the complainant's statement.

▶FIGURE 4-10
Glass fracture match of a rear tail light and assembly
Pieces of red tail light were found at the scene of a hit-and-run and matched with pieces still intact in the tail light assembly when the suspect vehicle was located. (Courtesy Mr. Ed Hueske and Ms. Sherry Bethune, Forensic Training and Consulting, LLC, 2007)

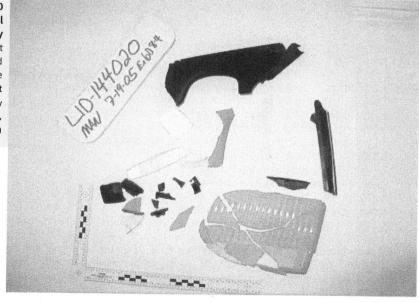

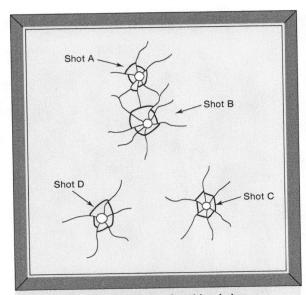

▲ FIGURE 4-11   Bullet holes found in window

Walking a beat in a downtown business section in the late evening hours, a uniformed officer heard an alarm go off and saw an individual round the corner and run toward him at full speed. On seeing the officer, the individual started to double back the other way and then stopped. As the office approached, the man started to flee, but he stopped when commanded to do so. The man then told the officer that he had observed two people standing in front of a jewelry store window take a brick from a shopping bag and throw it through the window. The person said that, on seeing this, he became frightened and ran. Subsequent investigation revealed that the person who had rounded the corner was in fact the perpetrator of the offense and that he had fled before obtaining any material from the display window, because a lookout had seen a police car responding to a call in an adjacent block and had given warning. Processing of the perpetrator's clothing revealed pieces of glass in the cuff of his pants sufficiently large to make fracture matches with glass at the scene.

It is essential that the crime scene technician and investigator understand the ways in which glass reacts to force. Often this knowledge is critical in determining whether a crime has been committed, establishing the sequence of action, and evaluating the credibility of statements given by parties at the scene. Before any glass or window pane is moved at all, it should be photographed

in detail to reflect the exact features of the existent glass fractures. Moving the evidence may cause fracture extensions that could change the conclusions of the investigator and laboratory analyst. At crime scenes involving automobiles, the utility of glass evidence may be compromised by rescue personnel working to free occupants and wreckers pulling involved vehicles to the side of the road.

This example underscore the importance of the investigator's paying particular attention to determining what occurred between the time of the crime and the time he/she arrived at the scene. A key question that the investigator must attempt to answer with glass and other types of evidence is whether the position and characteristic of evidence could have been altered by the suspect, a witness, the victim, emergency medical personnel, or another officer. Stated differently, do not assume that the position of evidence you locate is in its original position.

HANDLING GLASS EVIDENCE

Ordinarily, if glass evidence is to be processed for fingerprints, it will be done in the laboratory.[31] Tape should not be used to collect glass evidence in the field because it interferes with laboratory processing. As with other types of evidence, photography precedes the collection of glass evidence.

The physical properties used for comparison of known and questioned glass specimens are color, fluorescence, thickness, surface features, and curvature.[32] If glass is being submitted for comparison purposes, that is, to determine whether the particles may have originated from a common source, they are ordinarily small, and the following precautions should be taken: (1) glass evidence from combing hair should be done over clean paper; (2) clothing and shoes should be packaged separately, and in no case should the victim's and suspect's items be comingled in any way; (3) if clothing items are wet, air dry them in the manner previously described; (4) glass may be embedded in the skin and open wounds of victims and suspects, and recovery by qualified medical personnel may be required; (5) submit weapons and tools without disturbing glass evidence; (6) samples of laminated glass—for example, windshields, should be labeled "inside" and "outside" and separately packaged in leak proof containers; (7) if a vehicle is involved, use a vacuum to collect the glass from each area of the vehicle; evidence collected from different areas should be packaged separately, and a new vacuum bag should be used for each new area processed; and (8) known and questioned glass samples, and evidence from victims and suspects, should be shipped separately to avoid contamination. These types of evidence should be wrapped in clean paper and sealed in a rigid container, such as a box, or if sufficiently small, a plastic container. Do not submit the evidence in a glass container.

If door, window, or other framed glass is to be submitted for possible fracture matches, submit the entire frame

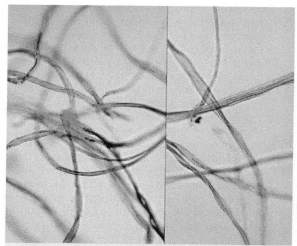

▲FIGURE 4-12 **Comparison of cotton fibers**
The victim, who was wearing a red shirt, was stabbed by a man. Fibers from the victim's shirt (*above*) were compared to fibers collected from the assailant's pants (*right*). The two sets of fibers were consistent in all respects, although this finding does not exclude other sources for the fibers on the assailant's pants. (Courtesy Chicago Police Department)

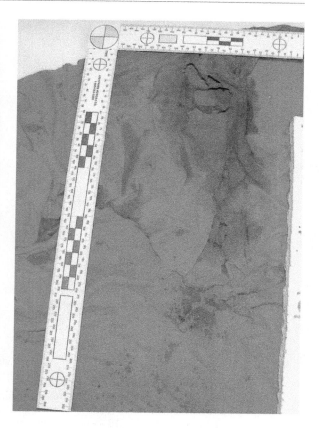

in which all glass originally existed, marking the sides of the frame to show which way is inside and outside, along with marking it "top," "bottom, "left," and "right." Broken pieces should be carefully packaged in separate containers to avoid breakage in transit. Depending on the sizes involved, it may be necessary to place the glass between sturdy pieces of cardboard or plywood.[33]

FIBERS, CLOTH FRAGMENTS, AND IMPRESSIONS

Fibers are of value as evidence because they incorporate such variables as material type, number of fibers per strand, number of strands, thickness of fibers and strands, amount and direction of twists, dye content, type of weave, and the possible presence of foreign matter embedded in them. When something composed of fibers, such as clothing, comes into contact with other clothing or objects, there is the opportunity for the exchange or transfer of fibers. Fibers may also be located on the body of the victim or the suspect, serving to connect one to the other (Figure 4-12).

Cloth fragments may be found at the scene of violent crimes or along the perpetrator's point of approach to, or exit from, a crime scene (Figure 4-13). They may be found on such diverse points as a chain fence, the splintered edge of a wooden building, or protruding nails. In hit-and-run offenses, cloth fragments may be found in the grille or undercarriage of the striking vehicle. Cloth impressions are found infrequently in investigations, usually on wet paint or some surface of a vehicle involved in striking a pedestrian.

Both fibers and cloth fragments should be packaged in a pillbox or in folded paper that is taped shut. Only on rare occasions will it be possible to obtain a cast of a cloth impression. This effort, however, should invariably be preceded by the taking of several photographs; at least one of these photos should show a scale to allow for comparisons at some future date.

STRING, CORD, ROPE, AND TAPE

String, cord, rope, and tape evidence is usually found in robbery, murder, rape, and kidnapping cases. It is also associated with accidental hangings by children and accidental

◄**FIGURE 4-13 Fabric match**
Physical matching (sometimes called *physical* fit or *jigsaw* fit) is powerful and incontrovertible evidence. Shown here is a fragment from a victim's clothing found in the grille of the suspect's vehicle involved in a hit-and-run case. The fabric fragment fitted the victim's raincoat and conclusively established the contact between the suspect's vehicle and the victim. (© The McGraw-Hill Companies, photographer Keith Eng)

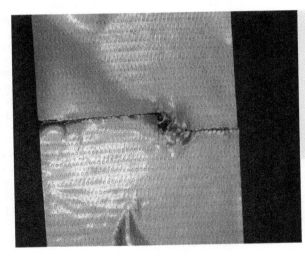

◄**FIGURE 4-14 Tape match**
In a particularly violent rape, the suspect used gray duct tape to tie the victim's hands and cover her mouth. The victim was left for dead, but she managed to crawl out an open window and seek help. The top portion of the photograph is the filament tape recovered from the victim's face covering her mouth. The bottom part of the photograph is the end of the tape roll found in the suspect's pocket. By showing that these two ends of the duct tape match, a physical match is established. (Courtesy Portland, Oregon Police Bureau)

sexual asphyxiations. String, cord and rope have essentially the same characteristics and share some characteristics of fibers. Known samples of these types of evidence can be compared to crime scene evidence on the basis of composition, diameter, color, and construction; if a tracer is present, it is possible to identify the manufacturer. There is some preliminary evidence if string, cord, and rope is made from plant material, and contains cells from the plant of origin, then DNA analysis techniques can exclude or include as a source remnants found in a suspect's possession as compared to a length used to bind a victim.[34]

In instances where the victim was tied, it may be possible to match the ends of the string, cord, rope, and tape with the rest of the roll in the suspect's possession (Figure 4-14). When rope evidence is removed from a victim or from anyplace, knots should never be severed. Instead, a place away from the knot should be cut and a piece of twine used to loop the two ends together. A tag should be attached to indicate that the investigator has cut the rope. Evidence about knot tier handedness and use of habitual knots has been scarce and conflicting. A 2010 study of 562 subjects did reveal differences in patterns of knot tying between left and right handers.[35] Ordinarily, because of its resilient nature, the packaging of this type of evidence poses no particular problem when standard procedures are followed.

FINGERPRINTS

Several different parts of the body—such as palms, fingers, toes, and the soles of the feet—have friction ridges that can form a "fingerprint." All such prints are collected, preserved, and identified using similar methods. But it may not be immediately apparent which part of a body made the print; as used here, "fingerprint" includes all prints made by friction ridges. Basically, a **fingerprint** is a replica of the friction ridges that touched the surface on which the print was found. These ridge characteristics are also called **minutiae.**

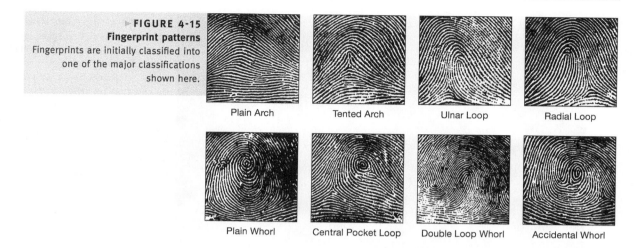

▶ FIGURE 4-15
Fingerprint patterns
Fingerprints are initially classified into one of the major classifications shown here.

Plain Arch   Tented Arch   Ulnar Loop   Radial Loop

Plain Whorl   Central Pocket Loop   Double Loop Whorl   Accidental Whorl

With just a few exceptions—persons with birth defects or amputations—everyone has fingerprints. This universal characteristic is a prime factor in establishing a standard of identification. Since a print of one finger has never been known to duplicate exactly another fingerprint—even of the same person or an identical twin[36]—it is possible to identify an individual with just one impression. The relative ease with which a set of inked fingerprints can be taken as a means of identification is a further reason for using this standard. Despite such factors as aging and environmental influences, a person's fingerprints do not change. This unaltering pattern is a permanent record of the individual throughout life.

BASIS FOR FINGERPRINT IDENTIFICATION

The ridge detail of fingerprints—including ends of ridges, their separations, and their relationship to one another—constitutes the basis for identification of fingerprints. There are as many as 150 ridge characteristics in an averaged-sized fingerprint.[37] The major **fingerprint patterns** are shown in Figure 4-15. About 65% of the population have loops, roughly 30% have whorls, and the remaining 5% have arches.[38] Points are identical characteristics that are found in fingerprints from known and questioned sources. Positive identification cannot be made when an unexplained difference appears, regardless of the points of similarity.

There is no reliable method for judging the age of latent fingerprints, although the context in which they are found may provide some information. However, both here and in England over the past decade, research has been conducted on how the chemical composition of latent fingerprints varies from the time they are deposited; there is also interesting work suggesting that the chemical composition of latent fingerprints may at some point allow us to make some statements about the approximate age of the donor.[39] The more immediate application of the research on the chemical composition of latent fingerprints will be improvements in the methods of developing them.

There is no standard requirement of print size for positive identification. It is necessary only that the partial print be large enough to contain the necessary points of individuality. This number may be found in an area as small as the flat end of a pencil. Thus, the rule whenever an investigator develops a partial latent print that appears to have only a few ridges is that it should be submitted to the laboratory.

Some persons erroneously believe that the points used for identification of the fingerprint occur only in the pattern area of the finger. In fact, all the different types occur outside the pattern area on the finger as well as on the first and second joints of the finger and the entire palm of the hand. They are also present on the toes and the entire sole of the foot; they may be found in any area where friction ridges occur.

LATENT FINGERPRINTS

Latent prints can be used in two different ways: (1) to refer to all three categories of prints identified below, in the sense that they have been found at the scene of the crime or on items of investigative interest—for example, a murder weapon recovered from a lake far from the primary crime scene—and (2) to refer specifically to latent/invisible prints. Ordinarily, the context in which the term is used helps in understanding which meaning is intended.

1. **Plastic prints** are three-dimensional; they are molded, indented, or impressed into some pliable surface (Figure 4-16). They are created when fingers touch material such as a painted surface that is still "tacky," oil films, explosives, edible fats, putty, dust, caulking, and similar surfaces.

2. **Patent/contaminated/visible prints** result after fingers, contaminated with foreign matter such as soot, oils, face powder, ink, and some types of safe insulation, touch a clean surface. The most common type of contaminated print results when a finger is pressed into a thin layer of dust before touching a smooth surface. Fingerprints that result from blood contamination are sometimes less distinct than those that result from other types of contamination. Patent prints are readily visible to the eye.

3. **Latent/invisible prints** are unseen or hidden. When a crime scene is processed for latent fingerprints, they are made visible by "developing" them, a process described later in this chapter. Latent prints are associated with the small amounts of body perspiration and oil that are normally found on the friction ridges. A latent fingerprint is created when the friction ridges deposit these materials on a surface.

CONDITIONS AFFECTING THE QUALITY OF LATENT FINGERPRINTS

The quality of latent fingerprints is affected by a number of conditions, including these:

1. *The surface on which the print is deposited:* The type of surface on which latent prints are left affects their durability and the type of process used to develop them. There are three broad categories of surfaces:[40]
   a. nonporous surfaces, which are not absorbent. These surfaces often appear polished and repel moisture. Examples include mirrors, glass, smooth ceramics, plastic, and painted wood. Prints on these types of surfaces are more susceptible to

damage, because they are on the outermost surface. Undisturbed, they might last for years.
   b. porous surfaces, which are absorbent, such as documents and cardboard. Prints on documents, for example, may be durable and fairly stable over a period of years or they can quickly fade or deteriorate beyond the point of being useful it they are subject to high humidity or if they become wet.
   c. semiporous surfaces, which don't fit easily into the previous two categories, because they both resist and absorb fingerprints, which may or may not soak into the surface. Semiporous examples include glossy cardboard, magazine covers, and some types of cellophane. The durability of prints on these surfaces is variable.

Textured surfaces, such as the "pebbled" effect of some computer monitors are both nonporous and porous, because the pebbled effect creates an inconsistent contact between the friction ridge skin and the surface, producing a discontinuous appearance when developed and a lack of fine detail.

2. *The nature of the material contaminating the fingerprint:* patent fingerprints resulting from contamination by soot, safe insulation, and face powder are quickly destroyed; those made with blood, ink, or oil can last longer periods of time under favorable conditions.[41]

3. *Any physical or occupational defects of the person making the print.*

4. *How the object on which the prints appear was handled:* The distance between friction ridges is very small, and if the finger moves even slightly, that ridge detail can be lost.

5. *The amount of the contamination:* When the finger leaving the print is very contaminated, both the ridge surfaces and their "valleys" get filled up, resulting in a smeared appearance with little value as evidence.

LOCATING LATENT FINGERPRINTS

Proper latent print processing begins with wearing latex, nitrile, or other suitable gloves.[42] Latent prints are such valuable evidence that extraordinary efforts should be made to recover them. The investigator must adopt a positive attitude about this, regardless of apparent problems or past failures.

It is imperative that the investigator thoroughly search all surface areas in and around the crime scene that might retain prints. Shining a flashlight at an oblique angle to the surface being examined is often helpful in this search. The fact that an individual may have worn gloves in no way lessens the need for a complete search. On occasion, gloves themselves leave impressions as individualized as fingerprints. Moreover, although unusual, it may be possible to develop a latent fingerprint on the inside of a glove recovered at a crime scene.[43] Particular attention should be paid to less obvious places, such as the undersides of toilet seats, toilet handles, tabletops, and dresser drawers; the surfaces of dinner plates and filing cabinets; the backs of rearview mirrors; and the trunk lids of automobiles. Frequently handled objects, such as doorknobs and telephones, ordinarily do not yield good prints. But because they are likely to have been touched, they should always be processed.

Never assume that the offender took precautions against leaving prints or destroyed those left. The commission of a criminal offense involves stress, and the offender may have made a mistake. If gloves were worn, for example, the suspect may have removed them for some operation.

It helps to attempt to view the scene as the criminal did. Such conditions as time of day, weather, and physical layout may suggest that certain surfaces should be more closely examined. In conducting the examination for latent prints in a burglary case, for example, the investigators should begin at the point of entry. For other crimes, such as the issuance of worthless checks, the point of entry often takes on less importance. Ordinarily, however, whatever the crime and its attending circumstances, reconstruction by the investigator gives direction to the search.

A person who is familiar with the environment, such as the owner of the building or the occupant of an apartment, may give valuable aid in obtaining latent prints. The person should be allowed to observe the scene so that he or she can indicate any items out of place or brought to the scene by the suspect.

When neither the ambient lighting nor the use of a bright flashlight reveals latent prints, other methods of searching for them—a forensic light or laser unit—may provide results. A **forensic light source (FLS)** is a powerful light source that has one or more specialized light capabilities, such as infrared (IR) or ultraviolet (UV) light capabilities. UV lights, in addition to causing naturally fluorescent/glowing prints to be visible, are useful in locating small amounts of body fluids, hairs, fibers, and other evidence too small to be visible to the naked eye. Historically, lasers had superior illumination capabilities, but their size and cost precluded their use in most law-enforcement agencies. With the recent arrival of less costly, handheld third-generation laser systems, which are green-light-based, laser systems are becoming more widely used in the field. Appropriate safety precautions prescribed by FLS and laser system manufacturers, for example, wearing approved goggles, should be followed.

METHODS OF DEVELOPING LATENT FINGERPRINTS

Plastic and contaminated prints require little or no development. However, there are numerous ways to develop latent prints. Four methods that investigators should be familiar with are (1) use of traditional powders, (2) use of fluorescent powders, (3) application of chemicals, and (4) cyanoacrylate or superglue fuming. The most common method of developing latent/invisible prints is through the use of traditional powders (Figure 4-17). Because it may be possible to obtain a DNA sample from a print, the method selected for development should not eliminate this possibility.

Traditional Powders

Commercially prepared **traditional powders** come in a number of colors, including black, white, silver, red, and gray. To provide a good contrast between the print and the background on which it has been made, darker powders are used to locate latent/invisible prints on lighter-colored surfaces, and lighter ones are used on darker backgrounds (Figure 4-17). There are also dual-use powders, which appear black when dusted on a light-colored surface and silver when applied to a dark one. The tip of the brush is gently placed into the wide-mouthed powder container and then lightly tapped to allow excess powder to drop away. Caution must be used when applying the powder to a latent print. Too much powder creates a print in which the details are difficult to identify. This is why powder is never sprinkled directly on the surface to be dusted. The entire area to be dusted should be covered with smooth, light brush strokes until the ridge detail begins to show. Then, the brush strokes should follow the contours of the ridges until the latent/invisible print is fully visible. Even if the first attempt to develop a print is not successful, a second one may be. The choices of brushes include tips made of fiberglass, feathers, and camel hair. Most latent print development is done with traditional powders.

◄**FIGURE 4-17 Locating prints**
A crime scene technician uses protective equipment while dusting for fingerprints. Several developed prints can be seen in the area the technician is dusting. **(Courtesy Nassau County, New York Police Department)**

Magnetic applicators may be used in lieu of a brush. A magnetic applicator has a magnet in its head and when placed close to a magnetic powder container, it attracts the powder, forming a virtual brush. Magnetic powders commonly come in black, gray, and white. There are also dual-use magnetic powders. Magnetic powders are only used on nonmetallic surfaces.

Fluorescent Powders

As mentioned earlier, low concentrations of some naturally occurring substances will cause a latent print to fluoresce, or glow, under FLS or laser illumination. To compensate for the typically low level of naturally occurring fluorescence, investigators can dust the area to be examined with a special **fluorescent powder,** which chemically enhances the print when viewed under FLS or laser illumination (Figure 4-18). Fluorescent powders are also available in several colors for use with a magnetic applicator.

CHEMICALS

A variety of chemicals are used to develop and enhance latent prints. These chemicals are applied by spraying or brushing the surface being examined, by fuming, or by dipping the object on which there may be prints in a solution.[44] Among chemicals in use are the following:

- Amido black is a dye sensitive to properties in blood and may be used with contaminated/visible prints involving blood. It has the capability to turn blood proteins to a blue-black color. It should not

be used as a presumptive test for blood, because it also reacts to other things.
- Gentian violet is a dye used to develop purplish latent prints on the adhesive side of almost any kind of tape.
- Ninhydrin was formulated in 1910 and proposed for use in developing fingerprints in 1954; this chemical is used to develop latent prints on paper and cardboard, producing purplish prints (Figure 4-19).
- DFO (1, 8-diazafluren-9-one) functions similarly to ninhydrin but is about three times more sensitive in developing latent prints on paper. The developed red-colored prints are immediately visible but paler than those produced by ninhydrin. DFO prints fluoresce under FLS and laser illumination. Both DFO and ninhydrin may be used on paper, but DFO must be used first to get any fluorescence.
- Small-Particle Reagent (SPR) is used for developing latent prints that have been immersed in water, such as when a perpetrator has attempted to dispose of a firearm used in a crime by throwing it into a river or lake. It is also used to develop prints on dew- or rain-soaked cars; on surfaces covered with a residue, such as salt from being on or near the ocean; and on waxed materials, plastics, tile, and glass. Developed prints appear dark gray on a light surface and light gray on a dark surface. Although SPR can be sprayed on an object, immersion of the object for about 30 seconds in an SPR solution produces better results.

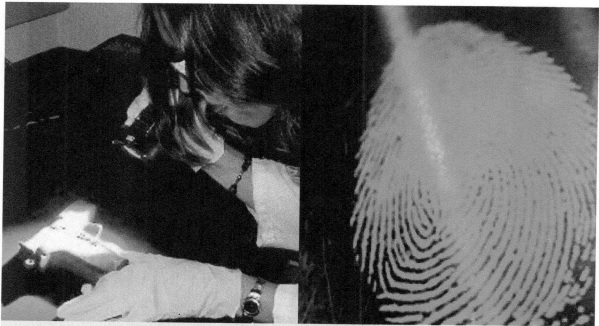

▲FIGURE 4-18   Reflected ultraviolet imaging system
The technician is holding a RUVIS SceneScope in her right hand, which is shaped a like a fat flashlight. The RUVIS operates on ultraviolet (UV) light and can locate objects that are naturally fluorescent. In this case, a .45 Colt semi-automatic pistol was dusted with fluorescent powder. This RUVIS has an attached camera, which photographed the fluorescing fingerprint on the pistol.
(*Left:* Courtesy HORIBA Jobin Yvon S.A.S., North Carolina Bureau of Investigation, State Crime Lab, Latent Evidence Section, *right:* Courtesy State of Utah Crime Lab)

- Rhodamine 6G is an excellent fluorescent chemical dye to use on metal, glass, leather, plastic, wood, and many other types of nonabsorbent surfaces. Rhodamine 6G may enhance latent prints already developed and also reveal others.
- After Super Glue fuming, Basic Yellow 40 can be effectively used on nonporous surfaces. It fluoresces well under alternative lighting. Ardrox and Basic Red 28 are also used following Super Glue fuming.

Cyanoacrylate (CA) or Super Glue Fuming

Super Glue fuming was developed in 1978 in Japan. The three factors associated with its rapid acceptance were ease of use, remarkable results, and low cost. The mechanics of

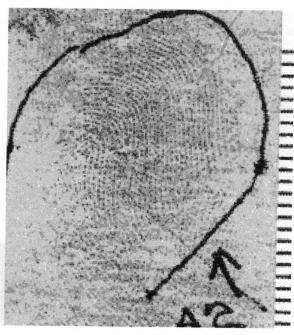

▶FIGURE 4-19   Ninhydrin developed print
Using ninhydrin is an excellent technique to develop latent prints on paper. In this case, a thumb print is raised on an envelope containing an extortion note. (Courtesy Wisconsin Department of Justice, Law Enforcement Services Division)

▲ **Figure 4-20   Portable Super Glue fuming chamber**
This portable Super Glue unit is being used to process a
weapon and liquor bottles at the scene of a murder-robbery
in New York City. Note that the chamber can be used in the
field or in the laboratory. (© Seth Gottfried)

fluorescent powders and Super Glue fuming. Success has
also been reported using combinations of these methods—
for example, fuming followed by the use of fluorescent
powders. There is no consensus method. Because of
potential health threats to living victims, investigators
need to be well-informed about the products they use. As
bodies decompose, the likelihood of developing latent
fingerprints on them is reduced.

Some authorities recommend after the medical examiner has released a body at the scene, it should be glue
fumed to preserve any latent prints while the body is
transported to the morgue. The body should not be
refrigerated until after further latent print development
efforts are completed. At the scene, there may be some
indication of specific handling of a body by the suspect—
for instance, placed in a pose or the victim's statement.
Key target areas for finding latent prints on the victim are
ankles, armpits, wrists, inner thighs, and neck. On living
victims areas of redness are a key indicator of handling.
Humidity and temperature levels can affect development
efforts and charts are available to determine the optimum
conditions for processing.[45]

COLLECTING AND PRESERVING LATENT PRINTS

Occasionally items such as beer cans or glasses that have
condensation on them need to be processed for prints.
Heat lamps or any other source of artificial heat should
not be used to dry the object quickly. Such objects should
be allowed to air-dry naturally. Similarly, articles that
have been frozen and need to be processed for prints
must be allowed to thaw and dry naturally. Whenever
reasonable to do so, the actual item on which the print
is located should be submitted for developing in the
laboratory.

Once a print is found it should be photographed
immediately with a rigid scale in view. The ruler allows
a one-to-one, or actual-size, picture of the print to be
made. This provides a permanent record of the print in
the event that it is accidentally altered or destroyed while
attempting to collect or transporting it.

Most latent prints are lifted with a clear strip of tape,
1½ inches to 2 inches wide, or with clear flap lifter after
they have been developed with powders. One end of the
clear tape is placed on the surface just before the latent
print appears. Pressure is then applied to progressively
lay the tape over the print, taking care not to leave air
bubbles. If air bubbles are accidentally created, the tape
should be carefully smoothed over to eliminate them. The
tape may be left on the object if the object is to be submitted to the laboratory.

Alternatively, the pattern of the print is lifted by pulling up the tape, starting at one end and moving progressively to the other end. Now the powder that shows the
print pattern is stuck to the sticky side of the tape. This
tape is then laid back down on an appropriately colored

Super Glue fuming are fairly straightforward. Cyanoacrylate (CA) is heated in a high-humidity chamber. As the
fumes condense, they develop white-colored latent prints
in 5 to 15 minutes. The developed prints may be further
enhanced with powders or soaked in chemicals that fluoresce under FLSs.

Super Glue fuming may be done by small Super Glue
fuming wands, in small portable chambers (Figure 4-20)
and in various sized chambers in the laboratory. On a
larger scale, entire rooms and automobiles are processed
using this method.

DEVELOPING LATENT FINGERPRINTS ON BODIES

The development of identifiable latent fingerprints on living victims and corpses has been accomplished using a
variety of methods, including tradition, magnetic, and

backing card. For example, assume that a latent print on a glass window is developed with dark powder.

MARKING AND IDENTIFYING PRINT LIFTS

When a latent print has been developed, lifted, and placed on a card, the card must be properly identified. Information recorded on the card should include the date, type of case, case number, address of the crime scene, name of the officer who made the lift, exact place of the lift, and type of object from which the print was lifted. Regardless of how well the latent print was developed and lifted, if the card is not properly marked with all the data required or if the fingerprint specialist is not furnished with the information required, the entire process may be wasted effort. In describing the exact place that the lift was made, it is sometimes helpful to draw a simple sketch of the object. The sketch should be made on the fingerprint card that is sent to the laboratory. The inclusion of corresponding numbers on both the lift and the sketch establishes the location of the latent print.

FORENSIC ODONTOLOGY

Forensic odontology has been defined as the intersection of dentistry and criminal law; it is a medical specialty relating dental evidence to investigation. The most common cases involve missing and unidentified persons (MUPs) cases, where unidentified human remains are found at a crime or death investigation scene.[46] In second place is the recognition, documentation, preservation, evaluation, interpretation, and comparison of bite mark evidence.

A forensic dentist may be able to make significant contributions to the following types of cases:

1. a head is found or there is an otherwise unidentifiable body;
2. a decomposing, burned, or skeletonized body is found;
3. sexual assault, child/elder abuse, domestic violence, and homicide cases involving aggressive and/or defensive bite marks. More rarely, bite marks may be self-inflicted as part of a staged crime.[47] Although bite marks are most frequently found on skin and in human tissue, they may also be located on pencils, styrofoam cups, food (Figure 4-21), and other objects.
4. identifying mass casualties of attacks and natural and industrial disasters—such as 9/11, the Indian Ocean tsunami (2004) that may have killed as many as 250,000 people, Hurricane Katrina (2005), and the Interstate 35 bridge collapse in Minneapolis (2007) (Figure 4-22). In Thailand, 75% of the 2004 tsunami victims were identified by forensic odontology;[48]
5. verifying a presumptive, or reasonably believed, identity—for example, Hitler, Eva Braun, and Mussolini during World War II and more recently al-Qaeda terrorists Abu Musab al-Zarqawi and Mohammed Atef.

IDENTIFICATION

Forensic odontology's normal approach to identifying MUPs is the comparison of postmortem or after-death dental remains with antemortem or predeath records, including written notes, radiographs/X rays, casts, bridges,

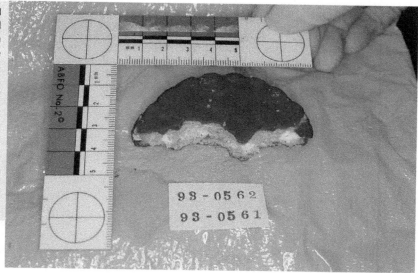

▶ **FIGURE 4-21**
Bite mark in food
A partially eaten "Moon Pie" bitten by one of the suspects in a double homicide. From the bite marks it can be determined that the individual making them had two non-equally protruding upper front teeth. Such information can play an important role in determining probable cause for arrest and/or search warrants.
(Courtesy Dr. Richard R. Souviron, DDS, ABFO, Chief Forensic Odontologist, Dade County Medical Examiner Department, Miami, Florida)

▲ **FIGURE 4-22   Identification of victims at disasters**
Cars and trucks lie in the wreckage of the I-35W bridge that spanned the Mississippi River in Minneapolis, Minnesota (August 1, 2007). Forensic odontology has been an invaluable tool in identifying the victims of disasters. (© AP Photo/The Minnesota Daily, Stacy Bengs)

fillings, and caps.[49] Morphological (shape and form) peculiarities of teeth can also help establish identity of MUPs.

Additionally, forensic dentists have established individual identity on the basis of "smiling photographs" (Figure 4-23). Some dentures are marked and can be traced to a particular owner, although the possibility that they were discarded at the scene must be eliminated. There is no set number of points required to establish a positive match; one unique feature may be sufficient.

The FBI maintains the National Dental Image/Information Repository (NDIR) on missing persons and unidentified remains and is adding dental information to the wanted persons file. Other sources of dental records include the military, health insurance carriers, local dentists, and community health clinics for indigent and low income persons and families. In some cases, it is useful to have a forensic artist prepare a likeness of the deceased, as he/she may have appeared in life, which can be done from as little as a skull. This image is placed in the newspaper with a public appeal for assistance in making an identity. Any suggestions as to identity may be checkable against dental records.

Searches for dental records may not be productive, because (1) some number of individuals under the age of 30 have no dental decay, and (2) individuals with decayed or missing teeth may never have sought treatment. In either case, there are no records of antemortem dental restorations that can be compared with the postmortem dental features of a victim.

When human remains are discovered in remote areas, clandestine graves, abandoned buildings, or under similar circumstances, the bodies may be in very "rough" shape, and animal predation may require treating a larger area as a crime scene. However, teeth are the most durable part of the body, and dental evidence may play a key role in these types of investigations. The longer bodies have been left unattended, the greater the probability that teeth have fallen out or otherwise been dislodged from their normal place. Violence to the victim may have accomplished the same thing. "Rough" body scenes are unpleasant, and investigators should be sure that every precaution is taken to recover loose teeth and other evidence associated with the scene. The addition of a forensic anthropologist, skilled in methodically processing human remains sites, to the investigative team should be considered, especially at burial sites and when the victim's body is skeletonized.

DENTAL PROFILING

When there is an unidentifiable victim and there are no antemortem or predeath dental records, the forensic dentist can help narrow the population pool to which the deceased belongs by **postmortem (after-death) dental profiling** by providing a variety of useful observations:[50]

1. Some teeth give us an idea of racial characteristics—for example, Native Americans and Asians have deep grooves in the inner aspects of their upper front teeth, called shovel-shaped incisors.
2. Age at time of death estimate—through 13 years old an approximation of age accurate to within six months is possible; from 14 to 25 years old a one year plus or minus window is possible; after age 25, scientific testing is usually required to establish an approximate age.
3. Gender—the morphology of teeth does not vary by gender, but analysis of dental pulp and the cranium can provide gender identification. There is also research on using the geometric relationships of teeth to establish gender; this method has achieved accuracy rates of 84% in controlled testing.
4. Suggestion of social class by the presence or absence of various types of dental care.
5. Opinions about habits, such as pipe smoking and nail biting.

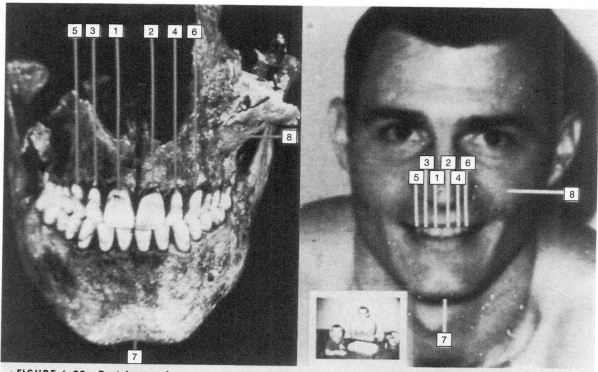

▲ **FIGURE 4-23** **Dental comparison**
The left photo shows upper and lower jaws of an unknown white male. Some bone loss (pyorrhea) and tobacco staining are evident. There were no fillings, decay, or missing teeth and no evidence of any dental treatment. The right photo is an enhancement and enlargement of a photo of the victim at his son's birthday party. His kidnappers/killers were sentenced to life terms. (Courtesy Dr. Richard R. Souviron, D.D.S., ABFO, Chief Forensic Odontologist, Dade County Medical Examiner's Department, Miami, Florida)

BITE MARKS

Investigators must be particularly alert to the possibility that bite-mark evidence exists, particularly when they are working sexual assault, child/elder abuse, and homicide cases. Female victims are most often bitten on the breast, buttocks, and legs during a sexual assault, whereas male victims are more likely to be bitten on the arms and shoulders. Bite marks on the arms and hands are usually defensive wounds caused when a person holds up his/ her arms to ward off an attacker.[51] Facial hair associated with bite marks may be transferred between attackers and victims; it should be collected consistent with the guidelines in the next major section, "Hair." In 99% of all violent rapes, victims are bitten at least once by their attacker (Figure 4-24).[52] The collection of bite mark evidence, when reasonably possible, should be left to a forensic dentist.

Bite marks may be mistaken for bruises, abrasions, indentions, or lacerations (Figure 4-25); most have an overall ovoid appearance. One or both arches of teeth may be present and there may be multiple, overlapping bites at the same location. Bite marks on skin should be processed quickly because they may be degraded by skin elasticity, the post mortem position of the body, and skin dehydration. Collecting bite mark evidence includes the following steps:

1. Document the bites using color photography; the shots should include general views establishing where the bites are on the victim, a medium-range photograph, and close-ups without and then with an American Board of Forensic Odontology (ABFO) #2 scale. Some labs request that the scales used be submitted with the evidence; in the absence of an AFBO #2, place two scales at right angles as close to the bite mark as possible without disturbing it. When possible, infrared and ultraviolet photos should also be taken.

2. Swab the *center* of each bite mark *twice* with a different sterile cotton applicator moistened with distilled water. Each swab should allowed to air dry and packaged in a paper envelop, sealed, and marked. Even if the prospects for collecting saliva seem

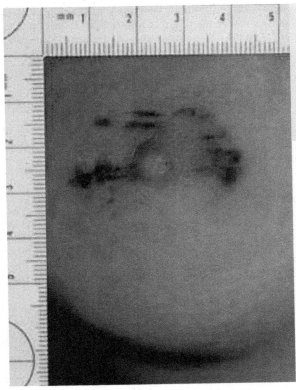

◄ **FIGURE 4-24   Bite mark on breast and nipple**
Bite marks are often found on victims of sexual abuse, rape, and violence. It is not uncommon that the suspect bites the victim as part of the sexual sadist ritual. Here, a bite mark is reflected on the breast and nipple of a sexual assault victim. First swab the area for traces of the suspect's saliva, which may yield DNA evidence. Photograph the bite mark and follow other guidelines set forth by the ABFO relating to bite mark evidence collection and preservation. **(Courtesy Forensic Denistry Online)**

3. When the bite area is within reach of the victim's dentition, a cast of his/her teeth should be taken.
4. Impressions of the bite area can be made using dental grade silicon impression material.
5. If the victim is deceased, the medical examiner's office may remove the block of tissue containing the bite mark and preserve it in formalin. To maintain the size and contour of the bite mark, it is attached to a custom-made ring prior to the tissue being removed.[54]

Although bruises and bite marks change color as time passes, this process is not linear and unvarying. Statements about bruise color and age of the injury should be regarded warily because they are opinions unsupported by science. A 2010 study of the ability of forensic experts to date the age of bruises showed them to be unreliable; however, they were better in placing sequential photographs of bruises from the same subject in the correct chronological order. These photographs were taken from the time they appeared until they disappeared.[55]

remote, the procedure should be followed; in a rare case saliva was recovered from the skin of a victim submerged in a slow-running river for 5.5 hours.[53] If the bite mark is made *through* clothing, the clothing is also a potential source of saliva to be processed.

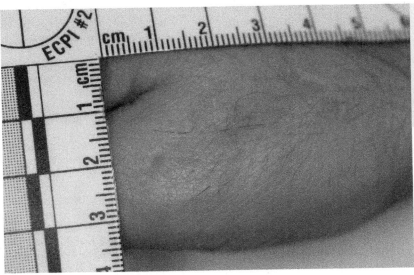

◄ **FIGURE 4-25**
Hand laceration by teeth
Laceration at base of suspect's thumb area caused by victim's defensive bite. Suspect grabbed victim from behind, trying to gag her with his hand. **(Courtesy Los Angeles Police Department)**

Before collecting evidence from a suspect, the legal authority to do so must be established; normally this is done by search warrant, court order, or consent. A request for consent and sometimes a court order will alert suspects and/or their attorneys to a pending examination and may provide sufficient time for suspects to alter their dentition—for example, have all teeth pulled. Two search warrants should be obtained to (1) seize the suspect's dental records and (2) collect evidence from the suspect. The application for the search warrant should specify what evidence will be collected using what methods, including saliva swabbing for DNA if appropriate to the fact situation.

Collection of evidence from the suspect is the responsibility of forensic dentists or technicians working under their supervision, who should describe the protocols that will be used to the suspect. Elements of evidence collection include:

1. The suspect's dental records subsequent to, or in closest proximity to the date of the bite mark.
2. A complete set of photographs.
3. A clinical examination, to include identification of misaligned, broken, or missing teeth; a determination of how long teeth have been broken or missing; restorative dental work; evidence of trauma and surgery; maximum mouth opening; periodontal condition and any loose teeth. A dental chart is usually prepared.
4. Two impressions of the upper and lower arches of the suspect's teeth.
5. Sample bite marks in a wax—for example, aluwax, Styrofoam, or other ABFO-approved material; suspects should not be physically forced into providing a standard/reference sample.[56]

The process of comparing bite marks with a suspect's dentition includes analysis and measurement of size, shape and position of the individual teeth.[57] From the impressions, a life-sized study model of the suspect's dentition is produced. At the broadest level of comparison, if the arch and shape characteristics do not match, the suspect can immediately be excluded. Most comparison methods rely on the use of overlays. The use of laser imaging in bite mark comparisons is very promising, producing a high level of three-dimensional details.[58]

HAIR

Hair evidence is often found because both victims and suspects can transfer it to each other or the scene; hair is easy to locate and recover, and durable.[59] It may be found on ski masks abandoned by armed robbers, in the head and pubic hairs of assailants and victims, clutched in the hands of victims, on clothing, and numerous other places. Hair evidence is primarily associated with violent crimes.

Microscopic examination of hairs can determine whether the origin is a fiber wig, animal, or human. A number of useful conclusions are *possible* from the microscopic examination of human hair, such as the:

1. racial characteristics of the donor—that is, European, Asian, or African;
2. somatic or body area origin of the hair—for example, eyelashes, pubic, scalp, and beard;
3. manner in which it was removed—for instance, if hair has an anagen/active growth root it suggests forcible removal;
4. damage to the hair—for example, by putrefaction, blunt force trauma, or burned;
5. types of drugs ingested and how recently;
6. presence of hair contaminates, including blood, semen, soil, pet hair, and soil; contaminates *may* suggest an occupation—for instance, automotive spray paint particles might indicate working in a body shop;[60]
7. hair treatment, including bleaching, shampoo residues, and dyes;[61]
8. determination of whether known and questioned hair samples could have a common origin (Figure 4-26).

Most often, when a reference to DNA and investigation is made, it is in the context that individual identification can be established. This is true with nuclear DNA (nDNA), which is passed from both parents to their offspring. Thus, if a hair has its root, or other tissue attached, then establishing individual identity is possible from nDNA. However, when investigators have recovered only a hair shaft, it contains a different type of DNA, mitochondrial or **mtDNA,** which is inherited only from the maternal line. It is not possible to establish individual identity with mtDNA, because other people along the same maternal lines share it. There is also the possibility of a random match. In contrast, some mtDNA is so rare that it is seen only once even in very large DNA databases. MtDNA can be used to exclude suspects, establish that the victim is not from a particular lineage (or that he/she is), all of which helps to focus investigative effort.[62]

When collecting hair standards, at least 50 should be cut at the skin from various portions of the head to assure that all shades of texture and color have been properly sampled; this number should be doubled for deceased individuals, and they should be pulled.[63] At least 20 standard pubic hair samples should be cut at the skin surface from various regions on a live person; double that number and pull them from deceased. Standard hair samples can be placed in a clean envelope, which is sealed and labeled.[64] Pill boxes, glass vials, and other tightly sealed containers are also acceptable in many labs.

The collection of questioned hair samples requires a clean piece of paper to be placed under the area to be combed. All areas of the pubic or other area should be thoroughly combed to dislodge foreign hairs and other materials.[65] When the process is completed, place the

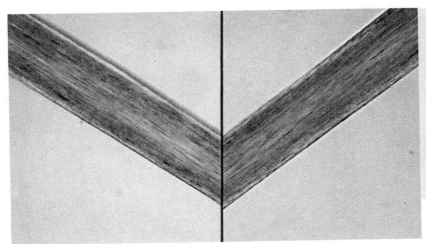

◄ **FIGURE 4-26   Hair analysis**
Photomicrograph of hair found inside a rape suspect's vehicle (*left*) is matched with a sample of hair from the victim (*right*). Note the darker shading of brown near the outside of each strand as a result of color added to the victim's hair. These types of peculiarities provide matches between the characteristics of hairs but not to the exclusion of a donor other than the victim. (Courtesy Texas Department of Public Safety)

comb on the paper, carefully fold it, and place the paper in an envelope. If samples are collected from several portions of the body, the comb should be changed between areas and each area packaged separately. Known and questioned samples should be packaged separately when submitted to the laboratory. The investigator should be present when qualified medical personnel collect samples. Before the process begins, the investigator should verify that the medical person understands the proper collection and packaging of samples.

Hair collection at the crime scene requires a different set of considerations regarding known and questioned samples:

1. Document by photos, the evidence log, and by diagram where the hairs were recovered.
2. Do not submit wet hairs to the lab; they should be allowed to air dry.
3. If they are firmly attached to an object, leave the hairs intact and submit the object.
4. When visible hairs are not firmly attached to an object or the object is too large to submit to the lab, carefully remove them with clean tweezers.
5. If hairs were possibly transferred to the victim's and/or suspect's clothing, keep their clothes apart. Package each article of clothing separately and submit to the laboratory separately.[66]
6. Do not overlook the potential probative value of animal hair; if a victim's pets were present at the time of the offense, samples should be pulled from them and handled in the usual manner.

BLOOD

Blood was class-characteristic evidence until the introduction of DNA analysis in the early 1980s. However, an initial study published in 2010 hints at the possibility that blood may have other important contributions to make. Blood samples from 195 people, from a few weeks to 80 years old were analyzed. The research reports the ability to identify age from blood, plus or minus 8.9 years.[67] However, even if confirmed, this capability may be five or more years away from common use. The identification of eye and hair color, skin pigmentation, height, and weight from blood analysis are also being explored.[68]

On average, an adult's body contains about 5 to 6 quarts of blood, and even small cuts can produce a lot of blood. At crime scenes, blood may be encountered in amounts ranging from small drops to large pools, in states ranging from fresh to dried, and in almost any place, including on floors, walls, ceilings, clothes, weapons, the suspect's and victim's bodies, and the exterior and interior of vehicles.

Because of the frequency with which blood is encountered and the fact that DNA analysis can provide individual identification (Table 4-1), officers need to be alert to locating and protecting this type of evidence. Moreover, they should wear appropriate PPE and take the other kinds of protective measures discussed in Chapter 3, "Investigators, the Investigative Process, and the Crime Scene."

THE APPEARANCE OF BLOODSTAINS

If blood at the crime scene is fresh and relatively uncontaminated, identifying it as blood is not difficult. If it is in some other condition, identifying blood merely by "eyeballing it" becomes increasingly difficult. Blood may appear as a rust-colored stain or have gray, black, green, or blue tints. It may also be mixed with earth, grease, paint, or other substances, making it difficult to see.

Very fine drops of blood can be located by viewing the surfaces concerned at an oblique angle close to the plane

TABLE 4-1	Sources of DNA Evidence	
EVIDENCE	POSSIBLE LOCATION OF DNA ON THE EVIDENCE	SOURCE OF DNA
Baseball bat or similar weapon	Handle, end	Sweat, skin, blood, tissue
Hat, bandanna, or mask	Inside	Sweat, hair, dandruff
Eyeglasses	Nose or ear pieces, lens	Sweat, skin
Facial tissue or cotton swab	Surface area	Mucus, blood, sweat, semen, earwax
Dirty laundry	Surface area	Blood, sweat, semen, vomit
Toothpick	Tips	Saliva
Used cigarette	Cigarette butt	Saliva
Stamp or envelope	Licked area	Saliva
Tape or ligature	Inside or outside surface	Skin, sweat
Bottle, can, or glass	Sides, mouthpiece	Saliva, sweat
Used condom	Inside or outside surface	Semen, vaginal or rectal cells
Blanket, pillow, or sheet	Surface area	Sweat, hair, semen, urine, saliva, dandruff
"Through and through" bullet	Outside surface	Blood, tissue
Bite mark	Person's skin or clothing	Saliva
Fingernail or partial fingernail	Scrapings	Blood, sweat, tissue

Source: *www.dba.Gov/Basics/Evidence_Collection/Identifying*, January 5, 2011.

of the surfaces. If the light is not strong or if the scene is dark, viewing the surfaces will be enhanced by shining a flashlight beam at the same oblique angle. Blood is naturally fluorescing and may be detected by the use of a FLS.

The drying time of blood depends on a number of factors, including whether it is on a porous or nonporous surface, its size and thickness, and the presence or absence of a fan or breeze. Higher temperatures hasten the drying time of blood, whereas increased humidity decreases it. Drying first appears at the edges of a bloodstain and works toward its center. A dried bloodstain will begin to pucker and crack from the edges inward after further drying. Thus, it is difficult to accurately estimate the age of bloodstains. Research has been carried out on dating the age of blood using changes in its chemical composition.[69]

USING BLOODSTAINS TO RECONSTRUCT THE CRIME

Bloodstains (known as blood spatter) may take many forms at a crime scene. These forms are not random but are produced by such factors as the type, location, and number of wounds inflicted; the type of weapon involved; movements by the victim while trying to escape, defend himself/herself, or attack the offender; changes in the location of the victim's body owing to its being moved by the offender or someone; and continuing postmortem violence to the body by the offender,

suggesting that the killer was in a state of rage and possibly knew the victim.

By studying bloodstain and spatter evidence, the investigator can learn significant facts that facilitate reconstruction of the crime. These facts include:

1. Direction in which blood droplets were traveling when they were deposited on the surface (Figure 4-27).
2. Distance from the source of the blood to the surface on which the droplets were found (Figure 4-28). An important fact to note concerning blood spatter is that blood droplets cannot exceed 4 feet in horizontal travel from a stationary point (for example, blood spatter from a direct gunshot wound); thus, the blood droplets in Figure 4-28 reflect vertical fall.[70]
3. Angle at which the droplets impacted (see Figure 4-29).
4. Direction and relative speed of blood trails.
5. Nature of the object used as a weapon.
6. Number of blows struck.
7. Relative locations of other persons, surfaces, and objects having droplets on them.
8. Sequence of events, if multiple events are involved.
9. Interpretation of blood-contact or blood-transfer patterns.
10. Estimation of the elapsed time for the event and the volume of bloodshed.[71]

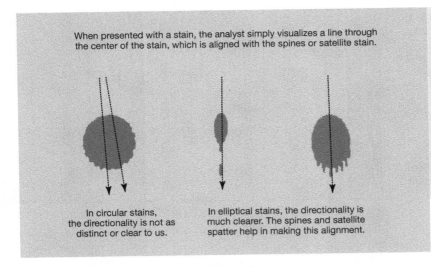

When presented with a stain, the analyst simply visualizes a line through the center of the stain, which is aligned with the spines or satellite stain.

In circular stains, the directionality is not as distinct or clear to us.

In elliptical stains, the directionality is much clearer. The spines and satellite spatter help in making this alignment.

◄ **FIGURE 4-27**
Directionality of blood droplet
To visualize or demonstrate directionality in a droplet, the analyst simply draws a line down the long axis of the stain, splitting it into two equal parts. This line is oriented to the scallops, spines, or satellite stains. (Source: Tom Bevel and Ross M. Gardner, *Bloodstain Pattern Analysis: With an Introduction to Crime Scene Reconstruction,* 2nd ed. [Boca Raton, FL: CRC Press, 2002], p. 146. Used by permission.)

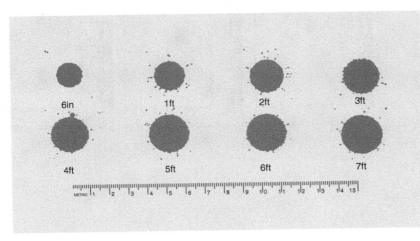

6in   1ft   2ft   3ft

4ft   5ft   6ft   7ft

METRIC 1 2 3 4 5 6 7 8 9 10 11 12 13 14 15

◄ **FIGURE 4-28**
Distance between bloodstain and source
Increasing diameter of bloodstains as a function of increasing distance fallen by single drops of blood from fingertips onto smooth cardboard (Source: Stuart H. James and William G. Eckert, *Interpretation of Bloodstain Evidence at Crime Scenes,* 2nd ed. [Boca Raton, FL: CRC Press, 1998], p. 21. Used by permission.)

LOCATING BLOOD EVIDENCE

The places at which the investigator will find bloodstains are virtually unlimited. For example, if a criminal homicide occurred indoors, blood might be found not only on the floor but perhaps also on the walls or even the ceiling. Ordinarily when perpetrators of violent crimes get blood on their bodies or clothing, they will attempt to rid themselves of it immediately. In some instances, they may be so repelled by the sight of blood on their hands that they will impulsively wipe it on a piece of furniture, such as a stuffed chair; if the fabric is multicolored or sufficiently dark, the stain may escape detection by the unobservant investigator. They may also attempt to clean bloodied hands before leaving the scene by using such surfaces as the reverse side of a small throw rug or the undersides of cushions on a couch.

At bloody scenes it is not uncommon for the suspect to have left a shoeprint on some hard, smooth surface. In turn,

it is likely that some of the blood may be found in the cracks and crevices of the suspect's shoe soles. This is important evidence, because it can tie the suspect to the scene with great certainty, particularly if DNA evidence from the blood can positively link the suspect to the scene.

Another way of locating blood evidence is use of a presumptive or preliminary field test (Figure 4-30). **Luminol,** a water-based spray, locates trace amounts of blood within 30 seconds, creating a blue glow after the lights are turned out. Luminol's disadvantages are that the glow is short lasting; it doesn't differentiate between human and animal blood, and it reacts to copper, some alloys, and certain bleaches. **Hemident** also does not distinguish between human and animal blood. In the presence of blood, it produces a dark blue/green appearance within seconds. **Hexagon OBTI** (Figure 4-31) distinguishes between animal and human blood in two to three minutes; however, it also displays sensitivity to the blood of higher primates. To have legal significance, all three of these presumptive tests

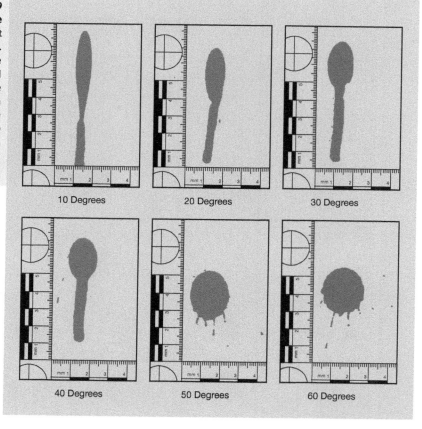

▶ FIGURE 4-29
Impact angle and stain shape
The range of droplet shapes that result from the varying impact angles. The more elliptical the stain, the more acute the angle of impact. Round stains indicate that the impact angle was closer to 90 degrees. (Source: Tom Bevel and Ross M. Gardner, *Bloodstain Pattern Analysis: With an Introduction to Crime Scene Reconstruction,* 2nd ed. [Boca Raton, FL: CRC Press, 2002], Color Figure 2. Used by permission.)

10 Degrees   20 Degrees   30 Degrees
40 Degrees   50 Degrees   60 Degrees

▲ FIGURE 4-30   **Use of BlueStar forensic**
Mop used by assailant in an effort to clean up blood from scene of an attack. The BlueStar reagent was sprayed on the mop, revealing presence of blood invisible to naked eye.
(Courtesy BlueStar Forensics)

must be confirmed by more elaborate testing procedures in the laboratory. Some presumptive tests for blood may interfere with DNA analysis, and so investigators need to determine whether the one they are contemplating using does so.[72] If yes, the collection of blood samples from the scene should precede presumptive testing. Alternatively, a small blood sample can be collected and tested.

Occasionally, in an indoor homicide, the perpetrator will remove the body to an outdoor area to avoid discovery and then will return to the scene and attempt to eliminate all traces of the crime. Typically, this involves washing hands and scrubbing or mopping the floor on which the body had lain:

An aggravated assault occurred between two friends who mutually agreed to misrepresent it as an accident. When the victim appeared at the local hospital for

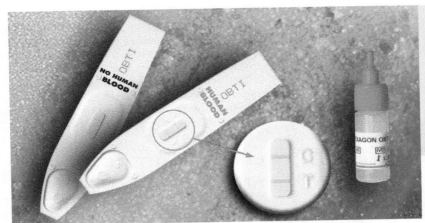

Blood is placed in the white collection tube, followed by the addition of the reagent in the red-capped bottle at right. If the test is functioning properly, but there is no human blood detected, a single blue line appears in the window. Two single blue lines denote the presence of human blood. (Courtesy BlueStar Forensics)

treatment, the police were summoned owing to the nature of the wounds and their locations, which suggested to the doctor that they were not accidentally inflicted. Investigators went to the scene and were told the accident happened outside while barbecuing. Granted permission to look inside the house, they found fresh blood underneath the faucets at the kitchen sink. Trace amounts of blood were found on the recently mopped floor between the back door and the kitchen sink. The location of the blood evidence was particularly pertinent, because the people involved alleged that the "accident" had happened in the backyard while they were barbecuing and that they had gone directly to the hospital. Although a solid investigation was conducted, no prosecution resulted due to a lack of cooperation from the victim and witnesses.

Before handling any blood evidence, investigators must document its location and physical state (for example, fresh) by some combination of notes, diagrams, video recording, and photographs. Other details may be pertinent to record as well, such as the temperature, humidity, or existence of multiple severe wounds but little blood. The last condition suggests that the person was killed somewhere else or that an attempt was made to clean the victim and/or scene, an action possibly indicating that the perpetrator had an attachment to the victim.

Blood Samples from a Known Source

Only qualified medical personnel should collect blood samples from a person. The following guidelines apply:

1. Draw two 5-milliliter samples of blood in purple-stoppered tubes, the insides of which are coated with EDTA, a preservative used to prevent coagulation.

2. If drug or alcohol testing is to be done, collect a 10-milliliter sample in a gray-stoppered tube, which contains a sodium fluoride (NaF) preservative.
3. Identify each tube with the date, time, collector's name, case number, subject's name, location at which drawn, and evidence number.
4. Do not freeze blood samples; the tubes may break. Refrigerate them, and use cold packs, not dry ice, to pack them for shipment to the laboratory.
5. Pack the blood tubes in special bubble packs, or wrap them in the same type of material.
6. After sealing the outer container or box, label it "Keep in a Cool Dry Place," "Refrigerate on Arrival," and "Biohazard."
7. Submit the samples to the laboratory as soon as possible.[73]

Fresh or Dried Blood on a Person

If there is fresh blood, absorb it on a clean cotton cloth or swab. If the blood is clotting or has dried, use distilled water to moisten a cotton cloth or swab and then absorb the blood with the moist surface. Leave a portion of the cloth or swab unstained as a control or blank sample. Let the cloth or swab air dry naturally. Do not place it in direct sunlight or next to a heat source, and do not use a hair dryer on it. These actions could cause the evidence to begin decomposing, thus reducing or eliminating its evidentiary value. Wrap the evidence in clean, dry paper, or place it in an envelope with sealed corners; plastic or airtight containers should not be used.

Fresh Blood on Surfaces or in Snow or Water

The procedure for collecting fresh blood from most surfaces is the same as that previously described for blood on a person. However, when blood is in a filled bathtub or some other body of water or when it is on snow, a different approach is required. For blood in water, recover the sample from the thickest concentrations of blood and clots whenever possible. When gathering blood from snow, eliminate as much snow as possible from the sample. Freeze it in a clean, airtight container, and submit the sample to the laboratory as rapidly as possible.[74]

Fresh or Dried Bloodstains on Garments and Objects

Allow fresh bloodstains on garments to air dry naturally; then fold the clothing with the crusts intact. Do not fold clothing in a way that creases bloodstains, since the creases may cause them to become dislodged. As you fold the clothing, place clean paper between each layer. Usually, bloodstained garments are found at the crime scene or retrieved from a hospital's emergency room.

Fresh bloodstains on a small movable item, such as a weapon, lamp, or door, should also be allowed to air dry naturally. The item is then submitted to the laboratory for processing; pack the item in clean paper in such a way that the paper does not rub against the bloodstains, since rubbing could alter or eradicate the bloodstain pattern.

When bloodstains are on a large immovable object, they can be collected, if fresh, by using the cotton cloth or swab technique or by cutting a large sample from a dried stain. If there are multiple stains on the object, use a new cloth or swab each time you switch from one stain to another; likewise, thoroughly clean the scalpel, razor blade, or knife you are using to cut dried samples when you switch from one collection area to another. In some cases, it may be necessary to cut a section out of the immovable object and transport it to the laboratory; do not forget the need for a control or blank sample.

Other Considerations in Handling Blood Evidence

During warm weather, especially during daylight hours, blood evidence should not be locked in car interiors or trunks, because heat could rapidly degrade the evidence. If dried-blood evidence is not submitted to the laboratory immediately the garments, objects, and/or samples taken should be refrigerated.

LABORATORY DETERMINATIONS

Under ordinary conditions, laboratory examination of blood evidence can determine the following characteristics about the source of the blood:

1. species (human, dog, horse, and so on);
2. gender;
3. blood type and DNA profile;
4. use of drugs or alcohol by the blood source;
5. presence of certain types of illnesses (for example, venereal disease);
6. presence of carbon monoxide;
7. whether the source was a smoker.

The importance of such determinations was highlighted when labor leader Jimmy Hoffa disappeared in 1975. He had told people he was meeting that night with organized crime figures. It was thought that someone close to Hoffa betrayed him because of bloodstains found in that person's car. However, laboratory examination confirmed the person's statement that the bloodstains were from fish he was taking home. Hoffa was declared dead in 1982; his body was never found.

LIP COSMETICS, DNA, AND LIP PRINTS

Laboratories can differentiate between many types of lip cosmetics, and this information can destroy a suspect's alibi that the lipstick on his shirt was deposited there by his girlfriend when it is consistent with the victim's and inconsistent with the girlfriend's.[75] An unidentified victim's lip cosmetics will supply enough material for a DNA profile of him/her about 80% of the time.[76] Lip print comparisons presently lack scientific validity.

FIREARMS

Firearm evidence is commonly encountered and includes single- and double-action revolvers, semi-automatic handguns, rifles, scopes, shotguns, rim- and center-fire ammunition, bullets, shot pellets and slugs, shell cases, gunshot residues, clips and magazines, firing-pin impressions, and extractor and ejector marks. Moreover, there may be blood, tissue, and/or fingerprints on firearm evidence, making it even more important to a case. Investigators must acquire a broad, working knowledge of firearm evidence for three primary reasons: (1) the frequency with which they will encounter it; (2) the value of such knowledge in a combat situation:

A metropolitan police department had just completed transition to the .40 caliber, semiautomatic, 16-shot (15 magazine, plus 1 chambered) Glock Model 22. Two revolver wielding gunmen robbed a bar and ran out the back door, where they were confronted by a patrol officer walking the alley. Several quick shots were fired as all three men scrambled to get behind some type of cover. After several more shots were exchanged, the officer had fired six shots. One of the gunmen yelled "He's out of ammo, Let's get him!" They left their cover and rushed the officer, who dropped both of them.

and (3) your personal safety and that of others—never assume that a firearm is unloaded, no matter who brings or hands it to you; that assumption could get you or someone else killed:

> It was late on the evening watch in a detective division and three investigators were sitting around talking. Two other investigators brought a man in who was not handcuffed and told him to sit down in front of a desk. One of them laid a revolver on the desk and said, "We're charging this guy with murder; watch him 'til we get back." A few minutes later, the suspect stood up, picked up the revolver, and killed himself in front of the three investigators.

LABORATORY DETERMINATIONS

The laboratory examination of firearm evidence may be able to provide answers to a number of important investigative questions.

1. Was This Bullet Fired from This Weapon?

Shotguns are smooth-bore weapons, but pistols and rifles have **rifling.** The **caliber** is the diameter of a bullet, whereas the **bore** (Figure 4-32) is the diameter of the barrel's interior between its opposing high sides, or **lands.** The low sides of the barrel's interior are called **grooves.** When a cartridge is fired, its bullet portion separates from it and passes through the barrel. Because the bullet's caliber is

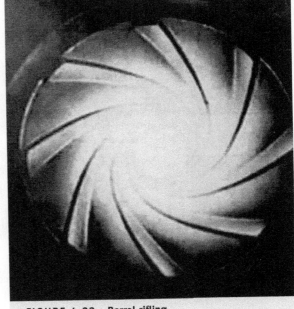

▲**FIGURE 4-33   Barrel rifling**
Cross-section photograph of the barrel of a 9-mm pistol with traditional rifling. Note how the lands and grooves "twist" to the right, spinning the bullet as it is propelled through the barrel of the weapon. Rifling allows the bullet to be much more aerodynamic, improving the accuracy and stability of the bullet in flight. (Courtesy Forensic Training and Consulting, LLC)

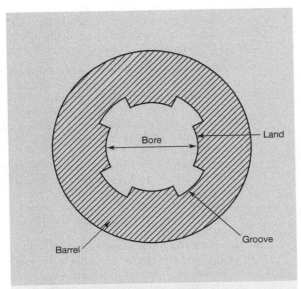

▲**FIGURE 4-32   Rifled barrel**
Important features of a rifled firearm's barrel

somewhat larger than the bore, the rifling grips the bullet, causing it to rotate, usually in a right-hand direction. The rotation increases the range and accuracy of the bullet (Figure 4-33.)

This rotation also creates striations on the bullet. Marks are also left on fired bullets from manufacturer defects and the use of a firearm. The combination of these distinctive scratches creates a "signature" on a bullet as it passes down a rifled barrel. A bullet recovered from a body can be compared to one fired from a suspect's firearm in a laboratory (Figure 4-34). Identification, however, is affected by the condition of the gun and that of the bullet or fragments. Although it is ideal to have the firearm, bullets themselves can yield important data. By matching striations on bullets recovered at different crime scenes, investigators can tie together information from several cases; the combined data may produce new leads and result in the clearance of the case.

In some cases, the striations on a bullet recovered from a decomposed body can be negatively affected by the interaction between the bullet material and the body tissue.[77] Conversely, an older revolver whose cylinders do not properly align may sheer off a portion of the bullet when fired, creating distinctive markings. Other aspects

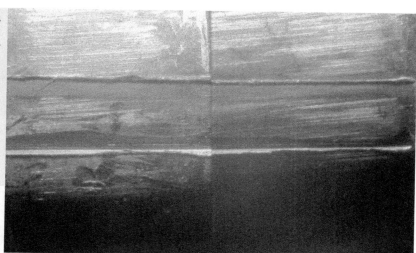

▶**FIGURE 4-34**
Bullet comparison
A drug user murdered his supplier in order to "cancel" his debt and obtain additional drugs. This is a photomicrograph of the bullet recovered from the body (*left*) compared to a bullet fired from the murder gun (*right*) after the revolver was recovered from a river by police divers. (Courtesy Royal Canadian Mounted Police)

of how individual-class firearm evidence is produced are discussed later in this section.

2. What Else Can Be Learned from the Bullet?

A fired bullet yields evidence of the class characteristics of the weapon that fired it with respect to the number of lands and grooves as well as their height, depth, and width. The class characteristics of a firearm are the design specifications to which it was manufactured; weapons of a given make and model will have the same class characteristics. The individual characteristics of the bore are found in the striae along the fired bullet. Examination of a fired bullet will suggest the type of weapon from which it was fired, whether the bullet is a hard-nose or soft-nose projectile, and the pitch and direction of twist within the barrel. Additionally, if the fired bullet is recovered in sufficient size, it may be possible, through weighing and measurement, to determine its caliber. Since bullets are often recovered as fragments, the caliber may only be implied; for instance, the weight may rule out smaller calibers. Although it is possible to determine the caliber of the bullet, some caution must be taken with respect to determining the bore of the weapon from which it was fired, since a smaller-caliber bullet can be fired through a larger-bore weapon.

Fired bullets are ordinarily damaged on impact. In some cases, you can see fabric impressions on the bullet's nose that were made as the bullet passed through the victim's outer garment. Additionally, there may be minute traces of blood, tissue, bone, fabric, or other such materials (Figure 4-35). Great care must be taken by the investigator not to destroy or in any way alter such evidence. When the fired bullet is to be recovered from the victim, the investigator should alert the attending medical personnel, if there is any doubt about their familiarity with proper handling procedure, as to the

irreparable damage that can be wrought by the careless application of forceps or other such instruments in removing the bullet.

Note that it is ordinarily not possible to make a positive identification as to whether pellets were fired from a particular shotgun. However, in extraordinarily rare circumstances involving smooth-bore firearms, it may be possible to make an individual identification on the basis of gross defects in the barrel.[78]

3. What Determinations Can Be Made from Cartridge Cases?

In contrast to a bullet, which is typically acted on only by the barrel, a cartridge case is subject to a number of different forces that make marks on it, any of which can produce individual-class evidence. Such marks include:

1. Striations made on the outside of cartridge case as it is loaded into the chamber in preparation for firing; these striations may be caused by the action of the magazine or by the slide action of the firearm.
2. A firing-pin impression made on the base of the cartridge case, which is created when the weapon is fired (Figure 4-36).
3. Marks are left on the cartridge case as the exploding gases that propel the bullet forward force the casing outward against the chamber wall and backward against the breach face of the weapon (Figure 4-37). The breach face is the mechanism that holds the bullet in the chamber.
4. **Extractor marks** made when the case is pulled out of the chamber and **ejector marks** made when the case is "kicked out," both of which are associated with semiautomatic and automatic weapons.

Markings made on cartridges by self-loading pistols can vary somewhat over a series of discharges. In laboratory

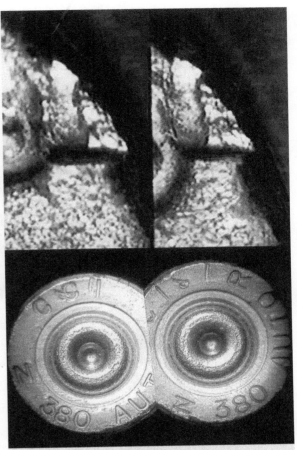

▲ **FIGURE 4-36**   **Firing pin impressions**
(*Top*) Photomicrograph showing comparison of questioned
and known firing-pin impressions of .22-caliber rim-fire
cartridge cases. (*Bottom*) Photomicrograph showing
comparison of questioned and known firing-pin impressions
on .380-caliber center-fire cartridge cases. Note the
significant differences between a rim-fire and a center-fire
cartridge: on the center-fire cartridge, the pin must strike
the center of the primer to ignite the powder; however, on
the rim-fire cartridge, contact may be anywhere around
the face of the cartridge. **(Courtesy Forensic Training and
Consulting, LLC)**

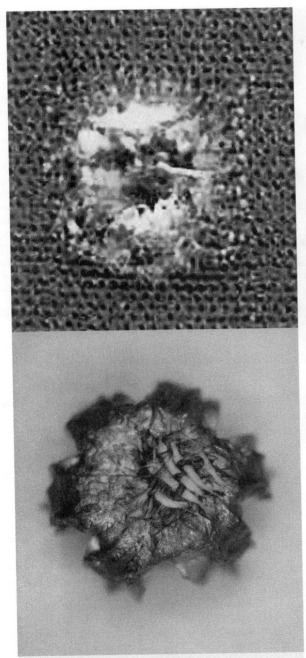

▲ **FIGURE 4-35**   **Fabric traces in spent bullet**
In some cases, the fabric of the garment being worn by the
victim can be found attached to the bullet. In this unique
homicide, the fibers from the sweater of the victim (*top*)
are found inside the flattened "mushroom" of the bullet
(*bottom*) recovered from the body. **(Courtesy Forensic Training
and Consulting, LLC)**

tests, the first and 250th cartridges fired by the same auto-
loader were identifiable as being made by the same
weapon, but some differences in individual characteristics
were observed.[79] Visualization of fingerprints deposited on
cartridge cases before the gun was fired can be problematic
owing to discharge heat and friction, but prints may be
recoverable.[80]

▲ FIGURE 4-37 Breach-face markings
Photomicrograph of the breach-face markings on two Speer 9-mm cartridge cases that were recovered at different locations at the scene of a murder. The victim was scheduled to testify in the trial of a drug dealer the next day. The murder is unsolved and under active investigation. (Courtesy Tennessee Bureau of Investigation)

What Miscellaneous Determinations Can Be Made by Examination of Firearms Evidence?

If a firearm is received at a crime laboratory several determinations beyond those mentioned may be possible. Does the weapon function properly, including safety features? Has it been modified to discharge in a manner other than designed, for example, for automatic fire? What was the shot trajectory? If the trigger pull on a weapon is of the "hair" nature, requiring only the slightest pressure to pull it, this would indicate that an accidental shooting was possible. Laboratory examination might reveal that a firearm is constructed—or malfunctioning—in such a way that it could discharge if dropped on its hammer, thereby giving more credibility to a claim that a shooting was accidental. Furthermore, even though invisible to the naked eye, obliterated serial numbers can sometimes be restored

by the laboratory, thus providing an additional investigative lead.

COLLECTING FIREARM EVIDENCE

A cardinal rule in handling weapons at the scene of a crime is that they should never be picked up or moved until they have been photographed and measurements have been made for the crime scene sketch. As in the case of many rules for criminal investigations and as discussed in an earlier chapter, there are several exceptions: (1) if rapidly deteriorating weather conditions, for instance, a driving rain/sleet/snow storm or quickly rising water, threaten the potential to recover fingerprint or DNA evidence from a firearm located outside, move it to a sheltered area; (2) at the scenes of aggravated assaults and murders, feelings run high, and there is a danger that an emotionally charged person may suddenly attempt to pick up a weapon and shoot another party; or (3) there may be some compelling safety need, such as un-cocking a weapon that is in potential danger of falling and discharging.

Following documentation, the process of collecting firearms evidence includes:

1. noting the position of the hammer and the slide, and safety, if applicable;
2. recording the description of rounds and empty chambers in a revolver (Figure 4-37);
3. removing cartridges from a revolver and packaging them individually;
4. noting for semi-automatic/automatic weapons whether there is a misfeed/jam, a chambered cartridge, an inserted magazine, and the number and description of each round in the magazine in their exact sequence;
5. removing any chambered round in a semi-automatic or automatic weapon and releasing the magazine—do not remove any cartridges from the magazine;
6. recording the serial number, not to be confused with patent or model numbers—to avoid manual transcription errors, some law-enforcement agencies and laboratories recommend dusting and lifting the serial number;
7. allowing any fresh blood on a weapon to naturally air dry;
8. placing metal objects recovered from water into a container filled with water from the same source.

In no case should a pencil or similar object be placed into the barrel of the gun to pick it up; this can dislodge evidence that may be in the barrel, such as tissue, blood, hair, or other trace evidence, and it can contaminate the barrel, thereby confusing the laboratory examiner.

To enhance the recovery of blood, tissue, and fingerprints, firearms evidence should be handled as little as possible consistent with the need to process it and "safe" the firearm. A victim is often the donor of blood and tissue on a firearm. Although a victim may grab a gun barrel and leave fingerprints, the more usual case is any fingerprints developed on a weapon or other firearms evidence are from the shooter, unless the victim's own gun has been used against him/her.

"Touch DNA" is a relatively new iteration in DNA analysis that involves skin cells rather than body fluids. When an assailant touches a weapon or rips the clothing from a rape victim, he/she may deposit some of his/her own outermost skin cells, which can establish individual identity. Requests for touch DNA examinations became so routine that some laboratories adopted a policy to conduct them only after all significant leads have been exhausted. Whether done in the field or the laboratory, the systematic swabbing of firearms evidence may produce blood, tissue, or touch DNA. Among the areas to which particular attention should be directed are serrated triggers, hammers, pistol grips, magazines, and safety mechanisms.

In rare situations it may not be possible to "safe" a firearm because of mechanical failure or damage, and in this case the laboratory should be contacted for guidance. The lab may recommend transporting the malfunctioning/damaged gun loaded, which is otherwise not done. Lacking such guidance, one can check with other resources, such as the local ATF office or a military installation.

MARKING AND PACKAGING FIREARM EVIDENCE

The FBI and many state crime laboratories do not recommend marking directly on firearms evidence. A gun should be tagged and placed in an approved firearms box. To secure the gun, place a strap over the barrel and another at the base of the hammer. Straps should never be placed inside the trigger guard. Magazines are another type of firearms evidence that is tagged. Smaller items—for example, cartridges and bullet fragments—should be placed separately in paper envelopes, sealed, and then put into a rigid container. Plastic wrapping or bags are not used with firearms evidence. If there is dried blood on any firearms evidence, a "Biological Hazard" sticker should be placed on the outside of the container.

TOOL MARKS

Tool mark evidence is commonly, but not exclusively, seen in burglaries at the point where a suspect attempted or achieved a forced entry. Figure 4-38 shows a case in which a pry bar was used as a murder weapon. In a rare case, a clod of soil at a gravesite had substantial details left by the digging tool. Later, when a suspect was identified, a mattock was found in the trunk of his car that

examiners concluded was used to dig the grave.[81] A mattock has a wooden handle of roughly 36–42 inches and a metal head, one end of which is a pointed "spike" and the other end looks like a hoe.

A **tool mark** is any impression, cut, gouge, or abrasion made when a tool comes into contact with another object.[82] When a tool and a softer surface come into contact with each other, the softer surface yields (Figure 4-39). The tool may create an impression in the softer surface, produce striations on it, holes through it, or cut/shear the item. Tools often leave microscopic markings that can be class or individual class characteristic evidence[83] (Figure 4-40). Additionally, contaminants on the tool and/or the surface affected may be transferred. Tools may simply require "elbow grease" to use or have a designed action, such as scissors or a bolt cutter. Tool mark examination includes locks and keys, for example, in an attempt made to open a lock with an unauthorized implement.

Tool mark examinations are conducted to:

1. identify the type of tool that made the mark or impression;
2. establish the action used to operate the tool;
3. specify the size and other characteristics of the tool;
4. identify unusual features—for example, a broken tip on a screwdriver;
5. establish whether two portions of a tool were ever commonly joined (Figure 4-41);
6. establish whether the evidence is suitable for comparison purposes;
7. determine whether "this" tool could have made "that" impression or mark. Alternatively, the examiner might report that the evidence is inconclusive or exclude the tool as a source for making an impression or mark.

In collecting evidence of tool marks, make every effort to obtain and submit the actual area for direct comparison. When this is not possible, a cast should be made. There are several good choices for casting tool marks, including Mikrosil. Tool marks should be photographed to establish their locations; however, the images have no forensic identification value. In no event should the investigator place a tool against a tool mark for size evaluation; doing so could lead to accidental cross contamination or result in the accidental destruction of evidence. When a tool is to be submitted to the crime laboratory for examination, the actual tool should be submitted; the making of test impressions or cuts is a function of qualified technicians in the laboratory. The importance of this last point is illustrated by the fact that under test conditions in the laboratory examiners found that when there was more than a 15-degree difference between the vertical angle at which a screwdriver was actually used and the comparison mark made in the laboratory, an improper finding of no identity from the same tool could result.[84]

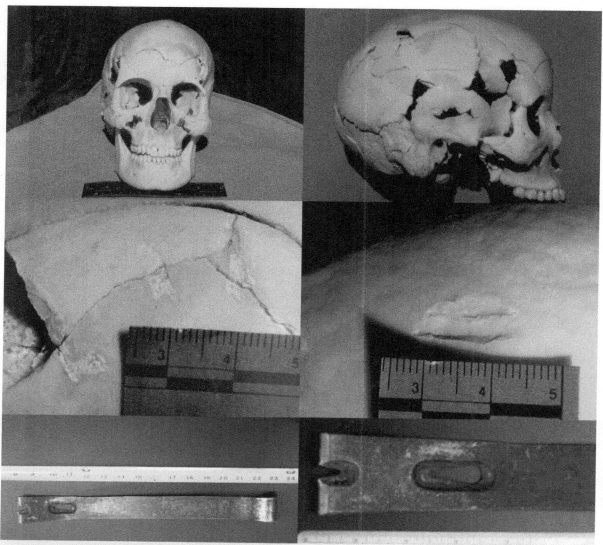

▲ FIGURE 4-38   Tool marks on human skull

A murder case in Arizona represents a unique tool match with wounds to the skull of the victim. The severely fractured skull and body of a young female victim were found in a freezer, presumably left there by the killer some two years before. Several tools were also found in the suspect's garage. By reconstructing the skull and carefully noting the unique types of wounds and marks, investigators determined that a pry bar was the murder weapon. Confirming the tool mark comparison and match were microscopic pieces of bone found on the prongs of the bar. (Courtesy Forensic Training and Consulting, LLC)

QUESTIONED DOCUMENTS

Loosely defined, a **document** is anything on which a mark, symbol, or writing is made for the purpose of transmitting a meaning. The mark, symbol, or writing may or may not be visible to the naked eye and may appear on surfaces other than paper. A disputed or **questioned docu-**ment is one whose origin or authenticity is in doubt.[85] The typical questioned document submission involves the comparison of a questioned document with a known sample[86]—for example, was this suicide note written by the deceased?

White-collar crimes generate most requests for handwriting examinations.[87] These tests typically involve checks,

▲**FIGURE 4-39   Screwdriver marks**
The photomicrograph on the left depicts microscopic striae on the head of a woodscrew left by a burglar attacking a door. The right side is a known or test impression made by the laboratory examiner using the screwdriver seized in the suspect's custody. Note that black-and-white photography is often used to highlight the striae.

credit cards, and other financial and legal documents (Figure 4-42). Although in a lesser volume, handwritten documents, such as schedules, plans, checklists, and bank robbery and ransom notes, may be part of the execution of violent crimes.

Document examiners analyze non-handwritten evidence as well, including writing instruments, inks, paper, and rubber stamps. Mechanical means of printing and the writings they produce are also within the purview of document examiners—for example, check writers, scanners, facsimile machines, photocopiers, computer printers, and, less frequently, typewriters.[88] Some mechanical means of printing are central to counterfeiting items such as receipts, driver's licenses, ski lift and sporting event tickets, academic transcripts and degrees, social security cards, and passports.

HANDWRITING SAMPLES AND EXAMINATIONS

Handwriting samples may be requested or nonrequested. Some state/regional laboratories provide booklets for collecting requested samples of signatures and extended writings. If such a tool is not available, there are some basic guidelines:

1. For requested samples, if only a signature is being sought, 15 to 20 should be collected from an individual, one to a page. If there is an extended questioned sample, for example, an extortion demand or death threat, the investigator should dictate the contents, obtaining at least five repetitions. No instructions as to format or other aspects of writing should be given—for instance, assistance with spelling words or punctuation—except if the questioned sample is printed or handwritten, the known sample should also be. The questioned samples are never shown to the person providing the known samples. As each page is completed, have the subject initial it; separate from those initials the investigator should

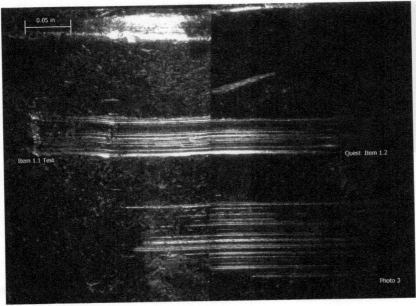

◄**FIGURE 4-40**
Comparison of plier marks
After breaking in, a suspect used pliers to dismantle cooper tubing to sell for scrap metal. This image compares marks found on the copper tubing at the scene with test marks made in the laboratory with pliers found in the suspect's possession.
(Courtesy Wyoming State Crime Laboratory)

▶ **FIGURE 4-41**
Fracture-match tool
While trying to pry open a window during an attempted burglary-rape, the suspect broke the kitchen knife he was using as a tool, leaving the end of the knife embedded in the window sill. The suspect was later found walking in a nearby park with the broken knife and handle in his pocket. A fracture match of the knife tip was made with the remainder of the knife handle. (Courtesy Albuquerque Police Department)

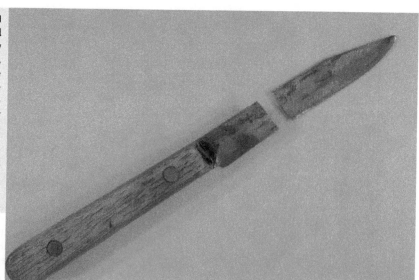

▶ **FIGURE 4-42**
A counterfeit marriage license
Note the differences between the "M" in "Robert M. Webster" and the "M" in "May," "March," and "Minister." Also, note the differences between the "3" and "4" in Webster's age and the same numbers elsewhere in the document. The differences in the type fonts as well as the gaps in the lines under the changed letters, left by whiting out the original entry, indicate a counterfeit document. (Courtesy Immigration and Naturalization Service, Forensic Document Laboratory)

Certified Copy of Record of Marriage

License No. __93-471__
Date issued __May 23, 1993__
Date filed __May 13, 1993__

I, CLARA HARTLEY WOODARD, County Clerk hereby certify that:
Mr. __Robert M. Webster__
of __110 Pine Street__ in the County of __Dade__
and State of __Florida__ of the age of __34__ years, and
Miss __Elizabeth Thomas__
of __201 Willow Lane__ in the County of __Dade__
and State of __Florida__ of the age of __22__ years
were united in Marriage
on the __3rd__ day of __March__ A.D. __1993__
in said County, at __Dade County Baptist Church__
by __Stevenson Edwards__ a __Minister__

Witnesses:
__Sandra Williams__
__Louis Hobbs__

I do hereby certify that the foregoing is a true and correct copy of the License and Certificate of Marriage as the same appears of record in my office.
IN TESTIMONY WHEREOF, I have set my hand and affixed my Official Seal, this __23rd__ day of __May__ A.D. 19 __93__.
__Clara Hartley Woodard__
COUNTY CLERK
By __Marian E. Ayers__ Deputy

SEAL

add his/her own initials, identifying number, and the date and time, and he/she should number the pages sequentially as they are completed.

2. Collect requested writings with the same class/type of writing instrument as was used in the questioned samples. If this is not known, use a black ballpoint pen. If the questioned is on lined paper, paper of the same size should be used to collect the known. As each signature or extended writing is completed it should be removed from the person's sight.

3. Nonrequested samples should be collected from existing documents created/signed closest to the time the questioned document was executed, because handwriting evolves over time. Among the sources for nonrequested samples are signatures on Miranda warnings; suspects' statement; notes to jailers; credit, employment, employment, insurance, and mortgage

applications; messages written on greeting cards given to others; and workers' compensation claims.

Nonrequested writings were not executed with the thought they would be scrutinized and therefore ordinarily are not disguised in any way. Disguised handwriting is problematic for document examiners, and it attracts more misleading and inconclusive rates of authorship opinions; one study concluded that the error rate for examiners in labeling a writing genuine or disguised was 4.3%.[89] A difficulty with nonrequested samples is locating sufficient high-quality signatures and extended writing material from the same time frame as the questioned samples.

Document examination is partially automated, using software such as CedarFox. Its capabilities include comparison of samples and searching handwriting databases to find potential matches, both of which must be confirmed by the examiner.[90]

LABORATORY DETERMINATIONS

In addition to the possibility of determining whether handwriting can be attributed to a particular person, laboratories *may* be able to:

1. Determine whether a document is authentic or counterfeit. In 1983, 62 volumes of diaries attributed to Adolph Hitler were purchased by a German publisher. Three handwriting experts concluded Hitler wrote them, although others disagreed. However, forensic analysis established the method used to produce the paper on which the diaries were written was not available until 1954, and the ink used was first manufactured in 1982.
2. Recover indented writing; if not visible to the eye, indented writings may be located by an electrostatic detection apparatus (ESDA).
3. Identify the class/type of the writing instrument, such as a ballpoint, felt-tip pen, or pencil.
4. Determine whether the inks of known and questioned samples have consistent characteristics—the Secret Service and the Internal Revenue Service maintain the International Ink Library with more than 9,500 samples.
5. Decipher charred, burned, or water-soaked documents.
6. Match the ends of cut/torn paper. A man handed a bank teller a note, "This is a robbery." He left

with money, but she retained the note. A week later, police executed a search warrant at the suspect's home, finding "This is a robbery" in indented writing on a pad. A portion of paper remaining in the pad also matched one end of the robbery note.[91]
7. Establish the source of paper through watermarks and other features.
8. Detect erasures, obliterations, and alterations to documents.
9. Determine whether one or more pages in a document were added subsequently to its original production.
10. Establish the relative age of a document.
11. Determine whether an office machine—for example, scanner, photocopier, typewriter, fax machine, or computer printer—is associated with a particular document. Often, the machine must have a defect or some unusual attribute to be distinguishable. However, there is substantial interest in developing "signatures" for scanners, printers, and digital cameras. One line of inquiry is looking at their intrinsic features to identify unique attributes; the alternative method is to embed microscopic codes, such as a serial number, on each page of output.

COLLECTING AND PACKAGING EVIDENCE

In many respects, all evidence collection is like the first rule of physicians: do no harm. Investigators should not attempt to reassemble torn or shredded documents; write on, trace, highlight, or underline portions of them; or make repairs to or fold them. Documents should be collected and processed using the following guidelines:

1. Wear gloves and use clean tweezers to handle documents.
2. Handle the documents as little as possible.
3. Use a transparent envelope if possible; otherwise, use a manila paper one.
4. Before placing the document in the envelope, fill out all required blocks of information on it and then slip it in the evidence and seal it.
5. Processing for latent prints and DNA is a laboratory responsibility.
6. Keep documents in a cool, low-humidity environment, out of the sunlight, until submitted to the lab.

KEY TERMS

bore	dental stone	fluorescent powder
caliber	document	forensic light source
concentric fracture	ejector mark	forensic odontology
class characteristics	extractor mark	fracture match
CrimeShoe	fingerprint	grooves
cross contamination	fingerprint patterns	Hemident

Hexagon OBTI
impressions
individual characteristics
known source
lands
latent prints
latent/invisible prints
Luminol
minutiae

MtDNA
Paint Data Query
patent/contaminated/visible prints
plastic print
postmortem (after-death) dental
    profiling
questioned document
radial fracture
residue prints

rifling
SoleMate
Super Glue fuming
tool mark
Touch DNA
traditional powders
TreadMate
unknown (questioned) sources

REVIEW QUESTIONS

1. What are class and individual characteristics?
2. How are known and questioned sources different?
3. What procedures would you follow to take soil samples?
4. How do you cast a shoe impression using dental stone?
5. What is the proper way to collect loose paint chips at a crime scene?
6. Radial and concentric fractures are different in what way?
7. What are minutiae?
8. How are plastic prints formed?
9. You are assigned to dust for latent fingerprints on a white refrigerator door using a traditional powder. How should you do this?
10. Forensic odontology can be an asset in what five circumstances?
11. What conclusions are possible from the examination of hair?
12. What is Touch DNA?
13. How would you attempt to locate "hidden blood" at a crime scene?
14. A revolver is found near a body at an indoor crime scene. What procedures should be followed for processing the revolver?
15. How do you collect a tool impression in a door-frame where a prying-type action was used to gain entry in a burglary?
16. What is a questioned document?

INTERNET ACTIVITIES

The FBI and other federal agencies have been working for more than 20 years to advance forensic standards and techniques. One mechanism to achieve these goals has been the creation of scientific working groups (SWGs) and technical working groups (TWGs). Alto-gether, there are perhaps 15 SWGs and TWGs, whose membership include both federal and state/local law-enforcement agencies that have produced important publications. Visit SWGs and TWGs at *www2.fbi.gov/hq/lab/html/swg.htm.*

◄ Officers interview suspects arrested for possession of cocaine outside a house where a search warrant has been served. Interview questions focus on suspects' knowledge of the drug-related activities occurring inside the house.

(© A. Ramey/PhotoEdit)

5

INTERVIEWING AND INTERROGATION

CHAPTER OBJECTIVES

1. Explain the similarities and differences between interviews and interrogations.

2. Discuss the objectives of interviewing and interrogations as well as the qualifications of interviewers and interrogators.

3. Understand the importance of selecting the right place and time for conducting an interview or interrogation.

4. Explain how an investigator should prepare for conducting an interview or interrogation.

5. Understand the importance of witnesses' motivations, perceptions, and barriers.

6. Assess the reliability of eyewitness identification.

7. Discuss witness intimidation and what can be done to effectively deal with it.

8. Explain the psychological dynamics that cause some people to confess.

9. Identify the principal reasons why false confessions occur.

10. Understand the limitations related to the use of admissions and confessions at trial.

11. Explain the impact of *Miranda* v. *Arizona* and other past and current landmark U.S. Supreme Court cases on law-enforcement interrogation.

12. Discuss the best indicators of detecting deception or truthfulness.

In every criminal investigation process, interviewing and interrogation are among the most important means of obtaining needed information about a crime. Both require a combination of artistry and skill that must be cultivated and practiced. However, not all people who possess information needed by the investigator are willing to share it. This is true in both interviews and interrogations. Witnesses may have various motivations and perceptions that can influence their responses during an interview. Their motivations and perceptions may be based on either conscious choices or subconscious stimuli. In addition, gaining information from specific demographic groups such as the elderly, those who do not speak English, or persons with physical infirmities requires unique skills on the part of the investigator. Situational characteristics such as the time and place of the interview or interrogation may also create challenges to eliciting information about a particular case. Each of these conditions must be effectively addressed in both interview and interrogation settings. The successful interviewer or interrogator must fully understand the techniques of interviewing and interrogation and be able to evaluate the psychological reasons why people are willing or reluctant to impart information. In this chapter we also examine many other important elements in the interviewing and interrogation process, including witness protection, false confessions, and the most recent U.S. Supreme Court rulings regarding the admissibility of confessions and the most effective methods for **detection of deception.**

INTERVIEWS AND INTERROGATIONS: SIMILARITIES AND DIFFERENCES

The success of an interview or interrogation depends on a number of personal characteristics and commitments of the investigator. Planning for and controlling the events surrounding both interviews and interrogations are important but are generally viewed as more critical to the success of an interrogation. Establishing **rapport,** asking good questions, listening carefully, and keeping proper documentation are elements common to both forms of obtaining information. Table 5-1 illustrates the similarities between interviews and interrogations.

TABLE 5-1	Similarities between Interviews and Interrogations
INTERVIEWS	**INTERROGATIONS**
Planning important	Planning critical
Controlling surroundings important	Controlling surroundings critical
Privacy or semiprivacy desirable	Absolute privacy essential
Establishing rapport important	Establishing rapport important
Asking good questions important	Asking good questions important
Careful listening	Careful listening
Proper documentation	Proper documentation

Besides the difference in purpose between interviewing and interrogation, many other distinctions exist. Of paramount importance are the myriad legal requirements that pertain to interrogations but are absent in interviews. Because of the criticality of confessions and their use in obtaining convictions, it is not surprising that numerous legal guidelines and standards apply in interrogations that would not be needed in interviewing witnesses or victims; these are all discussed in greater detail later in this chapter. Also, it is far more likely that a hostile and adversarial relationship will exist between an interrogator and a **suspect** than between an interviewer and a **victim** or **witness**. The differences between interviews and interrogations are noted in Table 5-2.

OBJECTIVES OF INTERVIEWING

Interviews are conducted in criminal cases for the purpose of gathering information from people who have, or may have, knowledge needed in the investigation. The information may come from a victim or from a person who has no other relationship to the criminal activity other than being where he or she was. But interviewing is not a haphazard process consisting of a list of questions. It is a planned conversation with a specific goal.

The job of the investigator-interviewer is to elicit from the witness information actually perceived through one or more of the witness's five senses—sight, hearing, smell, taste, and touch. In any given case, any or all of a witness's senses may be involved. For example, in a case involving a drug-related killing, a witness may see the perpetrator pull the trigger, hear the victim scream, smell the pungent odor of marijuana burning, taste the white

TABLE 5-2	Differences between Interviews and Interrogations
INTERVIEWS	INTERROGATIONS
Purpose is to obtain information	Purpose is to test information already obtained
Minimal or no preinterview legal requirements; no rights warning	Extensive preinterrogation legal requirements; rights warning required
Cooperative relationship between interviewer and subject likely	Adversarial or hostile relationship between interrogator and subject likely
No guilt or guilt uncertain	Guilt suggested or likely
Moderate planning or preparation	Extensive planning and preparation
Private or semiprivate environment desirable	Absolute privacy essential

Source: John Fay, unpublished notebook, American Society for Industrial Security, Workshop in Criminal Interrogation (Jacksonville, FL: ASIS, 1991), p. A1-1.

powdery substance later identified as heroin, and touch the victim to feel for a pulse.

Because, as earlier suggested, witnesses report perceptions based on their own interests, priorities, and biases, obtaining accurate and sometimes even voluntary information is not as easy to obtain as it may first appear. Investigators must always be sensitive to any of the psychological, physical and environmental influences as well as the motivations affecting witness perceptions.

At the outset of the interview, the person to be interviewed must satisfy three requirements of being a witness: presence, consciousness, and attentiveness to what was happening.[1] Presence and consciousness are relatively easy to establish in the interview process; attentiveness is more difficult. Yet all three elements are important to establishing the accuracy of a witness's perception.

OBJECTIVES OF INTERROGATION

Interrogation as opposed to interviewing is designed to match acquired information to a particular suspect in order to secure a **confession.** Whereas interviewing is primarily for the purpose of gaining information, interrogation is the process of testing that information and its application to a particular suspect.

There are four commonly recognized objectives in the interrogation process:

1. to obtain valuable facts;
2. to eliminate the innocent;
3. to identify the guilty;
4. to obtain a confession.

As the investigator moves from the preliminary task of gathering valuable facts to the concluding task of obtaining a confession, the difficulty of acquiring information increases. That difficulty, however, is rewarded by an increase in the value of the information. Figure 5-1 illustrates these relationships. In attempting to obtain a confession from a suspect, the interrogator also gains information about the facts and circumstances surrounding the commission of an offense. In seeking such information, the investigator must be concerned with asking the basic questions that apply to all aspects of the investigative process: Who? What? Where? When? How? and Why?

QUALIFICATIONS OF INTERVIEWS AND INTERROGATORS

The effective interviewer or interrogator must be knowledgeable in the art and science of criminal investigation and know how to use psychology, salesmanship, and dra-

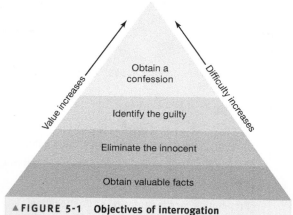

▲ **FIGURE 5-1   Objectives of interrogation**
(John Fay, unpublished notebook, American Society for Industrial Security, Workshop in Criminal Interrogation [Jacksonville, FL: ASIS, 1981], p. A2-1)

matics. Persuasiveness and perseverance are also essential to success. The interviewer or interrogator must make himself/herself easy to talk to. By the appropriate use of vocal inflection, modulation, and emphasis, even the Miranda warnings (discussed later in this chapter) can be presented to a suspect in a manner that does not cause the suspect to immediately assume a defensive posture. The words can be spoken without creating an adversarial atmosphere. The interviewer or interrogator must have a flexible personality and must be able to convey empathy, sympathy, anger, fear, and joy at appropriate times, but must always remain objective. The interviewer or interrogator must keep an open mind and be receptive to all information, regardless of its nature.

A positive, firm approach, an ability to inspire confidence, and knowledge of a broad range of topics of general interest all help establish dominance or control in an interview: Behavior—not words—that shows confidence, determines dominance.[2]

During an interrogation, the investigator must carefully evaluate each development while studiously avoiding the pitfall of underestimating the capabilities of the subject being interrogated. Screaming or shouting, belittling the subject or the information, sneering, and other such unplanned and uncontrolled reactions most often adversely affect the interrogation. The investigator must at all times maintain control of the interrogation without being openly domineering, by being a good active listener, by being serious, patient, and, most important, by being persistent and persuasive.[3] An ability to categorize the psychological and emotional traits being manifested by the suspect helps the investigator react in a manner that increases the possibility of conducting a successful interrogation, for it is the job of the interrogator to make it easy for a suspect to confess.

TIME, PLACE, AND SETTING OF INTERVIEWING AND INTERROGATION

Law-enforcement officers conduct interviews in a number of situations. The most common is the on-the-scene interview. Whether it is a routine traffic accident investigation or a major felony case, officers who respond to the scene should, at the earliest possible moment, seek out and identify individuals who may have knowledge of the event and whose information may contribute to the investigation. Such individuals, of course, include victims and other participants as well as uninvolved witnesses. Once witnesses have been identified, they should be separated from one another and, as much as possible, isolated from other people who may be loitering in the area (Figure 5-2). This prevents the witnesses from seeing or hearing irrelevant matters that may taint their actual knowledge. All witnesses should be interviewed as soon as practical, while their memory is still fresh, but this rule must be applied with discretion to take into account all circumstances.

▲ **FIGURE 5-2   Police interview witnesses separately**
A domestic violence complaint called to 911 by a neighbor who heard these people screaming at each other and what sounded like heavy objects being thrown around, hitting walls and the floor, brought these officers to the scene. It turned out to be an argument, but neither party committed a domestic assault or battery. (© Bob Daemmrich/The Image Works)

Although convenience of the witness is important to a successful interview, the interviewer need not relinquish the psychological advantage in selecting the time and place of the interview. It is not a good practice, for example, to rouse a witness from bed in the middle of the night. However, there are certain psychological advantages to questioning a witness at a law-enforcement agency rather than in the witness's own home or office. A witness may feel in a better position to control the interview in familiar surroundings. The investigator cannot let this happen; he or she must be fair but always be in command of the situation.

After taking into account the factors of immediacy, privacy, convenience, and control, and weighing the importance of each in the context of the total circumstances, the investigator may decide to interview witnesses at their homes or places of business. As a matter of courtesy, the investigator should attempt to make an appointment to ensure convenience, particularly for professional and businesspeople. Others, such as salespeople, office workers, and laborers, may be interviewed during working hours with approval of their supervisors.

Privacy is of the utmost importance in conducting interviews (Figure 5-3). Distractions tend to have an adverse effect on the interview and its results. The interviewer should insist on as much privacy as possible, but the circumstances of on-the-scene interviews often have to be recognized as a fact of life for the investigator, who can be expected to perform only to the best of his/her ability in the given case. Similarly, investigators are often called on to canvass neighborhoods and interview residents. In these instances, investigators often are in no position to influence the conditions under which the interview takes place. Noisy children, blaring television sets, nosy neighbors, and similar factors must be accepted.

The physical and emotional states of the witnesses are important when one is conducting or determining whether to conduct an interview. Cold, sleepy, hungry, physically uncomfortable, or intoxicated people generally prove to be unsatisfactory witnesses.[4] Similarly, persons suffering noticeable emotional problems can give, at best, highly questionable information. Most investigators can recognize this state and wisely choose to wait until the witness becomes lucid before conducting the interview.

Reinterviewing witnesses should be avoided if the reinterview is likely to produce nothing beyond the information given in the initial statement. Reinterviewing tends to become less and less convenient for witnesses, even though they may be friendly and cooperative. There may also be a tendency for reinterviewed witnesses to feel that the investigator does not know his/her job or was not prepared during the initial interview. To avoid this problem, the investigator should first tell the witness that the purpose of the interview is not to rehash old information and should then explain what new

▶ **FIGURE 5-3**
Interviewing a witness
This woman saw a purse-snatching incident occur on a main street in this city about an hour before this photo was taken. She is with one of the investigating officers explaining what she witnessed, describing the man who grabbed the other woman's purse and ran, and giving a statement. (© Mike Karlsson/Arresting Images)

information is being sought. The investigator should ask for the information in a manner that does not elicit a repetition of the previous interview. But investigators should not hesitate to conduct follow-up interviews when necessary, whether there was lack of skill in obtaining an initial statement, new information has developed, or the time or setting of the initial interview did not elicit the full attention of the witness.

Unlike the interview, which may take place in any number of different locations and at various times—which may or may not be advantageous to the investigator—interrogation is a process controlled by the interrogator. The interrogator is in command of the setting and governs the number and kinds of interruptions. The most critical factor in controlling the interrogation is to ensure privacy and to guarantee that any distractions, planned or otherwise, are controlled by the interrogator. Privacy may be used as a psychological tool; the suspect may feel more willing to unload his/her burden of guilt in front of only one person.

THE INTERROGATION ROOM

The traditional interrogation room should be sparsely furnished, usually with only two chairs. There should be no physical barriers, such as tables or desks, between the investigator and the suspect. From the officer's standpoint, such barriers may create an unwanted feeling of psychological well-being on the part of the suspect.

If there is a table or desk in the room, the chairs should be corner to corner rather than on opposite sides. This arrangement permits the interrogator to move both chairs away from the table and eliminate the barrier (Figure 5-4).[5]

Proximity in an interrogation can also be important. The suspect and the interrogator should be close enough to touch without being too close, without having any object such as a chair or desk between them. "It seems, for example, that around 27 inches is the limit of proximity for white American middle-class males . . . If you move closer, people become uncomfortable . . . farther

▲ **FIGURE 5-4**   **Interrogation room**
Note that the table and chairs can be easily moved so the table does not separate the interrogator from the suspect.
(© Mike Karlsson/Arresting Images)

away than 27 inches, you can't read a person's face well."[6] There are, however, considerable differences in the comfort zones of various ethnic groups, and interrogators must make it a point to know as much as possible about the unique psychological and cultural characteristics of the individuals they are most likely to encounter both in interviews as well as interrogations.

The two-way mirror, although still a useful tool for allowing others to observe the interrogation, is widely known and may cause some subjects to refuse to cooperate in the interrogation. If a two-way mirror is to be used, it should be small and unobtrusive. As a standard practice, the interrogation room should be equipped with a video or audio system that includes a recording device, unless prohibited by state law. (The use of electronic recording in interrogation is discussed later in this chapter.)

Although the traditional interrogation room just described is designed to ensure control and domination over the interrogation because of its privacy, security, and aura of authority, this approach does not impress the habitual or experienced offender, who understands the rules and standards of conduct of the classical interrogation room. If the offender is skilled and intelligent, he/she not only can cope with the psychological influences such a setting is designed to foster but perhaps also can become the dominant force, or at least be on the same psychological level as the interrogator. When this occurs, the skills of the interrogator become even more important.

PREPARATION FOR THE INTERVIEW OR INTERROGATION

The success of the interviewer or interrogator and of the interview or interrogation is often determined by the time and dedication committed to preparing for the conversation. The interviewer must become familiar with the facts of the case under investigation and with the victim. To carry out the four objectives listed earlier, the interrogator must learn as much as possible about the offense, the victim(s), and the suspect through the process of collecting, assessing, and analyzing data and theorizing about the motivations and thought processes of the suspect. This begins the formulation of a profile that will then dictate the initial approach the interrogator will take on first contacting the suspect.

THE WITNESS

If the interview is to be conducted with a witness other than the victim, the interviewer should find out as much about the witness as possible before the interview. This includes learning about the witness's motivations and

perceptions and any barriers that might exist. In some cases it might be advantageous to determine if a witness has a previous criminal record.

THE OFFENSE

It is necessary that the interviewer know specifically what crime or crimes were allegedly committed. This knowledge includes a working familiarity with the elements of each offense and some understanding of the kind of information necessary to prove each. Accurate information on the date, time, place, and method of the crime—including tools used, points of entry and exit, method of travel to and from the scene, complete description of any property involved, weapons used, modus operandi, and physical evidence recovered—is essential. The interviewer should also obtain a full description of the crime scene and the surrounding area. In addition, any and all possible motives should be identified.

THE VICTIM

The interviewer should learn as much as possible about the victim's background, the nature of the injury or loss, attitudes toward the investigation, and any other useful information, such as the existence of insurance in a property crime case. If the victim is an organization or a business, a determination of any practices that would make the organization a criminal target could be extremely valuable. If relevant, the interviewer should determine whether the business is insured against losses.

THE SUSPECT

The interrogator must evaluate the circumstances surrounding the conduct of the interrogation and must begin to evaluate the suspect. An effective interrogator understands that a successful interrogation cannot be organized and compartmentalized into a neat, orderly, step-by-step package. Rather, it is a combination of personality, behavior, and interpersonal communication skills between the interrogator and suspect. It is made up of verbal processes and the way they are communicated, nonverbal actions including **body language,** and personality characteristics that together might be characterized as a psychological fingerprint.[7] Only by understanding the interaction of all these variables can the interrogator effectively evaluate the interrogation process as it will be initiated and as it will be modified during the interrogation.[8] To begin the preparation, the interrogator should review the offense report, statement of witnesses, laboratory reports, all file information pertaining to the suspect, and other related data. It is also essential that the interrogator know all the elements of the offense involved. Failure to possess this information may preclude obtaining a complete confession, which, by definition, must contain **admissions** by the suspect to the commission of each and every element of the crime.

▲ FIGURE 5-5

Investigator preparing for interview/interrogation

This investigator is reviewing her notes one last time to insure she has all available information on and statements of witnesses, information and statements of the victim, lab reports, investigative materials, a knowledge of the elements of the offense, and as much information as is available about the probable suspect before beginning her interviews or interrogation. (© Spencer Grant/PhotoEdit)

WITNESSES: MOTIVATIONS, PERCEPTIONS, AND BARRIERS

There are many types of witnesses, and each has different motivations and perceptions that influence his/her responses during an interview. The motivations and perceptions may be based on either conscious choices or subconscious stimuli. The interviewer must learn to recognize, overcome, and compensate for these factors.

There is no way to categorize all personalities, attitudes, and other character traits. The variables are too numerous and individualized; the combinations are as complex as the human mind. Nevertheless, there are some basic groupings that can be mentioned:

- Some witnesses may be honest and cooperative and desire to impart information in their possession to the investigator. Despite these admirable qualities, however, the information may still be affected by other factors that influence all witnesses, such as age, physical characteristics, and emotions. It may be wise in most circumstances to interview this type of witness first to obtain basic information that can then be compared with later-acquired stories.

- Some witnesses may desire not to give any information in an interview regardless of what they know. Some may simply not want to get involved, while others may fear any contact with a law-enforcement agency, especially if they have had some earlier negative experiences with law enforcement. This is especially true of immigrants who have come from developing countries in which the police may have been corrupt. Others may not understand the significance of information they have, and some may not want to do anything that would aid law enforcement.

- Some witnesses may be reluctant to cooperate or be suspicious of the motives of the interviewer until a rapport is established and the investigator can assure the witness of his or her good intentions.

Because some witnesses may be deceitful and provide incorrect information, it is a basic principle that an investigator should never take a witness's explanation totally at face value but should obtain supporting information or evidence.

There may be other barriers that must be overcome in order to successfully interview someone who has knowledge of the circumstances under which a crime was committed. Language barriers, which may not initially be recognized as significant, may prevent the interviewer from obtaining any useful information; however, some people may be so talkative and provide so much information that their motives should be questioned, along

The investigation should reveal as much personal background information on the suspect as can be obtained (Figure 5-5). This information should include aliases, Social Security number, date and place of birth, education, marital status, employment history, financial history and current circumstances, prior offenses, past and present physical and mental health, any drug or alcohol abuse or addiction, relationship to the victim or crime scene, possible motive, biases and prejudices, home environment, sexual interests (if relevant), and hobbies. Additionally, the investigation and preparation for an interrogation should determine whether the suspect had the capability and opportunity to commit the offense and should confirm or disprove an alibi.

The interrogator should also obtain as much information as possible from other people involved to determine the suspect's attitude. This will enable the interrogator to anticipate levels of hostility or cooperativeness during the interrogation.

with the information they provide. A potential witness who may be under the influence of alcohol or drugs may or may not have information that could be used at trial; thus the condition of the witness is a major factor to be considered in assessing the value of any information obtained.

PERSONS WITH PHYSICAL INFIRMITIES

Interviewing an older person or any person with physical infirmities may present a unique set of challenges. The interviewer must have knowledge of and appreciation for the physical changes that may occur with aging and be able to effectively respond to those changes when conducting an interview.[9]

Visual Infirmities

Changes in vision that are related to aging vary widely from person to person. These changes are not strictly dependent on chronological age or general health, and excellent vision without glasses is sometimes maintained even in extreme old age. However, this last situation is an exception. About three-fourths of all older women and over half of all older men experience moderate to severe changes in visual functions. Those 65 or older account for half of all legally blind persons in the United States. The simple statistical probabilities are that an older person will have vision difficulties of one kind or another.

If the witness claims to have seen something, the investigator should ascertain if the witness had his or her glasses on, or contact lenses in.

Hearing Loss

Hearing loss resulting in a distortion of sounds generally is caused by changes in the inner ear. A person who suffers from a hearing loss must take advantage of every opportunity to use other skills in communicating, such as speech reading. Speech reading, often thought of as "lip reading," is the process of visually receiving cues from all lip movements, facial expressions, body posture, gestures, and the environment. Speech reading is a skill everyone has to a certain degree. It is only when hearing becomes impaired that this skill becomes important.

Interviewers will be able to communicate most effectively and interview hearing-impaired people by following these suggestions: (1) gain the person's attention; (2) speak to a person from a distance of 3–6 feet; (3) speak clearly; (4) control external noises as much as possible.

Competency of a Witness

The term *competency* refers to a witness's personal qualifications for testifying in court. Competency must be established before a witness is permitted to give any testimony. The witness's personal qualification depends on circumstances that affect his or her legal ability to function as a sworn witness in court. Competency has nothing to do with the believability of a witness's information.

Among the factors an investigator must evaluate in determining the competency of a witness are age, level of intelligence, mental state, relationship to individuals involved in the case, and background characteristics that might preclude the testimony of the witness from being heard in court. For example, in many jurisdictions, a young child cannot be a witness unless it can be shown that the child knows the difference between truth and imagination and understands the importance of being honest. Similarly, any person whose intelligence or mental state prevents him/her from understanding the obligation of telling the truth is not permitted to testify, regardless of the information he/she may possess.

Relationships among individuals involved in a case may also affect a witness's competency. Husbands and wives need not testify against each other, nor may attorneys testify against clients, doctors against patients, or ministers against penitents. Privileges vary by state. Background characteristics also may preclude a witness's testimony from being accepted in court. For example, some state laws forbid a convicted perjurer from testifying.

Possibilities such as those described in the preceding paragraphs mean the investigator must learn as much as possible about the witness before and during the interview.

RELIABILITY OF EYEWITNESS IDENTIFICATION

Eyewitness identification and other information provided by eyewitnesses to a criminal event are relied on heavily by both law enforcement and courts in the investigative and adjudication stages of our system of justice,[10] yet research indicates that eyewitness testimony is the most unreliable form of evidence and causes more miscarriages of justice than any other method of proof[11, 12] (Figure 5-6).

Research and courtroom experience provide ample evidence that an eyewitness to a crime is being asked to be something and do something that is not easily accomplished. Human perception is sloppy and uneven.[13] Existing research does not permit precise conclusions about the overall accuracy of the eyewitness identifications that are a common feature of criminal prosecutions, but research does lead us to conclude that identification errors are not infrequent.[14] Such errors are borne out by case studies in which the use of DNA evidence exonerated people who had been convicted on the basis of eyewitness identification.[15]

Many factors influence an individual's ability to accurately recognize and identify persons, and all of them depend on the circumstances under which the information is initially perceived and encoded, stored, and retrieved.[16] Eyewitness identifications take place in a

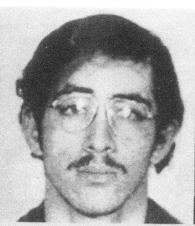

▲ **FIGURE 5-6   Look-alikes**
Mistaken identifications led to the arrests of two innocent men: Lawrence Berson (*left*) for several rapes and George Morales (*right*) for a robbery. Both men were picked out of police lineups by victims of the crimes. Berson was cleared when Richard Carbone (*center*) was arrested and implicated in the rapes. Carbone was convicted. He later confessed to the robbery, clearing Morales.
(From Scientific American, 1974, Vol. 231, No. 6, Reprinted by permission)

social context[17] in which the witness's own personality and characteristics, along with those of the target observed, are as critical as factors relating to the situation or environment in which the action takes place.

Thus, human perception and memory are selective and constructive functions, not exact copies of the event perceived. The gaps will often be filled in by the observer in order to produce a logical and complete sequence of events. A person is motivated by a desire to be accurate as she/he imposes meaning on the overabundance of information that impinges on her/his senses, but also by a desire to live up to the expectations of other people and to stay in their good graces. The eye, the ear, and other sense organs are, therefore, social organs as well as physical ones.[18]

Agreeing with this theory of eyewitness perception, one observer notes:

Studies of memory for sentences and pictures indicate that when we experience an event, we do not simply file a memory, and then on some later occasion retrieve it and read off what we've stored. Rather, at the time of recall or recognition we reconstruct the event, using information from many sources. These include both the original perception of the event and inferences drawn later, after the fact. Over a period of time, information from these sources may integrate, so that a witness becomes unable to say how they know a specific detail. In the end they only have a single unified memory.[19]

The gender, age, expectations, intelligence, race, and facial recognition skills of the witness are factors that individually may or may not influence the eyewitness

identification process but collectively or in combination with other variables are likely to have a bearing.[20] Facial attractiveness and distinctiveness, disguises, facial transformations, and the gender and race of the target (the person identified) are factors likely to influence identification.[21] Situational factors include such things as the presence of a weapon, exposure duration, and significance of the event in relation to all surrounding circumstances.[22]

Experts distinguish a number of factors that limit a person's ability to give a complete account of events or to identify people accurately. The following are among those factors:

- *The significance or insignificance of the event:* When an insignificant event occurs in the presence of an individual, it does not generally motivate the individual to bring fully into play the selective process of attention.
- *The length of the period of observation:* If ample opportunity is not provided for observation, the capability of the memory to record that which is perceived is decreased.
- *Lack of ideal conditions:* In situations where ideal conditions for observation are absent, the ability of the witness to perceive details is significantly decreased. Distance, poor lighting, fast movement, or the presence of a crowd may significantly interfere with the efficient working of the attention process.
- *Psychological factors internal to the witness:* A witness under stress at the time of observation may find this to be a major source of unreliability in his/her observations.

- *The physical condition of the witness.* If the witness is injured or intoxicated, this condition will affect his/her ability to provide complete and accurate information.
- *Lack of familiarity with members of another race or ethnic group.* Some of the most egregious cases of misidentification have occurred in those crimes which are interracial or interethnic in nature. These occur because in some cases the victim is not accustomed to dealing with members of the race or ethnic group of the assailant and is unable to distinguish important variation in facial characteristics. The more contact the victim has had with members of that race or ethnic group the less likely it is that a misidentification will occur.
- *Expectancy:* Research has shown that memory recall and judgment are often based on what psychologists term *expectancy*. This concept means that an individual perceives things in the manner in which he or she expects them to appear. For example, a right-handed eyewitness to a homicide might, in answer to a question and without positive knowledge, state the assailant held the gun in his right hand, whereas a left-handed person might say the opposite. Biases or prejudices are also illustrated by the expectancy theory, as is the classic problem associated with stereotyping.[23]

WITNESS INTIMIDATION

Citizens who witness or are victimized by crime are sometimes reluctant to report incidents to the police or to assist in the prosecution of offenders.[24, 25] Such reluctance may be in response to a perceived or actual threat of retaliation by the offender or his or her associates, or may be the result of more generalized community norms that discourage residents from cooperating with police and prosecutors. In some communities, close ties between witnesses, offenders, and their families and friends may also deter witnesses from cooperating; these relationships can provide a vitally important context for understanding witness intimidation. Particularly in violent and gang-related crime, the same individual may, at different times, be a victim, a witness, and an offender.[26] Historically, witness intimidation is most closely associated with organized crime and domestic violence, but has recently thwarted efforts to investigate and prosecute drug, gang violence and other types of crime.

FORMS OF WITNESS INTIMIDATION

Witness intimidation takes many forms, including:

- implicit threats, looks, or gestures;
- explicit threats of violence;
- actual physical violence;
- property damage;
- other threats, such as challenges to child custody or immigration status;
- confronting witnesses verbally;
- sending notes and letters;
- making nuisance phone calls;
- parking or loitering outside the homes of witnesses;
- damaging witnesses' houses or property;
- threatening witnesses' children, spouses, parents, or other family members;
- assaulting or even murdering witnesses or their family members.

Threats are much more common than actual physical violence and are in fact just as effective in deterring cooperation.[27] Although some witnesses experience a single incident of intimidation, it may also involve an escalating series of threats and actions that become more violent over time.[28] Other witnesses do not experience intimidation directly but rather believe retaliation will occur if they cooperate with police. Either way, they are deterred from offering relevant information that might assist the police and prosecutors. Particularly in communities dominated by gang and drug-related crime, residents have seen firsthand that offenders are capable of violence and brutality. Many witnesses also believe offenders will return to the community after relatively brief periods of incarceration or will be able to arrange for intimidation by others while they are incarcerated. In many cases the experience of actually having witnessed violence by the perpetrators or groups of individuals in the community lends considerable credibility to any threats and creates a general sense of fear that discourages cooperation with police.

RESPONSE STRATEGIES FOR ADDRESSING WITNESS INTIMIDATION

The following response strategies provide a foundation for addressing witness intimidation.

- *Form multi-agency partnerships.* The appropriate party to address the threat of witness intimidation may change as a case moves through the criminal justice system. For example, the police may be responsible for protecting or supporting witnesses at the outset a case, but the responsibility might later shift to the prosecutor when the case goes to trial.
- *Strengthen ties between police and the community.* Fostering cooperation of reluctant witnesses is a natural extension of community policing and community prosecution, which focus on engaging residents in preventing and responding to crime.[29] For example, mobile precincts can increase police visibility after a high-profile gang-related crime in an area where intimidation is likely to occur. Storefront precincts can increase the level of contact with residents and make it easier to provide encouragement and support.

- *Minimize the risk of witness identification when reporting crime or offering statements.* This is particularly true in neighborhoods where communitywide intimidation is a factor and residents may hesitate to cooperate with police at the scene of a crime, because they fear being labeled as an informant or a "rat." As a result, methods for reporting crime or offering witness statements that do not make cooperation obvious to observers are sometimes needed.[30]
- *Reduce the likelihood of contact between witnesses and offenders.* Most often, acts of intimidation are committed at a witness's home, workplace, or school, or during the normal course of the witness's daily activities. Minimizing the opportunities and avenues by which witnesses come into contact with offenders can reduce the incidence of intimidation. For example, wherever practical witnesses can alter their normal routines by varying the routes taken to work or school and making their schedules irregular and unpredictable.[31]
- *Transport witnesses to and from work and school.* Many witnesses feel vulnerable when traveling to and from work or school, or while attending to their business in the community. Police escorts during these times can deter offenders from making contact. However, such protection schemes consume significant police resources and may not be feasible for broad application.
- *Keep witnesses and defendants separated at the courthouse.* Other than at home, witnesses are most often intimidated in the courthouse, both while waiting to testify and while in the courtroom giving testimony. Not only must witnesses endure a face-to-face encounter with the defendant, but they may also be apprehensive about contact with the defendant's family and friends. Key danger areas include courthouse entrances, hallways, elevators, waiting areas, refreshment areas, and restrooms. Separate waiting rooms and entrances for witnesses and defendants can be useful.
- *Relocate witnesses.* Because it is unusual for offenders to travel outside their neighborhoods to intimidate witnesses, simply moving a witness to another location may effectively protect him or her from harm. Of course, the key to this strategy is to ensure that the new location remains confidential. Out of boredom, or because they are reluctant to sever ties with friends and family, the witnesses may unwittingly compromise the secrecy of their new locations.

DETERRING INTIMIDATORS

The following responses focus on actions that can be taken to deter intimidators.

- *Admonish intimidators.* When witnesses or victims tell police they are afraid or have experienced direct intimidation, police can visit the offender and his/her family and friends to caution them regarding their behavior and to explain the laws concerning witness intimidation and obstruction of justice. In court, judges should be vigilant about threatening gestures or actions and should admonish defendants or spectators who display such behaviors. Some jurisdictions educate judges about the types of courtroom intimidation that are exhibited by gang members, such as courtroom packing or wearing black.[32]
- *Request high bail and no contact orders.* In cases in which the risk of intimidation is significant, prosecutors can seek high bail to keep defendants in jail and away from witnesses. Where this strategy is used, bond hearings cannot be a mere formality; witness statements and risk assessments should be prepared in advance and presented in court. Prosecutors should seek release conditions that forbid contact with witnesses and victims and make sure that the consequences for violating such conditions are clearly articulated.

DOCUMENTING INTERVIEWS

Note-taking during an interview raises two primary concerns for the interviewer. First, it may occasionally be distracting or suspicious to a witness; witnesses may be reluctant to give information knowing it is being documented. Consequently, the investigator should tell witnesses that notes will prevent the need for subsequent interviews owing to lapses of the investigator's memory. This explanation usually reduces the reluctance of the witness. Second, the interviewer should avoid becoming preoccupied with taking notes, for this creates the appearance of inattentiveness. As important as notes may be, the interviewer should treat them as less important than conversation with the witness. Note-taking during the interview should be kept to a minimum, recording only salient details. As soon as possible after the interview, the investigator should complete the notes, before their memory wanes.

In many instances, witnesses should write or sign statements concerning the events of which they have knowledge. In many jurisdictions, law-enforcement officers are authorized to administer oaths so that such statements are sworn to or affirmed. The theory is that victims and/or witnesses are more inclined to be truthful if they are under oath and aware that charges of perjury could be lodged against them at a later date if they were determined to be lying.

The best form of documentation is electronic sound recording or a sound-and-visual recording of the interview.

TABLE 5-3	Comparison of Types of Interview Documentation	
TYPE	ADVANTAGES	DISADVANTAGES
Memory	Quick and easy	Limited absorption and recall
	Captures salient details	Most information lost shortly afterward
	Prevents need for reinterviewing	
Note-taking by interviewer	Sufficient in most cases	May distract or offend witness
	Captures salient details	May preoccupy interviewer, creating appearance of inattentiveness
	Prevents need for reinterviewing	
Handwritten or signed statements by witness	Useful if witness cannot testify	Request may be offensive to witness
	Can be used to impeach if witness changes story in court	Not necessary in routine cases
Electronic sound or sound-and-visual recordings	Relatively inexpensive	Not necessary except in the most important cases
	Some equipment portable	Generally not practical
	All information recorded in witnesses' own words	
	Does not rely on inaccuracies of memory or another's notes	
	Does not distract	
	Prevents unnecessary reinterviews	

Visual recordings are generally not practical when the interview is held anywhere other than at a law-enforcement agency, where equipment can be permanently situated. Audio recorders, however, are inexpensive, portable, and helpful in the majority of cases. The recorded interview has many significant advantages: all information is recorded in the witness's own words, details are not left to be recalled by human memory, concerns about detracting from the interview by note-taking are absent, interviewers may listen to the verbatim conversations over and over at a later time to be sure they have understood completely and accurately what was said, and the taped interview might avoid unnecessary reinterviews. The advantages and disadvantages of each type of documentation are shown in Table 5-3.

DOCUMENTING INTERROGATIONS

Documenting an interrogation consists of three main phases: note-taking, recording, and obtaining written statements. All three phases are geared to accomplishing two basic functions: first, retaining information for the benefit of the interrogator and the continued investigation and, second, securing a written statement or confession from the accused for later use as evidence in court.

THE USE OF ELECTRONIC RECORDINGS FOR INTERROGATIONS

The methods of keeping notes of interrogations is the same as described for interviews. Electronic recording of an interrogation is the best means of documentation. Audio, video, or a combination of both may be used, but case law and local requirements should be checked.

At present, 238 law-enforcement agencies in 38 states currently record custodial interviews of suspects in felony investigations. These agencies are located in every area of the United States and are quite diverse in size and individual practices. Following are some of the elements addressed in their respective policies as they relate to the use of electronic recordings for interrogation.[33]

- *Mandatory or discretionary:* Most agencies leave the recording decision to the discretion of the investigator in charge, although recordings are customarily made by the investigators in cases covered by discretionary policies.
- *When to begin recordings:* Most departments use either audio and/or video recording devices to record interrogations of persons under arrest in a police facility starting from the point when the *Miranda* warnings (discussed later in this chapter) are given until the interview is ended, with no intentional breaks or omissions in the recordings.
- *Crimes under investigation:* Most departments record only in "major" or "serious" felony investigations,

such as homicide, sexual assault, armed robbery, and other crimes against persons and those involving weapons. Many also record interviews in DUI, child abuse, and domestic violence investigations.

- *Equipment:* Some departments use multiple cameras from different views, while others use a single camera focused on the suspect.[34] Many departments are acquiring digital technology in order to improve picture resolution and conserve storage space.

- *Suspect's knowledge:* State eavesdropping laws govern whether suspects must be told they are being recorded. "One-party consent" laws allow the police to record without informing the suspects. "Two-party consent" laws require the police to obtain the suspects' consent. Most state laws permit police to record surreptitiously, although sophisticated suspects and repeat offenders may be aware without being told. Most departments inform suspects that the session will be recorded and/or place the recording equipment in plain view, although most of them are not required by state law to do so. Almost all investigators turn the recording devices off if the suspect declines to talk while being recorded.

BENEFITS OF RECORDING FOR POLICE OFFICERS AND PROSECUTORS

An electronic recording of suspect interviews has proven to be an efficient and powerful law-enforcement tool. Audio is good, but video is better. Both methods create a permanent record of exactly what occurred. Recordings prevent disputes about the investigator's conduct, the treatment of suspects and the voluntariness of statements they made. Investigators are not called on to paraphrase statements or try later to describe suspects' words, actions, and attitudes. Instead, viewers and listeners see and/or hear precisely what was said and done, including whether suspects were forthcoming or evasive, changed their versions of events, and appeared sincere and innocent or deceitful and guilty. An electronic record is law enforcement's version of instant replay.

Experience also shows that recordings dramatically reduce the number of defense motions to suppress statements and confessions. The record is there for defense lawyers to see and evaluate: if the officers conduct themselves properly during the questioning, there is no basis to challenge their conduct or exclude the defendants' responses from evidence. Officers are spared from defending themselves against allegations of coercion, trickery, and perjury during hostile cross-examinations.

The use of recording devices, even when known to the suspect, does not impede investigators from obtaining confessions and admissions from guilty suspects. When suspects decline to talk if recorded, the investigators simply turn the recorder off and proceed with taking handwritten notes.

Recordings permit investigators to focus on the suspect rather than taking copious notes of the interview. When investigators later review the recordings they can often observe inconsistencies and evasive conduct which they overlooked while the interview was in progress.

Electronic recording forces investigators to better prepare for conducting interrogations by:

- clarifying whether an interrogator missed something that requires further questioning;
- giving prosecutors a better understanding of cases, thereby fostering better charging decisions, plea-bargaining options, and case preparation;
- minimizing challenges by defense attorneys about the accuracy of the electronic recordings and the completeness of written confessions;
- reducing doubts about the voluntariness of confessions;
- jogging investigators' memories when they are testifying.

In addition, tapes can be reviewed and used as training aids for less experienced investigators who are attempting to develop their interrogation skills.[35]

THE WRITTEN STATEMENT

After the use of such recordings, the next-best form is a signed statement written in the first person by the suspect in his or her handwriting. Frequently, however, it is not possible to convince a suspect to prepare such a statement. Or perhaps the suspect cannot write.

Other forms in which statements may be admitted into evidence, listed in descending order of the credibility with juries, are these:

- a typed or handwritten statement by someone else that is signed in the accused's own hand;
- a typed or otherwise prepared statement that the accused does not sign but that is acknowledged in front of witnesses;
- the oral testimony of a person who was present and overheard the subject give a confession or admission.

In the last case, even though admissible, the testimony is likely to carry little weight with the jury. Table 5-4 lists the types of documentation in descending order of preference and the advantages and disadvantages of each.

The form and content of a written statement should include a heading, which incorporates the data identifying the circumstances under which the statement was taken, the body of the statement, and a verification. The statement should open with an indication of the time and place where it was taken, and an identification of the person giving the statement that includes his/her name, address, and age. The heading must also include a definite statement to the effect that the subject is giving the

TABLE 5-4	Comparison of Types of Confession Documentation (in Descending Order of Believability to Juries)	
TYPE	ADVANTAGES	DISADVANTAGES
1. Electronic video-audiotape or movie	May be required by legislative or judicial directive Shows all, including fairness, procedures, and treatment Easy to do Can be relatively inexpensive	May face legal constraints
2. Audio recording	Can hear conversations Can infer fairness	Some words or descriptions may be meaningless without pictorial support Necessitates identifying people and things involved
3. Statement written and signed in suspect's own handwriting	Can be identified as coming directly from suspect	Can't see demeanor or hear voice inflections Suspect may not agree to procedure
4. Typed statement signed by suspect	Signature indicates knowledge of and agreement with contents of statement	Less convincing than methods described above
5. Typed unsigned statement acknowledged by suspect	Contents of confession or admission are present Acknowledgment helps show voluntariness	Reduced believability of voluntariness and accuracy of contents
6. Testimony of someone who heard confession or admission given	Contents admissible	Carries little weight with juries

statement freely and voluntarily after having been appropriately advised of his/her constitutional rights.

The body of the statement, which acknowledges the subject's involvement in the crime under investigation, should, if possible, be phrased in the first person, allowing the suspect to include his/her own ideas in a free-flowing manner. However, if this is not possible or practical, then the question-and-answer format is permissible. The terminology used should include the words, grammar, idioms, and style of the person making the statement. The body of the statement should be arranged so that its content follows the chronological order of the subject's involvement in the case under investigation.

At the end, the statement should indicate that the suspect has read the statement or has had it read to him/her, that its contents and implications are understood, and that the suspect attests to its accuracy.

Other suggestions for the interrogator to keep in mind include:

- Each page of the statement should be numbered consecutively with an indication that it is page no. _____ of _____ pages. If the pages get separated, they can later be easily restored to order.

- The interrogator should ensure that each page is initialed by the subject. If the subject is unwilling to sign, the statement should be acknowledged by him/her. If the subject cannot write, another identifying mark may be used.

- On occasion an interrogator may encounter someone who says, "I'll tell you what I've done, but I'm not writing anything and I'm not signing anything." In such circumstances, the interrogator can explain that the suspect confessed, and the interrogator or some other person who heard the confession can go into court and testify about it. By preparing or signing a statement, the suspect protects himself/herself against the interrogator's testifying to something more damaging by changing the story in court (another good reason for electronic recording).

- If the suspect cannot read, the statement must be read to him/her, and the interrogator must ensure the suspect understands its contents before the suspect is allowed to attest to its accuracy.

- All errors in the statement should be corrected on the final copy and initialed by the suspect. The interrogator may accommodate the suspect by allowing small errors if this will help obtain the suspect's initials on each page of the statement.

- The interrogator should make sure the suspect understands all the words used in the statement. If some words are confusing, their meanings should be explained to the suspect and the suspect should be required to explain them back in front of witnesses in order to confirm this understanding.

- During the process of drafting and attesting to a statement derived through interrogation, there should be at least one additional witness who can testify to the authenticity of the statement and the circumstances under which it was obtained. After the suspect signs the statement in ink, the witnesses should sign their names, addresses, and positions.[36]

WHY PEOPLE CONFESS

It is human nature to talk. Most people cannot keep a secret. It has been estimated that 80% of all people will confess to a crime. There are two basic categories of people who tend to confess to crimes: (1) guilty parties who psychologically need to "get if off their chest" and (2) persons who are not guilty but who act under some urge to confess. It is to protect the latter category of people that some procedural safeguards are provided. For example, a conviction cannot be based solely on a confession. There must be some other independent corroborating evidence to support the conviction.

The psychological and physiological pressures that build in a person who has committed a crime or who suffers from feelings of guilt concerning any other type of conduct are best alleviated by communicating. Talking is the best means of communicating. Therefore, in spite of having been advised of certain protections guaranteed by the Constitution, some people feel a need to confess. Even confirmed criminals sometimes suffer from the same pangs of conscience as first-time offenders. However, fear of the potential punishments that await them contributes to their silence. Those who confess rarely regret it, for doing so gives them peace of mind. It permits them to look at themselves and life differently and to live with themselves. Most guilty individuals who confess are, from the outset, looking for the proper opening during an interrogation to communicate their guilt to the interrogator. The good interrogator will seek out and be able to recognize individuals who desire to confess and will approach the interrogation in such a way as to provide the accused with the proper opening and reason for the relief of the psychological and physiological pressures that have built up.[37] If it is human nature to talk, and if people cannot generally keep secrets, then the job of the interrogator is to make it easy for a suspect to confess.

FALSE CONFESSIONS

A false confession is an admission of guilt followed by a narrative statement of what, how, and why the confessor committed the crime. Over the years, confessions have been proven false in a number of ways, as when it is discovered that the confessed crime was not committed; when new evidence shows it was physically impossible for the confessor to have committed the crime; when the real perpetrator, having no connection to the defendant, is captured and implicated; and when DNA and other scientific evidence affirmatively establishes the confessor's innocence. Through these methods, and contrary to the widespread belief that people do not confess to crimes they did not commit, the pages of American history reveal large numbers of men and women who were wrongfully prosecuted, convicted, imprisoned, and sometimes sentenced to death on the basis of false confessions.[38]

Although many researchers have discovered large numbers of false confessions in recent years, it is not possible to project from these cases the frequency with which innocent people in general confess to crimes they did not commit. First, within the U.S. criminal justice system, the postconviction cases discovered by the Innocence Project[39] and others do not include the numerous false confessions that are disproved subsequent to arrest but before trial, those that result in a false guilty plea, those to minor crimes that attract no postconviction scrutiny, and those that involve juveniles in which confidentiality provisions are in place.[40] In a North American survey of 631 police investigators, respondents estimated from their own experience that 4.78% of innocent suspects confess during interrogation.[41]

Over the years, researchers have reported on numerous accounts of proven false confessions, producing a vast literature of case studies. As reported in books, newspapers, TV documentaries, and analyses of actual case files, these stories reveal false confessions occur with some unknown frequency, they share certain common features, and they seem more likely to occur in some types of people and under some conditions than others. From these descriptive analyses of specific instances and associations, one cannot draw conclusions about the causes of false confessions. Nevertheless, case studies of this nature have proven invaluable in the development of this area. By comparing and contrasting several known cases throughout history, for example, Kassin and Wrightsman[42] introduced a taxonomy that distinguished among three types of false confessions: voluntary, **coerced-compliant,** and **coerced-internalized.**

VOLUNTARY FALSE CONFESSIONS

Voluntary false confessions are those in which people claim responsibility for crimes they did not commit without prompting or pressure from police. Often this occurs in high-profile cases. For example, when Charles Lindbergh's infant son was kidnapped and killed in 1932, an estimated 200 people volunteered confessions. When "Black Dahlia" actress Elizabeth Short was murdered in 1947, more than 50 people confessed. In 2006 John Mark Karr confessed to the unsolved murder of JonBenet Ramsey. Researchers have not systematically studied these types of false confessions, in part because they are typically disproved at the outset by the confessor's ignorance and inability to furnish corroborating details about the crime. There are several reasons why innocent people might volunteer confessions, such as a pathological need for attention or self-punishment; feeling of guilt or delusions; the perception of tangible gain; or the desire to protect a parent, child, or someone else.

COERCED–COMPLIANT FALSE CONFESSIONS

In contrast, people may be induced to confess through the processes of police interrogation. In false confessions, the suspect capitulates in order to escape a stressful custodial situation, avoid physical or legal punishment, or gain a promised or implied reward. G. H. Gudjonsson[43] identified, based on a review of cases, some concrete initiatives for this type of confession, such as not being allowed to sleep, eat, make a phone call, go home, or, in the case of drug addicts, feed a drug habit. Like the results of classical forms of influence observed in psychological studies of conformity, compliance, and obedience to authority, this type of confession is an act of public capitulation and compliance by a suspect who knows he/she is innocent but perceives that the short-term benefits of confession (for example, being left alone, fed, or released) outweighed the long-term costs (for instance, a loss of reputation, conviction, and incarceration). This phenomenon was dramatically illustrated in the 1692 Salem witch trials, in which women confessed to witchcraft;[44] in *Brown* v. *Mississippi*, a classic case in which three black tenant farmers confessed to murder after they were whipped with a steel-studded leather belt; and in the infamous Central Park jogger case in 1989, in which five New York City teenagers confessed after lengthy interrogations, each claiming he expected to go home afterward. All the boys were convicted and sent to prison, only to be exonerated in 2002 when the real rapist gave a confession that was confirmed by DNA evidence.

COERCED–INTERNALIZED FALSE CONFESSIONS

Internalized false confessions are those in which innocent but vulnerable suspects confess and come to believe they committed the crime in question, a belief that is sometimes accompanied by false memories. Gudjonsson has argued that this kind of false confession results from "memory distrust syndrome," whereby people develop a profound distrust of their own memory that renders them vulnerable to manipulation from external cues.[45] Kassin likened this process of influence to the creation of false memories sometimes seen in psychotherapy patients. In both situations, an authority figure claims a privileged insight into the individual's past, the individual is isolated from others and in a heightened state of malleability, and the expert ultimately convinces the individual to accept a painful self-insight by invoking such concepts as dissociation or repression. The case of 14-year-old Michael Crowe, whose sister was stabbed to death, illustrates this phenomenon. After lengthy interrogations, during which Michael was misled by lies into thinking there was substantial physical evidence of his guilt, he concluded he was a killer: "I'm not sure how I did it. All I know is I did it." Eventually, he was convinced he had a split personality—that "bad Michael" acted out of jealous rage while "good Michael" blocked the incident from his consciousness. The charges against Crowe were later dropped when a drifter from neighborhood was found with the victim's blood on his clothing.[46]

RECOMMENDATIONS TO REDUCE THE POSSIBILITY OF FALSE CONFESSIONS

Given that false confessions do occur, even if rarely, police administrators need to ensure their investigators are properly trained in interrogation techniques that elicit the most accurate and truthful information from suspects. The following recommendations will do much to reduce the possibility of a false confession.[47]

- *Use police skill teams.* The teams should consist of seasoned interview specialists who, through training and actual interview experiences, possess the skills necessary to conduct successful critical interviews.
- *Provide mandatory police training.* Investigators must be made aware of the circumstances under which false confessions may be obtained. These include:
  —the suspect's desire to eliminate friends, relatives, and close associates from the investigative process;
  —the suspect's attempt to distract police from identifying other motives and/or suspects through a false confession, which is usually fraught with inconsistencies;
  —situations in which police officers provide too much information to the suspect, which the suspect may later repeat as part of a false confession. These include, among other things, the date and time of death, the location of the offense, the specific positioning of the body, wounds to the body, the instrumentation of death and so forth. Unless this kind of specific information has been released to the public by the media or through some other source, then only the police and the person(s) committing the crime should possess this kind of information.

- *Provide mandatory police training on special interview considerations in dealing with populations most vulnerable to false confessions.* These include juveniles, the mentally impaired, and individuals under the influence of alcohol and/or drugs.
- Police agencies that in the past have been involved in wrongful convictions based on false confessions should review existing policies and make the appropriate changes to eliminate the problem.
- Mandate that police conclude the interview by asking a series of questions that emphasize the voluntariness of the confession—that is, no coercion was used and the suspect was not under the influence of alcohol and drugs. Interviews should be concluded with questions that firmly establish the fairness and professionalism of the interviewing investigators. A simple yet very effective way to achieve this result is by asking such questions as: "Why did you decide to talk to me?" and "Why did you decide to talk to me now?"

ADMISSIBILITY OF CONFESSIONS AND ADMISSIONS

Before 1936 the only test for the validity and admissibility of a confession or admission was its voluntariness. However, the determination as to whether it was given voluntarily by the suspect was subject to very loose interpretation. There were no rules restricting the method by which law enforcement obtained "voluntary" statements. Physical violence, psychological coercion, empty promises, and meaningless guarantees of rewards were not considered objectionable procedures.

THE FREE-AND-VOLUNTARY RULE

The first notable incidence of U.S. Supreme Court intervention into interrogation practices came about in *Brown* v. *Mississippi*.[48] In this 1936 case, the Supreme Court held that under no circumstances could a confession be considered freely and voluntarily given when it was obtained as a result of physical brutality and violence inflicted by law-enforcement officials on the accused. The reaction to this decision by law enforcement was not unexpected. Many threw up their hands and claimed they could no longer function effectively because "handcuffs had been put on the police." However, as was true with many other decisions placing procedural restrictions on law-enforcement agencies, the police found they were able to compensate by conducting thorough criminal investigations.

Subsequent to the *Brown* decision, the Supreme Court, in a succession of cases, has continued to reinforce its

position that any kind of coercion, whether physical or psychological, would be grounds for making a confession inadmissible as being in violation of the **free-and-voluntary rule.** This includes such conduct as threatening bodily harm to the suspect or members of the suspect's family,[49] using psychological coercion,[50] engaging in trickery or deceit, or holding a suspect incommunicado. Investigators are also cautioned about making promises to the suspect that cannot be kept. All these practices were condemned in *Miranda* v. *Arizona* (discussed in much greater detail later in this chapter).[51] Despite the appearance that Miranda has eliminated all coercive techniques previously used in interrogations, this is not actually the case. What Miranda seeks is to abolish techniques that would prompt untrue incriminatory statements by a suspect. Thus, unlike physical coercion, psychological coercion, threats, duress, and some promises, the use of trickery, fraud, falsehood, and similar techniques are not absolutely forbidden. If such methods are not likely to cause an individual to make self-incriminating statements or to admit to falsehoods in order to avoid threatened harm, confessions or admissions so obtained are admissible.[52]

THE DELAY-IN-ARRAIGNMENT RULE

In 1943 the U.S. Supreme Court delivered another decision concerning the admissibility of confessions. Even though the free-and-voluntary rule was in effect in both the federal and state courts, another series of statutes seemed to have gone unheeded. Every state and the federal government had legal provisions requiring that after arrest a person must be taken before a committing magistrate "without unnecessary delay." Before 1943, if there was an unnecessary delay in producing the accused before a committing magistrate, the delay was merely one of a number of factors the courts were required to take into consideration in determining whether the confession was freely and voluntarily given.

The facts of **McNabb v. United States**[53] reveal that McNabb and several members of his family were involved in bootlegging. They were arrested after the murder of federal officers who were investigating their operation in Tennessee. McNabb was held incommunicado for several days before he was taken before a committing magistrate. He subsequently confessed, and the confession was admitted into evidence at his trial. He was convicted, but on appeal to the Supreme Court the conviction was reversed. The Court held that the failure of federal officers to take the prisoner before a committing officer without unnecessary delay automatically rendered his confession inadmissible. The significance of this case is that for the first time the Court indicated that failure to comply with this procedural requirement would render a confession inadmissible regardless of whether it was obtained freely and voluntarily. Thus, instead of examining the facts of the case to determine the voluntariness of the confession, the Court ruled, as a matter of law, that the procedural violation also rendered the confession inadmissible. The holding in the *McNabb* case was emphatically reaffirmed in 1957 by the Supreme Court in *Mallory* v. *United States*.[54]

As the mandate of the Supreme Court in the *McNabb* and *Mallory* cases had applicability only to federal prosecutions, the states were free to interpret their own statutes on unnecessary delay as they saw fit. Few chose to follow the *McNabb-Mallory* **delay-in-arraignment rule.** The majority have continued to require that there must be a connection between the failure of law enforcement to produce the accused before a committing magistrate without unnecessary delay and the securing of a confession.

INTERVIEWING AND INTERROGATION: LEGAL REQUIREMENTS

PREINTERROGATION LEGAL REQUIREMENTS

Preinterrogation legal requirements became of critical concern during the 1960s. As a result, the Supreme Court handed down a landmark decision that dramatically affected the conditions under which interrogations take place. The issue revolved around the Fifth Amendment protection against self-incrimination and the Sixth Amendment guarantee of the right to counsel, both as made applicable to the states through the due process clause of the Fourteenth Amendment.

MIRANDA V. ARIZONA

In *Miranda* v. *Arizona*[55] the Supreme Court, in a five-to-four decision, spelled out the requirements and procedures to be followed by officers when conducting an in custody interrogation of a suspect.

In March 1963, Ernest Miranda was arrested for kidnapping and rape. After being identified by the victim, he was questioned by police for several hours and signed a confession that included a statement indicating that the confession was given voluntarily. The confession was admitted into evidence over the objections of Miranda's defense counsel, and the jury found him guilty. The Supreme Court of Arizona affirmed the conviction and held that Miranda's constitutional rights had not been violated in obtaining the conviction because following the ruling from *Escobedo* v. *Illinois*[56] the year before, in which Escobedo's confession was ruled to have been improperly admitted because he asked to see his lawyer but was denied that right, Miranda had not specifically requested counsel. The U.S. Supreme Court, in reversing the decision, attempted to clarify its intent in the *Escobedo* case by spelling out specific guidelines to be followed by police before they interrogate persons in custody and attempt to use their statements as evidence. In clarifying the requirements of *Escobedo*, the Court felt compelled to include the Fifth Amendment requirements against self-incrimination in the decision. The guidelines require that after a person is taken into custody for an offense and before any questioning by law-enforcement officers, if there is any intent to use a suspect's statements in court, the person must first be advised of certain rights (Figure 5-7.) These rights include:

1. the right to remain silent;
2. the right to be told that anything said can and will be used in court;

THE EXPLANATION OF THE ADMONITION AND USE OR WAIVER OF YOUR RIGHTS	LA EXPLICACION DEL AVISO Y EL USO O NO DE TUS DERECHOS
1) You have the right to remain silent—you do not have to talk.	1) Tienes el derecho de quedar en silencio—no tienes que hablar.
2) What you say can be used, and shall be used against you in a court of law.	2) Lo que digas se puede usar y se usará en contra de ti en la corte de ley.
3) You have the right to talk with an attorney before you talk with us, and you have the right to have the attorney present during the time we are talking to you.	3) Tienes el derecho de hablar con un abogado antes de hablar con nosotros, y tienes el derecho de tener el abogado presente durante el tiempo que nosotros estamos hablando contigo.
4) If you do not have the funds to employ an attorney, one shall be appointed to represent you free of charge.	4) Si no tienes el dinero para emplear un abogado, uno sere fijado para que te represente, sin pagar.
5) Do you understand these rights as I have explained them to you, yes or no?	5) ¿Comprendes estos derechos como te los expliqué, si o no?
6) Do you want to talk to us about your case now, yes or no?	6) ¿Quieres hablar con nosotros de tu caso ahora, si o no?
7) Do you want an attorney present during the time we are talking to you, yes or no?	7) ¿Quieres un abogado presente durante el tiempo que estamos hablando contigo, si o no?

◄FIGURE 5-7
Warning-rights card in English and Spanish
(Courtesy Los Angeles County Sheriff's Department)

3. the right to consult with an attorney before answering any questions and the right to have an attorney present during interrogation;
4. the right to counsel. If the suspect cannot afford an attorney, the court will appoint one.[57]

SUSPECT'S RESPONSE: WAIVER AND ALTERNATIVES

It is common practice for the officer to ask the suspect if he or she understands the rights as they have been explained. If the answer is yes, then the officer may ask if the subject wants to talk with the officer. At this point, four alternatives are open to the suspect:

1. *The suspect may choose to remain silent,* not wanting even to respond to the officer's question. The courts have held that choosing to remain silent does not imply consent to be interrogated and no questions should be asked.
2. *The suspect may request counsel.* At that point, the investigator must not undertake any questioning of the suspect, for anything said will not be admissible in court. In *Edwards* v. *Arizona* in 1981, the Supreme Court held that no police-initiated interrogation may lawfully take place once the suspect has invoked the right to counsel unless, and until, an attorney has been provided or unless the defendant voluntarily begins to talk with the officers.[58] In **Minnick v. Mississippi** in 1990, the Supreme Court held that once counsel is requested, interrogation must cease; officials may not reinitiate interrogation without counsel being present, whether or not the accused has consulted with his or her attorney. The requirement that counsel be made available to the accused refers not to the opportunity to consult with a lawyer outside the interrogation room but to the right to have the attorney present during custodial interrogation. This rule is necessary to remove suspects from the coercive pressure of officials who may try to persuade them to waive their rights. The rule also provides a clear and unequivocal guideline to the law-enforcement profession.[59]

    The *Edwards* and *Minnick* lines of cases remained constant until the Supreme Court ruled in **Maryland v. Shatzer** in 2010. The facts involved an attempt by a detective to question Shatzer in 2003 about allegations that he had sexually abused his son. At the time Shatzer was in prison on an unrelated offense. Shatzer invoked his *Miranda* rights to have counsel present during the interrogation. The detective terminated the interview and the case was subsequently closed. Shatzer was returned to the general population. Another detective reopened the investigation three years later and attempted to interrogate Shatzer, who was still in prison. Shatzer

waived his *Miranda* rights this time and in 2006 made some inculpatory statements that were admitted at this trial for sexually abusing his son. Shatzer was convicted. After several appeals, which held the trial court was wrong to admit Shatzer's incriminating statements since he had previously asked for an attorney, the appeals courts held there was no exception once the request for an attorney had been made in accordance with the *Edwards* decision, since Shatzer was still being held in custody. The Supreme Court, however, agreed with the trial court, allowing the statements to be used against Shatzer. The Court reasoned that because Shatzer experienced a break in *Miranda* custody, lasting more than 2 weeks between the first and second attempts at interrogation, *Edwards* did not require suppression of his 2006 statements. The Court said that even though Shatzer was still in prison during the time between the 2003 and 2006 interrogations, he was in the general population, where he could have spoken with a lawyer during the 3-year break and was no longer in a police-dominated atmosphere on the sexual abuse case. Even though he was still in prison Shatzer resumed his "normal life."[60]

3. *The suspect may waive his or her rights and agree to talk with law enforcement without the benefit of counsel.* The waiver of rights is a sensitive topic for law enforcement, because it is the responsibility of law enforcement and the prosecutor to prove in court the waiver was validly obtained. A valid waiver must be voluntarily, knowingly, and intelligently given by the suspect. The burden is on the prosecution to prove that the suspect was properly advised of his or her rights, that those rights were understood, and that the suspect voluntarily, knowingly, and intelligently waived those rights before the court will allow the introduction of any incriminating testimony in the form of a confession. The waiver cannot be presumed or inferred. It must be successfully proved by the prosecution. Therefore, it is preferable for the investigator who secures a waiver of rights from a suspect to attempt to get the waiver in writing with sufficient witnesses to substantiate its voluntariness. Figure 5-8 is a sample waiver form. Most law-enforcement agencies also attempt to get individuals in custody to sign a rights waiver form as one more step to show a good faith effort to comply with the requirements of the *Miranda* ruling.

    However, a suspect who has waived his or her rights is free to withdraw that waiver at any time. If this occurs during questioning, the investigator is under a legal obligation to cease the interrogation at that point and either comply with the suspect's request for representation or simply cease the interrogation if the suspect refuses to talk.

YOUR RIGHTS

Date_____

Time_____

WARNING

Before we ask you any questions, you must understand your rights.

You have the right to remain silent.

Anything you say can and will be used against you in court.

You have the right to talk to a lawyer for advice before we ask you any question and to have him with you during questioning.

If you cannot afford a lawyer, one will be appointed for you.

Geauga County has a Public Defender. Before answering any questions, you have a right to talk with the Public Defender.

If you decide to answer questions now, without a lawyer present, you will still have the right to stop answering at any time. You also have the right to stop answering at any time until you talk to a lawyer.

Do you understand these rights? _____

Signed: _____

Witnesses:

_____

_____

WAIVER OF RIGHTS

I have read this statement of my rights and I understand what my rights are. I am willing to make a statement and answer questions. I do not want a lawyer at this time. I understand and know what I am doing. No promises or threats have been made to me and no pressure or coercion of any kind has been used against me.

Signed: _____

Witnesses:

_____

_____

Date: _____

Time: _____

◄ FIGURE 5-8   Rights waiver form (Courtesy Geauga County, Ohio, Sheriff's Department)

4. *The suspect may indicate a desire not to talk with the investigators.* At this point, law enforcement has no choice other than to refrain from attempting to interrogate the suspect concerning the events of the crime for which he/she has been arrested. In this event, the case must be based on independent evidence, which may or may not be sufficient to warrant prosecution. The U.S. Supreme Court's emphatic position on terminating interrogation once a suspect has invoked the right to remain silent was announced in 1975 in the case of *Michigan* v. *Mosley.*[61]

Since the responsibility is on the prosecution, supported by evidence provided by the investigators, to substantiate the voluntariness of the waiver and the propriety of the warnings given to the suspect, many law-enforcement agencies provide printed cards with the exact wording of the required warnings. They further recommend or require that when warnings are given they be read verbatim from the printed card. In this manner, the officer, when testifying in court, can positively state the exact words used in advising the suspect of his/her constitutional rights. Such a procedure avoids any confrontation with the defense as to the exact wording and contents of the *Miranda* requirements. But in 1989 in *Duckworth* v. *Eagen*, the Supreme Court held that it was not necessary that the warnings be given in the exact form described in the *Miranda* decision, provided the warnings as a whole fully informed the suspect of his or her rights.[62] This position was reaffirmed in a 2010 case *Florida* v. *Powell.*[63]

A person being subjected to **in-custody interrogation** often chooses not to answer any questions posed by law enforcement—or at least not until an attorney is present. When counsel is made available to the suspect before or during interrogation, it is almost universal practice for the attorney to advise the client not to say anything to the police. Therefore, the effect of the *Miranda* decision has been to reduce significantly the number of valid interrogations by law-enforcement agencies in this country today. For the most part, however, confessions obtained in compliance with prescribed rules are of better quality and are more likely to be admissible in court.

It must be impressed on investigators that the failure to properly advise a suspect of the rights required by *Miranda* does not invalidate an otherwise valid arrest, nor does it necessarily mean a case cannot be successfully prosecuted. Even in light of the line of court decisions indicating that *Miranda* warnings may not be required in all interrogation situations, good practice or departmental policy may require that all suspects in custody be advised of their rights.

IN-CUSTODY INTERROGATION

For investigators to understand the proper application of the *Miranda* requirements, it is essential they understand the meaning of in-custody interrogation. The *Miranda* case involved simultaneous custody and interrogation. Subsequent police actions revealed that all cases were not so nicely defined and the meanings of "in custody" and "interrogation" required clarification. Although it may be difficult to separate the custody from the interrogation in certain factual situations, the two concepts must be considered separately.

Custody

Custody occurs when a person is deprived of his/her freedom in any significant way or is not free to leave the presence of law enforcement. Analyses of case decisions show there is not yet a universally accepted definition of custody. Rather, case-by-case analysis is used to determine the applicability of the *Miranda* requirements (Figure 5-9).

MIRANDA AND MISDEMEANORS

The question of whether *Miranda* applies to misdemeanor arrests was the subject of controversy for many years. In 1984, the Supreme Court settled this issue. The Court ruled in *Berkemer v. McCarty* that *Miranda* applies to the interrogation of an arrested person regardless of whether the offense is a felony or a misdemeanor. The justices found that to make a distinction would cause confusion, because many times it is not certain whether the person taken into custody is to be charged with a felony or a misdemeanor.[64]

INTERROGATION AS DEFINED BY THE U.S. SUPREME COURT

For legal purposes, interrogation includes any express questioning or any verbal or nonverbal behavior by a law-enforcement officer that is designed to elicit an

▲**FIGURE 5-9**
Uniformed officer with handcuffed prisoner
In deciding when *Miranda* warnings are required, there is no universally accepted definition of "custody." In this, photograph, it is clear that this suspect is in custody between the officer leading him by the arm and the handcuffs; there is no doubt that the suspect is not free to leave. (© Cleve Bryant/PhotoEdit)

incriminating statement or response from the suspect of a crime. For many years following the *Miranda* ruling, there was considerable confusion over what constituted questioning or interrogation. For example, in a 1977 case the Supreme Court found that an impermissible interrogation occurred when an investigator delivered what has been called the "Christian burial speech" to a man suspected of murdering a young girl. While the suspect was being transported between cities, the investigator told the suspect to think about how the weather was turning cold and snow was likely. He pointed out how difficult it would be to find the body later. The investigator went on to say that the girl's parents were entitled to have a Christian burial for the little girl, who had been taken from them on Christmas Eve and murdered. Subsequent to this little speech, the suspect led the investigators to the spot where he had disposed of the body. The Supreme Court held this to be an interrogation within the scope of *Miranda*, even though direct questions had not been asked of the suspect.[65]

The Supreme Court faced the question of what constitutes interrogation for the first time in the 1980 case of *Rhode Island* v. *Innis*. In that instance a robbery suspect was arrested after the victim had identified him from photographs. The prisoner was advised several times of his constitutional rights and was being transported by three officers who had been specifically ordered not to question the suspect. During the trip, two of the officers were having a conversation about the case, and one commented how terrible it would be if some unsuspecting child found the missing shotgun (used in the robbery) and got hurt. The conversation was not directed at the suspect, nor did the officers expect a response from the suspect. However, the suspect interrupted the conversation and, after again being advised of his rights, led the officers to the shotgun. The Supreme Court stated the rule regarding interrogation as follows:

> We conclude that *Miranda* safeguards come into play whenever a person in custody is subjected to either express questioning or its functional equivalent. That is to say, the term "interrogation" under *Miranda* refers not only to express questioning, but also to any words or actions on the part of the police (other than those normally attendant to arrest and custody) that the police should know are reasonably likely to elicit an incriminating response from the suspect. The latter portion of this definition focuses primarily upon the perceptions of the suspect, rather than the intent of the police. This focus reflects the fact that the *Miranda* safeguards were designed to vest a suspect in custody with an added measure of protection against coercive police practices, without regard to objective proof of the underlying intent of the police.[66]

As a general rule, *Miranda* warnings need not precede routine booking questions that are asked in order to obtain personal-history data necessary to complete the booking process. As long as the questions are for that purpose and not a pretext to obtain incriminating information, *Miranda* warnings need not be given.[67]

MOST RECENT U.S. SUPREME COURT DECISION ON THE RIGHT TO REMAIN SILENT

On June 1, 2010 the U.S. Supreme Court's decision in the area of ***Berghuis* v. *Thompkins*** was decided and shines new light on issues surrounding both the invocation and waiver of the *Miranda* right to remain silent.[68, 69]

In *Berghuis*, Van Chester Thompkins was arrested in Ohio for a shooting that occurred approximately one year earlier in Southfield, Michigan. While in custody,

Thompkins was questioned by two detectives in a police interview room. At the beginning of the interrogation, the detectives presented Thompkins with a general set of *Miranda* warnings.[70]

To make sure Thompkins could understand English, one of the detectives asked Thompkins to read a portion of the warnings out loud, which he did. Thereafter, the detective read the rest of the warnings to Thompkins and asked him to sign the form, indicating that he understood his rights. Thompkins refused to sign the form, and the officers began interrogating Thompkins. "At no point during the interrogation did Thompkins say he wanted to remain silent, did not want to talk to the police, or wanted an attorney."[71]

With the exception of some minor verbal responses and limited eye contact, Thompkins remained silent for most of the 3-hour interview. Approximately 2 hours and 45 minutes into the interrogation, one of the detectives asked Thompkins if he believed in God. Thompkins said he did. The detective then followed up by asking Thompkins if he prayed to God. Thompkins said, "Yes." The detective then asked, "Do you pray to God to forgive you for shooting that boy down?" To which, Thompkins answered, "Yes." Thompkins refused to make a written statement, and the interrogation ended.[72]

COURT PROCEEDINGS

Thompkins filed a motion to suppress the statements he made during the interrogation and claimed his Fifth Amendment right to remain silent had been violated. The trial court denied the motion, and Thompkins's admission was used against him at trial. Thompkins was convicted of first-degree murder and sentenced to life in prison without parole.

Thompkins appealed.[73] The Michigan Court of Appeals rejected the *Miranda* claim, and the Michigan Supreme Court denied review. Thereafter, Thompkins filed a petition for a writ of habeas corpus in the U.S. District Court for the Eastern District of Michigan that was likewise denied. The U.S. Court of Appeals for the Sixth Circuit reversed the district court ruling in favor of Thompkins.[74] However, for the reasons set forth herein, the Supreme Court reversed the judgment of the Sixth Circuit Court of Appeals and found no *Miranda* violations.

RIGHT TO REMAIN SILENT—INVOCATION

In filing his motion to suppress the statements he made during the interrogation, Thompkins first argued he had invoked his right to remain silent by not saying anything for the first 2 hours and 45 minutes of the interrogation. If, in fact, he had invoked his right to remain silent, it is undisputed the officers would have been obligated to stop questioning.[75] However, Justice Kennedy, in writing the majority opinion, explained that Thompkins's mere silence in the face of questioning was not clear and unambiguous invocation of his right to remain silent.[76] The Court noted that, unlike its earlier ruling in *Davis* v. *United States* regarding the invocation of the *Miranda* right to counsel, it never had defined whether an invocation of the right to remain silent must be unambiguous. In *Davis*, the defendant initially waived his *Miranda* rights and was interrogated for 90 minutes before saying, "Maybe I should talk to a lawyer." The Court held that if a subject is unclear, ambiguous, or equivocal in requesting a lawyer, officers can ignore the reference and proceed with the interrogation.[77]

In *Berghuis*, the Court acknowledged "there is no principled reason to adopt different standards for determining when an accused has invoked the *Miranda* right to remain silent and the *Miranda* right to counsel at issue in *Davis*. . . . Both protect the privilege against compulsory self-incrimination . . . by requiring an interrogation to cease when either right is invoked." Moreover, the Court explained there are no practical reasons for requiring that an invocation of the right to silence be clear and unambiguous. Namely, "an unambiguous invocation of *Miranda* rights results in an objective inquiry that 'avoid[s] difficulties of proof and . . . provide[s] guidance to officers on how to proceed in the face of ambiguity.'"[78] Accordingly, *Berghuis* does for the invocation of the right to silence what *Davis* did for the invocation of the right to counsel—it mandates that an invocation of either *Miranda* right must be clear and unambiguous to be effective.

RIGHT TO REMAIN SILENT—WAIVER

Thompkins next argued that absent an invocation of his right to silence, his statements still should be suppressed because he never adequately waived his right to silence. Two portions of the original *Miranda* decision seem to tilt the scale in Thompkins's favor on this issue. First, the *Miranda* Court said, "a valid waiver will not be presumed simply from the silence of the accused after warnings are given or simply from the fact that a confession was in fact eventually obtained."[79] Additionally, "a heavy burden rests on the government to demonstrate that the defendant knowingly and intelligently waived his privilege against self-incrimination. . . ."[80]

However, the Supreme Court has clarified its position with respect to the waiver since the *Miranda* decision. The impact has been to keep *Miranda* focused on the right to refrain from speaking and to consult an attorney. As the Court in *Berghuis* noted: "The main purpose of *Miranda* is to ensure that an accused is advised of and understands the right to remain silent and the right to counsel. . . ."[81] Thus, "if anything, our subsequent cases have reduced the impact of the *Miranda* rule on legitimate law enforcement while reaffirming the decision's core ruling that unwarned statements may not be used as evidence in the prosecution's case in chief."[82]

DETECTION OF DECEPTION

Identifying deceit is so difficult that repeated studies begun in the 1980s show that most people—including judges, attorneys, clinicians, police officers, FBI agents, politicians, teachers, mothers, fathers, and spouses—are no better than chance (50–50) when it comes to detecting deception.[83, 84] It is disturbing but true. Most people, including professionals, do no better than a coin toss at correctly perceiving dishonesty. Even those who are truly gifted at detecting deception (probably less than 1% of the general population) are seldom right more than 60% of the time. Consider the countless jurors who must determine honesty or dishonesty, guilt or innocence, based on what they think are deceptive behaviors. Unfortunately, those behaviors most often mistaken for dishonesty are primarily manifestations of stress, not deception.[85] There is simply no single behavior that is indicative of deception—not one.[86]

This does not mean we should abandon our efforts to study deception and observe for behaviors that, in context, are suggestive of it. But a realistic goal is to be able to read nonverbal behaviors with clarity and reliability.

THE CRITICAL ROLE OF THE COMFORT/ DISCOMFORT EQUATION IN DETECTING DECEPTION

Those who are lying or are guilty and must carry the knowledge of their lies and/or crimes with them find it difficult to achieve comfort, and their tension and distress may be readily observed. Attempting to disguise their guilt or deception places a very distressing cognitive load on them as they struggle to fabricate answers to what would otherwise be simple questions.[87]

The more comfortable a person is when speaking with investigators, the easier it will be to detect the critical nonverbal discomfort associated with deception. The goal is to establish high comfort during the early part of any interaction or during the period of time characterized as "rapport building." This helps to establish a baseline of behaviors during that period when the person, hopefully, does not feel threatened.

ESTABLISHING A COMFORT ZONE FOR DETECTING DECEPTION

In pursuing the detection of deception investigators must be aware of their impact on the actions of suspects being interrogated and recognize how their behavior will affect the other person's behavior.[88] How the investigator asks the question (accusingly), how the investigator sits (too close or not close enough), how the investigator looks upon the person (suspiciously), will either support or disrupt the suspect's comfort level. It is well established that if a person's personal space is violated, he/she will have a tendency to act nervous. In addition, if a person is questioned in a prosecutorial tone, this will very likely negatively intrude on the questioning process.

DEFINING SIGNS OF COMFORT

Comfort is readily apparent in conversations with family members and friends. It is easy to sense when people are having a good time and are comfortable. While seated at a table, people who are comfortable with each other will move objects aside so that nothing blocks their view, and over time, they may draw closer so they do not have to talk as loudly. Individuals who are comfortable display their bodies more openly, showing more of their torsos and the insides of their arms and legs (they allow ventral access or fronting). In the presence of strangers, comfort is more difficult to achieve, especially in stressful situations such as a formal interview or a deposition. This is why it is so important for the investigator to create a comfort zone from the very outset and to facilitate beneficial interaction with the person to be questioned.

When we are comfortable, there should be *synchrony* in our nonverbal behavior. The breathing rhythm of two comfortable people will be similar, as will the tone and pitch of their speech and their general demeanor. If a person is standing while talking to someone, leaning to the side with his/her hands in pockets and feet crossed, most likely the person he/she is talking to will do the same. By **mirroring** (called isoparaxis) another person's behavior, he/she is subconsciously saying "I am comfortable with you" (Figure 5-10).

In an interview setting or any situation in which a difficult topic is being discussed, the tone of each party should mirror the other's over time if there is synchrony.[89] If harmony does not exist between the people involved, synchrony will be missing, which will be discernible: they sit differently, talk in a different manner or tone, or at the least their expressions will be at odds, if not totally disparate. Asynchrony is a barrier to effective communication and is a serious obstacle to a successful interview or discussion.

Obviously, displays of comfort are more common in people speaking the truth; because there is no stress to conceal and no guilty knowledge to make them uncomfortable.[90] Thus, the investigator should still be looking for signs of discomfort—when they occur and in what context—to assess for possible deception.

SIGNS OF DISCOMFORT IN AN INTERACTION

We all show signs of discomfort when we do not like what is happening to us, when we do not like what we are seeing or hearing, or when we are compelled to talk about things we would prefer to keep hidden. We display discomfort first in our physiology, owing to arousal of the limbic brain.[91] Our heart rate quickens, we per-

▲ **FIGURE 5-10   Isoparaxis (mirroring)**
Here is an example of isoparaxis: both people are mirroring each other and leaning toward each other, showing signs of high comfort. (Joe Navarro, with Marin Karlins, *What Every Body Is Saying* [New York: Harper Collins, 2008], p. 212)

spire more, and we breathe faster. Beyond the physiological responses, which are autonomic (automatic) and require no thinking on our part, our bodies manifest discomfort nonverbally. We tend to move our bodies in an attempt to block or distance ourselves from the source of our discomfort. We rearrange ourselves, jiggle our feet, fidget, twist at the hips, or drum our fingers when we are scared, nervous, or significantly uncomfortable.[92] We have all noticed such discomfort behaviors in others—for example, at a job interview or being questioned about a serious matter. These actions do not automatically indicate deception but do indicate that a person is uncomfortable in the current situation for any number of reasons.

When the investigator is attempting to observe discomfort as a potential indicator of deception, the best setting is one that has no objects (such as furniture, tables, desks, or chairs) between the person being observed and the investigator. Movements of the lower limbs are particularly revealing. Thus, if a person is behind a desk or table, the investigator should try to move it or get the individual to move away from it, because such an obstacle will block the vast majority (nearly 80%) of the body surfaces that need to be observed. In fact, the investigator should watch for the deceptive individual using obstacles or objects to form a physical barrier between the investigator and him/her. The use of objects is a sign that an individual wants distance, separation, and partial concealment, because the subject is being less open—which goes hand in hand with being uncomfortable or even deceitful. When it comes to questioning someone, the investigator can obtain more nonverbal clues while standing rather than sitting.

Other clear signs of discomfort seen in people during a difficult or troubling interview include rubbing the forehead; covering the throat; difficulty swallowing; clearing the throat; coughing; covering or twisting the mouth; biting or licking lips; yawning and sighs; itching and rubbing the nose, mustache, or beard; tugging at the ears or covering the ears; pulling the hair or grooming it; flushing of the skin or becoming extremely pale; squeezing the face; rubbing the neck; and stroking the back of the head with a hand. People may show their displeasure with the process by rolling their eyes in disrespect, picking lint off themselves (preening), or talking down to the person asking the questions—giving short answers, becoming resistant, hostile, or sarcastic, or even displaying microgestures with indecent connotations such as giving the finger.[93]

When making false statements, liars will rarely touch or engage in other physical contact with the investigator. Since touching is more often done by the truthful person for emphasis, such distancing helps to alleviate the level of anxiety a dishonest person is feeling. Any diminution of touching observed in a person engaged in conversation, especially while listening to or answering critical questions, is more likely than not indicative of deception.[94]

When observing a person's face for signs of comfort or discomfort, investigators should look for subtle behaviors such as a grimace or a look of contempt.[95] Also, they should check to see if the person's mouth is quivering, which is a clear indication of nervousness and discomfort. Any facial expression that lasts too long or lingers is not normal, whether a smile, a frown, or a surprised look. Such contrived behavior during an interview is intended to influence the investigator's opinion and lacks authenticity. Often when people are caught doing something wrong or lying, they will hold a smile for an unusual period of time. Rather than being an indication of comfort, this type of false smile is actually an indication of discomfort.

On occasion, when we do not like what we are hearing, whether a question or an answer, we often close our eyes as if to block it. The various forms of eye-blocking mechanisms are analogous to folding one's hands tightly across the chest or turning away from those with whom we disagree. These blocking displays are performed sub-

consciously and occur often, especially during a formal interview, and are usually related to a specific topic. Eyelid flutter is also observed at times when a particular subject causes distress.[96]

All these eye manifestations are powerful clues as to how information is registering or what questions are problematic for the recipient. However, they are not necessarily direct indicators of deceit. Little or no eye contact is *not* indicative of deception.[97] As a matter of fact, predators and habitual liars actually engage in greater eye contract than most individuals and will lock eyes with the person they are communicating with. Research clearly shows that psychopaths, con artists, and habitual liars will actually increase eye contact and consciously employed it, because they are aware it is so commonly (but erroneously) believed by many that looking someone straight in the eye is a sign of truthfulness.

However, there are cultural differences in eye contact and eye-gaze behavior that must be considered in any attempt to detect deception. For example, individuals belonging to many groups of people, such as Latinos, Asians and people from the Middle East, are often taught to look down or away when being questioned by individuals in a position of authority. This behavior is considered to be a gesture of respect and deference.[98]

Head movements can also be revealing. If a person's head begins to shake either in the affirmative or in the negative as they are speaking, and the movement occurs simultaneously with what they are saying, then the statement can typically be relied on as being truthful. If, however, the head shake or head movement is delayed or occurs after the speech, then most likely the statement is contrived and not truthful. Although it may be very subtle, the delayed movement of the head is an attempt to further validate what has been stated and is not part of the natural flow of communication. In addition, honest head movements should be consistent with verbal denials or affirmations. If a head movement is inconsistent with or contrary to a person's statement, it may indicate deception. While typically involving more subtle rather than exaggerated head movement, this incongruity of verbal and nonverbal signals happens more often than we think. For example, someone may say, "I didn't do it," while slightly nodding his/her head in the affirmative.

During discomfort, the limbic brain takes over, and a person's face can conversely either flush or lighten in color. During difficult conversations, the investigator may also see increases in perspiration or breathing, an accelerated pulsation of the carotid artery, and the person noticeably wiping away sweat or trying to control her/his breathing in an effort to remain calm. Any trembling of the body, whether of the hands, fingers, or lips, or any attempt to hide or restrain the hands or lips (through disappearing or compressed lips), may be indicative of discomfort and/or deception, especially if it occurs after the period of normal nervousness should have been dissipated.

However, indications of nervousness do not necessarily mean deception. The following case illustrates this point.

In a Florida case several years ago a suspect whom the investigators accused of sexual assault and murder was interrogated for 16 hours and eventually confessed. The statement was later suppressed by the judge and the charges were dropped. The suspect had become a prime suspect, because his face flushed and he appeared embarrassed during an initial interview, a reaction interpreted as a sign of deception. Investigators did not know the suspect was a recovering alcoholic with a social anxiety disorder that caused him to sweat profusely and blush in stressful social situations. These same characteristics that could have been interpreted as being signs of guilt in this case were characteristics of a person responding to extreme stress.[99]

A person's voice may crack or may seem inconsistent when being deceptive; swallowing becomes difficult as the throat becomes dry from stress and the person begins to swallow hard. These problems can be evidenced by a sudden bob or jump of the Adam's apple and may be accompanied by the clearing or repeated clearing of the throat—all indicative of discomfort. However, these behaviors are indicators of distress, not guarantees of deception. For example, many honest people who testify in court display these behaviors simply because they are nervous and not because they are lying. Even after years of testifying, many law-enforcement officers still acknowledge they get nervous on the witness stand. Thus it is important to remember that signs of tension and stress need to be deciphered within the context in which they are occurring.

PACIFYING BEHAVIORS

Although pacifiers, which are physical behaviors we use to calm ourselves, are not alone definitive proof of deception (since they can manifest in innocent people who are nervous), they do provide another piece of the puzzle in determining what a person may be truly thinking.

Reading Pacifying Nonverbal and Interpersonal Interactions

- *Expect some pacifying behaviors.* A certain level of pacifying behavior is normal in everyday nonverbal displays; people do this to calm themselves as they adapt to an ever-changing environment. Pacifying behaviors take many forms. When

stressed we might soothe our necks with a gentle massage, stroke our faces, or play with our hair. This is done automatically. Our brains send out the message "please pacify me now," and our hands respond immediately, acting in a way that helps make us comfortable again. Sometimes we pacify by rubbing our necks or our lips from the inside with our tongue, or we exhale slowly with puffed cheeks to calm ourselves. If a stressed person is a smoker, he/she will smoke more, if given the opportunity. If the person chews gum, she/he will chew faster. All these pacifying behaviors satisfy the same requirement of the brain—that is, the brain requires the body to do something that will stimulate nerve endings, releasing calming endorphins in the brain so that the brain can be soothed. As a general rule, men prefer to pacify by touching their face; women prefer to pacify by touching their clothing, jewelry, necklace, and neck.

- *Get a clear view.* To assure that no pacifying behavior will be missed, have nothing blocking the total view of the person. If, for example, the person pacifies by wiping his/her hands on his/her lap, the investigator would want to see this—which is difficult to observe when there is a desk in the way.

- *Expect initial nervousness.* Initial nervousness in the questioning process by the police is normal. For example, if an innocent person is being told by the police that he/she is considered a suspect in a murder or rape investigation, one would certainly expect a certain level of nervousness.

- *Get the person to relax first.* As questioning progresses, individuals should eventually calm down and become more comfortable. In fact, a good investigator will make sure this happens by allowing the person to relax before asking questions or exploring topics that might be stressful.

- *Establish a baseline.* Once a person's pacifying behaviors have decreased and stabilized to normal (for that person), the investigator can recognize that pacifying level as a baseline for assessing future behavior.

- *Look for increased use of pacifiers.* As the interview or conversation continues, it is normal for pacifying behaviors to increase (spike) in their frequency, particularly when they occur in response to a specific question or piece of information. For example, if a person is questioned about a crime and starts to ventilate his collar (a pacifier), that means that specific inquiry has caused a sufficient amount of stress to make the brain require pacification. This indicates the issue needs to be pursued further. The behavior does not necessarily mean that deception is involved but simply that the topic is causing the interviewee stress.

- *Ask, pause, and observe.* Good investigators, like good conversationalists, should not engage in staccato-fashion type questioning. Unfortunately, some false confessions (discussed earlier in this chapter) have been obtained because of sustained staccato-like questioning, which causes high stress and obfuscation and nonverbal cues. Innocent people have been known to confess to crimes and have even provided written statements in order to terminate a stressful interview when excessive or inappropriate pressure is applied.[100]

- *Keep the interviewee focused.* Investigators should keep in mind that many times when people are simply talking and telling their side of the story there will be fewer useful nonverbals used than when the investigator controls the scope of the topic. Pointed questions elicit behavioral manifestations that are useful in assessing a person's honesty.

- *Chatter is not truth.* One mistake made by both novice and experienced investigators is to equate talking with truth. When the person being questioned is talking, investigators tend to believe them. When the person is reserved, it is assumed they are lying. During conversation, people who provide an overwhelming amount of information and detail about an event or a situation may appear to be telling the truth; however, they may really be trying to obfuscate the facts or lead the conversation in another direction.

- *Stress coming in and going out.* A person with guilty knowledge will present two distinct behaviors in sequence. When asked a difficult question such as "Were you involved in the murder of your wife?" The first behavior will reflect the stress experienced when hearing the question. The person will subconsciously respond with various distancing behaviors including foot withdrawal (moving him away from the investigator) and may lean away or may tighten his jaw and lips. This behavior will be followed by the second set of related behaviors, pacifying responses to the stress that may include signals such as neck touching, nose stroking, or neck massaging as he ponders the question or answer.

- *Isolate the cause of the stress.* Two behavior patterns in series—the stress indicators followed by pacifying behaviors—have traditionally been erroneously associated with deception. This is unfortunate, because these manifestations need to be explained more simply as what they are—indicators of stress and stress relief—not necessarily dishonesty. No doubt someone who is lying may display these same behaviors, but individuals who are nervous also show them.

SPECIFIC BEHAVIORS TO CONSIDER IN DETECTING DECEPTION

Following are some specific behaviors to consider when one is attempting to determine if a subject is being deceptive.

- *Lack of emphasis in hand behaviors:* As noted social psychologist Aldert Vrij and others have reported, a lack of arm movement and a lack of emphasis are suggestive of deception.[101] Any sudden reduction in or change in movement reflects brain activity. When arms shift from being animated to being still, there is a reason, be it dejection or (possibly) deception.

  Deceptive individuals will tend to display less steepling of the fingers. The investigator should look for the white knuckles of the individual who grabs the chair armrest in a fixed manner as though in an "ejector seat." Many criminal investigators have found that when the head, neck, arms, and legs are held in place with little movement and the hands and arms are clutching the armrest, such behavior is very much consistent with those who are about to deceive, but again, it is not definitive (Figure 5-11).

- *Swearing to the truthfulness of assertions:* Interestingly, as individuals make declarative statements that are false, they will avoid touching not only other people but also objects, such as a podium or table. It is almost unheard of for a person who is lying to yell affirmatively, "I didn't do it," while pounding his/her fist on a table. It is not at all unusual for individuals who are not being truthful to immediately invoke the name of God and say such things as "I swear to God," or perhaps even invoke their children by making statements such as "if I'm lying may my children die or lose their eyesight," or some other ridiculously desperate plea to convince the interrogator they are not lying. The same psychological motivation for swearing is involved in the use of such expressions as "I have a spotless record" and "I am a very religious man, I couldn't do anything like that." Expressions of this type are frequently used by guilty subjects in an effort to lend forcefulness or conviction to their assertions of innocence. Also, what usually happens in this case is that there may be very weak, non-emphatic statements and gestures that are equally mild. People who are being deceptive lack commitment and confidence in what they are saying. Although their thinking brain (neocortex) will decide what to say in order to mislead, their emotive brain (the limbic system—the honest part of the brain) simply will not be committed to the ruse and therefore will not emphasize their statements using nonverbal

▲ **FIGURE 5-11   Flash frozen**
Sitting for long periods in a chair, as though flash frozen in an ejector seat, is evidence of high stress and discomfort. (Joe Navarro, with Marin Karlins, *What Every Body Is Saying* [New York: Harper Collins, 2008], p. 227)

▲ **FIGURE 5-12   The rogatory position (palms up)**
The palms-up, or "rogatory," position usually indicates that the person wants to be believed or wants to be accepted. It is not a dominant, confident display. (Joe Navarro, with Marin Karlins, *What Every Body Is Saying* [New York: Harper Collins, 2008], p. 228)

behaviors (such as gestures). The sentiments of the limbic brain are hard to override.

- *The rogatory position:* When people place their outstretched arms in front of their bodies, with palms up, this is known as the *rogatory* (or "prayerful") display (Figure 5-12). Those who worship turn their palms up to God to ask for mercy. This behavior is also seen in individuals who say something that they want you to believe. When a person makes a declarative statement, note whether the hands are palms up or palms down. During regular conversation in which ideas are being discussed and neither party is vehemently committed to a particular point, the investigator can expect to see both palms-up and palms-down displays.

However, when a person is making a passionate and assertive declaration such as "You have to believe me, I did not kill her," those hands should be face down (Figure 5-13). If the statement is made palms up, the individual is supplicating to be believed, and such a statement should be highly suspect. Although this interpretation is not definitive, any declarative statement made with palms up should raise serious questions about the truthfulness of the statement being made. People who are telling the truth do not have to plead to be believed; they make a statement, and it stands.

USE OF TECHNOLOGICAL INSTRUMENTS TO DETECT DECEPTION

POLYGRAPH

The first workable polygraph is attributed to John Larson (1892–1983) in 1921. Its use spread relatively quickly in policing circles, and since then it has been improved a

▲ **FIGURE 5-13   Palms-down position**
Statements made palms down are more emphatic and more confident than statements made with the palms up, in the rogatory position. (Joe Navarro, with Marin Karlins, *What Every Body is Saying* [New York: Harper Collins, 2008], p. 229)

number of times, such as by adding the use of computer scoring (Figure 5-14). The primary purpose of a **polygraph** examination is to determine if victims, suspects, and informants are being truthful or untruthful about what they say. The polygraph is an adjunct to, but never a substitute for, other methods of investigation. Other common objectives for polygraph examinations are determining the reliability of informants, eliminating suspects, and narrowing the scope of an investigation. Research on the accuracy of the polygraph varies, roughly from 64% (laboratory studies) to 98% ("real world" use). Such differences may in part be attributable to laboratory protocols in which one group is told to lie about a mock crime scene or other event and the other group tells the truth. When people are not in real jeopardy for lying they may not have the same physiological responses as those who are lying to avoid criminal culpability for a felony.

Polygraphs record indicators of a person's cardiovascular pattern and fluctuations, respiratory patterns and fluctuations, and changes in skin resistance or sweat on the fingertips. The three most common findings by an examiner are no deception indicated, deception indicated, and inconclusive.

A supervisor's approval is required before an investigator can have a person examined by a polygraphist. The investigator is obliged to work with the examiner in a number of ways, such as:[102]

1. Providing the examiner with the information obtained in the investigation that supports and justifies the use of the polygraph.
2. Giving the polygraphist copies of incident, supplemental, and other relevant documents.

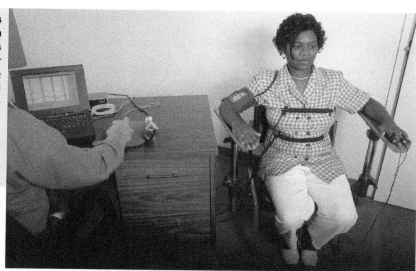

▶ **FIGURE 5-14 Polygraph examination**
Note that a blood-pressure cuff is attached to the subject's right upper arm; two pneumograph tubes are stretched across the chest and abdomen; and metal plates are attached to the index and ring fingers. Readings from these sources are displayed on the examiner's screen at the left side of this photograph.
(© Anna Clopet/Corbis)

3. Calling attention to evidence that the subject does not yet know the police have.
4. Making available background information on the subject, including criminal history and possible motives.
5. Advising of statements made by the subject to victims and witnesses, as well as alibis provided.
6. Giving news articles and other general information about the case.
7. Helping the examiner arrange for a sign-language interpreter or translator, as necessary.
8. Not trying to plan the procedures to be used, which is the purview of the examiner.
9. Not interrogating the suspect just before the examination.
10. Ensuring that persons authorized to be with the subject are present (for example, attorneys, parents, or legal guardians).
11. Promptly advising the examiner if the subject is going to be late or has cancelled.

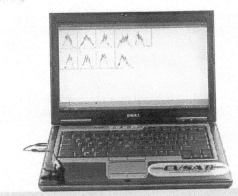

FIGURE 5-15
Computerized voice stress analysis system (CVSA)
Newly developed and released second-generation computerized voice stress analysis system (CVSA II) displayed on a laptop computer. (Courtesy National Institute for Truth Verification)

COMPUTER VOICE STRESS ANALYSIS

Computer Voice Stress Analysis (CVSA) was originally developed in 1988 by the National Institute for Truth Verification (NITV) and grew out of the Vietnam-era Psychological Stress Evaluator (PSE), which was used to differentiate between suspected Viet Cong and civilians. Around 1,600 police departments use the CVSA. The CVSA is small, easily portable, and, unlike the polygraph, does not require any attachments to the subject.

Basically, the CVSA notes microvariations in the audible and nonaudible portions of speech. As with the polygraph, reports of its accuracy have varied—for example, one laboratory study found that it was not significantly better than random chance, whereas NITV cited a number of studies showing much higher rates. Here, too, the earlier comments about the absence or presence of real jeopardy affecting the studies' outcomes apply.

The NITV spent many years and invested tremendous resources to develop an automated system to accurately quantify CVSA patterns with the goal of removing any subjectivity in evaluating CVSA charts. A new scoring algorithm has been developed and field tested in state and local law-enforcement agencies across the country. The charts under this new CVSA II (Figure 5-15), which was released in January 2007, reflect whether deception is or is not indicated. Field evaluations are showing a 96% accuracy rate for the new system, with a false positive rate of less than 1%.[103]

KEY TERMS

admission
Berghuis v. *Thompkins*
body language
coerced-compliant
coerced-internalized
computer voice stress
    analysis (CVSA)
confession
delay-in-arraignment rule

detection of deception
eyewitness identification
free-and-voluntary rule
in-custody interrogation
Maryland v. *Shatzer*
McNabb v. *United States*
Minnick v. *Mississippi*
Miranda v. *Arizona*
mirroring

polygraph
proximity
rapport
suspect
victim
voluntary false confession
witness
witness intimidation

REVIEW QUESTIONS

1. What are the similarities and differences between interviews and interrogations?
2. What are the four commonly recognized objectives in the interrogation process?
3. What are the qualifications of interviewers and interrogators?
4. What should an interrogation room look like?

5. What steps should an investigator take in order to prepare for an interview or interrogation?
6. Why is eyewitness testimony so unreliable?
7. What are the forms that witness intimidation can take?
8. What can the police do to deter individuals who would be inclined to intimidate witnesses?
9. What are the advantages of using electronic recordings for interrogation?
10. There are two basic categories of people who tend to confess to crimes. What are they?
11. Three categories of false confessions were discussed. What are they?
12. What recommendations were made to reduce the possibility of false confessions?
13. What was the first notable incident of U.S. Supreme Court intervention into interrogation practices by nonfederal law-enforcement officers?

14. What requirements are imposed on law-enforcement personnel by *Miranda* v. *Arizona*?
15. What are the facts and the significance of the U.S. Supreme Court case involving *Maryland* v. *Shatzer* in 2010?
16. What is the significance of the U.S. Supreme Court decision in the case of *Berghuis* v. *Thompkins*?
17. In the discussion of detection of deception a number of body positions were discussed: isoparaxis, flash frozen, rogatory position and the palms-down position. What is the significance of each of these positions as it relates to the detection of deception?
18. What types of measurements are employed by the polygraph and computer voice stress analysis to detect deception?

INTERNET ACTIVITIES

Much debate surrounds the fairness and effectiveness of eyewitness identification in police lineups. Go to *www.eyewitness.utep.edu/consult04A.html* and read the summary of the whitepaper regarding evaluating lineup fairness. What two aspects of lineup fairness should investigators consider? How similar to one another should the members of the lineup be?

6

FIELD NOTES
AND REPORTING

CHAPTER OBJECTIVES

1. Understand the importance of field notes.
2. List the six interrogatory investigative questions.
3. Understand formats for basic incident reports.
4. Explain techniques involved in writing effective reports.

5. Summarize the report approval and disposition processes.
6. Explain the purpose of follow-up investigation and supplemental reports.

Taking field notes and writing reports is considered a necessary evil by most law-enforcement officers and investigators. These tasks are not the most exciting or pleasurable parts of the profession. Yet, it cannot be overemphasized how important it is to perform these duties at the highest levels of accuracy and completeness.

This chapter examines several aspects of the field-note-taking and report-writing processes. After discussing field notes and the basic and primary questions that need to be asked in an investigation, it addresses the importance of completing well-prepared incident/offense reports. Incident-report formats vary among law-enforcement agencies. Despite the variation, however, there are common elements that should be included in all reports.

It is considered a standard practice that investigators should gain as much information as possible when arriving at the crime scene. Even facts and details that seem unnecessary at first may later prove to be highly valuable to the investigation. But this practice must be tempered with the following caution:

> determinations must be made as early as possible in the investigative process of what the case is about and what potential criminal charges may be filed, followed by what information the prosecutor will need to file formal charges, what the elements of the offense are, and, also important, what the prosecutor needs to prove a case. Equipped with this information, the first responders and follow-up investigators can pursue and focus on the investigation so that they can separate the important from the "nice to have" or superfluous information. Such an approach is appreciated by prosecutors.

FIELD NOTES

Field notes play a significant role in every criminal investigation. They provide a short written record of events, times, places, suspects, witnesses, and other information and are used as the basis for preparing incident/offense reports. The importance of taking effective and complete notes in every investigation, regardless of the offense, should not be underestimated. Because field notes are more reliable than a person's memory, they can be used as a source of specific facts and details that otherwise might be forgotten. Detailed field notes also reduce the need to recontact victims and witnesses regarding information that was overlooked or questions that were not asked in the initial contact. Finally, it is not uncommon for officers to testify in court several months or years after the conclusion of a particular investigation. Comprehensive field notes can not only help to refresh the

investigator's memory but also to strengthen his/her court testimony.

Field notes are the shorthand written record made by a police officer from the time she/he arrives at the scene until the assignment is completed. Field notes are more reliable than an officer's memory. It is probably easy to remember what you had for breakfast this morning, but what about your lunch five months ago?[1] Often an officer responds to several calls before he/she has time to write an incident/offense report on an earlier call. Even during that short time, some important details can be forgotten. The only way to prevent the possibility of lost information is to prepare thorough field notes.

Field notes are the primary information source for preparing the incident/offense report. Because the first-responding officer is usually the person who writes any incident report required by the situation, field notes are important, because they contain the information that forms the content of the incident report. Moreover, other

▲ FIGURE 6-1

Homicide investigators sharing information from their field notes

These investigators have just finished interviewing neighbor residents in an apartment building where a homicide occurred. The investigators are discussing the information gleaned from their interviews. One investigator is conferring on a cell phone with a third colleague in an effort to join the pieces of the event into a whole story. (© James D. DeCamp/ Columbus Dispatch)

officers who also responded may have taken actions or seen and heard things that are of investigative significance and for which there needs to be an investigative record. They will rely on their own field notes to write reports that supplement the incident report. Well-taken, detailed field notes are the wellspring for good incident reports.

Detailed field notes may reduce the need to recontact the parties involved. Once in a while, victims and witnesses get annoyed and even angry when they are recontacted by an officer who obviously didn't take good field notes when he/she talked to them earlier and therefore cannot complete the incident report without additional information. Comments such as "Weren't you listening to me?" or "You couldn't be very interested in my case, or you would have asked about this when you talked to me the first time" can be avoided by taking thorough notes. The follow-up investigator faces the possibility of similar comments when recontacting victims and witnesses: "Didn't you talk to the officer who took the report?" "With you guys, it looks like the left hand doesn't know what the right one is doing." Although follow-up investigators may be required by departmental policy to make such contacts, sometimes they may have to do so because of shortcomings in the incident report. (For more on this point, see Chapter 7, "The Follow-Up Investigation and Investigative Resources.")

Field notes can be used to defend the integrity of the incident/offense report. When an officer is testifying in a case for which he/she wrote the incident report, the officer can refer to field notes for assistance in recollecting the events. Most often, cases come to trial months or years after the incident report is written, so it would be rare for a testifying officer to remember everything about the event and all its details. In court, field notes are an indication of an officer's thoroughness as an investigator. Moreover, if at trial an officer is asked what sources of information were relied on in preparing the incident report, the notes add to the credibility of the report (Figure 6-1).

GUIDELINES FOR NOTE-TAKING

There are six main guidelines for taking notes:

1. Listen attentively, without interrupting the person who is speaking.
2. Intervene if the speaker is losing focus; bring the person back to the topic as gently as possible.
3. Review all specifics in your notes with the person providing the information.
4. Allow time for the person to consider the information you have stated and to verify it, correct it, or add information.
5. Add and/or correct information as needed.
6. Verify all changes in your notes with the speaker.[2]

NOTE-TAKING EQUIPMENT

Officers typically use small loose-leaf and spiral-bound notebooks for their field notes. Through experience they learn which sizes and types best suit the way they work.[3] Most officers use a ballpoint pen to write their notes. If you are going to write on the front and back of pages, do not use a heavy ink, as it "bleeds" through to the other side of a page, and you will not be able to use that side for note-taking. Number the pages separately for each case, and use some kind of case identifier, such as the case number, on each page so that the pages can be put back in order if they are accidentally separated. Officers should place a departmental business card, or duplicate its information, on the inside of the notebook used for field notes.

Entries in the notebook should be made on a chronological basis. If you are using a loose-leaf notebook, remove the pages when they are filled, place them in a sealed envelope with the covered time period noted on the outside, and insert new blank pages. If you are using a spiral-bound notebook, place the entire notebook in a sealed envelope and start with a new one. Too often, first-responding officers and investigators think it is all right to discard their field notes after they prepare the incident report. This is not a good idea. Frequently, in a later court proceeding, the officer/investigator will be asked to explain where or from whom he/she got the information contained in the incident report. If all the information and its sources are not contained in the incident report, the field notes made at the time of the investigation can often provide reliable answers to the questions asked.

Officers/investigators should not use case notebooks to record personal information such as a list of groceries to buy on the way home. Should such information mistakenly end up in the notes the officer/investigator takes to court, it can be used to embarrass the note-taker. The defense attorney has the right to inspect whatever the witness is using to refresh his/her memory and ask questions to insure that the witness is using the notes only to refresh memory, not to recall information totally forgotten. If the witness does not prepare for trial by studying the notes and case file beforehand, such a situation will become clear very quickly once the witness starts to testify.

SIX INTERROGATORY AND BASIC INVESTIGATIVE QUESTIONS

To gather needed information, first-responding officers and follow-up investigators should phrase all questions beginning with the six interrogatories—who, what, where, when, how, and why. Although no single set of questions can meet the investigative needs in all types of crime, following this format should provide the needed information for the officer/investigator to understand the chronological order of events as they occurred and to enable the preparation of a well-written and thorough incident report. Here are some examples of typical questions:

1. **Who**
   —was the victim?
   —discovered the crime?
   —reported the crime?
   —took the victim to his or her present location?
   —does the suspect associate with?
   —was last seen with the victim?
   —last saw the victim?
   —may be with the suspect when he/she is arrested?
   —are the witnesses connected with or related to?
   —had a motive and the means of committing the crime?
   —completed the crime scene entry and other logs?
   —processed the scene?
   —took what evidence where?
   —else may have heard, smelled, touched, or seen anything of investigative value?

2. **What**
   —crime was committed?
   —actions did the suspect take?
   —methods did the suspect use?
   —do witnesses know about the crime?
   —evidence is there?
   —tools or weapons were used?
   —actions did you take?
   —further action is needed?
   —information may victims and witnesses be withholding?
   —does the victim claim was stolen?
   —parts of the victim's account of the event match that of any witnesses, the appearance of the scene, and the physical evidence?
   —information (and evidence of what types) do you need to clear the crime?
   —knowledge, skills, or strength was needed?
   —other units or agencies are involved or need to be notified?
   —is the case about?
   —are the potential charges?
   —information does the prosecutor need to file formal charges or seek a grand jury indictment?
   —are the elements of the offense?
   —does the prosecutor need to prove the case?

3. **Where**
   —was the crime discovered?
   —was the crime committed?
   —were any tools, evidence, or recovered property found?
   —was the victim when the crime was committed?
   —is the victim now?
   —were the witnesses?
   —did the suspect go?
   —does the suspect frequent, live, and work?
   —is the suspect now?
   —was the suspect arrested?
   —was the evidence marked?
   —is the evidence stored?
   —might other witnesses be located?

4. **When**
   —were you dispatched, and when did you arrive?
   —was the crime discovered?

—was the crime committed?

—was the victim last seen?

—did help arrive, and what type was it?

—was the suspect arrested?

—did the suspect decide to commit the crime?

5. **How**

—was the crime committed?

—did the suspect get to and from the scene?

—did the suspect get the information needed to commit the crime?

—were tools and weapons obtained?

—was the arrest made?

—much injury was done to the victim?

—much damage was there to any premises involved?

—much money was taken, and what type of valuables?

—difficult was it to carry off the property that was stolen?

—is the suspect described by the victim and witnesses?

—closely do the descriptions of victims and witnesses match and diverge?

6. **Why**

—was the crime committed?

—were particular tools or weapons used?

—was the crime reported?

—was there a delay in reporting the crime?

—were the victim or witnesses reluctant to talk?

—were the victim or witnesses so quick to identify the suspect?

—am I uncomfortable with the victim's account and description of the suspect?

INCIDENT REPORTS

Despite the fact that **incident reports** are a crucial source of investigative information, writing them is often not a popular duty. One of the authors says that report writing "is not the favorite indoor sport of law-enforcement officers." The significance of this jest has serious implications. An incident report, like an investigative report, must tell a story. It must be written in such a manner that someone reading that report can understand what happened and can know the answers to the questions who, what, where, when, how, and why. Along with his/her memory, an officer/investigator must use the field notes taken to tell the story of the events. There are two indispensable elements of reports: (1) accuracy and (2) clear communication of the meaning that the writer intended.

More than a few excellent investigations have been wasted by an officer's failure to fully document what was done and not done. The case history that follows indicates the importance of recording all aspects of an investigation:

A burglary in progress was reported at a one-story doctor's office. As two officers moved to cover the building, a suspect was seen leaping from an office window carrying a small flight bag. The suspect ran from the scene, followed by one of the officers. He attempted to scale a fence. In the ensuing struggle, the suspect fell on the far side of the fence, breaking his arm. During treatment at a hospital, the suspect told the officer, in front of medical personnel, that he was going to claim his arm had been broken during questioning. He further indicated this would be an attempt to discredit the police, as he had only recently been released from the state prison and feared that such an immediate second violation would cause the court to invoke a stringent sentence upon conviction. Because many arrested people state that they are going to claim the police violated their civil rights, the officer regarded it as little more than a commonplace occurrence. Even though they did not relate directly to the investigation, the suspect's remarks and the identity of the persons witnessing them were included in the report as a matter of thoroughness. Subsequently, when the FBI investigated the matter of a possible violation of the suspect's rights, the allegation was easily refuted by corroborating statements from the medical personnel identified in the police officer's report.

A well-prepared incident report based on a thorough investigation of an offense can promote the rapid apprehension of the suspect, thus preventing further crimes and making the recovery of property more likely. The report also serves as the official memory of the department so that anyone who needs access to the file after the reporting officer or investigator is no longer available, can make sense of the report and the event.

Incident reports serve important operational and administrative purposes. When their data are combined, useful crime analysis reports can be produced, personnel assignments in the department can be properly aligned with the actual workloads, and geographic information system (GIS) data can produce informative maps showing, for example, where robberies with certain types of characteristics are being committed.

FORMATS FOR INCIDENT REPORTS

Although the exact layout for incident reports varies from one jurisdiction to another, all incident report forms have a "face" with blank spaces that must be filled in by the officer conducting the preliminary investigation. He/She enters basic case information in the blanks, such as information about the type of crime committed; the complainant, victim, witnesses, and offenders; and other details. Figure 6-2 shows a basic incident report.

CRN 01-____-____-_____   **Athens-Clarke County Police**   Page 1 of ____
INCIDENT REPORT   ORI - GA0290100

Press Hard - Multiple Copies   Press Hard - Multiple Copies   Revised 0900

From Date	From Time	To Date	To Time	☐ Complainant ☐ Victim No. ___ ☐ Witness No. ___	Premise Type	Case Status

Desires Personal Information Not Be Released

Premise Type
1. Highway
2. Serv. Station
3. Conv. Store
4. Bank
5. Commercial
6. Residence
7. School/Campus
8. All Other

Case Status
☐ Active
☐ Inactive
☐ Arrest -Adult
☐ Arrest-Juv.
☐ Ex. Cleared
☐ Unfounded
Status Date

Department Title Most Serious Criminal / Traffic / Ordinance Offense. See Table.   Zone

☐ Downtown ☐ AHA

Incident Location - Common Name   Address: No., Dir., St., Suffix, Apt.

☐ Athens ☐ Winterville ☐ Bogart

☐ Alcohol Related ☐ Drug Related ☐ Unknown
Type Of Drug(s) ☐ Amphetamine ☐ Barbiturate ☐ Cocaine ☐ Hallucinogen ☐ Heroin ☐ Marijuana ☐ Opium ☐ Methamphetamine ☐ Synthetic Narcotic ☐ Unknown ☐ Form:____
Solvability Factors: ☐ M.O. Present ☐ Physical Evidence ☐ Property Traceable ☐ Witness
Suspect Can Be: ☐ Named ☐ ID ☐ Located ☐ Described ☐ Vehicle ID

Complainant Information ☐ Juvenile ☐ Victim
Last / First
Middle / Suffix
Address: No., Dir., St., Suffix, Apt
City, State ☐ Athens, GA / Zip Code
Phone: Home / Work
Race ☐ M ☐ F DOB

Victim Information ☐ Juvenile ☐ State Of GA ☐ A.C.C.
Last
First
Middle / Suffix
Address: No., Dir., St., Suffix, Apt
City, State ☐ Athens, GA / Zip Code
Home / Work / Cell/Pager
Race ☐ M ☐ F DOB
Alias/Street Name
Employer / Occupation
☐ County Resident ☐ Student School
☐ Can ID Suspect ☐ Will File Charges ☐ Medical Treatment Hospital
Type / Extent Of Injury: ☐ Fatal Injury ☐ Broken Bones ☐ Gun/Knife ☐ Superficial Injury ☐ Sexual Abuse ☐ Other ☐ Property Damage/Loss ☐ Mental Abuse ☐ Threats

Witness 1 Information ☐ Juvenile
Last, First, Middle, Suffix
Address: No., Dir., St., Suffix, Apt
City, State ☐ Athens, GA / Zip Code
Phone: Home / Work
Race ☐ M ☐ F DOB

Witness 2 Information ☐ Juvenile
Last, First, Middle, Suffix
Address: No., Dir., St., Suffix, Apt
City, State ☐ Athens, GA / Zip Code
Phone: Home / Work
Race ☐ M ☐ F DOB

Reporting Officer

Offender 1 Information ☐ Juvenile
Last
First
Middle / Suffix
Address: No., Dir., St., Suffix, Apt
City, State ☐ Athens, GA / Zip Code
Home / Work / Cell/Pager
Race ☐ M ☐ F DOB
Alias/Street Name
Employer / Occupation
☐ County Resident ☐ Student School
OLN / State
Height / Weight / **Stranger To Stranger?** ☐ Yes ☐ No
Eye Color: ☐ Black ☐ Brown ☐ Blue ☐ Green ☐ Hazel ☐ Gray ☐ Other____
Hair Color: ☐ Blonde ☐ Brown ☐ Black ☐ Red ☐ Gray ☐ Salt&Pepper ☐ Other____
Offender's Vehicle Description ☐ Vehicle Searched
Tag / Year / State
Veh. Year / Make
Model / Style
Color-Top / Color-Bottom

☐ **Incident Recorded** ☐ Hand cuffed
Tape No. ☐ D. L. ☐ B. B.

Burglary Factors For Incident/Offense No.____
Forced Entry? ☐ Yes ☐ No ☐ Unknown ☐ Kicked ☐ Pushed ☐ Pry Tool ☐ Heavy Object ☐ Lock Tamper ☐ Cutting Tool
Point Of Entry? ☐ Door ☐ Window ☐ Roof ☐ Wall ☐ Attic ☐ Other ☐ Unk ☐ Front ☐ Rear ☐ Side ☐ Basement ☐ Move A/C
Point Of Exit? ☐ Same As Entry ☐ Other____
Structure Was: ☐ Occupied ☐ Unoccupied

Attached Documents:
☐ Incident/Offense Continuation
☐ Persons Form ☐ Juvenile Complaint
☐ Domestic Violence ☐ Property / Vehicle
☐ GCIC ☐ ABR ☐ Victim Notification

Emp. No. / Report Date / Approving Supervisor / Emp. No.

Incident /Offense 1 Code Section
☐ Attempted ☐ Committed
Title
Assault Factors ☐ Assault ☐ Theft ☐ DV ☐ Sexual ☐ Mental Subject ☐ Hate Crime ☐ Unknown
Weapon Type ☐ Gun ☐ Other ☐ Knife/Cutting Tool ☐ Hands/Fists/Etc.
Weapon Description
Offense Status ☐ Active ☐ Inactive ☐ Unfounded ☐ Arrest ☐ Ex. Cleared
Involved Suspect No.(s) / Victim No. (s)
Murder Circumstance

Incident /Offense 2 Code Section
☐ Attempted ☐ Committed
Title
Assault Factors ☐ Assault ☐ Theft ☐ DV ☐ Sexual ☐ Mental Subject ☐ Hate Crime ☐ Unknown
Weapon Type ☐ Gun ☐ Other ☐ Knife/Cutting Tool ☐ Hands/Fists/Etc.
Weapon Description
Offense Status ☐ Active ☐ Inactive ☐ Unfounded ☐ Arrest ☐ Ex. Cleared
Involved Suspect No.(s) / Victim No. (s)
Murder Circumstance

Incident /Offense 3 Code Section
☐ Attempted ☐ Committed
Title
Assault Factors ☐ Assault ☐ Theft ☐ DV ☐ Sexual ☐ Mental Subject ☐ Hate Crime ☐ Unknown
Weapon Type ☐ Gun ☐ Other ☐ Knife/Cutting Tool ☐ Hands/Fists/Etc.
Weapon Description
Offense Status ☐ Active ☐ Inactive ☐ Unfounded ☐ Arrest ☐ Ex. Cleared
Involved Suspect No.(s) / Victim No. (s)
Murder Circumstance

Incident /Offense 4 Code Section
☐ Attempted ☐ Committed
Title
Assault Factors ☐ Assault ☐ Theft ☐ DV ☐ Sexual ☐ Mental Subject ☐ Hate Crime ☐ Unknown
Weapon Type ☐ Gun ☐ Other ☐ Knife/Cutting Tool ☐ Hands/Fists/Etc.
Weapon Description
Offense Status ☐ Active ☐ Inactive ☐ Unfounded ☐ Arrest ☐ Ex. Cleared
Involved Suspect No.(s) / Victim No. (s)
Murder Circumstance

▲ **FIGURE 6-2**   **Basic incident report**
(Courtesy Athens-Clarke County, Georgia, Police Department)

NIBRS-COMPLIANT INCIDENT REPORTS

For more than a decade, a voluntary program has been moving law-enforcement agencies away from the basic incident-report format and toward a detailed format that documents much more data about an offense. This program, the **National Incident-Based Reporting System (NIBRS)**, was created as part of the **Uniform Crime Reports** and is administered by the FBI. It is in use in over 4,000 small and medium-size local law-enforcement agencies throughout the country, as well as a growing number of jurisdictions with populations in excess of 250,000. A large number of departments are working toward becoming NIBRS-compliant.

National crime reporting in the United States dates back roughly 70 years, to the time when the FBI began collecting and publishing annual "counts" of offenses in its Uniform Crime Reports (UCRs). Over the past 25 years, the desire for detailed, descriptive data about criminal offenses for crime analysis and other uses has necessitated a shift in incident-report formats. With this shift, which is still in progress, police agencies have started accumulating data about the relationship between victims and offenders, the role of drugs and alcohol in offending, and other factors. The availability of NIBRS data means that law-enforcement officials can more effectively allocate their resources to combat crime. Figure 6-3 reveals the level of detail in an NIBRS-compliant report, the last page of which is a continuation sheet for the chronological narrative. As computer technology continues to evolve, more and more of these reports are completed electronically (see "Computer-Generated Reports," below).

COMPUTER-GENERATED REPORTS

Since the 1980s, many law-enforcement vehicles have been equipped with **mobile computer terminals (MCTs)** (Figures 6-4 and 6-5). Although the terminals initially had limited capabilities and occasional reliability problems, MCTs have reduced demands on the overcrowded voice channels and enhanced officer safety. Technological advances continue to create new options and possibilities for the use of wireless systems in law-enforcement vehicles. Depending on the system and software used, current MCTs can do the following:

1. Provide consistently secure communications between 911 and law-enforcement units, and among law-enforcement units.
2. Allow officers to directly check important databases (rather than going through a dispatcher and waiting for a reply). They can access the National Crime Information Center (NCIC), as well as state and local systems. Officers can also receive information about newly wanted persons, including a facial composite likeness or mug shot. Outstanding warrants, court orders, stolen property inquiries, criminal and driving records, mug-shot files, crime analysis reports, and GIS maps of crimes and other incidents may all be directly available to the officer.
3. Enable officers in the field to write incident reports electronically, with full access to spelling- and grammar-checking tools. In modest systems, the reports are saved to a disk, from which they are printed at the station.

In addition to using MCTs, some agencies are using **iPhones and iPads** (Figure 6-6). iPads are particularly useful in traffic enforcement; they print a hard copy of the citation for the violator and send a digital copy to the station.

Agencies using wireless technologies have experienced significant productivity gains as the systems reduce the amount of time officers must spend on paperwork. In general, the time gained per officer ranges from 2.5 to 4 hours per day.

HANDWRITTEN REPORTS

Despite the widespread use of MCTs, many officers still write all their reports by hand, because their jurisdictions cannot afford MCT technology, have not made its acquisition a priority item in their budgets, or believe that the technology's cost outweighs its benefits. In actuality, when the formats of handwritten and MCT-generated reports are compared, the differences can be so slight that it is difficult to distinguish between the two.

Hand writing reports is slower, and officers do not have the advantages provided by spelling and grammar checkers. Moreover, if officers make mistakes, sometimes the only solution is to rewrite the page up to the point of the error and then continue with the correct information. Although officers writing incident reports electronically also make mistakes, recovery is much easier, because it is a simple matter to insert additional words, sentences, and paragraphs.

COMMON ELEMENTS OF INCIDENT REPORTS

Incident-report contents vary, ranging from the essential data in a basic incident report to the more extensive information in an NIBRS-compliant report. However, certain elements are common to most reports. The importance of obtaining as much detailed and complete information as possible for inclusion in the incident report cannot be over emphasized.

Name

The full names of complainants, witnesses, and other parties must always be obtained. In the recording of proper names, the first time an individual is referred to in a report the sequence of names should be last, first, middle. When a person mentioned in the report is commonly known to acquaintances by some name other than the

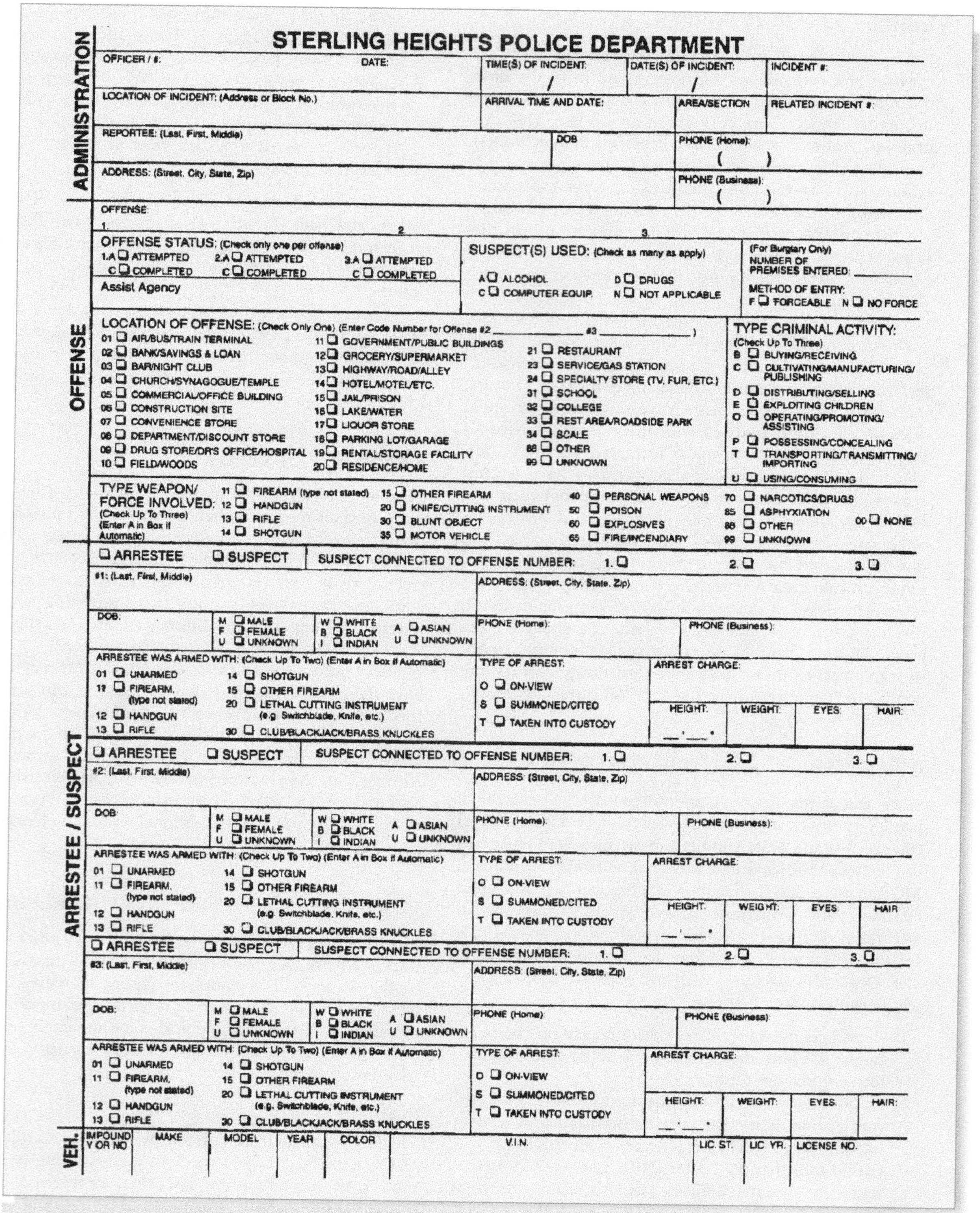

STERLING HEIGHTS POLICE DEPARTMENT

ADMINISTRATION

OFFICER / #: | DATE: | TIME(S) OF INCIDENT: / | DATE(S) OF INCIDENT: / | INCIDENT #:

LOCATION OF INCIDENT: (Address or Block No.) | ARRIVAL TIME AND DATE: | AREA/SECTION | RELATED INCIDENT #:

REPORTEE: (Last, First, Middle) | DOB | PHONE (Home): ( )

ADDRESS: (Street, City, State, Zip) | PHONE (Business): ( )

OFFENSE

OFFENSE: 1. 2. 3.

OFFENSE STATUS: (Check only one per offense)
1.A ☐ ATTEMPTED C ☐ COMPLETED; 2.A ☐ ATTEMPTED C ☐ COMPLETED; 3.A ☐ ATTEMPTED C ☐ COMPLETED
Assist Agency

SUSPECT(S) USED: (Check as many as apply)
A ☐ ALCOHOL D ☐ DRUGS C ☐ COMPUTER EQUIP. N ☐ NOT APPLICABLE

(For Burglary Only) NUMBER OF PREMISES ENTERED: ____
METHOD OF ENTRY: F ☐ FORCEABLE N ☐ NO FORCE

LOCATION OF OFFENSE: (Check Only One) (Enter Code Number for Offense #2 ______ #3 ______)
01 ☐ AIR/BUS/TRAIN TERMINAL
02 ☐ BANK/SAVINGS & LOAN
03 ☐ BAR/NIGHT CLUB
04 ☐ CHURCH/SYNAGOGUE/TEMPLE
05 ☐ COMMERCIAL/OFFICE BUILDING
06 ☐ CONSTRUCTION SITE
07 ☐ CONVENIENCE STORE
08 ☐ DEPARTMENT/DISCOUNT STORE
09 ☐ DRUG STORE/DR'S OFFICE/HOSPITAL
10 ☐ FIELD/WOODS
11 ☐ GOVERNMENT/PUBLIC BUILDINGS
12 ☐ GROCERY/SUPERMARKET
13 ☐ HIGHWAY/ROAD/ALLEY
14 ☐ HOTEL/MOTEL/ETC.
15 ☐ JAIL/PRISON
16 ☐ LAKE/WATER
17 ☐ LIQUOR STORE
18 ☐ PARKING LOT/GARAGE
19 ☐ RENTAL/STORAGE FACILITY
20 ☐ RESIDENCE/HOME
21 ☐ RESTAURANT
23 ☐ SERVICE/GAS STATION
24 ☐ SPECIALTY STORE (TV, FUR, ETC.)
31 ☐ SCHOOL
32 ☐ COLLEGE
33 ☐ REST AREA/ROADSIDE PARK
34 ☐ SCALE
88 ☐ OTHER
99 ☐ UNKNOWN

TYPE CRIMINAL ACTIVITY: (Check Up To Three)
B ☐ BUYING/RECEIVING
C ☐ CULTIVATING/MANUFACTURING/PUBLISHING
D ☐ DISTRIBUTING/SELLING
E ☐ EXPLOITING CHILDREN
O ☐ OPERATING/PROMOTING/ASSISTING
P ☐ POSSESSING/CONCEALING
T ☐ TRANSPORTING/TRANSMITTING/IMPORTING
U ☐ USING/CONSUMING

TYPE WEAPON/FORCE INVOLVED: (Check Up To Three) (Enter A in Box if Automatic)
11 ☐ FIREARM (type not stated)
12 ☐ HANDGUN
13 ☐ RIFLE
14 ☐ SHOTGUN
15 ☐ OTHER FIREARM
20 ☐ KNIFE/CUTTING INSTRUMENT
30 ☐ BLUNT OBJECT
35 ☐ MOTOR VEHICLE
40 ☐ PERSONAL WEAPONS
50 ☐ POISON
60 ☐ EXPLOSIVES
65 ☐ FIRE/INCENDIARY
70 ☐ NARCOTICS/DRUGS
85 ☐ ASPHYXIATION
88 ☐ OTHER
99 ☐ UNKNOWN
00 ☐ NONE

ARRESTEE / SUSPECT

☐ ARRESTEE ☐ SUSPECT | SUSPECT CONNECTED TO OFFENSE NUMBER: 1. ☐ 2. ☐ 3. ☐
#1: (Last, First, Middle) | ADDRESS: (Street, City, State, Zip)
DOB: | M ☐ MALE F ☐ FEMALE U ☐ UNKNOWN | W ☐ WHITE B ☐ BLACK I ☐ INDIAN A ☐ ASIAN U ☐ UNKNOWN | PHONE (Home): | PHONE (Business):
ARRESTEE WAS ARMED WITH: (Check Up To Two) (Enter A in Box if Automatic)
01 ☐ UNARMED; 11 ☐ FIREARM, (type not stated); 12 ☐ HANDGUN; 13 ☐ RIFLE; 14 ☐ SHOTGUN; 15 ☐ OTHER FIREARM; 20 ☐ LETHAL CUTTING INSTRUMENT (e.g. Switchblade, Knife, etc.); 30 ☐ CLUB/BLACKJACK/BRASS KNUCKLES
TYPE OF ARREST: O ☐ ON-VIEW S ☐ SUMMONED/CITED T ☐ TAKEN INTO CUSTODY
ARREST CHARGE: | HEIGHT: __'__" | WEIGHT: | EYES: | HAIR:

☐ ARRESTEE ☐ SUSPECT | SUSPECT CONNECTED TO OFFENSE NUMBER: 1. ☐ 2. ☐ 3. ☐
#2: (Last, First, Middle) | ADDRESS: (Street, City, State, Zip)
DOB: | M ☐ MALE F ☐ FEMALE U ☐ UNKNOWN | W ☐ WHITE B ☐ BLACK I ☐ INDIAN A ☐ ASIAN U ☐ UNKNOWN | PHONE (Home): | PHONE (Business):
ARRESTEE WAS ARMED WITH: (Check Up To Two) (Enter A in Box if Automatic)
01 ☐ UNARMED; 11 ☐ FIREARM, (type not stated); 12 ☐ HANDGUN; 13 ☐ RIFLE; 14 ☐ SHOTGUN; 15 ☐ OTHER FIREARM; 20 ☐ LETHAL CUTTING INSTRUMENT (e.g. Switchblade, Knife, etc.); 30 ☐ CLUB/BLACKJACK/BRASS KNUCKLES
TYPE OF ARREST: O ☐ ON-VIEW S ☐ SUMMONED/CITED T ☐ TAKEN INTO CUSTODY
ARREST CHARGE: | HEIGHT: __'__" | WEIGHT: | EYES: | HAIR:

☐ ARRESTEE ☐ SUSPECT | SUSPECT CONNECTED TO OFFENSE NUMBER: 1. ☐ 2. ☐ 3. ☐
#3: (Last, First, Middle) | ADDRESS: (Street, City, State, Zip)
DOB: | M ☐ MALE F ☐ FEMALE U ☐ UNKNOWN | W ☐ WHITE B ☐ BLACK I ☐ INDIAN A ☐ ASIAN U ☐ UNKNOWN | PHONE (Home): | PHONE (Business):
ARRESTEE WAS ARMED WITH: (Check Up To Two) (Enter A in Box if Automatic)
01 ☐ UNARMED; 11 ☐ FIREARM, (type not stated); 12 ☐ HANDGUN; 13 ☐ RIFLE; 14 ☐ SHOTGUN; 15 ☐ OTHER FIREARM; 20 ☐ LETHAL CUTTING INSTRUMENT (e.g. Switchblade, Knife, etc.); 30 ☐ CLUB/BLACKJACK/BRASS KNUCKLES
TYPE OF ARREST: O ☐ ON-VIEW S ☐ SUMMONED/CITED T ☐ TAKEN INTO CUSTODY
ARREST CHARGE: | HEIGHT: __'__" | WEIGHT: | EYES: | HAIR:

VEH.

IMPOUND Y OR NO	MAKE	MODEL	YEAR	COLOR	V.I.N.	LIC. ST.	LIC. YR.	LICENSE NO.

FIGURE 6-3 NIBRS-compliant incident report
(Courtesy Sterling Heights, Michigan, Police Department)

STERLING HEIGHTS POLICE DEPARTMENT - Part Two

OFFICER / #: DATE: SUPERVISOR / #: DATE: INCIDENT #:

VICTIM

VICTIM #1: (Last, First, Middle) PHONE (Home): PHONE (Business):

ADDRESS: (Street, City, State, Zip) DOB:

M ☐ MALE W ☐ WHITE A ☐ ASIAN
F ☐ FEMALE B ☐ BLACK U ☐ UNKNOWN
U ☐ UNKNOWN I ☐ INDIAN

AGGRAVATED ASSAULT/HOMICIDE CIRCUMSTANCES:

01 ☐ ARGUMENT
02 ☐ ASSAULT ON LAW OFFICER
03 ☐ DRUG DEALING
04 ☐ GANGLAND
05 ☐ JUVENILE GANG
06 ☐ LOVERS' QUARREL
07 ☐ MERCY KILLING
08 ☐ OTHER FELONY INVOLVED
09 ☐ OTHER CIRCUMSTANCES
10 ☐ UNKNOWN CIRCUMSTANCES

20 ☐ CRIMINAL KILLED BY PRIVATE CITIZEN
21 ☐ CRIMINAL KILLED BY POLICE OFFICER
30 ☐ CHILD PLAYING WITH WEAPON
31 ☐ GUN-CLEANING ACCIDENT
32 ☐ HUNTING ACCIDENT
33 ☐ OTHER NEGLIGENT WEAPON HANDLING
34 ☐ OTHER NEGLIGENT KILLINGS

TYPE OF VICTIM: (Check Only One)

I ☐ INDIVIDUAL G ☐ GOVERNMENT
B ☐ BUSINESS R ☐ RELIGIOUS
F ☐ FINANCIAL S ☐ SOCIETY/PUBLIC
P ☐ POLICE OFFICER U ☐ UNKNOWN
O ☐ OTHER

JUSTIFIABLE HOMICIDE CIRCUMSTANCE:

01 ☐ Criminal Attacked Police Officer and that Officer Killed the Criminal
02 ☐ Criminal Attacked Police Officer and Criminal Killed by Another Police Officer
03 ☐ Criminal Attacked a Civilian
04 ☐ Criminal Attempted Flight from a Crime
05 ☐ Criminal Killed in Commission of a Crime
06 ☐ Criminal Resisted Arrest
09 ☐ Unable to Determine/Not Enough Information

VICTIM CONNECTED TO OFFENSE NUMBER
1. ☐
2. ☐
3. ☐

INJURY TYPE:
N ☐ NONE F ☐ FATAL
B ☐ BROKEN BONES M ☐ MINOR INJURY
I ☐ POSS. INT. INJURIES O ☐ MAJOR INJURY
L ☐ SEVERE T ☐ LOSS OF TEETH
LACERATION U ☐ UNCONSCIOUSNESS

RELATIONSHIP OF VICTIM TO SUSPECT: (For multiple suspect relationships enter suspect number(s) in space before box)

01 ☐ SPOUSE
02 ☐ COMMON-LAW
03 ☐ PARENT
04 ☐ SIBLING
05 ☐ CHILD
06 ☐ GRANDPARENT
07 ☐ GRANDCHILD
08 ☐ IN-LAW
09 ☐ STEPPARENT
10 ☐ STEPCHILD
11 ☐ STEP-SIBLING
12 ☐ OTHER FAMILY
20 ☐ ACQUAINTANCE
21 ☐ FRIEND
22 ☐ NEIGHBOR
23 ☐ BABYSITTEE (baby)
24 ☐ BOY/GIRLFRIEND
25 ☐ CHILD OF 'BG' ABOVE
26 ☐ HOMOSEXUAL REL.
27 ☐ EX-SPOUSE
28 ☐ EMPLOYEE
29 ☐ EMPLOYER
30 ☐ OTHERWISE
31 ☐ VICTIM WAS SUSPECT
98 ☐ STRANGER
99 ☐ RELATIONSHIP UNKNOWN

Victim Residence
R ☐ Resident of the Community
C ☐ Resides in the County
S ☐ Resides in the State
O ☐ Out of state
U ☐ Unknown

WITNESS

NAME (Last, First, Middle) | ADDRESS (Street, City, State, Zip) | DOB | RESIDENTIAL PHONE | BUSINESS PHONE

PROPERTY

TYPE/CODE	QTY	DRUGS	PROPERTY DESCRIPTION - INCLUDE MAKE, MODEL, SIZE, TYPE, SERIAL #, ETC. DRUGS - INCLUDE TYPE, QUANTITY, MEASUREMENT	VALUE	DATE RECOVERED Month/Day/Year
/					
/					
/					
/					
/					
/					
/					
/					

TYPE PROPERTY LOSS/ETC.

0 NONE
1 STOLEN/RECOVERED
2 BURNED
3 COUNTERFEITED/FORGED
4 DAMAGED/DESTROYED
5 RECOVERED
6 SEIZED
7 STOLEN
8 UNKNOWN

PROPERTY DESCRIPTION CODE TABLE: (Enter Number in Code Column Above)

01 AIRCRAFT
02 ALCOHOL
03 AUTOMOBILES
04 BICYCLES
05 BUSES
06 CLOTHES/FURS
07 COMPUTER HARDWARE/SOFTWARE
08 CONSUMABLE GOODS
09 CREDIT/DEBIT CARDS
10 DRUGS/NARCOTICS
11 DRUG/NARCOTIC EQUIPMENT
12 FARM EQUIPMENT
13 FIREARMS
14 GAMBLING EQUIP.
15 HEAVY CONSTRUCTION/INDUSTRIAL EQUIPMENT
16 HOUSEHOLD GOODS
17 JEWELRY/PRECIOUS METALS
18 LIVESTOCK
19 MERCHANDISE
20 MONEY
21 NEGOTIABLE INSTRUMENTS
22 NON-NEGOTIABLE INSTRUMENTS
23 OFFICE-TYPE EQUIPMENT
24 OTHER MOTOR VEHICLES
25 PURSES/HANDBAGS/WALLETS
26 RADIOS/TVs/VCRs
27 RECORDINGS-AUDIO/VISUAL
28 RECREATIONAL VEHICLES
29 STRUCTURES-SINGLE FAMILY
30 STRUCTURES-OTHER DWELLINGS
31 STRUCTURES-OTHER COMMERCIAL BUSINESS
32 STRUCTURES-INDUSTRIAL/MANUFACTURING
33 STRUCTURES - PUBLIC/COMMUNITY
34 STRUCTURES - STORAGE
35 STRUCTURES - OTHER
36 TOOLS - POWER/HAND
37 TRUCKS
38 VEHICLE PARTS/ACCESSORIES
39 WATERCRAFT
77 PENDING INVENTORY
88 OTHER
99 SPECIAL

TYPE DRUG
01 = "Crack" Cocaine
02 = Cocaine
03 = Hashish
04 = Heroin
05 = Marijuana
06 = Morphine
07 = Opium
08 = Other Narcotics
09 = LSD
10 = PCP
11 = Other Halucinogens
12 = Amphetamines/Methamphetamines
13 = Other Stimulants
14 = Barbiturates
15 = Other Depressants
16 = Other Drugs
17 = Over 3 Drug Types
88 = Unknown

MEASUREMENT
WEIGHT
GM = Gram
KG = Kilogram
OZ = Ounce
LB = Pound

CAPACITY
ML = Millimeter
LT = Liter
FO = Fluid Ounce
GL = Gallon

UNITS
DU = Dosage Units/Items
NP = Number of Plants
XX = Not Reported

BIAS Y ☐ N ☐ #1 _____ #2 _____ #3 _____

FIGURE 6-3 NIBRS-compliant incident report (continued)
(Courtesy Sterling Heights, Michigan, Police Department)

STERLING HEIGHTS POLICE DEPT.

INCIDENT NO.

▲ **FIGURE 6-3   NIBRS-compliant incident report (*concluded*)**
(Courtesy Sterling Heights, Michigan, Police Department)

proper name or an apparent derivation, the nickname should also be provided. The full names and badge numbers of other officers/investigators should be reported, including those from other agencies who participated in the investigation.

Race or Ethnicity and Sex

Race or ethnic extraction should never be documented in such a manner as to cast aspersion on a person. Ordinarily race is indicated by use of one of the following abbreviations: W (White), B (Black), H (Hispanic), A (Asian or Pacific Islander), I (American Indian or Native Alaskan), and U (Unknown).[4] Sex is always designated by F for female and M for male. The proper sequence is race/sex—for example, W/F.

Age

On entries requiring only a person's age, it should be indicated as of the last birthday. However, the first reference to the individual in the narrative portion of the

▶ **FIGURE 6-4   Officer using a mobile computer terminal**
This officer, with his partner observing, is checking several databases to verify the existence of a warrant for an individual and checking the person's photograph through the state's drivers licenses database before they go to a house a block away to make an arrest. (© Joel Gordon)

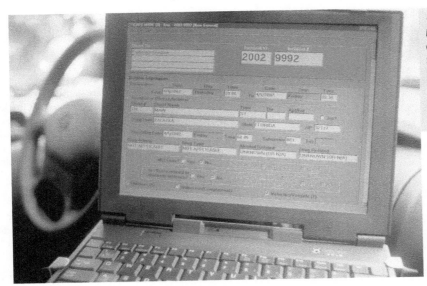

◄ FIGURE 6-5
Mobile computer terminal in a law-enforcement vehicle
Shows the initial screen with the blanks filled in by an officer as he starts entering the data to complete that portion of an incident report.
(© Joel Gordon)

▲ FIGURE 6-6
A Seattle police officer uses an iPhone for a report while working in a park in downtown Seattle, Wednesday, March 3.
(© AP Photo/Elaine Thompson)

report should give the exact date of birth, if known. For certain parties, such as an unidentified deceased person or a suspect whose identity has not been established, age may be approximated or given in a narrow span of years—for example, "approximately 32 years" or "approximately 31–33 years."

Physical and E-Mail Addresses

This information is particularly important, because it helps investigators to find people for additional interviews or related procedures. Each residence and business address should show the street number and, when applicable, the apartment, suite, or room number. If this information is not immediately ascertainable, the general location should be described in sufficient detail to make its whereabouts known. When military personnel are involved, the location information should include serial numbers, unit designations, and ship or installation, if applicable. If a person is only visiting a location, both temporary and permanent addresses should be obtained. E-mail addresses have become so common that they should be included in the report.

Telephone, Cell-Phone, and Pager Numbers

The telephone numbers of an individual should always be obtained, including area code, residence number, business number, and any extension number. Additionally, officers should inquire about and record any cell-phone or pager numbers.

Personal Description

Minimally, the following points should be included: sex, race, age, complexion, hair and eye color, physical defects, scars, marks, tattoos, build, and the nature and color of clothing worn.

Property Description

Elements useful in describing property are make, model, serial number, color, and type of material from which constructed. Other types of information may also be pertinent. Using the case of a stolen car as an example, the presence of stickers, cracked windows, articles hanging from the mirror, or loud engine noise would be additional information useful in locating the vehicle, and, of course, make, model year, color, vehicle identification number, and license plate state and number.

Occupation

The occupation of a person may be of some importance to an investigation. In the case of a suspect, it may establish familiarity with the use of certain types of equipment or procedures associated with a particular function, such as banking. It may also lend further credibility to the statement of a witness:

> A man exited from a restaurant as two suspects ran about 15 feet from the bank they had just robbed, entered a vehicle, and rapidly drove around the corner. Despite being presented with only a brief view of the car, the witness was able to give the police a fairly detailed description of it. At the trial, the defense was unsuccessful in casting doubt on the accuracy of the description, since the witness operated an automobile repair service.

Occupation is also useful in suggesting times when a person might be successfully and conveniently contacted by the investigator. An unemployed individual's ordinary line of work is to be given along with the notation "currently unemployed." College students or homemakers should be so designated. If the individual is employed, the occupation given in a report should be as specific as possible—for example, "brick mason" as opposed to "manual laborer."

Value

The value of property stolen may determine whether the offense is a felony or misdemeanor. For articles subject to depreciation, the fair market value should be used, unless the property is new or almost new, in which case the replacement cost should be used. On goods stolen from retail establishments, the merchant's wholesale cost, which constitutes the actual dollar loss, is the proper value to use. The value placed on nonnegotiable instruments such as traveler's checks or money orders should be the cost of replacing them; negotiable instruments, including bonds payable to the bearer, are valued at the market price at the time of the theft.

When the stolen property is subject to appreciation from the time of its acquisition by the owner—for example, limited-edition prints—the current fair market value is to be indicated.

The value of recovered stolen property ordinarily equals the valuation placed on it at the time of theft unless damaged, in which case it is to be established by the fair market value. In cases where the value of the stolen article is not readily ascertainable, the conservative estimate of the owner may be used.

Date

Many dates are used in a report, but officers/investigators must know what dates are most critical. Often, important dates needed by prosecutors to file formal charges are hard to find or are missing from reports. For example: it is more critical to know what date a motor vehicle was stolen rather than recovered. It is important to know what date a bad check was presented for payment or to be cashed (uttered) rather than the date it was returned from the bank and reported to law enforcement. In any investigation, learn which dates are most important to include in the report.

Time

For all official business, excluding general public and related information, most police agencies use the military system, or 24-hour clock, of hundred hours. Time runs from 0001 hours (12:01 A.M.) through 2400 hours (12 A.M.).

WRITING EFFECTIVE REPORTS: THE NARRATIVE

THE NARRATIVE

Almost always, there is more information to document than can fit on the face of an incident report. The additional information is entered in **narrative style** (Figure 6-7). There are a number of ways to organize the incident report to tell the story, but the narrative report generally makes the most sense if written in a chronological format beginning with the earliest thing that happened and progressing to the most recent fact or happening. The hardest part of writing a narrative is making sure that all the necessary information, including the smallest details, are transposed from the officer's/investigator's head and notes and recorded on paper. Doing a good job of report writing takes time, takes concentration, takes desire, and takes commitment. This sounds great on paper, but the realities of law enforcement often mean that an officer or investigator has calls backed up or a heavy caseload, and so the object is to write the shortest, most direct report possible. The belief is that very few cases ever go to trial, thus officers believe that the time and effort saved by writing short, direct reports are worth the risk. As we continue to point out in this chapter, the reality is that no one can predict which cases may later develop into something significant, where the quality of a report is critical. The account is written in the blank space on the reverse of the report's face or on a page referred to as "continuation," "investigative narrative," or "supplemental" (see Figure 6-7, a case that started as a missing-person report and turned into a criminal homicide investigation). Furthermore, even cases that are plea bargained require certain information to pass muster with the local prosecutor's office. It is of utmost importance that first-responding

Incident #   2002710051   Report Date: Wednesday, September 27, 2000
THERESA ANDREWS 23 YOA...5·7 BROWNISH RED HAIR 9 MONTHS PREGNANT.
COP ENTRY SENT OUT AT 16:51. 17:19 TELETYPE OHALLTERM SENT OUT. RIVERS WAS
CALLED AT 17:57

We received a call to go to 207 W. Riddle Ave. reference a missing person. Circumstances as stated by dispatch was that a female adult was missing from the home. It was reported that the husband came home from work, found the door open, his wife's belongings such as purse, keys, and cell phone at the residence. It was also reported that a person was to take a test ride in a vehicle for sale this morning.

Based on information given by dispatch I asked Detective Francis to accompany myself and Ptl. Wilmington to the residence. Upon arrival we were met by Mr. Andrews who was in the front lawn talking on a cell phone. He appeared to be upset but not frantic.

Upon speaking to him he stated that his wife paged him at work around 9:00 am this morning and told him that a lady was coming by to take a look and test drive their jeep that was for sale. The Pr stated that they have the jeep listed in trading times and were trying to sell the car. He stated that he tried to call back around noon or so and could not get an answer. He stated that he told her not to go with anyone, just get their driver's license and let them take a drive. Pr stated that upon arriving home he found the front door wide open. He stated that his wife's purse, house keys, and cell phone were in the house but she was gone as was the jeep.

The Pr described his wife as being 8 1/2 months pregnant and not feeling well. He stated that she has to be helped in and out of bed and that she had not been feeling well. Pr stated he had checked the hospital and was trying to phone the doctor to see if something had happened with the baby. The jeep was described as all black 1999 with soft top and Ohio Reg. CAB4351 and is a Wrangler type.

Ptl. Wilmington, Det. Francis and myself checked the interior of the house as well as the yard and garage area. No one was located. The house appeared to be very tidy with no signs of foul play or struggle. I instructed dispatch to place a COPS teletype, administrative teletype, and radio broadcast with the information. I also advised dispatch to enter Mrs. Andrews as missing as well as the vehicle.

▲ FIGURE 6-7   **Portion of an investigative narrative**

officers and follow-up investigators learn the minimum amount of information required by the prosecutor to enable her/him to do the basic filing of formal charges. It cannot be over emphasized that complaints by law-enforcement officers that prosecutors don't do a very good job are too often based on ineffective reports submitted by officers.

The incident report must also contain as much detail about the suspect as is known, including descriptive data, clothing, hair, complexion, language or accent information, and weapons displayed. All information from witnesses or other people interviewed, including details of the information provided, along with name and contact information needed by follow-up investigators and prosecutors, must be obtained. The report must include a listing of all evidence seized or found, with details about where it was found, by whom, who has control of it, how it was marked and recorded, and any other information necessary to protect the chain of custody.

If incidents reports are to serve the many uses to which they can be put, they must meet certain standards. Among the standards most usually cited are proper classification; complete, accurate, concise, objective, and fair information; and timely submission.[5] Keep the following guidelines in mind when you are preparing incident and investigative reports:

1. *Fill in all the blanks* on the incident report unless the information is not available or it is withheld, in which case this should be explained in the report. As discussed earlier, it is easier to get the necessary information at the scene than to try to recontact complainants and witnesses.
2. *Write the report in the first person*, using "I arrived at the scene at 1645 hours" as opposed to "Officer Morales arrived at the scene at 1645 hours." The reader of the report knows that Officer Morales wrote the report, and the officer's constant reference

to himself/herself in the third person (Officer Morales) is awkward. Although some departments require the use of the third person in reports, the trend in report writing is not to use it.

3. *Avoid unnecessary technical or legalistic jargon* such as "hereinafter," "point of fact," or "thereof," because you may convey a meaning that you do not intend or do not fully understand. Such jargon is a means by which your credibility can be attacked. Avoid writing statements of your own whose meaning you cannot fully explain. Certainly, if a suspect tells you, "I was abducted by aliens who implanted a control box in my head and they sent me commands to rob the pharmacy," you must faithfully record the statement even if you can't explain it—but the words are not your own.

4. *Write short sentences,* because they are less likely to be confusing to (or misunderstood by) readers, such as the prosecutor. A concise, "punchy" presentation of the facts makes it easier for the reader to "find the beef."

5. *Use short paragraphs* for the same reasons as those for writing short sentences.

6. *Support any conclusions you express with details,* because others who read the report, such as the prosecutor, need to know what facts shaped your thinking. Also, when a trial begins weeks, months, or even years later, you will have forgotten many facts. If you included them in the report, you will be able to refresh your recollection and provide convincing testimony.

7. *Don't repeat facts more than once,* unless doing so is required by your department's reporting format or policies. Duplication of entries wastes your time, and it creates the possibility that when you are distracted, tired, or in a hurry, your entries may conflict in some way with one another, calling your credibility into question.

8. *Check your spelling.* People who don't know you will form opinions of your capabilities on the basis of the reports you write and they read. Also, you are representing your department, so its reputation is on the line, because defense attorneys, judges, members of the news media, juries drawn from the community, and prosecutors read police reports. Misspelled words can change the meaning of a sentence or cause the meaning to be lost. Spell-checker software is an aid to accuracy, but it does not catch words that are spelled correctly but used inappropriately (for example, "E. Wazolewski took a write turn").

9. *Edit what you write.* Don't miss an opportunity to catch and correct your errors. Many people do this best when they read slowly and out loud, but you may find a system that works better for you. Taking the time to edit your report is more important than the system you use. If you are using a com-

puter, editing is far easier than writing several successive handwritten drafts of a report. Moreover, the software includes a spell checker, thesaurus, and grammar checker.[6] Editing can also catch errors in the use of macros. Agencies using computer programs generally have pre-prepared macros that an officer/investigator can use to cover a certain point in the report that can be used as a generalization, such as, "the arrestee was searched incident to the arrest, and cocaine was found on his person." In fact, after being arrested for DUI, the routine search of the arrestee did NOT produce cocaine or anything else that violated the law. On the witness stand, the officer had to admit that that information was in a macro he used, but, clearly, he did not edit his report. That failure was not lost on the defense attorney or on the jury.

Not infrequently a new investigator will, if only at the subconscious level, attempt to impress those who will be reading the incident report by writing in an elaborate manner in order to display mastery of the English language. However, persons reading the report will learn much, or perhaps all, they will ever know about the investigation from what has been written. Therefore, it is essential to write in a clear and uncluttered style; the report must be written not only so that it can be understood but, more important, so that it also cannot be misunderstood.

The report must be completely accurate. No detail should be added or deleted; the potential or actual consequences of such deviations, however innocent the motivation, are considerable. For example, at the scene of an armed robbery, a young investigator was conducting interviews necessary to prepare the original report. One of the questions he asked the victim was "Have you ever seen the perpetrator before this happened?" The response was "Yes, he works on the loading platform of the grocery on Sixth Avenue." Out of a desire to provide as much detail as possible, the investigator supplemented this statement with information from the telephone directory, writing a portion of the interview in the following manner:

The victim told the undersigned officer that the suspect works at Blake's Grocery Wholesale, located at 1425 Sixth Avenue, telephone number (813) 223-3291.

Later, the following exchange took place between the officer and the defense attorney in court:

Q **Defense Attorney:** *Officer, do you recognize this report?*
A **Officer:** *Yes, I do.*

Q **Defense Attorney:** *Did you prepare it?*
A **Officer:** *Yes, sir, I did.*

Q **Defense Attorney:** *Would it be fair to say that it represents your investigation?*
A **Officer:** *That is correct, sir.*

Q Defense Attorney: *Then, having conducted the investi-gation and having prepared the report, your testimony would be that it accurately and completely portrays your actions and what you learned?*

A Officer: *Yes, sir.*

Q Defense Attorney: *Would you read from page 2 of this report?*

A Officer: *"The victim told the undersigned officer that the suspect works at Blake's Grocery Wholesale, located at 1425 Sixth Avenue, telephone number (813) 223-3291."*

Q Defense Attorney: *Officer, the complainant in this case has already testified to the effect that she did not, in fact, tell you this. Why are you prejudiced toward the defendant in this case, and what else have you added to the report or subtracted from it in order to strengthen the state's case?*

Thus, a seemingly innocuous addition to a report reduced the credibility of the entire investigation. Clear communication and accuracy are the mainstays of effective reports. The absence of one diminishes the other.

In summary, the narrative is the most critical part of an incident/investigative report. It should tell a story from beginning—such as "Once upon a time"—all the way through to the end—"and they lived happily ever after." If the middle part of the story has holes in it, so the reader doesn't know how the story unfolds to get to the end, the report writer has failed to communicate what was intended.

SUPERVISORY REVIEW AND DISPOSITION OF INCIDENT REPORTS

By reviewing the reports written by subordinates, supervisors get a current picture of the quality of their officers' investigative efforts and report-writing skills. On the basis of such information, supervisors can give constructive feedback to subordinates, as well as make appropriate performance evaluations. To carry out this responsibility at the highest level, supervisors must carefully read their subordinate's reports for content, not just style and spelling. Supervisors must take the time to understand the investigatory process involved in the particular incident and make sure that the reports accurately address what is needed for a prosecutor to file charges and prove a case. With this knowledge, constructive feedback to subordinates has meaning.

In electronic systems, officers can often prepare reports while stopped between calls and routine. In such advanced systems, reports can be sent wirelessly to the supervisor. If the supervisor declines a report, it is sent back, with comments, to the officer, who resubmits it after addressing the comments.

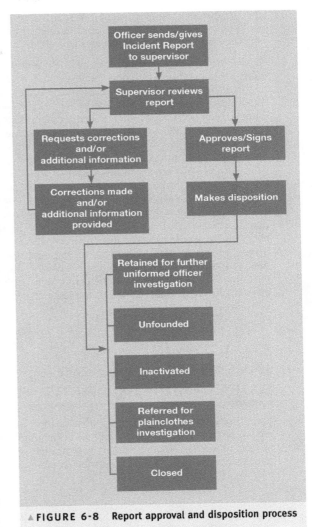

▲ **FIGURE 6-8** **Report approval and disposition process**

The approval process for handwritten incident reports is much like that described for MCT-generated reports. Several times during the shift, the officer's supervisor will call to meet with him/her to review any completed incident reports. If a report needs additional information or clarification, it is returned to the officer. Once the report is completed to the satisfaction of the supervisor and is accepted, the supervisor makes a disposition, signs the report, and takes it to the station for appropriate disposition.

After approving an incident report, the supervisor must make a **disposition** of it. As depicted in Figure 6-8, any of the following dispositions may be made:

1. The case may be retained for further investigation by uniformed officers.
2. It may be unfounded (that is, the complaint is false).

3. The case may be inactivated due to a lack of leads.
4. It may be referred to plainclothes investigators.
5. The case may be completed and closed.

To some extent, a department's situation and policies affect the supervisor's decision about which dispositions to use. If the Uniform Division is seriously understaffed and officers have been reduced to being "report takers" because they do not have time to conduct thorough preliminary investigations, rarely will a case be retained for further investigation. By policy or the strong will of the investigations commander, the authority to unfound a case may be reserved for an investigation supervisor. In addition, because copies of incident reports may be routinely routed to an investigations supervisor, a uniformed supervisor who has inactivated cases only to have an investigations supervisor reactivate them may be slow about doing anything other than referring them to the investigations division, especially if the reactivations have at least occasionally resulted in the cases being successfully cleared. Regardless of the disposition, copies of all completed and approved reports are sent to the records keeping section of the agency.

FOLLOW-UP INVESTIGATION AND SUPPLEMENTAL REPORTS

Periodically during the follow-up investigation, supplemental reports must be initiated. Ordinarily, supplemental, or follow-up, reports should be written no less frequently than every 10 days, and the continuance of a particular investigation beyond 28 days should require supervisory approval to ensure proper use of an investigator's time. The purpose of writing follow-up reports is to keep the file current as new or corrected information is gathered. Additionally, specific acts or accomplishments might require individual supplemental reports, such as the activation or cancellation of a pickup order or BOLO, the issuance of a search warrant, the arrest of a suspect, the complainant's discovery that additional property was stolen that was not noticed as missing at the time the incident report was made, the recovery of all or part of the property taken, or a change in the title of the offense owing to improper classification on the original report—for example, a strong-arm robbery reclassified as a purse snatch.

Other circumstances under which supplemental reports are required include (1) when the offense is unfounded, (2) when it is exceptionally cleared, meaning that the police know who the perpetrator is but are unable to pursue the case further owing to circumstances beyond their control, such as the death of the only witness, and (3) when the case is inactivated. If the supervisor reviewing the incident report inactivates it because of insufficient leads to warrant follow-up investigation, then a supplemental report is not required. However, if some follow-up work is done, no promising leads are developed, and the case is then inactivated, the person assigned responsibility for it must complete a supplemental report to substantiate the basis for inactivation.

As a general concluding note, case files inactivated may in later months or years receive further investigative work that is productive. Therefore, it is of considerable importance that at each stage of report writing care is exercised in presenting all available information.

KEY TERMS

disposition (of incident report)
field notes
incident reports

iPad, iPhone
mobile computer terminal (MCT)
narrative style

National Incident-Based Reporting System (NIBRS)
Uniform Crime Reports (UCRs)

REVIEW QUESTIONS

1. Identify and briefly discuss four reasons why field notes are important.
2. What are the six interrogatory investigative questions?
3. Briefly discuss the operational and administrative uses of incident reports.
4. How would you characterize the difference between basic incident reports and those that are

NIBRS compliant? (Check the Internet for additional information on how these reports differ.)
5. How are MCTs and PDAs being used in law enforcement?
6. After a uniformed supervisor accepts a report, he/she must make a disposition of it. What are five dispositions that might be made?

INTERNET ACTIVITIES

1. Learn more about NIBRS at www.icpsr.umich.edu/icpsrweb/NACJD/NIBRS/. Find out if your state has recently received any NIBRS grants. Read the brief report entitled, "Effects of NIBRS on Crime Statistics." How do NIBRS statistics differ from UCR data? What impact does NIBRS have on crime statistics? What factors need to be considered when one is comparing summary UCR statistics and NIBRS data?

2. Log onto your local, county, or state law-enforcement agency website and find out if the agency uses mobile computer terminals. If it does, in what capacity are they used? Are all patrol vehicles equipped with MCTs? Does the site provide any information on other data technology used by officers (PDAs, and so on)? If so, what?

► Two investigators reviewing the contents of an incident report with a patrol sergeant. Note that they are using good technique. One investigator focuses on the questions while the other takes notes.

(Courtesy Chief Jack Lumpkin and Sgt. David Leedahl, Athens Clarke County (Georgia) Police Department)

7

THE FOLLOW-UP INVESTIGATION AND INVESTIGATIVE RESOURCES

CHAPTER OBJECTIVES

1. Describe the use of solvability factors.
2. Explain the preparation of a case file.
3. Discuss reinterviewing victims and witnesses.
4. Describe the purpose and use of NamUs.
5. Summarize NCIC files and capabilities.
6. Explain LeadsOnLine.
7. Identify behaviors in which investigators should not engage with informants.
8. State the purposes of physical surveillance.
9. Describe how a photo lineup should be conducted.
10. Identify three potential indicators of a staged crime.

11. Describe the intelligence cycle.
12. Summarize the use of facial recognition software by law-enforcement agencies.
13. Identify the ways crime analysts link crimes.
14. Explain the role of the scientific method in crime scene reconstruction.
15. Describe the four factors on which criminal profiling focuses.
16. Summarize geographical profiling.
17. Provide four examples of remote sensing.
18. Identify four ways investigators use the Internet.

INTRODUCTION

Certain crimes, such as murder, rape, and child abuse, are always going to receive a follow-up investigation. To ensure that the use of investigative resources is warranted, other crimes are screened. Only those that have some promise for success receive a follow-up investigation. Investigators should be familiar with the numerous information sources and databases that are available to them. They should also have an understanding of special topics, such as conducting photo lineups and handling informants. These and related topics are covered in this chapter.

THE DECISION TO INITIATE A FOLLOW-UP INVESTIGATION

From Chapter 6, "Field Notes and Reporting," we recall that when an officer completes an incident report his/her immediate supervisor will review it and make one of several dispositions. The decision to inactive a case or refer it for further investigation is often made through the use of a case screening model, which requires the presence of sufficient solvability factors before a case can receive a follow-up investigation. **Solvability factors** are elements of information that have been demonstrated to correlate with higher probabilities of investigative success.

In some case screening models, solvability factors have different mathematical weights attached to them according to their potential to contribute to a successful investigation. These weights must total a certain number of points for a case to be referred for follow-up. In other models, the screener subjectively considers the solvability factors that are present and "other information" to make the decision. The solvability screening may be done by a patrol or investigative supervisor. Solvability factors usually include these questions:

- Is the suspect named?
- Can the suspect be identified?
- Is there a detailed description of the suspect?
- Is there significant physical evidence?
- Are other suspects named, identified, or described in detail?

- If a vehicle is involved, is there a license number or detailed description?
- Does the crime fit an established modus operandi or method of operation?
- Were deadly weapons displayed or used?
- To what extent was the victim physically harmed?
- What similarity is there to recently reported crimes?
- Will the victim be able to identify the suspect?
- Was traceable property taken?
- Are there reliable witnesses?
- Does the nature of the crime (for example, theft of explosives) necessitate a follow-up?
- Can a composite sketch of the suspect(s) be prepared?

THE FOLLOW-UP INVESTIGATION PROCESS

As a visual aid to follow-up investigators, some departments have checklists. Figure 7-1 is a "universal" checklist, meaning that it is not crime specific. Investigators draw a line through or enter Not Applicable or NA in portions of a universal checklist that are not applicable to a case they are handling. The steps involved in a follow-up investigation do not necessarily occur in an exact order. The specifics of each case will dictate how those steps actually unfold. For example, if a suspect is already in custody, the attempt to interrogate him/her will come much earlier than if an arrest is made much later. Generally, a follow-up investigation will include most of the following activities:

1. Departmental policies regarding follow-up investigation files vary but as a minimum require that a case file be prepared to organize the information that is immediately available—for example, the incident and supplemental reports. Over the course of an investigation the file will grow as lab reports, copies of checks, charge card records, and other data are received.

   Some agencies require an **investigative plan (IP)** showing what lines of inquiry will be pursued and any special resources needed—for instance, the assistance of a surveillance unit. As the investigation progresses, many factors can cause IPs to be

▶ **FIGURE 7-1**
Universal follow-up investigation checklist
(Courtesy of Chief Lynn Rowe and Lt. Rick Headlee, Springfield [Missouri] Police Department)

Activity	Activity Description	Date Completed	Notes
1.	Autopsy/Crime Lab Reports		
2.	Bank Records Reviewed		
3.	Crime Vict. Notif. Record		
4.	Criminal Case Report Form		
5.	Department of Corrections		
6.	Department of Revenue		
7.	Identification Unit Rpts.		
8.	Intelligence Reporting		
9.	Interview Informants		
10.	Mandatory: Notify Victim		
11.	Medical Records		
12.	NCIC Criminal History		
13.	Neighborhood Canvass		
14.	Pawn Shop Records Check		
15.	Photographic Lineup		
16.	Phys. Evid./Property Disp.		
17.	Polygraph Examination		
18.	Search Warrant App./Exec.		
19.	Search Warrant Return		
20.	S.P.D. Records Check		
21.	State Fingerprint Record		
22.	State Probation & Parole		
23.	Stolen Property Files		
24.	Surveillance Conducted		
25.	Suspect Miranda/Interview		
26.	Suspect: P/C Item/Arrest		
27.	Witnesses Interviewed		
28.	Other:		
29.	Other:		
30.	Other:		
31.	Other:		

revised, such as a newly identified witness who names a suspect or can describe where unrecovered physical evidence—for example, a handgun—is located. A case log may also be required, which is a chronological listing of what the investigator has done and the results.

Local prosecutors may have an effect on the paperwork for a follow-up investigation. For example, they may require a sheet that specifies the specific statutory crime to be charged, a list of each element needed to prove the crime, and the evidence supporting each element.

2. Read the offense report and any supplemental reports and become thoroughly conversant with them. As needed, contact or meet with the officer originating the report and those writing supplements to clarify information or resolve discrepancies. As a practical matter, this happens infrequently.

3. Get the criminal histories of named suspects. As appropriate, review the criminal histories of victims to assess the possibility for insurance fraud. "Victims" may file a false crime report to hide a theft they committed or to gain money by reporting a theft of something they never really had.

4. Obtain, as appropriate, the credit histories of key figures in the investigation.

5. Visit the crime scene if possible and review the visual documentation of the scene.

6. Review other incident reports that may be related.

7. Attempt to link suspects to other crimes by modus operandi (M.O.) analysis.

8. Examine the physical evidence (Figure 7-2) and review lab results as examinations are completed.

9. Contact victims and witnesses for in-depth interviews and search for other witnesses. If it has not already been done, conduct a neighborhood canvass (Figure 7-3). Review the names of people

▲**FIGURE 7-3   Neighborhood canvass**
An Allentown Police Department Detective going door to door, canvassing residents in an effort to find witnesses to a shooting. If he develops information, he can immediately inform other investigators using the departmental radio in his left hand. (© Dennis Wetherhold, Jr.)

interviewed to determine whether any have criminal backgrounds or are known associates of criminal figures. Evaluate to determine if a "witness" may be involved in the crime or has potential to become an informant.

10. Assess the credibility of witnesses and also people who are unusually helpful:

In a case involving the abduction of two girls on a rural road, a person known to the police brought much appreciated coffee and sandwiches to the mobile command center several times. Finally, someone decided that giving him access to the command center was not wise, and as an afterthought they ran a records check on him. A prior record for child molestation existed, and the man confessed to the abductions. He also related that he used what he heard in the command center to keep ahead of the investigation and also fabricated a story about seeing a car with an out-of-state tag cruising the road the day of the abductions.

11. Delivering death notices is an occasional duty, and it requires the utmost compassion. Preferably the law-enforcement chaplin should accompany the investigator—failing that possibility, the family pastor or close friend, if their identities are known. Such notices should not be delivered to juveniles. If a juvenile is the only person available, or the intended message recipient is not present, a written message, with no other details, to call the department should be left. When called, the officer should return to the address and personally handle the notification. Serious injury notifications may also be necessary, and departmental policies and circumstances dictate whether those contacts must be made in person.

12. If not already done, arrange the preparation of a drawing/likeness of the suspect. Releasing the likeness and some details about the crime may be necessary to solicit public assistance, and this often requires the approval of the investigator's supervisor. Before any information is released, it should be carefully scrutinized to ensure that people are not endangered and that it does not hinder the investigative effort—for instance, by alluding to tactics or avenues of inquiry.

13. Reevaluate the case periodically, especially as new information is received.

14. Disseminate information about the crime and suspects within the agency as needed or secure the assistance of specialists—for example, profilers.

15. Coordinate with other jurisdictions if there are substantially similar methods of operation or the suspect may be, or is, involved with crimes elsewhere.

Significant and serial offenses may lead to the establishment of short-term departmental or multi-jurisdictional task forces by commanding officers.

16. Explore lines of inquiry and pursue leads by using databases available through a variety of international, national, regional, private organizations, and your own department. (These databases are covered in more detail later in this chapter.)

17. Identify and interview known associates of the suspect who may have information.

18. Obtain any documentary evidence—for example, bank statements, hotel records, telephone calls, and credit card charges.

19. Conduct a custodial interrogation to obtain a documented confession, identify any codefendants, and evaluate the suitability of the suspect as a confidential informant.

20. Talk to informants as needed.

21. Use specialized investigative procedures if appropriate (for example, physical and technical surveillance, polygraph and psychological stress examinations, and photographic and physical line-ups).

22. Prepare necessary affidavits, apply for, and execute search and arrest warrants and make the required "returns" to the court specifying what action was taken.

23. Identify, locate, and apprehend the suspect, if he/she is not already in custody.

24. Recover stolen property.

25. Determine if the suspect's auto or other property is subject to seizure under federal or state laws. If so, refer to initiate seizure and condemnation procedures when appropriate.

26. File supplemental reports on the progress of the investigation as required by departmental policy (for instance, case status and the release of any property to the victim or his/her family).

27. Keep all records well organized.

28. Keep victim/victim's family informed on any changes in the status of the case.

29. Meet with the prosecuting attorney.[1]

REVIEWING THE INCIDENT AND SUPPLEMENTAL REPORTS

The incident and supplemental reports may answer many of the follow-up investigator's initial questions, such as: (1) how, when, and where the crime was committed, including a chronological description of the events; (2) the victim's identity and if appropriate, his/her medical condition and statement; (3) the number of suspects, if any are in custody, whether they are in the jail or a hospital, and their descriptions or identities; (4) whether composite sketches of suspects at large have been prepared and distributed; (5) the words spoken by suspects during the commission of the crime, spontaneous statements made by them following their arrest, and any post-Miranda statements made by them to the arresting officer; (6) the identities and statements of witnesses and any conditions noted, such any degree of drinking or appearance of having been using drugs; (7) the nature and value of the property stolen; (8) the types of physical evidence seized; and (8) description of any vehicles involved or a copy of an impound report for vehicles seized.

JAIL BOOKING REPORT

The jail booking report is created when a subject is in-processed at a jail. This jail may be part of the investigator's agency, or it may be operated by another entity, such as the sheriff. The booking report is often computer generated and may have an incident report integrated into it, as well as a color photo; fingerprints; and description of the subject's health and medications; his/her mental state (for example, drunk or verbally or physically combative); medical treatment received while in custody; a full description of the subject, including scars, marks, and tattoos; criminal history; employment and home addresses; aliases used; and an inventory of the personal effects seized by jailers during the in-processing. In particular, the personal effects may provide useful information.

Among personal-possession items often found are matchbooks; Zig Zag paper; condoms; business cards for the subject (and from his/her associates or people he/she recently met); foreign currency; identity and credit cards in several different names; scraps of paper with telephone numbers on them; and various types of lists. Such items may suggest places the subject habituates or recently visited, suggest possible personal habits and associates, identify countries recently visited, or connect him/her to other crimes.

In one case, an investigator went to the jail to interview a subject arrested for stabbing a man in a bar. Among the subject's personal possessions was a real-estate card from a woman murdered several days previously. Although the man initially denied knowing the woman or being in the area where she was killed, he finally admitted to the crime after being confronted with the real-estate card.

VEHICLE IMPOUNDMENT REPORT

If a suspect is arrested while driving a vehicle, the vehicle is inventoried and towed to an impoundment lot. Articles that appear on the inventory list may or may not have a relationship to the case. Moreover, the impounding officer may not recognize their significance, as can be the case with common tools that have been modified for use in burglaries. Thus, the impounding report should be carefully read. Under most circumstances, a follow-up investigator cannot search a car after it has been impounded without a search warrant issued on a showing of probable cause.

FIELD INTERVIEW/ INFORMATION REPORTS

A **field interview/information report (FIR)** is shown in Figure 7-4. Such reports are filled out when patrolling officers identify persons or vehicles that are suspicious to them but are not connected with any particular offense. These cards can establish whether a suspect was in the immediate area of a crime, how he/she was dressed at the time, what vehicle the suspect had access to, and who else was in the vehicle. On rare occasions, FIR cards have proved to be a suspect's best alibi witness.

TRAFFIC CITATIONS

As with FIR cards, traffic citations can link suspects to the vehicles they register and drive, as well as those to which they may have access. Access to the vehicles of others usually denotes a special relationship and may help identify girlfriends or boyfriends, criminal associates, relatives, or operators of particular kinds of businesses, such as used-car and scrap-metal firms. Traffic citations can also pinpoint where the operator was at a particular date and time. Occasionally, FIR cards are also written during traffic stops, so these two sources of information may be associated.

EXAMINING PHYSICAL EVIDENCE

The physical evidence should be viewed early in the investigation, because it may soon be forwarded to the crime laboratory for analysis. Actually seeing the evidence adds a level of specific understanding about each item of evidence as to its appearance, color, weight, damage done to it in the commission of the crime, modifications to weapons, and other matters. These observations may help the investigator make connections when he sees or hears a comment at a later stage in the follow-up.

REINTERVIEWING VICTIMS AND WITNESSES

Victims or their families should be contacted very early in the process. They often have questions about the status of the case, their rights, whether they need protection,

►FIGURE 7-4
Field interview/information report (FIR) card
(Courtesy of Springfield, Missouri, Police Department)

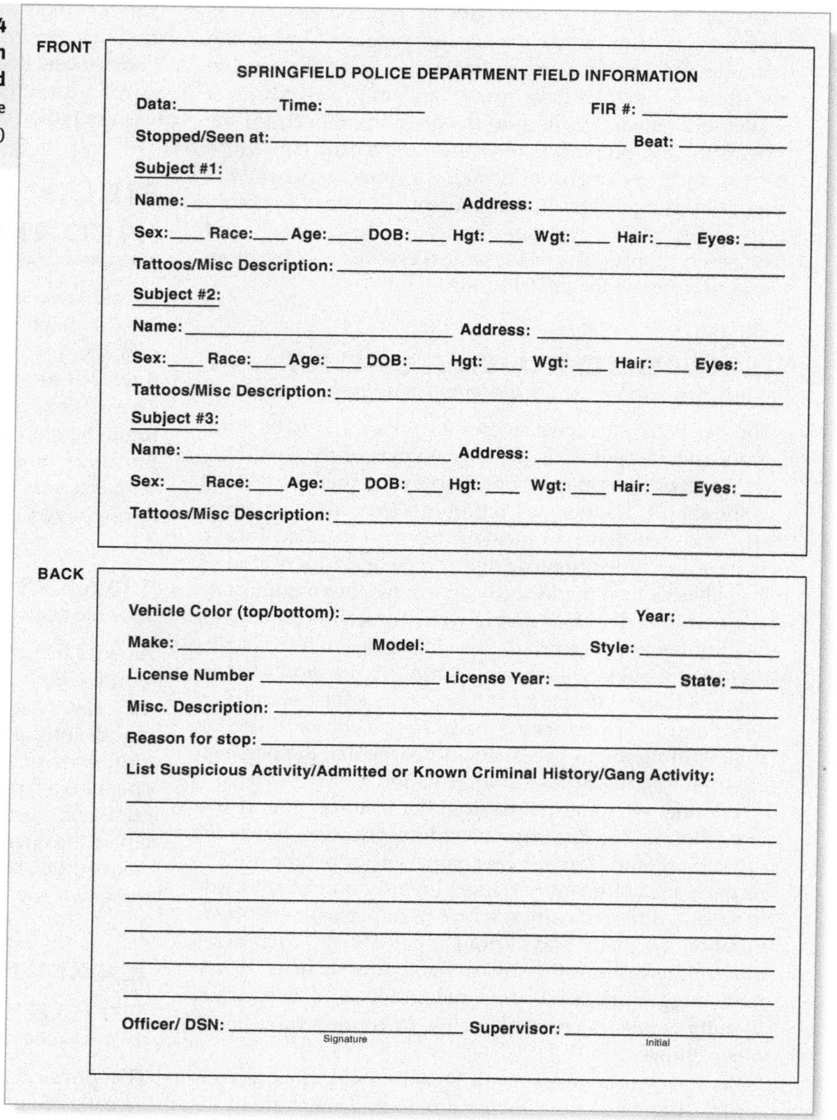

FRONT

SPRINGFIELD POLICE DEPARTMENT FIELD INFORMATION

Data: _____ Time: _____ FIR #: _____

Stopped/Seen at: _____ Beat: _____

Subject #1:

Name: _____ Address: _____

Sex: ___ Race: ___ Age: ___ DOB: ___ Hgt: ___ Wgt: ___ Hair: ___ Eyes: ___

Tattoos/Misc Description: _____

Subject #2:

Name: _____ Address: _____

Sex: ___ Race: ___ Age: ___ DOB: ___ Hgt: ___ Wgt: ___ Hair: ___ Eyes: ___

Tattoos/Misc Description: _____

Subject #3:

Name: _____ Address: _____

Sex: ___ Race: ___ Age: ___ DOB: ___ Hgt: ___ Wgt: ___ Hair: ___ Eyes: ___

Tattoos/Misc Description: _____

BACK

Vehicle Color (top/bottom): _____ Year: _____

Make: _____ Model: _____ Style: _____

License Number _____ License Year: _____ State: ___

Misc. Description: _____

Reason for stop: _____

List Suspicious Activity/Admitted or Known Criminal History/Gang Activity:

_____
_____
_____
_____
_____
_____
_____
_____

Officer/ DSN: _____ Supervisor: _____
        Signature   Initial

how a case gets processed through the criminal justice system, if they are eligible for victim's compensation for medical expenses or funerals, and, if they have been disabled by the crime, is there living assistance available to them. The investigator can answer some of these questions and then make sure the victims get linked to victim assistance entities, which may be state agencies. Some religious denominations also provide victims assistance on an ad hoc or other basis.

Recontacting victims and witnesses serves to confirm information in the incident or supplemental reports and to develop further information. Unfortunately, such contacts are sometimes met with questions such as "I already told the other cops everything I know. Why aren't you out looking for the guy that did this instead of bothering me with the same questions? Don't you cops talk to each other?" Experienced investigators let such frustrated comments politely roll off of their backs. "Look, I'm only trying to help you" has the potential to produce a downward spiral. It is better to "join" the victim or witness by using statements such as "I want to arrest the person that did this to you. In my experience sometimes victims or witnesses think of something else that is important, and rather than burden you with trying to find me, I thought it would be courteous for me to come to you." An often overlooked purpose of reinterviewing is to assess, if possible, the credibility of witnesses.

◄ FIGURE 7-5
Lead-assignment sheet
(Imprimus Forensic Services, LLC, copyright
2001. This form may be reproduced for law-
enforcement purposes only.)

Before any reinterviewing is done, the investigators should carefully assess what a witness said he/she:

- saw—under what lighting conditions, at what distance, for how long, and was the witness wearing any needed glasses or contacts? A fair question to an 18-year-old witness would be "How do you know it was a '57 Chevy Impala?"
- heard—for example, "I heard him hitting her." What facts support that conclusion? Any auditory problems? Wearing a needed hearing aid?
- smelled—"The man who raped me was wearing Old Spice shaving lotion or cologne." A key question is "How do you know that odor?"
- touched—a blind person touches her mugger's face and reports it was unshaven with a short vertical scar above the left eye. The investigator might ask for other examples of her tactile sensitivity. If she reads Braille proficiently, it is likely to be very good. Blindfolded victims may also have useful tactile data: "I traced the letters GHS and the number 87 on a jacket while in the trunk of the car."
- tasted—for example, a hospitalized woman says that her last meal "tasted funny, like almonds," a sign of cyanide poisoning. How is she familiar with that taste?

LEADS

Some leads turn out to be "good," whereas others are simply "dry holes" and an unproductive use of time. The truth is that both kinds chew up resources and must be followed up, because often we can't accurately tell one from the other.

The fact that an incident report specifically names a suspect does not mean the person actually committed the offense or knows anything substantive about it. Victims can be mistaken about a person's name, report their suspicions as "fact," or attempt to cause problems for someone they don't like or have had difficulty with in the past. Or, their theory about how the crime was committed is simply wrong:

A burglary victim called an investigator to explain that she thought the offenders were two employees of a firm that the apartment complex had hired to do some work in her apartment. The described suspects, names unknown, had been given a key to her apartment in order to perform the necessary work. The burglary had been committed eight days later, and there had been no forced entry. The apartment manager, when contacted by the investigator, vouched for the men but had not directly supervised their work. The owner of the firm employing the men testified to their long-standing reliability and a lack of similar allegations in the past. A message was left for the suspects to contact the investigator. The suspects called back about a half-hour later and gave the investigator all the information requested and described the work done on the victim's apartment in detail. The investigator checked their backgrounds and concluded the men were not likely to have been the offenders and closed the investigation.

Major cases, such as the murder of a community leader or a robbery with a large "score," typically require the combined efforts of a number of investigators, who report to the supervisor responsible for the case. A key responsibility of the case supervisor is coordination of information, especially with respect to making sure that leads are prioritized and worked and that the results are disseminated to all team members. One way this can be done, by hand or on a computer, is by using a lead-assignment sheet log (see Figure 7-5).

USING DATABASES

The use of databases allows investigators to rapidly close off some lines of inquiry, encourage the continuance of others, and suggest new ones. The available databases are international, national, multistate, state/regional/local, as well as private. The ones identified here are illustrative and not exhaustive, and other capabilities are mentioned within crime-specific chapters.

INTERNATIONAL

One of the most frequently used databases of the International Criminal Police Organization (Interpol) is MIND/FIND, which determines whether passports, identity cards, and visas have been reported lost or stolen.

NATIONAL

The Bureau of Alcohol, Tobacco, Firearms and Explosives (ATF) has **Arson, Explosives, and Incident System (AEXIS),** which contains information on arson, bombs, and misuse of explosives, including incident characteristics that can be useful in determining patterns, trends, and motives. ATF also operates the National Integrated Ballistics Information Network (NIBIN). ATF's law-enforcement partners use Integrated Ballistic Identification Systems (IBIS) capabilities to acquire images of firearms evidence that are uploaded to NIBIN to determine if the evidence is related to other cases[2] (NIBIN is further discussed in Chapter 8, "The Crime Laboratory"). The Treasury Department's Financial Crimes Enforcement Network (FinCen) provides information and analysis to law-enforcement agencies with respect to money laundering.

When first operational in the 1970s, the Drug Enforcement Administration's (DEA) El Paso Intelligence Center (EPIC) focused on drug, alien, and weapons smuggling in the Southwestern states bordering Mexico. Now using advanced technologies, EPIC has an international focus. DEA's **National Drug Pointer Index (NDPIX),** which began operating in 1997, alerts participating agencies of investigative targets they have in common.

Launched in 2009, the **National Missing and Unidentified Persons System (NamUs)** is a database administered by the National Institute of Justice. Presently there are an estimated 100,000 missing person cases and more than 40,000 sets of human remains that have not been identified.[3] NamUs is a free web-based tool accessible to everyone, including law enforcement, coroners/medical examiners, victim advocates, and families and friends. Considerable data remains to be uploaded into NamUS; only 2,800 missing people have been entered and just 6,200 sets of human remains. The number of cases resolved using NamUs is not large, possibly because it is a great untapped resource for investigators: in 2010, only 1,100 law-enforcement agencies had registered to use it. Some cases have been resolved by family members. A woman's sister had been missing for 22 years. Using NamUs, she discovered that her sister had been murdered and dumped alongside a highway in another state. Authorities there were unable to identify her, and she was buried as a "Jane Doe" in a pauper's grave. The sister was able to make the identification based on unique unicorn and rose tattoos on her murdered sibling.

The Department of Homeland Security's (DHS) Homeland Security Information Network (HSIN) develops and shares information about domestic terrorism threats and incident management with its partners at the federal, state, local, tribal, territorial, private-sector, and international level; its principal function is the dissemination of information and Sensitive But Unclassified intelligence (SBU).[4]

The FBI maintains the **National Crime Information Center (NCIC),** which is the most comprehensive documented criminal justice information system in the country. Established in 1967, its structure has been periodically refined. NCIC has provided the information critical to solving high-profile cases, including the 1968 murder of Dr. Martin Luther King, Jr., which led to the arrest of James Earl Ray. NCIC was also instrumental in the arrest of Timothy McVeigh on the same day as the 1995 Oklahoma City bombing. The NCIC database consists of 19 files that are available continuously to those with approved access:

1. *National Sex Offender Registry File (1999):* contains records on individuals who are required to register in a jurisdiction's sex offender registry.
2. *Unidentified Person File (1983):* includes deceased persons, recovered portions of dismembered bodies, remains from disasters, and living persons unable to identify themselves, such as infants or Alzheimer's victims. It is cross-referenced to the Missing Persons File.
3. *Missing Persons File (1975):* covers individuals, including children, who have been reported missing to law enforcement, and there is a reasonable concern for their safety. It includes those absent who have a proven physical/mental disability or are senile; persons missing following a catastrophe; and those unemancipated under their state law, usually persons under 18 years of age. Some file information may be disclosed to the National Center for Missing and Exploited Children (NCMEC), a nongovernmental but federally funded private corporation.
4. *U.S. Secret Service Protective File (1983):* has records containing names and other information on individuals who are believed to pose a threat to the U.S. President or others afforded protection by the Secret Service.
5. *Protective Order File (1997):* has records on individuals against whom protective orders have been issued. A protective order may be temporary or final and is issued by a civil or criminal court to prevent harassing, threatening or violent acts against a person by another or regulates communication, proximity or contact with the protected person.
6. *Foreign Fugitive File (1987):* has records on persons wanted by a foreign country for a crime that would be a felony if committed in this country.

7. *Gang File (2009):* has records on violent gangs, their members, and associates; originally was part of a previous file established in 1995.

8. *Known or Appropriately Suspected Terrorist (KST) File (2009):* Emphasis for this file was added with a Homeland Security Presidential Directive (HSPD-6) in 2003; records on known or suspected terrorists are maintained; originally it was part of a previous file established in 1995.

9. *Immigration Violator File (1996):* covers criminal aliens who have been deported, as well as aliens with outstanding warrants for removal.

10. *Supervised Release File (1999):* contains records on individuals on probation, parole, and supervised release, as well as persons released on their own recognizance or during pretrial sentencing/deferred prosecution, which allows certain first-time offenders the chance to avoid a conviction by adhering to parole-like restrictions.

11. *License Plate File (1967):* includes information pertaining to unrecovered license plates that have been reported stolen. In two-plate states where only one plate has been stolen, the victim must agree not to use the remaining tag.

12. *Identity Theft File (2005):* contains descriptive and other information that law-enforcement personnel can use to determine if a person is a victim of identity theft or if the individual may be using a false identity.

13. *Vehicle File (1967):* has records on unrecovered stolen vehicles, vehicles involved in the commission of crimes, and those that may be seized based on a federally issued court order. Articles stolen from vehicles—for example, radios and CD players, are entered in the article file.

14. *Boat File (1969):* unrecovered stolen boats with unique identifying numbers may be entered in this file; "boat" includes jet skis, canoes, kayaks, and sail boards.

15. *Vehicle/Boat Parts File (1999):* has records for unrecovered component parts stolen from a vehicle or boat.

16. *Gun File (1967):* includes records of serially numbered weapons that are recovered (abandoned, seized, or found), missing, or are believed to have been involved in a felony.

17. *Securities File (1968):* has records on serially numbered stolen, embezzled, counterfeit, or used-for-ransom securities.

18. *Wanted Persons File:* has records of individuals who have an outstanding warrant. This file also contains records for juveniles who have been judged delinquent and who have escaped from custody or supervision or who have absconded while on probation or parole. There are also records on juveniles who were charged with committing an act of delinquency that would be a crime if committed by an adult and who have fled from the state in which

the act was committed. Agencies may also enter temporary felony want records into this file. Temporary felony want records allow a law-enforcement agency to take prompt action to apprehend a person suspected of committing a felony when circumstances prevent the agency from immediately obtaining a warrant.

19. *Article File (1967):* contains records on unrecovered articles that have a unique serial number or other unique personal identifying number. Included are lost public safety, homeland security, and critical infrastructure identification items, such as badges, credentials, smart cards, and "dog tags." Illustrations of other articles that may be entered are livestock, toxic chemicals, tools, sports equipment, and musical instruments. To be entered, articles must meet one or more of three criteria: (1) have a value of $500 or more—but office equipment, televisions, and bicycles may be entered regardless of their value; (2) regardless of value, the article being moved interstate, or the seriousness of the crime dictates entry; or (3) regardless of the value of any item, the total value of the items stolen exceeds $5,000.[5]

The effect of NCIC can be seen in the following examples:

An officer noticed a man, with a small child in the front passenger's seat, driving his car too rapidly and weaving through traffic, causing other drivers to slam on their brakes. The officer stopped the vehicle and did a NCIC check on the driver. The subject was a registered sexual offender, who should not have been with a young child, was on parole in another state, and should not have left it.[6]

A patrolling officer saw a pickup pulling a sailboat. The brake lights for the trailer were either not working or not hooked up. The officer stopped the truck with the intent of getting this deficiency corrected. The driver nervously handed over his license. The officer noticed a second driver's license on the dashboard of the pickup. Both photographs matched the driver, but there were different names and birth dates on them. An NCIC check revealed that both names were aliases used by the man. He had a criminal history and was wanted in connection with a series of boat thefts. In his patrol car, the officer received the suspect's real name, his mug shot, a photograph of his tattoo, and a photograph of, and other data on, the boat attached to the suspect's truck, which was stolen.

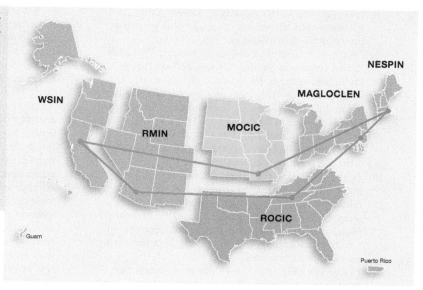

►FIGURE 7-6
RISS multistate centers
The members of RISS are the Western States Information Network (WSIN), the Rocky Mountain Information Network (RMIN), the Mid-States Organized Crime Center (MOCIC), the Regional Organized Crime Information Center (ROCIC), the Mid-Atlantic-Great Lakes Organized Crime Law Enforcement Network (MAGLOCLEN), and the New England State Police Information Network (NESPIN).
(Courtesy RISS)

The FBI also has other capabilities that support investigations. The purpose of the **National Center for the Analysis of Violent Crime** (NCAVC) is to provide behavioral-based analytical support to federal, state, local, and international law-enforcement agencies. The **Violent Criminal Apprehension Program (ViCAP)** is part of NCAVC and provides advice and support for a range of cases, including child abductions, serial, rapes and murders, and cybercrime. NCAVC and ViCAP are further discussed in Chapter 9, "Injury and Death Investigation." The **Next Generation Identification (NGI) Program** is developing a fuller set of biometric data. Missing, unidentified, and wanted persons may be identified by the National Image/Information Repository (NDIR). Law Enforcement Online (LEO) is a free secure communications portal for law-enforcement officers, first responders, criminal justice professional, and antiterrorism and intelligence agencies around the world. It is one way to broadcast alerts, and it has distance-learning opportunities, a multimedia library, and 540 special-interest groups. The groups are a way to share your expertise and benefit from the expertise of other people.

REGIONAL INFORMATION SHARING SYSTEMS (RISS)

There are six multistate centers in RISS (Figure 7-6). Each of the six centers, funded by the federal government, can tailor its services to the investigative and prosecutorial needs of its member agencies. The core services of all centers are information sharing, analytic services, loan of specialized investigative equipment, confidential funds, training conferences, and technical assistance. RISS communicates over its secure intranet, RISSNET. The RISS

National Policy Group consists of the Director and Policy Board Chairperson of each of the six centers. Law-enforcement agencies join their regional center based on its established application process.

Outside RISS, there are also a number of multistate databases, such as (1) the Alert-Emerging Threat Analysis Capability (ETAC), formed by a cooperative agreement between Missouri and Kansas law-enforcement agencies and governed by a Board of Directors consisting of one representative from each participating agency, and (2) the Western Identification Network (WIN), with Alaska, Montana, Oregon, Washington, Idaho, Nevada, Utah, and Wyoming as members of the consortium, as well as some local law-enforcement agencies in those states.[7] WIN was the first multistate Automated Fingerprint Identification System (AFIS) compact. AFIS, a capability pioneered by the FBI, uses high-speed computers to digitize, store, and compare fingerprint data and images. When possible matches are found, they are evaluated by expert examiners. The impetus for WIN came from (1) the recognition that people frequently moved among the member states and (2) smaller member states lacked the expertise and resources to create their own AFIS capability.

STATE AND LOCAL SYSTEMS

State information systems are robust; they contain files on over 100 million offenders. Simultaneously, they have some under-developed capabilities: only 19 state information systems accept photos of offenders' or wanted persons' scars, marks, and tattoos (SMTs).[8] State information systems include wanted, missing, and endangered persons; stolen property; driver's license and vehicle registration information; protective orders for juveniles and adults; state and local court information; Department of Corrections offender tracking; probation, parole, and supervised release data; prosecutorial information; and gang-related, juvenile justice, sexual-predator tracking, and other databases. Local systems serve a single jurisdiction, all the law-enforcement/criminal-justice agencies in a county, or a multicounty area.

NONPROFIT AND PRIVATE SOURCES

The Law Enforcement Intelligence Unit (LEIU) was formed in 1956 by 29 local and state law-enforcement agencies to exchange information about organized crime not available through normal police channels. LEIU originally excluded federal agencies, although that stance has been abandoned. In 2008, it changed its name to the Association of Law Enforcement Intelligence Units but kept its original acronym, LEIU. Its present focus is gathering, recording, and exchanging information about suspected or known criminal figures, groups, and businesses and terrorism.

Formed in 1966 as the Law Enforcement Teletype System (LETS) and incorporated as a not-for-profit in Delaware in 1973, LETS has morphed into the National Law Enforcement Telecommunication System (NLETS). Law-enforcement and other criminal-justice agencies use NLETS more than 1,000,000 times every day via 327,000 terminals.[9] In addition to providing secure channels for members' communication, NLETS also is a conduit for information and alerts flowing from the U.S. Department of Homeland Security (DHS). NLETS provides access to files from other states, such as those for wanted persons and concealed weapon permits; federal files, including the Federal Aviation Administration's (FAA's) aircraft registration data and tracking information; and the Canadian Police Information Centre (CPIC), which is similar to NCIC.

LeadsOnLine is a private subscription service used by more than 1,600 law-enforcement agencies. It provides access to transactions from thousands of reporting businesses, including scrap metal processors, secondhand stores, Internet drop-off stores, pawnshops, and eBay:

A husband listed a diamond ring for sale on Craigslist. A man made an appointment to come see the ring and along with several accomplices committed a home invasion robbery. While defending his son from violence the husband was killed. The invaders pawned the ring, which investigators located using LeadsOnLine, and the pawnshop records led them to the killers.[10]

Significant information about persons of interest is available for a fee from credit-reporting agencies such as Equifax, TransUnion, and Experian. Accurint for Law Enforcement (ALE) is an example of a group of high-end providers of information and information services that go beyond credit reports. Approximately 3,000 government entities use Accurint, which has access to 12 billion public records. It can quickly retrieve information about businesses and individuals, including current and former addresses, and links, such as to family members, neighbors, and associates. Among its capabilities is Person Alerts (PA); each time an individual who is a person of interest or fugitive appears in the database, the investigator is automatically notified.

Internet sites that can provide information about persons of interest are People Finder, Yahoo People Search, AnyWho, and BigFoot. The types of information vary somewhat from one site to another but include current and past addresses, possible relatives, birth dates, current telephone numbers, marriage and divorce information, litigation history, and e-mail addresses. WhoIs provides information about e-mail addresses both domestically and internationally.

Information about corporations can be obtained from each state's Secretary of State's Office. If a company uses a registered agent, some corporate information, such as officers, may not be available online, although some useful information about the corporation can be gleaned as a starting point. Dunn & Bradstreet can provide a Business Background Report, which provides summary coverage about the operations, history, and background of a company and its senior management; its Supplier Evaluation Report indicates the likelihood that a firm will cease doing business without paying its obligations in full or will seek debt relief under applicable federal and state laws.

Social network sites (SNS) are a category of websites that contain personal profiles and that may offer dating or other such services—for example, MySpace, FaceBook, MyYearbook, and Classmates. Legal restrictions apply to accessing some data, such as the names of people a victim was dating, but some useful information may still be gleaned from SNS files without a search warrant.

INFORMANTS

Informants provide information that is of investigative significance. They may expect to be paid or to receive consideration on charges pending against them or family members, or they cooperate for some other reasons. They may also be designated as confidential informants; some departments have adopted the term "cooperating individual" for them.

Law-enforcement policies generally identify activities that investigators should refrain from with informants. These includes socializing with them, becoming romantically involved, paying them without confirmation of the information, entering into a business relationship with them, accepting gifts, gratuities, or money from them, and loaning them money or accepting a loan from them. Policies also restrict who may be used as informants and determine whether prior special approval is required before they are used. Typically, restrictions apply to persons under 18 years of age, those who have been previously used and were not reliable, former drug-dependent individuals, and those on federal or state probation or parole (whose use as informants may require the approval of a judicial official).

An informant file, to which there is restricted access, consists of a recent photo of the informant, a complete informant sheet providing detailed information about him/her, copies of warrants and NCIC, and other items, including a criminal history, copies of cases in which the informant is a defendant, and debriefing reports following each meeting with him/her.

As a practical matter, some investigators run their own low-level informants, paying them out of pocket for their information or otherwise helping them. On the one hand, this is practical and works. On the other hand, an officer could be lured into a trap, and if he/she is killed, the department has to work the case in ignorance of the existence of the informant. Inexperienced investigators tend to contact informants too frequently or expect too much too quickly. To get inexperienced or lazy investigators "off their back," informants will "burn" them by knowingly giving them bad information. A more experienced investigator uses informants more judiciously:

A patrol officer passed a house in a rundown neighborhood near shipping docks. He heard screams and shouts through the screen door. Upon investigating he was told by a German seaman that "one of these whores stole my watch and wallet." Interviewing the woman alleged to be involved, the officer saw a small amount of marijuana on the bedside table. Several other "ladies" were also present in the house. The officer told the "mom" to have her "daughter" give the things back, which was done, and the seaman departed.

While talking to mom, the officer saw a picture of a boy on a table in the living room and asked about it. She proudly said it was her grandson, who lived with her and who was her "angel." The mom maintained a separate residence a few blocks away from her "office." The officer told the mom it would be regrettable if he had to arrest her, because the grandson would be placed in a foster home and be grown by the time she was released from prison. They reached an agreement.

Five months passed before the officer returned, seeking information about a local fugitive who had committed five burglaries of high-end jewelry stores. Three days later, based on mom's information, the suspect was arrested.

SURVEILLANCE

While some think of **surveillance** as "following," it actually means the continued observance of people, places, and things to obtain information of investigative significance. Most frequently surveillance is covert, although there may be occasions when it is made obvious in an attempt to spook subjects into making mistakes.

Surveillance is often broken into two types: physical and technical. Physical surveillance is personally done by one or more members of a surveillance team. Technical surveillance involves the use of various advanced technologies, including automatic vehicle tracking; pinhole cameras; acoustic, ultrasonic, and thermal image scanning; parabolic microphones; radio frequency (RF) bugs; and wiretaps. The balance of this section is devoted to physical surveillance.

PURPOSES OF SURVEILLANCE

Physical surveillance is carried out by people; it may be stationary/fixed/static or "rolling." At its simplest, it is done on foot, but it can also be done with cars, motorcycles, fixed-wing and rotary aircraft, boats, and rental apartments and offices. The purposes of surveillance include:

1. establishing the existence of a crime;
2. obtaining probable cause for a search warrant application;
3. apprehending suspects as they commit a crime;
4. identifying the associates of criminals and the places they frequent;
5. determining the reliability of informants;
6. providing protection for undercover officers and informants;
7. locating people, places, and things;
8. gathering intelligence about targets and premises prior to serving a warrant;
9. gathering intelligence on the activities of illegal groups and gangs;
10. preventing a crime by signaling police awareness of specific subjects.

PLANNING AND PREPARING FOR SURVEILLANCE OPERATIONS

Departmental policies and the applicable legal guidelines drive how the surveillance is conducted. In smaller agencies, investigators may have to do their own surveillance; in larger ones, there will be a unit with a title such as technical services to whom the work is "farmed out" or assigned.[11]

Planning the intelligence means making sure that the appropriate equipment is available (Figure 7-7) and safety and security measures are reviewed (Figure 7-8). Many investigators have been assaulted, wounded, and killed

Surveillance Kit Checklist

- Department two-way radio.
- Handheld portable radio with harness and fully charged spare battery.
- Mobile phone.
- Still camera with telephoto lens, adequate supply of film or other removable storage medium, and spare battery.
- Video camera with extra battery and removable storage medium.
- Stabilizing device, such as a portable tripod.
- Binoculars and portable infrared or thermal-imaging devices.
- Detailed road maps for the area.
- Compass or Global Positioning System receiver.
- Flashlight with extra batteries.
- Change of clothing with props, such as hats, to alter appearance, and other personal items, including toiletries.
- Food and water in a cooler.
- Cash, including coins to use at toll lanes requiring exact change, and toll passes.
- Extra set of car keys.
- Towels and glass cleaner.
- Equipment gear bag to hold preceding items.

◄FIGURE 7-7
Surveillance kit checklist
(John T. Nason, "Conducting Surveillance Operations," FBI Law Enforcement Bulletin, Vol. 73, No. 5, May 2004, p. 3)

Safety and Security Measures

- During a mobile surveillance, do not take unnecessary risks to keep up with a subject speeding, running red lights, or otherwise driving recklessly.
- While stationary, keep the vehicle windows closed and the doors locked.
- Regularly scan rear view mirrors to observe anyone or any activity to the rear.
- Alert other team members to any suspicious or unusual persons or activity in the area.
- In high-crime areas and in hours of darkness, remain in a heightened state of alert.
- Position vehicle to enable a rapid response to assist others if needed.
- Ensure vehicle has emergency equipment lights, siren, and first-aid kit.
- Keep identification, weapon, and ballistic vest accessible.
- Know and use challenge, password, and other appropriate safety measures to prevent friendly fire situation from developing.
- When leaving a vehicle to go on foot surveillance, fully secure the vehicle and equipment inside.

◄FIGURE 7-8
Surveillance safety and security checklist
(John T. Nason, "Conducting Surveillance Operations," FBI Law Enforcement Bulletin, Vol. 73, No. 5, May 2004, p. 6)

during operations, so risks must be assessed and the need for vigilance by all team members must be stressed. Additionally, all members of the team should be carefully briefed on such factors as:

1. The facts in the case.
2. Surveillance objectives.
3. Warnings about the subject, including any known drug use and possession of weapons.
4. The subject's previous experience with surveillance—whether he/she might be surveillance conscious and surveillance countermeasures may be used against the team.
5. Personal data about the subject, with photo, criminal history, associates, the vehicles of the subject and associates, locations the subject is known to visit, and whether the subject possesses unusual skills or abilities, such as being a martial arts practitioner or weightlifter.
6. Communication protocols for the team and descriptions of team members' roles (for example, photographer), and protocols for the keeper of the chronological surveillance log.

7. Before the surveillance, determination of which investigator should be sent into the area to assess conditions and to identify the "eye" or central observation point.

TERMINATION OF SURVEILLANCE OPERATIONS

There must be a periodic evaluation of whether a surveillance should be continued or terminated that includes the following considerations:

1. Have other cases arisen in which the use of surveillance is a better allocation of resources?
2. Is the operation providing important ongoing intelligence and evidence?
3. Does the continuation of the surveillance outweigh the increased risk of detection?
4. Can other investigative techniques or technical surveillance do the job at least as effectively?
5. Are there indicators that suggest threats to the team's safety?

GUIDELINES FOR CONDUCTING PHOTO LINEUPS, LIVE LINEUPS, AND FIELD SHOW-UPS

Eyewitnesses may be requested to see if they recognize anyone connected with the crime in one of three procedures: (1) a photo lineup, (2) a "live" lineup, and (3) a "show-up." Unlike the other two methods, one witness at a time views a single subject in a show-up. It is a technique that should only be used under the most exigent circumstances, because asking a witness to verify the identity of someone under law-enforcement control is inherently suggestive.[12]

The assigned investigator determines whether a case requires the use of a photo or live lineup and usually for all aspects of preparing them—for example, completion of a lineup creation form. That investigator also coordinates the process with witnesses, because they have some familiarity with him/her. The request to view a lineup should be kept factually neutral, such as "We'd like you to see a collection of photographs." Unless specifically asked by a witness, no mention of any suspect in custody should be made.[13] Several languages may be spoken in a community, and written witness instructions should be available in those languages. The investigator also needs to make sure that qualified language or American Sign Language (ASL) interpreters or other necessary accommodations are available. Sometimes the fact situation dictates whether a photo lineup or live lineup should be used:

A cab driver reported to the police that he had been robbed by one of his passengers. The cab driver made the report immediately after the suspect had fled on foot with the money. The driver reported that the suspect was a black male, approximately 25 years old, 6 feet 6 inches tall, 285 pounds, armed with a large nickel-plated type semiautomatic pistol. The man was wearing an orange shirt, blue jeans, and a white cowboy hat. Exactly $52.12 in cash had been taken.

Approximately 30 minutes after the crime was reported, the suspect was observed walking in the vicinity of the robbery by the same two officers who had taken the original report. The suspect was arrested by the police officers. A search produced a nickel-plated .45-caliber semiautomatic pistol and $52.12.

The investigator assigned to the case immediately knew that his only option was a photo lineup, because finding enough people for a live lineup who approximated the suspect in size, race, age, attire, and so forth would be very difficult.

In 2009 the Innocence Project released *Reevaluating Lineups: Why Witnesses Make Mistakes*. It identified numerous problems with existing photo, live, and show-up procedures and provided guidelines for using them in the future. Although these guidelines do not carry the weight of law by themselves, some states passed laws substantially mandating their use, and elsewhere many law-enforcement agencies adopted them. The processes described here are consistent with these "new" guidelines.

To avoid investigators giving subtle, unintended cues to witnesses, a "double blind" method of conducting photo and live lineups is now being widely used. The actual lineups are conducted by a trained lineup administrator who does not know who the suspect is or who the "fillers" are. In a photo lineup, fillers are photographs of people not believed to be involved in the crime. Administrators should be independent of the investigative unit—this is a good role for community volunteers and retired persons. The assigned investigator and anyone with knowledge of the suspect may not be in the same room as the lineup.

If several witnesses independently look at a lineup, the administrator may have some idea who the suspect is and potentially could unintentionally guide a witness to a particular identification, which is why such administrators require training. Alternatively, a different administrator could be used with every witness.

In addition to leading witnesses through a lineup procedure, the administrator has substantial record-keeping responsibilities. These often include, whether documented by video, audio, or in writing: (1) all identification and non-identification decisions, signed by the witness. If a signature is refused, the administrator records this fact and signs his/her own name; (2) the names of all persons present at the lineup and their affiliations; (3) the date, time, and location of the lineup; (4) the exact words used by the witness to identify the suspect; (5) the number of photos or individuals in the lineup; (6) the sources of all photographs or individuals used; (7) all photographs from a photo lineup; and in a live lineup, a photo or other visual recording of the lineup that includes all persons who participated in the lineup.[14] The administrator returns all photos and the result report to the assigned investigator. Depending on departmental policy and the results, the photos may be placed in the case file or the evidence room. After the lineup is completed, the investigator can be available to answer any witness's questions or to ask questions.

PHOTO LINEUPS

A **photo lineup** is a procedure in which a series of photographs are shown *sequentially* to a witness for the purpose of determining if he/she can identify the perpetrator of a crime. One practice is that as each photo is shown to a witness, he/she must make a decision about whether the person is the suspect before viewing the next photo. The

PHOTO LINEUP FORM

Case No: _____   Place: _____

Date/Time: _____   Assigned investigator: _____

Administrator: _____   Witness: _____

Others present: _____

ADMONITION

The lineup administrator will show you a collection of photographs. Look at all six photos before making any comment. You do not have to identify anyone. It is just as important to clear innocent persons from suspicion as it is to identify suspects. Individuals may not appear exactly as they did on the date of the incident. For example, head and facial hair are subject to change. Do not attach any significance to differences in the characteristics of photos. The person who committed the crime may or may not appear in these photos. If you recognize any person in the photos as the suspect, tell the lineup administrator and sign on the number below identifying the suspect. The lineup administrator cannot give you feedback on any identification you make. If you make an identification, please do not discuss the case with other witnesses or the media or indicate to them in any way that you have identified someone. Regardless of whether an identification is made, law enforcement will continue to investigate the incident.

ACKNOWLEDGEMENT

I hereby acknowledge that I have read the foregoing admonition and understand it.

Witness: _____   Administrator: _____

1. _____   2. _____   3. _____

4. _____   5. _____   6. _____

STATEMENTS/COMMENTS: _____
_____
_____
_____

Note: If an identification is made, ask the witness to state, in his/her own words, how certain he/she is of the identification. Record both identification and non-identification results in writing, including the witness' own words how sure he/she was.

◄FIGURE 7-9
Photo lineup form
(Garen Horst, Placer County California District Attorney's Office, 2010 Version, with some modifications)

second practice is to allow them to view all photos sequentially before any potential identification is made. There is some concern that allowing witnesses to see all photos sequentially before making a decision could contribute to some misidentifications, comparing photos a witness might point to the photo which *most appeared like the suspect*.

As a minimum, a photo lineup consists of six photographs—one of the suspect and at least five "fillers." Fillers are photographs of the same quality, size, shape, and type (black and white or color) of individuals who are similar in appearance—for example, sex, age, skin and hair color, facial hair, height, build, and other characteristics.[15] Although software may be able to make the background and lightening of photos similar, witness should be told not to attach any weight or significance to

such peripheral differences. Figure 7-9 is a Photo Lineup Form with instruction for witnesses, who are given the information individually in a private setting.

The photos are placed in the same position—for instance, middle of the page, in separate identical file folders that are numbered on the back for record keeping purposes and shuffled. The files are also shuffled before each new witness looks at them. The Innocence Project recommends having four blank files so the administrator doesn't know what the next file to be opened contains.[16]

If there are several witnesses, each is led separately through the process by the administrator. If there are multiple suspects, a separate photo lineup must be prepared for each suspect using different fillers; only one suspect can be in any single line up. If witnesses cannot be scheduled so they can be processed contemporaneously, without the opportunity for any personal contact with one another, a new photo lineup for each suspect must be prepared with different fillers for later witnesses. Even if a witness makes an identification, he/she should be guided to carefully consider any remaining photos. If a witness wants a second chance to view a photo lineup, wait at least 48 hours and then use another picture of the suspect wearing different clothes. If the posture of all the suspect and fillers is not standard, the suspect's picture should reflect him/her in a different posture. All new fillers must also be used.

Software is available to prepare a photo lineup and also produces the required recordkeeping documents. Because the computer selects the fillers, the investigator cannot be accused of selecting them in a manner that was intentionally biased against the suspect.[17]

LIVE LINEUPS

A **live lineup** is a process in which a series of "real people" are shown to an eyewitness to establish whether they can pick out the suspect (see Figure 7-10). All members of a lineup usually appear simultaneously, although there is some interest in sequential appearances. A suspect should be allowed to pick the order in which he/she appears. Requests from any attending defense attorney should be carefully considered and the request and its disposition documented by the administrator.

The suspect and at least four fillers are used, with the fillers selected on the same criteria as those used in a photo lineup. Some agencies prefer to use five fillers to make their photo and live lineup procedures parallel. If there are multiple witnesses, each one views the live lineup alone. The position of the suspect is changed in the lineup before each new witness to the same offense views it. If the witness has previously viewed a lineup involving a suspect and is asked to view another lineup with a second or subsequent suspect potentially involved in the same offense, the fillers must be entirely new each time.

The instructions to live lineup witnesses comport to those used in photo lineups, as does the need for the administrator to maintain strict neutrality. If any person in the live lineup is asked to perform a gesture, walk, or other movements, all others must individually do the same thing. The lineup administrator must be out of sight of the witness while conducting the lineup. The decision of the witness as to any identification must be conducted after the members of the lineup have left the room.

SHOW-UPS

When a crime occurs and fairly immediately thereafter officers stop a person suspected of being the perpetrator, they may lack probable cause to arrest him/her, but the offense is of such a severe or heinous nature that releasing the person may create a risk to public safety. Most **show-ups** involve a witness viewing one person stopped at or near the scene within a short time after the offense is committed.

If the victim is able or there is a witness, he/she might be taken separately to where the person in question is being briefly detained by the police. Most often this involves patrol officers. To view the person handcuffed in the backseat of a marked patrol car is tantamount to an accusation. Yet, having the person uncuffed, even if surrounded by officers, and standing near a marked patrol car, is only marginally better. It also raises concerns about officer safety and the possibility of escape. Show-ups in the field are problematic. If a warrant exists for some other offense, the person can be arrested, which will allow sufficient time to prepare a photo or live lineup.

The Innocence Project recommends that the person be taken to a neutral, noncriminal justice setting, to be viewed by the victim or a witness. All the cautions noted previously in this lineup section apply, except that only one person is viewed. Because a police investigatory stop and control of a person must be brief, there ordinarily will not be sufficient time to arrange a photo or live lineup that will sustain judicial scrutiny. Figure 7-11 is a show-up form; although it includes the use of an administrator, in some departments a patrol division supervisor or available investigator will fill this role.[18]

STAGED CRIME SCENES

Investigators should be open to the possibility that the offense they are investigating was staged. Staged crime scenes are not new. In the Bible, Joseph's brothers sold him into slavery and then dipped his robe in the blood of a goat they had killed to convince their father that Joseph had been devoured by a wild animal.[19] There are no official statistics on how often investigators encounter **staged crime** scenes, but there is some limited evidence that about 3% of all cases may involve some element of staging.[20]

One panel of experienced investigators concluded that the most common staged nonfatal crime was the false allegation of a sexual crime, followed by murder staged as a "burglary gone bad" or a robbery.[21] In part, the absence of statistics is due to the fact that when confronted with a staged crime scene, the police have simply unfounded the original report of a crime, reclassified it, or charged the person reporting it with filing a false report.

In recent years, some agencies have filed civil suits against the person falsely reporting a crime or staging a crime scene in order to recover costs of wasted investigative efforts. In addition to other charges that may apply to situations involving staged scenes, many states have

LIVE LINEUP FORM (Part 1)

Case No: _____   Date/Time: _____

Place: _____

Administrator: _____   Witness: _____

Others present: _____

ADMONITION

WHY WE'RE HERE: You were recently a crime victim or a witness to one. You will see a live lineup of five persons. There may be a person or persons in this lineup you recognize from the crime that brought you here today. The purpose of this form is to help you understand the lineup process and your role in it. Please carefully read all instructions. If you understand the instructions please sign at the bottom of this page. After you have seen the lineup, you will be asked to complete the other side of this form, which is about your experience in the lineup and sign it.

PERSONS PRESENT: An administrator will conduct the lineup. He/she is a "neutral" and doesn't know anything about the people in the lineup. The administrator cannot answer any questions related to them. Other people will be present who are not witnesses, however they are required to attend the lineup. If any of the other people present should ask you a question, you are not required to answer it.

WHAT YOU WILL SEE: You will be brought into a small, dimly lighted room (the lineup room). It has one-way glass separating it from the adjoining room. **While in the lineup room you cannot be heard or seen by anyone in the adjoining room no matter how close you get to the glass. You will be perfectly safe.** After you enter, the administrator will instruct you to look into the adjoining room. There will be five people who are similar in appearance and dress. They will be standing in a fully lighted room with their backs against a wall. There will be a number above each of them. Although you can see them, all they see is a mirror.

WHAT YOU SHOULD CONSIDER:

1. You are under no obligation to pick anybody from this lineup. Your only obligation is to be truthful. It is just as important to clear innocent persons from suspicion, as it is to identify suspects.

2. The **person** or **persons** involved in the crime **MIGHT or MIGHT NOT** be standing in the lineup.

3. Appearances can change over time (for example, head or facial hair may have grown or been cut, body weight may have been lost or gained, and height can be made to look different by slouching or standing very straight.

4. You might want to see the participants facing another direction. Please circle your choice below:

   Facing the wall   *Facing left*   *Facing right*

5. You might want to see the participants' gesture, walk, or make other movements. Please circle your choice below:

   Walk back and forth   Step closer to glass window   Any other movement, such as bend over at the waist or kneel down,

   please specify: _____

6. You might want the participants to repeat something you heard during the crime.
   Please write what you want them to say: _____

7. If you make an identification, neither the administrator nor others in the room can give you any feedback. Regardless of whether an identification is made, law enforcement will continue to investigate the incident.

TAKE YOUR TIME: Be sure to look carefully at each person and the number each is standing under. You may stand as close to the window or move back and forth as you want. **Remember, you cannot be seen or heard.** Again, if you want the lineup participants to do or say something, you only need to ask the administrator. When you are finished please inform the administrator and follow his/her instructions. If you have any questions or concerns, please talk with the administrator.

I hereby acknowledge and understand the foregoing admonition.

Signed: _____   Date: _____

▲ **FIGURE 7-10   Live lineup form (part 1)**
(Garen Horst, Placer County, California, District Attorney's Office, 2010 Version, with some modification)

LIVE LINEUP FORM (Part 2)

Case No: _____   Place: _____

Administrator: _____   Witness: _____

Others present: _____

Instructions: Please complete this form to the best of your ability, remembering the instructions that you were given. If you are unclear or uncertain about how to complete this form the administrator cannot tell you what to write. He/she can clarify the use of the form.

On _____, 2010, I viewed a live lineup of five persons. They were numbered 1 through 5. There are three statements below. Each statement has a box next to it. I checked the one box that describes my thoughts about the lineup. I also personally filled out the information asked for in the statement I checked. If I am unable to identify anyone, I will write a few sentences explaining why. I understand this is not a shortcoming on my part, but a reflection of my best judgement.

☐ **I AM CERTAIN** that person number _____ was the person who (describe what he/she did during the crime):

_____

_____

_____

_____

_____

☐ **I AM NOT SURE,** but I think person number _____ was the person who (describe what he/she did during the crime):

_____

_____

_____

_____

_____

☐ **I DID NOT RECOGNIZE ANYONE** in the lineup as being a person who was involved in the crime, because:

_____

_____

_____

_____

_____

YOUR LAST INSTRUCTION:
DO NOT DISCUSS THIS LINEUP IN ANY WAY WITH THE NEWS MEDIA. DO NOT DISCUSS THIS LINEUP IN ANY WAY WITH OTHER POTENTIAL WITNESSES, NOW OR IN THE FUTURE.

Signed: _____   Date: _____

▲ FIGURE 7-10 Live lineup form (part 2) (*concluded*)

SHOW-UP FORM

Case No: _____   Place: _____

Date/Time: _____   Administrator: _____

Witness: _____

Others present: _____

ADMONITION

As a witness, you will be asked to look at a person or persons. You are not obligated to identify anyone. It is just as important to clear innocent persons from suspicion as it is to identify guilty parties. You should not conclude that the person or persons you see committed the crime simply because they are present. Please be advised that I cannot give you feedback on any identification you make. If you make identification, please do not discuss the case with the news media or other witnesses or indicate to them in any way that you have identified someone. Regardless of whether identification is made, law enforcement will continue to investigate the incident.

ACKNOWLEDGEMENT

I hereby acknowledge that I have read the foregoing admonition and understand it.

Witness: _____   Officer: _____

STATEMENTS/COMMENTS:

_____
_____
_____
_____

Investigator's note: If an identification is made, ask the witness to state, in his or her own words, how certain he or she is of any identification. Remember to record both positive identifications and non-identification results in writing, including the witness' own words how sure they are.

◄ FIGURE 7-11   Show-up form
(Garen Horst, Placer County, California, District Attorney's Office, 2010 Version, with some modification)

laws dealing with fabricating false evidence and concealing, altering, or destroying evidence.

The essence of staging a crime scene is to misdirect investigators, usually away from the actual perpetrator. It may also be done for other reasons, such as protecting a family from embarrassment or financial hardship—for example, trying to make a suicide appear as an accident or a murder.[22] Most life insurance policies have a minimum waiting period, often two years, before suicides are covered. Assume that a man purchases a new life insurance policy, subsequently developed cancer, and commits suicide 23 months after the policy is issued. If his suicide is successfully staged as a murder, the family is financially protected.

Staging investigations focus on two questions: (1) what act is the staging intended to conceal, and (2) what was the motive for staging the crime, the determination of which usually leads to the perpetrator.[23] The staging motive is often one of self-preservation, to get away with the crime, or the previously mentioned avoidance of embarrassment or shame.[24]

Some staged crimes are so clumsy that they are immediately apparent. For example, a husband starts using meth and is secretly selling his wife's jewelry to buy it. To hide this fact, he breaks the window leading from the carport into the house to make it appear a burglary occurred. However, all the broken glass is on the carport—there is none on the inside of the house—meaning that the window was broken from the inside, not the outside. However, with so many crime investigation shows on television, people are learning more about police and laboratory capabilities and are becoming more sophisticated in staging scenes.

The first inklings of something being wrong may come from noticing that those who would seemingly be most affected by the crime, such as the murder of a spouse, display unusual behavior. Even allowing for the complexity of human behavior, when a surviving spouse treats the murder as an inconvenience, is only minimally distressed, or is even oddly undisturbed by it, investigators should be alerted. Stated somewhat differently, when there is an observable lack of congruence between the surviving spouse's affect and the murder, the cautious investigator wants to understand the reason for the gap.

Even when surviving spouses do not verbally express feelings of loss and despair to a significant degree, there are usually still nonverbal signs of distress—for instance, facial expressions, clutching their stomach, reaching for something to steady themselves or a chair to lower themselves into, moving their hands in circular motions as though they are trying to grasp the situation, and a mouth moving without the utterance of words suggest an inability to comprehend the loss.

In other staged situations, the investigator notes inconsistencies between the statements of the witness and the scene's physical evidence. These inconsistencies must be satisfactorily resolved, which may not be possible until the investigation gathers more information and receives the laboratory reports. Some staged crimes may be so successful that the case is closed and reopened only after the receipt of new information. For example, a new widow who came into a considerable amount of inheritance from the deceased is suddenly out partying continuously, immediately having an intense emotional relationship with someone, and cutting off contacts with the family's former friends and relatives, and rumors are surfacing about her previous affairs.

The best tool for identifying a staged crime is a thorough original and follow-up investigation. That documentation remains available and unchanging, needing only additional analysis.[25] Staged crime investigations profit from a logical process:[26]

1. Conduct a comprehensive and thorough review of the documented scene, which may be very time-consuming in violent crimes because of the abundance of evidence.

2. Carefully consider the victim's character, lifestyle, personal and professional associates, drug and alcohol use, normal hangouts, daily schedule and routines, physical condition, occupation, previous complaints to the police, and recent conversations with neighbors and friends. Is this information consistent with the scene and any behavior imputed to the victim; do any inconsistencies emerge that are significant?

3. Look at the incident from several perspectives. Does the reported sequence of events make sense—for example, why didn't the offender target the greatest threat first? Why did the greatest threat to the offender have the least amount of injuries? How did the husband escape a life-threatening injury or death while the assaults on his wife and children were fatal? Were the items taken from the scene valuable and easily removed, or did the offender take less valuable and odd items? Where were the stolen items before they were taken? How did the perpetrator know their location? Are the final positions of the bodies consistent with the location of

postmortem lividity (livor mortis), which is the settling of the blood to the parts of the body closest to the ground?[27] (Lividity produces a visible discoloration that is ordinarily reddish purple.

4. Identify and document in detail all possible indicators of staging.

5. Identify and document possible motives for the original act and for the staging. The person staging the scene is not someone who happened by and gratuitously changed things; it is almost always someone who knew the victim and had some association or relationship with him/her.

6. Determine who benefits from the original act and the staging.

COLD CASE INVESTIGATION

A **cold case** investigation, the most extreme form of a follow-up, is the reopening of an inactivated, unsolved case. "Cold" is a term that lacks precision, covering from months to many years. The most common type of cold case investigation is a murder or serial murders, followed by rapes.

Cold cases may have been inactivated because there were no more leads to pursue; forensic methods available now did not exist; more promising cases demanded attention; witnesses were reluctant to cooperate, were hostile, had vanished, died, or were murdered; and evidence was misplaced. Cases that are good candidates for reexamination are those that have some potential for overcoming these problems—for example, a new witness comes forward, or previously unrecovered evidence is located.

The work is challenging but has the potential to help families reach a resolution and to apprehend a significant predator. However, sometimes the victims or their families oppose a cold case investigation because they have "moved on" with their lives and don't want to revisit their painful past.

In 2001 the Los Angeles Police Department established a cold case unit, which started with 9,000 unsolved cases from the previous 20 years, most of which were not good candidates for activation; in the nine years that followed, approximately 100 offenses were solved.[28] Where staffing permits it, a dedicated staff of cold case investigators is believed to perform better than someone who is also carrying an active case load. The logic is that cold cases require a specialized type of investigation.

Like many other agencies, the Fayetteville (North Carolina) Police Department (FPD) had cold cases and resource constraints, and so they implemented an innovative solution pioneered by Professor Glover at St. Leo University, who involved students in reviewing cold cases. The FPD cold case unit consists of a supervising investigator from the police department and volunteers, including several retired and highly experienced investigators and

Professor Pauly, Methodist University, who had a long career in forensic investigation before becoming a faculty member. Carefully screened students who sign confidentiality agreements enter data to be analyzed by investigative software packages. The newly formed unit has not reported its first success.

INVESTIGATIVE SUPPORT AND ANALYTICAL TOOLS

FUSION CENTERS

Following 9/11, it was concluded that if the isolated parcels of information known about the terrorists and their activities before the attacks had been pooled and analyzed, the attacks may have been disrupted, mitigated, or prevented. As part of the overall response, fusion centers (FCs) were developed, staffed by multiple federal, state, tribal, and local agencies and private-sector entities (Figures 7-12 and 7-13). About 70 FCs are operational.[29] **Fusion**

▲ **FIGURE 7-12 Fusion center**
(Courtesy Office of the Governor of Kentucky, Kentucky Office of Homeland Security)

is defined as turning information and intelligence into actionable knowledge; it is the fundamental process by which homeland security and crime-related information and intelligence are shared.

The essence of FCs is the constant merging, analysis, and dissemination of information and data from many disparate sources, including hospitals and the epidemiological monitoring capabilities of the Centers for Disease Control; this information is used both tactically and strategically for homeland security and crime-fighting purposes.

FCs have resulted in a convergence of crime analysis and intelligence to produce real-time, immediately actionable information. The concentration of information in FCs has alarmed civil libertarians concerned about abuses, and at the state level there is some sentiment that the federal government's intelligence contributions need to be more timely and substantial. It is predictable that issues will arise in an effort of such magnitude, and those issues deserve serious consideration.

INTELLIGENCE UNITS

Although many law-enforcement agencies have an intelligence unit, this unit's capabilities vary from simply trying to keep files current to using sophisticated analytical techniques. Depending on local capabilities and the fact situation, investigators may find no to considerable helpful information in local intelligence files.

Intelligence consists of pieces of raw information that when collected, evaluated, collated, and analyzed form meaningful and useful judgments that are both timely and accurate.[30]

In terms of categories of intelligence, there are at least four types:

1. *Indicative intelligence:* Focuses on emerging and new criminal developments.
2. *Tactical intelligence:* Immediately actionable and often results in arrests.
3. *Strategic intelligence:* Gathered and analyzed over time and usually confirms newly discovered patterns of criminal activity.
4. *Evidential intelligence:* Factual, precise information that can be presented in court.[31]

THE INTELLIGENCE/ANALYTICAL CYCLE

The **intelligence/analytical cycle** is driven by the needs of the client or end-user, who may be the commander of a task force working a serial murder case or the supervisor of an investigation unit trying to find a pattern in a string of violent convenience-store robberies. It is the end-user who specifies the types of information he/she wants, and it is the responsibility of the intelligence unit to make sure that the end-user understands both the possibilities and the limitations of the intelligence process and its

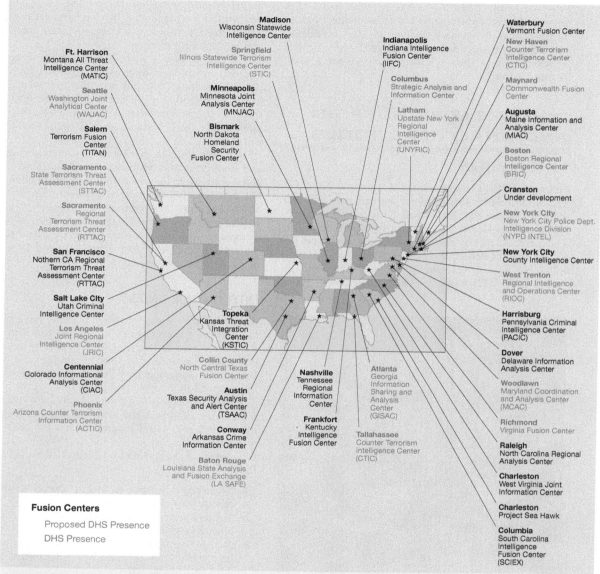

▲ **FIGURE 7-13**   **Map of current and planned fusion centers**
(Todd Masse, Siobhan O'Neil, and John Rollins, Fusion Centers: Issues and Options for Congress [Washington, D.C.: Congressional Research Service, July 6, 2007], p. CRS-93)

techniques. As depicted in Figure 7-14, the backbone of the intelligence/analytical cycle is a continuous six-step process,[32] which is discussed next.

1. PLANNING AND DIRECTION

The intelligence/analytical process must be managed throughout, from identifying the focus of the intelligence effort to delivering the finished product to the police unit requesting it. As a practical matter, finished intelligence often creates new questions during the reevaluation stage, which starts the process all over again.

2. COLLECTION

Collection is the gathering and managing of raw data, which is then analyzed to produce the finished product.[33]

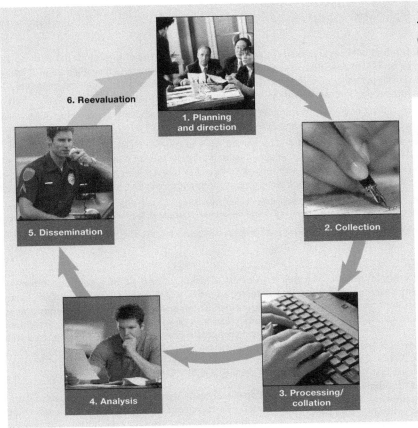

◀ **FIGURE 7-14**
The intelligence/analytical cycle
(U.S. Department of Justice, Department of Homeland Security, and The Global Justice Information Sharing Initiative, Fusion Center Guidelines [Washington, D.C.: July 2005], p. 26)

6. Reevaluation

1. Planning and direction

2. Collection

3. Processing/ collation

4. Analysis

5. Dissemination

3. PROCESSING

Processing converts raw information from all sources into a form that can be used by analysts.[34] This is accomplished by information management, which is the indexing, sorting, and organizing of raw data into files for rapid retrieval. It includes entering the data into a computer, checking the entries for accuracy, and collating paper files. One of the key considerations in processing is ensuring that the data-processing methods fit the analytical techniques that will be used.

4. ANALYSIS AND PRODUCTION

In the analysis and production step, the data that has been processed is translated into a finished intelligence product.[35] Analysts, who are subject-matter specialists (for example, organized crime, gangs, or terrorism), carefully scrutinize the data for timeliness, reliability, validity, and relevance. The role of the analyst is to combine the data and his/her analysis and judgment into a finished intelligence product that informs the end-user of the analyst's assessment of events and the implications of that assessment.

5. DISSEMINATION

The fifth element in the cycle is the dissemination of the finished intelligence report to the end-user who requested it.[36] The end-user can then make decisions or take actions on the basis of the intelligence provided.

6. REEVALUATION

It is crucial that the end-user provide feedback about the value of the intelligence so that there can be an ongoing cycle of improvement. Moreover, the finished intelligence report itself, the decisions made, and the actions taken all have the potential to create new questions that lead back to the first element, planning and direction, thus beginning a new intelligence/analytical cycle.

SURVEILLANCE CAMERAS AND FACIAL RECOGNITION SOFTWARE

Surveillance cameras (SCs) use continues to expand. In England, where there is an average of one surveillance camera for every 14 people, shoppers and workers are estimated to be caught on camera at least 300 times a

TABLE 7-1	Types of Crime Analysis
TYPE	DESCRIPTION
Tactical	Deals with recent offenses (for example, immediate to hours, days, or weeks) for the purpose of responding quickly to specific crimes; it provides uniformed officers and investigators with timely information (for instance, investigative leads) to guide their actions and apprehend offenders. Includes attempts to forecast where the next specific crime (such as burglary) will occur.
Strategic	Focuses on solving ongoing crime problems (months, quarters, or years) by matching police resources with crime, demands for service, and other variables.
Administrative	For police administrators, elected and appointed city and county officials, and others: analyzes crime and demographic, economic, geographic, and other factors on a long-range basis (quarterly, semiannually, or even multiyear) with respect to how they interact with one another. The information may be used in annual reports, policy-making, grant applications, and for other related purposes.

Synthesized from Crime Analysis Unit, "Types of Crime Analysis," Bernalillo County, New Mexico, Sheriff's Office, December 3, 2010, *www.bernco.gov*, and Crime Analyst, "Three Types of Crime Analysis," North Miami Police Department, December 3, 2010, *www.northmiamipolice.com*.

day.[37] In the United States there are 30 million SCs that record four billion hours of footage each week.[38] It is generally thought that people in this country are recorded 30 to 45 times daily. This footage can be "mined" to look for particular variables.

Malls may have hundreds of SCs inside and on the parking lots. They are also at ATMs, casinos, airports, downtown streets, "sit-down" and fast food restaurants, schools, dorms, grocery stores, football stadiums, and gyms, and they provide live monitoring of highway traffic. SCs are even in homes for security, although some also surreptitiously employ mini "nanny cams" to make sure their children are not being abused. Inevitably, SCs capture crimes in progress, providing investigative leads. Some retail giants, e.g. Target, quietly have established their own digital labs and work closely with investigators.

Facial recognition software (FRS) began being deployed by law-enforcement agencies during the 1990s. FRS has continued to evolve in terms of accuracy and the ways in which it is used. More advanced FRS can produce two- and three-dimensional facial images. Using advanced mathematical calculations, the face of an unknown person captured on camera can be compared to a known file photograph to make an identification. In 2010 the best-performing FRS had an error rate of 0.1 to 2.1%.[39]

FRS is being used by a growing number of states to ensure the identity of the person being licensed to drive. Some law-enforcement agencies compare SC photos of illegal activity with their departmental mug hot files. Impressionistically this procedure appears to have greater success with illegal check and credit card transactions at a counter. The subjects are relatively still in this setting, and there are multiple high-resolution images with which to work. FRS is also being used in homeland security efforts, such as at border-crossing stations. Some agencies have equipped patrol cars with facial recognition technology and digital cameras. During a two-year period, Pinellas

County (Florida) Sheriff's Office deputies in the field correctly identified 295 people who had lied about their identity.[40] There is ongoing research to determine whether other likeness of suspects—for example, artist's sketches and composite drawings—can reliably be used with FRS.

CRIME ANALYSIS

Crime analysis is the process of using systematic analytical methods to acquire timely and pertinent information on crime patterns and trend correlations.[41] The three general types of crime analysis are summarized in Table 7-1. Commonly used methods to link crimes include:[42]

- *Trends:* **Trends** are general tendencies in the occurrence of crime across large geographic areas over extended periods of time. They arise when areas become more conducive or less conducive to a particular crime or crimes. Trends can be associated with shifts in demography; for example, as a neighborhood ages, its residents may be seen as soft targets for muggings and home-invasion robberies. Trends can also stem from the creation of new targets; for instance, the presence of a new shopping mall increases the opportunities for shoplifting and thefts from, and of, vehicles

- *Patterns:* If the same crime is committed repeatedly over a short period of time, sometimes, but not always, by the same offender, it is a pattern. For example, outside a five-star restaurant, a number of female patrons who are leaving alone have their purses snatched.

- *Series:* In a **series,** the same type of crime is committed over a short period of time, probably by the same offender. For instance, in an affluent, gated residential community of 73 houses, six burglaries occur in nine days.

◀ **FIGURE 7-15 Hot blocks**
One way to see areas of interest larger than a hot spot is to highlight *hot blocks*, or areas where many incidents cluster. In this GIS map, auto thefts or recoveries occurred in tight groups. In the map, red spots indicate clusters of car thefts, and blue clusters represent recoveries.

- *Sprees:* When the same type of offense is committed at almost the same time by the same offender(s) it is called a spree. An example is the vandalizing of cars by a group of kids who spray-paint license plates while walking through a neighborhood.
- *Hot spots:* A **hot spot** is a location where various crimes are committed on a regular basis, usually by different perpetrators. An example is a bar where underage drinkers are served, there are numerous fights, user-level drug sales take place, prostitution flourishes, and patrons are occasionally mugged, robbed, or carjacked in the parking lot (Figure 7-15).
- *Crimogens:* A **crimogen** is either an individually known offender who is responsible for a large number of crimes or one victim who reports a large number of crimes. Examples include a career criminal and a convenience-store operator who reports gas drive-offs, shoplifting, robberies, assaults, and even thefts of entire ATM machines.

Crime-analysis reports, depending on their intended use and sensitivity, may be distributed at staff meetings, shift briefings, the departmental intranet, or other method.

The policies of most law-enforcement agencies require feedback from the users of the products to help determine the effectiveness of the unit. The weight of the new emphasis on intelligence gathering and tight budgets has resulted in some law-enforcement agencies creating a Crime Analysis and Intelligence Unit, combining what have historically been separate functions.

CRIME SCENE RECONSTRUCTION

Reconstruction of past events is routine in law enforcement. The first officer at a domestic violence call listens to the parties involved, examines any injuries, looks at the scene were the violence allegedly took place, evaluates the credibility of statements made by the parties involved and any witnesses, and in consideration of all the information available at that time makes a decision on the proper handling of it.

In contrast, crime scene reconstruction (CSR) involves more complex events, takes place over a longer period of time, integrates data from more varied sources, and uses a rigorous methodology to reach conclusions. The Association for Crime Scene Reconstruction (ACSR)

▶ FIGURE 7-16
The scientific method and CSR

STEPS IN THE SCIENTIFIC METHOD	RECONSTRUCTION APPLICATION
1. State the problem	IQ: Was the victim approaching or going away from VMS when she was shot?
2. Gather the relevant data	Crime scene photographs and diagrams; medical examiner's report; lab reports: bloodstain pattern analysis, ballistics.
3. Form a hypothesis	Victim was going away from VMS
4. Predict what the hypothesis would indicate if true	It would contradict VMS's account of incident: victim attacked him with a knife in her hand; he shot her with SW revolver in self-defense at a range of 18″; she turned around, staggered down the hallway and collapsed.
5. Test of hypothesis	1. Victim found 13 feet from VMS's alleged shooting position, near end of "L" shaped hallway. 2. No blood evidence at the point victim was allegedly shot. 3. No back spatter blood on revolver or VMS's person/clothing. 4. Bullet's entry point was the victim's back, through her nightgown. 5. High-velocity bloodstain pattern indicates victim was shot approximately 9' from VMS's position. 6. Lab test concluded victim could not have been shot at distance claimed by VMS.
6. State the conclusion	Victim was shot moving away from VMS's position at a distance of approximately 9 feet.

defines CSR as "the use of scientific methods, physical evidence, deductive reasoning, and their interrelationship to gain explicit knowledge of the series of events that surround the commission of a crime." There are different approaches to CSR, but they share common perspectives:

- data defines the conclusion;
- the context in which evidence is found, as well as its analysis, provides objective data;
- consider human testimony cautiously;
- effective forensic examination produces more refined data;
- what happened is not the only question—its sequence is also important;
- use "reverse engineering" to work backward from the evidence to develop an understanding of what happened.[43]

The different CSR approaches also ask four basic questions as each item of evidence is being considered:

- What is it?
- What function does it serve?
- What does it tell about the timing and sequence of events?
- What interrelationships does it have with other items of evidence?[44]

The **scientific method** is at the heart of all approaches to CSR. The steps of the scientific method and their application to CSR are identified in Figure 7-16. This illustration addresses a single investigative question (IQ).

The six steps of the scientific method are easily followed in a controlled laboratory experiment where there can be a single test point of a hypothesis before a conclusion is reached. However, in investigation we develop multiple hypotheses, often at different times—such as the victim was seated when shot; the suspect gained entry through the victim's rear door; the first of three shots fired through the glass window came from the inside; and the suspect returned to the scene and mutilated the victim's body. These hypotheses are not collectively tested at a single point in time but intermittently throughout the investigation as the appropriate information—for example, autopsy reports, surveillance camera images, and lab that require answers; thus, the employment of the scientific method produces an ever-expanding and self-correcting body of knowledge related to the crime.[45] This expanding body of knowledge may also introduce thorny new problems that require entirely new hypotheses. Assume a man's body is found next to his car in the parking lot behind a bar. The car door is open, the keys are near the victim's hand, and the scene suggests he was about to enter or leave his car when he was shot once in the chest and head. One rear trouser pocket is semi-turned inside out, and there was no wallet. The investigator's initial impression was that a lone gunman killed the victim in a robbery gone bad. Later, the autopsy report arrived, and bullets from two different caliber handguns were recovered from the victim. Before reading any further, the investigator entertains several new possibilities: One shooter using two different weapons? Two shooters? One shooter scared off before taking anything, and quickly thereafter an opportunistic criminal took the wallet and finished the possibly conscious victim off? Found wounded and killed by a spurned lover, who then staged a robbery by taking the wallet?

Despite such thorny problems, CSR goes forward using the discipline of the scientific method, blending empirical knowledge, gained from observation and deduction, and rationalism, inductive thought and reasoning,[46] particularly critical thinking. At its heart, critical thinking is an unremitting intellectual process that rejects evidence and conclusions that lack sufficient proof; it does not allow, for example, assumptions to masquerade as facts.[47] Key skills associated with critical thinking include analyzing, synthesizing, and evaluating.

One approach to CSR is Event Analysis (EA) model of CSR. "*Incident*" is any situation a reconstructionist is asked to investigate; the term is neutral and avoids the implicit assumption that a crime has been committed. An incident includes all of the activity from its beginning to its end.[48] Incidents consist of macro components, "*events*"; these, in turn comprise a series of actions, "*event segments*," that are much like a series of time-phased photographs.[49] The primary focus of EA is to identify as many event segments as possible; each event segment is a mini-conclusion based on the verifiable data associated with it[50] (Figure 7-18).

The scientific method is designed to eliminate other explanations and cannot establish a final, "absolute truth." Scientific methods and statements are open to re-examination, particularly in light of new data and new analytical techniques. An allied example is the number of people who were convicted by eyewitness testimony but freed years later by DNA analysis. What this means in investigation is that at the end of using the scientific method we have eliminated the impossible and implausible and what is left is a valid possibility. CSR does not deal with the "why" of crimes; that is the purview of criminal profiling, discussed next in this chapter.

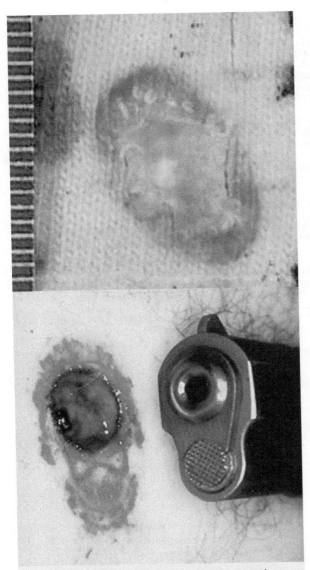

▲ **FIGURE 7-17** **Specific crime scene reconstruction** Suspect related he shot the victim from across the room. The victim's yellow sweater and skin reveal the shot was fired with the gun's muzzle in contact with the victim. There was also "blowback" evidence on the pistol, blood and tissue, from the victim. The physical evidence contradicts the suspect's story. (Courtesy Forensic Training and Consulting, LLC)

reports—becomes available (Figure 7-17). The testing, as well as the addition of new information, causes us to refine some hypotheses, discard others, and formulate new ones to test.

The scientific method is somewhat circular, because after we test a hypothesis, it often leads to new questions

▶ **FIGURE 7-18**

Illustration of event segment analysis

Case Situation:

Officers responded to call where a husband (TJM) returning home alone parked his BMW in the garage, closed the garage door, and entered the house through the door opening into kitchen. Although his wife was on an out-of-state trip, he expected his 17-year-old stepdaughter to be home. She was the only other person who would be in the house. He discovered "lots of blood" in her first-floor bedroom located in the home's west wing. TJM immediately went just outside the front door and used his cell phone to call 911. He did not reenter the house until arriving officers cleared it without finding anyone. The first arriving officer remained continuously with TJM, first outside the front door and later in the living room. Crime scene technicians arrived and began processing the scene. Soon thereafter, investigators reached the scene and 35 minutes later took TJM from the living room to the station, where he gave the statement used to describe this case situation.

Data Elements:

1. TJM brought BMW to scene.
2. TJM parked in garage.
3. TJM closed garage door.
4. TJM arrived alone at house.
5. TJM found blood in his stepdaughter's bedroom.
6. TJM immediately went outside the front door and called police on his cell phone.
7. First arriving officer stayed continuously with TJM, first outside the front door and later in the living room.
8. Other arriving officers searched but did not find anyone else in house.
9. Blood recovered from stepdaughter's room.
10. Visible blood droplets found on floor of master bathroom in home's east wing.
11. Blood found on inside of shower in master bathroom.
12. Blood found on rear bumper of BMW.
13. Blood found in trunk of BMW.
14. Blood noted in 5 and 9–13 above consistent with stepdaughter's DNA.

Event Segment:

Subsequent to stepdaughter's bleeding, TJM transferred her blood to the master bathroom and the BMW's bumper and trunk.

For detailed information about Event Analysis see Ross M. Gardner and Tom Bevel, *Practical Crime Scene Analysis and Reconstruction* (Boca Raton, Florida: CRC Press, 2009).

CRIMINAL PROFILING

Criminal profiling is also referred to by other terms, such as offender profiling and psychological profiling. It is the process of studying all available information related to a crime and developing a psychological portrait of the unknown offender. It has the potential to eliminate suspects, focus on one or several others, provide investigative leads, and be helpful in interrogations.

Profiling has a history of roughly 50 years. An early success involved "The Mad Bomber," who from 1940 until 1956 in New York City, with a "patriotic pause" during World War II, left over 30 bombs in public places. After reviewing the amassed evidence, psychiatrist James Brussels concluded:

He is a male, middle-aged, meticulous, largely self-educated, Slavic, Roman Catholic, has an Oedipal Complex, lives in Connecticut, and worked for Consolidated Edison or one of its subsidiaries. The police

would have to publicize the profile to draw the man out, and when apprehended he will be wearing a buttoned double-breasted suit.[51]

Drawn out by the publicity, George Metesky wrote letters to newspapers, which unintentionally contained clues that ultimately led to his arrest in 1957. Remarkably, he was wearing a buttoned double-breasted suit, and other aspects of the profile were also correct. Conversely, the profiles of the Washington D.C. snipers who terrorized that area in 2002 with their random murders were substantially off-target. Profiling is not an exact science and relies to a degree on the training, experience, and judgment of the profiler.

The FBI led the modern development of profiling beginning in the 1970s. Along with continually refining the methodology, the FBI produced one of the most widely recognized concepts of profiling, the organized-disorganized offender model (Table 7-2). Although many offenders fit neatly into the organized or disorganized

TABLE 7-2	Crime Scene Differences between Organized and Disorganized Sexual Homicides
ORGANIZED	**DISORGANIZED**
1. Offense planned; semblance of order before, during, and after the crime suggests aim of avoiding detection	Spontaneous offense, appears to be no plan to avoid detection
2. Victim frequently a targeted stranger in a location staked out by offender, to some extent victim is a target of opportunity; serial victims may share common characteristics, and offender may spend considerable time waiting for "right" victim	May know victim or select randomly, often familiar with location of crime
3. Personalizes victim	Depersonalizes victim; specific areas of the body may be selected for extreme violence; overkill or excessive force to face is often attempt to dehumanize victim
4. Offender may strike up conversation with victim as attempt to gain her confidence in order to capture victim without resorting to physical force	Minimal conversation aside from orders and directions
5. Scene reflects overall control	Scene random and sloppy, in great disarray
6. Demands submissive and compliant victim; may require certain reactions, e.g., fear and passivity during sexual activity	Sudden, overpowering violence to victim; offender uses a surprise blitz-style attack
7. Restraints used, e.g., ropes, chains, handcuffs, chemicals, belts, gags, blindfolds	Minimal use of restraints; victim killed quickly to avoid victim's getting the upper hand
8. Aggressive acts prior to death, weapon displayed, victim's life threatened	Any sexually sadistic acts follow death, e.g., mutilation of face, breasts, and genitals
9. Body hidden	Body left in view, often left in position killed
10. Weapons and evidence absent	Evidence and weapons often present, normally much physical evidence available
11. Transports victim or body, often using his or her vehicle	Body left at death scene

Source: Robert Ressler, Ann W. Burgess, and John E. Douglas, *Sexual Homicide: Patterns and Motives* (New York: Free Press, 1992), pp. 121–124, 131.

pattern, some of them reflect aspects of both patterns. A number of factors can lead to a mixed organized-disorganized crime: multiple offenders with different behaviors may be involved; a planned crime may deteriorate as unanticipated events unfold, such as being unable to control the victim; or the original motive may have been solely rape, but the victim's resistance (which may be successful) or the offender's changed emotional state may lead to murder. Youthful offenders or the offender's use of drugs and alcohol can also lead to a mixed scene.[52]

The FBI's Behavioral Science Unit continues to provide profiling services to other law-enforcement agencies. Profiling methods focus on the four factors that are briefly discussed below.

1. *Antecedent:* In this stage the profiler tries to understand the offender's mindset. What triggered the offender to commit the crime? Was he/she driven by fantasies about this victim, was it the characteristics of the victim and/or the location, was the

situation attractive—for example, would have a longer time to spend with the victim, did he/she act opportunistically or was it planned? What does the lack of planning or the items brought to the scene suggest?

2. *Method:* Although offenders may vary in how they commit a crime, often there is a pattern to it. They enter the victim's residence in a particular way, within a time range, on a particular day or two of the week, overpowering victims with a blow from a blunt instrument, binding them in a certain way using the same material to restrain them—for instance, duct tape, abusing them in a specific way or sequence, and suffocating them with a plastic bag over their heads.

3. *Disposal:* What the offender does with the victim after the offense may form part of a modus operandi or suggest things about the offender. A raped woman might be left tied to the bed, forced into a closet, or ordered to shower and restrained again.

If there are multiple murder victims the bodies may be cleaned up and positioned in sexual or other poses, as was done by Florida's "Gainesville Ripper." Bodies that are dumped in a National Forest, industrial park, or a particular segment of a river may indicate a familiarity with the area. Leaving bodies where they will be quickly found suggests a need for recognition.

4. *Post-offense behavior:* There may be no observable post-offense behavior, or the offender may contact the news media to publish obscure clues or rage against how the police are characterizing him, or send taunting letters to the police.

Although profiling has been an asset in many significant violent investigations, it has some detractors who in one way or another regarded it as pseudo-science. It was severely criticized in 2010, characterized as never having been a scientific process and essentially based on common sense intuitions and faulty theoretical assumptions that appear to be consistent with educated guesses and wishful thinking.[53] A more moderate criticism was raised in 2009, which called for a higher level of scientific validity.[54] These criticisms have not gone unnoticed, and multiple research efforts have been completed and others are underway to strengthen the scientific base.

GEOGRAPHICAL PROFILING

Geographic information system (GIS) software provides the capability to superimpose various types of data on a map. For example, a law-enforcement administrator might want to see where traffic citations are being written versus where accidents frequently occur, which could lead to a refocusing of the enforcement effort. **Geographic profiling** is a specialty that rests on the premise that given a sufficient number of crimes, with adequate information suitable for analysis, a probabilistic map of the area in which the offender's residence is located can be calculated. The size of the area depends on the amount and quality of data. Geoprofiling has also proven itself useful in locating insurgents responsible for planting improvised explosive devices and in border security (Figure 7-19).

Although others had worked on geographic profiling, the term was coined by Rossmo, a former Detective Inspector with the Vancouver (Canada) Police Department. While studying for his doctorate, he conceived of the idea of using geographic profiling to target the residence of offenders and was the central figure in developing the first software package to be able to do this. As in the case of other recently developed investigative technologies, geoprofiling is in a state of transition as refinements are developed. It is not a perfect tool, and its capabilities can be decreased if the number of cases in a series are roughly less than 5 or the crime linkage is inaccurate.[55]

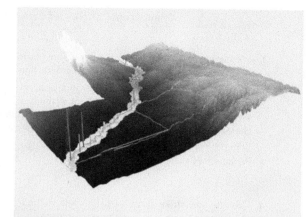

▲ FIGURE 7-19

Geoprofiling for illegal entries into the United States that resulted in criminal dispositions. The land of Mexico is to the left of the river (blue line); to the right is the United States. Note that the yellow line turns purple near the top of the image, showing an increase in elevation. Higher vertical lines portray more crossings made at that point. **(Courtesy Dr. Kim Rossmo, Center for Geospatial Intelligence and Investigation (GII), Texas State University, San Marcos)**

REMOTE SENSING

Remote sensing is the process of collecting and analyzing information about areas, objects, or events without being in contact with the focus of analysis.[56] Aerial surveillance was the first type of remote sensing; during the Civil War (1861–1865), officers were sent aloft in balloons to observe the disposition of enemy forces and report on what they saw. Some photographs were taken and used by commanders.[57] Today, aerial/visual sensing is conducted by manned space craft, satellites, rotary and fixed-wing aircraft, unmanned aerial vehicles (UAVs), and public surveillance cameras.

Aerial remote sensing can be used by law-enforcement personnel to detect illicit drug crops and clandestine labs, monitor airstrips, provide over-the-horizon (OTH) intelligence about drug smuggling boats and planes, quickly identify incipient forest fires, rescue lost hikers and mountain climbers, find airplane crash sites, locate fugitives and abducted persons, recover automobiles and other evidence from water systems, identify possible clandestine graves, as well as to provide investigative leads, the identification of suspects, and proof that the elements of a crime were committed.

Aerial surveillance platforms may be equipped with not only visual recording and transmitting capabilities but other sensor packages as well. Many police aircraft are equipped with Forward Looking Infrared Radar

◄**FIGURE 7-20**
NYPD officer working a German Shepherd trained to detect the odor of cadaver
The suspect confessed to having buried the victim in this area.
(© Susana Bates/New York Daily News)

(FLIR), which is a significant asset in tracking fugitives on foot at night through their heat signatures.

There are also numerous other remote-sensing capabilities, including (1) the use of canines to detect contraband and cadavers (Figure 7-20) and (2) ground-penetrating radar to locate clandestine graves, which is a process that is nondestructive to physical evidence. (3) Potential burial sites can be worked from the surface to a depth of several feet using metal detectors to search for items such as shell cases, projectiles, belt buckles, jewelry, buttons, and zippers. Advanced metal detectors with screens can show the depth of an item and estimate the probability that it is one type of artifact or another. (4) Radar-based through-the-wall surveillance (TWS) provides 3-D color images, including static objects and moving people, from a distance through walls as thick as 8 inches of concrete. This capability substantially reduces the danger to officers making high-risk entries into buildings to free hostages or apprehend violent offenders. Booby traps can also be identified, the number and locations of suspects determined, and other important tactical information provided. (5) Aquatic acoustic sensors can track boats smuggling drugs or weapons; and (6) smaller gamma-ray-based density meters can identify variations in the density of dashboards, tires, walls, and other surfaces. Such variations allow hidden compartments containing contraband to be identified, and larger gamma ray units can scan cargo (Figure 7-21).

TIME-EVENT CHARTING AND LINK ANALYSIS

Follow-up investigations often result in the accumulation of significant amounts of data. As a result, financial transactions, relationships, the importance of places,

◄**FIGURE 7-21**
Truck-mounted gamma-ray scanning the contents of a tractor-trailer
(© AP Photo/Jean-Marc Bouju)

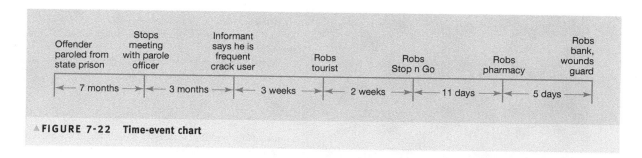

▲ **FIGURE 7-22 Time-event chart**

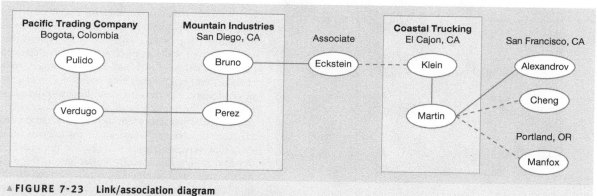

▲ **FIGURE 7-23 Link/association diagram**
Organizations are in boxes. Solid lines indicate confirmed relationships. Dotted lines are suspected relations.

events, telephone calls, and other data can be obscured and their importance overlooked, resulting in an unnecessarily protracted or unsuccessful investigation. Software has automated creating a variety of charts, saving investigative effort for other uses. Two commonly used investigative tools are time-event charting and link analysis.

A time-event chart is shown in Figure 7-22; it depicts the major events involving an offender paroled from the state prison. Time is shown as intervals between major events. The actual dates for events could be added to the chart. For seven months, he made his regularly scheduled meetings with his parole officer. Three months later, an informant described him as a frequent crack user. Three weeks after that, the parolee robbed a tourist. Over the next 30 days, he committed three more robberies, each time progressing upward to a more lucrative target. The choice of a pharmacy as a target gave him both money and drugs, which are the same as money on the streets. If he is selling drugs, informants may know of it. The interval between robberies is growing shorter, and the parolee has become violent. It is possible that he is pulling jobs while high, so the potential for further violence is great. Figure 7-23 is a link chart showing the relationships between individuals involved in importing drugs.

THE INTERNET

The possibilities of the Internet have not escaped law enforcement, which has been quick to use it for investigative, administrative, and public information purposes. For investigative purposes, the police use the Internet in many ways, such as:

1. Appealing to the public for information about specific crimes, often through "crime-stopper" programs.
2. Requesting information about missing children and adults.
3. Posting federal, state, and local most-wanted lists. These lists may be limited to the "top 10," or there may be separate most-wanted lists, such as a list for the most-wanted violent felons or burglars.
4. Soliciting information about individuals who are wanted as fugitives.
5. Alerting the public about jail and prison escapees and requesting information if they are sighted.
6. Requesting information about the identities of unknown subjects ("unsubs").
7. Showing photographs of recovered stolen property so that the owners can identify and claim it.
8. Providing crime-mapping capabilities so that investigators can approach their work with better information and citizens can be informed.

KEY TERMS

Arson, Explosives and Incident System
  (AEXIS)
cold case
crime analysis
criminal profiling
crimogen
facial recognition software (FRS)
Field Interview/Information Report (FIR)
fusion
geographical profiling
hot spot
intelligence/analytical cycle

investigative plan
LeadsOnLine
live lineup
National Center for the Analysis of
  Violent Crime (NCAVC)
National Crime Information
  Center (NCIC)
National Drug Pointer Index (NDPIX)
National Missing and Unidentified
  Persons System (NamUs)
Next Generation Identification (NGI)
  Program

photo lineup
remote sensing
scientific method
series
show-up
social network sites
solvability factors
staged crime
surveillance
trends
Violent Criminal Apprehension
  Program (ViCAP)

REVIEW QUESTIONS

1. How are solvability factors used?
2. How do you prepare a case file?
3. Why are victims and witnesses reinterviewed?
4. NamUs provides what capabilities?
5. What is NCIC?
6. How can LeadsOnLine help an investigation?
7. What things should you not do with informants?
8. Why conduct physical surveillance?
9. How should a photo lineup be conducted?
10. What are three potential indicators of a staged crime?

11. What stages make up the intelligence cycle?
12. How is facial recognition software being used by law-enforcement agencies?
13. How do crime analysts link crimes?
14. Why is the scientific method important to crime scene reconstruction?
15. Criminal profiling focuses on what four factors?
16. What is geographical profiling?
17. What are four examples of remote sensing?
18. In what ways can the Internet be used by investigators?

INTERNET ACTIVITIES

1. Visit "FBI Next Generation Identification (NGI) Overview" and read about the FBI's new emphasis on biometrics (*http://biometrics.org/bc2010/presentations/DOJ/pender-FBI-Next-Generation-Identification-Overview.pdf.*)

2. Go to the Center for Geospatial Intelligence and Investigation, Texas State University to learn more about geoprofiling (*http://txstate.edu/gii*).

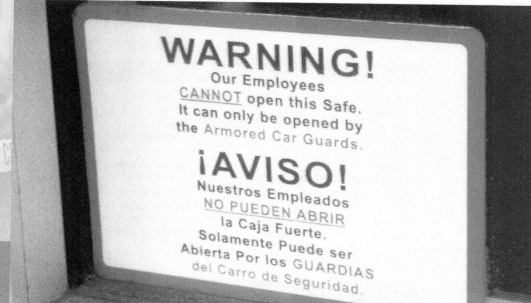

▶ In recent years, convenience store clerks, taxicab drivers, pizza delivery persons, etc. have been targeted in armed robberies. In response, "warning" signs in both English and Spanish (like the one at right) alert would-be robbers that minimal cash is on hand or accessible.

(© Joel Gordon)

13

ROBBERY

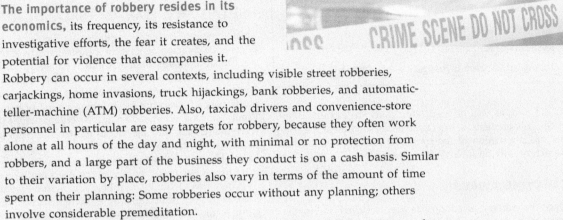

INTRODUCTION

The importance of robbery resides in its economics, its frequency, its resistance to investigative efforts, the fear it creates, and the potential for violence that accompanies it. Robbery can occur in several contexts, including visible street robberies, carjackings, home invasions, truck hijackings, bank robberies, and automatic-teller-machine (ATM) robberies. Also, taxicab drivers and convenience-store personnel in particular are easy targets for robbery, because they often work alone at all hours of the day and night, with minimal or no protection from robbers, and a large part of the business they conduct is on a cash basis. Similar to their variation by place, robberies also vary in terms of the amount of time spent on their planning: Some robberies occur without any planning; others involve considerable premeditation.

Because of the face-to-face confrontation between perpetrator and victim, the potential for violence is always present in a robbery. When violence does occur, it may range from minor injury to loss of life. Because of its personal and often violent nature, robbery is one of the crimes most feared by the public, a fear that may be heightened by perceptions of police inability to deal effectively with robberies. However, witnesses are often upset and may have seen the perpetrator only briefly—factors that sometimes limit how much they can assist the investigative process. These factors, coupled with the fact that most offenders operate alone, can make robbery investigations extremely difficult. Mitigating the investigative challenge are recent identification technologies that make it possible to quickly generate and distribute a likeness of a suspect. When security cameras are present and operating, they can also be of major assistance in providing leads.

In coping with a heightened sense of fear and alarm, robbery victims often seek guidance and advice to help prevent repeat victimization. Along with arresting suspects and recovering the victim's property, investigators and their departments can serve in a crime-prevention role. Providing the public with tips on what to do before, during, and after a robbery not only helps prevent robberies but also helps lessen the chance of repeat victimizations.

ELEMENTS OF THE CRIME

A **robbery** consists of these elements: the (1) taking and (2) carrying away of (3) personal property of (4) another, with (5) the intent to deprive the victim permanently, by (6) the use of force, fear, or threat of force.

TAKING

The property taken in a robbery must be taken illegally by the robber. Someone who has the right to take such property cannot properly be convicted of robbery. This illegal taking is called **trespassory.** The property must be taken from the custody, control, or possession of the

---

CHAPTER OUTLINE

Introduction

Elements of the Crime

Overview: The Offense, the Victim, and the Offender

Typology of Robberies

Responding to the Scene

Follow-Up Robbery Investigative Procedures

---

victim and, as will be seen later, from the victim's presence. This element of the crime is satisfied once the robber has possession of the property; until possession has occurred, only an attempt has taken place.

CARRYING AWAY

Once the element of taking has been satisfied, the robber must then carry away the property. This element can be satisfied simply by showing that the accused totally removed the article from the position that it formerly occupied. It is not necessary to show that any great distance was involved in the carrying away.

PERSONAL PROPERTY

The object of the robbery must be personal property as opposed to real estate or things attached to the land. Again, as in larceny (discussed in greater detail in Chapter 14), any tangible property and some forms of intangible property represented by tangible items, such as stocks and bonds, gas, electricity, minerals, and other such commodities, can be objects of robbery.

ANOTHER

The property taken must belong to another, not to the accused. This again relates to the first element of taking. If the taking is trespassory—illegal—then the property must be the rightful property of someone other than the robber.

INTENT TO DEPRIVE PERMANENTLY

Robbery is a crime of specific intent and requires that the prosecution establish, in court, that the defendant, at the time of taking the property by force or threat of force from the victim or the victim's presence, did, in fact, intend to deprive the victim of the use and enjoyment of that property permanently. In most cases, this fact can be concluded from the facts and the circumstances surrounding the case, but in specific-intent crime cases, juries are not permitted to assume this particular fact. Thus, the

police officer's investigation must be geared to establishing this as an essential element of the crime. The fact that force or the threat of force was used to secure the property from the victim is often enough to convince a jury of the accused's intent to deprive permanently.

USE OF FORCE, FEAR, OR THREAT OF FORCE

This element of the crime requires that the force or threat of force be directed against the physical safety of the victim rather than his or her social well-being. Thus, for example, a threat to expose some information that would be embarrassing to the victim unless a certain amount of money is paid does not satisfy this element of the crime. Proof that force was used or, at the very least, that threats were made such that the victim feared imminent bodily harm, is essential for successful prosecutions of robbery cases. However, the force used to separate the victim from his or her property in robbery need not be great.

When the victim of a robbery is seriously injured, there is usually little difficulty in convincing the investigator or the jury that force was used. However, difficulties may arise in the case of a victim who claims to have been robbed under the threat of force when no actual injury occurred. In this case, the skill of the investigator in determining the facts of the case becomes crucial to successful prosecution.

There are also more subtle situations in which the investigator must know legal requirements as well as investigative techniques. The typical purse-snatching case is an illustration. Often, the force element of the crime of robbery can be satisfied only by determining whether the victim attempted to resist the force used and, if so, the extent of that resistance. It is generally accepted by courts that a woman who puts her purse next to her on the seat of a bus without keeping her hand on it or loosely holds it in her hand is not the victim of robbery if someone quickly grabs the purse and runs. In these cases, the woman has not resisted. However, if she were clutching the bag tightly and someone managed to grab it from her after even a slight struggle, sufficient force and resistance would have occurred to constitute robbery. A good rule for the investigator to follow in cases of uncertainty is that the removal of an article without more force than is absolutely necessary to remove it from its original resting place constitutes larceny. If any additional force, no matter how slight, is used, it is then robbery, provided the object is taken from the presence or person of the victim. The property does not have to be held by the victim physically or be on his or her person. It merely has to be under the victim's control. "Control" in this sense means the right or privilege to use the property as the victim sees fit. Neither is it necessary or essential that the property be visible to the victim when the crime is committed.

When force is not used but a threat to the physical well-being of the victim is indeed made, it is not necessary that the victim actually be frightened to the point of panic. It is enough that the victim is reasonably apprehensive and aware of the potential for injury.

OVERVIEW: THE OFFENSE, THE VICTIM, AND THE OFFENDER

In terms of weapons used, a firearm is used in 40% of the incidents, a knife or other cutting instrument in 8% of the cases, and "some other weapon" in another 10% of reported robberies; the remaining 42% of the incidents are **strong-armed,** meaning no weapon was used.[1] An illustration of the use of "some other weapon" is the robbery of a convenience store by a man using a hypodermic needle filled with what he claims is AIDS-contaminated blood.

Together, this data reveals that approximately 6 of every 10 robberies are armed, and the balance are strong-armed. Armed robbers often carry two or more weapons. Because of this, officers must continue to exercise great caution when approaching a suspect who has thrown a weapon down.

About one-third of all robberies result in a physical injury to the victim.[2] Females are about 10% more likely to be injured than are males; Caucasians and African-Americans face nearly the same prospects for being injured.[3] Robbery is basically a stranger-to-stranger crime: 71% of the time the robber and the victim do not know each other.[4] About 60% of all robberies are committed by a single offender.[5] This factor tends to make robbery investigations more difficult: if the sole offender can keep his or her mouth shut, does not attract attention to him-/ herself or run with other criminals, and does not get a bad break, the offender can be hard to catch. Although a small number of victims fight back in some way, in 82% of robberies it is the offender who initiates violence.[6]

The objective of the confrontation between robber and victim is to get the victim's immediate compliance. In most situations, the mere showing of a gun will accomplish this. One offender reports: "Sometimes I don't even touch them; I just point the gun right in front of their face. I don't even have to say nothing half the time. When they see that pistol, they know what time it is."[7] A victim who hesitates or is seen as uncooperative may or may not get a warning.

Other robbers are less "tolerant" and when faced with uncooperative victims, they shoot them in the leg or the foot. However, for some offenders, injuring the victim is part of the thrill, the "kick" of "pulling a job." What type of violence is used and when it is used may form part of an identifiable modus operandi (MO). Such an MO can tie together several robberies, and the combined information from various investigations often produces significant investigative leads.

There is no question that being under the influence and committing robberies are intimately related. Victims

believe that 28% of those robbing them are high on drugs and/or alcohol.[8] Some offenders use alcohol to lessen their apprehension about getting caught. Robbery is basically an intraracial crime; in one study, blacks said that they were robbed by blacks 80% of the time, and whites said that they were robbed by whites 75% of the time.[9] Nationally, among those apprehended for robbery, 90% are males, 54% are blacks, and 19% are under the age of 25.[10]

Although no robbery is routine to victims, many cases are fairly straightforward to investigators. Some robberies, however, stand out because of unusual circumstances, as the following incidents illustrate:

A lone robber held up a bank and made off with $600. As police were chasing him, the robber crashed the stolen Chevrolet Suburban he was driving. It burst into flames, and the money burned up. Now being pursued on foot by a police officer, the robber tossed off his plaid jacket and escaped. The police found a napkin with a name and a telephone number in the jacket. With the bank's surveillance photos in hand, the police confronted the man identified on the napkin. In turn, he identified the robber as someone whom he had been letting sleep on his couch. An arrest was subsequently made in the case.[11]

Two thugs were cruising in a residential area looking for someone to rob. They spotted two men playing pool in an open garage. Blissfully unaware that the two men were off-duty police officers, the thugs approached them and placed a gun to one officer's head, and the officer began to struggle. The second officer pulled a weapon and shot both offenders.[12]

A teenage boy robbed a convenience store at knifepoint around 1:30 in the morning, taking money and merchandise and fleeing on foot. The police solved the case by following the offender's shoeprints in the freshly fallen snow straight to his home.[13]

Despite such variations, three styles of robberies—the ambush, the selective raid, and the planned operation—can be classified according to the amount of planning conducted by the perpetrators. The **ambush** involves virtually no planning and depends almost entirely on the element of surprise. A prime example is robberies in which victims are physically overpowered by sudden, crude force and in which "scores" are generally small.[14] The lack of planning does not mean, however, that there is no premeditation.

The **selective raid** is characterized by a minimal amount of casual planning. Sites are tentatively selected and very briefly cased, and possible routes of approach and flight are formulated. Scores vary from low to moderate, and several robberies may be committed in rapid succession.

The **planned operation** is characterized by larger "scores," no planned use of force, less likelihood of apprehension, and careful planning.

TYPOLOGY OF ROBBERIES

In addition to knowing the broad profile of the offense, the investigator must also be familiar with various types of robberies, such as the following.

VISIBLE STREET ROBBERIES

Approximately 5 of every 10 robberies happen on the street.[15] In 93% of the cases, the victim is alone[16] and typically on the way to or from a leisure activity within 5 miles of his or her home,[17] such as patronizing a nightclub or restaurant:[18]

> I'd watch people in bars and follow them. One time, I followed this guy and grabbed his tie and swung it down to the ground. And, uh, he hit his head, and that's when I took the money and ran.[19]

The victim is three times more likely to be confronted by a single perpetrator than by multiple perpetrators.[20] Youthful robbers are particularly likely to commit strong-armed robberies—also referred to as **muggings**—in which no weapons are involved and in which they suddenly physically attack and beat the victim, taking cash, jewelry, wallets, purses, and other valuables. As discussed earlier, purse snatching may or may not be a robbery. If a woman is carrying a purse loosely on her open fingers and someone grabs it and runs and she then experiences fear, robbery is not an appropriate charge, because the fear did not precede the taking. But if the same woman sees or hears someone running toward her and in fear clutches her purse, which is then ripped from her by the perpetrator, a robbery has occurred. If apprehended, the suspect would likely be charged with some degree of larceny, depending on the value of the object(s) being stolen. The penalty for larceny is generally much lower than that for the crime of robbery, and in many states if a firearm is used during the commission of a robbery the penalty is even more severe than for unarmed robbery.

Street robberies usually involve little or no planning by the perpetrators, who may have been waiting in one place for a potential victim to appear or walking around looking for someone to rob on the spur of the moment.

Because street robberies happen so quickly and often occur at night in areas that are not well lighted, victims often have difficulty providing anything more than a basic physical description. The description may be even more limited if the victim is injured either by a weapon or by a beating in a sudden, overpowering mugging.

Spontaneous street robbers may "graduate" to jobs that involve a certain amount of planning. For example, they may stake out ATMs or banks. In the case of ATMs, they may have decided that they are going to rob the first "soft-looking" person who is alone and driving an expensive car. In the case of banks, they may rob someone on the street whom they have watched long enough to know that the person is going to the bank to make a cash deposit or to use the night depository. Although people sometimes commit robberies for excitement or to be "one of the guys," for the most part they do it to get the money, which often goes to pay for drugs.

USE OF SURVEILLANCE CAMERAS TO PREVENT STREET ROBBERIES

The use of surveillance cameras to monitor the streets to prevent robberies and other crimes is becoming increasingly common. For example the Paterson, New Jersey, Police Department makes extensive use of surveillance cameras in their city. Currently they are using 18 surveillance cameras installed in high-crime areas throughout the city. The cameras can be moved to other locations within two hours as needed. They are also monitored around the clock by a police officer (Figure 13-1).

The monitoring officer can zoom in on a particular image as needed. These images are also recorded, so in the event something is missed officers can go back and replay the video for a closer examination. The cameras have captured several robberies in progress as well as drug transactions. The police department also reports observing drugs and weapons being discarded as police officers approach the suspects. The officers monitoring the surveillance cameras can inform officers at the scene what they have observed and direct them to areas where any contraband may have been discarded. The cameras have been characterized by one high-ranking police official as having one officer walking multiple beats.[21]

CARJACKINGS

During the 1960s, many cars were stolen as temporary transportation by youthful offenders who used them for "joyriding" and then abandoned them. In many states, the criminal statutes recognized both a felony auto theft

◀**FIGURE 13-1**
Use of surveillance cameras to prevent robberies
A Paterson, New Jersey, police officer is monitoring simultaneously 18 high-crime areas by the use of surveillance cameras. Each camera pans on a time sequence, produces high-quality video, and also allows the monitoring officer to zoom in on a particular location. The cameras can be moved to a new location within two hours.
(Courtesy Lt. Anthony Trainer, Paterson, New Jersey Police Department)

and a misdemeanor joyriding charge. Around 1970, there was a shift to stealing cars for their parts and an increase in stealing cars for resale here and abroad, after they had been "repapered," meaning that the vehicles were given new, false identities.

In conventional auto thefts, the car is removed surreptitiously, and there is no contact between the thief and the vehicle's owner. Before 1990, if an offender used a weapon to confront an owner and steal the person's car, the crime was simply classified as a robbery. But in 1990, with the number of such incidents increasing, the term **carjacking** was coined in Detroit to describe the growing numbers of this potentially violent type of confrontation between offender and victim.[22]

One explanation for the increase in carjackings is that such crimes are the result of too much success in the antitheft-device market, including tracking devices such as Lojack, the Club, computer chips in ignition keys, and motion sensors. A second explanation is that there is a widespread supply of potential victims, no skill is required, no inside information is needed, and the need for planning is minimal.

In terms of location, the most common places for carjackings to occur are at the victim's home, gas stations, ATMs, car washes, parking decks, shopping-center parking lots, convenience stores, restaurants, bars, offices, train stations, apartments, public transportation parking lots and at traffic-control signs and signals.

Carjackers tend to operate in small groups of two to five perpetrators. The modus operandi used is to quickly separate the person from the car. In some instances, doing so may be as quick and violent as using a brick to shatter the driver-side window of an occupied car and manhandling the occupant out of the vehicle. Mothers with children are particularly vulnerable when confronted by offenders who threaten to harm the children if the keys to the car are not given up immediately. One method of carjacking involves accidentally bumping the victim's car from the rear; when the driver gets out to investigate, one perpetrator pulls a gun, takes control of the victim's car, and flees, followed by his or her accomplices in the "bumper car." Another tactic is to use several cars to "box in" the target vehicle and then slow down gradually until it is stopped and the victim can be dealt with. Some carjackers target victims who drive into high-crime areas to buy drugs; some watch expensive cars in parking lots and then carjack them because they believe the victims are more likely to have jewelry and cash that can also be taken.

According to the FBI, the primary motives for carjacking are to acquire transportation away from the crime scene after robbing the driver, to get to and from another crime, such as another robbery or a drive-by shooting, to sell the car for cash, to trade it for drugs,[23] and to acquire temporary transportation. Whenever a carjacking takes place, the potential for a more serious crime exists.

Carjacking may also be a tool used by perpetrators to execute other crimes, which can lead to murder. For example, in one case a woman was carjacked and then forced into another car by the offenders. She was taken to a different location and raped. Later, she was forced to make several ATM withdrawals. Over the next several days, she was further abused and then executed by being slowly strangled with a coat hanger by one of the perpetrators while the others taunted her and cheered the executioner.

HOME-INVASION ROBBERIES

Home-invasion robberies (HIRs) typically target the person, rather than the residence, often selecting women and senior citizens.[24] Invaders often follow potential targets from shopping centers to their homes. They may enter the residence through an unlocked door or window, talk an unsuspecting victim into opening the door, or simply force the door open.

In some cases, the targets are "fingered," or identified, by others who pass information on to the invaders for drugs or money. Such offenders will also use deceit to gain entry into a residence. Home invaders may pose as police officers, water department employees, florists delivering bouquets, motorists who have "just struck your parked car," natural gas and electric company representatives, and "supervisors checking on your newspaper delivery service," to name just a few. The following case describes one such incident:

> Two men knocked on the door of a home and asked to use the telephone. After gaining entry by this ruse and casing the place, they decided the home was worth robbing. They returned that afternoon, forced their way in, severely beat the couple—who were in their late seventies—and left with valuables and the victims' pickup truck.[25]

AUTOMATIC-TELLER-MACHINE ROBBERIES

Automatic teller machines (ATMs) were introduced in the early 1970s, and their use has grown at a staggering rate since then. Today, there are approximately 12 billion ATM transactions annually.[26] At one point, robberies at these locations were so publicized that critics referred to ATMs as "magnets for crime" (Figure 13-2). However, the ATM robbery rate has dropped from 1 robbery per 1 million transactions during the 1990s to its present 1 per 3.5 million transactions.[27] A combination of factors account for this drop, including locating ATMs where customers have a high visibility of their surroundings, using landscaping of 24 inches or less in height, and keeping the ATM areas well-lit at night.[28] In addition, customers are becoming knowledgeable about self-protection measures and are adopting them. Despite such realities, public fear of being victimized at or near an ATM is substantial.

The ATM robbery victim is typically a lone woman who is using the machine between 8 P.M. and midnight.[29] To minimize the time spent with the victim and to avoid having to pressure the victim to make a withdrawal, many offenders simply wait until the transaction is completed before they pounce. Others confront the victim before the transaction, forcing her or him to make large withdrawals. Many victims report that they never saw the robber coming.

Offenders are most likely to work alone and are typically armed. They are usually about 25 years of age and tend to position themselves near an ATM, waiting for a likely victim to appear.[30] In addition to taking the cash and any valuables the victim has, offenders may carjack the victim's vehicle to flee the scene.

TAXICAB ROBBERIES

Taxi drivers have a higher homicide victimization rate than any other occupation in the United States and are also at great risk for robbery.[31] This is due to a combination of factors related to the nature of their job, including:

- having contact with a large number of strangers or people they do not know well;
- often working in high-crime areas;

▶ **FIGURE 13-2**
Automatic teller machines: natural target for robberies
Automatic teller machines are very popular today as a means of obtaining on-the-spot cash. At one point, robberies at these locations were so frequent that critics referred to ATMs as "magnets for crime." Placing ATMs in highly visible areas and improving surrounding lighting has led to a decrease in this form of robbery over the last few years. (© Syracuse Newspapers/David Lassman/Image Works)

◀ FIGURE 13-3
Robbery prevention sign on taxicab
Left photo depicts the typical location of a robbery prevention sign on a cab. Right photo provides a close-up of what the potential would-be robber would see upon approaching or entering the cab. The safety deposit box referred to in the photo is actually a heavy-gauge steel box bolted to the cab floor with a slot on top into which bills can be inserted. The box can be opened only by a key kept at the taxicab garage.

- usually carrying cash with them in an unsecured manner and handling money as payment;
- usually working alone;
- often going to, or through, isolated locations;
- often working late at night or early in the morning.

These risk factors, among others, have been mentioned in a number of studies of workplace homicide and violence in general.[32]

Crime-Prevention Strategies for Robbery of Taxi Drivers

Although the cab companies or individual drivers must be the ones to implement the crime-prevention strategies suggested below, crime-prevention specialists in the police department can be proactive and work with cab companies to assist in operationalizing some of these recommendations.

- *Provide physical barriers to separate drivers from passengers:* Bullet resistant screens or partitions should be installed, because they make it more difficult for robbers to carry out the robbery.
- *Record activity with security cameras in the cab:* Police and prosecutors can use the images to help identify and catch offenders and increase the evidence available for prosecution and conviction.
- *Use of an alarm to call for help:* Can be used to signal someone at a central location (taxi company or police station) if they are having trouble or they can be a "trouble light" on the vehicle itself that cannot be seen by the passengers. Alarms must be designed so that they can be triggered easily through the pressing of a toggle switch at the driver's foot, on the steering wheel, or on the radio itself.
- *Keep track of vehicle locations with automatic vehicle location (AVL) systems:* With global positioning satellite (GPS) systems, all that is required is the triggering of an alarm and the monitoring of that alarm signal by someone who can send help.
- *Put trunk latches on the inside of vehicle trunks as well as near drivers:* This feature is designed to reduce

the potential harm to drivers who may be locked in the trunk following the robbery incident. Trunk latches also permit drivers to open trunks without getting out of the cab, which may prove useful late at night if the driver does not think it is safe to exit the cab.
- *Eliminate cash payments:* Drivers should be encouraged to use payment systems that are cashless. These include:
  —Credit or debit cards.
  —Accounts accessible though mobile phones.
  —Accounts for regular customers, such as those used by restaurants, hospitals, and social services. (Authorized passengers merely sign the bill.)
- *Drop money off:* Drivers should be encouraged to drop off cash during their shifts. They can drop the cash at home, at cash machines, or at dispatching offices where the money can be secured until their shift is concluded. However, dispatching offices holding drivers' cash must be made secure against robbery as well.
- *Keep money locked up or out of sight:* Drivers can put money in a locked safe in the cab (Figure 13-3). If a safe is used it should be advertised on both the exterior and the interior of the cab. In addition, drop-off routines must be varied to prevent robbers from staking out drop-off locations and carrying out hold-ups as drivers leave their cabs.
- *Control who gets in:* Drivers can use a number of techniques to control who gets into their cabs by:
  —Keeping doors locked while drivers are waiting for the next fare.
  —Keeping windows rolled up enough to prevent someone from reaching in.
  —Limiting the number of passengers.
- *Find out the destination before moving:* One rule of thumb cited repeatedly is to determine passenger's destination "up front." It is seen as a sign of potential trouble if the passenger refuses to give a

destination at the beginning of the trip or changes destinations while en route.

- *Share destination information with others:* Drivers should keep as many people informed of their whereabouts as possible, especially where cameras or GPS systems are not used.
- *Limiting where the cab will make a drop off:* Drivers should be wary of making a passenger drop off in a dark, isolated, or out-of-the-way location, because these do not permit surveillance by others or allow the driver to see if someone is lurking at the destination.
- *Limit injury when a robbery occurs:* Taxi drivers are frequently advised to cooperate with those trying to rob them by handing over their money and not fighting back. Similarly, drivers should keep an extra key in a pocket to allow them to use their cab if the robbers have taken their keys. This is particularly important if they have been abandoned in a remote location and have no way of contacting the police or their dispatcher.

CONVENIENCE-STORE ROBBERIES

Convenience stores account for about 6% of all reported robberies. These stores do a great deal of business in cash, are often open 24 hours a day, have numerous locations, and typically offer little or no protection from robbers. Thus, it is not surprising that convenience-store workers are among the occupational groups having the highest risk for workplace violence.[33]

Specific Actions That Can be Taken by Retailers to Reduce Convenience Store Robberies

- *Maximize natural surveillance:* Employees should have an optimal view of the entrance and interior of the store.
- *Have multiple employees on duty during high-risk periods:* Businesses that remain open between 11 P.M. and 5 A.M. should use at least one of the following crime-reduction measures: two or more employees, bullet-resistant safety enclosures, a security guard, or a pass-through window to conduct business.[34]
- *Control access:* A consistent finding of studies involving the interview of convenience store robbers is that escape routes are a key factor to their target selection. Eliminating or at least limiting potential escape routes by using fences or landscaping is highly recommended.
- *Establish territoriality:* Stores in high-crime areas should discourage loitering as well as maximizing the existing lighting and design of their parking areas.
- *Train employees:* Training should include how to behave during a robbery had how to avoid violence.

- *Use cash-control procedure:* One 10-year study of convenience store robbers found that "80% of potential robbers can be deterred if a convenience store limits the amount of money kept in its cash register and this fact is conspicuously posted on the front door of the business."[35]
- *Install cameras and alarms:* The presence of CCTV monitors, clearly visible near cash registers, as well as signs that state surveillance equipment is in use, have been found to have some deterrent effect by increasing the robber's risk of identification.[36]

Police Robbery Prevention Recommendations for Convenience Stores

- *Provide robbery prevention and awareness training:* Police are in a prime position to guide businesses in crime prevention. They are typically the first point of contact after a robbery and can be particularly helpful to small businesses that may have limited access to other programs and must therefore rely more heavily on police to guide them in developing robbery prevention strategies.
- *Inspect convenience stores for compliance with robbery prevention measures:* Police might assume responsibility for regularly inspecting convenience stores to determine whether they have adopted either mandatory or voluntary robbery prevention measures.
- *Enforce prohibitions on loitering outside convenience stores:* Police should enforce loitering or trespassing statutes or ordinances that prohibit loitering (and panhandling) in order to keep opportunistic offenders away from potential victims.[37]
- *Conduct robbery stakeouts:* Police departments need considerable resources to be able to sustain the number of officers needed to await possible robberies in various locations over a long time. Unless there is specific information that a robbery is likely to occur, a stakeout will not be set up. However, if a stakeout is set up police officers must work with store employees to carefully plan out the tactics that will be employed if a robbery should occur. This is so because in the event a police officer does confront an armed suspect there is the potential for a shooting to occur. Therefore the clerk on duty must be carefully informed about what course of action to take in the event a robbery occurs.
- *Increase police patrols:* Because it takes a relatively short time to complete a convenience store robbery, the chances of thwarting one by increased patrols is not highly likely. However, if the decision is made to increase patrol, it must be based on a careful analysis of the patterns of convenience store robberies in a particular jurisdiction. On occasion, clear patterns do develop where a particular segment of a community is targeted. In such cases, the police may decide to saturate the area with marked patrol units in the hope of dissuading

individuals to commit the robbery. This in turn raises the possibility that the robbers will decide to move to another geographical area or even another police jurisdiction to commit robberies. In other cases, the police may decide to assign additional unmarked units to a particular geographical area that can respond very quickly if a robbery alert is activated in their area.

TRUCK-HIJACKING ROBBERIES

In the United States, cargo theft may be responsible for losses of $10 billion to $12 billion a year.[38] If so, the only crime category with a higher dollar loss is health-care fraud. The estimate for cargo-theft losses includes both cargo theft and truck hijacking. It is believed that hijacking accounts for a significant percentage of total cargo-theft losses, but because crime statistics on it are not kept, no one knows what the percentage really is. As cargo theft through hijacking has increasingly been recognized as a significant crime problem, there have been calls to gather statistics for it in the National Incident Based Reporting System (NIBRS). The FBI office in Long Beach, California, estimates that cargo-theft losses in that region are $1 million per day.[39] It should also be noted that truck hijacking is not a uniquely American problem. For example, in Argentina, truck hijackers are referred to as *piratas del asfalto* ("asphalt pirates").

The fact that accurate statistics are needed has not discouraged law-enforcement agencies from making important moves to combat this crime problem. Large agencies, such as the New Jersey State Police, have created Cargo Theft and Robbery Investigative Units, while others have adopted the use of multiagency task forces and Cargo Criminal Apprehension Teams (Cargo CATs). Additionally, specialized law-enforcement groups, such as the Western States Cargo Theft Association, exist to supply training and to exchange information on this subject.

Truck hijacking is committed by experienced armed robbers acting on inside information. Because transporting goods by truck generates a substantial written record, there are many points at which insiders can learn the nature of a cargo and when it will be moved. Many truck hijackings happen in or near large cities, because it is easy to dispose of the goods there. If there is a seaport, the goods taken may also be quickly on their way to a foreign country within hours. The contents of some hijacked trucks are off-loaded to another truck or several smaller trucks and may be in several other states by the time the investigation is getting started. Hijackers take what is valuable, with a preference for cargoes that are easy to dispose of and hard to trace. Examples include loads of clothing and high-tech equipment components, which may each have a value of $500,000 or more.

A number of truck hijackings involve collusion on the part of the driver with those committing this specialized form of robbery. The driver may be bribed or given some portion of the cargo for his or her personal use. In a variation of this, hijackers give drugs to drivers and provide them with women and then coerce the drivers into cooperating by threatening to cut off their supply of drugs and women, to give a spouse photographs of the driver's liaisons with other women, or to expose the driver's use of drugs to employers.

Drivers of rigs may be confronted at roadblocks, or "detours," set up by hijackers. They may be forced from the road or accosted by the hijackers as they enter or leave truck rest stops. Some drivers have been tricked into stopping to help a "disabled" motorist. In more brazen moves, hijackers may invade truck parks, seize or kill security personnel, and take the trucks that they have targeted.

BANK ROBBERY

Although this portion of the chapter focuses primarily on bank robberies, many of the investigative and crime-prevention suggestions set forth herein (some of which have already been discussed) can also be applied to large retail businesses, small convenience stores, jewelry stores, appliance stores, and so forth. This includes methods of escape, escape routes, target selection, and robbery prevention.[40]

Distinguishing Professional and Amateur Bank Robbers

Bank robberies and, for that matter, most robberies do not appear to be well-planned offenses committed by professional criminals; instead, increasing evidence suggests that many bank robberies are spontaneous and opportunistic crimes that are often acts of desperation.[41–48]

Because most bank robberies are committed by solitary, unarmed, and undisguised offenders, they can be considered the work of amateurs rather than professionals. In contrast, it is the less common armed bank robberies that more often involve multiple offenders and the use of disguises.[49–51] Distinguishing bank robberies as the work of amateur or professional robbers provides important insight about the risks or robbery in selecting crime-prevention strategies most likely to be effective.

To a great extent, bank robbers can be classified as amateur or professional based on known characteristics of the robbery—the number of offenders, use of weapons and disguises, efforts to defeat security, timing of the robbery, target selection, and means of getaway (Table 13-1).

Method of Escape

The method of escape further distinguishes amateur from professional robbers. Cars are not the sole means of escape; many offenders escape on foot or even by bicycle, at least initially.

Getaway vehicles are more prevalent when there are two or more offenders: 72% of robbery teams use vehicles, which reflects some degrees of planning.[52] In contrast, 58% of solitary robbers escape on foot. Two factors

TABLE 13-1	Distinguishing Professional and Amateur Bank Robbers	
	PROFESSIONAL	**AMATEUR**
Offenders	• Multiple offenders with division of labor • Shows evidence of planning • May be older • Prior bank robbery convictions • Travels further to rob banks	• Solitary offender • Drug or alcohol use likely • No prior bank crime • Lives near bank target
Violence	• Aggressive takeover, with loud verbal commands • Visible weapons, especially guns • Intimidation, physical or verbal threats	• Note passed to teller or simple verbal demand • Waits in line • No weapon
Defeat Security	• Uses a disguise • Disables or obscures surveillance cameras • Demands that dye packs be left out, alarms not be activated, or police not be called	
Robbery Success	• Hits multiple teller windows • Larger amounts stolen • Lower percentage of money recovered • More successful robberies • Fewer cases directly cleared • Longer time from offense to case clearance	• Single teller window victimized • Lesser amounts stolen • Higher percentage of money recovered • More failed robberies • Shorter time from offense to case clearance, including same-day arrests • Direct case clearance more likely
Robbery Timing	• Targets banks when few customers are present, such as at opening time • Targets banks early in the week	• Targets banks when numerous customers are present, such as around midday • Targets banks near closing or on Friday
Target Selection	• Previous robbery • Busy road near intersection • Multidirectional traffic • Corner locations, multiple vehicle exits	• Previous robbery • Heavy pedestrian traffic or adjacent to dense multifamily residences • Parcels without barrier • Parcels with egress obscured
Getaway	• Via car	• On foot or bicycle

Courtesy Deborah Lamm Weisel, *Bank Robbery*, U.S. Department of Justice, Office of Community Policing Services, 2007.

discourage solitary robbers from using vehicles: without an accomplice to drive the vehicle, it must be parked and quickly accessible to the robber; further, solitary robbers typically select targets that are convenient, such as those close to their residence making a car unnecessary. In contrast, professional bank robbers appear willing to travel farther than other robbers, perhaps because there are fewer banks than other types of commercial targets or because banks tend to be clustered geographically and are open for fewer hours.[53, 54]

Escape Routes in Target Selection

Because many bank robberies are the work of amateurs, it may appear that robbers randomly select targets. They do not. Instead, robbers select targets primarily based on their concern with getting away from the robbery quickly.

Although much effort to reduce bank robbery has focused on bank interiors and security measures, most bank robbers do not feel they are at risk of apprehension during the commission of the crime. Instead, robbers assume there will be easy access to cash and that the robbery will be completed quickly. Thus, robbers for the most part are relatively unconcerned about alarms and cameras, neither of which will slow their escape.

A robber's choice of target is shaped by two escape features: the type of transportation available and the ease and number of escape routes.[55–63] Because offenders prefer choices during flight, they tend to select targets that have more than one escape path.

Solitary offenders typically cannot escape in a vehicle because of the logistics of parking and retrieving a vehicle. Thus, solitary offenders typically escape on foot.

In contrast, multiple offenders typically escape in a vehicle—often stolen just before the robbery to reduce the likelihood that the vehicle has been reported stolen by the owner.

BANK ROBBERY PREVENTION

Following are some of the actions banks can take to reduce the likelihood of robberies and minimize their losses.

- *Limiting cash access:* Cash in banks is available at teller windows—the most frequent target of robbers—and safes. Most banks have cash management policies, such as removing cash from the teller drawers when it reaches a predetermined amount, a fairly common practice among convenience stores as well. Some banks use vacuum systems to quickly and efficiently remove cash from teller drawers.

- *Using dye packs:* Exploding **dye packs** are widely used by banks to prevent stolen money from being used. Dye packs stain both the robber and the cash, preventing use of the money and aiding in the detection of the robber. Many dye packs are supplemented by tear gas, which is triggered by an electromagnetic field near the bank exit door. When the tear gas explodes, the robber is effectively immobilized (Figure 13-4).

- *Slowing the robbery:* Because bank robbers want the crime to proceed quickly, some banks have adopted strategies that are intended to slow the pace of the robbery. A slow robbery may increase the suspect's perception of risk and will sometimes cause the robber to abandon the crime.[64, 65] For example, interior obstacles such as revolving doors and customer service counters can slow the robber's escape; timed safes and withdrawal limits on cash-dispensing machines can further extend the duration of the robbery.

- *Employing greeters:* Bank employees known as greeters welcome customers and reduce the anonymity of a would-be robber; this face-to-face interaction may discourage a robbery before it occurs. Greeters should be trained to be alert to suspicious behavior. They are more likely to discourage amateur robbers than professional robbers.

- *Use of security guards:* There is disagreement regarding the effectiveness of bank security guards.[66–68] Guards are expensive, and they may also create an environment that makes customers fearful. Some research suggests that guards reduce the risk of bank robbery.[69–71] However, some studies also suggest that the presence of the armed guards increases the risks of violence during a robbery.[72–74]

- *Warning likely offenders:* Bank robbers tend to overestimate the amount of money they will get from a robbery, to underestimate the likelihood of arrest, and to be unaware of the sentences they face if convicted. Thus, some banks and trade associations have developed publicity campaigns designed to educate would-be offenders about the low take,

▲ **FIGURE 13-4   Exploding dye packs**
Exploding dye packs are widely used by banks to prevent stolen money from being used. When they explode, the dye packs stain both the robber and the cash, thereby preventing use of the money and aiding in the detection of the robber. Many dye packs are supplemented by tear gas that is triggered by an electromagnetic field near the bank exit door. When the tear gas explodes, the robber will be effectively immobilized. (Courtesy 3SI Security Systems)

high capture rate, and other perils of a career in bank robbery.[75]

- *Using tracking devices:* Some banks conceal electronic **tracking devices** with the robbery money, thus aiding police in locating offenders. Tracking devices use low-voltage transmitting microchips with transponders. However, tracking devices are intended to increase the chance of apprehending offenders, so they are not likely to prevent robberies from occurring.

- *Using bait money:* **Bait money** is cash with sequential serial numbers that are recorded by the bank. When the money reenters circulation, police track its use in hopes of locating the suspect. Bait money is already widely used by banks.

- *Offering rewards:* Some banks actively publicize "most wanted" bank robbers, displaying their surveillance photos and offering rewards for information leading to their capture. Banks use

▶ **FIGURE 13-5**

Bank surveillance camera

A bank surveillance camera captures the image of a man who has just entered the bank for the purpose of committing a robbery. He concealed a gun inside his hat. The man had entered the bank earlier in the day to case it for a robbery. At that time he was observed by an alert bank teller who had previously seen a bank surveillance photograph of the man which had been shown to her by law-enforcement officials several days before. The bank surveillance photo shown to her was of a man who had previously committed a bank robbery. She recognized the man and the police were contacted. The police then staked out the bank parking lot. The man returned several hours later, committed the robbery, exited the bank, entered his car at which time he and his companion were arrested. (Courtesy Arlington, Texas Police Department)

websites, local silent witness programs, and tip lines to publicize crimes and to seek out offenders. There are also national tip organizations that coordinate information about highly mobile robbers.

- *Upgrading electronic surveillance:* Bank surveillance cameras are in widespread use: 98% of robbed banks have interior surveillance cameras. However, cameras do not appear to reduce robberies. Many bank robbers are not deterred, because they simply do not believe they will be caught. Others believe that cameras can be thwarted with a disguise or by covert behavior or that cameras can be disabled, such as with spray paint; or they simply do not think about cameras at all.[76–78] However, sometimes electronic surveillance can have unanticipated benefits. For example, one alert employee in a Texas bank noticed a man hanging around the bank lobby and thought she recognized him from a photograph she had been shown several days before by law-enforcement officials. The picture of the individual, who had held up other banks, was being shown to bank employees in the general area. The individual did not stay in the bank very long, but when he left the alert bank employee contacted the police who then started to surveil the bank parking lot. Several hours later the man returned to the bank. His partner remained in the car while he walked inside the

bank to commit the robbery. Once again, his image was captured by the surveillance camera, depicted in Figure 13-5. The man can be seen concealing what would turn out to be a gun in his hat. The police were not able to prevent the robbery, but once the man exited the bank and entered the getaway car, police officers were able to converge in their vehicles and to place both men under arrest. Thus, one possible strategy for bank robbery prevention could be to obtain bank surveillance photographs of individuals who committed bank robberies and show them to bank employees in the same general area in order to alert them to what the potential robbers look like. As it turned out, the individual and his partner confessed to robbing seven other banks in a half dozen nearby towns.

- *Rapidly activating alarms:* Although alarms lead to the arrest of bank robbers in only about 6% of crimes, there is evidence that prompt activation increases apprehension rates. Some bank employees do not activate alarms until after the robber has left the premises. This is so because of safety concerns about the employees and customers in case the police trapped the robber inside the bank thus creating a potential hostage situation and violence. In other cases, the delay might be due to panic or to comply with instructions made by the robber.

- *Installing bandit barriers:* The FBI recommends that banks install bullet-resistant glass **bandit barriers** between tellers and customers. Such devices are also becoming fairly common in convenience stores, especially those that operate 24 hours a day and

◄**FIGURE 13·6   Bandit barriers**
Bandit barriers may discourage some bank robbers and also increase the safety of bank employees. Such devices are also becoming fairly common in convenience stores, especially those that operate 24 hours a day and are located in high-crime areas. (Courtesy Clear Security Systems. www.clearsesecuritysystems.com)

are in high-crime areas (Figure 13-6).[79] Although most of these are permanent installations, some bandit barriers "pop up" when activated by tellers or when an object crosses the counter.

- *Installing access control vestibules:* Access control vestibules—also known as man-catcher vestibules or man-traps—are a specialized form of access control device. These devices can be used to scan potential customers for weapons before they access the bank interior; others are designed to be manually activated by tellers.

- *Hardening targets:* Banks have employed a wide variety of **target-hardening strategies** that are designed to make the bank interior appear inhospitable to would-be robbers. These include revolving doors, increased distance between entrances and teller stations, higher teller counters, queuing and other physical barriers, and single-door entrances and exits.[80–82]

- *Consider the possibility of an inside job:* When a bank robbery does occur, investigators should consider the possibility of the robber having received assistance from someone inside the bank. One interesting case occurred recently in the Atlanta, Georgia, area. A Bank of America was held up by two young women identified as the "Barbie Bandits." These two young women, who would eventually be identified as Heather Johnston and Ashley Miller, both 19, were photographed by a bank security camera and subsequently identified by people who recognized them when their pictures were shown on local television (Figure 13-7). Their

◄**FIGURE 13-7   Bank robbery: inside job**
This photo depicts two young women, Ashley Miller (*left*) and Heather Johnston (*right*) both 19, dubbed by the media "the Barbie Bandits." Their images were captured on a bank surveillance camera wearing sunglasses and reportedly giggling throughout the robbery. The bank robbery occurred in the Atlanta, Georgia, area. The video camera images were broadcast on local television and the two young women were identified by viewers who knew them. As it turned out the robbery was actually an inside job in which the two women conspired with a convicted drug dealer and a bank teller who worked in the bank they robbed. (© AP Photo/Cobb County Police Dept.)

arrest and the subsequent investigation led to the arrest of two additional accomplices—namely, a convicted drug dealer, Michael Darrell Chastang, 27, and a Bank of America teller, Benny Allen III, 22. The four had conspired to commit the theft and divided the money after the crime was committed.

RESPONDING TO THE SCENE

In route to the scene of a robbery call, the officer must ensure that all information available from the dispatcher has been obtained, including the answers to the following questions: What is the exact location of the offense, including the type of business? Is the offense in progress? How many suspects are involved? What type of and how many weapons were displayed? What description of the suspect is available? By what method and in what direction did the suspect flee? What is the description of the means of transportation used by the suspect?

In approaching the scene, the officer must be alert for several possibilities:

- The dispatcher may provide information on the suspects' escape, such as their direction in fleeing from the scene and whether they were on foot or in a vehicle.
- Information about the target, MO, suspects, vehicles, weapons used, and other factors in recent robberies may help the responding officer recognize the suspects if they are moving away from the scene on the street along which the officer approaches, even if the dispatcher cannot supply any specific information other than the nature of the crime.
- The fleeing suspects may, as the officer approaches them on the way to the scene, abruptly turn off, fire at the officer, or otherwise suddenly reveal themselves.

The primary tactical objectives of officers responding to a robbery call are public safety, officer protection, and tactical control of the scene. Secondary objectives include conducting the preliminary investigation, apprehending perpetrators, and recovering property. Arriving at the scene unobserved by the suspects facilitates the achievement of both primary and secondary objectives. It also allows tactical control and the element of surprise to pass from the robbers to the police. Units assigned to a robbery call should plan and coordinate the actions to be taken at the scene. Because the perpetrators may have police scanners, care should be taken with respect to radio transmissions. Arriving officers should not give away their exact positions and should refer to buildings by prearranged letter designations

(for example, "the A building").[83] They can never assume that the robber(s) have left the scene; for example, robbers have been known to hide near or at the scene, seeking to escape detection. Responding units should approach separately on streets parallel to that on which the robbery occurred or is occurring, using emergency lights but not sirens. The use of emergency lights permits more rapid progress through traffic. The reason for not using a siren is that the sound may panic suspects near or at the scene, triggering violence or hostage taking. It is believed that 9 out of 10 hostage situations that develop out of robberies occur because of a too visible first-responding officer.[84]

However, remember that most states require a police vehicle responding in an emergency mode to have both its emergency lights and siren activated. Thus, when the tactically correct decision is made to deactivate the siren, the officer's driving must be adjusted accordingly, because now the motoring public no longer has the benefit of "hearing" the approaching police vehicle and being able to yield to it.

At a distance of three to five blocks from the scene in an urban area and much farther in rural settings,[85] the emergency lights should be turned off to avoid possible detection by a lookout. The police officer should begin to smoothly decelerate, thus avoiding engine noise, squealing tires, or "emergency" stops that could give away the police car's arrival.

The first officer on the scene must quickly "size up" the area to gather any possible intelligence, including location of the robbers, lookouts, and escape vehicles. The locations of the perpetrators are particularly important given the fact that such criminals may have automatic and other weapons—which they are willing to use. Actually identifying the **lookouts** may be difficult; two officers in New York, for instance, were killed by a lookout disguised as a nun.[86] The officer should leave his or her car quietly and move—unobserved—to a protected position to watch, where possible, two sides (for example, north and east) of the building. One of these sides should be the exit most likely to be used by the robbers. Moving unobserved does not necessarily imply moving quickly. Running into position may invite passersby to "rubberneck," giving away the officer's location.[87] Before moving to any position, the officer should make sure the background of that position, when viewed from the perpetrators' positions, does not silhouette him or her.[88] The officer in the second unit should take the same precautions as the first in moving into position. The second officer's responsibility is to cover the two remaining sides (for instance, the south and the west). Both officers should keep their vehicles and portable radios at low volume to avoid being detected. The primary and backup officers should be sure that their positions in the lines of fire do not endanger each other.

Also, when moving into their respective unobserved positions, officers must not get inside of, that is, between, any possible lookouts and the robbery scene. Such a position would leave them vulnerable to fire from several sides.

Both in approaching the scene and at the scene, officers should avoid action, physical, or situational stereotyping.[89]

ACTION STEREOTYPING

Action stereotyping occurs when the officers' expectations are set to see one thing, which closes their minds to other eventualities. For example, the responding officer may expect the suspect to come rushing out of the store, hop into a car, and speed away. Although this may be the case, there are also other possible behaviors:

> Two robbers who confessed to over 20 "quick mart" robberies had been apprehended during a police surveillance. While being interrogated, the pair revealed that they had come close to being caught on several occasions when responding units arrived at the scene very quickly. They said they had escaped apprehension at those times by simply walking away in a normal manner. This proved to be an embarrassment for one officer who remembered the pair walking past his car. This officer said that they just appeared to be "normal" citizens and that there was nothing extraordinary about them.[90]

PHYSICAL STEREOTYPING

Physical stereotyping is an officer's expectations that the robber will look like a particular type. Such stereotypes may allow the suspect to escape or be fatal to officers:

> An officer entered a convenience store in response to an alarm; his gun was drawn, but he started to put it away when he didn't see anything out of the ordinary. As he approached the two clerks behind the counter, the younger one yelled a warning: the other "clerk" was an armed robber whose appearance—he was 60 years old—did not fit with the officer's stereotype of a robber.[91]

Another aspect of physical stereotyping is that investigators may have difficulty believing witnesses' descriptions. For example, we expect bank robbers to be relatively young adults and vigorous. However, in northern Colorado nearly a decade ago, an 82-year-old man known as the "salt-and-pepper bandit" was arrested for a string of bank robberies; in another case, a 105-pound 70-year-old woman donned a black plastic bag as a disguise and robbed a bank, declaring, "There's a bomb here; give me the money, no bells, no sirens."[92]

SITUATIONAL STEREOTYPING

In **situational stereotyping,** the officers' previous experience with, and knowledge of, a particular location increases their vulnerability:

> A silent alarm went off at a bar; the call was dispatched, and as the assigned unit drove toward the bar, the two partners joked about the inability of the owner to set the alarm properly, since he was continuously tripping it accidentally, creating frequent false alarms. The officer operating the police car parked it in front of the bar, and as the two officers began to saunter casually up to the front door of the bar, two suspects burst out with guns in hand and began shooting. Miraculously, neither officer was hit. One of the suspects was wounded and arrested at the scene; the other one escaped and was not apprehended until several weeks later.

Returning to some earlier points: although the suspects may be observed fleeing the scene or may reveal themselves in some manner to the officer assigned to respond to the call, such encounters do not take place with any regularity. In addition, deviating from the assignment to become engaged in a "pursuit," instead of proceeding directly to the call, is often unproductive. In such instances the "suspect," especially one driving an automobile, may merely be acting in a suspicious manner because he or she may have committed some minor traffic violation and is fearful that the officer is going to write a traffic citation. The officer actually assigned to the robbery call should not normally deviate from the assignment without significant reason; the officer's responsibility is to get to the scene and to get accurate, detailed information for the preliminary pickup order or BOLO as rapidly as possible. When the officer does this, more resources are then brought to bear on the offense, and the likelihood is reduced that other officers may unknowingly stop armed suspects for what they think is only a traffic violation.

If not assigned to the call as the primary or backup unit, other officers should not respond to the scene. Instead, they should patrol along a likely escape route such as entrances to expressways. They should avoid transmitting routine messages, because the primary unit will need to transmit temporary pickup orders or BOLOs concerning the offense.

If available, helicopters have the potential of being helpful in robbery investigations when a good description of the vehicle in which the robbers fled is included in the BOLO. Helicopters can cover territory rapidly. Flying at 500 feet, a helicopter provides observers accompanying the pilot with an excellent observation platform. Approximately 75% of all pursuits aided by a helicopter are successful.[93]

FOLLOW-UP ROBBERY INVESTIGATIVE PROCEDURES

To standardize the ways in which robberies are investigated, departments should have a standard operating procedure (SOP) that deals specifically with this crime. It is also extremely important that both the responding officer(s) and follow-up investigator are thoroughly familiar with this procedure. The specifics of the Robbery SOP naturally vary from jurisdiction to jurisdiction because of the sizes of communities and the number of investigative specialists that are available. However, we have attempted herein to provide a broad model from which an investigative procedure can be developed by an agency irrespective of its size or the number of investigative specialists it has.[94]

INITIAL INVESTIGATION

Although it may not always be possible, an on-duty investigator (preferably one who works robberies) should be available to respond to the scene of all reported robberies. If, however, a police department does not normally have investigators respond to the scenes of all robberies, then certain criteria must be set forth. They should respond when:

- requested by a uniform supervisor;
- a victim or witness has been seriously injured;
- a suspect has been apprehended;
- a suspect has been identified;
- victim(s) have been tied up or incapacitated for an extended period of time;
- large sums of money or property have been taken;
- the robbery has occurred inside a residence;
- a carjacking has occurred;
- leads with a high solvability factor are present and will be lost by a delayed response.

Specific Responsibilities for the Robbery Investigator

- Assume responsibility for the investigation.
- Ensure that proper preliminary investigative action has been taken by uniformed personnel, and take additional steps as necessary.

- Interview victim(s) and witness(es) in detail.
- Collect physical evidence.
- Canvass the area and document the names and addresses of all persons interviewed and include a summary of their observations.
- Determine if identifiable property has been taken (serial number, bait money, and so on), and ensure that this information is entered into the National Crime Information Center (NCIC).
- Determine if a cell phone has been taken, and identify the cell number, subscriber, and carrier information.
- Display photographs of known offenders and suspects to the victim(s) and witness(es). Request that they respond to the Robbery Bureau to view photographic files if necessary. If identification is made: have the victim(s) and witness(es) sign and date all photographs identified. Number and initial those photographs shown with the identified photograph(s) and preserve them as evidence for court presentation by placing them in an envelope sealed with evidence tape in the case file.
- Obtain notarized identification statements from individuals who are visitors or when the investigator believes that such a statement will enhance the possibility of prosecution.
- Follow up all available leads to a proper conclusion before terminating the initial investigation.
- When the investigation leads to the identification of a suspect, make record checks before obtaining an arrest warrant. It must be determined that the suspect was not incarcerated at the time of the offense.
- If verification of custody or detention dates is made, make a computer printout part of the case file. In instances where confusion exists concerning the subject's confinement, verification must be obtained from the appropriate governmental agency. When received, this information will be documented in the investigator's report.
- Discuss the case with the state's prosecutor and obtain an arrest warrant(s) in a timely manner.
- When applicable, consult appropriate federal law-enforcement agencies (for example, FBI, ATF, and so on) regarding the potential for filing federal charges against the suspect(s).
- If the subject is at large, and an arrest warrant has been issued, conspicuously display all relevant information along with a photograph at key locations within police headquarters. Also distribute wanted fliers to uniform patrol officers as well as other investigators.
- Upon notification that a wanted subject has been taken into custody outside the police jurisdiction, the applicable supervisor shall evaluate the case and, if appropriate, request that Robbery Bureau personnel be utilized for the extradition. If Robbery Bureau personnel are not used, the lead investigator shall

coordinate any investigative activity that is necessary immediately upon return of the subject and before the subject is booked into the jail.

- Review and analyze all reports prepared in the preliminary phase.
- Reinterview victim(s) and witness(es) if it appears there may be information that was not obtained owing to incomplete questioning or insufficient recall of the event. Occasionally, witnesses will remember some detail and not go to the "trouble" of looking for the police department's listing. Therefore, the investigator should leave a card with his/her name and departmental phone number.
- Return to the crime scene at exactly the same time of day the offense was committed and attempt to locate additional witnesses; at the same time, reconduct the neighborhood check. When conducting a neighborhood check, officers must be certain to record the names of all witnesses interviewed in order to avoid any type of duplication with other investigators who may be assisting on the case. In the event that possible witnesses are not at home, this, too, should be recorded to ensure that they are contacted later. It is imperative that every person who was in a position to have possibly witnessed the crime be contacted and interviewed.
- Make an attempt to tie the offense to other robberies, because the combined information from several offense reports may result in sufficient detail to identify the perpetrator.
- Review any pertinent departmental records, reports, or database.
- Seek additional information from other sources (for example, uniformed officers, informants, other investigators, other agency investigations, or informational/intelligence bulletins).
- Review the results of laboratory examinations.
- Determine the involvement of subject(s) in other crimes.
- Prepare the case for presentation to the Prosecutor's Office.
- Assist in the prosecution as required.

False Robbery Report

A file check should be made of the victim's name in case the person has a history of making crime reports. For instance, certain types of businesses—such as economy gasoline stations and convenience grocery stores—may not conduct even a minimal background investigation of employees. Given the availability of cash and long periods of isolation during the night hours, an untrustworthy employee will occasionally pocket cash for personal gain and cover its absence by claiming a robbery was committed. A file check on the complaining witness may suggest such a pattern. For example, one of the authors, who was a robbery investigator, routinely checked the police records

of robbery victims. In one instance, he found that a clerk employed at a convenience store, who regularly changed jobs, had allegedly been the victim of an armed robbery three times at three different convenience stores during an 18-month period, and in each case the suspect reportedly had the same identical physical description, said the same exact words when demanding the cash, and carried the same type of firearm. Naturally, this caused considerable suspicion, and when the victim was confronted with this string of "coincidences" he was unable to explain how it occurred and adamantly denied he was stealing the money. He was asked to take a polygraph examination to verify the authenticity of these robberies but refused. His employer was notified of the pattern of previous robberies as well as his reluctance to cooperate, and he was subsequently dismissed from his job.

The following represent two additional examples of false robbery reports.

Two teenage clerks were shot in a robbery at a Quick Mart convenience store. Despite the clerk's wounds, investigators were suspicious about the incident. After further questioning by the police, both "victims" admitted they made up the story about being robbed to conceal their theft of $400 and shot each other to make it look more convincing.[95]

A woman told officers that a laughing man put a gun against her 2-year-old daughter's head and robbed her at an ATM. The victim also reported that no one else was around the ATM when the incident happened at 7:52 A.M. Investigators initially thought it was highly unlikely that nobody else was at the ATM around the time of the alleged robbery. They checked the transactions at the ATM and found that a man had used the ATM just 4 minutes before the robbery and did not see anyone matching the robber's description. Moreover, the man did not immediately leave the ATM after he had finished his transaction. Based on this evidence, it was established that the woman had made up the story because she wanted some attention.[96]

GENERATING A LIKENESS OF A SUSPECT

The likeness of a suspect should be created and distributed as rapidly as possible. There are a number of methods available to create a likeness. One of them is through the use of a police artist (Figure 13-8). Several software programs can be used to generate suspect likenesses, including Sirchie's ComPhotoFit Plus Color[97] (Figure 13-9).

▸ **FIGURE 13-8**
Facial likeness of a robbery suspect created by a forensic artist along with a police mug shot showing the resemblance
The photo on the left depicts a facial reconstruction completed by Police Artist Gil Zamora, working with a robbery victim. The photo on the right depicts the police mug shot of the robbery suspect at the time he was arrested. As can be seen, the similarities are remarkable. (Photos courtesy of police artist Gil Zamora and Lt. Rick Martinez. San Jose California Police Department)

▸ **FIGURE 13-9**
Sirchie's ComPhotoFit Plus Color
The composite facial reconstruction photo on the left is a computer-generated composite sketch of a robbery suspect. The photo on the right, which is remarkably similar, depicts the photo of the suspect at the time he was booked into the county jail. The facial reconstruction was made with Sirchie's ComPhotoFit Plus Color. (Courtesy Laurie A. Ward, Crime Scene Administrator and Sheriff Grady C. Judd, Jr. Polk County Sheriff's Office, Bartow, Florida.)

KEY TERMS

action stereotyping
ambush
bait money
bandit barriers
carjacking
dye packs

home-invasion robbery (HIR)
lookouts
muggings
physical stereotyping
planned operation
robbery

selective raid
situational stereotyping
strong-armed robbery
target-hardening strategies
tracking devices
trespassory

REVIEW QUESTIONS

1. What are the elements of the crime of robbery?
2. Give a profile of visible street robberies.
3. When is purse snatching a robbery?
4. Give three explanations for the increase in carjackings.
5. Discuss how home invaders operate.
6. What are the two occupations in which a person has the greatest danger of being the victim of a violent crime on the job?
7. How are drivers confronted in truck-hijacking robberies?
8. Discuss the characteristics that distinguish professional from amateur bank robbers.
9. Discuss the multiple techniques that can be employed in bank robbery prevention.
10. Explain action, physical, and situational stereotyping.
11. Why is it important to have a standard operating procedure for robbery investigations?
12. Why should a file check be made of the victim in a robbery case?

INTERNET ACTIVITIES

1. Most large police agencies in the United States have robbery investigation units. Find several such agencies in your region. What is the total number of officers assigned to these units? What are the units' functions and responsibilities? Is there information concerning the numbers of robberies that are investigated and/or cleared? Is any robbery prevention information provided? Websites such as *www.officer.com* provide information to both local and international police agencies.
2. Go to the website *www.forensicartist.com* and learn more about how forensic artists generate the likenesses of people through age composition, composite drawing, and facial reconstruction.

► After determining no one was home, two burglars broke into a home through the rear entrance. They removed more than $100,000 in valuables. The homeowner's surveillance camera captured one of the burglars carrying a signed and framed Michael Jordan basketball jersey.

(Courtesy Ft. Lauderdale Police Department)

14

BURGLARY

CHAPTER OBJECTIVES

1. Describe the characteristics of different types of burglaries.

2. List the characteristics of professional and amateur burglars.

3. Outline the steps in the burglary investigation checklist.

4. Specify actions officers responding to burglary in-progress calls should take.

5. Recognize burglary tools.

6. Identify the types of evidence to collect in safe burglary cases.

7. Explain the laws and methods associated with attacks on ATMs.

8. Profile burglaries of cars, recreational vehicles, and trailers.

9. Discuss indicators at different types of burglary scenes that may suggest juvenile subjects.

10. Briefly describe methods of reducing the risk of residential and commercial burglaries.

INTRODUCTION

The two most striking aspects of burglary are its frequency and economic impact. In 2009 burglaries averaged one every 14.3 seconds.[1] There were an estimated 2,199,125 burglaries reported, and, although the number reflects a 1.3% decrease compared to 2008, victims suffered an estimated $4.6 billion in lost property. The average loss per burglary was $2,096.[2] In spite of the reduction in the number of burglaries, the offense accounted for 23.6% of the estimated number of property crimes committed in 2009.[3] The clearance rate for burglaries was a low 12.5%, and only 299,351 people were arrested for burglary in 2009.[4] Thus, burglary is a crime of major importance and concern. Because such items as credit cards and checks may be taken in burglaries, the offense tends to spawn subsequent or secondary crimes, such as frauds and forgeries. Investigating these crimes can sometimes lead back to the identity of the burglars; to illustrate, during the breaking and entering of a convenience store, "scratch-off" lottery tickets were stolen. When the burglar attempted to cash in a few winners at another convenience store, he was videotaped by the security camera. After placing his picture in the newspaper the police quickly learned his identity, and the man was arrested. Burglaries also have the potential to turn into violent crimes, for example, when home owners or workers return unexpectedly.

Many homes and businesses have alarms, but the alarms may be affected by improper installation, faulty equipment, or user errors. Unfamiliarity with the system or not allowing for roaming pets results in 10%–25% of all automatic alarm calls being false ones; if all false alarms were eliminated, the result would be 35,000 officer days per year being available nationally to redirect toward genuine problems.[5] Many jurisdictions have responded to this situation by allowing one free false alarm and then charging the owner for subsequent false alarms on a flat-fee or escalating-the-charge basis for each subsequent false alarm.

People often think of burglaries as involving just homes and businesses, other structures may also be covered by many state burglary laws, including recreational vehicles, railroad cars, houseboats, airplanes, and automobiles.[6] Some states also have created a **coin-operated machine burglary** charge to cover vending machines outside of businesses. Unlike other types of burglaries, this offense is typically a misdemeanor; in states that lack such an offense category, the charge is for larceny, with the level of offense being determined by the value of the property stolen.

Various aspects of burglary are summarized in Table 14-1. Most burglaries are through a door rather than a window. In general, commercial establishments are attacked at the rear at night, whereas homes are mostly victimized during the day at the front door. There is some evidence that, as the geographical distance between burglaries shortens, the likelihood of there being a serial offender increases; this is true, respectively, for residential and nonresidential burglaries.[7] When the same home is burglarized a second time shortly after 30 days from the initial incident, it

CHAPTER OUTLINE

Commercial burglaries are also committed through other points of entry, such as skylights and chopping a hole in a roof. In certain situations, such as strip malls, burglars will break into one business and then enter the others by knocking through connecting walls. As ATMs have become more widely available, such businesses as convenience stores have been broken into by people driving stolen vehicles as large as dump trucks through the glass doors. Once inside, burglars can grab an ATM and some store goods and be gone in 2–7 minutes. Day burglaries of homes tend to follow a pattern: the owners are often at work or running errands, and neighbors are used to seeing delivery people, campaign workers, and others approach front doors. So, seeing someone at a front door is not an abnormal occurrence that compels attention. Furthermore, front doors are often recessed, limiting visibility; burglar alarms are often not set; and many front doors can be quickly kicked in, facilitating the burglar's quick entry and exit.

Burglars may work alone—as illustrated by the Spiderman case discussed later in this chapter—or in organized groups or gangs. There are numerous cases of professional people becoming burglars, and burglars can be roughly categorized as professional and amateurs by their level of skill. Many juveniles and teenagers commit burglaries, including those involving cars. One study concluded that prolific burglars also shoplift, perhaps to supplement their income, to obtain goods they cannot get through their burglaries and to "lay low" when the risk of burglarizing may be perceived as too high.[9]

When police officers respond to a burglary-in-progress, officers must be alert when approaching the scene, both

may be by the same offender seeking to steal items left behind during the first offense—for example, something too big to take, or perhaps the first time the burglar did not know a fence, or perhaps he/she came back to steal items the resident bought as replacements (for example, televisions or video equipment) for losses in the first burglary.[8]

TABLE 14-1   Burglary Facts

Type of Premises Attacked

Residential	72.6%
Nonresidential	27.4%

Types of Attacks

Forcible Entry (e.g., used pry bar to break glass and enter)	61.0%
Unlawful Entry (e.g., through open door or window)	32.6%
Forcible Attempt	6.5%

Time of Attacks	Residential	Nonresidential
Day	37.2%	9.1%
Night	20.2	11.6
Unknown	15.1	6.7

Cases Cleared (Arrests and Exceptionally Cleared): 12.7%

Arrested Offender Demographics

Race	Gender	Age	
White 66.5%	M 85.1%	Under 15	6.9%
Black 31.7	F 14.9	Under 18	25.3
All Other 1.8		18 & over	74.7

Source: FBI, Uniform Crime Reports 2009, issued in 2010. See *www.fbi.gov/UCR/CIUS 2009*, Tables 41, 42, and 43, and Burglary definition page.

to protect themselves and to avoid rushing past look-outs or burglars driving calmly from the scene. At the scene, officers may have to tactically clear the building before their investigation can begin. This should never be attempted until adequate backup and specialized units, such as Canine, have arrived. During the preliminary investigation, officers have to consider the possibility of a crime staged for filing a false insurance claim; in particular, when there are fires at scenes, officers may need specialized assistance to determine if the fire is accidental or coincidental, set by the burglars to destroy evidence, or arson. In the end, a burglary is a burglary, but officers should examine each scene while being alert to all possibilities. The number of safe burglaries has lessened as we've progressed into a "cashless society," but officers still need to have a basic understanding of them to prevent the accidental destruction of evidence.

Burglars sell much of what they steal to support their lifestyle or trade the merchandise for drugs, tips from insiders about new burglary opportunities, or sex. Thus, as police try to recover stolen property, they come into contact with criminal fences and must check pawnshop records, local sales ads, swap meets, and eBay-type outlets.

THE OFFENSE AND OFFENDERS

From humans' earliest times, thieves existed and committed what we recognize as burglaries. The elaborate tombs of the Egyptian pharaohs, designed to send the rulers into the next world in splendor, contained magnificent treasures. They also contained elaborate security features to protect those riches. Yet they were often plundered by thieves of that time.

The nature of burglary has stayed the same over time, but *how* it is committed constantly changes, largely as an influence of technological advances and architectural design. For example, now virtually extinct in the United States are such specialized methods of burglary as entry through coal chutes—because people in this country heat mainly with electricity, natural gas, and even solar power. As municipalities began requiring the use of fire escapes, they were appended to the outside of apartment buildings. This created a new method of burglary—the "step-over." Although people would place bars or other barriers over apartment windows by the fire escape, they would neglect to protect other windows. The step-over artist would go up a fire escape to the apartment to be hit and then step over from the fire escape to the ledge of a window that was unprotected. As interior fire escapes became more common, the opportunities to be a step-over artist gradually declined, although they certainly still exist. A slight variation on the step-over method is still in practice: parents send children as young as five years old to do the step-over and then open the apartment door from the inside to let in the parents, who plunder the premises.

In the last 20 years, a method of burglary that has gained in popularity is one in which the offenders steal a car and drive it through the front door of a gun, jewelry, or other type of store. Once inside, they quickly grab what they can, exit, get picked up by a confederate (who is often operating another just-stolen car), flee the scene, and then abandon the stolen car. This method is essentially an aggravated case of the well-known **smash-and-grab,** in which a perpetrator throws a brick or concrete block through the plate-glass window of a jewelry store, seizes what can immediately be reached, and then gets away from the scene as quickly as possible.

Some targets selected for burglaries require more than just crude force; they demand a high level of skill and daring. A former Army paratrooper who stole some $6 million in cash, jewelry, and credit cards was dubbed "Spiderman" by investigators, because he specialized in burglarizing high-rise apartments—a total of 132 of them—before he was apprehended (Figure 14-1). To reach his targets, Spiderman would climb as many as 30 stories

▲ **FIGURE 14-1   The Spiderman burglar**
Man arrested as Spiderman gives a media interview at jail. His attorney is the man wearing the white coat, and a reporter takes notes in the background. Investigators claim that $6 million was taken during Spiderman's "career."
(© AP Photo/Wilfredo Lee)

on the *outside* of the buildings—without any climbing equipment.[10] Initially, investigators had difficulty even considering this method of approaching the target, because its use seemed too improbable.

Some burglaries require careful planning and coordination. For example, thieves stole merchandise from parked Susquehanna Railroad freight cars four times in three months, netting as much as $100,000. The men used 30-inch bolt cutters to force entry into the cars. Once inside, the merchandise was "selected," and walkie-talkies were then used to summon gang members driving gutted vans, which were then used to haul the loot off. To stay ahead of the police, the ring monitored a police scanner. After surveillance of the tracks failed to produce any results, officers were pulled off of that assignment, and the burglars went back to work. However, a man walking his dog at 9:30 P.M. spotted the men on top of the freight cars and alerted police, who were able to make arrests at the scene.[11]

Although some burglars prefer to work alone to maximize profits and to avoid the possibility that their partner(s) will "roll over on them" if arrested by the police on burglary or other charges, others work in gangs. These gangs vary in composition (for example, from juveniles, to members or affiliates of organized crime, to those having ethnic or foreign ties). In one particular crime wave involving a Tennessee burglary gang, investigators were sure juveniles were involved because of the nature of the items being taken, but they were nevertheless shocked to later learn that the two members of this "gang" were both less than 13 years old. The MO was for the 12-year-old boy to boost the 10-year-old girl through a broken window, and she would then open the door and let her "partner" into the home.[12]

In Chicago in another case, a long-time burglar, with reported mob connections, operated his "crew" for 30 years. When the leader was arrested, more than $2,000,000 in jewelry and stolen property was found in his home. A member of the crew virtually signed his presence at burglaries by always taking expensive Lladro porcelain figurines and adding them to his personal collection. Part of the "formula" used so successfully by the gang for decades was that after spotting a potential victim, they would bribe a public official to run the mark's auto tag so they could immediately know where he/she lived, after which they would begin to accumulate information before making their move. The gang was also successful in identifying restaurant owners who skimmed money from their businesses and accumulated large sums of cash in home safes.[13]

In the New York City area, 52 men from Colombia operated the "Codewise Crew" burglary ring, committing 6–12 burglaries a day. The gang operated in groups of three members, spotting residences that looked easy and striking in the mid-afternoon when families were often not home. Lookouts would communicate with the inside man, advising him of detection threats. The men would meet at a bar in the morning and later go pull their burglaries. Ultimately, the gang's downfall occurred when some members got reckless about how they operated, leading to their arrest.[14] Another illustration of a major crime gang/group with foreign ties is Yugoslavian, Croatian, and Siberians (YACs). YACs have operated along the Eastern seaboard, specializing in burglarizing ATMs in supermarkets, which may have $100,000 in them at any time, and the safes of buildings thought to have large amounts of cash on hand, such as bars and restaurants.[15]

Although burglars are often thought to be poor and uneducated, relying on that profile may cause investigators to overlook professionals who are also burglars.

A former police officer pleaded guilty to 16 felony counts involving a string of residential and commercial burglaries he committed while on duty. Just a month before entering his plea, the 18-year law-enforcement veteran was granted a disability pension after experts testified at his retirement hearing that he suffered from an obsessive-compulsive disorder that led to his pathological gambling.[16]

A church organist was arrested for committing three burglaries of churches and synagogues in which religious items of gold and silver valued at $25,000 were stolen. Following his arrest, the suspect confessed to having burglarized 500 such places, taking articles worth $2.5 million. There was little hope that any of the stolen property would ever be recovered, since it was believed to have been melted down and sold. Police were led to the suspect when a drifter was arrested for disorderly conduct. In the drifter's duffel bag, religious articles were found. He admitted having stolen them from the suspect, who had provided him with shelter for the night.[17]

Although burglars may be classified according to a number of variables, such as preferences for premises to be attacked and types of property that they will, or will not, take, the most useful classification is skill. Conceived as a continuum, the two extremes would be the amateur burglar and the professional. The largest number of burglars would be clustered toward the less-skilled end of the continuum, with progressively fewer toward the skilled end.

Professional burglars may commit only a few offenses per year, going for the bigger "scores," as in the following cases:

The FBI, working with Brazilian police officials, recovered three Norman Rockwell paintings valued at over $1 million. Nearly 25 years earlier, they were stolen from the Elayne Galleries in St. Louis Park, Minnesota. No one knows how the Rockwells ended up in Brazil. The thieves have never been caught.[18]

Space Coast Credit Union employees came to work on a Monday morning to find a hole in the roof over the vault and more than $100,000 missing. The police had responded to the alarm that went off at 12:30 and 1:30 Sunday morning, but they could not see the roof from the parking lot or the highway, nor could they find anyone with a key to the premises so that they could check inside. Several months before, a bank was successfully attacked using the same method of operation. In that case, the burglary was described as "the biggest financial loss in our city."[19]

However, professional burglars can also be quite active, committing a large number of offenses:

Members of a burglary ring were arrested for committing some 1,000 burglaries over a three-year period. They selected shops, businesses, and fast-food restaurants that would have anywhere from several thousand to $75,000 on hand. The targets included McDonald's, Pizza Hut, Burger King, and Dunkin Donuts.[20]

Although many professional burglars may commit only a few offenses a year, they are of considerable interest to investigators because of the large value of cash or property taken and their intimate knowledge of sophisticated fencing systems, which are often detected, and therefore investigated, only following the apprehension of a professional. In addition to the big score, the hallmark of the professional is the thorough planning that precedes each burglary. Professionals usually refuse to place themselves in jeopardy for anything other than sizable gains and do so only after weeks or even months of painstaking study of the target selected. Knowing exactly what they want in advance, professionals do not ransack premises. Thus, if they have employed surreptitious methods of entry, articles taken may not be missed for some time. Working nationally, or at the very highest professional level, internationally, this type of burglar often operates for long periods of time without being arrested.

When arrested, such burglars are usually released without being charged owing to a lack of physical evidence, coupled with their own skill in responding to the questions of investigators. When operating in elegant hotels or apartment buildings, the professional will use a businesslike appearance and manners to talk his way out of a situation. Should an occupant return unexpectedly, the burglar may pull out forged credentials identifying him as the building's security officer and say he found the door ajar and was just beginning his investigation. Or he may pretend to be drunk, ask for directions to some similarly numbered room, and stagger away acting confused.

However, if these or similar ploys fail, or if the burglar's real intent is apparent, the professional will employ violence if necessary to escape:

A well-known cardiologist was shot to death when he walked into the burglary of his home in a fashionable section of Washington, D.C. The police arrested a man who was alleged to be a "superthief" for the crimes. Upon searching the suspect's swank suburban home, the police found some $4 million worth of stolen property. It took the police 472 man-hours and 400 legal-size pages to count, tag, and describe the property. The 18-foot truck in which the seized property was transported away contained 51 large boxes and two smelters that were believed to have been used to melt down precious metals.[21]

Amateur burglars often operate on the basis of impulse or react to suddenly presented opportunities. Such burglars tend to work not only in one city but often in a relatively small segment of it. Amateurs may cruise in cars looking for businesses to victimize, prowl hotels seeking unlocked doors, or try to locate doors whose locks can be easily slipped using a credit card. While amateurs may occasionally enjoy a relatively big score, it is the absence of preplanning that sharply differentiates them from professionals. If they are narcotics addicts, amateurs must often work four or more days per week, committing several offenses each day, in order to support their habits. Even if they are not addicts, this may still be necessary to support their lifestyles. Frequently using sheer force to enter, amateurs crudely ransack businesses or residences to find anything of value. Occasionally, unlike their discerning professional counterparts, they take costume jewelry in the belief that they have found something of considerable value. When confronted by an unexpectedly returning business owner or occupant of a residence, amateurs may become immediately violent, and secondary crimes, such as murder or rape, unintended in the original offense, can occur. Finally, amateur burglars often have lengthy records and are frequently in and out of jail.

THE LAW

The crime of **burglary** generally consists of the following elements: (1) breaking and (2) entering (3) a dwelling house or other building (4) belonging to another, (5) with the intent to commit a crime therein. The common-law crime of burglary necessitates that the act be committed in the nighttime. This element has been deleted in a number of state statutes.

Burglary and related offenses are classified as crimes against the habitation, dwelling, or building itself; no force need be directed against a person. The breaking element may be satisfied through acts that constitute a breaking into, a breaking out of, or a breaking within. Generally, the slightest force used to remove or put aside something material that makes up a part of the building and is relied on to prevent intrusion, for example, doors or windows, constitutes breaking. This element can be satisfied whether accomplished at the hands of the perpetrator, through the use of some inanimate object like a brick, or by the participation of an innocent third party. Similarly, the element of entry is satisfied once the slightest intrusion has taken place by the perpetrator, an inanimate object, an animal, or an innocent third person.

The character of the building at which the breaking and entering takes place largely determines the type of offense committed. The most serious offense is often breaking and entering of a dwelling house, that is, a place used by another person as a residence. The nature of the dwelling itself is not determinative but, rather, the manner in which it is used. Hence, a hotel room can be considered a dwelling house.

The other major ingredient controlling the nature of the crime is the intent with which the perpetrator unlawfully breaks and enters the building. The more serious the crime intended to be committed after entry, the more serious becomes the breaking and entering itself. Thus, breaking-and-entering which is done with the intent to commit a felony carries a higher sentence in many states.

APPROACHING THE SCENE AND INITIAL ACTIONS

When responding to a burglary-in-progress call, uniformed officers should drive rapidly while avoiding excessive noise, such as the dramatic but unnecessary use of the siren. The last several blocks to the scene should be driven at lower speeds for two reasons. Doing so eliminates the possibility that the squealing tires of the police vehicle will give the perpetrators, if still on the scene, the advantage of crucial seconds of warning. Additionally, lower speeds allow opportunity for observation. A vehicle driving away from the vicinity of the scene may be seen and its description and license plate number noted as a possible investigative lead. Under such conditions,

late-model, expensive cars, such as Cadillacs and Lincolns, should not be discounted. Burglars often select these, not only because of the large amounts of equipment and stolen property such cars can hold but also because they recognize that the police often behave respectfully to the occupants of these vehicles, because of the implied social status.

When dispatched to a burglary-in-progress call, the uniformed officer working alone should attempt to coordinate his/her arrival time and position with the backup unit. This will enable the officers to secure the building immediately. One unit can arrive positioned so it can watch two sides of the building—for example, the north and east sides—while the other unit can observe the west and south sides. When a two-officer unit is dispatched to a burglary-in-progress call, the operator of the police vehicle should drop his or her partner off in a position to view two sides of the building and position the vehicle to allow observation of the remaining two sides. When working alone, if it is necessary to begin checking the exterior of the building immediately, the uniformed officer should drive around it to determine whether there is a readily observable break. If this is not possible, the officer should check rapidly, but cautiously, on foot. When a flashlight is used during hours of darkness, it should be held away from the body, because the suspect is most likely to aim at the light source if firing at the officer. If a point of entry is established, under no circumstances should an officer attempt to enter, as entering would needlessly expose him or her to extreme danger. Most burglars prefer to be unarmed because, in many states, breaking and entering while armed is a more serious offense than an unarmed breaking and entering. However, occasionally burglars are armed and willing to use their weapons to avoid apprehension:

A woman whose home overlooked the back of a shopping center saw two people break into a dress shop through the rear door. She called 911, who gave the call out as a burglary in progress, subjects on the premises. A motorcycle officer who was returning to the station at the end of his shift heard the call, which was assigned to a patrol unit, and swung by to back them up because he was close to the scene. The woman, still connected to 911, gave a running account of what happened. The motorcycle officer arrived first and pointed his motorcycle lights at the rear door. Instead of maintaining his position and waiting for assistance, he walked up to the door—fully silhouetted by his own lights. As he stood in the doorway, he was shot three times and collapsed. As the officer lay dying, one of the perpetrators stood over him and emptied his pistol into him. This death should not have occurred. It was caused because the officer used a tactically unsound procedure and because he encountered armed subjects willing to shoot it out with the police. Both subjects were arrested at the scene. Follow-up investigation revealed that they had a major incentive to use deadly force against the police—they were wanted on murder charges in two other states.

The fact that no point of entry is determined by riding or walking around the building does not mean that a forcible entry has not occurred. Whenever possible, the roof should be checked, particularly vents and skylights. Even if there is an alarm sounding, there may not be a burglary. Alarms frequently malfunction, particularly during inclement weather. However, officers must never become complacent about checking premises with a reputation for false alarms. If a breaking and entering has occurred, additional cars, if available, should be brought into the general area. Burglars often park their vehicles some blocks from the building to be attacked, and the perpetrator may not yet have had time to flee the area. "Lovers" parked in the general area should not go overlooked by the police. Burglars often use couples as lookouts or have their girlfriends remain in the car while they commit the offense. The perpetrator may have reached the car but have been unable to flee the immediate area; the use of a "just parked lovers" story may allow him to escape detection.

If a burglary has been committed and the police department has a canine unit, the uniformed officer at the scene should request its presence before entering the building. The alarm servicing company ordinarily sends a representative to the scene fairly rapidly to provide officers with access to the building. If there is no alarm, then the owner must be contacted either from information usually posted on the door or from other sources. Before beginning the crime scene search, officers must thoroughly check the building to ensure that the burglar is not hiding on the premises. To achieve the proper degree of caution, the building check should be conducted as though it were known that the burglar was still there.

Figure 14-2 is a **burglary investigation checklist;** it makes no distinction between the tasks associated with initiating the incident report and those associated with the follow-up investigation, so that the entire scope of investigative tasks can be seen at once.

INVESTIGATIVE CONSIDERATIONS AT THE SCENE

Caution must be exercised to avoid the accidental destruction of physical evidence while attempting to make a determination of whether the burglar is still in the building. Officers should be sensitive to the possible presence of physical evidence but not act in a manner that might jeopardize the most important thing—the officer's safety. If gross physical force has been used in gaining entry, the point of attack is easily established (Figure 14-3). However, one cannot assume that it is also the point of exit. Often burglars will break into a building at a particular point and then leave by opening a door. Where gross physical force is used, the point of attack is of particular importance because examination of it may yield the types of physical evidence discussed in Chapter 4, "Physical Evidence." In combination, the determination of the points of attack and exit will suggest the avenues of approach and flight traveled by the perpetrator, which also must be explored for the possible presence of physical evidence. Officers must be particularly attentive for unusual signs that may be of investigative value. Juvenile burglars commonly commit destructive acts of vandalism (Figure 14-4). Also, age may be suggested from the choices of what is taken and what is left behind:

When I started hustling . . . didn't know much, like what crap be really worth and how to get bills for it . . . at first alotta stuff I just leave back . . . just grabbed things for me . . . like a nice coat or small crap you can just walk with and sell quick for cash . . . like a gun . . . main thing for me was getting some bills so I could high-cat around and get stuff . . . Nike shoes. I couldn't walk around with no stereo or TV . . . had to leave the big stuff.

The sudden removal of trophies or other prized possessions by their owner from a business or residence, followed by a burglary for the purpose of committing arson, should raise certain questions in the investigator's mind. Further, the weight or dimensions of property taken in a burglary may suggest, if only roughly, the number of people involved in the offense. Articles or tools left behind, combined with other specifics of the crime, may be useful in the identification of an MO.

Many commercial establishments keep check imprinters on their premises. A not uncommon occurrence is for a burglar to gain entry to a commercial building, tear several checks from the company checkbook, imprint them, and cash them the next day. Thus, it is of particular importance to have the proprietor ensure that no checks have been taken. Normally, when a burglar employs this practice the checks will be taken from the very rear of the book or from several different series in order to lessen the likelihood of detection.

▶ FIGURE 14-2
Burglary investigation checklist*

Completed	Tasks
_____	Determine use of premises (e.g., residence versus commercial), point of entry and if different, point of exit. Was entry forced or unforced? What is missing?
_____	Who discovered the burglary? When? What was he/she doing when discovered? Did he/she touch or move anything? What? Why?
_____	Is the victim the complainant versus a neighbor or employee? Victim assistance? Are there independent witnesses?
_____	Is there any significant time gap between when discovered and when reported? Why?
_____	Who knows when the last time the premises was secure? When?
_____	Was any alarm set or not set? Who is responsible?
_____	What physical evidence is there? Entry tool(s) left behind? Is crime scene processing warranted under department policies/procedures?
_____	Are there exterior/interior surveillance cameras? Working? Why not? Get videos if available. Review past tapes to identify suspect casing the premises.
_____	Is there evidence the crime was staged (e.g., possible insurance fraud)?
_____	What actions did the suspect(s) take in entering, while inside, and leaving?
_____	Does the item(s) taken suggest more than one suspect and vehicle (e.g., 50″ HDTV taken)?
_____	Does the scene suggest some inside knowledge of the premises (e.g., perpetrator went right to where item stolen was versus the scene being "tossed")?
_____	Were any acts of sexual deviancy committed (e.g., masturbated in victim's underwear, defecated on bed or elsewhere, or cut crotches out of victim's underwear)?
_____	Does the type of entry and articles stolen suggest juveniles are involved (e.g., change, condoms, alcohol, Nintendo games, costume jewelry taken, real jewelry left behind, only small articles taken for which a vehicle is not needed to transport)? Was school out? Were known juvenile offenders in the area absent from school?
_____	Does the method of entry and articles stolen suggest unusual skills or special knowledge (e.g., safe successfully attacked using a single method versus several different types of unsuccessful attacks, good jewelry taken, costume items left behind)?
_____	What precautions did the suspect(s) take to avoid detection? Were alarms and cameras disabled? Does the neighborhood check reveal possible lookouts? Were telephones or walkie-talkies left behind? Was phone on premises used? What number(s) was called?
_____	Have residential victims determine if checks are missing; have commercial owners determine if checks are missing from rear of business checkbook. Was checkwriter taken, or does its present position suggest its use while suspect(s) was on the premises?
_____	View evidence/enter identifiable stolen items in database.
_____	Check intelligence, field interview reports, and other databases. Check with crime analysts to determine if the MO is identifiable to an individual. Check with other investigators to see if cases they are working on may be related. Also contact other area agencies for the same reason. Read follow-on reports from lab examining evidence.
_____	Check pawnshop records (Figure 14-10).
_____	Visit flea markets and swap meets. Check newspaper for sale ads, and also eBay.
_____	Check suspect information (e.g., verify name, aliases used, criminal history, address, employment, associates). Obtain current photo, prepare photo pack, check for warrants, and issue BOLO.
_____	Check jail records and interview/interrogate suspect in custody.
_____	Schedule polygraph/Computer Voice Stress Analyzer (CVSA) examinations.
_____	Obtain arrest and search warrants as needed; file returns.
_____	Respond to information requests from District/State Attorney.

Source: Authors' experience, with some elements added from Universal Case Checklist, Assistance Chief of Police (Retired) Bill Proffitt, and Sergeant Karen Eichler, St. Petersburg, Florida, Police Department.

*This list does not distinguish between steps taken gathering information for the incident report and the follow-up.

RECOGNITION OF BURGLARY TOOLS

Most often, when tools used in the commission of a burglary are recovered at the scene, they are not very different from those found in many households. A partial list of **burglary tools** includes knives, screwdrivers, crowbars, tire irons, pipe wrenches, chisels, sledgehammers, hacksaws, bolt cutters, axes, and glass cutters. In the crude smash-and-grab burglary, where the display window of a jewelry store is broken and articles immediately available are taken, the "tool" may be as unsophisticated as a

◄ **FIGURE 14-3 Broken front door**
The burglary of this residence was accomplished by prying the front door open. The burglar first made an unsuccessful attempt to remove the deadbolt lock. When this failed, he simply pried the door open, as evidenced by the marks along the door's right edge. (Courtesy Chief Rick Boren and Sgt. Doug Shafer, Columbus (Georgia) Police Department)

brick in a paper sack. However, tools left at the scene may have been subject to certain adaptations to facilitate their use in a burglary. Screwdrivers or crowbars may be carefully sharpened or shaped to increase their effectiveness in attacking doors and windows; nippers can be transformed into lock pullers if they are honed in a manner that permits firmer biting ability on exposed lock edges. Burglars will also apply masking tape in the shape of a cone to the end of a flashlight so that it emits only a very thin light beam.

Apprehension of a suspect not in the act of burglary but in possession of lock picks (Figure 14-5), specially modified tools (Figure 14-6), or standard tools that can be used in burglaries may permit a felony charge of possession of burglary tools. Some states require that a person have a prior conviction for burglary in order for this charge to be placed. Even where this requirement does not exist, proof of intent to commit burglary is essential for conviction.

◄**FIGURE 14-4 "Tossed" home office**
A heavily "tossed" home office. The chaotic scene suggests amateur burglars and, more particularly, juvenile perpetrators who became frustrated looking for things they could easily carry away. More seasoned offenders, for example, would have methodically searched the filing cabinet at the left of the picture from top to bottom or bottom to top. The open drawer in the middle of the cabinet suggests a more random approach. (Courtesy Chief Dwayne Orrick, Cordele (Georgia) Police Department)

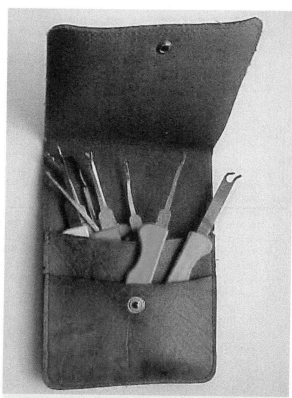

▲ **FIGURE 14-5   Lock tools**
An assortment of lock picks in a leather case. Such tools are commonly sold on the Internet for as little as $15 to $20 for a group of four to five picks. (Courtesy Major Tolbert and Lt. Richard Zapal, Savannah Chatham Metropolitan Police Department)

▲ **FIGURE 14-6   Snip-ez**
Battery-operated scissors modified to use as an electric lock pick. The scissors were removed, and a lock pick was mounted in their place. (Courtesy Major Tolbert and Lt. Richard Zapal, Savannah Chatham Metropolitan Police Department)

SURREPTITIOUS ENTRIES

Occasionally, the investigation of a burglary cannot establish a point of entry or exit. What happens in such instances is in large measure determined by the knowledge and thoroughness of the investigator, who may initiate a report indicating "entrance by unexplained means," decline to take a report owing to lack of evidence, or take a report knowing that, because of departmental policy, it will subsequently be designated "unfounded." Complaints of this nature frequently involve surreptitious entries—that is, a burglary has occurred, but there was no apparent force used. Excluding the case of closed but unlocked doors, the most common explanations are that the door was "loided," the lock was picked, or the premises were victimized by someone who has an unauthorized possession of a key.

Loiding is the act of slipping open or shimming, by using a strip of celluloid, a spring-bolt lock that does not have an antishim device. Technically, a spring bolt without an antishim device should be considered a privacy device, rather than a security device. Simply stated, **picking** is a process of manipulating a lock into an unlocked position using picks rather than a key. When picking is suspected as the means used to gain entry, the lock should be submitted to the laboratory for examination. By examining the lock, the laboratory will be able to determine whether or not the lock was picked. From the marks alone on a lock, the laboratory cannot state the type of picking device used, except in general terms. If, however, a pick is seized as evidence, it is possible to make an individual identification by comparing the marks on the lock with test marks made by the seized pick. To facilitate the reassembly of the lock after its examination by laboratory personnel, the key should also be submitted. The laboratory cannot determine whether a lock was loided, owing to the lack of physical evidence associated with this technique.

Officers must be familiar with privacy and security devices, because this increases their investigative effectiveness and the credibility of their testimony, assists in the construction of MO files, generates data to support crime prevention legislation, and allows them to talk knowledgeably before community groups.

IMPORTANCE OF THE TIME FACTOR

An important aspect of taking burglary reports is attempting to determine when the offense took place. Typically, burglaries are reported from several hours to a number of days after they are committed. Late reporting is largely attributable to the circumstances of businesses being closed for the weekend and home owners being away for short trips or extended vacations. Summer communities, populated by people living some distance away who visit their mountain or lakefront vacation homes only intermittently, represent a large problem for the police. Such residences are particularly vulnerable to burglars, who may take all the furniture and dispose of it several months before the offense is even detected. In such instances, the estimate of the time frame in which the offense occurred will of necessity be very broad. Frequently, however, it is possible to identify a range of time during which the perpetrator attacked the premises; the range can then be correlated with other data to provide investigative leads and to include or exclude certain persons as suspects. For example, a person known to employ an MO similar to the one used in a particular offense would be a suspect. If, however, a field interrogation report was initiated on him some distance away from the scene at about the same time that the offense occurred, his presence there would have been virtually impossible, thus excluding him as a suspect. While this example is an unusual occurrence, its essence is important. As the time range in which the offense could have taken place narrows, other information becomes more useful.

SAFE BURGLARIES

TYPES OF SAFES

Safe burglaries have been declining for decades. In part, this is due to the prevalence of cashless transactions (for example, buyers using debit and credit cards) and target-hardening measures taken by home owners and businesses. Nonetheless, investigators need to have a basic understanding of safes and the types of evidence associated with them so evidence is not accidentally destroyed.

Many older safes are still in use, as well as numerous new ones that include such features as electronic locking bolts and entry through the use of a personal password or by swiping one of the owner's credit cards. In general, there are two broad categories of safes:

1. *Fire-resistant safes*, which historically had square or rectangular doors and were intended primarily to protect stored money and documents from being destroyed in a fire (Figure 14-7). Such safes also provide a minimum level of burglary protection. These safes have a light metal skin with insulation between their inner and outer walls.

2. *Money chests or burglar resistant safes*, which historically often had round doors, were made of heavier metal and were insulated to provide fire protection. As safe-construction methods continued to evolve, the use of square or rectangular doors became common on burglar-resistant safes. Burglar-resistant safes (Figure 14-8) are sometimes referred to as combination safes, because they have an outer fire-resistant chamber combined with a smaller inner chamber, usually referred to as a money chest. Financial institutions use large walk-in vaults that offer substantial fire and theft protection for stored documents, provide safety deposit boxes to customers, and protect cash and other financial instruments.

There is variety in the labels that safe manufacturers give their products, including security chest, executive safe, top-opening, under counter, wall, personal, and drawer and cash management, which is used in businesses that need to track which employees used the cash drawer. Companies also often employ different terminology: one manufacturer may use "money chest" to denote small

◀**FIGURE 14-7**
Fire resistant safe that was successfully attacked
This is a small fire safe weighing about 99 pounds; no dimension (height, width, depth) is greater than 19 inches. The burglar laid the safe on its back to get better leverage when attacking it. Note the pry marks on the bottom edge of the safe and shoe prints on the floor to the right of the safe. The hinge pins on this type of safe are unprotected and were removed during the attack. (Courtesy Chief Rick Boren and Lt. Ronnie, Columbus (Georgia) Police Department)

▶ **FIGURE 14-8 Gardall safe**
Fire and burglar resistant safe. Note the heavy metal phalanges protecting the hinge bolts. To facilitate use of the safe during the day when it may be necessary to open it several times, once the combination lock and handle has been used to open the safe it can be closed and opened using a key in the lock to the right of the combination dial. (Courtesy Athens (Georgia) Key and Lock)

safes that are attached to the frame of houses, whereas others simply use the term "safe" to identify their line of burglar-resistant safes. Thus, when investigating a burglary where the victim says the "safe" was attacked, they may be using the term imprecisely.

Since 1913 the underwriters laboratory (UL) has tested safes and categorized them according to the level of protection they provide. These categories are commonly found on labels inside the safe. For example, a safe with a "tl-15" label means that it is resistant to attack by a burglar using common handheld and electrical tools for 15 minutes. UL also uses labels for fire-resistant capabilities. For instance, the highest level of a "type class 150" label provides fire protection to the safe's contents for up to 4 hours at 2,000° while maintaining an interior temperature of not more than 150° F. Knowledge of these labels allows investigators to have some sense of how much time a burglar spent compromising a safe.

ATTACK METHODS FOR SAFES

Knowledge of methods of safe attack is important, because it allows the investigator to make judgments about the skill and knowledge of the perpetrator and thus narrow the focus of the investigation. The methods of safe attack include the punch, pulling, the peel, the rip, blasting, drilling, burning, manipulation, the pry, and the carry-off. Some of these methods are encountered infrequently, but they are included here, because in the few instances when they are used, investigators must be prepared to respond properly.

SAFE-BURGLARY EVIDENCE

The scenes of safe burglaries are usually rich with physical evidence. Broken parts of screwdrivers, pry bars, drill bits, and other equipment offer the possibility of making a fracture match with the remaining portion in the suspect's possession. If a drill and bit are seized from a suspect, marks on drill-bit shavings recovered at the scene can be compared to those made by the equipment seized. Drilling is noisy, so safe crackers may make special sound-deadening boxes in which to place their drills. The materials used have the potential to be matched with the remaining material in the suspect's possession. Bolt cutters recovered from the suspect's home can be tested in the laboratory to see whether the striae made match those on chains, padlock hasps, or fences at the burglary site. Slag seized at the scene of a burning job can be analyzed for consistency with samples obtained from the suspect's car or home. At some burglaries, opportunities to locate DNA evidence exist: offenders may have left hats with dandruff in the sweatbands; may have cut themselves accidentally when using equipment, leaving blood; may have left their saliva on water or other bottles they brought to or used at the scene; or may have used the bathroom but forgot to flush, leaving urine. They may have used company telephones to make calls, providing investigative leads, and one cannot ignore the possibility of finding latent prints and impressions. Whenever an attack on a safe has exposed the safe insulation, samples should be collected as evidence.

Depending on the circumstances, particles of insulation may be found on the perpetrators' tools, their clothing, under their fingernails, in their shoes, pants cuffs, or pockets, on the floormat of their car, or embedded in their shoes. In a number of cases, safe insulation has been found in the nail holes of shoe heels several weeks after the commission of the offense.

It is the variation among insulations that makes them valuable as class evidence. Many safes made before 1930 contain an insulation of natural cement made by burning to a powder certain claylike limestones, used without gravel or cement only as safe insulation. A number of more recently made safes use an insulation of diatomaceous earth, portland cement, and vermiculite mica—a combination used only in safe insulation. Many brands of safes contain distinctive insulation, samples of which are kept in the FBI laboratory files. It is, therefore, possible to compare insulation found on a suspect's tools or person with those in the file and name the make of safe from which it came. Some safe manufacturers use material for insulation, such as gypsum mixed with wood chips, which is not peculiar to safe insulation. In such instances, however, laboratory examination can establish consistency, or the lack thereof, between insulation samples from the scene and from the suspect.

As a final note on the value of safe insulation as evidence, establishing intent is important in charging a person with **possession of burglary tools.** Tools found with what can be conclusively established as safe insulation on them may be the basis for providing that intent.

ATM ATTACKS

Some premises are burglarized for the purpose of attacking ATMs inside buildings—for example, gas stations, convenience stores, fast-food restaurants, and bank and credit union lobbies. Stand-alone ATMs in convenience and other types of stores may not be bolted to the floor and weigh roughly 200 pounds.[22] Amounts of money in these ATMs vary based on recent servicing and use, but typical losses range in the area of a few thousand dollars.[23] The store hosting the stand-alone ATM, which is often a private venture as opposed to being one that is bank-operated, may be conventionally burglarized, and then the stand-alone ATM is physically carried off to a waiting panel truck, a truck with a lift, a pickup, or a U-Haul-type truck. These vehicles are often stolen and may have separately stolen license plates on them.

In some surveillance photos, offenders can be seen entering with a hand truck/dolly to help move the stand-alone ATM with greater ease. Several other methods of burglarizing premises and stealing stand-alone ATMs are also used. In smash and grabs, heavy trucks (such as a dump truck in one case) are driven right through the glass doors,[24] the ATM is snatched up, loaded into the vehicle, and then taken to a place, such as a wooded area, where it is opened. Insurance companies report that carry-off attacks on ATMs result in so much damage to the unit that it is a total loss.[25] From an investigator's point of view,

ATM attacks may yield considerable forensic evidence, including tire and shoe impressions, tools and tool marks, fingerprints on dropped currency, beer cans, blood from skinned hands, and food wrappers. Some businesses no longer have stand-alone ATMs, because they attract crime, the premises suffers damage that needs to be repaired, retail floor space is taken up by the ATMs, and items are also stolen.[26] To prevent the loss of business, ATM owners are making use of some new measures, including placing GPS tracking devices in the machines and using Fog Security Systems, which emit a heavy, impenetrable fog that lasts several hours and makes suspects simply bolt the premises as soon as they can.[27]

Different from stand-alones are the ATMs that are located at the drive-throughs of banks or are embedded in walls outside of banks, pharmacies, apartment buildings, or other structures. Embedded ATMs tend to be operated by banks. Attacks on these ATMs, depending on the applicable state laws and prosecutorial discretion, may be charged as a burglary or as a larceny to the amount of the property stolen. Also, some ATMs enjoy the protection of Title 18, United States Code 2113(b): "Whoever takes and carries away with the intent to steal or purloin, any property or money or other thing of value exceeding $1,000 belonging to, or in the care, custody, control, management, or possession of any bank, credit union, or any savings and loan association . . ." may be fined and/or imprisoned for up to 10 years. Thus, in some ATM cases there may be concurrent jurisdiction between the FBI and the local enforcement agency.

Embedded ATMs carry more cash than the stand-alones, because they are intended for use by a much larger population. Attacks on these range from the crude to the bizarre. There have been reports of heavy trucks backing into them at high speed to jar them loose or to allow heavy chains to be attached to them.[28] After the chains are affixed, the trucks accelerate forward, ripping the ATM out. Suspects have also used acetylene torches on embedded ATMs[29] and tried blasting at them with shotguns.[30]

In addition to solving burglaries involving ATM attacks through the follow-up investigation, many arrests are made by alert officers patrolling the area, aided by the stores' use of silent alarms (which means police cars are responding to the scene without the burglars knowing it) and by neighbors and bypassers who witness unusual activity and call the police.

RESIDENTIAL BURGLARY

Earlier in this chapter, we noted that residential burglaries were primarily committed during the day, with the front door being the point of attack. Black home owners are victimized at a higher rate than is any other group.[31] The younger the head of a household is, the more likely that the residence will be burglarized.[32] As shown in Table 14-2, the losses associated with residential burglaries

TABLE 14-2	Home-Burglary Victimizations by Amount of Loss

AMOUNT OF LOSS	PERCENTAGE OF BURGLARIES
No loss	1.2%
Less than $50	10.5
$50–$99	4.2
$100–$249	14.4
$250–$499	11.7
$500–$999	11.3
$1,000 or more	30.8
Not known/not available	15.9

Source: Bureau of Justice Statistics, Criminal Victimization in the United States—2007. Washington, D.C.: U.S. Department of Justice, December 2007; Internet edition without page numbers, Table 85. Most recent statistics as of December 2010.

are not intrinsically significant. However, to many households, even relatively small losses are devastating. Moreover, when you consider the residual feelings of the victims, there is another type of loss: victims feel as though their privacy has been violated. They often struggle psychologically afterward to regain a sense of security in their own homes.

Many burglars are amateurs in the sense that even though they may commit the crime numerous times, they often act on impulse, driven by the need for money:

Usually when I get in my car and drive around I'm thinking, I don't have any money, so what is my means for money? All of a sudden I'll just take a glance and say, there it is, there's the house! . . . Then I get the feelin', that very moment that I'm moving then.[33]

Some burglars report that "legitimate" financial emergencies are the only reason they resort to breaking in:

Usually what I'll do is a burglary [or a couple of them] if I have to . . . helps get me over the rough spot until I can get it straightened out. Once I get it straightened out, I just go with the flow until I hit a rough spot where I need the money again . . . The only time I would go and commit a burglary is if I needed money at that point in time. That would be strictly to pay light bill, gas bill, rent.[34]

Although such cases clearly exist, burglaries are more often committed for other reasons:

I might find somebody with some good crack . . . while I'm high I say damn I want me some more of that good shit. Go knock a place off, make some more money, go buy some more dope.[35]

I use the burglary money for gifts for young ladies—flowers or negligee or somethin'. Some shoes . . . put them shoes on, them pumps . . . then watch 'em dance nude.[36]

See I go steal money and go buy me some clothes . . . See, I like to look good. I likes to dress . . . own only one pair of blue jeans 'cause I like to dress [well].[37]

Burglary is excitin' . . . it's just a thrill to going in undetected and walking out with all their shit . . . like going on a treasure hunt.[38]

From these quotes, it can be seen that burglars tend to commit their crimes for four broad reasons: (1) keeping themselves and their families fed, clothed, and sheltered; (2) keeping the party going; (3) keeping up appearances so that they can look better off financially than they are; and (4) keeping adventure in their lives.[39]

Whereas amateur burglars act on impulse, the more professional burglars are, the less likely they are to take chances. They develop information on their own or pay tipsters for it. They may simply cruise well-to-do neighborhoods looking for opportunities or follow expensive cars to their homes. Once they have identified a preliminary target, they begin a "workup," watching the house until they have become familiar with the people who live there, their daily routines, the absence or presence of alarms and dogs, views of possible attack points from other homes in the area, and the frequency of private and public police patrols.

One way of developing information on their own is simply to read the newspapers. Wedding announcements often reveal that a couple will honeymoon in another city or country and then reside in whatever community. With a little effort, burglars can often find out the couple's address and burglarize the home, stealing wedding gifts and other items, while the victimized partners are blissfully enjoying their honeymoon. Other types of announcements that might provide similar opportunities include funeral arrangements and gala charity events or parties, which many wealthy people can be expected to attend. Butlers and maids can get lists of the people attending such events. Tipsters—sometimes called "spotters," "fingermen," "noses," or "setup people"—provide another source of information that can be used in selecting homes for burglaries. For example, insiders at cruise ship operations can provide passenger lists. Medical personnel know when patients will be in their offices for appointments. Workers in various occupations such as telephone installers and flower delivery workers, enter numerous homes legitimately and have the chance to size up opportunities. Coworkers know when their bosses are going on vacation. Insurance office personnel know which homes' contents have been heavily insured and which may have special riders attached for silverware or other valuables. Armed with such information, professional burglars reduce the risk of apprehension and increase the probability of "making a nice haul."

Homes are burglarized during the day because that's when the occupants are most likely to be gone—working, attending school, or running errands. The same generally holds true with many neighbors, who might otherwise witness the attack. Burglars do not want to attract attention to themselves, but they also do not want a confrontation with an occupant. If they have learned the home's telephone number, they will call to see if anyone is there. While an answering machine encourages some burglars, it makes others leery of going ahead, fearing that someone is home and using the machine to screen the calls.

Alarms and dead-bolt locks are a deterrent to amateur burglars but not to more professional ones. Residential burglars usually do not have to carry an assortment of tools because so many targets are "soft." Often, they carry little other than workman's gloves and a large screwdriver or small pry bar (Figure 14-9). If they cannot easily effect entry at the front door, they will try to enter through the garage—which is ideal because they are out of sight—or a rear window. Most home burglars go straight to the bedroom, because that's where most people keep small valuables, such as jewelry, cash, furs, and guns. The master bathroom is also where most people keep their prescription drugs. As their experience builds up, burglars will begin to check the "clever" places where people hide their valuables, including in freezer compartments and behind towels in linen closets. If they have an accomplice, they will call him or her to bring the vehicle into which televisions, DVD/Blu-Ray Players, stereo systems, tools, and other valuables are loaded. Table 14-3 shows the seven types of property most commonly taken in burglaries.

▲ FIGURE 14-9   **Pry marks on residence's front door**
Pry marks left on the front door frame of a residential burglary. This is a general orientation photograph; close-up photographs of the marks with a ruler alongside them would also be taken. The positions of the pry marks would also be documented by notes and a sketch, using precise measurements. Ideally the marks would be cut from the door frame to be able to make comparisons with tools that may subsequently be found in the possession of a subject arrested for the crime. Failing that, they could be cast using Mikrosil, Silmark, or some similar putty. The drying times for putty varies, most drying in 5–8 minutes in normal temperatures and 12–15 minutes when very cold. **(Courtesy Chief Rick Boren and Sgt. Doug Shafer, Columbus (Georgia) Police Department)**

CAR, RV, AND TRAILER BURGLARIES

In most states, breaking into cars, recreational vehicles (RVs), and trailers constitutes a burglary. **Car burglars** tend to be juveniles, teenagers, and young adult offenders. Many entries by these offenders are done by simply opening unlocked car doors; others involve breaking a window to reach inside and take whatever is available.

TABLE 14-3	Property Most Frequently Taken from Homes with Reported Losses
PROPERTY	**PERCENTAGE OF CASES**
Portable electronic and photographic gear, jewelry, clothing, and other personal effects	42.5%
Household furnishings	12.8
Tools, machinery	12.1
Cash	11.1
Purse, wallet and credit cards	6.5
Bicycles and their parts	4.2
Firearms	2.2

Bureau of Justice Statistics, *Crime Victimization in the United States, 2007 Statistical Tables*. Washington, D.C.: U.S. Department of Justice, December 2007, Table 84. Most recent statistics as of December 2010.

Unlocked trunk releases are also pulled and items in the trunk stolen. Some street-wise suspects carry a spark plug with them, which when thrown hard easily breaks a car window. Additional "tools" include tire irons, slim jims, or other pry-bar type instruments, hammers, door lock punches, or whatever is handy, such as portable signs and rocks.

Typical items taken include visible change, wallets left in the center console and purses left on the floor board, car electronics, CDs, speed detectors, laptops, cameras, and cellular phones. Juveniles and teenagers often do more damage than is necessary in removing dashboard electronics. When valuable, but larger items, such as golf clubs, are left behind, the lack of a vehicle to transport them out of the area and/or the inability to sell them quickly also suggests youthful offenders. People of all ages on drugs commit auto breaking-and-enterings (B&Es), stealing items that they can quickly convert to cash to support their drug use. Wherever cars are parked, they can become a target. Apartment complexes, sorority and fraternity houses, and mall, mass transit, campus, and employee parking lots offer plentiful targets that allow offenders to quickly commit a larger number of car burglaries. Cars that are burglarized on railroad cars and new car sales lots tend to suggest more experienced car burglars. In most jurisdictions, car burglaries increase sharply around Christmas time, when shoppers leave many packages in plain view in their vehicles.

Modest pop-up campers may cost in the $5,000–$10,000 range, whereas RVs can top out at $1.5 million. Burglaries at dealerships tend to focus on electronics, and often the damage to the RVs is greater than the amount of the property stolen. Many RV burglaries occur at RV storage sites and along interstate and major state highways, because those routes are typically used by travelers. Pop-ups are often attacked in state or national parks when the owners are away hiking, photographing, hunting, or fishing. High-end RVs often have safes where the owners keep valuables and sometimes surprisingly large amounts of cash. High-end RVs have also been the target of home invasion–style robberies.

In addition to apprehensions made by patrol officers viewing crimes in progress, such crimes are often foiled or solved by reviewing surveillance data, targeting repeat offenders, owners returning unexpectedly to their vehicles, perpetrators bragging about their success, juveniles displaying their goods to classmates at school, suspects stopped for traffic offenses with the stolen property in plain view in the rear seat, and the use of "bait cars" by police.

INVESTIGATING CRIMINAL FENCES AND OTHER OUTLETS FOR STOLEN PROPERTY

Criminal **fences** or receivers are persons who knowingly purchase stolen property at a fraction of its cost and then resell it at a considerable profit (but still at a "really good" price) to the consumer. Fences usually buy at 10%–20% of an item's actual cost or may simply set a flat price for the goods—for example, $700 for a particular year, make, and model of car. How "hot" the goods are and how quickly they can be safely resold are also factors in setting the price. When confronted with someone who bought property that later turned out to be stolen, officers must determine whether the purchaser acted in good or bad faith. Among the indicators of a buyer's lack of good faith are

1. paying a price below that of a "good bargain";
2. purchasing from persons who are not known to them;
3. buying from persons whom they don't know how to recontact;
4. accepting items without a receipt;
5. buying property that bears an obliterated identification number or from which the number has been removed;
6. purchasing articles that have unusual property control numbers on them, such as those identifying the owner as a state agency;
7. having a past history of receiving stolen property;

The most basic notion of a fence is that after committing a burglary or another crime (for example, hijacking a truckload of clothing), the thief takes the merchandise (for instance, a television) to the fence and says, "How

INVESTIGATING CRIMINAL FENCES AND OTHER OUTLETS FOR STOLEN PROPERTY   393

much will you give me for it?" Although this approach is still used, fencing has become considerably more complicated, and there are numerous types of fences,[40] as shown by these examples:

- *Amateurs fences*, who usually do fencing intermittently, have limited resources and may buy stolen goods for resale to friends, as gifts to girlfriends, or for their own personal use.
- *Store owners and individuals*, who often buy only the goods for which they have placed an order with the thief or only from a thief who works for them relatively full time. Such thieves may also work as freelancers or as members of gangs, some of which are ethnically based, in multistate areas.

Theft of luxury clothing items, such as leather coats and upscale designer-label clothing, is a growth industry. The property may be stolen in burglaries or some other type of crime, including "mopping," another term for shoplifting. The clothing is then sold to fences or underground boutiques. Inside one drab family residence in Queens, police uncovered over $500,000 in stolen clothes. Said one detective, "The inside of this place looks like Macy's."[41]

Pakistani owners of a convenience store also led a three-state ring of thieves. They recruited 200 professional shoplifters and illegal Pakistani immigrants with promises of a better life and plenty of money to send home. Members of this group stole over-the-counter cosmetics, computers, DVD players, jet skis, pharmaceuticals, and anything else they could get their hands on. The merchandise was taken to a warehouse where it was repackaged and sent to coconspirators in two different states and in Pakistan. Competition to "bring in the most" was intense. One thief, enraged that another thief had brought in more than he had, hired thugs to beat up the higher-performing member of the gang. Gang cohesion was also reduced when some members "skimmed" some items for themselves, reducing the "take" for the rest of them. As investigators "rolled" individual gang members, the investigation snowballed, resulting in the eventual recovery of $450,000 in cash and $1.6 million in stolen goods.[42]

- *Professionals*, who have substantial bankrolls, do business with a select clientele known by them or reliably referred to them, may work for long periods without being caught, and usually have several locations at which to store their purchases.
- *Occasional or opportunistic fences*, who normally conduct their businesses legally (for example, as garages or **pawnshops**) but who from time to time "turn a deal" (Figure 14-10).
- *Providers of illicit goods and services*, such as those who trade drugs and access to prostitutes for stolen merchandise.

◄**FIGURE 14-10**
Pawnshops: Legitimate businesses or fencing operations?
Fences are persons who knowingly purchase stolen property for a fraction of its cost and then resell it at a considerable profit. Pawnshops suffer a continuing image problem from the illegal conduct of fencing by some of its operators. Most, if not all, jurisdictions have enacted statutes and ordinances in an effort to regulate how pawnshops conduct their business. (© Randy Faris/Corbis)

► **FIGURE 14-11**
Police raid uncovers stolen bicycles and other property
A police raid on a fencing operation in an inner-city neighborhood recovered a great deal of stolen property, some of which the police are inventorying in this picture. The operators of the fence paid for stolen goods with cash, drugs, and access to prostitutes.
(Courtesy Major Tolbert and Lt. Richard Zapal, Savannah Chatham Metropolitan Police Department)

- *Technology-proficient fences*, who do their business on the Internet. Some of these "fences" are the thieves themselves:

Two career thieves who may have committed as many as 100 burglaries in Massachusetts and New Hampshire sold approximately $30,000 worth of their booty on eBay. They had another $70,000 in stolen property that they also planned to sell there when police arrested them.[43]

Many fences can operate for long periods of time without being detected because they are often "invisible" until some situation creates the need for police to take a closer look at individuals and/or locations (Figure 14-11). Outlets for stolen property include swap meets, flea markets, for-sale advertisements in local newspapers, secondhand furniture stores, eBay and other Internet outlets, and overseas venues, often in third-world countries. In some instances, knowledge about fencing operations comes to the police under more unusual circumstances:

Two men approached a police sergeant with an offer of a $25,000 cash bribe in return for destroying physical evidence that tied them to a robbery. They were given some items and appeared satisfied with having bought themselves a cop. However, the officer was actually working the two men with the knowledge and support of his department and the local FBI field office. Ulti-mately, the two men and their associates were linked to warehouse burglaries and container thefts that totaled more than $3 million in stolen goods, and they had acted as fences for stolen laptop computers.[44]

From a policy viewpoint, the police know that the more the receiver markets can be disrupted or eliminated, the greater the likelihood that there will be some reduction in burglary and other offenses, whose profits depend on the availability of these illicit markets. Plainclothes officers quietly visit swap meets, flea markets, and other likely outlets, looking for known burglars or their associates offering merchandise for trade or sale. Such locations may be good candidates for the use of facial recognition software. Articles being offered are examined for possible signs of being stolen, such as missing or newly attached serial numbers. Arrested burglary offenders are always asked, "What did you do with the stuff you took?" When squeezed between facing almost certain prison time and giving their fences up, some will barter the information for a more lenient sentence. Because drug users usually steal to support their habits, whenever they are arrested, they are going to be asked, "What can you give me?" Their answers to this question may help identify drug dealers, fences, and other types of offenders.

Once in a great while, such questioning may yield a professional, big-time fence, but more frequently this is not the case. Professional fences usually screen their customers carefully and have worked with them over a period of years. Moreover, an arrested offender knows that by giving up a big-time fence, he/she will risk getting "wacked" for talking. Thus, the more usual case is that offenders try to get away with giving up "little fish."

Once a suspected fence is detected, officers work the case, investigating to confirm or disconfirm the fencing operation. When this is accomplished, officers attempt to broaden the case and apprehend more than just the offenders in front of them. This often entails both physical and electronic surveillance to identify the places fences frequent and who their associates are. An undercover officer may then be assigned to begin frequenting these places, covertly gathering additional information and/or attempting to develop a relationship with the fence and his/her associates. This method is also used when active burglars are targeted for arrest and surveillance is initiated. At some point, arrest and search warrants will be issued. When multiple locations and perpetrators are involved, raids executing the warrants should be conducted simultaneously to prevent offenders from slipping away.

As an industry, pawnshops suffer a continuing image problem from the illegal conduct of some operators. When the illegality was perceived as a serious problem, state statutes and local ordinances were enacted to regulate their shops' conduct, and this has reduced the number of pawnshops acting as fences. Usually these laws require that the pawnshops provide the names and addresses, and in some instances fingerprints, of persons pawning property, along with a full description of the property. In some locations, all secondhand dealers of property must provide the same type of information. In both instances, this must ordinarily be done within 24 hours of each transaction. Because of the temptations created by the high profits that can be gained by buying and selling stolen property, pawn and other second-hand dealers are closely scrutinized. State investigative agencies and many individual agencies maintain pawnshop databases to monitor secondhand merchandise transactions:

> While entering information in the database, an officer working with the burglary squad noticed that a subject had sold an expensive loose diamond to a local used-jewelry store. She also noticed that the subject had previously sold expensive jewelry to the same business. In the sale that had attracted the officer's attention, the subject had received $10,400 for the diamond. On the transaction slip from the jewelry store, it was noted that the seller lived in a nearby jurisdiction and worked as a plumber, so the officer contacted the police department there to find out if any high-priced jewelry thefts had occurred. She was not successful there, but ultimately she found a department in the area where investigators had noted a pattern in which the subject did plumbing jobs, and subsequently there would be missing jewelry from the homes he had worked in. Eventually, the diamond, actually valued at $63,000, was matched with a victim's ring from which the plumber had pried it.[45]

> In another case, the same officer noted that the home of one of the department's employees had been burglarized, resulting in the loss of a camera, zoom lens, and credit card. While processing transaction slips, she found a pawnshop that had taken in the camera and zoom lens, along with a diamond ring and bracelet, which had been purchased with the stolen credit card. Investigation revealed that the subject selling the articles to the pawnshop had an extensive criminal background and lived within a few blocks of the employee. On the basis of this and other evidence, he was arrested and the property recovered.[46]

Police **sting operations** are an effective means of combating fences, identifying active criminals, penetrating criminal organizations, and recovering property. In a typical sting, officers set up a legitimate-appearing "front" business in which they slowly develop a reputation as being fences. As all transactions are videotaped, a great deal of intelligence is gathered that can be used in their current investigation or in collateral ones. Alternatively, the officers may do business in a different type of setting and use a warehouse located elsewhere to store the stolen property:

> An FBI agent, a cooperating witness, and participating local departments ran a fencing operation out of a Brooklyn social club. The "drop" for the merchandise was a warehouse they had rented at another location. This undercover operation resulted in the indictments of 39 individuals on charges of selling stolen property, drug trafficking, gun dealing, and loan-sharking. Over $5 million in property was recovered, including a hijacked truckload of designer gowns valued at more than $1 million.[47]

In Chapter 7, "The Follow-Up Investigation and Investigative Resources," the enhanced capabilities of NCIC 2000 were discussed. The NCIC databases are of great importance for investigators, particularly since images of stolen property have been added. This new capability enhances the opportunity to recover stolen property.

THE INVESTIGATOR'S CRIME PREVENTION ROLE

While at the scene of a burglary, investigators should tell the victims the precautions they can take to decrease the likelihood of their being "hit" again.

► FIGURE 14-12
Sample office security checklist
(Source: Courtesy Bolen Industries, Hackensack, New Jersey, with modification)

	Yes	No
1. Do you restrict office keys to persons who actually need them?	☐	☐
2. Do you keep complete, up-to-date records of the disposition of all office keys?	☐	☐
3. Do you have adequate procedures for collecting keys from terminated employees?	☐	☐
4. Do you restrict duplication of office keys, except for those specifically ordered by you in writing?	☐	☐
5. Do you require that all keys be marked "Do not duplicate" to prevent legitimate locksmiths from making copies without your knowledge?	☐	☐
6. Have you established a rule that keys must not be left unguarded on desks or cabinets, and do you enforce that rule?	☐	☐
7. Do you require that filing-cabinet keys be removed from locks and placed in a secure location after opening cabinets in the morning?	☐	☐
8. Do you have procedures that prevent unauthorized personnel from reporting a "lost key" and receiving a "replacement"?	☐	☐
9. Do you have some responsible person in charge of issuing all keys?	☐	☐
10. Are all keys systematically stored in a secured wall cabinet either of your own design or from a commercial key-control system?	☐	☐
11. Do you keep a record showing issuance and return of every key, including the name of the person, the date, and time?	☐	☐
12. Do you use telephone locks or access codes to prevent unauthorized calls when the office is unattended?	☐	☐
13. Do you provide at least one lockable drawer in every secretary's desk to protect personal effects?	☐	☐
14. Do you have at least one filing cabinet secured with an auxiliary locking bar so that you can keep business secrets under better protection?	☐	☐
15. Do you leave a night light on?	☐	☐
16. Do you record all equipment serial numbers and file them in a safe place to maintain correct identification in the event of theft or destruction by fire?	☐	☐
17. Do you shred all important papers before discarding them in wastebaskets?	☐	☐
18. Do you lock briefcases and attaché cases containing important papers in closets or lockers when not in use?	☐	☐
19. Do you insist on identification from repair people who come to do work in your office?	☐	☐
20. Do you deposit incoming checks and cash each day so that you do not keep large sums in the office overnight?	☐	☐
21. Do you clear all desks of important papers every night and place them in locked fireproof safes or cabinets?	☐	☐
22. Do you frequently change the combination of your safe to prevent anyone from memorizing it or passing it on to a confederate?	☐	☐
23. When working alone in the office at night, do you set the front-door lock to prevent anyone else from getting in?	☐	☐
24. Do you have the police and fire department telephone numbers posted and handy?	☐	☐
25. Do you check to see that no one remains in hiding behind you at night if you are the last to leave the office?	☐	☐
26. Are all windows, transoms, and ventilators properly protected?	☐	☐
27. Do you double check to see that all windows and doors are securely locked before you leave?	☐	☐
28. Are all doors leading to the office secured by heavy-duty, double-cylinder, dead-bolt locks?	☐	☐
29. If your office is equipped with a burglar alarm system or protected by a guard service, do you make sure the alarm equipment is set properly each night?	☐	☐
30. Do you have a periodic security review by a qualified security expert or locksmith?	☐	☐
31. Are computer access codes and/or selected files password-protected on a need-to-know basis?	☐	☐
32. Are all computer disks and tapes containing sensitive, client, or secret information maintained under controlled conditions during the day and locked securely at night?	☐	☐

REDUCING THE RISK OF COMMERCIAL BURGLARY

Many of the suggestions provided in the next section for preventing residential burglaries also apply to businesses. In addition, operators of businesses should be told to prevent easy access to their roofs by securing all vents and roof openings; to use security-providing locks, frames, and doors properly; to light the exterior of the building; to use, if feasible, an alarm system and surveillance camera; to use a money chest rather than a fire-resistant safe; and to set the safe in concrete in open view at a place that can be lighted at night. Completion of the office security checklist in Figure 14-12 serves two purposes: It provides the owners with useful information about how to improve their security, and it may provide important investigative leads, particularly if a surreptitious entry is involved.

REDUCING THE RISK OF RESIDENTIAL BURGLARY

To protect their residences as well as businesses, when appropriate, occupants should do the following things when they are on vacation or otherwise away:

1. Stop delivery of mail and newspapers, or arrange for a neighbor to pick them up daily.
2. Arrange for a special watch on their premises by patrol officers.
3. Use timers to turn on lights and radios at various times to make it look like the residence is occupied.
4. Ask reliable neighbors to immediately report any suspicious activity to the police.
5. Ask a trusted neighbor to come over occasionally and change the position of drapes, blinds, and other things.
6. Put up "Beware of Dog" signs, or if they really have a dog, ask someone to take care of it in the home whenever feasible.

For day-to-day security, occupants can take other actions that will help them avoid being burglary victims or, if they are victimized, will help reduce their losses:

1. Create an uninviting target: use motion-sensor lights, purchase an alarm system, use dead-bolt locks on solid doors mounted in steel frames, and place locks on windows.
2. If possible, avoid placing valuables where they can be seen through windows.
3. Cut plants low around doors and windows so that burglars can't conceal themselves while breaking in.
4. Grow thorny plants around places where someone might attempt to force an entry.

5. Don't leave ladders or tools lying around in the yard or clothes on an outside line—a thief who initially may have thought of just taking them will see the greater opportunity they create.
6. Don't tell strangers about your comings and goings.
7. Don't allow strangers to use your telephone, and don't give your correct number to anyone who claims they are calling by mistake; instead, ask the caller whom he/she was trying to reach at what number. Baby-sitters and children should be instructed to do the same thing.
8. Don't keep spare keys in the usual places—under the mat, over the door, and in flower pots. Burglars know these places.
9. Don't go out to run a quick errand without locking all doors, including garage doors.
10. Engrave valuables with special identifying numbers. Alternatively, mark them with small translucent decals that have your special identification data on them. These microdots are about the size of a speck of pepper and are virtually invisible to the naked eye.
11. Keep strong control over your keys. It may be helpful to leave them for service workers or give them to maids, but at the cost of greater risk exposure.
12. Don't leave notes on the door saying where you have gone or when you will be back.
13. Get to know your neighbors; they'll be more likely to respond faithfully to requests to "watch my place while I'm gone."
14. When new snow is on the ground, back out of your driveway and pull back in several times; do the same walking in and out of your door. This makes it harder for burglars to figure out if you are home.
15. To enhance recovery of your property if you are victimized, take pictures of valuables and record makes, models, and serial numbers of your property.

KEY TERMS

amateur burglars
ATM attacks
burglary
burglary investigation checklist
burglary tools
car burglars

coin-operated machine burglary
fences
loiding
pawnshops
picking
possession of burglary tools

professional burglars
safe
smash-and-grab
sting operations
theft of luxury

REVIEW QUESTIONS

1. Describe the dimensions of the crime of burglary.
2. What is the profile of persons arrested for burglary?
3. How are professional and amateur burglars distinguished?
4. What are the elements of the crime of burglary?
5. What considerations are important in approaching the scene of a burglary?
6. How are attacks on ATMs committed?

7. The text noted that black home owners and younger people are victimized more frequently than others. What are some possible explanations for this?

8. What signs at a burglary scene may suggest juvenile perpetrators?

9. How are fire-resistant safes and money chests differentiated?

10. What special actions are required if there are explosives at a burglary scene?

11. How do burglars get their information?

12. With respect to the possible illegal receiving of stolen property, what are some indicators of the absence of good-faith purchasing?

13. Explain two investigative approaches to locating fences.

14. What measures can home owners and business operators take to lessen their chances of being burglarized?

INTERNET ACTIVITIES

1. The two most famous burglaries in American history are usually referred to by one word, "Watergate." What were these burglaries about, and what was their ultimate importance?

2. To learn how different police agencies across the country are attacking burglary problems go to

www.cops.usdoj.gov (the Community Oriented Policing Services [COPS] website), click on "Resource Information Center (RIC), and enter "burglary" in the search field.

◀ In 2008, store surveillance video captured a Florida woman shoplifting. Police investigators later discovered that the woman was part of an extensive shoplifting ring comprising approximately 18 family members. The group allegedly stole more than $100 million worth of merchandise over a five-year period.

(© AP Photo/Bedford, N.H. Police Department)

15

LARCENY/THEFT AND WHITE-COLLAR CRIME

CHAPTER OBJECTIVES

1. Distinguish between tangible and intangible property.

2. State the difference between petit/petty and grand larceny.

3. Define, from two different perspectives, white-collar crime.

4. Explain why so little property from larceny/thefts is recovered.

5. Contrast organized retail theft and organized retail crime.

6. Explain methods of identity theft and the uses made of stolen identities.

7. Explain credit card and check frauds.

8. List different types of frauds, scams, and cons.

9. Define and describe methods of money laundering.

10. Describe security and investment frauds.

11. Identify and summarize telephone scams.

12. Outline common telemarketing and postal frauds.

This chapter deals with two groups of crimes: larceny/theft and white-collar crime. The traditional definition of larceny/theft is the unlawful taking and carrying away of the tangible personal property of another with the intent to permanently deprive that person of his interest in the property. **Tangible personal property** means things that have both a physical existence that can be touched and intrinsic value—such as jewelry, lawn mowers, cameras, laptop computers, televisions, furniture and clothing, and collectibles such as coins and civil war uniform buttons.

In contrast, **intangible property** has value, but it is more abstract—such as stocks, bonds, checking and saving accounts, and other types of financial instruments, as well as patents and copyrights. State statutes have historically addressed the theft of intangibles through specific statutes, which supplemented the existing larceny statutes. Larceny essentially incorporates the elements of the crime of robbery, except the element of the use of force, threat, or fear is not included (see Chapter 13, "Robbery"). Additionally, although robbery is a face-to-face crime, the law does not require that the victim of a larceny be present at the time of a crime. However, the victim may be present as illustrated by purse snatching, pickpocketing, and an owner driving home from work in time to see a stranger pick up his daughter's bicycle from the lawn of his home, toss it in the back of a SUV, and drive away.

Larceny/theft is often divided into **grand larceny** and **petit or petty larceny;** the former is a felony and the latter a misdemeanor. The difference between the two is the value of the property stolen, which varies by state; the dividing line between the two is often that if the value of the property stolen is $1,000 or more, it is a felony. In some states, larceny/theft statutes are divided into grades or classes of offending, such as Class A, Class B, and so on; the gradations of offenses are usually based on the amount of loss to the victim, and the legal penalties are tied to the grade or class of the theft.

Many states have also enacted specifically titled larceny/theft statutes that reflect special aspects of their economy, such as "timber theft or fraud," or special problems, for example, "transit fare evasion, identity theft" or "organized retail theft" to distinguish between prosecutions that are aimed at rings of professional shoplifters causing significant losses and that have more serious penalties versus those directed at the teenager who "lifts or boosts" a CD, tube of lipstick, or shirt (Figure 15-1) and is charged with "theft from retail merchants," a lesser shoplifting offense.

CHAPTER OUTLINE

Introduction
The Offense and the Offender
Elements of the Crime
Shoplifting and Organized Retail Crime (ORC)
Identity Theft and Follow-On Crimes
Credit Card Fraud
Check Fraud
Counterfeiting
Frauds, Scams, and Cons
Money Laundering
Security and Investment Frauds
Telephone Scams
Telemarketing and Postal Frauds

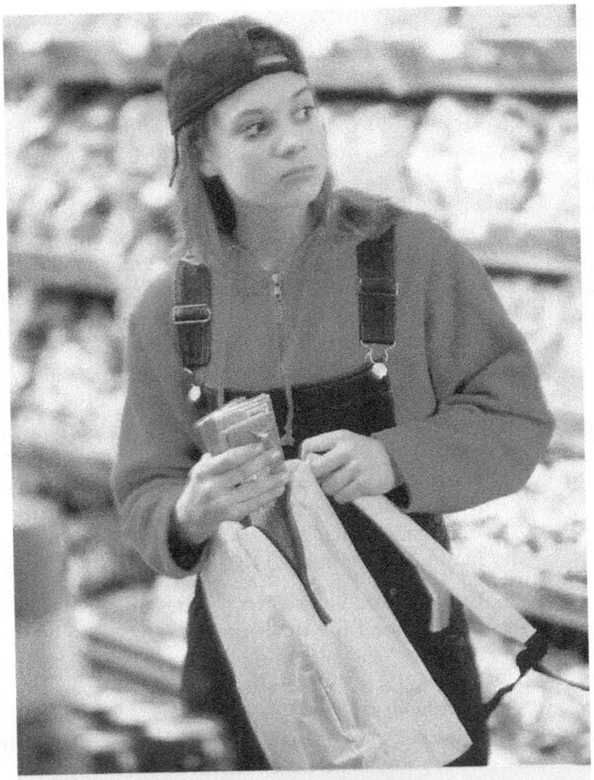

▲**FIGURE 15-1 Theft from retail merchant**
Teenage shoplifter takes one last look around before concealing merchandise in her backpack. (© Benelux)

The term *white-collar crime* was coined in 1939 by sociologist E. H. Sutherland. His white-collar criminals were characterized by respectability and higher social status, which they used to commit more complex offenses such as **fraud** and **embezzlement,** as opposed to street crimes. Now, almost 70 years later, the U.S. Department of Justice defines **white-collar crime** as nonviolent, illegal activities that rely on deceit, deception, concealment, manipulation, breach of trust, subterfuge, or illegal circumvention. Note that Sutherland's definition was based on the characteristics of the offender versus the present orientation of white-collar crime being the characteristics of the actions taken by the offender.[1] There is no set of laws titled "white-collar crime." It is a construct, useful for how we think about such crimes, but offenders are often charged with larceny/theft crimes, such as theft by fraud. Many of these crimes are investigated and prosecuted at the federal level. For instance, the FBI investigates theft crimes that involve the transportation of stolen property across state lines, the U.S. Postal Inspectors investigate mail and wire fraud, and the U.S. Secret Service investigates fraudulent credit cards and checks drawn upon payment and financial systems of the United States. In addition, the Secret Service is charged with the enforcement of counterfeiting and fraud statutes aimed at preserving the integrity of United States currency, coin, and financial obligations.

Statistically, pickpockets are not a large problem in the United States; the crime accounts for only about one-half of 1% of all larceny/thefts, but losses are still serious to victims. Abroad, pickpockets flourish in all major cities, such as Rome, Beijing, Bangkok, Paris, Berlin, and London. In foreign countries, tourists lose not only their valuables but often their passports, which interrupts their vacations while they seek to get a replacement. The crime flourishes where people congregate at peak hours, such as transportation centers, along crowded streets, and at sporting events.

Children as young as five and six years old are trained as pickpockets in some foreign countries. There are schools in South America from which, in order to graduate, the would-be pickpocket must "lift" items from all the pockets of a mannequin dressed in a three-piece men's suit. Each pocket is guarded with a bell that cannot ring if the "student" is to pass. Pickpockets may work alone, although a "crew" of three is common: one distracts the mark (for example, drops something, bumps him/her, or feigns a medical emergency or accident), another takes the valuables, which are immediately handed to a third accomplice, who quickly slips away. A seasoned operator can take the wristwatch off your arm without you realizing it; in Oslo, Norway brazen pickpockets even lifted the wallet of the Chief of Police. Some very skilled pickpockets morph over to shoplifting expensive jewelry because of the higher values. Investigators should exercise caution when arresting pickpockets, a small number of whom turn violent when apprehended. They should also be on-guard for assaults from previously unnoted accomplices.

Most victims had exposed valuables, such as their wallet, within the 30 minutes before their victimization; pickpockets study the crowd and carefully select their target. Women are more likely to be victimized than men are, whereas men are more likely to be the perpetrators. Secondary crimes included credit card fraud and withdrawals from the victim's ATM account, because the victim's personal identification number (PIN) was written down in the wallet.[2]

THE OFFENSE AND THE OFFENDER

Although the number of larcenies decreased by 9% in 2009 estimates, a larceny/theft occurs every 5.0 seconds, a rate of nearly three times that for burglary,[3] and the average loss is $864.[4] This crime bears a low clearance rate; only 21.5% are resolved by arrest of exceptional means.[5] A little over half of all larceny/thefts were of items valued at $200 or below.[6] Larceny/theft is often an opportunistic act; fishing rods and tool boxes are taken from open beds of pickup trucks parked at a Sam's Club, or a thief loitering at an airport notices that someone waiting for a flight is distracted and takes her purse, carry-on luggage, or laptop. Many items are taken from motor vehicles or acquired through shoplifting tactics as indicated in Figure 15-2. Overwhelmingly, these offenses are committed by young, white males.

Because small items of low value are often stolen and there are frequently no leads, many larceny/theft cases are simply inactivated after the incident report is taken, and they receive no investigative follow-up. This fact accounts for the reality that the recovery in property in larceny/theft is low; in only 3.7% of all such cases is at least some property recovered. However, 4.7% of the time all of the property is recovered, often from offenses with larger losses and significant leads.[7]

ELEMENTS OF THE CRIME

Although the traditional definition of larceny is still operative in some states, others have eliminated the distinction between the theft of tangibles and intangibles and created more comprehensive larceny/theft statutes to cover both types of losses. Such statutes drop the former "tangible personal property of another" and use "property

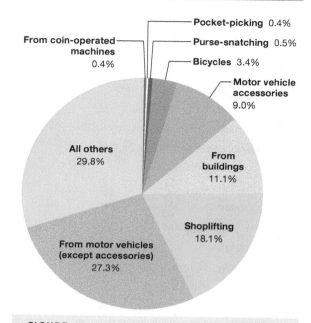

▲ FIGURE 15-2 Larceny-theft distribution, 2009
(Uniform Crime in the United States, 2009 [Washington, D.C.: FBI, 2010], www2.fbi.gov/ucr/cius2009/documents/index.htm)

of another," to cover the loss of a wide range of things, such as stocks and bonds, services—such as electricity, natural gas, television cable, high-speed Internet access, tickets to the symphony and sporting events, lawn mowers, paintings, hotel rooms and rental cars, computer software and information files, cash and jewelry. To illustrate, in some states the failure to return a rental car within 72 hours of the agreed-on time in the lease is evidence of intent to commit larceny/theft.

The person from whom the property is taken in a larceny/theft need not own it and may simply be the custodian of it. Although he/she is the victim of the crime for reporting purposes, if the property is recovered it is returned to the owner. If there is no recovery, the owner receives the fair market value from his/her insurance company.

The broader larceny/theft laws recognize that the taking may be accomplished in a variety of ways, such as:

1. **theft by trick,** such as con games and swindles;
2. **theft by receiving stolen property,** meaning knowingly receiving and disposing of property he/she should have known or knew was stolen;
3. **theft by deception**—for example, the removal of a price sticker from one item for sale and replacing it with a less expensive sticker;[8]
4. **theft by fraud,** illustrated by the unauthorized use of another's credit card, using someone else's medical insurance card or Social Security number to get benefits, and "pump and dump" stock schemes,

whereby a stock is heavily promoted—after the stock runs up in price, its promoters dump it;

5. **theft of services,** covering such things as "skipping out" on hotel, restaurant, and bar bills, or illegally connecting or reconnecting an electrical meter.

In states with comprehensive larceny/theft laws, the crime of embezzlement has often disappeared, because the language of the larceny/theft law usually provides a means to bring charges for that conduct, often by a crime titled **theft by conversion.** Where it remains, the elements of embezzlement are the same as the traditional larceny charge, with the addition that a person who has been entrusted with something of valuable converts it to their own purpose or use in contravention of his/her legal obligation.

SHOPLIFTING AND ORGANIZED RETAIL CRIME (ORC)

SHOPLIFTING

In the United States, **shoplifting** produces losses of $33.1 billion annually with an average loss of $120.[9] Security experts calculate that for every $40 dollars stolen, only one dollar of merchandise is recovered. A significant problem is that there is no single profile of a shoplifter; they can be ordinary people or professional thieves.[10] Slightly more men (55%) than women (45%) shoplift, although women take higher-value items, juveniles account for roughly 33% of all cases.[11] These types of offenses are most likely to occur on Saturdays (18%) and Fridays (15%), and 60% of all cases occur between noon and 6:00 P.M.[12] There are also seasonal variations in shoplifting, with spikes in activity just before students go back to school in August, before Christmas, Easter, and when schools are letting out for summer. There are five types of shoplifters: (1) kleptomaniacs or those who have a compulsion to steal; (2) amateurs, who steal on impulse or because of peer pressure; (3) professionals, who are the least numerous but produce the largest losses; (4) drug users, who steal to support their habit, often selling what they take to criminal fences; and (5) "desperate straits" people, such as vagrants or the homeless and mothers who cannot afford items for their babies.

Retail establishments combat shoplifting by a combination of prevention strategies, such as sales staff greeting customers to make them feel singled out, posting signs about prosecuting shoplifters, placing expensive items in locked cases, putting on display only one of a pair of items, keeping aisles uncluttered to facilitate observation, roving employees and uniformed security officers, using electronic tags, and placing dummy surveillance cameras in plain sight. In recent years, "clamshell blisters" have gained popularity. This type of packaging seals a product in a clear plastic container, which allows 360-degree visibility of the product and is difficult to open. Retailers also use a strategy of apprehension that involves the use of observable, real surveillance cameras, "spy cameras" (for example, inside of clocks, smoke detector sprinklers, and heads of mannequins), observation ports, and the use of store security to work the floor. *Source tagging* is used widely—merchants place a small insert between the pages of a book or in a package of tools; the tag emits a narrowband radio frequency that triggers an alarm if the item has not been scanned.

Investigators working a shoplift detail should be alert for customers in a retail establishment who (1) avoid contact with sales personnel; (2) pick up a small item and wander about the store because they may finally palm it, and leave; (3) "have their heads on swivels" to assess their opportunity to steal; (4) wear baggy clothing or coats in weather not requiring it; (5) distract sales personnel or serve as shields so their partner can take and conceal items; (6) make repeated trips to fitting rooms, sometimes to wear store merchandise out under the clothes they wear; and (7) carry large handbags or push strollers in which items can quickly be concealed.

Theft by employees includes such activities as the removal of products, supplies, merchandise, money, data, information, and intellectual property.[13] Estimates vary across studies, but roughly 50% of all shoplifting is done by employees. The annual cost of embezzlement and employee theft is between $20 and $90 billion and upward of $240 billion if thefts of intellectual property are included; it is believed that 30%–50% of all business failures are caused by embezzlement and employee theft.[14]

ORGANIZED RETAIL CRIME (ORC)

Shoplifting has long suffered from the misperception that it is "small-time crime." Yet, its previously noted annual losses of $37.4 billion dwarf the combined annual losses of burglary ($4 billion) and motor vehicle theft ($7.9 billion).[15] Recognition of such facts has led to important new initiatives in combating shoplifting and other crimes against retailers. In 2006 legislation was signed creating an Organized Retail Theft Task Force at the FBI and mandating the creation of a public database on retail theft. A related database already exists, the National Retail Federation's (NRF) Retail Loss Prevention Intelligence Network (RLPIN), which was designed with the assistance of the FBI and other law-enforcement agencies.

Two terms that have emerged recently are **organized retail theft (ORT)** and **organized retail crime (ORC).** ORT refers to the problem of significant losses to retailers caused by crews or rings of often mobile professional shoplifters. ORC has emerged as a broader term and includes not only professional shoplifters but also other associated problems such as thefts from merchandise distribution centers, truck hijacking, credit card fraud, counterfeit goods, and the fences and other outlets for stolen merchandise.

Target is one of the largest retail stores in the United States, operating more than 1,700 stores in 49 states nationwide and employing more than 350,000 people. Target has focused their attention on organized retail crime (ORC) by developing a specialized investigative model. The Target model focuses on forensic evidence in four primary areas:

- clarification of images from video;
- photographic comparisons;
- suspicious and suspect vehicle identification;
- latent fingerprint identification and comparison with other crimes involving Target.

After a meticulous and time consuming investigation comparing criminal activity in multiple states via their real-time investigative process, the Target investigative team discovered a string of broken X-Box and PlayStation 3 game consoles that were fraudulently returned to retail stores in multiple locations. The team discovered a sophisticated and well-organized ring of criminals that were purchasing new game consoles at retail stores, removing the working hard drives, replacing them with broken hardware and counterfeit serial numbers, and returning the malfunctioning systems for a full refund. They then sold the new machines through various online auction websites. The Target team was able to positively identify the thieves actively working in several states. Criminal felony indictments eventually stopped the multimillion-dollar ORC ring.[16]

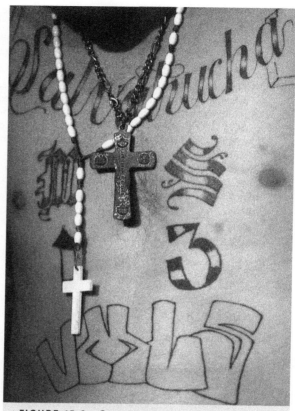

▲ **FIGURE 15-3 Gang tattoos**
(© Yuri Cortez/AFP/Getty Images)

ORC offenders range from independent, loosely tied together crews to more organized entities, including traditional crime families to the ultraviolent transnational gangs such as Mara Salvatrucha (MS-13). While some ORC groups may essentially specialize in crimes against retailers, others, like MS-13, have diverse interests, including alien, drug, and gun smuggling. One MS-13 leader has called for gang action against volunteer border patrol groups, such as the Arizona Minutemen, because that state is often a gateway into the United States from Mexico for their activities. Some ORCs run by persons with ties to Middle Eastern countries wired "profits" to Jordan, Egypt, and Palestine, where they were allegedly used to finance terrorist organizations such as Hamas and Hezbollah; tracing the money once it reaches unfriendly foreign countries has proven difficult, but it seems clear that some ORC profits are used to finance terrorism.[17]

Some of the most violent organizations, MS-13 members have long worn their numerous tattoos with pride (Figure 15-3). However, continued pressure from federal, state, and local investigators has resulted in a number of indictments and convictions of the easily identifiable gang members. Consequently, some MS-13 leaders have quietly encouraged members to be less ostentatious with the tattoos.

ORC offenders are known to have paid illegal immigrants, the homeless, and drug addicts to steal items for them (for example, $1.00 for each can of baby formula). Because some of the people in these categories might shoplift on their own, it is difficult for investigators to know exactly what they are dealing with when they make some shoplifting arrests. Yet, it is important to try to find out not only from a case investigation standpoint but also because of the potential national security implications.

Some ORC operations have their own warehouses chock full of stolen goods, which are sold through controlled convenience stores and neighborhood stores, flea markets, and other outlets, as well as shipped to unsuspecting wholesalers. Some stolen goods have expiration dates ("use by" or "use before") on them, such as diabetes-testing and teeth-whitening strips, batteries, baby formula, condoms, pharmaceuticals, and food products. The public health is endangered when expiration dates on stored stolen products are altered to make them marketable. This endangerment also exists when other items, such as frozen dinners, are allowed to thaw and then are refrozen or stored at improper temperatures before being sold.

COPPER AND OTHER PRECIOUS METAL THEFT

As the price of copper rises above $4.00 per pound, the number of thefts from electrical companies, construction sites, utilities, telephone lines, cell towers, air conditioners, transformer units, and even catalytic converters in newer model cars also dramatically increases (Figure 15-4). Copper and other precious metal (for example, platinum, gold and silver alloys, zinc) thefts have become so prolific that in 2008 the FBI developed a specific intelligence report focused on the theft of copper as a major threat to critical infrastructure within the United States.[18] According to the report, the theft of copper and other precious metals is conducted by individuals as well as organized transnational groups that work independently and in loose association with large fencing operations and the sale of contraband. The theft of these metals is spurred by several important factors:

- Since 2001 the price of commodities (especially copper) has dramatically climbed from $1 per pound to over $4 per pound on the Comex division of the New York Mercantile Exchange. As a result, the number of thefts as well as the monetary loss from such thefts has skyrocketed across the country.
- The trade and sale of copper is poorly regulated and is fueled by supply and demand at a global level. With robust economies and national building programs, the countries of China and India have spiked the demand for copper. Thieves can easily sell raw copper to metal shops and recyclers capitalizing on these higher spikes in price.
- There is little means to associate stolen raw copper to a specific crime scene. Therefore, even if large caches of copper wire or gold alloy are located and found, tying these products to a specific case is almost impossible.
- The theft of copper and other precious metals is relatively new, and various database development, focused task-force operations, and laws designed to capture important scrap-metal transactions have only recently been implemented by local and federal law-enforcement agencies to curb the problem.

One of the newest and most important scrap-metal tracking systems developed to assist law enforcement is the LeadsOnline Metal Theft Investigative System (MTIS). The electronic reporting system records important seller information that is collected by recyclers and scrap-metal dealers—such as an image of the driver's license and vehicle of the seller, type and quantity of the metal sold, digital images of fingerprints, and, of course, pictures of the seller as well as the metal being sold.[19] The MTIS is being used in several areas (New York City, Dallas, San Francisco, and the entire State of Arkansas) with more than 3,000 law-enforcement users and is bolstered by recent state legislation that requires all scrap-metal dealers and pawn shop owners to report large-quantity copper

▲ **FIGURE 15-4**   **Copper theft**
Transformers contain approximately 50 lbs. of copper with the potential to yield $200 of profit if sold to a scrap-metal dealer. (© Ultimate Group, LLC/Alamy)

and precious metal sales to the police. The MTIS is compatible with NCIC and is an official eBay partner, and serves as an important means to investigate copper and other precious-metal thefts across multiple jurisdictions.

INVESTIGATIVE POINTS

When investigating a larceny/theft, investigators should consider the following strategies.[20]

- Gather a detailed list of the stolen items, including serial numbers and photos.
- Assess the modus operandi compared to other crimes within close geographic proximity.
- Examine other reports and field interviews for suspicious individuals, vehicles, and activity in the area.
- Check pawn shops and chop shops.
- Obtain and review surveillance video.
- Collect intelligence by carefully questioning arrestees charged in unrelated offenses after Mirandization and obtaining information on the offense for which they are charged.
- If the stolen property is a cell phone, laptop, or iPad, it may be tracked via GPS.

IDENTITY THEFT AND FOLLOW-ON CRIMES

Identity theft, which began to emerge as a problem in the 1990s, has been called the "crime of the new millennium."[21] The normal daily activities of consumers include purchasing tickets and merchandise online, cashing checks, using credit and debit cards, and renting videos—all of which result in information being shared. At all points where personal data is collected, processed, or stored, there are opportunities for identity theft.[22] Identity theft may be the fastest growing crime of any kind in our society. In 2009 almost 8 million Americans were victimized by this crime with combined individual costs and losses to businesses placed at nearly $50 billion.[23] The person whose identity is stolen is one victim; the businesses that suffered losses owing to the criminal use of the stolen identity represent another group of victims. Estimates of the cost to individual victims to clear their names vary, but sources maintain that it requires as few as 24 to as much as 600 hours of effort and from $80 to $1,500 worth of lost earnings to correct credit and other related problems. Over 1,300 victims have been the subjects of criminal investigations, arrests, or wrongful convictions.[24]

Identity crimes involve two types of criminal acts: (1) identity theft and (2) the **follow-on crimes** that occur, such as credit card and check fraud.

HOW IDENTITY THEFT OCCURS

Abundant opportunities exist for identity thieves to get the personal information of people they victimize. Among methods used to obtain data are these:

1. Stealing wallets and purses containing identification, bank, credit, membership, and other types of cards.
2. Stealing mail, which provides bank and credit statements, preapproved credit offers, Social Security numbers, and other personal data. Some thieves follow mail carriers at a distance and then steal from mailboxes that appear to have just had a large stack of mail delivered. Alternatively, they might cruise affluent neighborhoods looking for raised red flags on mailboxes and stealing outgoing correspondence.
3. Going to the Post Office and completing a change of address form to divert mail to another location.
4. Rummaging through the victims' trash, or the trash of businesses, to "mine" for personal data—a practice described as **dumpster diving.**
5. Fraudulently obtaining the victim's credit report by posing as a potential landlord or employer.
6. Stealing personal identification from the victim's home.
7. Opportunistically using information from lost wallets and purses.
8. Family members, relatives, roommates and acquaintances misappropriating information.
9. Stealing personal data assistants (PDAs) and smartphones, such as Blackberries and iPhones, and laptops and tablets; this area may become more significant in the future, because more than one spyware virus for PDAs and smartphones are known to exist.
10. Obtaining personal information by hacking into home and business computers or by such tactics as downloading spyware programs. (Identity thieves posing as a legitimate business duped an Atlanta-area company out of personal information for perhaps as many as 400,000 people nationally.[25])
11. Stealing information from employers, medical and insurance offices, student records, and other locations or bribing corrupt employees to provide the victims' personal data.
12. Scamming victims out of personal information on the Internet is done by a technique known as **phishing.**[26] Two common phishing scams are sending an e-mail to potential victims that appears to be from a legitimate source, such as eBay, AOL, Yahoo, Best Buy, Wells Fargo, a credit card company, or a bank, and asking that they update their account information data. The second method involves using an e-mail to notify victims they have won a prize, such as the Canadian or Netherlands Lottery, but need to pay a processing fee to receive it, thereby tricking the victims into completing an accompanying credit form.[27]

    There are numerous variations on these two methods. One is an e-mail promising a free credit report subject to the recipient completing a personal information form. A second method is an e-mail from the U.S. Internal Revenue Service offering an $80 credit if they will participate in an online satisfaction survey, Form IR-2007-148, which also requires the disclosure of personal information.

    Any time a possible victim reports an unsolicited e-mail contact from the IRS it is a phishing attack, because the IRS neither initiates unsolicited contacts that way nor does it ask for passwords and other related information. Other bogus forms falsely attributed to the IRS include IR-2007- ending in 49, 75, 104, 109, or 116. Victims should be directed not to open attachments associated with such e-mails and to report the attack to *phishing@irs.gov.* Since this mailbox was established in 2006, more than 30,000 taxpayers have reported 400 separate phishing incidents.
13. **Shoulder surfing,** or watching and listening from a nearby location as victims identify themselves and use credit cards or write checks or are punching in their long-distance calling-card numbers.[28]
14. Using technology, such as skimmers, to obtain personal data. **Skimmers** are pager-sized data collection devices that cost roughly $300. These are attached

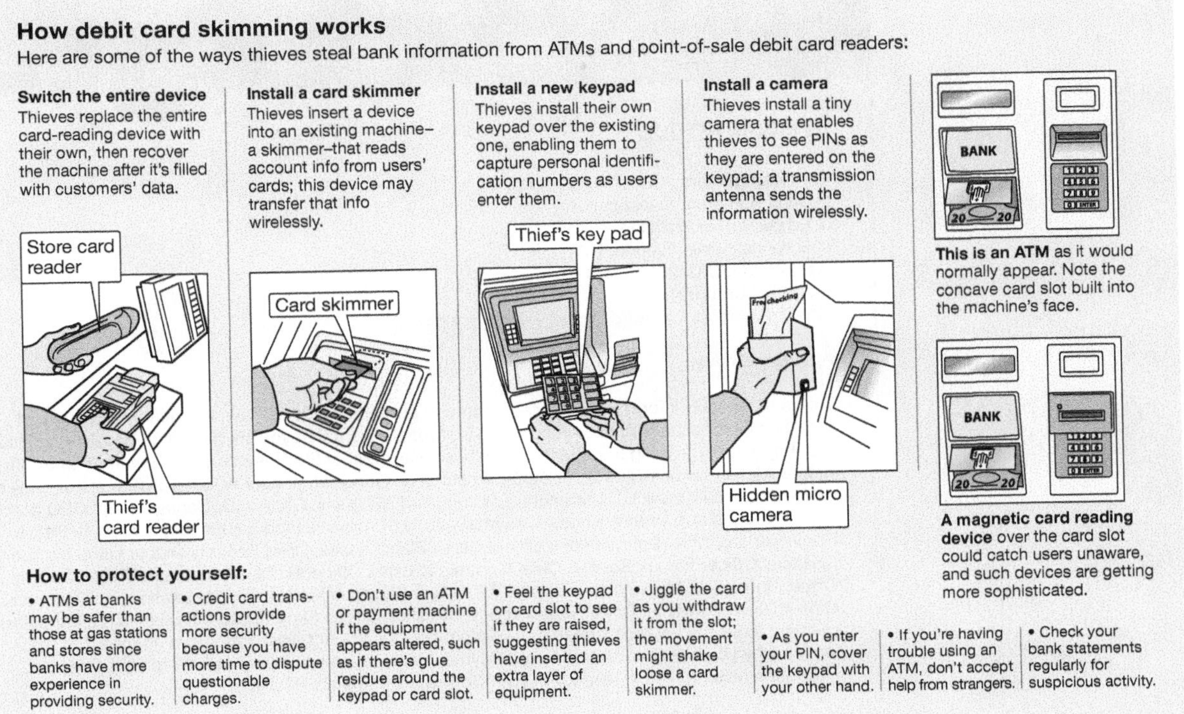

How debit card skimming works

Here are some of the ways thieves steal bank information from ATMs and point-of-sale debit card readers:

Switch the entire device
Thieves replace the entire card-reading device with their own, then recover the machine after it's filled with customers' data.

Store card reader

Thief's card reader

Install a card skimmer
Thieves insert a device into an existing machine— a skimmer—that reads account info from users' cards; this device may transfer that info wirelessly.

Card skimmer

Install a new keypad
Thieves install their own keypad over the existing one, enabling them to capture personal identification numbers as users enter them.

Thief's key pad

Install a camera
Thieves install a tiny camera that enables thieves to see PINs as they are entered on the keypad; a transmission antenna sends the information wirelessly.

Hidden micro camera

BANK

This is an ATM as it would normally appear. Note the concave card slot built into the machine's face.

BANK

A magnetic card reading device over the card slot could catch users unaware, and such devices are getting more sophisticated.

How to protect yourself:

- ATMs at banks may be safer than those at gas stations and stores since banks have more experience in providing security.
- Credit card transactions provide more security because you have more time to dispute questionable charges.
- Don't use an ATM or payment machine if the equipment appears altered, such as if there's glue residue around the keypad or card slot.
- Feel the keypad or card slot to see if they are raised, suggesting thieves have inserted an extra layer of equipment.
- Jiggle the card as you withdraw it from the slot; the movement might shake loose a card skimmer.
- As you enter your PIN, cover the keypad with your other hand.
- If you're having trouble using an ATM, don't accept help from strangers.
- Check your bank statements regularly for suspicious activity.

▲ **FIGURE 15-5　How debit card skimming works**
(Identitytheft911, Wells Fargo Bank, Los Altos [Calif.] Police Department, *San Jose Mercury News; Dallas Morning News*, October 20, 2010, p.21a.)

---

to the telephone line running between a business's legitimate card swipe and a telephone jack. During what appears to be a normal transaction, the skimmer reads and stores the data, which is retrieved later by the user. There are also portable skimmers through which waiters and clerks can run victims' cards while they are in the back of the restaurant. More difficult to detect is "skimmer bug" software that can be inserted into point-of-sale terminals. These bugs store the data read in the terminals' circuitry, and then the modem is used to send the data to the thieves' computers. Some banks have found dispensers filled with bank pamphlets attached to the side of their ATMs. What they discovered is that these thief-placed dispensers actually contain miniature cameras that record the names, debit card numbers, and codes of ATM users[29] (Figure 15-5).

15. Employing *card trappers*. One example of this involves attaching a false card slot to the front of the ATM. As legitimate users enter their codes, shoulder surfers wait nearby or use binoculars or a camera with a telephoto lens to get the accounts' access codes. Unable to retrieve their cards, custom-

ers leave the ATM, and the thieves have both the access codes and the ATM cards.[30]

16. Picking up discarded computers. From these, thieves recover sensitive files between 33% and 50% of the time.[31]

17. Sending a fraudulent letter and IRS-like form to nonresident aliens who have earned income in the United States. The form is an altered version of IRS Form W-8BEN, "Certificate of Foreign Status of Beneficial Owner for United States Tax Withholding." This form asks for many types of personal information and account numbers and passwords. United States citizens receive a similar phony IRS Form, W-9095, the intent of which is also identity theft.

18. An innovative and novel twist on sending a letter from the IRS, is the new scam-letter from the FBI that informs the recipient that they have been the "victim" of a fraud and that the FBI is investigating their case. The unsuspecting individual is then asked for important personal information on which further fraud and theft scams can be conducted. These letters can be received via e-mail or the postal mail and can be quite elaborate (Figure 15-6).

OFFICIAL NOTICE

FBI Headquarters in Washington, D.C.
Federal Bureau of Investigation
J. Edgar Hoover Building
935 Pennsylvania Avenue, NW
Washington, D.C. 20535-0001
Tel: 203-413-1789
http://www.fbi.gov/libref/directors/directmain.htm

Attn: Beneficiary,

This is to officially inform you that it has come to our notice and we have thoroughly investigated with the help of our Intelligence Monitoring Network System that you are having an illegal Transaction with Impostors Claiming to be Mr. Tito Mboweni Republic of the Reserve Bank Governor Of South African,Maria Ramos ABSA Bank CEO ,Christo Luus General Manager ABSA BANK, none officials of ABSA Bank, FNB Banks, Dr. Mamphela Ramphele FNB, Kevin Chaplin,Dr Danny Jordan CEO of the 2010 fifa world cup,Dr Irvin Khoza: Chairman, 2010 fifa organization committee, Joseph S. Blatter Fifa President, Chief Competitions Officer Derek Blanckensee, Chief Security Officer Linda Mti, Chief Financial Officer Farouk Seedat, Chief Communications Officer Richard Mkhondo, Chief Operations Officer Nomfanelo Magwentshu, Chief IT & T Officer Phumlani Moholi, Chief Marketing and Commercial Officer Derek Carstens, Chief Transport and Logistics Officer Skhumbuzo Macozoma,are Impostors claiming to be the Federal Bureau of Investigation. During our Investigation, we noticed that the reason why you have not received your Payment is because you have not fulfilled your Financial Obligation given to you in respect of your Contract/Inheritance Payment.

Therefore, we have contacted the Federal Ministry of Finance on your Behalf and they have brought a solution to your problem by coordinating your payment in total USD$11,000.000.00 in an ATM CARD which you can use to withdraw money from any ATM MACHINE CENTER anywhere in the world with a maximum of $4000 to $5000 United States Dollars daily. You now have the lawful right to claim your fund in an ATM CARD. Since the Federal Bureau of Investigation is involved in this transaction, you have to be rest assured for this is 100% risk free it is our duty to protect the American Citizens, European Citizens, Asian Citizen and UK. All I want you to do is to contact the ATM CARD CENTER Via email for their requirements to proceed and procure your Approval Slip on your behalf which will cost you $300.00 only and note that your Approval Slip which contains details of the agent who will process your Transaction.

CONTACT INFORMATION
NAME: Mrs. Michelle Isaac
EMAIL: mrsmichelleisaac@yahoo.cn
Telephone Numbers: + 27 730-385-679

Do contact Mrs. Michelle Isaac of the ATM CARD center with your details:
FULL NAME:
HOME ADDRESS:
TELL:
CELL:
CURRENT OCCUPATION:
BANK NAME:

So your files would be updated after which he will send the payment Information's which you'll use in making payment of $300.00 via Money Gram

▲ FIGURE 15-6   Scam-letter
A scam-letter can be very sophisticated. Note the "official notice," the seal of the FBI taken from their website, and the picture of Robert Mueller. Most interesting is the "note" attached to the letter that informs the receiver to forward any "impostors" to the official FBI "ATM Card Center."

Transfer for the procurement of your Approval Slip after which the Delivery of your ATM CARD will be affected to your designated home Address without any further delay. Mrs. Michelle Isaac will reply you with the secret code (3898 ATM CARD).

We advice you get back to the payment office after you have contacted the ATM SWIFT CARD CENTER and we do await your response so we can move on with our Investigation and make sure your ATM SWIFT CARD gets to you. Thanks and hope to read from you soon.

FBI Director Robert S.Mueller III.

Robert S. Mueller, III
Director
Since *September 4, 2001–Present*

Note: Do disregard any email you get from any impostors or offices Claiming to be in possession of your ATM CARD, you are hereby advised only to be in contact with Mrs. Michelle Isaac of the ATM CARD center who is the rightful person to deal with in regards to your ATM CARD PAYMENT and forward any emails you get from impostors to this office so we could act upon and commence investigation.

▲ **FIGURE 15-6   Scam-letter (*concluded*)**

19. Calling a home and telling the person that because he or she failed to come to court as required by "the jury duty summons sent to their residence" that the judge is going to issue a bench warrant for his/her arrest. When the panicked recipient of the calls insists no such summons was sent, the "Clerk of the Court" says "perhaps there has been a mistake, let's verify some information" and gets enough personal information to commit identity theft.

20. Offering "debt consolidation" services by phone, promising the unwary that by working with the holders of their credit cards, they can immediately get up to 50% of their debt immediately forgiven, and the one remaining monthly payment "will be less than 20% of the total you are paying now; all I need to get you started right now is your credit card numbers."

21. In yet another scheme, scammers are stealing Social Security numbers assigned to children who do not have bank accounts. The stolen Social Security numbers are then used to develop phony credit profiles, credit cards, bank accounts, and identification. Thieves run up huge debts that will never be paid off. These schemes unfortunately are quite successful and go undetected for long periods of time, until the rightful owner of the Social Security number applies for credit; if that person is a child, it may be years before the scheme is ever detected.

The U.S. Department of Education's (USDOE) Office of Inspector General reports that some students are receiving calls from people falsely claiming that they represent USDOE and offering them scholarships or grants. This financial assistance can be immediately obtained for a $249 processing fee that the student can pay with their credit card number. The USDOE does not charge a processing fee for financial assistance.[32]

FOLLOW-ON CRIMES

Once armed with enough stolen personal identification data, the process of identity theft is executed and follow-on crimes are committed by:

1. Calling credit card companies, asking them to change the address "your" bill is mailed to and quickly running up charges on accounts. The victim

may be unaware of any problems for a month or more. This practice is called **account takeover.**

2. Opening up new, fraudulent, credit card accounts using the victim's name, banking information, Social Security information, and other data. The first hint of trouble for a victim may be when a card company or collection agency calls because the "account" is in serious arrears.

3. Establishing new accounts for wireless telephone service, which go unpaid.

4. Opening bank accounts on which they write worthless checks.

5. Using counterfeit checks and debit cards to drain victims' banking accounts.

6. Purchasing cars by taking out loans using the victim's name, defaulting on payments and then fleeing with what is now a stolen vehicle.

7. Using the victim's identity if involved in an automobile accident, stopped for a traffic violation, or arrested by the police. If released by the police or bonded out of jail following an arrest, they don't show up for any required court appearance and an arrest warrant is issued in the victim's name.[33]

8. Fraudulently obtaining other types of identification, including passports, drivers' licenses, Department of Defense cards, and Social Security numbers.

9. Committing mail, investment, telemarketing, and Social Security frauds.

From the preceding list, three main patterns of identity theft can be established: (1) financial identity theft, when the thief uses the information for financial gain; (2) criminal identity theft, whereby the imposter provides someone else's name to law-enforcement officers issuing a traffic citation or conducting a criminal investigation; and (3) identity cloning, which permits the thief to establish a "new life."[34] In Chapter 7, the use of visual link analysis software was discussed and an application of it shown. Figure 15-7 demonstrates the use of this technique applied to an identity theft. In terms of main patterns of identity

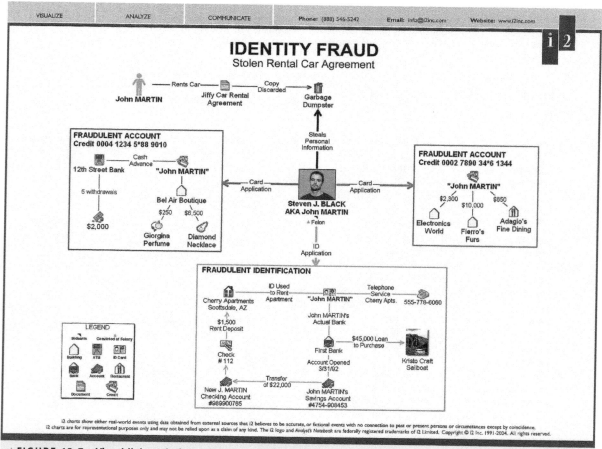

▲ **FIGURE 15-7** Visual link analysis applied to identity theft case

theft, the thief, Steven Black, is involved with two patterns: (1) financial identity theft and (2) establishing a "new life."

INVESTIGATION OF IDENTITY THEFT AND FOLLOW-ON CASES

From an investigatory view, the co-entwining of identity theft and follow-on crimes almost invariably means investigating multiple crimes, with a number of victims. Additionally, these crimes may be committed in many different jurisdictions, requiring careful case coordination and information sharing among the investigative agencies involved. All states and the District of Columbia have specific identity theft statutes;[35] Federal jurisdiction comes from United States Code, Title 18, Section 1028, The Identity Theft and Assumption Deterrence Act of 1998. This means there is often joint jurisdiction in identity theft cases. Depending on the nature and the specifics of the case, federal agencies with which state and local investigators may work include the FBI, the Secret Service, the Social Security Administration, the Post Office, and Homeland Security. In deciding whether there will be federal or state jurisdiction, one consideration will be the level of seriousness and extent of harm, with the most flagrant cases often becoming the responsibility of the jurisdiction with the most substantial criminal penalties.

Figure 15-8 summarizes how personal information is obtained by identity thieves. Note that the "big three," which account for more than 50% of cases, are lost/stolen wallet, checkbook, or credit card; friends/acquaintances/relatives with access; and corrupt employees with access

to the information. Unless the available information dictates otherwise, the big three may initially provide fruitful avenues for the investigation. Eighty-five percent of victims report that their first realization about the theft comes from a negative contact[36] (for example, a credit card company soliciting payment of past due amounts) or a collection agency. This means investigators are responding to calls where victims are angry, confused, and worried about their financial futures and personal reputations. Another immediate difficulty for the investigator is that most identity thefts and the follow-up crimes come to light only one to six months after they began,[37] meaning that victims' recollections about how and when the identity theft occurred may not be very helpful and that documentary evidence is of vital importance in working the case.

Figure 15-9 is an identity theft and follow-on crimes checklist, with emphasis on the unique types of determinations which need to be made.

CREDIT CARD FRAUD

The link between identity theft and credit card fraud was established earlier in this chapter. However, there are also other types of credit card frauds. Altogether these frauds create losses of $2 billion globally according to the Federal Trade Commission. Credit card fraud is particularly prevalent in this country because Americans hold 71% of all credit cards issued worldwide.[38] Credit card fraud has become so lucrative that some organized crime rings and drug dealers have shifted their "careers" to engage in it because it is simple to execute and quickly

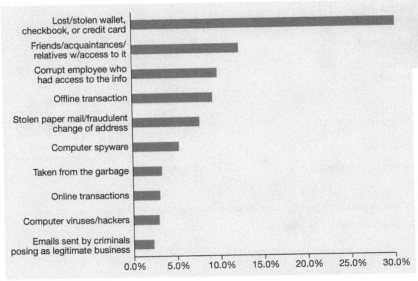

◀ FIGURE 15-8
How was victim's personal information obtained?
(© 2005 Javelin Strategy & Research)

Completed	Task	Completed	Task
	How did victim become aware of identity theft?		Opening utility/phone accounts in victim's name?
———	Fraudulent charges on credit card bill(s)	———	Unauthorized withdrawals from victim's bank accounts?
———	Received bills for accounts not opened		
———	Found irregularities in credit report	———	Loans taken out in victim's name?
———	Contacted by creditor demanding payment	———	Access to/withdrawals from securities/investments accounts?
———	Denied a loan		
———	Sued for debt victim did not incur	———	Obtaining government benefits in victim's name?
———	Not receiving bills from legitimate accounts	———	Obtaining employment in victim's name?
———	Received legal filing, such as bankruptcy	———	Obtaining medical services or insurance in victim's name?
———	Denied employment		
———	Driver's license suspended for violations not committed	———	Committing crimes attributed to victim?
		———	Check fraud?
———	Incident report completed naming victim as suspect	———	Passport/Visa fraud?
		———	Other (specify).
———	Victim advised of warrant or arrested		
———	Other (specify): _____		*To assist in pinpointing when and by whom ID was stolen or compromised, determine whether in the last 6 months if:*
———	What date did victim become aware of ID theft?		
———	When reported? Explain any gaps.	———	Victim carried social security daily.
———	When did the first fraudulent activity begin?	———	Kept PINs and passwords in wallet or purse.
———	What is the presently known chronology of fraudulent activities?	———	Had mail stolen. What? When? Get any reports.
		———	While away, mail kept at Post Office/collected by someone else.
———	Assign victim the responsibility for describing in as much detail as possible activities associated with all fraudulent activities.		
		———	Traveled on business or pleasure outside of home vicinity. When? Where?
———	What is the full name, address, birth date, and other identifying information that the fraudulent activities were committed under?	———	Mail diverted by forwarding request to Post Office or in a way unknown to the victim.
		———	Expected new credit card which did not arrive. Get particulars. Issuer contacted by victim? Report made?
———	What documents and identifying information were stolen or compromised? If known, when?		
———	Credit card: list banks, contact information, and account numbers.	———	Garbage was stolen or gone through.
		———	Left stamped payment bills in unlocked mailbox.
———	ATM card: contact information and account numbers.	———	Service providers (maids, delivery, electricians, etc.) in home.
———	Get voided check or checking account number, bank info, and contact information.	———	Placed documents with personal information in garbage without shredding—e.g., envelopes with victim's name on them, bank statements, payroll stubs.
———	Brokerage and/or stock account numbers: who holds accounts, contact information.		
———	Passport: obtain all relevant information, including country issuing.	———	Placed pre-approved credit cards and "convenience" checks in garbage without shredding.
———	Driver's license or license number; state issuing.		
———	State identity card: number, state issuing.	———	Threw ATM and credit card receipts away without shredding.
———	Social Security card or number, get number.	———	Shared PIN and password information with someone else.
———	Birth certificate (identify state and locality issuing), number.	———	Home/office/car burglarized? When? Reported? If not, why?
———	Resident alien green card or other documents, get all particulars.	———	Checkbook, wallet, purse stolen.
———	Bank and other account password/secret word, such as mother's maiden name.	———	Provided personal information to service providers—e.g., blood collection agency, financial adviser, took out auto/health/life insurance. Identify, get details.
———	Other (specify).		
———	Unknown.	———	Copy of credit report issued to someone claiming a legitimate business interest or using victim's name.
	To the best of the victim's knowledge, what crimes have been committed?		
———	Use of victim's actual credit cards or numbers without authorization?		
———	Opening new credit card accounts in victim's name?		

continued

FIGURE 15-9   Identity theft/follow-on crimes checklist

Completed	Task	Completed	Task
_____	Victim authorized a business to obtain credit report information. Which? When?	_____	What information does the victim have about the suspects?
_____	Some personal information was available on the Net—e.g., genealogy or school reunion site.	_____	Run records checks on suspects identified by victim.
_____	Gave personal information to telephone solicitor, telemarketer, "government worker" working door-to-door, charitable organization, entered contest, or to claim prize supposedly won.	_____	Have the victim list all banks which have legitimate accounts, identify accounts which have fraudulent activities.
_____	Made legitimate purchase, but clerk was out of sight with card during transaction.	_____	Have the victim list all legitimate credit card companies and banks which have issued credit cards, identify those with fraudulent activities.
_____	A new credit card account was just opened by the victim.	_____	Have victim specify all legitimate utility company accounts, identify those with fraudulent activities.
_____	Victim's home/property was refinanced.	_____	Have victim identify all legitimate loans, leases, and mortgages, list those with fraudulent activities.
_____	Victim provided information to obtain lease.		
_____	Victim opened new utility account(s).	_____	Have victim list all merchants with whom he/she has a store credit account—e.g., pharmacies and department stores. List all fraudulent activities.
_____	Victim applied for occupational or other license or permit.	_____	Have victim list all financial institutions where fraudulent accounts were opened.
_____	Victim took out new loan or finished paying one.		
_____	Victim applied for government benefits.	_____	Victim should list all fraudulent documents obtained in his/her name.
_____	Victim was featured in local paper, industry publications, on Internet, school site.	_____	Provide assistance to the victim by suggesting he/she contact the three major credit reporting companies, Equifax, TransUnion, and Experian, as well as financial institutions, the Department of Motor Vehicles, Social Security, and other entities. Victim should do this immediately by phone and follow up within 48 hours with letters, asking for return receipts.
_____	Online purchases were made using victim's credit card.		
_____	Released information to family member/friend.		
_____	Over the past 6 months, what purchases did the victim make from which sites, when, and for what merchandise?		
_____	Have the victim list all persons, businesses, nonprofits, or others to which he/she provided Social Security number.	_____	Provide any agency ID Theft Victim Assistant packages available. This information should include web addresses, such as the one at the Federal Trade Commission, which provides detailed guidance and sample forms and letters to use. Advise victim to log and carefully file all correspondence and return receipts from the Post Office.
_____	Does the victim have his/her Social Security number imprinted on checks?		
_____	Get a list of all places such checks were tendered.		
_____	Has victim or others written his/her Social Security and driver's license numbers on checks tendered? List all such instances.		
_____	Are identity crimes affecting the victim's business?		
_____	Whom does the victim identify as possible suspects? For what reasons?		

(Source: This information was adapted from content on an undated "Identity Theft" compact disk prepared by the Secret Service, United States Postal Inspection Service, and the International Association of Chiefs of Police.)

▲ **FIGURE 15-9   Identity theft/follow-on crimes checklist** (*concluded*)

profitable.[39] Figure 15-10 illustrates a credit card fraud which simply involves the illegal use of the victim's credit card.

The quickest exact growing sector of credit card fraud may be the counterfeiting of credit cards; the continuing availability of new technologies has helped counterfeiters produce exact replicas of bona-fide cards, including the so-called "hidden" security features, such as holograms, used by legitimate credit card issuers.[40] One source of the necessary equipment is the Far East; another is corrupt vendors. A Canadian vendor was arrested for supplying equipment to thieves and terrorist organizations as part of a multimillion dollar credit and debit card ring.[41] In the advanced payment scheme, the accounts created by credit cards that were obtained through yet-to-be detected thefts, identity theft, or counterfeiting are overpaid by the "card holder," with a bad check. The money is then quickly withdrawn by a cash advance before the check clears the bank. There are also other scams associated with credit cards. In the advanced fee scheme, a person with poor credit pays in advance to have their record "repaired." Other variants of advanced fee schemes involve victims paying by credit card to have a company find them new jobs, work-at-home employment (such as stuffing envelopes), scholarships, and low-cost car or other loans. These offers may appear in newspaper ads, be delivered by the postal service, or appear in the victim's e-mail inbox. Once victims have been taken in by a credit card or other type of fraud, criminals compile lists with their names to sell to other defrauders, including those who contact the victims with an offer to recover their lost assets.

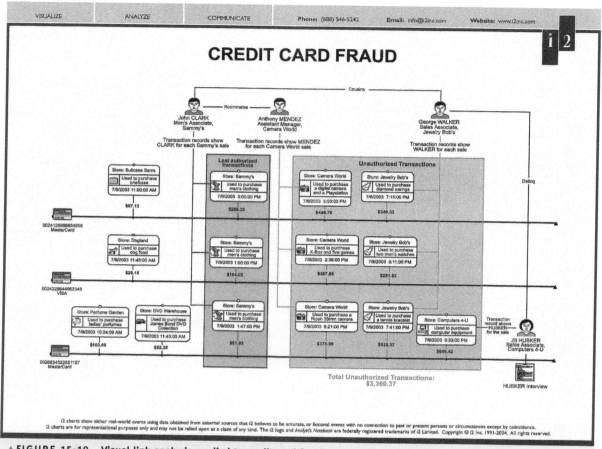

▲ FIGURE 15-10   Visual link analysis applied to credit card fraud
(© i2 Incorporated, 1991–2004. All rights reserved.)

CHECK FRAUD

Check fraud (Figure 15-11) is the forgery, alteration, counterfeiting, or knowing issuance of a check on an account that is closed or has insufficient funds to cover the amount for which the check is written.[42] People may innocently "bounce" a check because of nonsufficient funds owing to a math error in their checkbook or mistiming a deposit. Investigation and prosecution rarely happen, because the check is made good, and the necessary fees are paid.

Others write checks they know are no good and cannot cover; people leaving one state for another may write a bad check because they think there is no consequence; and others write checks on accounts they or others have closed. **Check kiters** open accounts at several banks, knowingly, issuing a check that overdraws their account at Bank 1 and then depositing a check in that account from their Bank 2 account to cover the first worthless check.

This process is repeated with ever-increasing amounts until the scheme falls apart because it cannot be continued indefinitely. An employee with the standing authority to issue checks may sign unauthorized checks or forge the manager's or owner's signature. Among the signs that an employee in a position of trust such as bookkeeper or business manager may be or is committing check based crimes are these:

1. checks made payable to the business or to cash by customers are deposited in an account the employee controls;
2. replacement checks to the employee are issued when there is no need to do so, for example, the original check was not lost;
3. payroll advances to the employee are not subtracted from the next paycheck;
4. there is no documentation explaining why checks are made payable to "Cash" or what happened to them;

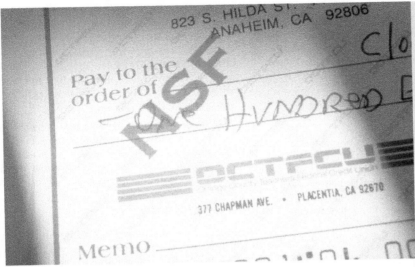

◄FIGURE 15-11
NSF stamped check
For one reason or another, 40% of all Americans are without a credit card and are totally dependent on paying bills with a written check. With an estimated 30 billion checks written annually, it is remarkable that only an estimated 1.2 million checks were not honored owing to "not sufficient funds" (NSF). NSF checks that are not made good are often sold to collection agencies for 80% or more of their face value. NSF checks are "bad checks," and the issuer may be subject to criminal charges, which may be a misdemeanor or a felony, depending on the amount for which the check was written. The amount separating these charges varies from one state to another. (© Tony Freeman/PhotoEdit)

5. the employee is reimbursed for unexplained expenses;
6. the employee keeps promising to show the business owner the bank statements, but it never seems to happen;
7. vendors and suppliers are complaining about slow and late payments.

Altogether, check fraud produces losses of some $24 billion annually,[43] and in addition to the practices previously described, others involve more sophisticated techniques. In one, an individual learns that he/she has gotten a job applied for online, which offers "signing bonuses" of $2,500 or more to "new hires." The "new employer" advises the "employee" that by mistake a larger amount in the $19,000 to $50,000 range has been sent to the employee, who is instructed to keep the signing bonus but wire the remaining funds to the employer, often at a European location. Of course, the job doesn't really exist, and the check sent by "mistake" is fraudulent. Because the "new employee" deposited the check originally, it is his/her responsibility to make it good. A wrinkle on this technique is when someone shows up to buy a car or other large-ticket item with a counterfeit cashier's check from a bank or a credit union that was "made out for too much," and the unsuspecting seller not only gives the buyer a check for the difference but also allows the suspect to drive off with the car, which may be quickly sold, creating an additional profit for the suspect. Very good counterfeit checks can be produced by using around $10,000 to purchase a computer system and software. It is estimated that counterfeit checks account for about $1 billion in annual losses.

Checks can be altered by washing them in commonly available chemicals and then dried with little damage to the checks. This process removes ink from the check. The checks can then be scanned into a computer, many copies can quickly be printed, and the checks cashed for the amounts desired by the "payees," who are in on the scheme and may be using identification obtained through identity theft.

Listed below are some of the indicators that a check has been altered or counterfeited:

• There is no perforated edge; most checks should have perforation on one edge.
• The routing and fractional routing numbers are inconsistent and/or do not match the location of the bank listed on the check.
• The check contains spots or stains.
• The word "VOID" appears.

COUNTERFEITING

Although we most often associate counterfeiting with currency, there is a vast range of other types of counterfeiting, including stamps, checks, bonds, and securities, as well as ski lift, sporting event, rodeo, and concert tickets. None of these are just-emerging crimes; the 1966 Beatles concert in Cleveland was plagued with this problem.

Gangs counterfeiting Universal Product Codes (UPC) have been operating a number of years. UPC codes help with inventory control and proper pricing at the point of sale where cashiers scan in the price. In particular Wal-Mart, Lowe's, and Home Depot have been hard-hit, with

Wal-Mart's losses reaching $1.5 million.[44] The modus operandi was to counterfeit UPCs in large numbers at print shops or by using personal computers, enter the stores and affix these UPCs over real ones, thereby lowering the price of the item that would be scanned in at the point of sale:

A kitchen faucet worth $169 would suddenly wear a UPC code indicating the price to be $39 or a lighting fixture's price would shift from $249 to $55.[45] Later the same day at a different location for the same retailer, another person would show up—with the phony UPC removed—and get a refund for the actual amount; doing this several times per day easily netted $1,000 to $1,500 daily. False identifications were presented at the refund counter, including English or Irish passports.[46]

FRAUDS, SCAMS, AND CONS

The economic turndown and resulting recession since 2008 has heralded a new wave of frauds, scams, and cons. While the largest of these frauds involved investment and "Ponzi" schemes (discussed later in this chapter), a notable rise in not only the individual number but also the financial losses associated with fraud has been reported.[47] Losses ranged from a few hundred dollars attributed to classic charity cons to over $150 million dollars associated with the largest Medicare fraud in history.

VENDOR FRAUD

Virtually every unit of government and business are dependent on outside vendors who supply such things as office supplies, equipment, vehicles, merchandise for retail, and consulting services. Vendor fraud costs businesses more than $400 billion in losses annually. Among the fraudulent practices used by vendors are these:

1. Bidders colluding to set bids at a higher than warranted price per unit and bidders concealing they are insolvent or have a record of defaulting on their bids.
2. Providing employees in the procurement office with cash and other types of bribes, such as trips in exchange for being the winning bidder.
3. Substituting lower-costing or counterfeit goods to fulfill the terms of a bid.
4. Consultants or contractors overstating the number of days worked or the amount of materials required to do the job.
5. Submitting bogus invoices for office supplies or other goods in the hope they will be paid.

6. Bogus Yellow Page advertising. In the minds of most people the "Yellow Pages" are legitimate ads in the local telephone directory; however, because the phrase was never copyrighted or registered others can use it. Fraudsters may offer "yellow page" advertising and either produce just a few one-page copies for the subscribers or simply abscond with the money.

In large corporations, these crimes may be investigated internally and the information turned over to the police, or the police may be invited in at an earlier stage. In units of government, the agency having jurisdiction will investigate instances of criminal fraud by bidders.

CHARITY AND DISASTER FRAUDS

There are some 70,000 charities. Unfortunately, a very small number are frauds and create two types of problems: (1) people are scammed out of their money and do not get a tax deduction, and (2) public confidence in charities is undermined, making it harder for legitimate charities to raise funds for important causes. Sham charities are skillful at their pitches, using words that suggest good causes; included are terms such as veterans, hunger, children, and orphans. They also often use names that are similar to those of legitimate charities and religious organizations. These pitches are made in person at homes, with buckets at intersections, through the mail, and Internet solicitations. In the aftermath of the 9/11 attacks (2001), the earthquakes in Turkey (2004), the Indian Ocean Tsunami (2004), and Hurricanes Katrina (2005) and Earl (2010), sham charities used the tragic events to line their pockets.

INSURANCE FRAUD

Insurance frauds can be **hard fraud** or **soft fraud**.[48] Hard fraud is when someone deliberately fakes an injury, accident, theft, arson, or other loss to illegally collect from insurance companies.

Virgil made a car collision insurance claim, stating that he had been trying to avoid a deer and crashed into a wall. The insurer deemed the car a total loss, and the claim was paid. Later, the insurance company learned that Virgil's son Brian was driving the car even though he was not covered by the policy. Both were arrested on one felony count of insurance fraud.[49]

In contrast, soft fraud, also called opportunity fraud, involves normally honest people who tell "little white lies" and collect reimbursements to which they are not entitled, as in the case when the value of the items reported stolen in burglary is overstated. Too, insurance companies have been known to scam insurers by charging them more than is warranted or declaring bankruptcy and going out of business when faced with a flood of claims they cannot pay following a natural disaster. Other types of insurance frauds are discussed next.

Arson Fraud

Chapter 19, "Arson and Explosives," addresses arson fraud. Here, a case is offered because it illustrates the point that such frauds can go tragically wrong.

> Helen hired two local teenagers to "torch" her Tampa restaurant, Gram's County Kitchen, so she could collect insurance money. However, fumes from the gasoline the teenagers poured in the restaurant accidentally ignited, causing an explosion. One died and the other was permanently scarred.[50]

Automobile Fraud

One source of automobile fraud is staged accidents, which include the **swoop and squat,** the **drive down,** and the **paper accident.** In the swoop and squat, a car quickly cuts in front of a legitimate motorist, hits the brakes, and creates a rear-end collision for which repair and fake medical claims can be made (Figure 15-12). The drive down involves waving to another driver to go ahead and make a turn in the intersection or elsewhere and then driving into the car, making it appear that the struck vehicle is at fault. Paper accidents are exactly that: no

accident has taken place. Collusion is required by a body shop operator, who may even provide a wrecked car for the adjuster to inspect. By only filing for the cost of repairs, which are not done, the amount paid by the insurance is not out of line and therefore not scrutinized closely. Naturally, the insured and the body shop owner split the money for the repairs. Owners who cannot make their car payments, which often involve luxury cars, arrange to have them stolen, and the insurance pays for the car. Then the car is sent to a chop shop. The owner protects his/her credit record and receives some money from the chop shop profit. To make false claims of injuries in accidents believable, the collusion of a doctor is necessary. In one very aggressive case, a chiropractor had "runners" out scouting for accidents and recruiting people to his practice, where false treatment bills were submitted to insurers and false medical records were created to submit to insurance companies.

HEALTH-CARE AND MEDICARE FRAUD

Annual health-care costs are estimated to be $2.2 trillion; the magnitude of spending is a magnet for fraud.[51] Estimates of the dollar loss attributable to fraud range from 3%–14% of annual expenditures.[52] The most commonly affected agencies in health-care fraud are two federal programs: (1) Medicare, which provides comprehensive care for the disabled and people 65 or older, and (2) Medicaid, a provider of services for low-income people.[53]

Perhaps the most common health-care fraud scheme is billing for services never provided. This is done by making claims for services, equipment, and tests not actually rendered, by filing claims for tests on patients who had, but did not show up, for appointments or by using

◄**FIGURE 15-12**
The classic "swoop and squat" auto accident fraud occurs when the perpetrator rapidly pulls in front of a car and then hits the brakes. The victim vehicle then rear-ends the other car, after which significant medical and auto damages are claimed. The victims of these types of crimes often drive more expensive makes, such as Mercedes-Benz, BMW, Porsche, Cadillac, and the like.
(© Christof R. Schmidt/F1 Online/Photolibrary)

patient information to file entirely fictitious claims.[54] Other fraud methods used by medical providers:

1. Filing duplicate claims.
2. "Upcoding" or using billing codes for more expensive tests or longer office visits than actually occurred.
3. "Unbundling charges," which is the practice of charging separately for each component of service. This produces a greater claim than if the service was properly billed as one single charge.
4. Misrepresenting the diagnosis in order to get paid for services not covered by the health plan or to charge for costly tests not actually provided.
5. Performing unnecessary tests;[55] a Massachusetts orthopedic surgeon routinely gave patients potentially harmful X rays and steroid injections they didn't need so he could falsely bill Medicaid. In less than three years, one patient was X rayed 74 times and given steroid injections on 112 occasions.[56]
6. Billing using the names of people who are deceased.
7. Charging for home health aide visits which were not made.

Others involved in health-care fraud are employers and employees. Employers may enroll employees who are actually not eligible in plans or change the dates of employment or termination to expand the dates of coverage. Members enrolled in health plans may alter the documents they submit in order to get a greater reimbursement than they are entitled to or to let someone else use their plan identification to obtain services.[57] An often overlooked effect for many types of medical fraud is that a person may end up with a false medical history, which may affect their ability to get life insurance or alter how they are subsequently treated medically.

Schemes to defraud the Medicare system are not limited to unscrupulous employees and medical providers. In 2009 alone, federal investigators uncovered over 2,000 cases of healthcare-related fraud[58]—with a portion of these perpetrated by organized criminal enterprises. In 2010 investigators exposed a massive fraudulent billing scheme perpetrated by an Armenian-American organized crime ring known as the Mirzoyan-Terdjanian Organization. The scam, dubbed "Diagnosis Dollars," involved more than 73 individuals working in conjunction across the United States to defraud the system out of $163 million dollars. The group not only opened over 120 fake clinics, they also stole the identities of Medicare beneficiaries and healthcare providers, frequently opening bank accounts in the names of the doctors whose identities were stolen.[59] To date, it was the largest Medicare fraud scheme ever perpetrated by a single criminal enterprise and represents the vulnerability of not only Medicare, but other American financial systems (for example, Social Security, State welfare programs, food stamp programs, unemployment systems) that may be compromised from an organized attack (Figure 15-13).

The Mirzoyan-Terdjanian Organization represented a very sophisticated and select group of high-level criminal from the former Soviet Union. The primary leader, Armen Kazarian was identified as a leading member of the "Vory v Zakone," a term that means "thief-in-law" and refers to members of the Russian organized crime cartel composed of former members of the secret police and intelligence agency (KGB) of the Soviet Union, popularized by the 2007 hit movie, *Eastern Promises*.

The Food and Drug Administration (FDA) identifies another type of health-care fraud: "It is the deceptive promotion, advertising, distribution, or sale of articles represented as being effective to diagnose, prevent, cure,

► FIGURE 15-13
Investigators discuss the complexities of the largest Medicare fraud in history, resulting in the arrest of 73 individuals, some connected to the "Vory v Zakone" or Russian Mafia. (© New York Daily News Archive/Getty Images)

treat, or mitigate an illness or condition, or provide a beneficial effect on health, but has not been scientifically proven safe and effective for such purposes."[60] Products identified as such by the FDA may also cause serious health problems. Some of these products are counterfeit drugs with no therapeutic value; others claim they can produce rapid weight loss, or cure skin cancer, Alzheimer's disease, rheumatism, hardening of the arteries, diabetes, improve virility, and eliminate gangrene and prostate problems.

WORKERS COMPENSATION FRAUD

The most common worker compensation fraudulent claim is when people falsely claim that they were injured on the job. They may have actually been injured while away from the job, faked the injury while working, or have an actual injury about which they report exaggerated symptoms. In New York, 18 people, including several teachers and a chiropractor, were arrested for defrauding the workers compensation system out of $550,000, because they were seen working other jobs while receiving benefits.[61] In addition to state workers compensation agencies being defrauded, cases may also involve insurance companies providing disability coverage.

MORTGAGE FRAUD

An array of fraudulent practices related to the real estate and mortgage industry have also been recently exposed. According to the Federal Bureau of Investigation, mortgage fraud schemes typically involve misrepresentations, false statements, or exclusions related to the property or the prospective buyer. These often take form as inflated appraisals, false loan applications, kickbacks, and straw buyers which are manifested in reverse mortgage and foreclosure rescue schemes, illegal property flipping, builder bailout scams, and air loans.[62]

Investigators are often made aware of these schemes through Suspicious Activity Reports (SAR) provided by federally funded banks and other financial institutions. The information in SARs can supply officials with leads to direct their investigations.[63] Additionally, the Federal Bureau of Investigation created the Financial Intelligence Center (FIC) to boost investigations of alleged mortgage fraud. Through the use of various technologies and data exploitations tactics, the FIC provides analyses of intelligence and financial databases.[64] Task forces comprised of federal, state, and local law-enforcement agencies also exist in "high-threat" locations and are utilized in the effort to combat mortgage fraud schemes.[65]

HOME IMPROVEMENT AND REPAIR FRAUDS

Common home improvement and repair scams include unneeded roofing, gutter, plumbing, chimney, or other repairs or replacements; paving driveways with a thin surface that quickly cracks; using materials and methods that do not meet local building codes; substituting cheap paint for higher-quality paint; not replacing rotted or missing decking when roofing; charging for more expensive shingles or for more bundles of shingles than were actually used, or not replacing valley gutters and shingles in places that are hard for the owner to see; using whitewash instead of paint; and "free" home, furnace, or other inspections that turn up "serious problems." Often, the "inspector" causes the damage that needs to then be repaired. These scams are usually worked going door-to-door using high-pressure sales and scare tactics, particularly with older people. Mention may be made that they just finished a job "nearby" and have leftover materials so "I can make you a good deal." Representations will be made that "we are having a sale and I can knock 20% off of the bottom line," although the actual price is never specified. The "vendor" usually refuses to provide a written estimate or contract and evades giving information about the location of his business. Natural disasters, including tornados, hurricanes, floods, and mud slides often bring out packs of repair scammers who prey on people desperate to get their lives back in order.

These scam artists often ask for a down payment or the whole amount and are never seen again; do the work in a substandard manner or not at all; or urge the victim to make temporary repairs that are poorly done when more substantial work is needed, only worsening a problem.

The Federal Trade Commission recommends dealing only with licensed and insured contractors, checking references and consumer affairs agencies for complaints about the vendor, getting recommendations from family, friends, and coworkers who have used contractors, not doing business with door-to-door solicitors, obtaining several bids from reputable contractors, and not using homes as financing collateral because owners may end up losing them.

INTERNET FRAUDS AND SCAMS

The fastest growing area of theft and larceny involves the myriad of frauds and scam on the Internet. These range from the common, unsolicited Nigerian 419 scams and "lottery winner" e-mails that almost everyone who has ever used the Internet has received, to the more sophisticated auction frauds that now threaten legitimate corporations such as eBay, PayPal, and Western Union. According to the Internet Crime Complaint Center (IC3) website, complaint submissions increased 33% in 2008 and estimates for 2009 approach another 30% increase from the previous year. The Internet Crime Complaint Center (IC3) is a unique partnership between the FBI, the National White Collar Crime Center (NW3C), and the Bureau of Justice. Its primary purpose is to serve as a vehicle to receive, develop, and refer criminal complaints regarding the rapidly growing area of cybercrime.[66] Cybercrime is specifically addressed in Chapter 17; however, this section discusses the various larceny and fraud crimes stemming from Internet use.

IC3 reports that **auction fraud** (including nondelivery of merchandise and/or payment) was by far the most reported Internet offense in 2008 and 2009, accounting for over 58% of referred complaints. Auction fraud involves the misrepresentations of a product advertised for sale through an Internet auction site or the nondelivery of products purchase through an Internet auction site.[67] These types of crimes commonly fall within three broad categories:

- **Overpayment fraud** targets the seller. A seller advertises a high-value item—such as a car or a computer—on the Internet. A scammer contacts the seller to purchase the item, then sends the seller a counterfeit check or money order for an amount greater than the price of the item. The purchaser asks the seller to deposit the payment, deduct the actual sale price, and then return the difference to the purchaser.
- **Wire-transfer schemes** start with fraudulent and misleading ads for the sale of high-value items being posted on well-known online auction sites. When buyers take the bait, they are directed to wire money to the crooks using a money transfer company. Once the money changes hands, the buyer never hears from them again.
- **Second-chance schemes** involve scammers who offer losing bidders of legitimate auctions the opportunity to buy the item(s) they wanted at reduced prices. They usually require that victims send payment through money transfer companies, but then don't follow through on delivery.[68]

Many of these auction frauds are committed by perpetrators living in a foreign country, such as South Africa or Romania. Consumers should exercise extreme caution when the seller posts the auction as if he resides in the United States, but then responds to the victim outside the United States. The perpetrators almost always request that funds be wired directly to him or her via Western Union, MoneyGram, or bank-to-bank wire transfer to addresses outside the United States. These services have virtually no recoverable recourse and sadly, provide dead-end leads for local police investigators. Finally, consumers should be wary if the deal "sounds too good to be true." Unfortunately, it usually is! Local police investigators should make sure that the victim files a complaint with the IC3, as well as provides security alerts to eBay or PayPal, if those sites were involved. Each provides a strong security alert and fraud prevention program as well as a list of "tips" for would-be buyers.[69] A common auction fraud report, filed in August 2010 is as follows:

I was sold a stolen vehicle on eBay. The seller indicated that he had recently moved to South Africa to start a new business and that he "had to sell his relatively new Beemer" for $10,000. I thought it was a great deal, so I wired the money to the seller (in South Africa) after checking him out on the Internet. He indeed had a number of business listed worldwide and a new one on his website in South Africa. I sent the money via Western Union, because I did not want to pay the state sales tax and I figured that the deal would go through, since the car was being shipped from Houston and I lived in Dallas, not even two hundred miles away. When I received the "bill of sale" on the vehicle, it was from one of the seller's businesses and not in his personal name. The problem was . . . of course . . . when the vehicle arrived, so did the police who informed me that the 2008 BMW was stolen and had to be impounded. I guess the deal was too good to be true![70]

Internet Gambling and Lottery Scams

While the Unlawful Internet Gambling Enforcement Act was passed in 2006 by Congress, essentially making all forms of gambling via the Internet illegal, a number of underground Internet sites still exist. The sites are "offshore," meaning that they are hosted in foreign countries, making enforcement very difficult. Further, the extent to which some of these sites are honest also appears to be an open question, as so many are beyond the reach of gaming regulatory agencies and American law enforcement.

Most Internet frauds involving gambling are usually based on phony letters announcing you as a winner (Figure 15-14). In these types of scams, the victim is notified of his/her "winnings" and is requested to provide confidential information on which false identifications are developed and/or more sophisticated identification theft schemes are placed into motion.

Nigerian 419 and Black Money/Wash-Wash Schemes

The **Nigerian advanced fee scam** begins with a potential victim getting an unsolicited fax, e-mail, or letter that purports to be from a current or former Nigerian governmental official or a relative of such. The recipient is told that a "confidential source has recommended the contact." The con takes its name from Chapter 42, Section 419, of the Laws of the Federation of Nigeria and Lagos, which deals with advanced fee frauds. Millions of U.S. dollars are available through an over-invoiced deal with the Nigerian national Petroleum Company, the recovery of unclaimed insurance money, money from a dead or defeated former government official, or other such spin.

From: POWERBALL NOTIFICATION <pabet4us@yahoo.co.uk>
Date: October 23, 2010 12:57:16 PM EDT
To: undisclosed recipients
Subject: Check Your E-mail

FROM THE DESK OF THE PROMOTIONS MANAGER
POWERBALL LOTTERY E-GAMES PROMOTIONS,
Accredited Claim Agent-
29 Colmore Row,
Birmingham, B3 2EW
United Kingdom
www.powerball.com

23th October, 2010.

Attn: Lucky Winner,

RE: AWARD WINNING EMAIL NOTIFICATION!!!

We wish to notify and congratulate you on the selection of your email ID as the jackpot winning entry in the Powerball E-Games Promotions, being the inaugural edition of our new e-lottery program. Your email ID identified with winning No. 10, 17, 18, 26, 43, 47 and was selected among the winning email ID's in the draws held today using the latest version of the Computer Random Selection System (CRSS) from the 50,000 promotional entries submitted by our international software support/affiliate companies.

You have been awarded with the jackpot promotional cash prize of $1,000,000.00 (One Million United States Dollars Only) credited to Reference Numbers PB/EGP/60961/OV. You will join the other two winners from Nigeria, Your payment will be made through our Nigerian payment center, since we have two winners already from Nigeria. Your winning cash prize has been transferred into an ATM VISA CARD to curtail the risk of carrying huge amount of money around. You shall receive your winning cash prize as an international ATM VISA Card which you shall cash in your country. To immediately process the claims of your prize award, please contact your assigned claims agent:

Name: Mohammed Hakim Ali
E-mail: mohammedhakim1949@hotmail.com
TEL: +2348060850444

To facilitate the claims of your winnings, you are advised to provide the claims officer assigned to you with the following details for processing the payment of your winnings:

Name:
Address:
Telephone Number:
Email Address:
Occupation:
Nationality:
Social Security Number:
Bank Name:
Bank Address:
Account Number:
VISA or MASTERCARD Bank:
Account Number:
Reference Number:
Award Prize Amount:

Once again, congratulations from all our staff on your promotional prize winning

Patricia Riley (Mrs.)
Coordinator; Powerball E-Games Promotion.

▲**FIGURE 15-14   Internet "winners" notification**
Note the important and confidential information requested from this unsolicited e-mail.

▶ FIGURE 15-15
Partially cleaned $100s in
the Nigerian "wash-wash"
advanced fee scheme
(© Eduardo Munoz/Reuters/Corbis)

The letter writer wants the victim's help in investing in the United States and will pay handsomely for it, up to 30% of the "total." Another 10%–15% of the money will be set aside to pay for miscellaneous expenses in getting the money transferred. The victim provides personal information, including bank account numbers to facilitate the movement of funds from Nigeria to this country. The personal information is not immediately abused; later it may be sold or employed in another type of fraud. The victim is pressured into sending money to cover unanticipated costs, which continues as long as the victim sends money. The money requests to the victim are accompanied by official-looking government and bank documents with embossed seals and verification stamps, all of which are counterfeit or phony.

"Wash-wash" (Figure 15-15) is what Nigerian cons call the black money scheme, also an advanced fee scam. It may be run in conjunction with a 419 or as a stand-alone con. The con reports that the dollars he is trying to get into this country have been treated with a chemical that turned them black, disguising their true value; in order to be able to wash the $100 bills clean so they can be used, special, expensive chemicals must be bought, and the victim must pay for them. A meeting is set up outside the United States, to avoid the higher risk of arrest. The victim flies there to actually see the money that will be "cleaned and divided." The meeting is conducted in a hotel room or other location. The con has a specially treated bill that is black, and he uses the "small amount of special cleaning chemicals he has left" to demonstrate the process, and the bill is partially cleaned. This process is actually very cheap and on the order of a sleight-of-hand trick. The victim advances several thousand dollars to buy the chemicals; but then, the vial is "accidentally left in a cab or broken." So, the victim advances more money. This is repeated as many times as the victim pays up and then the fraudsters disappear, allegedly to get the chemicals themselves.[71]

OTHER FRAUDS: PIGEON-DROP AND BANK-EXAMINERS CONS

Confidence games are practiced by individuals who understand human nature, gain the mark's trust by being good listeners, and through smooth talking, set the hook, and run the scam. As many as 70% of con games may be run against the elderly, who are often very trusting. Among the most enduring con games are the pigeon-drop scheme and the bank-examiner scheme.

The **pigeon drop** is run in many variations; commonly, two cons operate it. The first one strikes up a conversation with the mark on a street filled with shops or at a mall. The job of the first con is to make a "quick connection" with the mark and gain his/her confidence; they talk about the mark's family or whatever is comfortable. The second con approaches with a story of having just found an envelope filled with a lot of money and asks them if it belongs to them. When the envelope is opened, there will be some paperwork suggesting that it came from drug sales or other illegal activity. After asking the first con and the mark what should be done with the money, the mark is lead to the conclusion that all three should share it. Because there is no identification in the envelope, the money cannot be returned, and there is no real harm because the person who lost the money is dishonest. The two cons, quickly joined by the mark, talk about all the things they could do with the money. One of the cons calls his/her employer, who is an "attorney."

TABLE 15-1	Internet Scams in 2009	
SCAM	TYPE OF SCAM	DESCRIPTION
"Hitman Scam"	E-mail extortion	An e-mailer claims to have been sent to assassinate a victim, but the victim would be spared if he/she wires money overseas.
Astrological reading scam	Spam or pop-up message	A victim receives a free reading but is enticed into paying for a full reading to learn about something favorable about to happen.
Economic stimulus scam	Telephone call and online	A recorded phone message that sounds like President Barack Obama directs victims to websites requiring online applications and $28 in fees to receive a large sum of stimulus money.
Job site scam	Online	Victims are persuaded to provide personal information or copies of payroll checks only to find their bank account drained.
Fake pop-ups for antivirus software	Online	Victims click on fake pop-up ads warning them about threatening viruses on their computers and end up downloading malicious computer codes or viruses.

Source: *2009 Internet Crime Report* (Washington, D.C.: U.S. Department of Justice, 2010) and "Dallas Summit Target Cyber Crime," *The Dallas Morning News*, May 2, 2010, p. 18A.

The attorney advises that the money be put in "his firm's" trust account while a due diligence search is made to find the owner of the lost money. Additionally, the mark and the two cons are to provide a sum of money, as a show of good faith until the found money can be distributed, which will also be placed in the mythical trust account. After the mark withdraws his good faith money, the lawyer may take the group to lunch and take control of all of the money. The victim—the pigeon—has thus lost all the money he withdrew from the bank.

The **bank-examiner con** often begins with a call to the mark's home in which the caller identifies himself as a bank examiner who relates there is some apparent wrongdoing at the bank, and the assistance of the mark is solicited in finding out who it is. The mark is asked to withdraw some money from his/her account and then to meet the examiner at a nearby location. The bank examiner may be accompanied by "Sgt. Jones," who flashes a badge and praises the mark for his help. The bank examiner gives the mark a counterfeit cashier's check to replace the funds withdrawn but asks him/her not to deposit it for the week it takes to complete the investigation. By then, the scam has been run several times in that community, and the con men are long gone before the mark finds out that the check is bogus.[72]

Pigeon-drop and bank-examiner frauds are often started via the Internet. Unsolicited e-mails and other communications are transacted between the victim and the con through e-mail as well as the telephone. Clearly, the ubiquitous nature of the Internet has aided in new and various forms of scams that will undoubtedly continue to evolve over the years. Table 15-1 reveals recent variations of scams via the Internet.

VICTIMS OF FRAUD: SENIOR CITIZENS

Senior citizens are particularly susceptible to being the victims of a variety of fraud schemes, including Medicare fraud, telemarketing and funeral scams, counterfeit prescription drugs, Internet scams and cons, and phony reverse mortgages. For instance, many senior citizens are new to the Internet and unaware of the potential for fraud and scams associated within its use. They often come from a social genre that "trusted" their neighbor and believe that the government "protects" them from criminal predators. They often believe that scams and cons are relatively rare and that most people are honest in their business dealings. These are characteristics of the "greatest generation," who fought in World War II and who believe that most people are basically honest and technology is well-regulated . . . criminals are often viewed as street thugs that involve themselves in relatively minor crimes like shoplifting and other thefts. Most senior citizens polled continue to believe that violent crime is relatively rare in our communities and that the police can prevent most crime.[73]

From the perspective of a scammer, senior citizens are ideal victims for a number of reasons. First, they generally have good credit and a sizable savings. Second, elderly victims are not as likely to report being a victim

▶FIGURE 15-16
Senior citizens are often the victim of scams and cons
Federal and local police are trying to better educate senior citizens through individual workshops, Senior Citizen Police Academies, and general e-mails and postal mailings focused on fraud prevention. (© Tom Carter/ Index Stock Imagery/Photolibrary)

of fraud because they may not realize they were conned; if they do acknowledge their victimization, they may not report it, owing to embarrassment or shame. Third, even if they were to report the crime, some senior citizens can be poor witnesses, based on their limited ability to recall information. Moreover, a significant time lapse between the scam and discovery of the crime makes details of the event more difficult to remember.[74] Senior citizens account for a large amount of the victims to frauds and cons—so much so, that the FBI has focused considerable attention on educating senior citizens in an attempt to lower their victimization (Figure 15-16).

MONEY LAUNDERING

Criminals want to launder money to avoid prosecution, increase their profits, avoid seizure of their accumulated wealth, evade paying taxes whenever possible, and appear legitimate.[75] In laundering cases prosecuted, 60% of the money came from embezzlement or fraud, 17% involved drug trafficking, and 7% involved racketeering or customs charges.[76] **Money laundering** is the illegal practice of filtering "dirty" money or ill-gotten gains through a series of transactions until the money is "clean," appearing to be proceeds from legal activities. The United States Criminal Code defines money laundering as the concealment of the source and/or the destination of money, which has usually been gained through illegal activities.[77] Worldwide money laundering activity is estimated to be $1 trillion each year.[78] Money launderers have access to all the speed and ease of modern electronic finance to move funds globally. Thus, substantial cooperation and information sharing among law-enforcement agencies are

essential to identify the sources of illegal proceeds, trace the funds to specific criminal activities, and confiscate criminals' financial assets.[79]

At the risk of oversimplifying a complex subject, money laundering involves three distinct steps: (1) **placement,** (2) **layering,** and (3) **integration** (Figure 15-17).[80]

PLACEMENT

Placement is the process of placing unlawful proceeds into legitimate financial institutions or systems. Transactions are kept to $10,000 or less to avoid triggering the requirements of the federal Bank Secrecy Act (BSA, 1970). The BSA obligates institutions to report single transactions exceeding $10,000 to the U.S. Department of Treasury's Financial Crimes Enforcement Network (FinCen). FinCen is one of the Treasury's primary agencies to establish, oversee, and implement policies to prevent and detect money laundering. It also provides intelligence and analytical support to law enforcement. With FinCen's leadership, a meeting of financial intelligence units (FIUs) was held in 1995 in Brussels. An outgrowth of this meeting was the formation of the Egmont Group, which is an international network of FIUs dedicated to information sharing and coordination.

The BSA also requires a report when one entity makes multiple deposits exceeding $10,000 in a single day. In 1996, under regulatory authority granted by the Annunzio-Wylie Money Laundering Act (1992), the U.S. Treasury adopted a rule requiring banks and other depository institutions to report to FinCen any *suspicious* activities involving $5,000 or more.

Placement is often done by **smurfing,** or making multiple deposits of cash or buying multiple bank drafts,

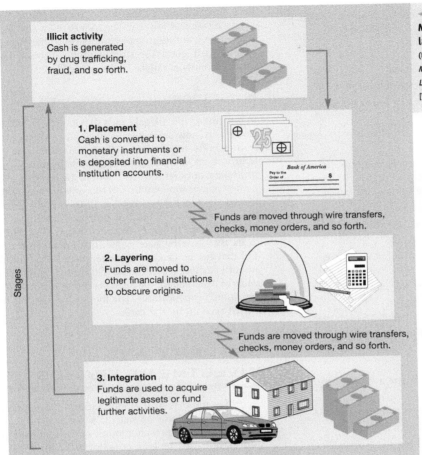

◄ FIGURE 15-17
Money laundering: Placement, layering, and integration
(United States General Accounting Office, *Money Laundering: Extent of Money Laundered Through Credit Cards Is Unknown* [Washington, D.C.: 2002], p. 7)

Illicit activity
Cash is generated by drug trafficking, fraud, and so forth.

1. Placement
Cash is converted to monetary instruments or is deposited into financial institution accounts.

Funds are moved through wire transfers, checks, money orders, and so forth.

2. Layering
Funds are moved to other financial institutions to obscure origins.

Funds are moved through wire transfers, checks, money orders, and so forth.

3. Integration
Funds are used to acquire legitimate assets or fund further activities.

Stages

which are checks issued by one bank against funds deposited in that bank that authorize a second bank to make payment to the entity named in the draft. One or more individuals conduct these transactions, often at multiple financial institutions. Other methods include buying money orders or travelers' checks at one institution, depositing them at another and using cash to buy chips at a casino, participating in gambling activities, and then cashing in the chips for a casino check. As a general matter, casinos withhold federal income tax at a 25% rate on winnings above $5,000. Placement has also been facilitated by bribing bank officials to ignore FinCen reporting requirements (which is increasingly difficult) by purchasing entire banks and operating them as part of a criminal enterprise and using "safe haven" **off-shore accounts** in some 60 nations that advertise "untraceable" financial services. These nations include the Cook Islands, Egypt, Guatemala, and Ukraine. In these jurisdictions, launderers may buy a "shelf company" that has been registered for years and open accounts into which illegal funds are deposited. Laws in the Seychelles Islands provide immu-

nity to depositors from all outside criminal charges, even if it is known the money came from criminal acts. The only government requirement is that investors not engage in illegal activities in the Seychelles Island chain.[81]

Another method of placement is the Colombian **black market peso exchange (BMPE).**[82] Colombian drug dealers export drugs to North America and Western Europe. Sales of drugs produce vast amounts of money in the currency of the countries in which the drugs are sold. The drug cartel contacts a peso broker, who will give it pesos for the currency held in foreign countries for roughly 80 cents on the "dollar." The cartel thus has its money, and the BMPE must now pick up the money and get it placed into the banking systems of the respective countries. In the final phase, the broker advertises to Columbian importers that they have foreign funds available to buy goods from other countries. On behalf of importers, the BMPE purchases goods from foreign manufacturers whose goods are shipped to the Caribbean or a South American country. These goods are then smuggled into Colombia to avoid expensive tariffs. Once the goods are

TABLE 15-2	Indicators Associated with Accounts Used for Money Laundering

1. Smurfing

2. Unusual underlying business plan

3. Account holder's wealth atypical for his/her profile

4. Unusually high rates of return for low-risk business activity

5. Reactivation of dormant account, often with increasingly large deposits

6. Questionable, unrealistic, or conflicting explanation of business plan or account activity; account holder has lack of knowledge about the field his/her business is in

7. Unnecessarily complex transactions

8. Disbursement of funds by several checks when one would do

9. Account holder has criminal record or suspicious associates

10. Account holder has defensive stance when asked about account activity

11. True beneficiary of account is deliberately concealed

12. Last-minute changes in fund transfer instructions

13. Account holder is discovered to use false/stolen identification

14. Account revenue is atypical for size and nature of business

15. Funds transferred to personal or relative's accounts

16. Account behavior changes without explanation

17. "Tidy" or rounded sums used to pay for commodities

18. Business lacks normal documentation

Source: No author, *FIUs (Financial Intelligence Units) in Action: 100 Sanitized Cases*, London: Egmont Group, 2000, drawn from a 170-page document.

sold, the broker is paid in pesos, which are then deposited into a legitimate banking system.

Money from illegal sources also still gets laundered in the traditional way. Front businesses—such as bars, restaurants, night clubs, and vending machine companies—and illicit source funds are commingled with legitimate revenue, with taxes being paid on all of it. These front businesses may be owned by criminals or be ones that they control. Indications of accounts being used for money laundering are summarized in Table 15-2.

LAYERING

Layering involves converting the funds placed into other assets or moving them to other financial institutions, the purpose of which is to further distance the funds from

their illegal source; these assets include bonds, stocks, works of art and jewelry. The money may also be wired to another institution to pay into a controlled account for non-existent goods or simply move through multiple other accounts anyplace in the world.[83]

INTEGRATION

In integration, the illegal funds that have been placed and layered are now clean and are virtually indistinguishable from wholly legal money. They are then used to buy luxury items or to invest in legitimate business ventures, real estate, or other sectors.[84] Both in the layering and integration phases some credit card accounts are used, although the actual extent is not known. In this country, the practice appears limited, but it is practiced through off-shore banks.[85] These banks offer anonymous ATM and credit cards that bear no user name, just an account number, and that can be used worldwide; there is no limit on the amount of money that can be withdrawn daily. The cards must be "preloaded" or deposits made to cover 200% of anticipated expenditures. The money not spent is held in a trust account by the bank.

SECURITY AND INVESTMENT FRAUDS

Securities fraud is any manipulation or deception that affects the purchase or sale of a security and usually includes the misrepresentation or omission of significant information. In general, a security is an investment instrument from which an investor expects to derive financial benefit through the efforts of others.[86] Illustrations include stocks, bonds, and other financial instruments. The two primary laws governing the securities industry and protecting investors are the Securities Act of 1933 and the Securities Exchange Act of 1934, both of which have been amended through the years.[87] In addition to these federal laws, each state has statutes and regulations pertaining to securities transactions, and the various stock and commodity exchanges also have regulatory requirements.[88]

In the 1987 movie *Wall Street*, the character Gordon Gekko soothingly intones at a stockholders' meeting, "Greed is good," which seemed to become the order of the day for some individuals and corporations. In 1990 Michael Milken, the "junk bond king," pled guilty to securities fraud and related charges and paid a fine of $600 million, thereby avoiding the more serious charges of racketeering and insider trading.

Formed by a merger of two companies in 1985, energy trading company Enron quickly soared owing to the deregulated energy markets, becoming the seventh largest corporation in this country. By 2000, Enron had filed for bankruptcy, brought down by some five years of using

▲ **FIGURE 15-18   Bernie Madoff**
Madoff pled guilty to a federal indictment alleging that the former securities broker dealer carried out one of the largest Ponzi schemes, defrauding his clients out of an estimated $64 billion. He pled guilty in June 2009 and was sentenced to 150 years in prison. (© AP Photo/Kathy Willens)

accounting methods that concealed massive losses, leading to a downward estimate of its net value by $1.1 billion. The scandal caused thousands of employees to lose their retirement savings and resulted in massive losses to investors. Its activities led to the conviction of some Merrill Lynch and Arthur Anderson officials, prison terms for some Enron officials, one of whom pled guilty to conspiracy to commit money laundering and conspiracy to commit wire fraud. The Board of Directors paid a $168 million fine to settle charges that they failed to adequately protect investors.

In 2008 federal officials investigated and arrested former NASDAQ chairman, Bernie Madoff, on charges of securities fraud (Figure 15-18). Madoff operated an asset management firm that, for decades, used the funds from new clients to pay profits and redemptions to existing clients. Often using his social networks to attract new investors, Madoff eventually defrauded his clients out of $64 billion, representing the largest investment fraud in history.[89] The number of dollars lost in the fraud is mind boggling! To place this number into perspective, compare the dollar loss in the preceding year, according to the 2007 FBI Uniform Crime Report.[90] According to the FBI, there were 9.8 million crimes against property in the United States in 2007, which included about 2.2 million burglaries, 6.6 million larcenies, and about 1.1 million car thefts—totaling a mere $17.6 billion in losses.[91] Put another way, the dollar loss for all property crimes in 2007 represented only a fraction (about 20%) of the total loss suffered by investors from the Madoff scheme! Even if 2007 was an "off year" for crime, to get a realistic picture of the magnitude of this crime: Bernie Madoff's fraud would essentially equal the monetary losses from all conventional property crimes against U.S. citizens for three years![92] There has been some retribution and repayment of loss since 2008. Madoff pled guilty and was sentenced to 150 years in prison, and in December 2010 federal authorities revealed that many Madoff's victimized clients may regain about half of their losses as a result of seized property and assets by the federal government.[93]

Bernie Madoff's investment fraud was brought to light the same year that was fictional character, Gordon Gekko reappears in the sequel, *Wall Street: Money Never Sleeps*; in this movie, Gekko hawks his new book entitled, "Greed is Good!" The cynical nature and devastation of monetary loss from Bernie Madoff's investment fraud provide the backdrop to the movie, which highlights one of the oldest and most successful cons: the Ponzi Scheme.

PONZI/PYRAMID SCHEMES

Carlos "Charles" Ponzi formed the Security Exchange Company in Boston in 1919 and promised to double people's investments in the company within 90 days (Figure 15-19). For early investors, this actually happened, because he used the deposits of subsequent investors to pay for the money doubling of previous investors. Eventually the scheme collapsed, because recruitment of new investors could not be sustained. Ponzi was arrested, convicted, and imprisoned for various crimes. This type of investment fraud is still practiced today and is referred to as a **Ponzi scheme, pyramid scheme,** or endless **chain scheme.** The ruse is based on "greed" and attempts to lure would-be investors into a program that promises or guarantees extraordinarily high returns. As in the initial Ponzi fraud, the scheme actually appears to be working in the beginning, as investors receive monetary "returns on investment," however; these returns are not based on profits from a working corporation or stock fund, but rather from new investors entering the program. The entire scheme fails when additional investors cannot be enticed into the scheme. It is usually at this time that the fraud becomes apparent as the perpetrator suddenly vanishes, taking all of the remaining investment money. Sudden stock market downturns and a slowing economy also quickly reveal Ponzi schemes as investors withdraw their money from the program, causing a rapid acceleration of payout and revealing the fraudulent nature of the scheme. This is precisely why so many Ponzi and pyramid schemes have come to light in the past few years, as the U.S. Stock Market dipped to its lowest point in decades in 2008 and the U.S. economy

▲ **FIGURE 15-19 Ponzi schemes**
Carlo Ponzi (1882–1949) immigrated to the United States, where he swindled thousands of investors out of millions of dollars. He was deported to his native Italy in 1934 and at one point worked for the dictator Mussolini. In 1949 he died penniless in Brazil. The scam he developed is timeless; in 2007 Norman Hsu was charged with defrauding investors out of at least $60 million in a massive Ponzi scheme and with making illegal political contributions. (© Bettmann/Corbis)

attesting that they were not promised anything for participating in the program (although each is led to believe that they all will become receivers). As the following sections indicate, Ponzis can be run in many different ways.

PUMP AND DUMP SCHEMES

The U.S. Securities and Exchange Commission describes **pump and dump** schemes, which are also called "hype and dump manipulation," as involving the touting of a company's stock through false and misleading statements to the market place often by using the Internet.[94] After distributing favorable, but false, information to drive up the price of the stock (the pump), the price of the stock rallies by its being bought. The pump or hype may include urging potential investors to "buy now before it is too late," suggestions that the recommendation is based on "inside" knowledge, or that an "infallible" economic model identified the stock.[95]

The pump is often done with microcap stocks, issued by the smallest companies, over half of which have capitalizations of less than $1.25 million.[96] Thus, "microcap" means companies that have micro capitalizations. Microcap stocks are traded in the over-the-counter (OTC) market, which has no listing standards. This is in sharp contrast to the great amount of information on companies whose stocks are traded on the major exchanges. Therefore, detailed, accurate information about the company is usually not available for victims who need such data in the face of a pump hustle.

AFFINITY FRAUD

Affinity fraud is run on groups of people who share some affinity to one another, such as religious, ethnic, and professional groups and groups whose members have a high sense of friendship and trust in one another.[97] The scammers often recruit the most respected members of the group to help promote the program, which offers "guaranteed returns." The use of such members makes it easier to recruit victims, and when it is apparent that the group has been defrauded, it may choose not to report the victimization to spare the respected member and the group embarrassment. The investment fraud can be run as a Ponzi scheme or as one of many other iterations:

continues to suffer a major recession. Table 15-3 lists some of the more infamous cases within the last few years. To would-be investors, the best adage may again well be, "if it sounds too good to be true, it usually is!"

As with most frauds, there are numerous variations in the Ponzi and pyramid routines. For example, these schemes may be run as "gifting clubs" or "women empowering women" programs. Eight new participants, called *givers*, are recruited, and each "gifts" the "receiver," who is the person at the head of the pyramid, with $2,000. When the receiver has $16,000 in hand, the pyramid splits, and the eight new participants move upward in the pyramid, each hoping eventually to become the receiver; to do so requires each of them to recruit new entry-level givers.

New participants in pyramid schemes are often required to sign confidentiality agreements requiring them not to discuss the specifics or the names of participants and

African-American groups were approached by a company that was portrayed as being successful and having more than $36 million in assets, when in fact it had a negative net worth of more than $27 million. The company promised to insure all investments made, and make a 30% tax-free return. Eventually, groups were conned out of $52 million before the company was stopped; the defendant later pleaded guilty to conspiracy to commit securities fraud.[98]

TABLE 15-3 Who's Been Accused in Recent Alleged Ponzi Schemes and Similar Scams

The stock market plunge in September and October, 2008, revealed a number of Ponzi and Pyramid type frauds; some of the more infamous frauds and schemes are listed here.

	R. ALLEN STANFORD	SHAWN MERRIMAN	NICHOLAS COSMO	ARTHUR NADEL	STEPHEN WALSH, PAUL GREENWOOD	WEIZHEN TANG	RAY M. WHITE	MARVIN RAY COOPER
Age	58	46	37	76	62, 64	50	50	32
Location	Texas and Antigua, West Indies	Aurora, CO	Hauppauge, Lake Grove and Queens, NY	Sarasota, FL	Sands Point, NY, North Salem, N.C.	Toronto	Mansfield, TX	Honolulu, HI
Company or companies	Stanford Financial Group, Stanford International Bank and others	Market Street Advisors	Agape World, Agape Merchant Advance	Scoop Management, Scoop Capital and others	Westridge Capital Management, WG Trading Investors and others	Oversea Chinese Fund, WiWin Capital Management and others	CRW Management	Billion Coupons, Billion Coupons Investment
Alleged length	At least 1999–09	1994–09	2004–09	1996–09	2006–09	2009–09	2007–09	2007–09
Amount raised from investors/clients	More than $8 billion	$17 million–$20 million	$370 million	$60 million	At least $553 million	$50 million–$75 million	At least $10.9 million	More than $4.4 million
Number of investors/clients	About 50,000	At least 38	More than 1,500	More than 100	Universities, public pension and retirement plans	More than 200	More than 250	At least 125 (many members of the deaf community)
Personal expenses	At least $1.6 billion in personal loans	Masterpieces by Rembrandt, Rubens, and other artists	Jewelry, hotel and limousine bills, youth baseball league	More than $1 million in wire transfers to private accounts	Homes, horse farm, collectible Steiff teddy bears	NA	Real estate and car-racing activities	Flying lessons, $1 million home, computer equipment

Source: Court filings by federal prosecutors and records from the Securities and Exchange Commission, Commodity Futures Trading Commission, FBI and U.S. Postal Inspection Service. Web Bryant, "Economic Troubles Reveal Plague," USA Today, April 17, 2009, p. B-1.

PAY PHONES/ATM MACHINE INVESTMENTS

Another type of investment fraud involves coin-operated, customer-owned telephones (COCOTs) or ATMs,[99] which investors "purchase" at $5,000–$7,000 each. They are then "leased" back to a management company for five years; the company collects rental fees from telephone companies or banks, maintains the machine, and pays the investor monthly profits. The profits promised are a 12.5%–15% annual return.[100] These offers usually come from life insurance agents or other persons not licensed to sell securities, and the investment is not properly registered. This type of investment is inherently risky, because the companies making the offers often have weak balance sheets; the realistic downside is that companies cannot provide the services promised, the phones or ATMs are never purchased, or the investment offer is actually being run as a Ponzi scheme.[101] This type of fraud became so prevalent that 26 states acting in concert took legal action on behalf of 4,500 investors who lost an estimated $76 million.[102]

ONE-YEAR CALLABLE CERTIFICATES OF DEPOSIT

The stock market has been volatile in recent years, and many older investors have fled it looking for more stable investments, such as certificates of deposit (CDs). CDs issued by local banks insured by the Federal Deposit Insurance Corporation (FDIC) have long been a trusted investment, because they are covered for losses up to $100,000. In purchasing a CD, the buyer agrees to invest a fixed amount for a fixed time. In return, the issuing entity agrees to pay the purchaser interest at regular intervals.[103] In addition to banks, CDs are now sold by national and regional brokerage firms and independent sales people or "deposit brokers." These brokers can sometimes negotiate a higher interest rate for their customers on the promise of bringing a certain sum of money to the bank.[104]

Unscrupulous sellers of CDs often trumpet the higher rates of interest to be paid but do not explain to investors about the terms used, thus misleading them. For example, a **one-year callable CD** has a "one-year call provision," meaning that the entity issuing the instrument can choose to call (terminate it by redeeming) a CD before its maturity date. The option to call a CD is with the bank and not with the investor. However, investors typically may not understand this language or are misled about its meaning, thinking that after a year of earning interest they can terminate their investment and use the money any way they want. Not only can they not do so, penalties for early withdrawal may amount to 25% or more. There are numerous cases across the country of investors in their 90s being sold CDs by unscrupulous entities that do not mature for 20–30 years. In addition to selling people unsuitable investments, these "brokers" may not be working with an FDIC institution but acting as the agent

for other investors, or the investor is not told that they own only a portion, and not all, of the CD. Moreover, some CD programs are operated as pyramid schemes, with the early investors receiving "Ponzi payments."

PROMISSORY NOTES

A **promissory note** is essentially a short-term written I.O.U. that promises to pay its holder, the investor, the fixed amount invested plus a fixed amount of interest at some specified date in the future.[105] Although promissory notes can be legitimate investments, those that are mass-marketed, sold door-to-door, or promoted on the Internet or through telemarketing are often scams, which amount to some $300 million annually. Most promissory notes have to be registered as securities with the Securities Exchange Commission and in the states where they are to be sold, but notes with maturities of nine months or less may be exempt from being registered. Therefore, when notes are not registered and mature in nine months or less, it is another sign that a scam may be in the offering instead of a great investment opportunity. Legitimate corporate promissory notes are not usually sold to the general public, but to sophisticated buyers who conduct a due diligence search before investing.[106]

The fraudsters recruit a sales staff with lucrative commissions ranging from 20%–30%; frequently, life insurance agents known and trusted in the community are recruited for this role.[107] These agents do not have a license to sell securities and rely solely on the information their employer provides, which later turns out to be false or misleading.[108] Enticed by promises of a 15% or 20% return on an "insured, guaranteed, no risk investment" and dealing with someone who is familiar to them, few victims ask any tough questions.[109] The pitch may include statements that reinforce the notion that this is a no risk investment, there is substantial collateral, and the investment is insured against loss. The money raised by the promissory notes may be needed to "open oil wells that were capped years ago because they were unprofitable to operate then, but new technology now makes it profitable to bring them on line." The notes may also be associated with activities such as "bringing out new products, funding a new television show, helping a real estate company acquire prime land for development, modernizing a Mexican gold, Colombian emerald, or South African diamond mine, or financing an e-commerce venture."

The fraudsters may simply take the money and run, leaving their unwitting sales agents to face charges, or operate the investment fraud as yet another variation on a Ponzi scheme. Promissory note fraud is also run as a type of affinity fraud.

PRIME BANK NOTES

International defrauders invented the prime bank note investment scam, which promises extremely high yields in a relatively short period of time.[110] They claim to have special access to investments that are usually "limited to only the very wealthy." The yields promised range from 5% per month to hundreds of percent annually. Victims are told that their money will be pooled to trade in prime bank notes, prime bank guarantees, prime bank debentures, letters of credit, bank purchase orders, zero coupon bonds, or other official sounding instruments.[111] Victims believe that such instruments can be purchased for a steep discount and then quickly resold for a substantial profit. They may also be advised that the profits are so vast that the International Money Fraud or the Federal Reserve Bank requires that a certain percentage of it be spent for charitable relief in third-world countries or elsewhere, which adds respectability to the pitch. The funds are actually sent to overseas banks in Geneva, London, or elsewhere. From there, they are transferred to off-shore institutions, where they are laundered, and the victims' money disappears. As is frequently the case in many types of frauds, this one can also be operated as a Ponzi scheme. Although individual investors are frequently victims, units of government are sometimes reeled in by the scheme—for example, the city of Clovis, New Mexico, lost $3.5 million in a prime note investment fraud.

VIATICAL SETTLEMENTS

Viatical settlements were developed during the 1980s, in part to help dying AIDS patients pay their bills; their life insurance policies were bought by investors for less than the face value of the policy, and the investors had their money returned and a profit made upon the death of the insured.[112] Later, the practice was extended to others, especially the elderly. Because some people live longer than their medical diagnosis suggests is possible, and because new treatments are constantly developed that extend the life of the insured, this is a risky venture even when operated legitimately.[113]

Viatical settlement frauds are conducted in many guises—for example:

> The National Medical Funding Company placed ads in gay publications soliciting terminally ill patients to sell their life insurance policies. The company never bought the policies; instead, they used the information from applicants to fabricate phony viatical contracts, which were then sold to Arizona investors as fully insured 12- to 16-month investments that paid 14% or more. As investors started complaining about bounced checks and payments that never arrived, the fraud was identified, with investors losing $13 million.[114]

TELEPHONE SCAMS

Unrelated to telemarketing fraud are three scams related to telephone billing, such as: (1) 1-900 and foreign exchange numbers, (2) the Mexican collect call scam, and (3) cramming.

1-900 AND FOREIGN EXCHANGE NUMBERS

Scammers will leave a telephone message or send an e-mail from someone offering to engage in phone sex, telling the recipient they have won a prize (which may end up being only a few dollars), telling them that a family member is sick, or some other bogus message. The return number may be a 1-900 (pay for service calls, some of which may be legitimate), 809 (Dominican Republic), 284 (British Virgin Islands), 876 (Jamaica), or some other three-digit code.[115] While international calls normally require a "011" prefix, calls to the just-identified countries, Canada, and some other Caribbean countries do not. The recipients think they are making a domestic long-distance call, but they are actually being connected to a number outside the United States and are billed at international call rates. Return callers often have to wade through automated menus and hear "dentist office" music to keep them on the line. These scams average $35 per call or more, which appears on the victims' telephone bills. Victims' vulnerability can be greatly reduced if they determine what country the three-digit prefix designates.

MEXICAN COLLECT CALL SCHEME

The Mexican collect call scam originated in that country, preys upon Hispanic consumers, and is basically a reverse of the scheme just described. The telephone rings and a voice, using the correct names of family members, says this is an emergency collect call, and the caller accepts the charges only to discover a stranger is on the line talking about something entirely different.

CRAMMING

It is entirely legal for phone companies to bill consumers for certain types of services as part of their regular telephone bill. **Cramming** is the practice of placing unauthorized, misleading, inaccurate, or deceptive charges on the victims' telephone bills, which may be accidental but is often intentional. Categories of cramming include voicemail, long-distance service, paging, Internet access, memberships, and pornography. Worldwide, pornography is a $97 billion industry, $13 billion of which is earned in the United States; a full 25% of all search engine requests involve pornography.[116] It did not, however, become a major industry simply by providing "free pornography." One source of its revenue is cramming—for example, visitors to some porn sites read that they can "download" movies for free; but the next month there is a charge on their telephone bill. Similarly, another common "cram" used in the porn industry is to request age verification through a VISA or MasterCard number. However the following month, there is a charge on their card for access to the porn website. There is virtually no recourse, since many of these sites are hosted in foreign countries. Much worse, the billing continues on a month-to-month basis until the victim contacts their credit card company. Yet in other cases, the "good" credit card numbers are sold to others and the fraud continues. The victim is forced to close their account and in the most vicious of cases, the victim's credit history is diminished for nonpayment of services.

TELEMARKETING AND POSTAL FRAUDS

Many of the types of frauds discussed earlier in this chapter can be run as telemarketing and postal frauds. These two mediums of communication are a means of reaching massive numbers of potential victims quickly. Table 15-4 identifies the top 10 telemarketing frauds, a number of which were discussed earlier in this chapter. Note that many of these top 10 telemarketing schemes are variations on advance fee frauds. It is estimated that consumers lose $40 billion to telemarketing annually, and one out of six consumers is cheated each year.

In the postal or mail fraud content that follows, some scams not already covered are described. Remember that these can also be run by other means, such as telemarketing. Included in postal scams are real estate, franchise scams, unsolicited merchandise, fees for normally free services, and phony inheritance cons. The top five postal frauds are (1) free prize schemes, (2) foreign lotteries, (3) pyramids scams, (4) investment frauds, and (5) work-at-home cons.[117]

LAND FRAUD

Offerings to sell parcels of land arrive in the mailboxes of potential victims, describing wonderful land on which

TABLE 15-4	Top 10 Telemarketing Scams		
NUMBER	SCAM	PERCENTAGE OF ALL COMPLAINTS	AVERAGE LOSS
1	**Fake Check Scams** Consumers paid with phony checks for work or items sold, instructed to wire money back. These have been the #1 telemarketing scam reported two years running.	58%	$3,854.78
2	**Prizes/Sweepstakes** Requests for payment to claim prizes that never materialize.	14%	$6,601.40
3	**Advance Fee Loans** False promises of business or personal loans, even if credit is bad, for a fee upfront.	5%	$1,583.02
4	**Lotteries/Lottery Clubs** Requests for payment to claim lottery winnings or get help to win, often foreign lotteries.	3%	$8,417.61
5	**Phishing** Calls or e-mails pretending to be from a well-known source, asking to confirm personal information.	2%	$149
6	**Magazine Sales** Con artists misrepresent cost of subscriptions or pretend to be the publisher offering renewals.	1.5%	$118.79
7	**Credit Card Offers** False promises of credit cards, for a fee, even if credit is bad.	1.5%	$292.58
8	**Scholarships/Grants** Scammers falsely promise to help get scholarships or government educational grants, for a fee.	1.4%	$532.28
9	**Buyers Clubs (not travel or lottery)** Charges for memberships in discount buying clubs consumers never agreed to join. This is the first time Buyers Clubs have appeared in the top 10 telemarketing list since 2004.	1%	$99.35
10	**Nigerian Money Offers** False promises of riches if consumers pay upfront to transfer money to their bank accounts. This once popular scam has not made an appearance in our top 10 telemarketing list since 2002.	1%	$1,687.50

Source: National Fraud Information Center, 2010.

---

to build vacation cabins or retirement homes or even just to hold as a "prime investment." The letters and brochures are slick and the language is glowing. Potential buyers should check with other brokers in the area or see if there are complaints against the person or company making the offer. This may simply be a version of an advanced fee scheme, or the land is worth very little because it is far from utility connections or cannot be built on without enormous costs because it is on the side of a steep ridge or mountain. Once they purchase the land, victims cannot resell it for even a fraction of what they paid for it.[118]

FRANCHISE CONS

Franchise offers arrive in the mail touting fast food or quick printing business opportunities that require a substantial investment. These offers mention brand names, such as FedEx/Kinko's or McDonald's, which are familiar to people or "soon to be very big in this area of the country." Using the cover of appearing to be a legitimate business opportunity, con men drain money from victims for application and other fees and then disappear.[119]

UNSOLICITED MERCHANDISE

People may receive gifts in the mail they didn't request, such as key chains, return address labels, and pens. Accompanying the gift is a postcard that suggests the sender's affiliation, such as recording for the blind, scholarships for students, and after-school programs. Money may not be directly solicited by the postcard, but many people send a check, thinking of it as payment for the gift or a small donation. Recipients of unsolicited merchandise have several alternatives: (1) if unopened, they can return it to the sender, which the Post Office does for free; (2) if opened and the contents are unattractive, throw them away, and (3) if opened and the merchandise is attractive, keep it without any obligation.[120] If recipients elect either of the last two options, they may get a high-pressure call or even a visit. In both cases, they should hang up, or not talk to the visitor or allow him/her inside the home. They are under no obligation to pay for unsolicited merchandise.

FEES CHARGED FOR NORMALLY FREE SERVICES

Many services are available for free from the government or other legitimate organizations. A mail come-on hopes that you are unaware of these services and offers to provide them for a fee. Victimization schemes include child-support collection, unclaimed income tax refunds, and filing for property tax exemptions, all of which are run as advanced fee frauds.[121]

MISSING RELATIVES

One of the cruelest frauds is the **missing person fraud,** which plays on victims' hopes of locating a missing loved one. The con men read the newspapers and visit official police sites where there are Internet postings soliciting information about missing persons, including personal information and the circumstances surrounding the disappearance. The fraudsters send a letter in which they pose as "people recovery specialists," offer phony credentials as former FBI, CIA, or other governmental agents, tout their national and international contacts, provide false accounts of successes, including recovering people from cults, and mention their access to special databases.

Once the offer is accepted, preliminary information is gathered by telephone, an advance fee is required, a face-to-face meeting is scheduled, and the fraudsters are never heard from again. Alternatively, they may come back with some vague information, which to follow up on involves some costs that require an additional sum of money.

PHONY INHERITANCE SCHEMES

Everybody fantasizes about winning the lottery or inheriting some money from a distant relative. Con men know this and fuel our fantasy with letters delivered to our mailboxes from **"estate locators"** or **"research specialists,"** which purport to be efforts "to locate the heirs of a substantial sum of money." These letters are, like other mail frauds, sent out in the thousands to unwary recipients who are asked to pay $30 or more for an "estate assessment."[122] This scam may also ask for personal information as the first step in an identity theft.

KEY TERMS

account takeover
affinity fraud
auction fraud
bank-examiner con
black market peso exchange
  (BMPE)
chain scheme

check kiters
cramming
drive down
dumpster diving
embezzlement
estate locators
follow-on crime

franchise offer
fraud
grand larceny
hard insurance fraud
identity theft
intangible property
integration

434 CHAPTER 15 LARCENY/THEFT AND WHITE-COLLAR CRIME

layering
missing person fraud
money laundering
Nigerian advanced fee scam
off-shore accounts
one-year callable certificates of
    deposit (CD)
organized retail crime (ORC)
organized retail theft (ORT)
overpayment fraud
paper accident
petit or petty larceny
phishing

pigeon drop
placement
Ponzi scheme
promissory note
pump and dump
pyramid scheme
research specialists
second-chance scheme
shoplifting
shoulder surfing
skimmers
smurfing
soft insurance fraud

swoop and squat
tangible personal property
theft by conversion
theft by deception
theft by fraud
theft by receiving stolen property
theft of services
theft by trick
viatical settlement
white-collar crime
wire-transfer scheme

REVIEW QUESTIONS

1. Shoplifting is often thought of as a "small time" crime. Is this true or false?
2. Why is so little property stolen in larceny/thefts recovered?
3. How does a three-person pickpocket operation work?
4. Give two definitions of *white-collar crime.*
5. List eight ways identity thieves can get a victim's personal information.
6. What are organized retail theft and organized retail crime?
7. After identity theft is committed, follow-on crimes occur. Identify five types of follow-on crimes.
8. What is smurfing?
9. What is shoulder surfing?
10. What are upcoding and unbundling charges used for?
11. What is the most common type of worker compensation fraud?
12. How does the swoop and squat method work?
13. Describe a viatical settlement fraud.
14. Why is it difficult to know how honest Internet gambling sites are?
15. How are bank-examiner and pigeon-drop cons run?
16. What is money laundering, and why do criminals want to do it?
17. What are pump and dump schemes?
18. How are prime bank and promissory note frauds operated?
19. Identify and discuss two telephone/pager scams.
20. The missing person fraud is cruel. How is it run?

INTERNET ACTIVITIES

1. Visit the website for the National Association of Shoplifting Prevention (NASP) at *www.shopliftingprevention.org/main.asp*. Search through the website and learn about "shoplifting addiction." Discuss the addictive qualities of committing petty crimes, including shoplifting. What can be done to stop this vicious cycle?
2. Visit the website of the Federal Trade Commission at *www.ftc.gov* and click on the link entitled "Identity Theft." Discuss the steps that you can take to "deter, detect, and defend" against identity theft. List at least three other Internet sites that provide detailed information about what to do if you become a victim of identity theft.

◀ Today, many vehicles are stolen primarily to be stripped for their parts. Once stripped for parts, such vehicles are abandoned, leaving owners with expensive repair bills.

(© Joseph Sohm, ChromoSohm Inc./Corbis)

16

VEHICLE THEFTS AND RELATED OFFENSES

CHAPTER OBJECTIVES

1. Identify types of motor vehicle theft.
2. List techniques for disposing of stolen motor vehicles.
3. Describe challenges associated with the theft investigation of heavy equipment and farm equipment.
4. Identify major investigative resources.
5. Discuss methods for assisting in the identification of a recovered vehicle.
6. Describe vehicle fire-investigation methods.
7. Explain vehicle and equipment theft-prevention approaches.
8. Assess title and registration issues related to marine theft.
9. Discuss aircraft and avionics theft and relevant identification and investigative techniques.

Motor vehicle theft is one of the most significant issues facing law enforcement today. In 2009 there was one motor vehicle theft every 39.7 seconds.[1] The number of motor vehicle thefts in the United States has been decreasing since 2000. With the collapse of communism and the opening of free-market economies in eastern Europe, auto theft has become an enormous problem. This, coupled with the increase in fraudulent insurance claims and other factors, has created a real challenge for law enforcement. In addition, investigating motor vehicle thefts can be difficult, and in some cases very complex, for several reasons.

When investigating vehicle theft, officers must determine the reason for the theft. Vehicles may be stolen temporarily, for example, for use in the commission of other crimes such as robberies or drive-by shootings, after which the vehicles are abandoned. Often, the stolen vehicle is not reported as such, because it is considered secondary or incidental to the robbery or drive-by shooting. Other reasons for theft can include joyriding, professional theft, and fraudulent schemes.

Professional thieves use a variety of means such as chop shops, stripping, salvage switches, and export to other countries to dispose of stolen vehicles. Once a vehicle has been chopped or stripped, trying to identify particular stolen vehicles and/or parts can be extremely difficult. However, this seemingly formidable task has been made easier in part by the creation of standardized vehicle identification number systems. Finally, investigators are often faced with situations where the perpetrators are not strangers or professional thieves but the owners themselves.

Given limited law-enforcement resources and an economically difficult time, vehicle theft may not be considered a top priority. Nonetheless, investigators have many major resources and organizations at their disposal. This chapter provides an overview of several of these resources, such as the National Insurance Crime Bureau and the American Association of Motor Vehicle Administrators, as well as the information they can provide. Although motor vehicle theft is the main topic of this chapter, also addressed is the theft of other high-value items, such as heavy equipment; commercial vehicles and cargo; marine vehicles; and aircraft and avionic equipment. We also discuss prevention programs that can help minimize the theft of motor vehicles and other items.

MOTOR VEHICLE THEFT

The number of motor vehicle thefts in the United States for 2009, as reported by the FBI, was 794,616, with a national loss of $5.2 billion in vehicle value. Of the total thefts, 72.1% were automobiles. Although 56.8% of stolen vehicles are later recovered, only 12.4% of the cases are cleared by law-enforcement agencies. Of these cases cleared by arrest or exceptional means, 14.7% were under 18 years of age, 82.3% were male, and 61.1 % were white.[2]

Other statistics for 2009: The average value of vehicles stolen was $6,505. The number of reported thefts decreased by 17.1% from the previous year,[3] 35.7% when compared with 2005 figures,[4] and 31.5 % when compared with 2000 figures.[5] Although these decreases look significant, some of the change could be caused by changes in reporting procedures, changes in crime classifications at local levels, more or fewer agencies reporting their statistics for central processing, or a variety of other reasons. Despite the decreased numbers, motor vehicle theft remains a problem of national concern.

MISCELLANEOUS STATISTICS AND NOTES

- According to the National Insurance Crime Bureau, there were 60,763 motorcycle thefts in the United States in 2008; 18,422 motorcycles were recovered, resulting in a recovery rate of 30%.[6]
- National and international rings, particularly those in cities near ports, export vehicles to countries all over the developing world, where they can be sold for three or more times the price for which they are sold in the United States.
- Since the collapse of communism in eastern Europe, the theft of motor vehicles has skyrocketed. More than 2 million vehicles are stolen annually in Europe. Many are illegally exported to developing countries, particularly in the Middle East.

- The theft of airbags and the resale of stolen salvaged airbags is still a major problem. One company that insures about 20% of the cars in the United States annually pays out over $10 million because of stolen airbags. Several states have enacted legislation that is largely ineffective because there is no national system in place to identify and respond to this problem. The National Insurance Crime Bureau (NICB) has been spearheading a drive to develop strategies for attacking this problem.
- Heavy-truck and tractor-trailer thefts are on the increase. The insurance industry annually pays out over $18 million because of commercial-vehicle theft, excluding cargo losses. California and Florida have the highest number of tractors stolen, while California, Texas, and Florida are ranked as the top three for trailer theft.

Auto Theft—Myths

- Auto theft happens to other people, not to me.
- Auto theft is a victimless crime. Insurance companies pay the costs.
- Most of the vehicles stolen are new models, so I don't need to worry if my car is a couple of years old.
- Most stolen vehicles disappear forever, because they are either exported or cut up into pieces.
- When an auto thief is caught, punishment is severe.

Auto Theft—Facts

- It is estimated that in 20%–30% of auto thefts, the operator has left the keys in the car.
- Everyone with comprehensive insurance pays for auto theft and fraud through increased premiums, even if he/she never has a vehicle stolen. According to the National Insurance Crime Bureau, consumers pay $300 per year just for insurance fraud.[7]
- Punishment for auto theft is not swift and sure.
- The theft of older-model cars is prevalent. For example, in 2007 the National Insurance Crime Bureau reported the top 10 most stolen vehicles in the United States were model years 1989–2004.[8]
- Everyone's tax dollars pay the cost of fighting auto theft, including the costs of components of the criminal justice system.
- Auto theft is not a victimless crime. Insurance does not pay for the victim's insurance deductible, work loss, inconvenience, emotional trauma, and time loss (estimated to average more than 40 hours, which include making telephone calls; filling out police reports; purchasing a replacement vehicle; completing insurance claim forms; and dealing with licensing and registration problems, vehicle inspection, and repairs, which may take many weeks if parts have to be ordered).[9]

▲ **FIGURE 16-1   Thief breaks car window**
The professional car thief is motivated by high profits and relatively low risk of apprehension. These thieves use a variety of means for entering locked cars, including breaking windows to open locked doors. The professional thief can break into a car, start it, and drive away in as little as 20 seconds. (© Premium Stock/Corbis)

TYPES OF THEFT

Motor vehicle thefts generally fall into one of four categories: temporary theft, joyriding, professional theft, or fraud.

Temporary Theft

The term **temporary theft** is not used to imply that the crime is not serious but to distinguish joyriding from something more ominous. Of growing concern are the thefts of vehicles specifically for use in the commission of other crimes such as robberies or drive-by shootings, after which the vehicles are abandoned. These thefts are on the increase and, when reported, are often recorded only as the underlying crime rather than also as a motor vehicle theft, thereby skewing the actual theft figures.

Joyriding

Joyriding is most often engaged in by teenagers—15–19 years old—who steal a car simply to drive it around before abandoning it. Among the reasons teenage joyriders cite for the thefts are that joyriding makes them feel important, powerful, and accepted among their peers; it's fun and exciting; they did it on a dare; it relieves boredom and gives an adrenaline rush; they don't feel like walking; they want to impress girls; to make money by stripping cars and selling the parts; to get even with parents, or to escape family problems; and it was done as part of a gang membership or initiation. Since many youngsters are not professionals, they fre-

quently target vehicles that are easy to steal and generally lack any antitheft devices. The large number of apprehensions in this age category may be due to the arrests of joyriders.

Professional Theft

In **professional theft** (Figure 16-1), the car thief is motivated by very high profits and generally low risk. The profits to be gained are second only to those from drugs. Anyone who has ever purchased a replacement part for a car is aware that the cost of replacing all the parts of a vehicle is much higher than the original cost of the entire vehicle. The professional can often sell the parts of a stolen car for up to five times the original assembled value. Considering what the thief "paid" for the vehicle, the profit margin is substantial.

However, professionals do have costs in operating their "businesses." It is not infrequent for professional thieves to employ and train youths to steal cars. Often a youth is paid a set amount, several hundred to several thousand dollars, for each theft. The amount varies depending on the make, model, and year of the vehicle. There are even "training schools" in some areas of the country where juveniles and young adults are taught how to steal cars, trucks, motorcycles, and other vehicles. The professional thief, for example, can break into a locked, high-priced car, start it, and drive it away in as little as 20 seconds.

Fraud

Although certain types of theft involve fraud perpetrated on innocent purchasers, the major category of **vehicle fraud** as described here does not actually involve the theft of vehicles by professionals or even strangers. The various types of vehicle fraud are generally committed by the owner or someone acting on behalf of the owner, with the underlying purpose of profiting at the expense of an insurance company.

The NICB estimates that anywhere from 15% to 25% of all reported vehicle thefts involve some type of fraud and that a vast majority of them involve fraudulent insurance claims. Insurance crime is an enormous problem, and its true magnitude is almost impossible to pinpoint. The associated crimes of identity theft and credit card fraud, both of which have reached epidemic proportions, make the fraud problem even more complex.

In addition, some insurance experts estimate that between 16 and 35 cents of every dollar in premiums paid by the public for motor vehicle insurance is used to pay fraudulent claims or to fight fraud. The NICB says that if the amount of insurance claim fraud and vehicle theft occurring in the United States represented a corporation, it would rank in the top 25 of the Fortune 500 and be called a growth industry. In addition, insurance fraud is on the rise, because it is an easy crime to successfully commit. Insurance companies, even those with highly qualified special investigation units whose function is to investigate suspected cases of fraud, must be concerned about potential liability resulting from lawsuits if someone is wrongly accused or a claim is wrongly denied. The fact that insurance companies are believed to have a great deal of money—deep pockets—makes these companies even more susceptible to civil suits and potential liability and, in turn, even more cautious.

Fraudulent auto-theft claims are not the only type of fraud to which the insurance industry is subjected, but they account for a significant part of the overall fraud. Fully 10% of all property and casualty claims are either inflated or outright fraud. Estimates are that fraudulent insurance claim payouts are $100 billion annually. This amount fluctuates, since it is well recognized that fraud increases as the economy worsens.

METHODS OF OPERATION— THE PROFESSIONAL

To turn a profit, professional thieves use a variety of means to dispose of stolen motor vehicles. Among the most common are chop shops, quick strip, salvage switches, export, and cloning.

Chop Shops

Very simply, a **chop shop** is a place where stolen vehicles are disassembled for resale of their parts (Figure 16-2). The operators and employees of chop shops cut stolen motor vehicles apart with torches, power saws, and other tools, sometimes in as little as 8–9 minutes. They alter or dispose of the parts that are potentially traceable and sell the untraceable parts to repair shops or salvage yards.

▲ **FIGURE 16-2   Interior of a chop shop**
A chop shop such as the one pictured here is a place where stolen vehicles are disassembled for resale of their parts. Stolen vehicles are cut apart in as little as 8 minutes in these chop shops. Parts are then sold to repair shops or salvage yards. Sometimes the repair shop operator is in collusion with the thief or the chop shop. **(Courtesy National Insurance Crime Bureau)**

Sometimes the parts buyers are unsuspecting. Often, the salvage yard or repair shop operator is in collusion with the thief or the chop shop. In fact, a chop shop may well direct the theft of a specific type of motor vehicle in order to "fill an order" for a specific part needed by a repair shop or salvage yard.

A modification of the typical chop-shop operation is as follows:

> Thieves steal a car, disassemble it carefully so that the parts are not damaged, have the remainder conveniently recovered and disposed of through a salvage sale, buy the salvage, reassemble the vehicle with all its original parts, and sell the vehicle, which has already been classed as a recovered theft and is no longer considered stolen.

Quick Strip

In a **quick strip,** a vehicle is stolen and stripped mainly for valuable accessories such as seats, stereos, car phones, and tires. These items are attractive to thieves because they normally do not contain any identifying numbers, thus making them difficult to identify and easy to dispose of.

Salvage Switch

Generally, a **salvage vehicle** is one that has been damaged or wrecked to such an extent that the cost of repairing it is beyond its fair market value. Thus, its primary value in the legitimate market comes from the sale of its undamaged parts. To the criminal, however, the value of a salvaged vehicle is far greater than its parts. The real profit is made after the criminal buys the salvage, provided it is accompanied by the certificate of title and the vehicle identification number (VIN) plate. Often the offender does not even want the vehicle and leaves it at the salvage yard from which it is purchased or disposes of it elsewhere. The thief then steals a vehicle identical to the wreck, changes the VIN plate, and sells the stolen vehicle, with a matching title, to an innocent purchaser or to a purchaser who is offered such a "good" price that no questions are asked. Through the **salvage switch,** the thief is able to disguise and dispose of stolen vehicles in the legitimate market.

Export

Vehicles manufactured in the United States are extremely popular in other countries. The sale of American-manufactured vehicles can also be highly profitable. Vehicles manufactured in other countries for sale in the United States are also stolen for export. Buyers in foreign nations often pay double the purchase price for quality cars, some of which is due to high tariffs. The NICB estimates that 13% of all vehicles stolen in the United States are illegally exported.[10] Mexico and Central and South

American countries are among the most popular but certainly not the exclusive destinations for stolen U.S.-manufactured vehicles. It has been estimated that as many as 20,000 stolen or embezzled cars, trucks, buses, motorcycles, and other vehicles are transported into Mexico each year. This amounts to 6.6%–10% of the estimated number of stolen vehicles exported each year.

Contributing to this problem are the limited, although effective, controls exercised by Mexican customs and the few effective controls exercised by the United States over southbound traffic entering Mexico. The volume of traffic going into Mexico makes it almost impossible to inspect and investigate all vehicles. Many stolen vehicles are also taken to Canada. Some are resold, but many are exported to their final destinations. Exports account for a growing percentage of unrecovered stolen vehicles, and the problem is even greater in port cities.

With the collapse of communism and the opening of free market economies in eastern Europe, auto theft has grown to become an enormous international problem. According to Interpol, auto theft has become the second largest source of terrorist funding.[11]

Cloning

Vehicle cloning is a crime in which stolen vehicles receive the identity of nonstolen, legally owned vehicles of the same make and model. This is accomplished by counterfeiting labels, stickers, VIN plates, and titles to make the stolen car look legitimate. Illicit profits from vehicle cloning in the United States are estimated by the NICB to be in excess of $12 million each year. Many high-priced, luxury vehicles are objects of cloning.[12]

Cloning is not confined to the United States. Many offenses have occurred in Mexico, Canada, and the United Kingdom. Exportation of legitimate vehicles is also used by professional thieves to clone vehicles. Once exported, the VIN number and other counterfeit indicia appear on stolen, cloned vehicles titled and registered in one or more states. These vehicles are referred to as being "reborn." Often, multiple copies of the counterfeit indicia will appear on stolen vehicles and, unless the vehicles are thoroughly inspected by trained investigators, these stolen vehicles are almost impossible to identify as being fraudulent. Many of the stolen, cloned vehicles are then exported to such popular destinations as Eastern Europe, Russia, the Caribbean, the Dominican Republic, Central and South America, and the Far East.[13] The NICB says that cloned vehicles are also used to facilitate drug trafficking, money laundering, and for transportation to and from crime scenes by organized crime.[14]

Many of the fraudulent theft schemes described in the next section apply equally to the cloning of a vehicle.

FRAUDULENT THEFT SCHEMES

Fraudulent auto-theft claim schemes fall into three major categories: false-vehicle schemes, in which no vehicle exists or the vehicle is not owned by the criminal; false-theft schemes; and inflated-loss-theft schemes.

False-Vehicle Schemes

False-vehicle schemes are particularly prevalent where insurance companies are lax or have ineffective programs to verify the existence of a vehicle before issuing an insurance policy. As a general rule, this type of fraud is planned well in advance of obtaining insurance coverage. The criminal purchases a policy that has a provision covering loss by theft. In fact, the vehicle does not exist except on paper, has already been salvaged, or does not belong to the person who buys the insurance. Most often, the vehicle insured is a recent model. Some time later (generally within three months, to hold down the cost of the insurance coverage purchase) a theft report is filed with a law-enforcement agency, and a claim is made to the insurance company.

Several modifications of the salvage switch, described earlier, are illustrative of false-vehicle schemes. Once a salvaged vehicle is purchased, insurance coverage is obtained. After a short time, a theft-loss claim is filed for the vehicle, which, of course, was in "excellent condition."

In some jurisdictions, a **salvage title** may be issued. This does not necessarily prevent false-theft claims on salvage; it merely channels the process in a different direction. One way the criminal avoids the problems associated with the issuance of salvage titles is by **washing,** or laundering, the title. This is done by fabricating the sale of the vehicle and transferring the title to an alleged purchaser in another state that does not issue salvage titles or does not carry forward a "brand" on the title issued by another state. The "buyer" then obtains a clean title in that state and transfers it back to the insured either directly or through several other people or businesses to make it appear to be a legitimate transaction. Then, with a clean title, the insured files a theft claim.

In another technique, the salvage buyer falsifies the necessary support documentation so that it shows the salvage vehicle as being completely rebuilt or restored and thereby obtains a "clean," or regular, title. The thief may not even bother to get a clean title; upon filing a claim for the alleged theft, he/she may simply contend that the vehicle was rebuilt or restored but was stolen before the insured could file the necessary paperwork to obtain a nonsalvage title.

In still another version of the salvage switch, the VIN plate may be attached to a rented or borrowed car of the same make and model and, along with the certificate of title, may be presented to and inspected by an agent of the company from which coverage is sought. After the policy is issued, the salvage vehicle VIN plate is removed and the vehicle is returned to the person or company from which it was borrowed or rented.

Presenting a counterfeit or stolen certificate of title or manufacturer's certificate of origin (MCO) as the basis for having a policy issued on a **"paper vehicle"** or on a stolen vehicle with a concealed identity is another technique for defrauding insurance companies through the filing of false-vehicle claims. A manufacturer's certificate of origin is the original identification document issued by a vehicle's manufacturer, somewhat like a birth certificate. It accompanies the vehicle through its delivery to a new car dealer until it is first sold to a retail purchaser, after which the MCO is surrendered to the jurisdiction issuing the first certificate of title in the name of the retail purchaser.

A variation on the counterfeit- or blank-title scheme is the altered title, whereby the criminal manages to conceal the existence of a lienholder who may have already repossessed the vehicle because of missed payments. A theft report is then filed along with the fraudulent insurance claim.

It is not uncommon to find the following scenario in a fraudulent claim on a false vehicle:

Henry Johnson owns a late-model full-size car. The vehicle is paid for and Johnson has the title in his possession. Johnson decides to sell the car. After he has it advertised for a few days, he receives a satisfactory offer from a person who pays cash and takes the car to another state to have it titled and registered. Johnson signs the title over to the buyer, who takes possession of the vehicle and drives it to his own state of residence. The next day, Johnson, claiming he can't find his car title, applies for a duplicate title in his own state. The title is issued and is branded with the word "duplicate." Although it may take several weeks to receive the duplicate title, the process may still be faster than it takes for the buyer's home state to issue a new title to the buyer and send the original of Johnson's title back to his state for official cancellation. Upon obtaining the duplicate title, Johnson files a theft claim with his insurance company and surrenders the duplicate title to the company in exchange for the theft-loss payment. After learning of the scam, the insurance company goes looking for Johnson and finds that all the information he provided was false, and he has disappeared not only with the insurance money but also with the money he made from selling the vehicle. Normally, the issuance of a duplicate title renders the original or any previously issued duplicate void, but this fact was unknown to the buyer of Johnson's car or to the buyer's home state, where he applied for a title in his own name.

False-Theft Schemes

As opposed to the many different fraudulent schemes in which no vehicle exists, in a **false-theft scheme,** the vehicle does exist and is in fact owned by the person who has obtained the insurance policy. The primary reason why an owner would file a phony theft-loss is generally either to avoid liability for some conduct that resulted from the use of the vehicle or to reduce or avoid some financial loss. The specific motivation leading to the filing of the fraudulent claim may exist at the time the policy coverage is obtained or may result from circumstances that develop later.

Among the vast number of motivations—and there are as many motivations as there are false claims—for filing false theft-loss claims are these:

- To cover or avoid personal responsibility for a hit-and-run accident. The owner reports the car stolen (before the police come to question him or her) and subsequently files an insurance claim.
- To replace an old vehicle that just doesn't look good or drive smoothly any longer.
- To replace a "lemon" that can't be sold for a decent price.
- To obtain money for another vehicle that is in need of repair or replacement.
- To avoid loss of the vehicle without receiving any financial gain—for example, through repossession caused by a default of payments or in response to a court order to transfer the title to a former spouse after a divorce.
- To end costly car payments or repair bills.
- To avoid the hassle of selling.
- To obtain a more favorable interest rate on a car loan.
- To break a restricting car lease.

As noted at the outset of this chapter, fraud may be committed by the insured acting alone or with another person or persons. When a vehicle owner conspires with others, the fraud is often referred to as an "owner give-up." Examples of both solo and give-up false-theft schemes include these:

- The vehicle is abandoned and later reported stolen (Figure 16-3).
- The vehicle, which may have been previously damaged or had some major mechanical defects, is reported stolen. Shortly afterward, it is recovered, and the insured claims that the damage or defects were caused by the theft.
- The vehicle is sold to an out-of-state buyer, and then a duplicate certificate of title is applied for and used to file the claim—just as in the Johnson scenario, reported earlier.
- The vehicle is not stolen but is hidden before the theft report and before the claim being filed. After the loss is paid, the vehicle can be returned to use, stripped, sold, chopped for parts, taken out of state, or otherwise disposed of.
- The vehicle is dumped in water, a method of causing damage that is increasing in use. This is often referred to as car dunking or vehicle dumping.

▶ FIGURE 16-3
Vehicle abandoned in false-theft scheme
Vehicle owners have been known to file false theft reports on their cars, often to avoid liability for some conduct associated with the vehicle or to reduce or avoid financial loss. The owner typically attempts to abandon the vehicle in a location beyond the scope of a general search conducted by the police. (© Chinch Gryniewicz, Ecoscene/Corbis)

Such vehicles generally cannot be repaired economically even if recovered.

- Vehicle burying is another way that owners dispose of unwanted vehicles—for example, an employee at the Charlotte/Douglas International Airport in North Carolina was charged with insurance fraud after police unearthed his car from the ground at a remote, wooded edge of the airport. After his attempts to sell the car met with no success, the insured, who worked as a landscaper at the airport, decided to use a backhoe to dig a pit and bury his car inside. He then reported the car stolen in order to collect an insurance settlement.[15]
- Vehicle arson is another form of fraud that is planned beforehand and is motivated by a desire to collect on an insurance policy either to make a profit or to solve a financial problem. (Vehicle arson will be covered in more detail later.)

Inflated-Theft-Loss Schemes

In contrast to the preceding schemes, in the **inflated-theft-loss scheme** the vehicle actually exists, actually belongs to the insured, and actually is stolen. The fraud occurs when the insured makes a false claim concerning the physical or mechanical condition of the vehicle when it was stolen; actually causes some damage or removes some parts on recovery of the vehicle but before it is inspected by the insurance company; claims there were expensive parts on or improvements made to the vehicle before it was stolen; or, if no follow-up inspection is conducted by the insurer, claims certain damage occurred that actually did not happen.

One frequently used scam has the insured enter into a conspiracy with a repair shop, after a stolen vehicle is recovered, to allege that damages were caused during the

theft. The damages do not exist. The vehicle is immediately "repaired" before the insurance appraiser has the opportunity to inspect the vehicle, and the repair shop insists that the insurer accept the repair bill, possibly using a photo of a wrecked vehicle of the same make and condition as the vehicle "before repair." A spinoff of this basic scenario has the repair shop show the appraiser an actual wrecked vehicle in its possession of the same make and model as the insured's car.

The inflated-theft-loss claim also extends to vehicle contents. The claimant alleges the vehicle contained valuable clothes, cameras, golf clubs, and other "new" items of considerable value when it was stolen.

Defrauding the Owner and the Insurer

Sometimes the owner is not involved in the fraud, and both the owner and the insurer become victims, as illustrated in the following example:

An individual leases a vehicle from a rental company and, during the rental period, reports the vehicle stolen to both the police and the rental company. Shortly after, the renter again calls the police and reports that the vehicle was recovered, using some excuse such as his coworker took it to the store or he forgot where he parked it the night before because he had had too much to drink. Consequently, the police never enter the "stolen" report into the National Crime Information Center (NCIC). Conveniently, the renter fails to notify the rental company, which assumes that the law-enforcement agency entered the theft into NCIC. The thief may have several days' or longer use of the vehicle before the victims can put the whole story together.

Some vehicles are exported by owners for the purpose of filing and collecting on fraudulent theft claims.

Another type of export fraud occurs when a vehicle owner makes multiple copies of proof-of-ownership documents to present to the Bureau of Customs Enforcement officials and exports his or her vehicle. After the vehicle arrives at its foreign destination, the VIN plate is removed and mailed back to the owner, who steals a car of the same make and model, switches the VIN plate, and, using the additional copies of ownership documents, exports the stolen vehicle. This is another variation of cloning.

As illustrated by the preceding examples, people who engage in insurance fraud are limited only by their imaginations. They are able to change tactics as quickly as law-enforcement agencies and the insurance industry devise methods for combating current fraud schemes.

THEFT OF HEAVY CONSTRUCTION EQUIPMENT

Heavy construction equipment (or, simply, **heavy equipment**) is commonly referred to as **off-road equipment**. The National Crime Information Center (NCIC) received 16,291 reports of commercial equipment thefts in 2006, with annual loss estimates as high as $1 billion. The recovery rate is only 28%. Insurance claims have been increasing at an annual 10%–20% rate for the past decade. The national average for a used piece of construction equipment is $135,000. The states with the highest theft rates are Texas, California, North Carolina, and Florida. California, Texas, and Florida have the highest recovery rates.[16]

Off-road equipment is stolen for the following reasons: its high value, a demand for the equipment, low security, low risk, and high rewards.[17] Thieves may steal on order, for stripping, or for export. One offender was caught with a notebook filled with photographs he had taken of machinery on various farms. When interrogated, he stated he had roamed the countryside obtaining the photographs in the notebook. The notebook was then used as a "sales catalog" when meeting with prospective buyers and as a means of instructing thieves working with him as to exactly what equipment from a particular location was to be taken. This arrangement made it possible for the equipment to be consigned or

sold before it was even stolen, minimizing the amount of time that the equipment was in the thieves' hands and therefore their risk.

The theft of off-road equipment and the investigation of the thefts cause numerous problems for owners, manufacturers, and law-enforcement agencies. Title or registration generally is not required for such equipment, and owners have traditionally resisted such requirements for several reasons. They fear that the title and registration records could be used to levy taxes on expensive items of property and that such a financial burden would have to be passed on to their consumers. Further, they believe that registration requirements would impede their ability to move the equipment rapidly and freely around the country.

Owners are also victimized by the problem of inventory control. Construction equipment is often spread over several miles of job site or over several job sites and may be left idle for days or weeks at a time in isolated areas. Thus, when the professional thief is overcome by the irresistible temptation, it is often days before the theft is noticed and reported to the police.

Another issue that compounded the construction equipment theft problem until recently was the fact that off-road equipment, unlike conventional motor vehicles, had no standard, permanently affixed identification number. Historically, each manufacturer had its own system of identification, and the numbering systems could vary from 4 to as many as 15 alphanumeric digits. On January 1, 2000, the 237 manufacturers of heavy equipment throughout the world (including the big four U.S. manufacturers—Case, Caterpillar, Deere, and Ford) began using a standardized 17-character **product identification number (PIN)** on all new equipment models[18] (Figure 16-4). The definition of "new model" will not necessarily change by calendar year. Consequently, it will take a few years before the standardized 17-character PIN becomes uniformly applied.

In at least one instance, the PIN is now more difficult to counterfeit than has been the case in the past. The new PIN plate on Caterpillar equipment is laser-engraved on black anodized aluminum and has a bar code and a microprinted security feature—the PIN number.[19]

Heavy equipment is also easily stolen; a single key may be used to start all models produced by a particular manufacturer, and where key locks are in place, the machinery can be jumped by placing a pocket knife or screwdriver across the electrical posts on the starter. Although manufacturers offer antitheft devices, they are costly items that add substantially to the base price of the equipment.

The unfamiliarity of most law-enforcement officers with the nature, identity, and terminology of construction and farm equipment is among the principal problems faced by law enforcement. Few agencies have anyone with the expertise to identify specific machines or to locate and interpret identification numbers (Figure 16-5).

►FIGURE 16-4
Product identification removed from stolen piece of construction equipment
The Product Identification Number (PIN) had been removed from this piece of construction equipment and, following its recovery, an NICB special agent was able to identify the unit by other partial numbers so it could be returned to its rightful owner. (Courtesy National Insurance Crime Bureau)

►FIGURE 16-5
Illustrations of heavy construction equipment

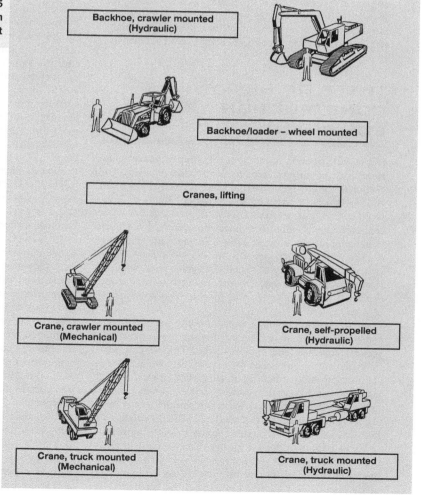

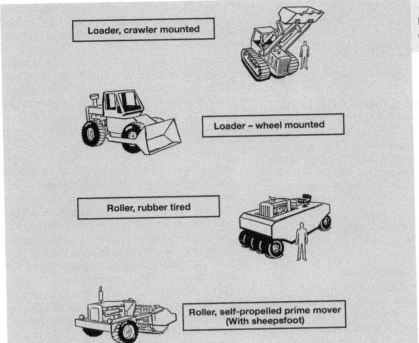

◄ FIGURE 16-5
Illustrations of heavy construction equipment *(continued)*

COMMERCIAL-VEHICLE AND CARGO THEFT

The insurance industry pays out about $18 million every year because of **commercial-vehicle theft.** It is difficult to convert this figure to the number of vehicles stolen, because commercial-vehicle theft data is incorporated into the overall motor vehicle theft statistics. Suffice it to say, the number is significant and rising. Additionally, it is estimated that the actual number of cargo thefts is 20% more than reported.

The theft of cargo from, or in, commercial vehicles—is a rapidly growing criminal enterprise. Although not a separate crime in itself, **cargo theft,** in the United States, is estimated as accounting for as much as $25 billion in direct merchandise losses each year.[20] As an aside, cargo theft is just one aspect of a larger problem called *cargo crime,* which also includes smuggling, counterfeiting, and product piracy. Total direct merchandise losses from all cargo crime are estimated as approaching $60 billion per year.[21] The products most vulnerable to cargo crime, in general, and cargo theft, in particular, are assembled computers, computer components and software, electronic products, cigarettes, and fashion apparel, packaged foods, appliances, and seafood.

In January 2010 the FBI announced that a cargo-theft data element was adopted in the national uniform crime reports program. This means state and local agencies need

to begin capturing and reporting this date to the FBI. The new program called Cargo Net provides that state UCR programs will have 18–24 months to implement needed software changes to begin collecting the data on the state level.[22]

INVESTIGATIVE TOOLS AND TECHNIQUES

Vehicle theft investigation is a fairly technical and sophisticated specialty. An effective investigator needs experience and expertise. Despite the fact that vehicle theft may not be among the offenses receiving the highest priority for the allocation of limited resources by a law-enforcement agency, there are thousands of specialists in the United States and elsewhere whose expertise is available to any investigator or street officer needing assistance. Often, these resources are just a telephone call away.

In any specialized investigative field, one is not born an expert and cannot become an expert without extensive training and experience. So it is with vehicle thefts and related crimes. Individuals who possess the expertise, such as highly skilled investigators, cannot assume that uniformed officers with general policing responsibilities have any knowledge about the field beyond their limited exposure in an academy setting. Thus, if investigators are anxious for patrol officers to perform some initial investigative tasks, the investigators should offer to teach those officers how to perform the desired tasks.

MAJOR INVESTIGATIVE RESOURCES

Automatic License Plate Recognition Systems (ALPR)

Automatic License Plate Recognition Systems (ALPR) can be installed in law-enforcement vehicles or at permanent locations on streets or highways. The technology allows thousands of vehicle license plates to be checked in short periods of time, limited only by the number of vehicles available to check. The ALPR checks each license plate against lists of stolen cars (with license plates), BOLOs, Amber Alerts, and others. The City of Long Beach, California, after a couple of years checked almost 7.5 million license plates. They recovered over 1,000 stolen vehicles and made over 200 arrests.[23]

National Insurance Crime Bureau

The **National Insurance Crime Bureau (NICB)** is not a law-enforcement agency that investigates auto thefts and arrests offenders in the traditional sense. Rather, the NICB is an information-gathering and dissemination body and a law-enforcement assistance agency. In this regard, its special agents do investigate professional theft rings and other auto-theft cases in conjunction with local, state, and federal law-enforcement agencies.

Beginning in 1912 with the efforts of a few individuals representing different insurance companies that joined forces to disseminate information on stolen motor vehicles, the cooperation gradually spread and evolved into several independent regionalized and, later, national groups. This growth limited communication and interaction. Duplication of efforts and costs, along with the creation of considerable confusion among law-enforcement officials in deciding whom to contact for information, led to the initial consolidation of all existing auto-theft information agencies and organizations into the National Automobile Theft Bureau (NATB) in 1912. In 1965 the NATB was completely nationalized and centralized.

Late in 1991 a merger took place between the NATB and the Insurance Crime Prevention Institute (ICPI), and on January 1, 1992, the National Insurance Crime Bureau was formed. The NICB now has approximately 150 investigative field agents working with another 800 fraud investigators who work for individual insurance companies.

The NICB is not a government organization. It is a not-for-profit organization operated by, funded by, affiliated with, and serving approximately 1,000 associated insurance companies nationwide. It supports engineering, research, and experiments aimed at reducing vehicle theft and fraud and is a recognized national voice for law enforcement and the insurance industry on legislative matters.

The NICB assists in the identification of vehicles and helps educate law-enforcement officers in investigative techniques of vehicle identification, fraud, and theft. Online Insurance Crime Training for Law Enforcement, including material on vehicle theft fraud, can be found at *www.nicbtraining.org.*

In addition to the expertise of its field personnel, the computerized records developed and established by the NICB, and now maintained and administered by the Insurance Service Office, Inc. (ISO), a private company, are invaluable investigative aids. These database services include:

- *Insurance theft file:* More than 1,000 insurance companies report stolen vehicles. Theft records from the Canadian Automobile Theft Bureau (CATB) and most European countries are also maintained and include all types of vehicles, off-road machinery, boats, parts, and accessories. The records contain full ownership and insurance information.

- *Salvage file:* Salvage vehicle reports are received from insurance companies on vehicles for which there has been a loss settlement and the company has taken the title. These vehicles are generally sold through salvage pools or to salvage buyers. The file contains information on both sellers and buyers of salvage.

- *Export file:* The U.S. Customs Service and others send copies of export declarations for entry into the system. The information aids in the detection of illegal exports and of fraudulent theft reports on exported vehicles in cases where a subsequent stolen vehicle report is filed.

- *NCIC mirror image and purge file:* All active and inactive theft records on vehicles and boats housed in NCIC are also contained in the mirror image file. In addition, vehicle theft records purged from NCIC since 1972 for a variety of reasons are provided to NICB on a daily basis and are entered into the system as a permanent record. The file is an important and time-saving tool for law enforcement.

- *Information-wanted file:* When a purchaser skips out on payments to a finance company that has purchased physical-damage insurance on the vehicle from one of the NICB sponsoring member companies, the information is made available to law-enforcement agencies investigating the vehicle as a suspected stolen unit.

- *Inquiry file:* When a law-enforcement agency makes an inquiry on a vehicle for an investigation, any subsequent information received or any inquiry on the same vehicle from another person or agency will be passed on to the original inquirer.

- *Shipping and assembly file:* This file holds the shipping and assembly records for most automobiles; light-, medium-, and heavy-duty trucks; semitrailers; motorcycles; and snowmobiles produced for sale in the United States and Canada.

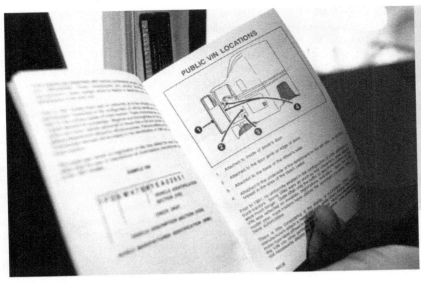

- *Impound file:* An increasing number of states are now collecting and reporting impound records to NICB for entry into this file. The file helps clear many stolen records and is a valuable investigative tool.
- *VINASSIST:* This NICB program, provided to law-enforcement agencies at no cost, defines, edits, evaluates, and corrects vehicle identification numbers, a process that greatly aids law enforcement in positively identifying specific recovered motor vehicles.
- *All-claims database:* With this database, claims filed against participating member insurance companies can be compared to detect possible fraudulent claims, including auto theft–related insurance fraud.

The NICB is organized into nine geographic areas, with its headquarters in the Chicago suburb of Palos Hills, Illinois, serving as the Area 1 office. The other offices serving major metropolitan and surrounding locales are in Seattle; Los Angeles; Dallas; Tampa; Washington, D.C.; New York; Columbus, Ohio; Hartford, Connecticut; and Chula Vista, California.[24]

Since 1919 the NICB or its predecessor, the NATB, has annually published the *Passenger Vehicle Identification Manual* (Figure 16-6), which contains the following information:

- federal motor vehicle theft prevention standards;
- explanation of vehicle identification numbers;
- VIN plate attachment and location;
- federal safety certification labels;
- passenger vehicle and light-duty truck VIN structure;
- motorcycles and all-terrain vehicle VIN structure;
- general information on snowmobiles and boats;
- vehicle shipping and assembly record information.[25]

Every five years, the NICB also publishes the *Commercial Vehicle Identification Manual,* which contains the following information:

- world manufacturer identification codes;
- model year identifier;
- truck-tractor identification;
- commercial-trailer identification;
- off-road equipment identification.[26]

In 2010 the NICB published *Heavy Equipment Identification Manual,* which contains:

- product identification number locations;
- types of construction equipment.[27]

Insurance Bureau Canada (IBC)

Known formerly as the Canadian Insurance Crime Prevention Bureau, the Insurance Bureau Canada has been functioning since 1923 but became an independent division within the Insurance Council of Canada on January 1, 1998. It is to Canada what NICB is to the United States. IBC is supported by over 90% of private-property and casualty insurers. Within the organizational structure of IBC are found the Canadian Automobile Theft Bureau (CATB) and the Canadian Police Information System, the sister organization of NCIC. IBC is headquartered in Toronto, Ontario. It has four regional offices, located in Innisfall, Alberta; Toronto; Montreal, Quebec; and Halifax, Nova Scotia.[28]

International Association of Auto Theft Investigators

Another resource available to the investigator is the International Association of Auto Theft Investigators (IAATI) and its regional affiliated chapters, which are located in many parts of the world, including Europe and Australia. With a current membership of almost 3,800 representing more than 35 countries, IAATI was formed in 1952 for the purpose of formulating new methods to attack and control vehicle theft and fraud. Its members represent law-enforcement agencies, state registration and titling agencies, insurance companies, car rental companies, the automobile manufacturing industry, and other interested groups. International and regional training seminars are held throughout the year. As with many such organizations, it is a great network of specialists all willing to assist any investigator or officer who requests help.

State Organizations

Many states have organizations consisting of auto-theft investigators who meet regularly to exchange intelligence information and learn new methods of combating the problems of theft and fraud.

National Crime Information Center

Another valuable resource for the investigator is the FBI's National Crime Information Center (NCIC). Online inquiries can be made to NCIC's vehicle or license plate files to check on records for stolen vehicles, vehicles wanted in conjunction with felonies, stolen component parts, and stolen license plates. In addition, a request can be made for an off-line search, which is a tool designed to assist an investigator by providing lead information. For example, an investigator attempting to track a stolen vehicle that is known to be traveling across the country can request an off-line search to see if any stolen inquiries had been made within a specific time frame on that vehicle. A hit would identify the time and location from which the inquiry was made, thus providing a lead to locating the vehicle.

The original NCIC system held more than 40 million records in its 17 databases and processed more than 2 million transactions a day, but it was more than 30 years old. An updated, new-generation system, NCIC 2000, was implemented in July 1999. It has all the advantages of the old system plus impressive new capabilities such as image processing, whereby mug shots, other photographs, signatures, and identifying marks can be electronically submitted; single-finger fingerprint matching, including storing and searching for right-index fingerprints; a linkage field, whereby multiple records concerning the same criminal or the same crime can be automatically associated; and several new databases, including the Convicted Persons on Supervised Release Database, the Convicted Sexual Offender Registry, and the SENTRY file of persons incarcerated in federal prisons. These can all be accessed through NCIC 2000.[29]

The NCIC databases can be used for many different purposes. For instance, through the linkage function, an inquiry on a gun can also identify a wanted person or a stolen car. Since vehicle information can be included in the Convicted Sexual Offender Registry, a traffic stop

with an inquiry on the license plate may identify an individual as a registered sexual offender.[30]

Special Investigative Units

In the mid-1970s Kemper Insurance Company created the first special investigative unit (SIU) for insurance companies. Its primary purpose was to investigate potentially fraudulent auto-theft claims. There are more than 800 SIU investigators employed in the insurance industry working fraud claims. Approximately 80% of the insurance companies now have SIUs. The agents and units work with and train insurance adjusters to detect oddities and "red flags" indicating potential fraud. The SIUs also work closely with law enforcement by lending assistance in investigations—providing computer information, claims histories, and statements of insureds made under oath.

The priorities of the NICB agents primarily assigned to fraud cases changes as new problems arise. The current priority is Medicaid Fraud.[31]

AAMVANET

The AAMVANET computerized communication network links state and provincial agencies on matters of highway usage and highway safety. The system was initiated by and for the **American Association of Motor Vehicle Administrators (AAMVA).** The AAMVANET corporation, a subsidiary of AAMVA, is working with the FBI to coordinate efforts to create the **National Motor Vehicle Title Information System (NMVTIS).** Beginning in 1992, AAMVANET developed the prototype for NMVTIS. Through NMVTIS, any inquiry receives a complete and up-to-the-minute history of a vehicle, including whether it was reported stolen, salvaged, or exported or is otherwise incapable of being the subject of a new transfer. In addition to inquiry capability, the system prevents the laundering of titles between states for the purpose of removing brands such as those that appear on salvage, flood-damaged, rebuilt, or unrepairable vehicles. Currently, with the exception of Illinois, all states are either fully operational, partially online, or providing data by batch.[32] The ultimate goal of the developers is to provide a system whereby a potential purchaser of a used vehicle will be able to inquire about the status of the vehicle before making a final commitment to purchase.

Government Agencies

In virtually all state governments, organizations or entities exist that possess information of value to investigators. Specifically, motor vehicle and driver's license offices, insurance fraud investigative units, and fire and arson investigative units may provide valuable information or assistance.

Manufacturers

Manufacturers are one of the most important resources an investigator can cultivate and turn to for assistance, particularly as they relate to the content and location of numbers on vehicles or parts. Domestic and foreign automobile manufacturers are generally most supportive of an investigator's inquiries, as are the Harley-Davidson Motorcycle Company and the John Deere, Case, and Caterpillar companies, which manufacture construction and farm equipment. This list is not meant to be exhaustive. Help will generally be given by any manufacturer when requested.

North American Export Committee

In an effort to stem the tide of stolen vehicles being exported from the country, the NICB, U.S. and Canadian Customs, Royal Canadian Mounted Police, Insurance Bureau Canada, and Miami-Dade Police Department in Florida, along with other law-enforcement agencies, the insurance industry, and other interested parties, established the North American Export Committee in 1995. The committee investigates ways in which the exporting of stolen vehicles could be slowed without impeding commerce at port facilities.

Shipments of vehicles occur in two ways—some vehicles are rolled on and then rolled off a ship, and some are shipped in containers. These are quite different concepts requiring entirely different approaches. U.S. Customs is charged with the responsibility of checking the paperwork on vehicles to be exported, and the paperwork must be received by Customs three days before a vehicle can be shipped. Only limited resources are devoted to this responsibility, however, because Customs is more concerned about property coming into the country and about commodities, other than vehicles being exported. Customs' role has become even more limited after 9/11. It was moved from the Treasury Department to the Department of Homeland Security and was reorganized. Customs inspectors are now part of the Bureau of Customs and Border Protection (CBP), whereas the law-enforcement agents are part of the Bureau of Immigration and Customs Enforcement (ICE). Either Customs or local law-enforcement checks the paperwork, physically examines as many of the vehicles as possible, and enters the VINs into a computer that transmits all those checked to databases with NICB, NCIC, OCRA (Mexican law-enforcement database), a rental car database, and a motor vehicle liens database. Overnight, the list is run against the export, stolen, salvage, and VIN verification files of NICB and the other databases. The next morning, an exceptions report is available to the submitting agencies so that the "trouble messages" (problems) can be checked out before the vehicles are shipped. At the Port of Miami, trouble messages occur on approximately 20% of the exports. Such electronic reporting is now used at 80 ports in the United States.[33]

Containerized vehicles present a different set of problems. There are over 8 million containers exported from the United States in a year. No manifest is going to acknowledge that a container has one or more stolen vehicles. Checking a container, even if it meets a predetermined set of conditions called a profile, is hot, sweaty work—the unloading and reloading take hours—and it interferes with commerce. Stolen vehicles are usually found in the front or middle of a container, with goods packed all around them. To make enforcement more productive, an efficient, effective, and economic method of looking inside containers had to be found.

Science Applications International Corporation developed a device that examines and photographs the contents of a container as it is passing through a gamma ray. In mid-1998, the corporation, in cooperation with the Miami-Dade County Multi-Agency Auto Theft Task Force and on behalf of the North American Export Committee, tested this equipment for a 90-day period at the Port of Miami in what is called the **Stolen Auto Recovery (STAR) System** (Figure 16-7). Before the 90 days were up, more

◄ **FIGURE 16-7**
Stolen vehicle recovered through gamma-ray scan
This stolen vehicle was located when the container in which it was found passed through a gamma-ray scan at the Port of Miami. The container's manifest reported its contents as household goods. (Courtesy Miami-Dade Auto Theft Task Force)

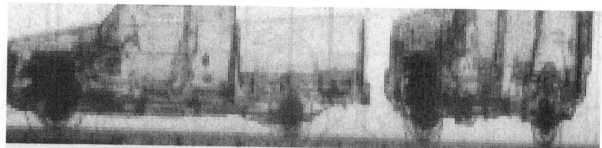

▲ **FIGURE 16-8   Gamma-ray scan showing two utility vehicles**
Advances in technology have assisted in the discovery of stolen vehicles being exported from the United States aboard ships. Science Applications International Corporation has developed a device that examines and photographs the contents of a container as it is passed through a gamma-ray scan. These units cost around $270,000, are very transportable, and are easily installed in one day's time. **(Courtesy Miami-Dade Police Department)**

than 7,700 containers were scanned in less than 6 seconds, each while it continued to move. A total of 630 vehicles were identified, and six stolen vehicles were recovered, valued at $217,000. There were no false identifications, and the flow of commerce was not impeded. The units cost around $270,000, are very transportable, are easily installed in one day, and the gamma-ray scan preserves a video image of the contents of the container (Figure 16-8).

Because of the success of the STAR System, Florida committed to installing a total of 10 systems across the state (at least three additional ports on Florida's east coast have been equipped).[34] Unfortunately, Miami-Dade reorganized its port facility and changed 4 lanes into 16 lanes of ingress onto the port. The money was not available to continue the gamma-ray scan technology at that location.

There are other technologies available. The use of X-ray equipment has been made safe. Portels is an X-ray system that scans from both the front and back of a container and gives an even higher definition picture than does the gamma-ray system. It is manufactured by AS&E and uses what is called "Backscatter" technology to allow X rays from both the front and rear portion of a container going through the system. The company also manufacturers a mobile system that can be mounted on a van with the equipment inside. The van can pull up to a stack of containers at a port and within seconds see sufficient contents to determine if vehicles or other items that may be contraband are inside. The equipment can "inspect" containers stacked three high.[35] VACIS is another system using X-ray technology. Customs and Border Protection has 40 of these units installed at U.S. ports and Canada; Mexico and Arizona have these units at border crossings.[36]

Canada has developed a task-force operation at the port in Vancouver, British Columbia, using this technology, with data transfer to the Canadian Insurance Crime Prevention Bureau. Early results were the recovery of 12 vehicles, all stolen from the province of Ontario.[37] The North American Export Committee also committed to the

further development and implementation of the National Motor Vehicle Title Information System (NMVTIS).

National Equipment Register

The scope of the theft of heavy construction equipment has led manufacturers, dealers, and insurers to support the development of a national database of stolen equipment and provide the services of law-enforcement specialists in the recovery of stolen equipment. The National Equipment Register (NER) facilitates the identification of lost and stolen equipment and the return of such equipment to owners and insurers and promotes due diligence in the purchase of used equipment, thereby deterring the trade in stolen equipment. The NER owner database has 7 million records, and its databases are connected to the databases of the Insurance Services Office, Inc. (ISO), the organization that provides all the computer services for the National Insurance Crime Bureau (NICB). In February 2008 NER, ISO, and NICB formed an alliance to strengthen the ability of the insurance industry to recover stolen heavy equipment.[38] The NER is available to law enforcement 24/7 at a toll-free telephone number for advice on where to locate product information numbers, check on the status of stolen equipment, and identify and locate owners of recovered equipment. If requested, NER can provide on-site assistance to law enforcement. The organization provides training seminars (for example, equipment recovery) for law-enforcement and theft-prevention sessions for equipment owners.[39] (NER can be reached at 212-976-1805 or by e-mail at info@nerusa.com. NER also has a website, *www.nerusa.com*.)

Indicators of Theft and Fraud

NICB publishes lists and pocket guides for law-enforcement officials on the suspicious conduct of people or the status of vehicles that should cause the officer/investigator to make a closer inquiry to determine if a vehicle is stolen or if fraudulent conduct is afoot. Similarly, NER has recommendations about suspicious conduct of people or circumstances that should lead to further inquiry about possible heavy-equipment theft.

LOCATING AND HANDLING VEHICLES

In recent years some investigators have gotten seriously ill while performing their jobs. Locating and handling the recovery of vehicles and parts can be very dangerous. Often, an investigator will climb or crawl around, through, and over wrecks, in a remote area of a salvage yard in order to locate or identify a vehicle part. Not only is the physical work dangerous, but, unknowingly, the investigator may be exposed to toxic waste, which can cause permanent physical damage. Gloves should be worn at all times, along with protective clothing and a mask or breathing device, when encountering the unknown. Similarly, when investigating a vehicle fire, investigators must take precautions, because toxic chemicals may be around that can cause serious long-term illness owing to exposure.

VEHICLE IDENTIFICATION

Often the most difficult and time-consuming task facing an investigator is the identification of a recovered vehicle. Although there are a number of ways by which motor vehicles can be identified, including a description by year, make and model, or license number, these items are easily generalized or alterable. For the investigator, identification is made by numbers affixed to, or inscribed on, the vehicle.

Since 1954 American automobile manufacturers have used a **vehicle identification number (VIN)** instead of an engine number as the primary means of identification. However, before 1968 VINs, although usually inscribed on metal plates, were not uniformly located on vehicles, nor was there any standard method for attaching a **VIN plate** to a vehicle (Figure 16-9). On varying makes and models, VIN plates were affixed with screws or rivets or were spot-welded on doors, doorposts, or dashes. Since 1968 VIN plates on almost all domestic and foreign cars have been attached to the left side of the dash on the instrument panel in such a fashion as to be visible through the windshield. Corvettes, before 1984, had the VIN plate attached to the left-side windshield post. Tractor and semitrailer manufacturers still lack consistency in the placement of VIN plates, as do construction and farm equipment manufacturers in the placement of product identification numbers (PINs).

VIN plates still are attached by a variety of methods. Several foreign manufacturers use a round-head "pop" rivet made of aluminum, stainless steel, or some plastic material. A six-petal "rosette" rivet made of aluminum or stainless steel has been used on General Motors products since 1966, on Chrysler-manufactured vehicles since 1968,

Round-head "pop" rivet aluminum, stainless steel, or plastic

Used on early General Motors vehicles prior to 1965 after departure from "spot weld" method of attaching VIN plates. Still used by most foreign manufacturers.

"Rosette"-type rivet 6 petals, aluminum, or stainless steel

Used by General Motors Corp. since 1965, Chrysler Corp. since 1966, and Ford Motor Co. since 1970. There have been instances when round-head rivets were used at some assembly plants but only on very rare occasions.

"Rosette"-type rivet 5 petals, aluminum

Used by Toyota since 1985, except for the 1985 Corolla front-wheel drive, diesel, and 1989 and 1990 Cressida models, which have round aluminum rivets.

Sheet-metal screws

Screws are occasionally used to attach VIN plates on some imported vehicles.

Note: From 1974 to the present, some manufacturers have used VIN plates with both concealed and exposed rivets.

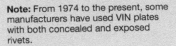

FIGURE 16-9   Attaching VIN plates

(National Insurance Crime Bureau, 2001 Passenger Vehicle Identification Manual [Palos Hills, IL: NICB, 2001], p. 46. Used with permission of NICB.)

and on Ford units since 1970. Sheet-metal screws are still occasionally used on some imports (Figure 16-9).

The use of a public VIN is designed to provide a positive, individualized means of identifying a motor vehicle. The 1981 adoption of a standardized 17-character VIN for all cars manufactured in or sold in the United States was certainly a forceful step in that direction. Previously, General Motors used a 13-digit VIN, Ford and Chrysler each used 11 characters, and imports used a host of other lengths. The standardized 17-character configuration is required of all imports manufactured for sale in the United States. The first 11 characters of the standardized VIN identify the country of origin, manufacturer, make, restraint system, model, body style, engine type, year, assembly plant, and a mathematically computed

452   CHAPTER 16 VEHICLE THEFTS AND RELATED OFFENSES

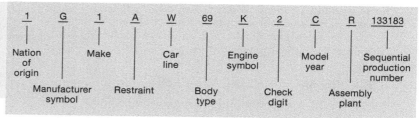

▶ FIGURE 16-10
Example of 17-digit VIN system
(National Insurance Crime Bureau, 2001
Passenger Vehicle Identification Manual
[Palos Hills, IL: NICB, 2001], p. 46. Used with
permission of NICB.)

▶ FIGURE 16-11
**World Manufacturer Identification
Codes**
(Courtesy of NICB, Palos Hills, Illinois)

Code	Manufacturer	Code	Manufacturer
JH4	ACURA	1LN	LINCOLN
ZAR	ALFA ROMEO	SCC	LOTUS
1AM	AMERICAN MOTORS	ZAM	MASERATI
SCF	ASTON MARTIN	JM1	MAZDA
WAU	AUDI	WDB	MERCEDES BENZ
12A	AVANTI	1ME	MERCURY
ZBB	BERTONE	WF1	MERKUR
WBA	BMW	JA3	MITSUBISHI
1G4	BUICK	JN1	NISSAN
1G6	CADILLAC	1G3	OLDSMOBILE
1G1	CHEVROLET	VF3	PEUGEOT
1C3	CHRYSLER	ZFR	PININFARINA
2E3	EAGLE PREMIER	1P3	PLYMOUTH
JE3	EAGLE SUMMIT	1G2	PONTIAC
VF1	EAGLE MEDALLION	WPO	PORSCHE
SCE	DELOREAN	VF1	RENAULT
1B3	DODGE	SCA	ROLLS ROYCE
ZFF	FERRARI	YS3	SAAB
ZFA	FIAT	SAX	STERLING
1FA	FORD	JF1	SUBARU
KMH	HYUNDAI	JS3	SUZUKI
JHM	HONDA	JT2	TOYOTA
JAB	ISUZU	WVW	VOLKSWAGEN
SAJ	JAGUAR	YV1	VOLVO
1JC	JEEP		

check digit that is used to verify all the other characters in the VIN. The last six characters are the sequential production number of the vehicle (Figures 16-10 and 16-11). The letters "I," "O," "Q," "U," and "Z" are not used so as to avoid confusion with similar-looking numbers.

Under the standardized 17-character system, the check digit is always the ninth character in the VIN and is calculated using the formula process illustrated on the worksheet depicted in Figure 16-12. By assigning specified numerical values to each letter and number, and then multiplying and dividing, the appropriate check digit can be determined and matched with the check digit on the VIN in question to ascertain whether there are any flaws

in the construction of the VIN such as altered or transposed characters.

The tenth character of the VIN represents the year of manufacture or vehicle model year. The letter A was used to designate 1980, B for 1981, and so on. Without the letters "I," "O," "Q," "U," and "Z," the remaining 20 letters, followed by the use of numbers 1 to 9, establish a 30-year cycle before the possibility of an exactly duplicated VIN could result from the normal manufacturing process (Figure 16-13).

On some newer vehicles, VIN plates also have a bar code that contains all the information represented by the alphanumeric characters of the VIN (Figure 16-14). The

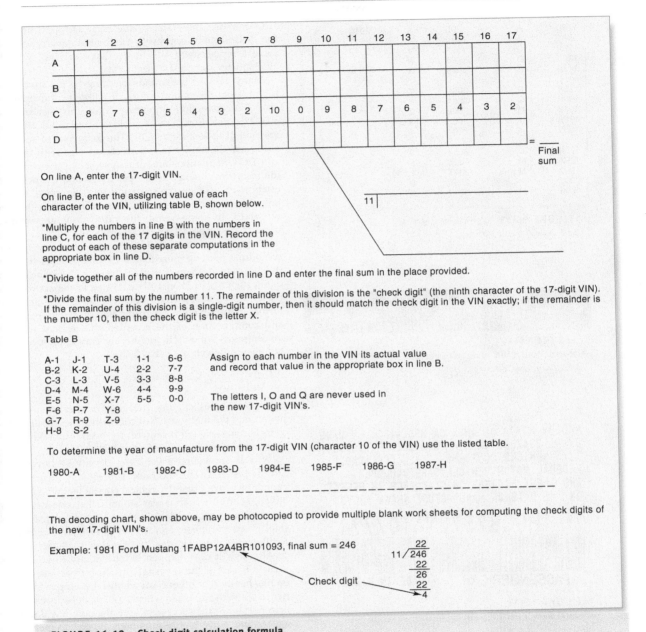

On line A, enter the 17-digit VIN.

On line B, enter the assigned value of each character of the VIN, utilizing table B, shown below.

*Multiply the numbers in line B with the numbers in line C, for each of the 17 digits in the VIN. Record the product of each of these separate computations in the appropriate box in line D.

*Divide together all of the numbers recorded in line D and enter the final sum in the place provided.

*Divide the final sum by the number 11. The remainder of this division is the "check digit" (the ninth character of the 17-digit VIN). If the remainder of this division is a single-digit number, then it should match the check digit in the VIN exactly; if the remainder is the number 10, then the check digit is the letter X.

Table B

A-1	J-1	T-3	1-1	6-6	Assign to each number in the VIN its actual value
B-2	K-2	U-4	2-2	7-7	and record that value in the appropriate box in line B.
C-3	L-3	V-5	3-3	8-8	
D-4	M-4	W-6	4-4	9-9	
E-5	N-5	X-7	5-5	0-0	The letters I, O and Q are never used in
F-6	P-7	Y-8			the new 17-digit VIN's.
G-7	R-9	Z-9			
H-8	S-2				

To determine the year of manufacture from the 17-digit VIN (character 10 of the VIN) use the listed table.

1980-A   1981-B   1982-C   1983-D   1984-E   1985-F   1986-G   1987-H

The decoding chart, shown above, may be photocopied to provide multiple blank work sheets for computing the check digits of the new 17-digit VIN's.

Example: 1981 Ford Mustang 1FABP12A4BR101093, final sum = 246

$$\begin{array}{r} 22 \\ 11\overline{)246} \\ 22 \\ \hline 26 \\ 22 \\ \hline 4 \end{array}$$

Check digit

▲ **FIGURE 16-12** **Check-digit calculation formula**
(Courtesy of National Insurance Crime Bureau)

Federal Safety Certification Label found on the door post of most vehicles, has been required since 1970, and now includes the full VIN and bar code (Figure 16-15).

Gray-Market Vehicles

When the U.S. dollar is strong overseas, it becomes economically feasible for individuals to purchase motor vehicles in other countries and have them shipped to the United States for sale, resale, or personal use. This effort can be profitable even though it may cost up to several thousand dollars apiece to "legalize" the vehicles for use in the United States. Since such vehicles are not manufactured for sale in this country, they are not constructed to meet U.S. emission control or safety standards, nor do

1980	A	1995	S	2010	A
1981	B	1996	T	2011	B
1982	C	1997	V	2012	C
1983	D	1998	W		
1984	E	1999	X		
1985	F	2000	Y		
1986	G	2001	1		
1987	H	2002	2		
1988	J	2003	3		
1989	K	2004	4		
1990	L	2005	5		
1991	M	2006	6		
1992	N	2007	7		
1993	P	2008	8		
1994	R	2009	9		

▲ FIGURE 16-13 Vehicle model year
(National Insurance Crime Bureau)

▲ FIGURE 16-14
General Motors VIN plate with bar code
(IAATI-SE newsletter, 1997)

▲ FIGURE 16-15
Federal Safety Certification Label with bar code
(IAATI-SE newsletter, 1997)

they have a 17-character standardized VIN. If **gray-market vehicles** are brought into this country legally, a bond for each must be posted with Customs and Border Patrol (CBP) until such time as the appropriate modifications have been made to bring the vehicle into compliance with the U.S. Environmental Protection Agency (EPA) emission control requirements and the safety standards promulgated by the U.S. Department of Transportation

(DOT). When these steps have been accomplished and the modifications approved, the federal government will issue a replacement VIN plate that conforms with the 17-character standard.

Many vehicles are found operating on the streets and highways of this nation before, or without conforming to, the legal conversion requirements for gray-market vehicles. The operation of these vehicles is unlawful, and they are subject to seizure by CBP. The frequency of such seizures and the ability to ensure compliance with the EPA and DOT regulations are, of course, a direct function of the resources devoted to the programs and the priorities established. Not unlike state and local agencies, federal law-enforcement programs also suffer from limited resources. In some years, the number of gray-market imports has approached 100,000 vehicles.

The nonconforming VIN on a gray-market vehicle is sometimes nothing more than a Dymotape label stuck on the left-side dash and visible through the windshield. Often such a VIN is on a plate riveted in the appropriate place, but its construction does not satisfy the accepted format requirements. Learning the proper appearance and configuration of the accepted VIN format will aid investigators not only in identifying gray-market vehicles but also in detecting altered VINs.

Attempts to Conceal the Identity of Vehicles

Salvage switches, cloning, defacing, or altering numbers are among the many ways of concealing the identity of a vehicle, thus making it difficult for even a trained investigator to accurately identify a vehicle.

Why is concealing a vehicle's identity so important? Simply put, if a vehicle cannot be positively identified, it cannot be proven that the vehicle was stolen, when it was stolen, or from whom it was stolen. Thus, one who is in possession of such a vehicle cannot be prosecuted as a thief. Even the most careful thief has extreme difficulty totally concealing the identity of a stolen vehicle.

Although it does happen, total inability to identify a vehicle is rare if the investigator doesn't hesitate to call on his/her own or others' knowledge, training, and experience. Knowing how and when to call on outside resources is important to the successful investigation. NICB special agents and other highly qualified law-enforcement officers know how and where to look for clues to a vehicle's identity.

The public VIN on the dash is not the only number that identifies a specific vehicle. The VIN may be stamped in several different places on the vehicle's body, frame, or component parts. The location of some of these secondary numbers is not a big secret, but others, referred to as **confidential VINs,** are stamped into frames or bodies in places supposedly known only to the manufacturer and to law-enforcement agencies and officers who are specialists in vehicle identification and auto-theft investigation, such as NICB special agents. Various other parts such as

◄FIGURE 16-16
Motor number on motorcycle
The Suzuki motorcycle with the ground VIN was easily identified using the motor number (shown here).
(Courtesy National Insurance Crime Bureau)

engines and transmissions will be given an identification number when manufactured, but, because they are distinct component parts, often manufactured in different locales from the final assembly plant, the numbers may be totally different from the VIN. However, documents created and maintained by the manufacturer, and provided to NICB, can be checked to determine the VIN of the vehicle in which the part was installed.

Other parts or components of a vehicle manufactured or subassembled elsewhere may be designed to fit a specific vehicle. In such cases, the part may have a serial number that is related to, but not identical to, the VIN. It may have a number that is a derivative of the VIN or that's formed from parts of the VIN, the same way a T-top may need to be matched to a vehicle of a specific body type denoted by the sixth and seventh characters of the VIN and the six-digit sequential number. Numerous combinations are possible and plausible; again, this is where the manufacturer's records become indispensable (Figure 16-16).

The numbers often used to match parts so as to foster accurate assembly of a vehicle may be written on components with pen, pencil, chalk, marking pen, or crayon. It does not matter what they are written with, as long as there are numbers that can lead an investigator to the end result of positively identifying a vehicle. Frequently, the various components subassembled elsewhere in the same plant or shipped from other plants will be accompanied by production order forms or written orders containing the VIN or a derivative number, which matches the parts for assembly. After the parts are matched and assembled, the production form has no use and may be left in some nook, cranny, or crevice of the assembly. If the investigator knows where to look, such a document may often be found and thus lead to vehicle identification.

Federal Safety Certification Label

All cars distributed in the United States since 1970 must have a **federal safety certification label.** This sticker, in addition to the required certification statements, also contains the vehicle's VIN. If the sticker is removed, it leaves behind a "footprint" that often shows the word "void." Obviously, if the correct sticker is in place and the correct public VIN shows through the windshield, the VINs should match.

The shape and size of the labels, as well as the materials from which they are constructed, vary among manufacturers. More common among domestic manufacturers is a paper label covered with a clear Mylar-type plastic.

The label is bonded to the vehicle with a mastic compound. Construction is such that the label should be destroyed if removal is attempted. Some foreign manufacturers construct the certifying label out of thin metal and attach it with rivets. In either case, security against removal and replacement is not absolute. However, investigators are encouraged not to use the VIN on the safety certification label as absolute proof of vehicle identification. The federal safety sticker will be located on the driver's door or on the doorpost and, in recent years, also includes a description of the vehicle and VIN on a barcode.

Federal Legislation

In an effort to reduce auto theft by easing the process of vehicle identification, Congress enacted the **Motor Vehicle Theft Law Enforcement Act** of 1984. Title I of the law requires that manufacturers place additional permanent identification numbers on up to 14 major parts of certain car lines. The car lines are selected every year for each manufacturer by the National Highway Traffic Safety Administration

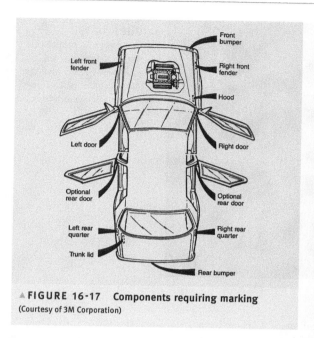

▲ FIGURE 16-17 Components requiring marking
(Courtesy of 3M Corporation)

AUTO MANUFACTURERS NAME	VIN LABEL	RDOT LABEL
Ford/US		R Ford DOT
Audi		Audi R DOT
Ford/Germany		R Ford DOT
Mercedes Benz		R Mercedes DOT
Porsche		R Porsche DOT
VW		VW R DOT
Renault		R ◇ DOT
Ferrari		R Ferrari DOT
Maserati		R Maserati DOT
Saab		R SAAB DOT
Nummi/US		New United Motor R DOT
Honda		R Honda DOT
Isuzu		R Isuzu DOT
Mazda		Mazda R DOT
Mitsubishi		R Mitsubishi DOT
Subaru		Subaru R DOT
Toyota		TOYOTA R DOT

▲ FIGURE 16-18
Original- and replacement-part labels for selected manufacturers
(Courtesy of 3M Corporation)

(NHTSA), the federal agency charged with setting the standards for the administration of the law. The car lines chosen each year for **parts marking** are those designated as high-theft lines. The parts requiring the additional identification are the major parts that are normally most sought after in a chop-shop operation and include: the engine; transmission; both front fenders; hood; both front doors; front and rear bumpers; both rear quarter panels; decklid, tailgate, or hatchback (whichever is applicable); and both rear doors (if present) (Figure 16-17).

The numbers must either be inscribed on the designated parts or be printed on labels attached to the parts. Labels must tear into pieces if removed; if completely removed, they must leave a "footprint," which becomes visible through certain investigative techniques such as using an ultraviolet light. The standards apply to the major parts of the designated new car lines and to replacement parts for the same car lines. The new-part labels must have the manufacturer's logo or other identifier printed on them and must use the full 17-character VIN for identification (Figure 16-18); if, however, a VIN derivative of at least 8 characters was being used to identify the engine and transmission on a particular covered line on the effective date of the law, that practice may continue. The identifier on covered replacement parts must carry the manufacturer's trademark, logo, or other distinguishing symbol, the letter "R" to reflect replacement, and the letters "DOT" (Figure 16-18). The labels are to be affixed to the part on a surface that is not normally exposed to damage when the part is installed, adjusted, removed, or damaged in an accident. When the part is removed from the vehicle, the label or inscription must be visible without disassembling the part.

The law limits the application of the requirements to no more than 14 production car lines for any one manufacturer, and the costs to the manufacturer for compliance cannot exceed $15 per vehicle, excluding the costs of marking the engine and transmission.

There is an exemption in the law, called a "black-box" exemption, which allows NHTSA to exempt from compliance with the standards up to two car lines per year for any single manufacturer if the vehicle line is equipped by the manufacturer with a standard equipment antitheft device determined by NHTSA to be as effective in deterring and reducing vehicle theft as would be compliance with the parts-marking requirements of the theft prevention standard.

The intent underlying the passage of the law, the promulgation of standards, and the marking of original and replacement parts was to reduce auto theft by ostensibly making it more difficult for the thief to conceal the identity of major parts, by providing fewer significant parts that would be untraceable, and by making it easier for law-enforcement investigators to identify stolen parts.

Having determined that the parts-marking program initiated in 1984 was effective, Congress passed the Anti-Car Theft Act of 1992, which continued and extended the program. The 1992 legislation also called for the U.S. Attorney General to conduct an initial evaluation, in 1997, of the effectiveness of the program in inhibiting chop-shop operations and deterring motor vehicle theft, with the objective of extending the parts-marking program to all lines (makes and models) by the end of 1997. The study recommended continuance of the program. The act required a long-range review of the program in 1999. In addition to evaluating whether chop-shop operations were affected and theft had been deterred, the study was to determine whether the black-box exemptions were an effective substitute for parts marking in substantially reducing motor vehicle theft.

The act also required repair shops to check the VIN on all parts against a national file. Previously, this was the NCIC stolen-vehicle file, but the FBI, by direction of the act, established the National Stolen Parts Motor Vehicle Information System (NSPMVIS). Other provisions of the law made armed carjacking a federal crime; doubled the maximum penalty for importing, exporting, transporting, selling, or receiving a stolen vehicle; and directed U.S. Customs to spot-check vehicles and containers leaving the country.

To carry out the study mandate of the 1992 legislation, the Attorney General directed the National Institute of Justice to commission a study on the effectiveness of the parts-marking program. The report, released in 2000, concluded that the available evidence warrants application of the parts-marking standard to all motor vehicle lines. The decision was, in large measure, based on estimates and the absence of negative information. The study estimated that parts marking costs manufacturers about $5 per vehicle.[40] The study also concluded that 33–158 fewer cars are stolen per 100,000 marked cars because of parts marking.[41] The research was unable to establish whether antitheft devices installed in vehicles were an effective alternative to parts marking.[42]

Manufacturers urged the Attorney General not to expand the program, but the Attorney General listened to law-enforcement investigators who identified four ways that parts marking provides assistance. First, thieves often remove, alter, or obliterate the VIN plate and other numbers, but as long as one part number remains intact, the vehicle can be identified; this enables the owner to be identified and facilitates proving that the vehicle was stolen and securing an arrest. Second, auto-theft investigators in many jurisdictions have been given authority to seize parts or vehicles when markings have been removed or destroyed. Third, the absence of markings causes investigators to inquire further, and such investigations often lead to larger stolen-vehicle cases. Fourth, in jurisdictions requiring inspections of rebuilt vehicles before issuing a new certificate of title, a determination can be made as to whether stolen parts are being used in the rebuilding process.[43]

VIN Editing and Reconstruction

In any investigation, even when it appears that the VIN has not been altered or defaced, the investigator must check the validity of the identifying numbers. Using the worksheet in Figure 16-12 will verify the correctness of the check digit only as compared with, and calculated from, the other 16 characters. A VIN edit computer program available at many law-enforcement agencies and state motor vehicle regulatory offices can readily determine if the entered VIN is "good." If the VIN is invalid, computer programs can analyze the available information and at least narrow the valid possibilities of a correct VIN. Such programs replace what formerly was a long drawn-out manual process accomplished by checking manufacturers' records. VINASSIST, available from NICB, is one such program and is currently being used by over 10,000 insurers and law-enforcement agencies. As noted earlier, the program edits, evaluates, and corrects vehicle identification numbers.

VIN Restoration

The restoration of manufacturers' serial numbers altered or obliterated from metal is a process that can be performed by an investigator with the proper material at hand (Figure 16-19). There is no mystery involved in number restoration as long as the investigator is willing to do the necessary preparation and has the patience to await results that are often slow in developing.

When a die is struck on metal, the molecules beneath the die are compressed, and it is on these compressed molecules that the restoration mediums are applied. The type of metal surface dictates which of the three primary methods of restoration—heat, acid, or acid and electricity—should be used. In the heat process, an oxygen-acetylene torch is used on cast iron only. An electrolytic process in which 5–6 volts of electricity at 2–3 amps are used in conjunction with a solution of hydrochloric acid is generally used on steel. For the etching of aluminum, one solution of potassium hydroxide and a second of hydrochloric acid and mercuric chloride are applied using a cotton or fiberglass swab.

Regardless of which type of surface is involved and which restoration process is used, the surface must be

►FIGURE 16-19
Obliterating a VIN
From the appearance of the marks, the VIN was ground off with an electric grinder. (Courtesy National Insurance Crime Bureau)

►FIGURE 16-20
Vehicle Identification Number restored after use of acid on this aluminum part
This restoration identified the vehicle, which led to the identity of the owner from whom the vehicle was stolen. (Courtesy National Insurance Crime Bureau)

painstakingly prepared. All paint, oil, grease, or other foreign matter must first be removed by using any solution that will work, including paint remover and acetone (Figure 16-20). The surface is not to be scraped with a wire brush, knife, or any other tool, since one major purpose of preparation is to eliminate scratches and grind marks. Depending on how badly the surface is defaced, it may need to be polished with emery paper, a mill file, or a high-speed sanding or polishing disk to remove scratches or gouges. Polishing the surface to a mirror-like finish is desirable. Sometimes careful preparation of the surface will make all or some of the numbers visible.

Documenting the surface before beginning the restoration process is advisable. This can be done by photograph-ing the area to be restored, dulling the shine with the use of fingerprint powder or carbon paper, and then taking a tape lift of the area (similar to lifting a fingerprint from a metal surface) and/or making a large-scale drawing of the area. It is always advisable to check with the manufacturer to ascertain the structure of the numbers used on a factory identification number if it is not already known. For example, the investigator should ask whether Os are rounded or squared and if 3s have rounded or flat tops. Such information can assist the investigator in determining whether visible numbers are valid.

If the heat process is to be used on cast iron, the ignited torch should be slowly moved back and forth over the area to be processed and gradually brought closer to the surface in a manner that will not crack the block. When the top of the blue cone of the flame is being moved back and forth about half an inch above the surface, the surface will soon reach a cherry-red color. When that happens, the torch should gradually be drawn away from the surface until it is about 6 inches away, all the while being slowly moved back and forth. After the surface has cooled, it should be very lightly polished with emery paper to remove the carbon deposits. The restored numbers should show up as a lighter color than the surrounding metal. If no numbers appear, either too much of the metal was removed and restoration will not produce results or the surface was not heated to a high-enough temperature, in which case the process should be repeated.

In the electrolytic process of restoring numbers on steel, two pieces of number 12 or 14 braided wire, 18–24 inches in length with alligator clips attached to the ends, along with a 6- or 12-volt battery, are needed. Direct current may be used if a battery is not convenient. One wire should be connected to the positive pole, with the other end grounded somewhere near the area to be restored. The other wire, connected to the negative pole, should have a swab dipped in acid solution attached to the other end; the swab should be moved one way only over the surface until any numbers are restored. The acid, speeded by the electricity, eats the surrounding metal surface until the numbers (if not totally destroyed) are revealed. In this and all acid-processing techniques, drawings or sketches should be made as individual numbers or letters are revealed because they may fade before more heavily ground characters are restored. Once the process is completed, the surface should be neutralized with water, dried, and coated with oil to prevent rust. In using any acid, good ventilation is imperative.

Good ventilation is also necessary in the acid process of restoring numbers on aluminum. Using potassium hydroxide solution and a swab, the surface area should be brushed in one direction for about 1 minute. The surface should then be dried and brushed with a solution of hydrochloric acid and mercuric chloride in the same direction for 2 minutes. The surface should be dried again. This process constitutes one application. Often, results will appear after two to four applications, but repeated applications may be made as often as necessary.[44]

INVESTIGATION OF VEHICLE FIRES

Along with the general increase in crimes in the United States has come an increase in automobile fires. Many of the criminal fires occur when stolen vehicles have been stripped of valuable parts and the rest is burnt to destroy the evidence. However, as in other fire investigations, the investigator first must eliminate natural and accidental causes of fire.

Before beginning the physical investigation of a vehicle fire scene, the investigator must understand that the crime scene examination includes both the vehicle and the area in which it was burned. Hence, the investigation must follow established principles by first recording the scene. Photographs should be taken immediately, before there is any disturbance of the crime scene (Figure 16-21). Measurements must be taken to establish the exact location of the vehicle in relationship to fixed objects, crossroads, houses, and so on. A description should be noted regarding the terrain, nearby roadways, and weather conditions (including prevailing wind directions).

A thorough search should be made of the area for tire-tread marks, footprints, cans, bottles, other containers,

◄**FIGURE 16-21**
Photographing and documenting burned vehicle
A fire investigator photographs and documents the burned vehicle as part of his investigation. This process is essential in preparing for any subsequent prosecution of the arsonist. (© AP Photo/Daily News, Geoff Crimmins)

unusual residue or materials, old tires, matches, or any other item that may be related to the case. Samples should be taken of soil, which may contain evidence of flammable liquids. When found, each item should be photographed before being moved, and then it should be properly packaged and marked as evidence.

An inspection of the salvage must be completed for information on the origin and possible motive for the fire. Generally, investigators inspect the burnt automobile before contacting the owner, and the inspection is made as soon after the fire as possible. The inspection starts where the fire apparently originated. In accidental fires, this will normally be the part of the vehicle that is the most badly damaged from the intensity of the heat. Accidental fires usually spread in diminishing degrees from the point of origin according to prevailing conditions. Conditions include direction and velocity of wind and/or materials on which flames feed, such as gasoline in the tank, woodwork, or other similarly flammable parts of the vehicle. When there are significant variations in these patterns, arson emerges as a possibility. Arson fires started with flammable materials usually show intense heat in more than one place. The investigator should carefully note the extent of the fire and its path. This information may prove valuable in the later questioning of the owner or witnesses.

The car also should be inspected for the removal of equipment such as stereo, heater, air horns, fog lights, and so forth. Notice should also be made of other irregularities such as old tires on new cars or missing spare tires.

Inspection of the Fuel System

The investigator should determine whether the cap to the gas tank was in place at the time of the fire. Sometimes gasoline to start the fire is siphoned from the tank, and the cap is carelessly left off. If the cap is blown off, it will show effects of an explosion. The drain plug in the bottom of the tank should be checked. In addition, if it was removed or loosened before the fire, there might be evidence of fresh tool marks, especially pliers' marks, on it.

The gas lines should be examined for breaks between the tank and the fuel pump. Breaks should be examined for tool marks. Some arsonists disconnect the line below the tank to obtain gasoline to start the fire and fail to replace the line.

Gasoline to start the fire is sometimes obtained by disconnecting the line from the fuel pump and running the starter. If the fuel pump is melted, there should be evidence of fire on the sidepans. If the fuel pump was disconnected to allow the gasoline to run out and then be set on fire, there may be carbon deposits inside the gas line at the fuel pump.

The investigator should establish whether parts of the fuel pump are missing. If key parts of the fuel system are missing, and the owner says that the vehicle was running at the time of the fire, then there is strong reason to suspect arson. This is true regardless of whether the vehicle is equipped with a mechanical pump in a low-pressure carbureted system or an electric pump in a high-pressure fuel-injected system.

Inspection of the Electrical System

A short circuit in the electric wiring is the most common excuse offered for automobile fires. The chances of a modern automobile's burning up from a short in the wiring are negligible. Engineers have virtually eliminated this hazard. If a fire in fact did start from malfunctions in the electrical system, there generally is enough evidence to substantiate it.

The wires near where the fire started should be inspected. If the wires are not melted completely, a short can be located. A short melts the strands of wire apart and causes small beads of melted wire to form on the ends. Wires that are burned in two have sharp points. If the fire started in an electrical system, the system must be close to a flammable substance for the fire to spread. If a fire started from a short while the motor was running, the distributor points will be stuck or fused.

Inspection of the Motor, Radiator, and Parts Under and Near the Hood

The only possible place for an accidental fire to start at this location is around the fuel pump or carburetor and at the wiring. Any evidence of a fire on the front lower part of the motor not attributable to these parts indicates the use of flammables. If lead is melted from any lower or outside seams of the radiator, this is strong evidence of flammables. The fan belt does not usually burn in an accidental fire.

Gasoline on the motor sometimes causes the rubber cushions for the front of the motor to show evidence of fire. This evidence does not occur in accidental fires.

The radiator should also be checked. A badly burned lower right corner indicates that the gas line from the fuel pump to the carburetor was disconnected, the starter was run to pump out gasoline through the fuel pump, and then the gasoline was set on fire.

Inspection of the Body

The body of the car is usually so badly burned as to afford little evidence. However, signs of the intensity of heat sometimes point to the use of an inflammable. An excessive amount of flammable material may run through the floor of the car and burn underneath, causing oil or gasoline soot to form on the underside of the car. An examination should be made for this soot. If the hood was raised during the fire, the paint on the top panels may be blistered but not be burned off where the two panels touched. If the wind was blowing from the rear of the car to the front, the paint should be burned for almost the length of the hood. The radiator core will be burned, but there will not have been enough fire at the rear of the car to do much damage to the gasoline tank. If the paint on the hood is burned only an inch or so from the rear toward the front, this would indicate that the wind was blowing from the front of the car toward the rear, in which case the gasoline tank may be badly damaged but the radiator will be intact.

CONTACT WITH THE OWNER

An investigation must be made of the car owner for evidence of intent, motive, and opportunity, and the owner must be questioned to establish his or her knowledge of the fire and to verify information. Before interviewing the owner, the investigator should learn as much as possible about him/her. This information may prove quite useful during the interview. The importance of preplanning the interview cannot be overemphasized. The more facts the investigator has available, the greater the probability of a successful clearance or later conviction.

Information should be obtained from the owner about the details of the purchase, such as date, cost, trade-in, down payment, amount of mortgage due, payments past due, name of salesperson, and so forth. The investigator should also inquire about the general condition of the car at the time of the fire and ask about defects, mileage, presence or absence of unusual equipment, and recent repairs.[45]

PREVENTION PROGRAMS

Each year new and innovative approaches to the prevention and the detection of crime and the apprehension of offenders are developed. Some of these are related to investigative techniques, whereas others are high-tech equipment developments that are designed to reduce the vehicle theft problem or assist law-enforcement officers in their efforts. Other strategies are available to reduce the incidence of fraud.

AUTO THEFT

Law-enforcement officers and agencies in a number of jurisdictions now rely on integrated communications and computer networks of the FBI, state, and local police to identify and locate stolen vehicles. One unique system uses a small device called a micromaster, which is installed at random in a vehicle's electrical system. The micromaster is a microprocessor-controlled transceiver with its own unique code.

If a vehicle is stolen, the owner reports the theft to the local police in the usual way. The owner also tells the police that the vehicle is equipped with a micromaster. The police then announce through normal channels and the National Crime Information Center that a micromaster-equipped vehicle has been stolen. A computer then activates a transmitter that sends a signal with the stolen vehicle's own code. (The present system can manage up to 8 billion discrete micromaster codes.) The signal activates the micromaster's transceiver, and starts sending a signal identifying it as a stolen vehicle. The activation and tracking of the micromaster signal is under the control of

law-enforcement authorities. They have a homing device or, more recently used, GPS tracking system that gives them information about the location of the car. The system also allows police officers to identify micromaster signals and determine whether the stolen car has been involved in a crime.[46] LoJack is probably the best known system in use. Some of these tracking systems rely on signal relay towers, whereas others use a satellite-enhanced global positioning system (GPS) method of tracking. The law-enforcement vehicles are equipped with tracking computers that bring up street maps that pinpoint the location and direction of travel within a very close proximity.

Many vehicles are now being manufactured with anti-theft locks, starter disengagement systems (called *ignition kill switches*), and various other devices in an attempt to reduce the attractiveness of a particular model to the thief. Some of these are models that qualify for the black-box exemption to the labeling standards established under the guidelines of the Motor Vehicle Theft Law Enforcement Act of 1984.

In recent years, a number of private concerns have begun marketing antitheft devices that can be used effectively on older vehicles. It should be noted at the outset that no device can absolutely prevent motor vehicle theft, and one should look askance at any product or brand of product that is represented to be an absolute theft preventive.

Theft deterrent devices are of two types—passive or active. With a **passive system,** the driver does not need to do anything to activate the system, though he or she may be required to do something to deactivate the system. An **active system** requires that the operator do something every time the vehicle is driven or parked.

Audible alarm systems may be either passive or active and may be effective if anyone pays attention when an alarm is activated. Because some systems activate easily when someone passes the vehicle, a strong wind blows, or lightning strikes half a mile away, many people pay little attention, beyond a passing glance, to a vehicle with an alarm blaring. Escape from the vicinity of the noise is more important than determining if a theft is occurring. The alarms are treated more as an annoyance than as a theft deterrent.

A boot is an active device installed under a front tire that prevents the vehicle from being moved until the boot is removed. Other active devices can key lock the transmission or the brakes.

Many communities have instituted decal "alert" programs that provide decals for vehicles registered with the local law-enforcement agency and authorize any law-enforcement officer to stop the vehicle and question the driver if the vehicle is observed on the streets during certain hours (such as 2 A.M. to 6 A.M.).

A fuel shut-off device, which blocks the fuel line, may be activated by removal of the ignition key or by the throwing of a switch.

A case-hardened steering-column ignition lock that cannot be removed using a conventional slide hammer or lock puller can be effective, as can a case-hardened steel protective cap that fits over the ignition lock to prevent extraction of the ignition lock cylinder. The cap fastens to a steel collar that fits around the steering post and over the ignition lock. The ignition key fits through a slot in the cap.

Several manufacturers install a microchip or transponder in the ignition key that must be electronically read when inserted into the ignition in order for the vehicle to start. Early versions of some of these systems had only a few combinations, which could easily be defeated if a thief could procure a set of masters with all the combinations. However, General Motors' PASS-KEY III and Ford's Passive Anti-Theft System (PATS), as well as the newer systems on many other domestic and foreign-made brands, use much more advanced and sophisticated electronic systems that are deterring theft.

General Motors' OnStar system uses GPS to track vehicles whose drivers need assistance. OnStar can now slow down a stolen vehicle. The Stolen Vehicle Slowdown (SVS) service is an enhancement to the normal stolen vehicle assistance program offered by OnStar. When an OnStar equipped vehicle is stolen, OnStar can provide the vehicle's exact GPS location to law enforcement. They would also notify law enforcement if the slowdown service is available. When law enforcement has sight of the stolen vehicle, the OnStar operator can flash the lights of the car to verify that law enforcement has the correct vehicle. If necessary, law enforcement can request a slowdown. OnStar will then send a signal to the vehicle that causes the throttle input to be ignored. As a result, the vehicle will start slowing down to idle speed. All other systems of the vehicle continue to act normally.[47]

A steel or an alloy post, rod, or collar may attach to the steering wheel, which can be extended and locked in place. The device prevents the steering wheel from making full rotations. This type of active device can be an effective deterrent to theft if used properly, but it is obviously ineffective if the operator of the vehicle forgets or considers it an inconvenience to install it each time the vehicle is left unattended.

VIN etching is a process that helps identify vehicles recovered by the police after a theft has occurred. As noted earlier, thieves often attempt to conceal the identity of stolen vehicles by grinding numbers. When the VIN is permanently etched, using acid, on all the vehicle's windows, the identifying numbers are often overlooked by the thief or require that the thief remove all the window glass to prevent identification, a major task a thief may not be willing to undertake.

Some programs focus on the responsibilities of vehicle owners to do their part in preventing vehicle theft. The Michigan affiliate of the American Automobile Association implemented a law providing that if a car is stolen and the keys are anywhere in the passenger compartment, the owner, in addition to absorbing his or her insurance deductible, also absorbs an extra $500 plus 10% of the value of the vehicle. The total amount is deducted from the amount of the insurance payment made on the theft loss claim. The responsibilities of owners are also reflected in a survey initiated by the NICB that consists of scoring answers to some questions and taking necessary preventive actions on the basis of the total score. This is called a *layered approach to theft deterrence* (Figure 16-22).

Some other prevention techniques include these:

- If a lighter receptacle is used for a radio, telephone, or radar detector, remove the item when leaving the vehicle and reinsert the lighter. Thieves look for empty receptacles.

FIGURE 16-22
The layered approach
(Courtesy of National Insurance Crime Bureau)

1 Location

City population	Points
Over 250,000	8
250,000 to 100,001	6
100,000 to 50,001	4
50,000 to 10,000	2
Under 10,000	0

2 Vehicle style

Vehicle owned	Points
Sports car	5
Luxury car	4
Sport-utility	4
Sedan	3
Passenger van	1
Station wagon	0

3 Vehicle age

Age of vehicle	Points
0 to five years	1
Six to eight years	2
Nine-plus years	0

4 Bonus point

Add 1 point to your score if you live near an international port or border.

Your score tells how many layers of protection your vehicle needs. For example, if your vehicle scored a 4, the chance of theft is considered low and it should have a first layer of protection. If your vehicle scored a 12, it should have first, second and third layers. The scores:

Layer 1 (0 to 4 points)
Common sense—Remove keys from the ignition, lock the doors, close all windows, park in lighted areas.

Layer 2 (5 to 10 points)
Visible or audible deterrent—Steering wheel locks, steering column collars, theft-deterrent decals, tire locks, window etching.

Layer 3 (11 to 14 points)
Visible immobilizer— Smart keys, fuse cutoffs, kill switches, and starter, ignition or fuel disablers.

Layer 4 (15 to 16 points)
Tracking systems

- Always lock the vehicle and remove the keys.
- Lock valuables in the trunk. Do not leave personal identification or credit cards in the vehicle.
- Do not leave a vehicle running while unattended.
- Photocopy registration and insurance papers and carry them on your person, not in the glove compartment.
- Park in a garage or in a well-lighted, heavily traveled area.
- When parking at a curb, turn the wheels toward the curb and use the emergency brake. This makes the vehicle harder to steal.
- Do not hide spare keys in or on the vehicle.
- Write the name of the owner and the VIN in crayon under the hood and in the trunk.
- Drop business cards down window channels into door interiors. This will make later identification easier.

Theft of vehicles from new- and used-car dealers is not a new phenomenon. Sometimes the dealership knows a vehicle is missing, such as when a vehicle taken on a test drive is not returned. Other times, if an inventory is large, a vehicle may be stolen overnight and not missed for several days. Employee theft is also a problem. Key control is an essential crime prevention practice for a dealership. Keys should be kept in a locked cabinet with only a few people having access. Keys that are out for demonstration or sales purposes must be monitored. Controls should be so tight that no one can take a key and get a duplicate made. Customers should never be allowed to test-drive a vehicle without a salesperson going along. Display lots should be well lighted, and barriers should be erected that permit access and good observation from outside but are sufficient to deter theft at night and when the dealership is closed. Officers who are familiar with the concepts of crime prevention through environmental design should be consulted.

CAR RENTALS

Car rental companies are generally knowledgeable about motor vehicle theft and techniques of prevention, but an investigator would be wise to understand some basics. In daily rental, the company is handing over the keys of a car to a person no one in the company has seen before or knows anything about. The rental agreement should be completely filled out, and the picture and information on the renter's driver's license should be carefully checked to make sure it matches the description of the person to whom the vehicle is being rented.

Rental companies generally require a credit card even for a cash rental. This not only serves as a good indication that the customer is a responsible person but also helps ensure that the contract will be paid. The employee of the rental company should make sure the credit card is current and check it against the driver's license to make sure the same name is on both documents.

Theft of rental vehicles generally occurs when a vehicle is not returned after it has been rented. At least one national rental company is in the process of installing tracking systems, as described earlier, which are traceable using radio-wave or GPS systems.

HEAVY EQUIPMENT

Tiny transponders that act as identification devices are now available. The device can be glued anywhere on the vehicle. Some agencies are experimenting with injecting the transponder into tires of construction equipment. If attempts are made to completely conceal or alter a stolen vehicle's identity, a receiver can accurately distinguish the vehicle from all others.

Owners of construction equipment are also encouraged to take the following actions:

- Use security devices such as ignition locks, stabilizer arm locks, and fuel shut-off valves.
- Record all product identification numbers, and participate in equipment identification programs.
- Photograph all equipment, paying particular attention to unique features such as dents, decals, and scratches, to aid in later identification.
- Leave equipment in well-lighted and fenced areas at job sites and equipment yards.
- Know the location of all construction equipment at all times.
- Keep law enforcement informed about where equipment is located and how long it will be maintained in a particular location.
- Take extra precautions on weekends. Most equipment thefts occur between 6 P.M. on Friday and 6 A.M. on Monday.
- Do not leave keys in any equipment that uses keys, and lock all machines that can be locked when not in use.
- Immediately report suspicious activity (such as a stranger taking photographs of equipment) to law-enforcement officials.

Other methods of reducing or preventing theft of off-road equipment are available. Programs are available through private enterprise whereby heavy equipment can be registered, with each piece being assigned its own identification number. The equipment is "decaled" with its own number welded on at several locations. Should a law-enforcement officer become suspicious, the dispatcher can call a toll-free number and remain on the line as the company calls the owner to verify the location of the equipment.

FRAUD

The prevention of fraud can best be accomplished by knowing some things about both the insured and the vehicle. "Know your insured" is always sound advice for an insurance agent. Getting good identification on the person, learning why the person selected a particular agent or agency, and finding out how the insured learned of the agent or agency can all be useful in helping to determine whether the act of insuring is legitimate. Knowing about the insured vehicle is equally important in the fight against fraud.

Perhaps the most profound fraud prevention effort ever initiated is the preinsurance inspection program, particularly when photographs are required. Deceptively simple in concept and application, it is amazing that fewer than half a dozen states have even considered, much less adopted, mandatory legislation. The concept requires that before a vehicle can be insured, it must be physically inspected by a representative or an agent acting on behalf of the insurer.

A simple inspection requirement can immediately eliminate or substantially reduce two of the most prolific tactics in committing insurance fraud. First, it virtually eliminates the false-vehicle theft, which is normally based on insuring a "paper," or "phantom," car—in other words, a vehicle that does not exist—and subsequently reporting it stolen in order to file against and recover on an insurance policy. Second, a well-written preinsurance report can substantially reduce fraudulent claims about theft of expensive equipment on a vehicle or claims that damage actually present before issuance of the policy occurred when the substandard vehicle either was involved in a reported accident or was stolen.

Photographs supporting an inspection report make the program particularly effective, and color photographs are even more revealing. Photographs can show the exact condition of a vehicle at the time a policy was issued so as to dispel fraudulent damage claims filed later. It is recommended that at least two photographs be taken from diagonal corners so that one picture shows the front and one side of the vehicle and the other photo shows the rear and other side. These two photos will eliminate false damage claims, but there remains the question of proving that the photos are of the insured vehicle and not simply one of the same year, make, and model. To resolve this concern, a few of the jurisdictions having inspection programs require that a third photograph be taken of the federal motor vehicle safety certification label (often called the EPA label), which is usually found on the left door. This label contains, among other information, the vehicle identification number, which, as noted earlier, is the specific identifier for that vehicle as distinguished from all other vehicles. This reverifies the number contained in the written report, thus avoiding or explaining inadvertent omissions or the accidental transposition of numbers.

An inexpensive instant-developing camera and film can be used for the program. In 1977 New York became the first state to enact legislation mandating photographic inspection before the issuance of insurance policies. The program initially required that two photographs be taken

from a 180-degree angle, but the law was amended in 1986 to require the third photo of the federal motor vehicle safety certification label. Massachusetts was the next state to adopt a preinsurance inspection program. Legislation followed thereafter in New Jersey and Florida, although not all these states have equally effective legislatively mandated programs. In addition to these states, two insurance companies have their own photographic inspection programs. Neither GEICO nor State Farm will insure a noninspected vehicle.

Is the program effective? Although it is difficult to measure how much crime (insurance fraud) is deterred by a photo inspection program, it has been estimated that in the state of New York, reduction in costs and in insurance fraud claims has saved well over $100 million, and these savings have been passed on to insurance buyers through premium reductions. Although insurance premiums have not actually been reduced in New York, the overall increase in premiums in that state has amounted to less than half the national average.[48]

ODOMETER FRAUD

One of the most costly consumer frauds of modern times is **odometer fraud,** also known by various other names, including odometer tampering, rollbacks, and clocking. The National Highway Traffic Safety Administration (NHTSA) estimates that over 3 million cars are clocked each year and that the cost of this fraud to American consumers surpasses $3 billion annually.

The most susceptible vehicles to odometer tampering are those that are relatively new with exceptionally high mileage. Of the total number of passenger cars sold in the United States each year, approximately half are sold to car rental or leasing companies or to others for business use. Each year, at least 4 million of these late-model high-mileage cars are replaced. Those that are taken off lease or are no longer used for business purposes find their way into the used-car market.

The reason for odometer rollbacks is to increase the value of used vehicles on the market. Obviously, a car with fewer miles should bring a higher price than one with high mileage. It has been conservatively estimated that on a small or intermediate-size car, the sales value increases $50 for each 1,000 miles that the odometer is set back; in larger vehicles, the value increases to around $65 per 1,000 miles the odometer reading is reduced. Thus, a late-model car that is clocked from 70,000 miles to 30,000 miles can increase its value to the seller by $2,000 to $2,600. This amounts to a nice additional profit for persons inclined to indulge in such deceitful conduct.

Besides the obvious profits to the seller of clocked vehicles, the costs to the purchaser can be even greater in the form of potential unanticipated safety problems and increased repair costs. Since cars are generally the largest purchase made by people after the cost of a home, the condition of a car and the anticipated costs for repair and maintenance figure prominently in the decision of whether to buy a particular car. But when the odometer has been clipped, mileage is not a dependable guide for estimating potential maintenance costs, since such a vehicle will be more costly to maintain and more likely to need expensive repairs. If the purchaser-owner is unable to afford the higher costs, the quality of maintenance and repairs may suffer, along with the safety and roadworthiness of the vehicle.

Because of the proliferation of this fraud, most states have created some type of investigative unit to deal with odometer tampering by accepting complaints from citizens and determining if there is any basis for enforcement action. In addition, there are national and federal agencies and organizations actively engaged in enforcing laws and trying to prevent odometer and title fraud. NHTSA has an odometer fraud investigation arm. They work on multiple state large-volume cases. The Department of Justice attorneys prosecute the cases investigated by NHTSA. The National Odometer and Title Fraud Enforcement Association comprises investigators from the member states, NHTSA investigators, federal prosecutors, and interested auctions and dealers. State investigators can be most helpful in local investigations.

When examining a late-model low-mileage vehicle that is suspected of being clocked, the investigator should check for extensive wear on the brake pedal, the driver's seat, and the seals around the trunk. Does the extent of wear conform to the claimed mileage? A check should be made for service stickers on the door, on the doorpost, and under the hood. If present, a date and odometer reading may be present; missing stickers may suggest tampering. The odometer wheels should be in alignment, should not rotate freely, and should not be scratched or nicked. Any of these conditions may be indicative of a rollback and warrant further inquiry. The investigator should order a vehicle history file through the state's motor vehicle titling agency and then check with each

successive owner (including individuals, dealers, and auctioneers), obtain all odometer disclosure statements, piece together an odometer history, and attempt to determine if there has been a rollback. If a rollback seems likely, the investigator should determine the possessor of the vehicle when it was clocked. Standard investigative techniques should then be applied.

Title fraud is as big a part of the odometer rollback problem as is the act of clocking. Title alteration, discarding of title reassignment forms to complicate the tracing of ownership, manufacturing of false reassignments, and title laundering are criminal acts that violators often engage in to support and cover up odometer rollbacks.

To mandate better record keeping, reduce the opportunity for odometer tampering, and assist law enforcement in the investigation of cases, Congress enacted the **Truth in Mileage Act** in 1986. This act, along with amendments made in several subsequent years, attempts to improve the paper trail of odometer readings by requiring more tightly controlled documentation and recording of odometer readings each time that ownership of a vehicle changes. The law attempts to close loopholes that permit the inception of fraudulent title schemes and to reduce the incidence of title washing between jurisdictions by requiring all states to adhere to strict record-keeping criteria, thus avoiding schemes to create confusing paper trails that intentionally avoid jurisdictional boundaries of courts and law-enforcement agencies.

MARINE THEFT

Marine theft is a serious problem to the boating community (Figure 16-23). It includes the theft of boats, boat trailers, outboard motors, jet skis, and all equipment associated with boating or water activities. Marine theft is a "shadow crime." It is real but difficult to define because of the lack of accurate statistical information. The main reporting mechanism, the *Uniform Crime Report* (UCR), compiled and reported annually by the Federal Bureau

◄ FIGURE 16-23
Marine police on lookout
Marine theft, which includes theft of boats, trailers, and all associated equipment, is a serious problem in the boating community. In communities that have extensive waterways, local police often have a marine patrol unit that provides routine patrol and investigates theft of marine equipment. (© Bonnie Kamin)

of Investigation, enters the theft of an outboard motor in the burglary index, the theft of a boat trailer in the vehicle file, and other related thefts in different categories. As a result, the magnitude of the marine theft problem is hidden in other crime indexes. Marine insurance theft data are similarly disjointed because there are many types of policies—home owners', business, inland marine, yacht—that provide coverage for marine equipment. Nevertheless, it is estimated that nationwide losses resulting from marine theft exceed $250 million annually.

The majority of thefts occur from homes, businesses, or dry storage facilities. A boat and outboard motor on a boat trailer can be stolen in a matter of seconds by a thief who simply backs up to the trailer, hooks up, and drives away. Although locking mechanisms are available for boat trailers and may deter the amateur thief, such devices are easily overcome by the professional.

Theft by water is accomplished simply by towing the boat away with another boat or by starting the motor and driving away. Boats powered by outboard motors, under 25 horsepower, usually do not have keyed ignition switches. However, even on larger boats, a dozen master keys will start virtually any marine motor, whether outboard or inboard.

Approximately 87% of all boats stolen are under 20 feet in length. Of these, boats of 16 feet and less constitute 65% of the thefts. The National Crime Information Center reports over 27,000 boat thefts entered into the computer system. Law-enforcement experts agree that most thefts are not investigated thoroughly (if at all) because of the difficulty investigators experience understanding marine equipment identification numbers and the lack of available ownership information.

Because of the absence of accurate statistical data, law enforcement is somewhat hampered in its efforts to address the problem. Consequently, there is a general lack of knowledge about marine theft and a resulting lack of commitment of resources to address the problems. In many agencies, marine theft reports are assigned to the auto theft or burglary unit and are treated as low-priority items.

Why are boats stolen? The number-one reason is profit. Marine theft is a high-profit, low-risk crime. Most often, a boat, motor, and trailer are stolen and sold as a package at a fair market value. To reduce the possibility of identification, some organized theft rings operate a chop shop, switching stolen motors, trailers, and boats or selling them separately.

There is also a lucrative market for the exportation of stolen outboard motors. In Central and South America, a used outboard motor will sell for more than a new motor in the United States. In addition, as in auto theft, insurance fraud may be involved in 25% or more of the reported marine thefts.

The increase in marine theft has often been linked by the media to drug trafficking. Experts tend to disagree. If, in fact, 87% of the boats stolen are under 20 feet in length,

it is unlikely that these are being used for drug trafficking. Boats 30 feet and longer could very well be involved in drug trafficking, but such thefts constitute only 3% of the problem. Of course, larger boats are also targets for professional thieves because of their high value. However, there may be some legitimate linkage between the theft of outboard motors and the drug problem. A 300-horsepower outboard motor, which retails for over $15,000, can be sold without any ownership documents.

Most small boats are stolen not by professionals but for the personal use of the thief or, occasionally, for joyrides. This is particularly true in the theft of personal watercraft. Approximately 20% of all boat thefts involve personal watercraft stolen by juveniles for their own use. Only occasionally are boats stolen to be used as transportation in other crimes, such as burglary of a waterfront home or business.

HULL IDENTIFICATION

Effective November 1, 1972, the Federal Boating Safety Act of 1971 required boats to have a 12-character **hull identification number (HIN).** Before this, boat manufacturers assigned whatever numbers were needed for their own production records. The HIN was subsequently codified by federal regulation. The promotion of boating safety was the original purpose for the HIN. It enabled the U.S. Coast Guard to identify "batches" of boats produced by a manufacturer that failed to meet certain production standards. This consumer protection function soon became secondary after titling and registering authorities began using the HIN assigned to a boat to identify ownership in much the same manner as the VIN is used for a motor vehicle.

Although manufacturers are required to affix each HIN to the outside of the boat's transom in a "permanent manner" so that any alteration or removal will be evident, in reality this is rarely enforced. Many manufacturers attach the HIN using a plastic plate pop-riveted to the transom. This can be easily removed and replaced with a false HIN. Some manufacturers of fiberglass boats place the HIN on the outer layer of the gelcoat using a "Dymo label"–type device during the molding process. However, this can easily be scraped or gouged out by a thief with a screwdriver or knife. A professional thief will replace the removed HIN with automotive body filler that often matches the color of the gelcoat. Then, by stamping a false HIN into the body filler, it appears that the HIN was affixed by the manufacturer and the alteration often goes undetected. An additional problem occurs when the Coast Guard allows a manufacturer to alter a HIN on any boat that remains in inventory by changing the production dates or model year to reflect a newer model year. Even for an experienced marine investigator, it is difficult to recognize whether a HIN was altered to cover a theft or modified by a manufacturer to reflect a newer model year.

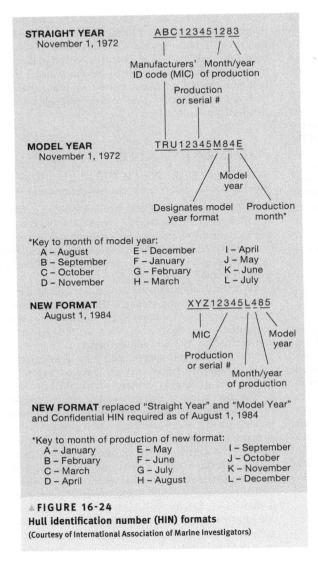

STRAIGHT YEAR
November 1, 1972

ABC123451283

Manufacturers'   Month/year
ID code (MIC)   of production

Production
or serial #

MODEL YEAR
November 1, 1972

TRU12345M84E

Model
year

Designates model   Production
year format   month*

*Key to month of model year:
A – August   E – December   I – April
B – September   F – January   J – May
C – October   G – February   K – June
D – November   H – March   L – July

NEW FORMAT
August 1, 1984

XYZ12345L485

MIC   Model
year

Production
or serial #

Month/year
of production

NEW FORMAT replaced "Straight Year" and "Model Year"
and Confidential HIN required as of August 1, 1984

*Key to month of production of new format:
A – January   E – May   I – September
B – February   F – June   J – October
C – March   G – July   K – November
D – April   H – August   L – December

FIGURE 16-24
Hull identification number (HIN) formats
(Courtesy of International Association of Marine Investigators)

Figure 16-24 shows the three different HIN formats approved by the Coast Guard. The straight-year and model-year formats were used from November 1, 1972, until August 1, 1984, when a new format replaced them. The only differences between the three formats are the last four characters. In the straight-year format, the last four characters reflect the calendar month and year of production. In the model-year format, the ninth character is always the letter "M" followed by the model year and a letter indicating the month of production. The newer format, optional starting January 1, 1984, and mandatory as of August 1, 1984, uses the ninth and tenth characters to reflect the calendar month and year of production and the eleventh and twelfth characters to represent the model year.

The first three characters of the HIN are the manufacturer's identification code (MIC), assigned to each manufacturer by the Coast Guard. Since 1972, over 13,000 MICs have been assigned. Many codes have been reassigned after the original company went out of business. Because of this, it is very difficult even for the most experienced marine investigator to remain familiar with all the manufacturer's codes. In addition, large conglomerates such as Mercury Marine and Outboard Motor Corporation have purchased many boat manufacturers and used manufacturer's identification codes assigned to the parent corporation for multiple boat lines.

The middle five characters of the HIN are used as production numbers or serial numbers assigned by the manufacturer. Although the letters "I," "O," and "Q" cannot be used, any other letter can be used in combination with numbers. These "production" numbers can and often are repeated on a monthly basis for an entire year. Whereas the automobile VIN has a 30-year uniqueness and a check digit to avoid unintentional or deliberate omission of numbers and intentional or unintentional transposition of numbers, the HIN does not yet have these features.

TITLE AND REGISTRATION ISSUES

There are approximately 12 million pleasure boats in the United States. Roughly 160,000 of these are federally registered by the Coast Guard and are referred to as "documented." Ownership and financial disputes over **documented vessels** can be resolved in the federal courts. The remainder of the pleasure boats are registered and/or titled by each state, except Alaska, in which registration issues are regulated by the Coast Guard.

Over 30 states require that boats be titled, but only a few states require the titling of outboard motors. Even in titling states, many boats are exempted by being less than a specified length or powered by less than a specified horsepower of motor. More than half the titling programs are administered by wildlife or natural resource agencies. The remainder are operated by motor vehicle agencies.

Many jurisdictions that title boats do not have computerized ownership records or do not retain the information for more than one year. The boat registration or title files in only a few states can be accessed using the National Law Enforcement Telecommunications System (NLETS). The inability of an investigator to obtain ownership information in a timely and efficient manner makes boat theft investigation very difficult.

NCIC BOAT FILE

As noted earlier, over 27,000 stolen boats are included in the NCIC system, under the title "Boat File." The Boat File, one of the 17 NCIC 2000 files, records information on stolen boats, boat trailers, and boat parts. Information in the file is retrievable on an online basis by entering the registration or document number, the hull identification number, or the assigned NCIC number. Unless otherwise removed or located, information in the Boat File is maintained for the balance of the year of entry, plus four years. The exception to this is records that have no boat hull identification number or other number assigned by the owner that can be used for identification purposes. These remain in the file for only 90 days after entry.

The boat theft problem may be much greater than what the NCIC statistics display. There is no mandate requiring that boat thefts be entered into NCIC and, because of the difficulty of reporting, many thefts are not entered. According to marine theft experts, new edits installed in the NCIC Boat File in late 1993 contained errors, causing valid entries to be rejected and further discouraging the entry of stolen boat information by law-enforcement agencies. Another major flaw in the system is that NCIC does not enter all the Coast Guard–assigned manufacturer's identification codes and, in some cases, has assigned codes that are not those recognized by the Coast Guard.

INVESTIGATIVE RESOURCES

Marine theft investigations are often complex and time-consuming. With the difficulty in obtaining ownership information, the tens of thousands of boat manufacturers, and the lack of computerized theft information, the success of an investigation is often predicated not on what the investigator knows but on whom he or she knows to contact for assistance. A major resource is the International Association of Marine Investigators. This organization has over 2,000 members who network with other law-enforcement officers and agencies and insurance investigators throughout the United States, Canada, Europe, the Caribbean, and Central and South America. The organization holds an annual training seminar on marine theft issues.

PREVENTIVE MEASURES

There are several ways a boat owner can lessen the possibility of marine theft. For example, one individual who used to make his living by stealing boats and reselling them recommended that any boat with an electric starter should have a toggle switch that shuts off the electrical system when in the off position. The switch can be located under the dash or behind a panel. Typically, when a thief attempts to start the boat and cannot, the thief assumes that it is malfunctioning and gives up the effort to steal it.

To discourage theft, a boat owner may want to remove a vital engine part when the boat is left unattended. Trailered boats are more easily stolen than boats in the water. The best way to protect boats on trailers is to keep them out of the sight of thieves. They should be parked behind a house or behind or inside a garage where they cannot be seen from the street.

Owners should never leave boats where they will tempt a potential thief. If a boat appears difficult to steal,

the thief will seek an easier victim. The owner should never leave the keys or the registration on board when the vessel is not attended. Outboard motors should be bolted through the hull and secured with clamping locks. If the owner is to be away from the place where the boat is stored for an extended period of time, the engine should be disabled or one or more wheels should be removed from the trailer.

AIRCRAFT AND AVIONICS THEFT

With approximately 225,000 general-aviation aircraft in the United States, the theft of aircraft and burglary leading to the theft of avionics are certainly not as prevalent as motor vehicle theft. Nonetheless, they are significant criminal problems that law-enforcement investigators may encounter[49] (Figure 16-25).

In 2009, 7 aircraft were stolen, valued at $150,000. Through the end of October, 2010, 5 aircraft, valued at $225,000, have been stolen. These numbers sound small compared to the 56 aircraft stolen in 1991, but it is still significant.[50] It is believed that many of the thefts are going to Mexico and being used by the drug cartels. Aircraft owners are being strongly advised not to fly to Mexico and preferably stay away from the border.

The theft of aircraft electronic equipment, or **avionics,** can be a highly lucrative enterprise for thieves. Avionics include all the electronic radio and navigation equipment on board an aircraft—easily valued at over $10,000 in even the smallest aircraft. Many pieces of avionics look similar and can be accurately identified only by referring to the model number and/or name. Part of the difficulty encountered by many law-enforcement officers is their unfamiliarity with such pieces of equipment. In 2009 there were 34 aircraft burglaries in which 97 items were stolen worth $312,000. As of October 31, 2010, there have been 24 burglaries in which 47 items worth $126,000 were stolen.[51]

There are many reasons for equipment burglaries. One of the prime reasons is the lack of security at airports and the indifference on the part of many sales outlets regarding the identification and sources of used equipment. In addition, although most avionics contain stickers and plates identifying the manufacturer, model number, part number, and even the serial number, these are often easily removed and in some cases are just stick-on labels.

Most modern avionics are designed to be easily removed from the aircraft panel to facilitate frequent repair and maintenance of the equipment. Stolen avionics are often resold through the used-parts market or to persons who need the items and are willing to overlook the source of such reasonably priced equipment.

Much of the stolen avionics equipment is exported to other countries. Some is resold using counterfeited

◄ **FIGURE 16-25**
Stolen aircraft crashes into bank building
The theft of aircraft in the United States is a relatively rare event. However, breaking into an aircraft to steal electronic parts is relatively simple, since both door locks and ignition locks on many private planes can easily be picked. Thefts of aircraft are most likely to occur at airports that are poorly lit and unattended at night. The aircraft in the picture was stolen by a juvenile from a small airfield and ultimately crashed into a downtown bank building. (© Chuck Sutnick/Tampa Fire Rescue/Getty Images)

VIN labels and VIN plates. Other equipment is switched so that the stolen equipment is never discovered, as illustrated by the following example: A thief will identify the type of equipment desired in a specific aircraft at a specific airport. The thief or thieves will then locate the same type of equipment in another aircraft at another airport. At the time of theft, the electronic equipment will be removed from the first aircraft and placed in the second aircraft after the second aircraft's equipment has been removed. The equipment from the second aircraft is then sold on the market; normally, the owner of the second aircraft doesn't even know the equipment is missing because the same material, stolen from the first aircraft, has been installed in his or her craft. The theft of equipment from the first aircraft is reported, but it is never recovered because it is already comfortably installed in aircraft number two.

RESOURCES

An investigator who is unfamiliar with aircraft and aircraft thefts should not hesitate to obtain assistance from those who have the necessary expertise. It is advised that before undertaking a significant investigation, an investigator should visit a local airport, contact airport management, aircraft companies, flight schools, and so forth, to learn basic information about aircraft, avionics, and the theft of both. The Aviation and Crime Prevention Institute located in Hagerstown, Maryland, is an excellent source of assistance and support for law-enforcement officers involved in the investigation of aviation theft.[52] The mission of the institute is to reduce aviation-related crime through information gathering, communication with law enforcement and the public, and education programs in theft prevention and security awareness.

THEFT TECHNIQUES

The techniques thieves use to steal aircraft and burglarize aircraft for the avionics equipment are not that much different from, and most frequently parallel to, those used for stealing automobiles. Of course, if theft of the aircraft is the objective, it is unlikely that the thief will gain access by smashing a window. Indeed, smashing a window is generally not necessary. Perhaps the weakest security point of any aircraft is its locks. Most aircraft manufacturers use a limited number of key combinations, and a single key may open many aircraft of the same make. Occasionally, one manufacturer's key will open an aircraft of a different manufacturer.

Both door locks and ignition locks can easily be picked, and generally there are no antitheft devices on aircraft. Many of the more expensive aircraft don't even use ignition keys, so the only requirement for the thief is to enter the cabin.

Many of the techniques used to cover the theft of aircraft are similar to the processes used to conceal the theft of motor vehicles. The following illustrates a salvage switch involving aircraft: A thief decides on the type of aircraft desired and then purchases a total wreck of a similar aircraft from a junkyard. Rather than the certificate of title and VIN plate that come with a motor vehicle, the wrecked aircraft comes with its VIN plate and log book (a document required by the Federal Aviation Administration [FAA] that records the aircraft's history and repair record). The thief then steals (or has stolen) an aircraft of the same year, make, and model; switches the VIN plate; and installs the log book. After the thief adapts the registration markings and ensures that colors match the wrecked aircraft, the salvage switch is complete.

Thefts of aircraft are most likely to occur at airports that have poor lighting and are unattended at night, especially if they have little or no security, have no control tower, and perhaps are not even fenced.

AIRCRAFT IDENTIFICATION

Aircraft have the same basic identification information as do motor vehicles. The major difference is that aircraft are regulated under a federal licensing system, whereas motor vehicles are regulated under state licensing systems. All aircraft are identified by a registration number, which is similar to a license plate number; a VIN; and make and model. The U.S. registration numbering system is part of a worldwide system under which each country has a letter and/or number code. In the United States, the code begins with the letter "N." Consequently, all U.S.-registered aircraft display an N number.

Most registered aircraft receive their N numbers when they are manufactured. It is possible for the purchaser of a used aircraft or of an aircraft currently being built to request a special N number. Such requests are processed by the FAA.

The N number is found on each side of the aircraft or on the vertical tail in large or small letter and numeral combinations. In some cases, such as on older aircraft, the N number may be displayed on the underside of one wing and the topside of the opposite wing. Helicopters have the N number displayed under the nose or undercarriage.

Most aircraft have a small plate on the instrument panel with the plane's N number on it. An investigator can look at the plate and determine whether the plate number matches the N number displayed on the exterior of the aircraft. If the plate is missing, further investigation is warranted.

Although each aircraft has a VIN, manufacturers design their own numbering systems, and the location of a VIN plate varies depending on the make. For example, on Cessna aircraft the VIN plate is found on the doorjamb; the door must be open to see the plate. The VIN plate on most single-engine and small twin-engine Beechcraft planes can be found on the right side above the wing flap; large Beechcraft planes have the VIN plate inside the main-cabin entry door frame. On Piper aircraft the VIN plate is usually found on the lower side of the tail on the aircraft's body.

As in any attempt to identify a vehicle, a vessel, or aircraft, the investigator should understand the construction process well enough to know whether and where to look for identifiers. When aircraft are built, many of the parts are subassembled elsewhere in the plant, and such subassemblies are marked with the VIN number in Magic Marker or pencil so that the aircraft can later come together at the main assembly point. If the plate is missing, the investigator should look under seats, under carpeted areas, in inspection panels, and elsewhere for ID numbers relating to the VIN.

When trying to locate a VIN plate in aircraft other than those previously mentioned, the investigator should look in some of the most common locations, such as on the doorjamb on either side of the plane, on the lower tail section on either side of the plane, on the body where the main wing is attached, near the nose wheel, or on the lower body. In other words, when in doubt, the dedicated investigator will look over the entire aircraft in an attempt to find the attached plate, which will provide make, model, and VIN information.

THEFT PREVENTION TECHNIQUES

Following are a few examples of the theft-deterrent devices available and the actions an aircraft owner can take, some without cost, to reduce the chance of theft of the aircraft or the avionics.

- There are a number of alarm systems on the market, and some even have a pain generator, a second piercing alarm inside the cockpit that is most aggravating to the human ear.
- Ignition kills, which require entry of a security code into the control panel in the cockpit, are available. If the pilot fails to get the code right after a specific number of tries, the engine-starting circuits are disabled and, in some cases, a siren will sound.
- There should be a prearranged password known only to crew members and the airport operator. Thus, a person who calls and directs that the plane be prepared for flight must know the password in order to get the plane readied. This technique has prevented the theft of many aircraft.
- A wheel-locking device, or "boot," prevents the plane from being towed or from moving under its own power.
- More secure locks can be installed.
- Airplanes should be parked at night at airports that are well lighted, fenced, and otherwise provided with security. Window covers should be used to conceal avionics.
- Avionics equipment should be checked to ensure that it is the manufacturer-installed equipment. Each piece should then be marked with a dot, paint, engraving, or scratch, and a detailed inventory should be made and recorded.
- Propeller chains and locks are available.
- Instrument panels can be equipped with a locking bar or locking cover.
- Flight operations personnel at airports should be given a list that identifies each crew member and other persons permitted to be around the plane or to authorize service over the phone.
- Airport authorities should have a central point of contact available 24 hours a day.
- Vital aircraft records should not be kept in the aircraft.

active system (theft deterrent)
American Association of Motor Vehicle
  Administrators (AAMVA)
Automatic License Plate Recognition
  System (ALPR)
avionics
cargo theft
chop shop
commercial-vehicle theft
confidential VIN
documented vessel
false-theft scheme
false-vehicle scheme
federal safety certification label
gray-market vehicle

heavy equipment
hull identification number (HIN)
inflated-theft-loss scheme
joyriding
marine theft
Motor Vehicle Theft Law Enforcement
  Act (1984)
National Insurance Crime Bureau
  (NICB)
National Motor Vehicle Title Information
  System (NMVTIS)
odometer fraud
off-road equipment
"paper vehicle"
parts marking

passive system (theft deterrent)
product identification number (PIN)
professional theft (of vehicle)
quick strip (of vehicle)
salvage switch
salvage title
salvage vehicle
Stolen Auto Recovery (STAR) System
temporary theft (of vehicle)
title fraud
Truth in Mileage Act (1986)
vehicle fraud
vehicle identification number (VIN)
VIN plate
washing (of title)

REVIEW QUESTIONS

1. Describe a chop-shop operation.
2. How does a salvage switch work?
3. Distinguish false-vehicle, false-theft, and inflated theft-loss schemes.
4. What is a "paper" vehicle?
5. How is a certificate of title "washed"?
6. What are some of the factors contributing to the theft of off-road equipment?
7. What is the National Insurance Crime Bureau, and what functions does it perform for law enforcement?
8. Why is vehicle identification the most difficult and time-consuming task faced by an investigator in an auto theft case?
9. Why do vehicles have a standardized identification numbering system?
10. What was the purpose behind passage of the Motor Vehicle Theft Law Enforcement Act of 1984?
11. Describe the three basic methods for restoring vehicle identification numbers.
12. Describe some of the principal investigative steps in determining whether a vehicle fire is an accident or arson.
13. Describe the workings and benefits of a photographic preinsurance inspection program.
14. What is odometer fraud, and why is it a significant offense?
15. Discuss the nature and seriousness of marine theft.
16. What are avionics, and why is avionics theft prevalent?

INTERNET ACTIVITIES

1. Check the web to see if your state has law enforcement and/or insurance organizations that specialize in the investigation of motor vehicle and other related thefts. What types of investigative services do they provide? Are auto theft statistics available for your state? Does the site have auto theft prevention information? If you were a criminal investigator, what other information do you think should be available on the site?

2. Learn more about the export of stolen motor vehicles and other items by logging on to the U.S. Customs site at *www.cbp.gov* and the North American Export Committee site at *www.naexportcommittee.org*. The latter website also has several related links to insurance fraud and vehicle theft prevention.

A

A Child Is Missing (ACIM) This program, started in 1997, was created to assist law enforcement officers in locating missing children, as well as disabled and mentally challenged individuals, and elderly persons, such as those suffering from Alzheimers.

AAMVANET Maintained by the American Association of Motor Vehicle Administrators, this computerized network allows U.S. and Canadian agencies to share information about driver's licenses and motor vehicle matters.

accelerant In fire starting, any flammable fluid or compound that speeds the progress of a fire. Also called a *booster*.

account takeover A follow-on crime to identity theft. In this scenario, the possessor of your identity changes where your bill is being mailed to and quickly runs up charges before you are aware of the problem.

action stereotyping Occurs when an officer expects an event to unfold in a particular way; it can result in the officer's failure to see the event the way it actually occurred.

active system A type of vehicle antitheft device which requires that the driver do something to activate and deactivate the system every time the vehicle is parked or driven.

administrative log A written record of the actions taken by the crime scene coordinator, including assignments and release of the scene.

admissibility A legal criterion used to determine whether an item of evidence can be presented in court; requires that the evidence have relevance, materiality, and competence.

admission A person's acknowledgment of certain facts or circumstances that tend to incriminate him or her with respect to a crime but are not complete enough to constitute a confession.

advance-fee scheme These are operated in a bewildering variety of ways; goods, services, or a portion of a fortune are promised contingent upon the person being contacted paying an advanced or "up-front" fee. The essence of these is always (1) you pay before receiving anything, and (2) you never receive anything, unless it is a smaller amount designed to "hook" you into coming up with a really large advanced fee.

affidavit A sworn, written statement of the information known to an officer that serves as the basis for the issuance of an arrest warrant or a search warrant.

affinity fraud These include many different types of frauds perpetrated upon groups such as church members who know and trust each other, and have an affinity for one another. Often, a person of high status in the group, such as its pastor, president, or a member of the governing board will be recruited and will unknowingly help further the scheme by endorsing it.

affirmation The process in which a witness acknowledges that he or she understands and undertakes the obligation of an oath (i.e., to tell the truth with a realization of the penalties for perjury); a means of establishing a witness's competence.

agrichemical Any of various chemical products used on farms; includes pesticides, fertilizers, and herbicides.

agroterroism The use of biological agents as weapons against the agricultural and food supply industries.

algor mortis The decrease in body temperature that occurs after death.

alligatoring The checking of charred wood, which gives it the appearance of alligator skin.

alternative light systems (ALSs) Portable lasers and handheld ultraviolet lighting used to locate physical evidence at the crime scene; particularly helpful in locating trace evidence.

amateur burglar Burglars who operate on the basis of impulse or opportunity, with no planning. Often use sheer force to enter, ransacking the premises for anything of value. May become violent if detected and commit secondary crimes (e.g., murder, rape).

Amber Plan A voluntary partnership between law enforcement agencies and broadcasters to activate an urgent news bulletin in the most serious child abduction cases.

American Society of Crime Laboratory Directors (ASCLD) An international society devoted to maintaining the highest standards of practice at crime laboratories; conducts an accreditation program for laboratories and education programs for lab personnel.

Americans with Disabilities Act (ADA) A federal law which establishes the workplace rights of those with perceived or actual disabilities.

amido black A dye that is sensitive to blood and thus is used in developing fingerprints contaminated with blood.

amphetamines Stimulants that increase blood pressure as well as heart, respiratory, and metabolic rates; produces decreased appetite, hyperalert senses, and a general state of stress that lasts a prolonged period.

anger-excitation rape-murder This crime is designed to inflict pain and terror on the victim for the gratification of the perpetrator. The prolonged torture of the victim energizes the killer's fantasies and temporarily satisfies a lust for domination and control.

anger-retaliatory rape-murder This type of planned murder involves overkill. It is an anger-venting act that expresses symbolic revenge on a female victim.

anthrax An acute infectious disease with three forms (cutaneous, intestinal, and inhalation), which differ in the means of their transmission, symptoms, and lethality; also, a biological agent.

anthropometry Developed by Alphonse Bertillon in the late 19th century, the study and comparison of body measurements as a means of criminal identification.

archaeological looting The illegal, unscientific removal of archaeological resources from public, tribal, or private land.

arrest The process of taking a person into legal custody to answer a criminal charge.

arrest warrant A judicial order commanding that a particular person be arrested and brought before a court to answer a criminal charge.

assignment sheets Written reports completed by persons assigned tasks at a crime scene that document what they have done and found.

associative evidence Bidirectional evidence that connects the perpetrator to the scene or victim, or connects the scene or victim to the perpetrator.

ATM attacks The seizure and removal of ATMs from their rightful location to another place where they can be broken into, or the attempted or successful act of breaking into them where they are located. Applicable state statutes vary, so such attacks may be charged as a larceny or a burglary depending on the location of the crime.

attack code A malicious software program intended to impair or destroy the functioning of a computer or a network resource.

autoerotic death Death from accidental asphyxiation as a result of masochistic activities of the deceased. Also called *sexual asphyxia.*

Automated Fingerprint Identification System (AFIS) A computerized system, maintained by the FBI, that stores and compares millions of fingerprints and is used to find matches for identification purposes.

autopsy The medical examination of a body to determine the time, and cause, of death; required in all cases of violent or suspicious death.

avionics The electronic equipment (e.g., radio, navigation) on an aircraft.

B

bank examiner con A tried-and-true trick to separate unwary people from their money. The scam usually unfolds this way: A con identifying themselves as a bank examiner or police officer approaches a person with a tale about how someone is embezzling money at the bank and help is needed to identify that person. The victim is asked to withdraw money from their account and then meet the bank examiner who gives them a "cashier's check" for the money withdrawn. The victim is told not to deposit the check for a week in order that the investigation not be compromised. This action is repeated with other victims during the week and then the cons disappear along with the money they collected, leaving the victims holding worthless "cashier" checks.

barbiturates Short-, intermediate-, and long-lasting depressants (e.g., secobarbital, amobarbital) that when stopped abruptly can cause convulsions and death; nicknamed after the capsule or pill color, or the manufacturer's name.

basic yellow 40 Used after superglue fuming, a dye that causes latent prints to fluoresce under alternative lighting.

battered-child syndrome The clinical term for the mental difficulties sustained by a physically abused child.

behavioral evidence analysis (BEA) A deductive and evidence-based method of criminal profiling.

be-on-the-lookout (BOLO) Part of the preliminary investigation, a notification broadcast to officers that contains detailed information on suspects and their vehicles.

Bertillon, Alphonse Recognized worldwide as the father of personal identification; he developed anthropometry.

Biggers-Brathwaite Factors Test A test that balances the reliability of eyewitness identification (as determined by five factors specified by the Supreme Court) with the corrupting effect of any suggestive procedures; enables a highly reliable identification to be used in court even if something jeopardized the fairness of the identification procedure.

biological agents Certain microorganisms and toxins produced by organisms (e.g., smallpox, anthrax, plague, botulism) that cause human illness or death and could be used as terrorist weapons; typically slower acting than chemical agents.

black market peso exchange (BMPE) A sophisticated method of money laundering which is typically operated to convert drug or other illicitly gained money into funds which appear to be from legitimate sources.

bobbies A colloquial term used in reference to British police constables; derived by the public from the first name of Sir Robert Peel, whose efforts led to the creation of the first metropolitan police force in London.

body language Gestures, demeanor, facial expressions, and other nonverbal signals that convey, usually involuntarily, a person's attitudes, impressions, truthfulness, and so on.

bone rustlers Unauthorized fossil hunters, who loot public and private lands.

bore The diameter of a gun barrel's interior between its opposing high sides (the lands).

Bow Street Runners Established by Henry Fielding in 1748, a group of volunteer, nonuniformed home owners who helped catch thieves in London by rushing to crime scenes and beginning investigations, thus acting as the first modern detective force. By 1785, some were paid government detectives.

brands On livestock, registered combinations of numbers, letters, marks, and shapes that establish unique identifications.

buccal swab Sterile cotton swabs used to obtain saliva from the mouth of a suspect for DNA analysis.

burden of going forward In a criminal trial, the responsibility of the defense to present enough evidence to create a reasonable doubt of guilt in the jurors' minds; an optional burden, as the defense is not required to present any evidence.

burden of proof In a criminal trial, the requirement that the prosecution establish the defendant's guilt beyond, and to the exclusion of, every reasonable doubt.

burglary The crime of breaking and entering a house or other building belonging to another with the intent to commit a crime therein.

burglary checklist A police-generated written list of investigative steps which begin with the arrival of the first officer at the scene through prosecution.

burglary tools Tools used in the commission of a burglary; often are ordinary household tools, but may be modified for increased effectiveness in breaking and entering.

burn indicators Any effects of heat or partial burning that indicate a fire's rate of development, points of origin, temperature, duration, and time of occurrence and the presence of flammable liquids.

C

cadaveric spasm The instantaneous tightening of an extremity or other part of the body at the time of death. Also called *death grip.*

caliber The diameter of a bullet; somewhat larger than the bore of the weapon from which the bullet is fired.

car, recreational vehicle, and trailer burglaries The act of breaking and entering such places to commit an unlawful act therein. These acts may, depending on the state and fact situation, be chargeable as a burglary or as a larceny. Their inclusion in the burglary chapter is predicated by the fact that regardless of what charge is actually made, the techniques used to gain entry and the investigation of these acts is kindred to burglaries generally.

cargo theft The theft of items from or in commercial motor vehicles.

carjacking The crime of taking a motor vehicle from the motorist or passenger, or from his or her immediate presence, by use of force, fear, or threat of force, with the intent to temporarily or permanently deprive the owner of its use.

catalytic combustion detector A portable device that oxidizes any combustible gases in a sample; used to detect residues of flammable-liquid accelerants at fire scenes. Also called *sniffer, combustible-gas indicator, explosimeter,* and *vapor detector.*

chain of custody The witnessed, unbroken, written chronological record of everyone who had an item of evidence, and when each person had it; also accounts for any changes in the evidence.

charging The act of formally asserting that a particular person is to be prosecuted for a crime.

charring The scorching of materials by fire; used to deduce the direction of fire spread by comparing relative depths of char throughout the scene.

check kiters People who open accounts at several banks and then knowingly write a bad check on their account at bank 1 and then cover it with a bad check written on their account at bank 2 and so on. Eventually the scheme falls apart because the sums keep getting larger and larger and cannot be maintained indefinitely.

chemical agents Rapidly acting substances (e.g., mustard gas, sarin, V agents) that produce a variety of incapacitating symptoms or death; as weapons, can cause mass casualties and devastation.

chemical explosions Explosions in which a high-pressure gas is produced by reactions that involve changes in the basic chemical nature of the fuel; commonly caused by the burning of hydrocarbon fuels (e.g., natural gas, gasoline, lubricating oils).

child pornography The sexually explicit visual depiction of a minor (as defined by statute); includes photographs, negatives, slides, magazines, movies, videotapes, and computerized images.

chop shop An illegal operation at which stolen cars are disassembled and their traceable parts altered or disposed of so that untraceable parts can be sold to repair shops, salvage yards, and indiscriminate buyers.

Christian Identity theology A right-wing philosophy expressing the superiority of the white Aryan race over the forces of Satan (people of color and Jews). Central to the CI belief is a distortion of the Bible supporting the creation of "pre-Adamites," or people of color, the sexual union of Eve and Satan in the Garden of Eden giving rise to the Jewish race, and the future physical battle of Armageddon between Aryan people and the forces of Satan (Jews and non-whites).

clandestine drug laboratories Illicit operations that produce a variety of illegal drugs for sale and distribution; due to the chemicals, processes used, and workers' inexperience, police and firefighters, as well as the public, can face severe danger on location.

class characteristics Characteristics of physical evidence that are common to a group of objects or persons.

cleared by arrest The classification assigned to an offense when the suspect has been arrested and there is sufficient evidence to file a formal charge.

cloning (1) The creation of a second legitimate vehicle by counterfeiting or duplicating identification numbers and ownership documents.

cloning (2) The illegal programming of cellular phones by overwriting their access codes with the codes of legitimate cellular customers; done through a personal computer or cloning "black box."

cocaine A natural stimulant extracted from the leaves of the coca plant; illegally sold as a white, translucent, crystalline powder, which is often adulterated.

codeine An opiate in tablet, liquid, and injectable forms that produces less analgesia, sedation, and respiratory depression than morphine.

CODIS *See* **Combined DNA Index System.**

cognitive interview technique An interviewing approach in which a witness is asked to recall events and details in different ways as a means of fostering the witness's recollections.

cold case investigation Assigning detectives to examine cases that went unsolved, which includes using new advanced technology that was unavailable before to analyze old evidence, and re-interviewing witnesses who were previously hostile. In some cases, the original detectives assigned the case were simply overworked and could not allocate enough time to properly work it.

Combined DNA Index System (CODIS) Developed by the FBI, a database of convicted-offender and known- and unknown-subject DNA profiles that is used to find matches and to link unsolved crimes in multiple jurisdictions.

commercial-vehicle theft The theft of vehicle tractor units and trailers.

competency (of a witness) A witness's qualification for testifying in court, which depends on circumstances that affect the person's legal ability to function as a sworn witness (e.g., age, mental state).

component swapping A fraudulent practice in which manufacturers (e.g., of computers) use parts from the lowest-cost supplier but do not inform consumers that the parts are nonstandard.

computer abuse Any intentional act involving knowledge of computer use or technology in which the perpetrator could have made a gain and the victim could have experienced a loss; includes acts that may not be covered by criminal laws.

computer crime Any illegal act in which knowledge of computer technology is used to commit the offense.

computer manipulation crime Any act that involves changing data or creating records in an electronic system for the purpose of facilitating another crime, typically fraud or embezzlement.

computer vandalism The unauthorized removal of valuable information from a computer system, thereby preventing the legitimate user or owner from having access to that information.

Computer Voice Stress Analyzer (CVSA) A method of lie detection originally developed in 1988 by the National Institute for Truth Verification (NITV). By 2004, some 1,400 agencies were using it instead of the polygraph. The CVSA notes microvariations in the audible and non-audible portions of speech to identify deception. The CVSA is presently the first significant challenge to the dominance of the polygraph in 85 years.

concentric fracture lines Lines that roughly circle the point of impact in a glass window.

confabulation In hypnosis, the subject's fabrication of recollections to fill in gaps in his or her actual memory.

confession The acknowledgment by a person accused of a crime that he or she is guilty of that crime and committed every element of the offense; must exclude any reasonable doubt about the possibility of innocence.

confidential VIN A duplicate vehicle identification number stamped into a vehicle's frame or body in a place known only to the manufacturer and law enforcement specialists in vehicle identification and auto theft investigation.

contact burns Burns on the skin caused by contact with flames or hot solid objects (e.g., irons, cigarettes).

contaminated/visible prints Prints created when fingers contaminated with blood, face powder, or a similar material touch a clean surface.

corpus delicti evidence Evidence that substantiates elements whose commission or omission must be demonstrated to have occurred in order to prove a case.

crack or rock cocaine *See* rock cocaine.

cramming The intentional process of placing unauthorized, misleading, inaccurate or deceptive charges on the victims' telephone bills. While telephone companies may legally place such charges on your bill on behalf of other companies, it is also a method by which scams can also be run by those other companies.

credibility (of a witness) That quality of a witness that renders his or her testimony worthy of belief; established in terms of presence, consciousness, and attentiveness during interviews.

credit repair scam A type of advanced fee scam in which people with bad or poor credit are promised their records can be cleansed of negative entries. New credit cards may also be promised as part of the scam.

crime The commission of any act that is prohibited, or the omission of any act that is required by the penal code of an organized political state.

crime analysis The use of systematic analytical methods to acquire timely and pertinent information on crime patterns and trend correlations; subdivided into administrative, strategic, and tactical analysis.

crime laboratory A scientific organization that analyzes material collected from crime scenes and suspects to help determine whether a crime was committed and, if so, how, when, and by whom it was committed.

crime scene The location at which a crime was committed.

crime scene control The procedure of limiting and documenting access to the crime scene to ensure that physical evidence is not accidentally or deliberate altered or removed. The procedure begins with the arrival of the first officer at the scene and continues until the scene is released from police control.

crime scene entry log sheet A written chronological record of all persons who enter and leave the crime scene and the times they do so, along with their reason for entering.

crime scene release The end of crime scene processing and the return of the premises or area to the owner or another responsible person; determined by the scene coordinator.

crime scene search patterns Used to locate physical evidence at a crime scene; there are five patterns: spiral, strip/line, grid, zone/quadrant, and pie/wheel.

criminal enterprise homicide A murder committed for material gain.

criminalistics The application of scientific disciplines, such as geology, physics, chemistry, biology, and mathematics, to criminal investigation and the study of physical evidence.

crimogens (1) An individually known offender who is responsible for a large number of crimes; (2) one victim who reports a large number of crimes.

cross-contamination In a trial, the questioning of a witness who was initially called by the opposing party.

cross-examination In a trial, the questioning of a witness who was initially called by the opposing party.

cryptanalysis software Software used to intrusively access secured information by breaking down encryption.

crystal violet A dye used to develop latent prints on the adhesive side of almost any kind of tape.

crystallized methamphetamine A long-acting stimulant originally in pill or injectable form (*crystal meth, speed*) but now in a smokable, odorless version (*ice*); in solid form, resembles an ice chip but liquifies when lighted.

cyberstalking The crime of harassing or threatening victims by means of electronic technologies (e.g., through e-mail and Internet chat rooms or news groups).

cyberterrorism The use of electronic tools to disrupt or shut down critical infrastructure components, such as energy, transportation, and government operations.

D

dactylography The study and comparison of fingerprints as a means of criminal identification; first used systematically for that purpose in England in 1900, but a means of identification since the first century.

date-rape drugs Drugs that facilitate rape by debilitating the victim; they include Rohypnol, GHB, and many depressants and benzodiazapines.

Daubert v. Merrell Dow Pharmaceuticals, Inc. A 1993 case in which the Supreme Court held that the admissibility of an expert's testimony or a scientific technique's results depends on a preliminary assessment, made by the trial judge, of the principles and methodology involved.

decoys A police officer who is disguised to resemble the type of victims who are being targeted for robbery. This is especially true for street robberies.

deductive reasoning The thought process that moves from general premises to specific details—for example, a hypothesis about the crime is developed and then tested against the factual situation to arrive at a conclusion.

defense wounds Wounds suffered by victims while attempting to protect themselves from an assault; often inflicted by a knife or club.

delay-in-arraignment rule Based on a 1943 Supreme Court decision, the principle that the failure to take a prisoner before a committing magistrate without unnecessary delay will render his or her confession inadmissible even if it was freely obtained.

dental identification The identification of an individual on the basis of dental records (or, sometimes, "smiling" photographs); performed by a forensic dentist, who compares before-death records with after-death findings to see if there is a match.

dental stone The preferred material for casting tire, footwear, and foot impressions; stronger and faster setting than plaster of paris and provides more detailed impressions.

deoxyribonucleic acid (DNA) A nucleic acid consisting of the molecules that carry the body's genetic material and establish each person as separate and distinct.

depressants or sedatives Drugs that depress the central nervous system, reducing tension and inducing sleep; can cause, in chronic use, loss of balance, faulty judgment, quick temper, and in overdose, unconsciousness and death.

detention A temporary and limited interference with a person's freedom for investigative purposes. Also called *investigative detention, street stop,* and *field interrogation.*

DFO (diazafluren-9-one) A very effective chemical for developing latent prints on paper; produces red prints that may be visible to the naked eye and that fluoresce under most laser and alternative lighting.

digital forensic analysis The process of acquiring, preserving, analyzing, and presenting evidentiary electronic data relevant to an investigation or prosecution.

direct examination In a trial, the questioning of a witness by the party that calls the witness to testify.

disposition (of incident report) After approval of an incident report, the determination of how the case will be handled (i.e., unfounded, inactivated, retained for investigation by officers, referred to plainclothes investigators); usually made by the supervisor of the officer who wrote the report.

document Anything on which a mark is made for the purpose of transmitting a message.

documented vessel A boat that is registered by the U.S. Coast Guard.

domestic terrorism The use or threatened use of violence against persons or property by a group (or an individual) whose operations are entirely within the victims' nation, without foreign direction, and are done to further political or social objectives.

Drug Enforcement Administration (DEA) Created in 1973, this federal agency is responsible for enforcing laws on illicit drugs and fighting international drug traffic; also trains state and local police in investigative work regarding illegal drugs, surveillance, and use of informants.

due process Fairness.

due process clause The title of clauses appearing in both the Fifth and Fourteenth amendments to the Constitution of the United States.

dumpster diving Going through people's trash for the purpose of finding sufficient sensitive information to commit identity theft.

E

EDTA A preservative used to prevent coagulation.

effective fire temperatures In structural fires, identifiable temperatures which reflect physical effects that can be defined by specific temperature ranges.

embezzlement The misappropriation or misapplication of money or property entrusted to one's care, custody, or control.

emotional approach An interrogation technique in which the interrogator appeals to the suspect's sense of honor, morals, family pride, religion, and so on; works better with women and first-time offenders.

encryption A means of data security in which the data are scrambled into nonsense for storage or transmission and then unscrambled, as needed, by legitimate users.

Enderby cases Two rape-murder cases in England that involved the first use of DNA typing, in 1987, in a criminal case. DNA samples recovered from both victims led to the release of an innocent man and the subsequent arrest and conviction of the killer.

estate locators and research specialists These cons approach people by mail, purporting to be looking for heirs to a substantial fortune. In order to determine their eligibility, victims are asked to pay an "estate assessment fee" up-front, another variation on an advanced-fee scheme. This scam may also be operated as part of an identity theft operation.

evidence Anything that tends logically to prove or disprove a fact at issue in a judicial case or controversy.

evidence recovery log A chronological record of each item of evidence, listing who collected it, where and when it was collected, who witnessed the collection, and whether it was documented by photos or diagrams.

evidential intelligence Factual, precise information that can be presented in court.

evidentiary privileges Certain matters of communication that defendants and other witnesses can rightfully have barred from disclosure in court; classified as professional, political, social, and judicial.

exceptionally cleared The classification assigned to an offense when a factor external to the investigation results in no charge being filed against a known suspect (e.g., the death of the suspect).

exchangeable traces Particulates, lubricants, and spermicide added to condoms by manufacturers; can help identify particular brands and indicate condom use.

excusable homicide The killing of a person in which the slayer is to some degree at fault but the degree of fault is not enough to constitute a criminal homicide.

exigent circumstances An exception to the requirement that law enforcement officers have a search warrant; occurs when there is a compelling need for official action and there is no time to get a warrant.

expert witness A person who is called to testify in court because of his or her special skills or knowledge; permitted to interpret facts and give opinions about their significance to facilitate jurors' understanding of complex or technical matters.

exploits Software programs written to take advantage of security holes or "back doors" and thereby provide the user with illegal access to computer files.

explosion A physical reaction characterized by the presence of high-pressure gas, confinement of the pressure, rapid release of the pressure, and change or damage to the confining structure, container, or vessel as a result of the pressure release.

eyewitness identification The identification of someone or something involved in a crime by a witness who perceives the person or thing through one or more senses.

F

facial identification systems Manual kits or computer programs for preparing a likeness of a suspect; creates a composite from individual facial features.

facial recognition software Any of various computer programs that compare video images of persons' faces (taken by cameras at arenas, airports, hotels, and so on) with mug shots of known offenders for the purpose of identifying and apprehending wanted persons.

false-theft scheme An insurance fraud in which the owner of a vehicle reports it stolen but has actually hidden or disposed of it.

false-vehicle scheme An insurance fraud in which a person insures a vehicle that: does not exist; has already been salvaged; or belongs to someone else and later reports the vehicle stolen.

farm equipment Motorized equipment used on farms and on lawns; usually does not require a title or registration. Also called *off-road equipment*.

FBI Child Abduction and Serial Murder Investigative Center (CAS-MIRC) Provides investigative support through coordination and providing federal resources, training and application of multidisciplinary expertise, and to assist federal, state, and local authorities in matters involving child abductions, mysterious disappearances of children, child homicide, and serial murders across the country.

FBI Crime Laboratory A comprehensive forensic laboratory that conducts a broad range of scientific analyses of evidence and provides experts to testify in relation to analysis results; offers its services without charge to state and local law enforcement agencies.

federal safety certification label The sticker certifying a vehicle's safety, including its VIN; usually located on the driver's door or doorpost.

felonious assaults An assault committed for the purpose of inflicting severe bodily harm or death; usually involves use of a deadly weapon.

felonious homicides Killings that are treated and punished as crimes; includes murder and manslaughter.

felony A serious violation of the criminal code; punishable by imprisonment for one or more years or by death.

fences/receivers Individuals & businesses which knowingly buy, sell, or dispose of stolen merchandise, vehicles, financial instruments, and other things of value.

field interview/information report A form on which a patrolling officer notes details about a person or vehicle that seems suspicious but is not connected with any particular offense.

field notes The shorthand written record made by a police officer from the time he or she arrives at a crime scene until the assignment is completed.

Fielding, Henry Chief Magistrate of Bow Street in London beginning in 1748. In 1750, he formed a group of volunteer, non-uniformed homeowners, who hurried to the scene of crimes to investigate them. These "Bow Street Runners" were the first modern detective unit. In 1752, he created *The Covent Garden Journal*, which circulated the descriptions of wanted persons.

Fielding, John The brother of Henry Fielding. Following Henry's death in 1754, John carried on his work for 25 years, making Bow Street a clearing house for crime information.

Financial Crimes Enforcement Network (FinCen) Part of the Department of the Treasury, an agency responsible for investigating major financial crimes (e.g., money laundering); provides assistance to law enforcement agencies.

fingerprint classification A system used to categorize fingerprints on the basis of their ridge characteristics.

fingerprint patterns Patterns formed by the ridge detail of fingerprints; primarily loops, whorls, and arches.

fingerprints Replicas of the friction ridges (on palms, fingers, toes, and soles of the feet) that touched the surfaces on which the prints are found.

flame ionization detector A device that produces ionized molecules in proportion to the amount of combustible organic gases in a sample; used to detect residues of accelerants at fire scenes.

fluorescent powders Powders, dusted on areas being examined, that chemically enhance latent prints viewed under UV, laser, or alternative light illumination.

follow-up investigation The process of gathering information after the generation of the incident report and until the case is ready for prosecution; undertaken for cases receiving a supervisory disposition for further investigation.

footwear impressions Impressions that result when footwear, feet, or tires tread on a moldable surface such as earth, clay, or snow.

footwear prints Prints that result when footwear, feet, or tires contaminated with foreign matter such as mud, grease, or blood are placed on a smooth, firm surface (e.g., a floor, a chair, paper). Also called *residue prints*.

forensic entomology The study of insects associated with a dead body in order to determine the elapsed time since death.

forensic odontology A specialty that relates dental evidence to investigation.

forensic pathology The study, by physicians, of how and why people die; can also include examination of the living to determine physical or sexual abuse.

forensic photograph analysis The comparison of photos from a security surveillance camera with file pictures of suspects to identify a perpetrator or acquire information about him or her.

forensic science The examination, evaluation, and explanation of physical evidence in terms of law.

fracture match The alignment of the edges of two items of evidence, thereby showing that both items were previously joined together.

franchise fraud Scam in which people are conned into believing they are purchasing a legitimate franchise, such as a copy shop, convenience store, fast food restaurant, or other business.

free inspection fraud Most often, this type of fraud is associated with home repair or improvement scams, although it is also operated using automobiles. A person appears at your home promising a free inspection of your heating and cooling system, gutters, chimney, roof shingles, or your entire home. Serious defects are found and scare tactics are used to maneuver victims into correcting the situation "right away." Any actual damage is caused by the inspector, who may ask for an advance fee to buy materials or who offers a great deal because they have "just finished a job nearby and have some materials left over." Any work actually done is shoddy, uses inferior materials, and does not meet local building codes.

free-and-voluntary rule Based on a number of Supreme Court decisions since 1936, the principle that the exertion of any kind of coercion, physical or psychological, on a suspect to obtain a confession will render the confession inadmissible.

freehand forgery Written in the forger's normal handwriting, with no attempt to mimic the style of the genuine signature.

freezer crimes Thefts of livestock (usually only one or a few animals) in which the motivation is food rather than profit.

Frye v. United States A 1923 federal case which established that the results of a scientific technique would be admissible only if the technique had gained general acceptance in its field. (Per *Daubert*, this was superceded by the federal rules of evidence.)

G

Galton, Francis Galton published, in 1892, the first definitive book on dactylography, *Finger Prints*, which presented statistical proof of their uniqueness and many principles of identification by fingerprints. Charles Darwin's cousin.

gamma hydroxybutyrate (GHB) A central nervous system depressant used to perpetrate sexual attacks; mixed into a victim's food or drink, can induce relaxation or unconsciousness, leaving the victim unaware of the attack; can also cause seizures or death.

gas liquid chromatograph (GLC) A portable device that separates a sample gas into measurable components; used to detect residues of accelerants at fire scenes.

geographic profiling An investigative strategy in which the locations of a series of crimes (or, sometimes, the scenes of a single crime) are used to determine the most probable area of the offender's residence.

Girard, Stephen Bequeathed $33,190 to Philadelphia to develop a competent police force. In 1833, the city passed an ordinance creating America's first paid daytime police department.

Goddard, Calvin A U.S. World War I veteran and physician, he is widely considered to be most responsible for raising firearms identification to a science and for perfecting the bullet-comparison microscope.

Goddard, Henry One of the last Bow Street Runners, who in 1835 made the first successful identification of a murderer by studying a bullet recovered from a murder victim. In the case, a bullet mold with a noticeable defect was found at the suspect's home; this defect corresponded to a defect found on the recovered bullet.

gray-market vehicles Vehicles purchased abroad and shipped to the United States; may require modifications to meet U.S. emission control and safety standards.

grooves In a firearm's rifled bore, the low cuts that separate the higher lands.

Gross, Hans Austrian prosecutor who wrote the first major book on the application of science to investigation in 1893.

group cause homicide Involves two or more people with a common ideology, who sanction an act committed by one or more of the group's members that results in another person's death.

H

hacker's dictionary A software program that provides unauthorized access to computer systems by generating millions of alphanumeric combinations until it finds one that matches a password.

hacking or cracking The process of gaining unauthorized entry into a computer system.

hallucinogenic drugs Natural or synthetic drugs that distort perception of objective reality and, in large doses, cause hallucinations; can lead to unpredictable effects based on user and environment.

hard and soft insurance frauds Hard fraud is when a person fakes an injury, loss, accident, theft, arson, or other loss to illegally collect from an insurance company. Soft frauds are when people tell "little white lies" to increase the amount of an actual loss for which they will be compensated by their insurer.

hashish A natural hallucinogen, derived from resinous secretions of the cannabis plant, that is more potent than marijuana; sold in soft lumps and usually smoked in a small hash pipe.

hashish oil An extremely potent hallucinogen, derived by distilling THC from marijuana, that produces a high from a single drop; smoked in a cigarette or glass-bowled pipe, or ingested in food or wine.

hazardous wastes Solid, liquid, sludge, and manufacturing by-product wastes that are ignitable, corrosive, reactive, and/or toxic; may pose a serious threat to human health and the environment if improperly managed.

hearsay Testimony by a witness that repeats something which he or she heard someone say out of court and which the witness has no personal factual knowledge of; inadmissible in court.

heavy equipment Heavy construction equipment; usually does not require a title or registration. Also called *off-road equipment*.

Hemident A reagent used in preliminary or presumptive field tests to check for the presence of blood.

Henry system Devised by Edward Henry, the fingerprint classification system that facilitated the use of fingerprints in criminal identification; adopted in England in 1900 and today used in almost every country.

hepatitis B (HBV) and hepatitis C (HCV) Viruses present in blood (and, for HBV, other bodily fluids) that attack the liver and can lead to death; a health hazard at scenes where bodily fluids are exposed.

heroin (diacetylmorphine) An opiate that is much stronger than morphine and often causes death due to its purity or diluents; an odorless, crystalline white powder, which is usually sold diluted and is injected.

home-invasion robbery (HIR) A crime in which one or more offenders deliberately enter a home to commit robbery; characterized by gangs who target individuals rather than residences and use violence to terrify and control their victims.

homicide The killing of a human being by another human being; can be felonious or nonfelonious.

hot spots A location where various crimes are committed on a regular basis, usually by different offenders. Also called a *hot dot*.

hull identification number (HIN) Identification number assigned to boats.

human immunodeficiency virus (HIV) The blood-borne pathogen, also present in other bodily fluids, that can progress into AIDS, which reduces the body's defenses against diseases and leaves victims vulnerable to infections from which they die; a health hazard at scenes where bodily fluids are exposed.

hypercompliance In hypnosis, the situation in which the desire to please the hypnotist or others leads the subject to provide information that does not reflect his or her actual memories.

hypersuggestibility In hypnosis, the subject's heightened degree of suggestibility, which creates the possibility of the hypnotist's influencing the subject, intentionally or inadvertently, to give false information.

hypnosis A state of heightened awareness in which subconscious memories may surface that can be of help to an investigation.

I

identity theft The assumption of another person's identity for use in fraudulent transactions that result in a loss to the victim; accomplished by acquiring personal information about the victim (e.g., date of birth, address, credit card numbers).

immersion burns Burns on the skin that occur when part or all of the body falls into, or is placed into, a tub or other container of hot liquid.

impeachment In a trial, the process of discrediting or contradicting the testimony of a witness to show that he or she is unworthy of belief.

incendiary mechanism A fire-starting mechanism that consists of an ignition device, possibly a timing device, one or more plants to accelerate the flame, and, often, trailers to spread the fire; can be mechanical or chemical.

incest Broadly, any sexual abuse of a minor by an adult who is perceived by the minor to be a family member; also, under some statutes, sexual activity between closely related adults.

incident report The first written investigative record of a crime, usually compiled by the uniformed officer assigned to the call, who conducts the preliminary investigation.

incised and stab wounds Wounds inflicted with a sharp-edged instrument such as a knife or razor; typically narrow at the ends and gaping at the center, with considerable bleeding. Also called *cutting wounds.*

in-custody interrogation The legal condition under which the *Miranda* warnings are required, although case decisions vary on the definitions of "custody" and "interrogation."

indicative intelligence Information pertaining to emerging and new criminal developments; may include fragmentary or unsubstantiated information, as well as hard facts.

individual characteristics Characteristics of physical evidence that can be identified as coming from a particular person or source.

inductive reasoning The thought process that moves from specific details to a general view; e.g., the facts of a case are used to arrive at a logical explanation of the crime.

infant abduction The taking of a child less than one year of age by a nonfamily member; classified by the FBI as kidnapping, although the motive is usually to possess the child rather than to use the child as a means for something else (e.g., money, sex, revenge).

inflated-theft-loss scheme An insurance fraud in which the owner of a stolen vehicle reports a greater financial loss— based on alleged current value, damage, or stolen parts— than is the case.

infrared spectrophotometer A device that identifies samples by recording the amount of infrared light that passes through them; used to detect residues of flammable-liquid accelerants at fire scenes.

Integrated Automated Fingerprint Identification System (IAFIS) Maintained by the FBI, a national online fingerprint and criminal-history database with identification and response capabilities; may be accessed by local law enforcement agencies.

intelligence/analytical cycle A five-part process designed to produce usable information for the client.

international terrorism The use or threatened use of violence against persons or property by a group (or an individual) whose operations transcend national boundaries and are done to further political or social objectives.

interrogation A conversation between an investigator and a suspect that is designed to match acquired information to the suspect and secure a confession.

interrogatory questions Who? What? Where? When? How? And Why?

interviewing The process of obtaining information from people who have knowledge that might be helpful in a criminal investigation.

investigative psychology A criminal-profiling approach based on interpersonal coherence, significance of time and place,

criminal characteristics, and the offender's criminal career and forensic awareness.

investigator An official who gathers, documents, and evaluates evidence and information in the investigation of a crime.

iodine A dye used in developing latent prints on porous (particularly paper) and nonporous surfaces; one of the oldest and most proven means of locating prints.

J

Jacob Wetterling Crimes against Children and Sexually Violent Offender Registration Act A 1994 federal act requiring that states create and maintain registries of sex offenders. See also **Megan's law.**

jail booking report A document containing complete personal information about a suspect, including a photograph, fingerprints, and a list of the suspect's personal property at the time of booking.

joyriding The theft and use of a motor vehicle solely to drive it, after which it is abandoned; usually committed by teenagers.

judicial notice An evidentiary shortcut whereby the necessity of formally proving the truth of a particular matter is eliminated when that truth is not in dispute.

justifiable homicide The necessary killing of a person in the performance of a legal duty or the exercise of a legal right when the slayer is not at fault.

K

ketamine A synthetic hallucinogen that produces hallucinations, excitement, and delirium of less intensity and shorter duration than the effects of PCP and LSD; sold as liquids, tablets, or white powder, and injected, smoked, or ingested in a drink.

kinesics The relationship between body language (limb movements, facial expressions, and so on) and the communication of feelings and attitudes.

Kirk, Paul A biochemist, educator, and criminalist; wrote *Criminal Investigation* in 1953; helped to develop the careers of many criminalists.

known samples (1) Standard or reference samples from known or verifiable sources; (2) control or blank samples from known sources believed to be uncontaminated by the crime; (3) elimination samples from sources who had lawful access to the crime scene.

L

lacerations Wounds inflicted by blunt objects such as clubs, pipes, and pistols; typically open and irregularly shaped, bruised around the edges, and bleeding freely.

lands The high sides in a firearm's rifled bore.

laser illumination A method of developing latent prints in which lasers are used to illuminate a crime scene, causing otherwise-undetectable fingerprints to fluoresce when viewed through a special lens.

latent/invisible prints Fingerprints created when friction ridges deposit body perspiration and oil on surfaces they touch; typically invisible to the naked eye.

Lattes, Leone Made a key discovery in forensic serology in 1915, which permits blood typing from a dried blood stain.

Law Enforcement Online (LEO) Maintained by the FBI, an intranet system through which enforcement officers can communicate, obtain critical information, and participate in educational programs and focused dialogs.

layer-checking technique In arson investigation, the process of examining the strata of debris, working through to the floor; may indicate the sequence of burning.

left-wing terrorists Terrorists who usually profess a revolutionary socialist doctrine and view themselves as protecting the people against capitalism and imperialism.

LEO *See* **Law Enforcement Online.**

letter of transmittal In the context of criminal investigation, it is the letter which accompanies physical evidence to the crime laboratory; its elements include the identity and locator information of the submitting individual, the case facts, examinations requested, and other related information.

lifted-prints log A written record of lifted-prints evidence that contains the same type of information as that listed in the evidence recovery log.

lifters Various materials and devices used to "lift" evidence, especially fingerprints and footwear prints, from a surface and preserve it; include flap, electrostatic, rubber-gelatin, and clear-tape lifters.

ligature strangulation Pressure on the neck applied by a constricting band that is tightened by a force other than body weight; causes death by occluding the blood vessels that supply oxygen to the brain.

lineup A procedure in which a number of similar-looking persons, including the suspect, are shown simultaneously or sequentially to a witness who may be able to identify one of them as the perpetrator; can also be conducted with photos.

link analysis he process of charting or depicting temporal and other data gathered during a criminal investigation to uncover and help interpret relationships and patterns in the data.

livestock Farm and ranch animals raised for profit.

livor mortis Soon after death, a purplish color that appears under the skin on the portions of the body that are closest to the ground; caused by settling of the blood.

Locard, Edmond Researcher interested in microscopic evidence; all crime sense today comes under the presumption of Locard's Principle—that there is something to be found.

logic bomb A computer program that uses illegitimate instructions or misuses legitimate instructions to damage data structures; operates at a specific time, periodically, or according to other instructions.

loiding The act of slipping or shimming, by means of a celluloid strip or credit card, a spring-bolt lock that does not have an antishim device.

lookout Accomplices of a robber who watch for police and may provide armed backup for the offender.

lysergic acid diethylamide (LSD) A semisynthetic hallucinogen that produces mental changes lasting up to 12 hours; taken as drops on a sugar lump or blotted paper, was popular in the 1960s and is now making a comeback among juveniles.

M

macroscopic scene The "large view" of a crime scene, including things such as locations, the victim's body, cars, and buildings.

manslaughter A criminal homicide that is committed under circumstances not severe enough to constitute murder but that cannot be classified as justifiable or excusable.

marijuana A natural hallucinogen, derived from certain hemp plants, that produces a dreamy, carefree state and an alteration of sensory perceptions; in the form of crushed dried leaves and flowers, it is smoked or eaten in food.

marine theft The theft of boats, boat trailers, outboard motors, jet skis, and all equipment associated with boating or water activities.

mechanical explosions Explosions in which a high-pressure gas is produced by purely physical reactions; commonly caused by steam (e.g., the bursting of a steam boiler).

media statement Information released to the news media; must not prejudice the suspect's right to a fair and impartial trial.

Megan's law An amendment to the Jacob Wetterling act, legislation requiring that states disclose information about registered sex offenders to the public.

meperidine (Demerol) A synthetic narcotic that in illicit use is usually injected but can be taken orally; the first synthetic opiate.

mescaline A natural hallucinogen, derived from the peyote cactus, that produces hallucinations for up to 12 hours; ground into a powder and taken orally.

meth labs Illegal laboratories that manufacture methamphetamine; range from industrial-size organizations to oneperson tweeker labs, with prevalence skyrocketing due to the availability of "recipes" and chemicals via the Internet.

methadone A synthetic narcotic used to maintain a heroin addict at a stable level of opiate use during and after withdrawal from heroin; administered orally, thus reducing dangers from injection.

methaqualone A strong depressant that can cause poisoning and convulsive comas; removed from the legal U.S. market; street versions are usually counterfeit.

methcathinone A psychomotor stimulant chemically similar to methamphetamine but more potent, often producing extreme paranoia; usually a white or off-white powder that is sold pure and snorted. Also called *cat* and *goob*.

methylenedioxy methamphetamine (MDMA) or **ecstasy** A hallucinogen that produces reduced inhibitions, euphoria, light hallucinations and can result in paranoia and psychosis; sold as a white powder, with usage increasing alarmingly.

Metropolitan Police Act (1829) An act of Parliament that created the London Metropolitan Police, the first centralized, professional police force in Britain, which soon became the international model of professional policing.

microscopic scene A crime scene viewed in terms of specific objects and pieces of evidence associated with the crime, such as knives, guns, hairs, fibers, and biological fluids.

minutiae The characteristics of friction ridges on palms, fingers, toes, and soles of the feet.

Miranda v. Arizona The 1966 case in which the Supreme Court established that law enforcement officers must advise a person of his or her constitutional rights before beginning an in-custody interrogation.

mirror To match a person's words, actions, and mannerisms in order to eliminate communication barriers, foster trust, and create the flow of desired information.

misdemeanor A violation of the criminal code that is less serious than a felony; often punishable by imprisonment for no more than one year and/or a fine of no more than $500.

missing person frauds A particularly cruel type of advancedfee scam. Cons gather information on missing persons and then contact relatives explaining how they might be able to find the person for an up-front fee.

mitochondrial DNA (mtDNA) DNA found in the mitochondria of a cell; inherited only from the mother, it thus serves as an identity marker for maternal relatives.

mobile data terminal (MDT) An electronic system in a police car that provides features such as secure communication with 911, and among police units, direct access to national and local databases, and computer functions (e.g., e-mail, Internet access, computing, word processing).

money laundering The process of making illegally obtained money seem legitimate by filtering it through a business and falsifying the business's accounts and invoices.

morgue A crime lab that determines cause of death; when the cause is questionable or is other than a known disease, conducts analyses that produce investigative information.

morphine An opiate in tablet, capsule, and liquid form (but usually injected) that produces euphoria, drowsiness, and relaxation; provides the medical standards by which other narcotics are evaluated.

Motor Vehicle Theft Law Enforcement Act (1984) Federal legislation requiring that manufacturers place permanent identification numbers on major parts of certain car lines.

mugging *See* **strong-armed robbery.**

Mulberry Street Morning Parade Instituted by Chief Detective Thomas Byrnes in New York City in the late 1800s, an innovative approach to criminal identification in which all new arrestees were marched each morning before detectives so that the detectives could make notes and later recognize the criminals.

Munchausen syndrome by proxy (MSBP) A psychological disorder in which a parent or caretaker attempts to elicit medical attention for himself or herself by injuring or inducing illness in a child.

N

narrative style In incident reports, the officer's written chronological account of events at the crime scene from the time he or she arrived until the assignment was completed.

National Center for the Analysis of Violent Crime (NCAVC) Operated by the FBI, an organization that provides investigative and operational assistance to agencies dealing with violent crimes; consists of the BEA, CASMIRC, and VICAP.

National Crime Information Center (NCIC) The FBI's online system of extensive databases on criminals and crime; available to federal, state, and local agencies.

National Incident-Based Reporting System (NIBRS) An FBI program for crime reporting that features a detailed report format documenting far more data than does a basic incident report; involves voluntary participation, but made mandatory by some states.

National Institute-Based Reporting System The FBI's *Uniform Crime Reporting System (UCR)* began in 1929 and its focus is on reporting the types and numbers of crimes.

National Integrated Ballistic Information Network Program (NIBIN) A joint program of the ATF and the FBI, a computerized database of crime gun information that stores images of ballistic evidence (projectiles and casings), against which new images are compared for identification.

National Motor Vehicle Title Information System (NMVTIS) Under development; a computerized database that will include complete histories of vehicles in all states and will prevent title laundering between states.

NCAVC *See* **National Center for the Analysis of Violent Crime.**

NCIC *See* **National Crime Information Center.**

neighborhood canvas A systematic approach to interviewing residents, merchants, and others who were in the immediate vicinity of a crime and may have useful information.

neuro-linguistic programming (NLP) An approach used in interviewing and interrogating that emphasizes establishing rapport, through mirroring, as a means of improving communication and thus obtaining useful information.

NIBRS *See* **National Institute-Based Reporting System.**

ninhydrin A chemical used in developing latent prints on paper and cardboard; produces purplish prints, making it unsuitable for use with money.

NMVTIS *See* **National Motor Vehicle Title Information System.**

nuclear DNA DNA found in the nucleus of a cell; inherited from both the mother and the father.

O

oath A formal attestation in which a witness swears to tell the truth on the basis of his or her belief in a supreme being and acknowledges a realization of the penalties for perjury; a means of establishing a witness's competence.

odometer fraud The crime of rolling back a vehicle's odometer so that it shows a lower mileage than is the case, and obtaining or altering paperwork to support the fraud. Also called *odometer tampering, rollback,* and *clocking.*

off-road equipment Heavy construction equipment and farm equipment.

off-shore accounts Accounts in so-called safe-haven foreign banks, often operated by small island-nations which promise untraceable financial services.

one-year callable certificates of deposit Unscrupulous sellers tout these certificates of deposit (CDs) (which trumpet high rates of interest), but mislead or do not explain to investors about the actual terms of the investment.

opiates Drugs derived from the opium poppy (e.g., opium, morphine, heroin, codeine).

opium An opiate in the form of blackish-brown, pungentsmelling beads of dried fluid, which are smoked; produces drowsiness and relaxation and is the source of morphine, heroin, and codeine.

organized/disorganized offender patterns A criminalprofiling approach in which offenders are categorized as organized or disorganized on the basis of personal and crime scene characteristics. Mixed organized-disorganized crimes reflect aspects of both patterns.

Osborn, Albert In 1910, wrote *Questioned Documents,* still considered one of the definitive works on document examinations.

OxyContin A powerful narcotic consisting of oxycodone, a morphinelike drug, in a time-release formulation that, when crushed and snorted or injected, produces an intense heroinlike high; the latest drug of choice among addicts and teenage abusers.

P

packet sniffers Computer programs designed to monitor network communications and selectively record sensitive information (e.g., passwords, credit card numbers); used by hackers and, with a court order, by the FBI.

palo verde seedpod case A 1992 murder case in Phoenix, Arizona in which DNA analysis of plant evidence was used for the first time in criminal proceedings to help secure a conviction.

"paper vehicle" A vehicle that does not exist but is insured on the basis of a counterfeit title or manufacturer's certificate of origin so that it can later be reported stolen.

paralanguage Characteristics of speech—such as volume, pitch, tone, and tempo—that communicate, often unconsciously, meanings and attitudes of the speaker that may not be evident in the words themselves.

parts marking The process, mandated by law, of attaching VIN labels to the major parts of vehicles in high-theft lines.

passive system (theft deterrent) A type of vehicle antitheft device which activates automatically but may require that the driver do something to deactivate the system.

Peel, Robert *See* **bobbies.**

peremptory challenge The limited number of race and gender-neutral challenges each side has in a criminal case to excuse a juror for any other reason.

personal cause homicide Homicide motivated by a personal cause, which ensues from interpersonal aggression. The slayer and the victim(s) may not be known to each other.

personal protection equipment (PPE) Equipment and clothing designed to protect individuals at high-risk crime scenes from injury and infection.

phencyclidine (PCP) A hallucinogen in powder (angel dust), tablet, liquid, leafy mixture, and rock-crystal forms that produces unpleasant effects and can cause extreme violence and strength; as a street drug, often adulterated and misrepresented, yet usage is increasing notably.

phishing E-mails or letters soliciting personal and account information with which the collector can commit identity fraud or sell the information to someone who will commit that crime.

photographic log A written record listing the photographs taken at a crime scene and detailing who took them, where and when they were taken, and under what conditions.

photographing The primary means of documenting a crime scene.

phreakers People who misuse telephone systems through a variety of fraudulent methods that make it seem as if long-distance service and airtime are being legitimately purchased.

physical stereotyping Occurs when an officer expects that the robber will fit a preconceived description; can result in the escape of a suspect or harm to the officer.

pigeon drop con Another old, but effective scam in which one con strikes up a conversation with someone on the street. Another con approaches them with a bag of money, which is from some illicit source, which he/she just found. After talking about what they could do with the money, one of the cons calls his/her boss, an "attorney" who meets them. The attorney says they will be able to keep the money after they do a reasonable search for the owner, but that "good faith money" must be put up. After the mark puts up his/her money, the cons disappear with it.

PIN *See* **product information number.**

Pinkerton, Allan Formed the Pinkertons in 1850 along with Edward Rucker; the only consistently competent detectives in the United States for over 50 years.

placement, layering, and integration The three main phases of laundering money from illicit sources so it can take on the appearance of legitimate income.

plaintiff In a civil case, the party that was allegedly wronged and that files the lawsuit.

planned operation A robbery that involves careful planning and no planned use of force; has less likelihood of apprehension and generates a large score.

plant In arson, the material placed around the ignition device to feed the flame.

plastic prints Prints created when fingers touch moldable material, such as newly painted surfaces, the gum on stamps, putty, and the sticky side of adhesive tape.

poaching The illegal taking or possessing of game, fish, and other wildlife.

"police spies" In early nineteenth-century England, a derogatory term used in reference to plainclothes detectives; coined by persons who feared that the use of such officers would reduce civil liberties.

polygraph A mechanical device that records physiological changes that occur in a person while he or she is being questioned, with deviations from normal readings indicating deception; can be used only with subject's voluntary consent. Also called a lie detector.

Ponzi/pyramid fraud Basically this involves recruiting people who are promised great returns on their money. The early investors are paid with the money from later investors. The scheme always collapses because the recruitment of investors cannot be sustained and the cons will ultimately steal the funds for their personal use.

Popay, Sergeant Dismissed from London's Metropolitan Police in 1833 for infiltrating a radical group and advocating the use of violence after he acquired a leadership position. Today, we would call Popay's call for violence entrapment.

positive match In DNA analysis, an identical match of a suspect's DNA with that found on evidence at the crime scene.

power-assertive rape-murder A series of acts in which the rape is planned but the murder is an unplanned response of increasing aggression to ensure control of the victim. The acts within the rape assault are characterized by forceful aggression and intimidation.

power-reassurance rape A planned single rape attack followed by an unplanned overkill of the victim. Motivated by an idealized seduction and consequent fantasy, the killer focuses on acting out a fantasy and seeks verbal reassurance of his sexual adequacy.

preferential child molester A person who molests children because he or she has a definite sexual preference for children.

preliminary investigation The process undertaken by the first officer (usually a patrol officer) to arrive at the scene of a crime; includes assessment, emergency care, scene control, a BOLO, scene determination, incident report, and, sometimes, evidence procedures.

preponderance of evidence The burden of proof in civil cases; requires only that the evidence presented by one side be seen by the jury as more believable than the evidence presented by the opposing side.

primary scene The location at which the initial offense was committed.

probable cause A condition in which an officer has suspicion about an individual and knowledge of facts and circumstances that would lead a reasonable person to believe that a crime has been, is being, or is about to be, committed.

procedural criminal law That branch of criminal law that defines what can and cannot be done with, or to, people.

product identification number (PIN) PIN stands for product identification number.

professional theft (of vehicle) The theft of a vehicle to fill a specific order or to resell the parts.

promissory notes Essentially short term I.O.U.s which promise to pay its holder, the investor, the fixed amount invested, plus a fixed interest at some future specified date. While these may be operated legally, many such investments are simply frauds and the money disappears.

proof The combination of all the evidence in determining the guilt or innocence of a person accused of a crime.

Property Insurance Loss Register (PILR) An insurance industry database that lists the insureds in burglary and theft claims and everyone with an insurable interest in fire claims; detects repeated patterns of claim activity.

proximity The amount of space between the participants in a conversation—neither too close, which causes discomfort, nor too far apart, which causes a loss of connectivity.

psilocybin and psilocin Natural hallucinogens, derived from certain mushrooms, that produce hallucinations for about 6 hours; taken orally.

psychological autopsy An analysis of a decedent's thoughts, feelings, and behavior, conducted through interviews with persons who knew him or her, to determine whether a death was an accident or suicide.

pump and dump A scheme where glowing, but false, information about a stock is widely distributed, often through the Internet, and the rapid buying of it "pumps" the price of the stock up. Once pumped, the fraudsters "dump" the stock for a quick profit.

puncture wounds Wounds inflicted with piercing instruments such as leather punches, screwdrivers, and ice picks; typically small, with little or no bleeding.

pyromaniacs Arsonists who lack conscious motivation for their fire setting.

Q

quick strip (of vehicle) The process of removing from a stolen vehicle valuable parts (e.g., seats, stereos, tires) that have no identifying numbers and thus can be easily sold.

R

radial fracture lines Lines that move away from the point of impact in a glass window.

rape or sexual battery The crime of having sexual relations with a person against her or his will; with a person who is unconscious or under the influence of alcohol; or with someone who is insane, feeble-minded, or under the age of consent.

rape-murder Murder that results from or is an integral part of the rape of the victim; either an unplanned response (of increasing aggression or panic over sense of failure) or a planned act (of revenge or sadism).

rapid response deployment or quick action deployment (QUAD) An intervention approach in which patrol officers are trained in the principles and tactics of rapid deployment for critical incidents so that responding officers can take action immediately rather than wait for a SWAT team.

rapport In interviews and interrogations, the harmonious relationship with the witness or suspect that must be established by the investigator to foster trust and meaningful communication.

rebuttal In a trial, the optional process in which the prosecution, after the defense has closed its case, presents new evidence or calls or recalls a witness; it occurs at the discretion of the prosecution.

re-cross-examination In a trial, the requestioning of a witness initially called by the opposing party.

redirect examination In a trial, the requestioning of a witness by the party that called the witness.

reflected ultraviolet imaging system (RUVIS) Lighting and imaging system in which ultraviolet light applied to undetected fingerprints is "bounced" back, highly intensifying the prints.

refurbishment fraud A practice in which working components from damaged or returned items (e.g., a computer) are used in the construction of new items or are resold as new items.

revenge-motivated arson Fires set in retaliation for some injustice, real or imagined, that is perceived by the offender.

rhodamine 6G An excellent fluorescing chemical for enhancing developed latent prints and revealing others; used on metal, glass, plastic, wood, and other nonabsorbent surfaces.

rifling The lands and grooves in the rifled bore of a firearm.

right-wing terrorists Terrorists who usually espouse racial supremacy and antigovernment or antiregulatory beliefs; they often hold antiabortion and survivalist views and call for paramilitary training in "militias."

robbery The crime of taking and carrying away the personal property of another by means of force, fear, or threat of force, with the intent to permanently deprive the owner of its use.

rogues' gallery Instituted by the New York City Police Department in 1857, a display in which photographs of known offenders were arranged by criminal specialty and height for detectives to study so that they might recognize criminals on the street.

Rohypnol A benzodiazapine used to perpetrate sexual attacks; mixed into a victim's food or drink, can induce sedation, memory impairment, or unconsciousness, leaving the victim unaware of the attack. Also called *flunitrazepam*.

root kits Exploit packages that enable computer-system intruders to maintain the highest level of access by installing back doors and secret accounts and altering logs and basic system services.

rough sketch A drawing made at the crime scene; not drawn to scale, but indicates accurate dimensions and distances.

rules of evidence Federal evidentiary rules which state that scientific, technical, or other specialized knowledge is admissible if it will help the trier of fact understand the evidence or determine a fact at issue.

S

safes Locked receptacles for protecting valuables; classified as fire-resistant safes (offering protection from fire but minimum security) or money chests (providing security and reasonably good protection from fire).

salami slice A computerized-theft technique in which dollar amounts are automatically rounded down and the difference is diverted to the perpetrator's special account.

salvage switch A method of disguising a stolen vehicle whereby the title and VIN plate of a salvage vehicle are transferred to an identical stolen vehicle, which can then be sold in the legitimate market.

salvage title The title issued to an insurance company after it has paid a total-loss claim; remains with the vehicle until it is destroyed.

salvage vehicle A vehicle that has been damaged to such an extent that the cost of repairing it is more than its fair market value.

scald burns Burns on the skin caused by contact with hot liquids, either through spills/splashes or immersion; most common type of burn injury to children.

Scotland Yard The original headquarters of the London Metropolitan Police, so-called because the building formerly housed Scottish royalty. Since 1890, the headquarters have been located elsewhere, but have been still known as New Scotland Yard.

search The process of looking for evidence of a crime.

search and seizure The process of looking for evidence of a crime and taking that evidence into the custody of a law enforcement agency.

search warrant Written authorization by a judge allowing law enforcement officers to look for specified items of evidence of a crime in a specified place.

secondary scenes The locations of all events subsequent to, and connected with, the event at the primary scene.

selective raid A robbery that involves a minimal amount of casual planning and may be repeated several times in rapid succession.

semen A grayish-white fluid produced in the male reproductive organs and ejaculated during orgasm; has a chlorinelike odor and dries to a starchlike consistency.

series A crime characteristic in which crimes of the same type are committed over a short period of time, usually by the same offender.

sex offenses Crimes related to sexual activity; classified as serious (e.g., rape), nuisance (e.g., voyeurism, exhibitionism), and mutual consent (e.g., adultery, prostitution).

sexual homicide In sexual homicide, a sexual element (activity) is the basis, or the sequence of, acts leading to the death.

shaken-baby syndrome (SBS) Severe intracranial trauma caused by the deliberate application of violent force (shaking) to a child.

Shoeprint Image Capture and Retrieval System (SICAR) Computer software that classifies, archives, and identifies shoeprints.

shopping cart fraud A computer crime in which the offender selects purchases at an online store, saves a copy of the purchase page and lowers the prices, and then submits the altered page and continues the checkout process.

shoulder surfing When identity thieves stay close enough to people using their credit cards, pins, telephone calling cards, and writing checks that they can gather sensitive identity information.

situational child molester A person who molests children because the opportunity exists to do so or because of his or her inadequacy, regressed personality, or desire for experimentation; does not have a sexual preference for children.

situational stereotyping Occurs when an officer's knowledge and experience with a location creates the expectation that the present situation will be the same as past situations; increases the officer's vulnerability.

sketching The process of drawing a crime scene using rudimentary methods; sketches made can be "rough" or "smooth."

skimmers Data collection devices through which credit cards are passed. When used illegally, they are employed to obtain the credit card numbers used by customers so credit card and/or identity theft can be committed.

small-particle reagent (SPR) A chemical used in developing latent prints on objects that have been immersed in water, dew- or rain-soaked cars, surfaces covered with a residue such as ocean salt, waxed materials, plastics, tile, and glass.

smooth bore A bore without rifling; characteristic of most shotguns.

smooth sketch A finished sketch of the crime scene, often drawn to scale using information contained in the rough sketch.

smurfing A method associated with money laundering. Multiple deposits of cash are made at different accounts in different banks or bank drafts are bought; the transactions are kept under $10,000 to avoid the bank rendering a required report of the transaction to federal authorities.

snow print wax An aerosol wax sprayed on footwear impressions in snow to tint the highlights so that the impressions can be photographed before being cast.

solvability factors Used to screen and evaluate the information in an offense/incident report to determine if there is sufficient information to warrant a follow-up investigation. Such factors include whether suspects are named, the existence of significant physical evidence, the use or display of deadly weapons, and similarities to recently reported crimes.

spalling The breakdown in the surface tensile strength of concrete, masonry, or brick that occurs when exposure to high temperatures and rates of heating produces mechanical forces within the material.

speedballing The simultaneous ingestion of heroin (a depressant) and cocaine (a stimulant); produces a euphoric rush followed by a drowsy or depressing effect. Can cause convulsions and death.

sperm Tadpolelike organisms that are contained in, and travel through, semen to fertilize the female egg.

spill/splash injuries Burns on the skin that occur when a hot liquid falls from a height and splashes onto the body.

spontaneous heating An increase in temperature that results from a natural process; caused by chemical action, fermentation, or oxidation.

spontaneous ignition The catching afire of materials subjected to spontaneous heating; usually requires several hours to several months of oxidation or fermentation.

sprees A crime characteristic in which crimes of the same type are committed at almost the same time by the same offender.

STAR *See* **Stolen Auto Recovery System.**

stimulants Drugs that directly stimulate the central nervous system, producing excitation, alertness, wakefulness, and, sometimes, a temporary increase in blood pressure and respiration rate; in overdose, can cause hallucinations, convulsions, and death.

sting operations In combating fences, this is a tactic in which undercover officers pose as fences in a "front" business to gain information. Such operations have proven to be an effective means of identifying criminals, penetrating criminal organizations, and recovering property.

Stolen Auto Recovery System (STAR) A method of examining and photographing the contents of shipping containers, by means of gamma rays, while they are entering a port or being loaded onto a vessel; used to identify stolen vehicles being shipped abroad.

stop and frisk A limited pat down of the outer clothing of a person encountered by a law enforcement officer when the person is acting suspiciously, and the officer, concerned about safety, seeks to determine if the person has a weapon.

strategic intelligence Information gathered and analyzed over time that usually confirms new or recently discovered patterns of criminal activity.

striae Tiny furrows made by the action of a tool on an object's surface (e.g., marks left on a door's hinge from an attempt to force the door open with a pry bar).

strong-armed robbery A robbery in which the perpetrator attacks and beats the victim but no weapons are involved.

subpoena A written order commanding a particular person to appear in court at a specified date and time to testify as a witness.

substantive criminal law That branch of criminal law dealing with the elements that describe and define a crime.

sudden infant death syndrome (SIDS) The sudden and unexpected death of an apparently healthy infant, usually during sleep, the cause of which has yet to be determined.

superglue fuming The process of heating cyanoacrylate in a high-humidity chamber so that the condensing of the resultant fumes develops any latent prints.

surrebuttal In a trial, the process in which the defense, after a rebuttal by the prosecution, presents new evidence or calls or recalls a witness; permitted only if the prosecution conducts a rebuttal.

surreptitious entries Burglaries in which no apparent force is used and thus a point of entry or exit cannot be established; may indicate loiding, picking, an unlocked door, a perpetrator with authorized access, or an occupant-staged crime.

surveillance The secretive and continuous observation of persons, places, and things to obtain information concerning the activities and identity of individuals.

swoop and squat One of several varieties of auto fraud. In this version, a person suddenly swoops in front of the car you are driving and hits his/her breaks, causing you to rear-end them. The person then claims medical injuries were caused by you and your insurer usually pays the "victim."

synthetic narcotics Narcotics that are chemically related to opiates but that are produced entirely within laboratories; primarily used as painkillers.

T

tack The equipment used with horses (e.g., saddles, bridles, horse blankets).

tactical intelligence Information that implies immediate action and can lead to arrests or the collection of additional information; may be derived from surveillance, informants, and intelligence analysis.

telephone record analysis time-event charting An intelligence technique in which telephone records are compiled and analyzed to obtain information on the relationships between the subscriber and the numbers called.

testimony A witness's oral presentation of facts about which he or she has knowledge.

threat assessment The process of determining the risk level posed by a threat and whether law enforcement should be called in and a criminal prosecution pursued; includes evaluation of the threatener.

title fraud For motor vehicles, any act that involves altering, laundering, or counterfeiting a title or title reassignment form; often engaged in to support and cover up odometer rollbacks.

T-men Agents of the Bureau of Internal Revenue (which enforced Prohibition), so-called because the bureau was part of the Department of the Treasury.

tool mark Any impression, cut, gouge, or abrasion made when a tool comes into contact with another object.

totality of the circumstances In determining the applicability of the *Miranda* warnings, an approach that takes all the circumstances into consideration, rather than imposing a strict interpretation based on formal procedures.

trace evidence Evidence that is extremely small or microscopic in size or is present only in limited amounts.

trace evidence vacuum A vacuum which gathers small (even microscopic) evidence at the crime scene. Examples of evidence gathered by it include hairs and fibers.

traced forgery Created by tracing over a genuine signature, commonly found on fraudulent (questioned) documents such as contracts, checks, and monetary instruments.

tracing evidence Evidence that helps identify and locate the suspect.

traditional powders The basic powders, available in a number of colors, that have been used for decades for developing latent fingerprints.

trailer In arson, any substance used to spread the fire from the plant to other parts of a room or building.

trends A general tendency in the occurrence of crime across a large geographic area over an extended period of time.

Trojan horse Any computer program that is altered or designed to perform an unwanted or malicious function while appearing to perform a routine or benign function.

Truth in Mileage Act (1986) Federal legislation that requires more tightly controlled documentation and recording of odometer readings each time ownership of a vehicle changes.

T/S/D crimes Any illegal acts involving the treatment, storage, and disposal of hazardous wastes.

tuberculosis A chronic bacterial infection, spread by air, that usually infects the lungs and can lead to death if untreated; a health hazard for anyone in contact with high-risk individuals such as drug addicts and homeless persons.

tumbling The illegal altering of a cellular phone's microchip so that its access codes change after each call, making it difficult to trace the fraudulent user; done through a personal computer.

U

ultraviolet fluorescence A technique in which a darkened fire scene is illuminated with an ultraviolet lamp so that certain substances glow; used to detect residues of accelerants and to locate the point of a fire's origin.

unbundling A medical fraud technique in which each component of service is separated and billed separately, creating a higher charge than if properly billed as a single category of service.

unknown or questioned samples (1) Recovered crime scene samples whose sources are in question; (2) questioned evidence that may have been transferred to an offender during the commission of a crime and may have been taken away by him or her; (3) questioned evidence recovered at multiple crime scenes that associates a particular tool, weapon, or person with each scene.

upcoding A type of medical fraud in which patients and insurers are billed for longer office visits than occurred, or are billed for more expensive tests which were never done.

V

vehicle canvass A systematic approach to documenting every vehicle in the immediate vicinity of a crime as a means of locating the suspect's vehicle.

vehicle fraud Any fraudulent activity involving motor vehicles; includes theft of vehicles, fraud perpetrated on purchasers of vehicles, and fraud committed by owners (or persons acting on their behalf) against insurance companies.

vehicle identification number (VIN) The 17-character identification number assigned to every car manufactured or sold in the United States.

venire The large panel of potential jurors from which a trial jury will be picked.

viatical settlements Though some viatical settlements are operated legally, many are scams. An example of a viatical settlement is when people's life insurance policies are bought for less than face value. The seller thus has access to cash and the buyer makes a profit on the difference between the face value of the policy and the amount paid to the insured.

VIN *See* **vehicle identification number.**

violation In some states, this is a minor transgression of the law, often punishable by a fine of no more than $250 (e.g., littering).

Violent Criminal Apprehension Program (VICAP) FBI unit whose mission is to facilitate cooperation, communication, and coordination between law enforcement agencies and to provide support in their efforts to investigate, identify, track, apprehend, and prosecute violent serial offenders.

virus A malicious program that is secretly inserted into normal software or a computer's active memory and runs when the host runs; causes effects ranging from annoying messages and deletion of data to interference with the computer's operation.

Vollmer, August Often thought of as an administrator, Vollmer's other contributions are towering: he helped John Larson develop the first workable polygraph in 1921 and established in Los Angeles in 1923 America's first full forensic laboratory.

Vucetich, Juan Worked on the use of fingerprints in Argentina. In 1894, he published his own book on the subject, *Dactiloscopia Comparada.*

W

washing (of title) The process of fabricating a vehicle's sale to a purchaser in a jurisdiction that does not issue salvage titles or carry title brands forward, thereby obtaining a clean title on the vehicle.

weight (of evidence) The amount of believability a jury gives to the testimony of a witness or the presentation of an item of evidence.

West case A 1903 incident in which two criminals with the same name, identical appearances, and nearly identical measurements were distinguished only by fingerprints, thus significantly advancing the use of fingerprints for identification in the United States.

white-collar crime Any illegal act committed by concealment or guile, rather than physical means, to obtain money or property, avoid payment or loss of money or property, or obtain business or personal advantage. While these may be operated legally, many such investments are simply frauds and the money disappears.

witness A person who has firsthand knowledge regarding a crime or who has expert information regarding some aspect of the crime.

worm A malicious program that attacks a computer system directly, rather than infecting a host program; spreads rapidly through the Internet or e-mail.